WORLD DIRECTORY OF MINORITIES

MINORITY RIGHTS GROUP

Other recent titles from St James Press include the following:

Political Parties of the World, edited by Alan J. Day (1988), ISBN 0–912289–94–5, $85.00

Elections Since 1945: A Worldwide Reference Compendium, general editor Ian Gorvin (1989), ISBN 1–55862–017–6, $150.00

Trade Unions of the World, 1989–90 (1989), ISBN 1–55862–014–1, $85.00

Religion in Politics: A World Guide, edited by Stuart Mews (1990), ISBN 1-55862-051-6

Political and Economic Encyclopaedia of the Pacific, edited by Gerald Segal (1990), ISBN 1–55862–033–8, $85.00

WORLD DIRECTORY OF MINORITIES

ST. JAMES INTERNATIONAL REFERENCE

Edited by the
MINORITY RIGHTS GROUP

Preface by
ALAN PHILLIPS
(Executive Director, MRG, UK)

Regional Introductions by
DR PATRICK THORNBERRY

Main Compilers
MIRANDA BRUCE-MITFORD
HUGH POULTON (Eastern Europe)
DR JOHN RUSSELL (USSR)
KAYE STEARMAN

Other Compilers
SALLY BADEN, DUNCAN FISHER, JUDY KENDALL, GAVIN LEWIS, SHARON NILES

St J

ST. JAMES PRESS
CHICAGO AND LONDON

WORLD DIRECTORY OF MINORITIES

Published by Longman Group UK Limited, Westgate House,
The High, Harlow, Essex, CM20 1YR, United Kingdom.
Telephone (0279) 442601
Telex 81491 Padlog
Facsimile (0279) 444501

Published in the USA and Canada by St James Press,
233 East Ontario Street, Chicago 60611, Illinois, USA

ISBN   0-582-03619-4 (Longman)

1–55862–016–8 (St James)

British Library Cataloguing in Publication Data
Minority Rights Group
   World directory of minorities. – (Longman international reference).
   1. Social minorities   2. Ethnic minorities
   I. Title
305

ISBN 0–582–03619–4

Typeset by Quorn Selective Repro Ltd., Loughborough, Leics.
Printed and bound in Great Britain by Richard Clay Ltd., Bungay,
Suffolk

CONTENTS

MAPS

PREFACE

This *World Directory of Minorities* is being published at the beginning of a new decade when worldwide interest in and concern about minorities has reached unprecedented levels. The reduction in tension between East and West together with *glasnost* and *perestroika* in the USSR has led to a recognition that many contemporary conflicts are caused by a failure to enable minorities to participate fully within nation states. In 1988, according to the Uppsala University Department of Peace and Conflict Research, only 12 of the 111 major armed conflicts throughout the world involved the armies of two countries, while a majority of the remainder involved conflicts between minorities and majorities.

It has become evident that minorities must be better understood and their rights respected if these groups are to contribute positively to the social and economic development of nation states. The United Nations Human Rights Sub-Commission on the Prevention of Discrimination and Protection of Minorities, which has for so long marginalized minority issues to a late item of its agenda, has now appointed a Special Rapporteur on Minorities.

Consequently, MRG accepted the invitation to collaborate with Longman to produce this Directory, in order to promote understanding of minorities. The resulting *World Directory of Minorities* is a unique reference book, a hitherto neglected field for directories. This Directory should be an important reference not only for academics and students in a range of disciplines but also for those in development bodies, United Nations agencies, refugee organizations and others who work with minorities. It will be a valuable reference source for journalists and the media and can provide helpful quick briefings for business people and travellers.

The Minority Rights Group has published over 80 substantial reports in the last 20 years on minority rights throughout the world to meet its aims of:

- Securing justice for minority groups suffering discrimination by educating and alerting public opinion throughout the world.
- Helping to prevent problems from developing into dangerous and destructive conflicts.
- Fostering international understanding of the factors which create prejudiced treatment and group tensions.

These reports are significant references in their own right. Nevertheless, this Directory adds to and complements this field of scholarship, and the work of MRG and other human rights agencies. In one easily accessible volume it contains over 160 entries covering hundreds of named minorities, provides succinctly updated versions of MRG's own reports and other publications, while adding a large number of new entries that have not been previously published.

It would be misleading to claim that this Directory — or any similar publication — could be entirely comprehensive, and naïve to suggest that it could be totally objective. The subject material, with its concentration upon the experience of minorities, means that inevitably minorities receive attention rather than the constraints or problems of states or governments. The *World Directory* covers the majority of larger minorities throughout the world; it concentrates however on those groups on which MRG has undertaken prior research. A number of smaller minorities have not been included as it was not our intention to provide a comprehensive coverage of all groups, however small, but to ensure that each entry has been properly researched and provides valuable information and a greater understanding on their situation. We have endeavoured to ensure that there is a consistency in the type of information included in each entry and the style of presentation. We hope that this will be a living Directory and we would strongly encourage contact to be made with us by researchers who believe that they could introduce us to a body of research that will ensure a more comprehensive coverage in the future.

The introduction to each region by Dr Patrick Thornberry, a distinguished international lawyer, puts each section into the context of the international and constitutional legal obligations of the state and gives some indication of how well or poorly individual states live up to such obligations.

The quality of the reference can be attributed to the understanding of the authors who were invited to produce MRG's original reports, and the compilers and authors who summarised, updated and researched the entries; their names are found on the title page of the Directory. It is also due to the hard work and dedication of Miranda Bruce-Mitford, the chief compiler, and Kaye Stearman, Deputy Director of the Minority Rights Group, who has drawn upon her many years of experience in this highly complex area. She was supported very effectively by the "backstage staff" at MRG who provided the encouragement and help to ensure that tight deadlines were met, including Jim MacSweeney, Majid Majidian Talaghani, Allam Hanano, Carole McEwan, and Kathy Fundukian.

Finally our grateful thanks to the Niwano Peace Foundation of Tokyo who provided some financial support towards research costs for this Directory. Their contribution demonstrates that concern for human rights and minorities is truly global.

It is our intention that this Directory should not only further understanding on minorities but also strengthen our constituency of support. Consequently, we would encourage anyone who uses this Directory and wants to promote the rights of minorities to contact MRG, describing their interests and the way they may help.

Alan Phillips   *Minority Rights Group*
Executive Director   *379-381 Brixton Road*
Minority Rights Group   *London*
October 1989   *SW9 7DE, UK*

HOW TO USE THIS DIRECTORY

Minorities

In general this Directory follows the definition of "minority" given by Professor Capotorti, Special Rapporteur to the Sub-Commission for the Prevention of Discrimination and Protection of Minorities:

> "a group numerically inferior to the rest of the population of a state, in a non-dominant position, whose members — being nationals of the state — possess ethnic, religious or linguistic characteristics differing from those of the rest of the population and show, if only implicitly, a sense of solidarity directed towards preserving their culture, traditions, religion or language."

Given the huge scope of the topic the selection is inevitably limited — mainly to minority groups who have been considered as such for at least two generations (40 to 50 years). Thus many newer immigrant groups and refugees are excluded from this Directory, although MRG considers the situation of these groups to be within the normal scope of its work. This Directory has also excluded other groups of MRG concern such as women, children, gays and lesbians, mentally ill people etc.

Regions

The entries have been divided into 11 world regions, each with some historical, political and cultural unity as regards the experience of minorities. This may lead to problems where contiguous areas are in different regions, e.g. Greece in Eastern Europe and Turkey in the Middle East, even though some of their minority situations stem from common historical antecedents. Cross-referencing at the end of each entry should help the reader in these cases.

Each region has an introduction which outlines the international and national legal instruments pertaining to minorities, the treatment of minorities and any important themes typical of the region.

Entries

Entries within each region are arranged in alphabetical order. Most are listed under the names or names of minority/minorities; sometimes when a number of minorities are involved or a situation is sufficiently complex, it is listed under the name of the country, e.g. Burma (Myanma), Uganda; once again in alphabetical order.

Each entry is presented in a fairly standard format, with a few salient facts about the group at the beginning: alternative names, location, population, percentage of population, religion and language. The length of the entires varies from 200 to over 5,000 words and the longer entries are divided by sub-headings.

At the end of most entries there are cross-references to entries which the reader might wish to refer to, because they contain further information about this or a similar minority situation.

At the end of the book there is an index listed under the main name of the entry and the alternative name of the minority group. Entries under a country name, e.g. Uganda, are found under Uganda (minorities of).

Appendices

The appendices at the end of this Directory are referred to in the Regional Introductions and are either UN and other international legal instruments which are important for human rights and minorities rights or national instruments such as constitutions, agreements or resolutions which illustrate points in the introductory sections or entries.

Sources

The vast majority of information in these entries comes from MRG's own reports (82 in number by the end of 1989) and the three volumes of "World Minorities" published by MRG/Quartermaine Press between 1977 and 1980, updated where necessary from the UK press and other resources available to MRG. In addition we have drawn upon information published by other organizations, especially non-governmental research units and human rights organizations, and in particular the following:

   Amnesty International (London)
   Cultural Survival (Cambridge, Mass., USA)
   El Colegio de Mexico (Mexico City)
   International Alert (London)
   International Movement Against All Forms of Discrimination and Racism (IMADR) (Tokyo)
   International Working Group for Indigenous Affairs (IWGIA) (Copenhagen)
   Survival International (London)

  and information sent to MRG by minority and human rights organizations worldwide.

Acknowledgments

All the maps in this book (with the exception of the map of Belgium on p. 71) have been supplied by the Minority Rights Group, and the Publishers are grateful to MRG for permission to reproduce them. The map of Belgium was provided by Carpress International Press Agency. Copyright remains with MRG/Carpress respectively.

NORTH AMERICA

The North American region described in the following entries displays continuities and discontinuities in the treatment of minorities. The area is characterized by dominance of European-descended peoples: British, Dutch, French, Spanish, and, in the case of Greenland, Danish. The relationship between these immigrants and other peoples produces a number of distinct types of minority. In the first place, despite sustained waves of immigration, the indigenous inhabitants of the region have not been entirely displaced. If their numbers have been reduced drastically through war, disease, famine, policies of assimilation and even genocide in the centuries since 1492, their presence endures. Their voice and grievances are now heard more powerfully than ever since they have learned the lessons of organization, publicity and propaganda. A second group results from rivalries among the European powers in settlement and conquest, leaving descendants of one power in a minority: this is the situation of such as the French-speakers of Canada, principally the Quebecois, determined to preserve intact their French cultural inheritance. A third group consists of those whose origins lie in the slave systems practised in the past, creating a distinct class whose members have striven for a state based on principles of equality and non-discrimination and the rectification of historical injustices. The States under consideration have also developed a "tradition" of immigration, so that minority communities emerge through the domination of newer arrivals by longer established and powerful groups: the position of Hispanic minorities in the United States falls into this last category.

North America has powerfully influenced thinking on minorities questions in terms of a critique of segregation, and positive support for policies of non-discrimination, affirmative action, and the "melting-pot" of races and cultures. Assumptions about equality and non-discrimination as the primary desiderata of an enlightened minorities policy have been incorporated into international and constitutional law. The elements of human rights incorporated in the United Nations Charter (see *Appendix 1.1*) and the Universal Declaration of Human Rights (see *Appendix 1.2*) represent the first fruits of this approach to the protection of minorities in international law. Many State constitutions have incorporated chapters on fundamental rights using the Universal Declaration as a model.

Instruments on Minority Rights

The American Convention on Human Rights is not a relevant instrument: the States in the area are not parties; the Convention is mainly applicable to South and Central America (see introduction to that section). Regional human rights obligations may arise indirectly through membership of the Organization of American States which sponsored the American Declaration of the Rights and Duties of Man. This instrument contains only a basic non-discrimination provision in Article 2: "All persons are equal before the law and have the rights and duties established in this Declaration, without distinction as to race, sex, language, creed or any other factor." However, the States are also, with the exception of the USA and Haiti, parties to the International Covenant on Civil and Political Rights, with its important Article 27 on minorities (see *Appendix 1.3*). Canada, Denmark and Haiti are parties to the Convention on the Prevention and Punishment of the Crime of Genocide (see *Appendix 1.4*): the United States has signed, but not ratified, both of these treaties.

The protection of minorities is secured principally through constitutional and sub-constitutional law. Different "styles" of protection are exhibited: Canada, Denmark and the United States serve as examples.

The Canadian Charter of Rights and Freedoms (Part I of the Constitution Act 1982) (see *Appendix 1.5*) gives detailed linguistic and educational rights as well as basic non-discrimination provisions including a commitment to affirmative action. Thus, Section 16(1) provides: "English and French are the official languages of Canada and have equality of status and equal rights and privileges as to their use in all institutions of the Parliament and Government of Canada." The sections on official languages are followed by sections on "Minority Language Educational Rights". The Charter also refers to the aboriginal peoples of Canada. Thus, Section 35 of the Constitution Act 1982 states: "(1) The existing aboriginal and treaty rights of the aboriginal peoples of Canada are hereby recognized and affirmed." The treaties agreed by the ancestors of the Indians are not regarded as international in character but are affirmed nonetheless. Canada has attempted to transcend a narrow conception of its own nature and history through a commitment to multiculturalism considered as a necessary strengthening of federalism. The Constitution of Canada, Section 27, provides that the document is to be ". . . interpreted in a manner consistent with the preservation and enhancement of the multicultural heritage of Canadians".

Denmark provides examples of two methods of minority protection: the treaty relating to a specific group (see section on Western Europe and Scandinavia), and an extensive provision on autonomy or Home Rule applied to Greenland (see *Appendix 1.6*), the principle of which is that Greenland constitutes a special-status community within the Kingdom of Denmark. Home Rule is not the result of an international treaty, but stems from the delegation by the Danish *Folketing* (Parliament) of some of its powers in the field of administration, fisheries, conservation, education and culture, health, internal transport and environmental protection. Greenlandic is formally recognized as the primary language of Greenland, though provision is also made for instruction in Danish. In general, "external", international powers reside with Denmark, and "internal" matters may be dealt with by Greenland.

The United States has endeavoured to deal with minorities issues through the concept of universal human or civil rights. The American Declaration of Independence of 1776 states ". . . We hold these truths to be self-evident — that all men are created equal; that they are endowed by their Creator with certain inalienable rights; that among these are life, liberty and the pursuit of happiness . . .". The first ten Amendments to the Constitution comprise the Bill of Rights, which, *inter alia*, forbids the establishment of religion. The 13th Amendment prohibits slavery; the 14th Amendment provides that no state shall deprive any person of life, liberty or property without due process of law, "nor deny to any person within its jurisdiction equal protection of the laws". The *Plessy v. Ferguson* Supreme Court decision in 1896 provided official sanction for racial segregation through its "separate but equal" doctrine, but this was reversed in 1954 by *Brown v. Board of Education*, holding that "separate" was inherently unequal. The Civil Rights Act of 1964 outlawed discrimination in voting, employment, federally assisted programmes and public facilities. The United States' courts have, however, equivocated on affirmative action as a remedy for past racial injustice and inherited disadvantage. The total thrust of policy has been to favour integration or assimilation of groups into the American way of life, though recent movements to, for example, bilingual education for Hispanic groups, demonstrate some change in paradigm towards a multicultural approach or at least a more genuine equality of opportunity for the different ethnic groups. Official policy in relation to Indian groups has gradually moved from recognition of independent status, through assimilation/genocide to what appears to be a better recognition of the distinct characteristics and contribution of the groups to the social whole (see *Appendix 1.7*). This benign movement is, however, subject to inconsistencies of official intentions.

Treatment of minorities

The reports in this section provide a critique of State policy and practice. A positive attitude by Governments towards their minorities, expressed in terms of legal regulation, is only a crucial first step in ameliorating conditions among the groups: more enlightened policies must be matched by implementing action.

In any case, some public goals for minority groups remain open to question. In the case of many indigenous peoples, continuing pressures of assimilation and acculturation are maintained by States: the opening in 1991 of native lands in Alaska to outsiders, with all the attendant threats of accelerated attacks on Inuit culture, is only one example. The indigenous peoples of Canada and the United States figure at the bottom of almost every indicator of social deprivation. The result is suicide, alcoholism, murder at rates considerably above those for non-indigenous. The factor of cultural loss is crucial, and individuals continue to lose their sense of identity. The struggle for land rights, including compensation for deprivation, is a key to the restoration of dignity and self-respect, in view of basic economics and the reverence in which many indigenous peoples hold the lands of their ancestors.

The situation of other minority groups, such as Blacks and Hispanics, while perhaps lacking the continuing poignancy of the fate of the indigenous, is also severe. Proclamations of equality and justice are not matched by practice. For many immigrant groups, the promise of an open society full of opportunity matures into the reality of the ghetto. Some minority groups, such as the Japanese-Americans, have done conspicuously well in material terms, though at the price of surrendering cultural distinctiveness. In order to advance in society, it still appears that minorities are required to accept the values and world view of the majorities, to the loss of both sides in terms of potential mutual enrichment.

The treatment of minorities in North America does not at present suggest the darkest picture in the contemporary world. There are, however, ongoing threats and difficulties for groups of considerable magnitude, including that of survival as identifiable entities. Many of the greatest injustices — slavery, genocide — are past, but the effects endure and mutate into more subtle injustices. Freedom, equality, self-respect and the respect of society, remain distant horizons for many.

American Indians

Alternative Names: **Various Indian nations and clan names**
Location: **throughout USA, especially west and south-west**
Population: **approximately 1.5 million**
% of Population: **0.63%**
Religion: **various**
Language: **English and various Indian dialects**

There are approximately one-and-a-half million Indians living in the USA today. They are descendants of the original inhabitants of North America and do not represent a homogenous group but have different social, cultural, economic, and linguistic characteristics. The Bureau of Indian Affairs (BIA), which supervises all Indian affairs in the United States, recognizes 283 tribes in the mainland United States. These tribes receive special federal services, and trusteeships for their lands and assets based on treaties signed in the nineteenth century. Tribes range in size and character with reservations of more than 22,000 square miles and populations of more than 130,000 to tiny bands of less than 100 with a few acres, to those who on outward appearance are almost indistinguishable from their white neighbours. Some Indians live in cities and towns and therefore cease to be eligible for BIA services. Additionally there are some groups who identify themselves as Indian but are not officially recognized as such. These are tribes who had their status terminated in the 1950s and 1960s or those groups that never had federal status at all.

Background and history

Before European discovery and settlement there were perhaps three million Indians in present-day USA, with 600 distinct societies ranging from tiny hunting and gathering bands to sophisticated agricultural nations. Indian societies were generally small communities of only a few hundred people, divided by distance and traditional hostilities. Even at their zenith the larger nations numbered only approximately 60,000 individuals. Each group adapted to their own environments, and had distinct cultures, economies, beliefs and customs.

The Atlantic and Pacific seaboards were the most densely populated. The west coast and northwest had an abundance of fish, game, and wild plants, so the groups in these areas had prosperous, settled communities with rich cultures. The eastern seaboard was populated by farming nations whose people lived in permanent well ordered towns, and were usually organized into confederacies for mutual defence. Westward, across the Appalachian mountains, lived smaller more scattered migratory groups who usually depended on hunting, supplemented by a small amount of agriculture. Further west in the great plains region lived societies that depended primarily on hunting, while in the south-west between the southern plains and present day California lived the Pueblo peoples whose civilizations were influenced by the great indigenous civilizations of Central America and Mexico. They had adobe towns and cultivated the earth. This region was also home to the wandering bands of Navajos and Apaches. The Great Basin region, in what is now present day Utah and Nevada, was the poorest area. It was populated by tiny migratory bands of 15-20 people.

In the larger societies there were hereditary hierarchies and elementary policing systems but in general decisions were reached by consensus and individuals who disagreed with the decisions of the group could leave to join another tribe or form a society of their own. Religion played a very important part in the life of the Indians. They believed in influential spirit forces as well as a cosmic unity, that embraced man, animals, plants, and the elements. They had a reverence for the land and adapted their cultures to the peculiarities of their environments. The notion that the earth was their mother was a literal belief. They had an immense knowledge of nature and the resources of their own areas and their diet was more varied and plentiful than in Europe.

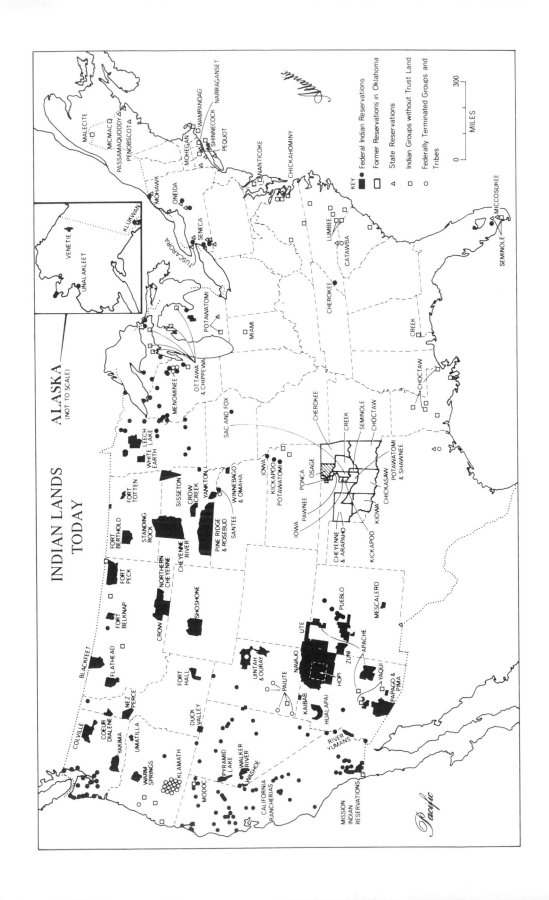

INDIAN LANDS TODAY

ALASKA
(NOT TO SCALE)

VENETIE

UNALAKLEET

KLUKWAN

KEY

● Federal Indian Reservations

■ Former Reservations in Oklahoma

△ State Reservations

□ Indian Groups without Trust Land

○ Federally Terminated Groups and Tribes

300

MILES

Pacific

Atlantic

MALECITE

MICMAC

PASSAMAQUODDY

PENOBSCOT

MOHEGAN

WAMPANOAG

SHINNECOCK

NARRAGANSET

PEQUOT

MOHAWK

ONEIDA

NANTICOKE

CHICKAHOMINY

TUSCARORA

SENECA

LUMBEE

CATAWBA

POTAWATOMI

OTTAWA & CHIPPEWA

MIAMI

CHEROKEE

CREEK

MICCOSUKEE

SEMINOLE

CHOCTAW

MENOMINEE

LEECH LAKE

WHITE EARTH

FORT TOTTEN

SAC AND FOX

CHEROKEE

CREEK

SEMINOLE

CHOCTAW

SISSETON

CROW CREEK

YANKTON

WINNEBAGO & OMAHA

SANTEE

IOWA

KICKAPOO

POTAWATOMI

OSAGE

PONCA

IOWA

PAWNEE

POTAWATOMI & SHAWNEE

CHICKASAW

KIOWA

FORT BERTHOLD

STANDING ROCK

CHEYENNE RIVER

PINE RIDGE & ROSEBUD

CHEYENNE & ARAPAHO

KICKAPOO

IOWA

FORT PECK

NORTHERN CHEYENNE

SHOSHONE

CROW

FORT BELKNAP

FLATHEAD

BLACKFEET

COLVILLE

YAKIMA

COEUR D'ALENE

NEZ PERCE

UMATILLA

FORT HALL

UINTAH & OURAY

PAIUTE

DUCK VALLEY

KAIBAB

NAVAJO

UTE

PUEBLO

ZUNI

HOPI

APACHE

MESCALERO

YAQUI

PAPAGO & PIMA

HUALAPAI

RIVER YUMANS

MISSION INDIAN RESERVATIONS

WARM SPRINGS

KLAMATH

MODOC

PYRAMID LAKE

WALKER RIVER

WASHOE

CALIFORNIA RANCHERIAS

European conquest and settlement

The first European conquerors were the Spanish who in 1598 declared the territory of the Pueblos in the south-west to be part of the Spanish empire, established the capital of Santa Fe and forced the Pueblos to work as slaves. The Pueblos later rebelled and were successful but 12 years later all the Pueblo tribes except the Hopi were again subdued. By 1656 the Spanish had also established settlements in Florida. Meanwhile the Dutch established a trading colony in Manhattan and the French established Port Royal in modern Nova Scotia.

By the end of the seventeenth century the French, who enjoyed relatively peaceful relations with the Indians (because their primary interest was the fur trade and not land acquisition), had spread out from Canada down along the Illinois river to the mouth of the Mississippi. The British had meanwhile founded Jamestown in Virginia. Less than a century later the English had colonies stretching from Maine to the Carolinas. In New England as well as in Virginia relations between the Europeans and the Indians were at first friendly. The Indians helped the early colonists to survive, sometimes even providing protection and the Europeans gave iron implements and goods to the Indians. By the 1630s the colonists had become self-sufficient. There was increased immigration and as a result they encroached further onto Indian territory.

The Europeans had a devastating effect on the Indians. They brought diseases that wiped out whole Indian populations. By 1662 a long stretch of the New England coast had been depopulated and whole communities wiped out. Over-hunting caused the extermination of fur-bearing animals from region to region and trade with the Indians eventually bred dependence on European trade goods, iron tools and weapons which were clearly superior to the implements of the Indians.

It was inevitable that the three European powers would fight over ultimate control of the territory and between 1689 and 1763 they were fighting among themselves. It was the Indians, however, who were most affected by these wars. Indians had turned against each other to aid their European allies. Some tribes were wiped out by other Indian tribes. At the end of these wars many of the tribes east of the Mississippi were destroyed. The end result was that Indian land was confiscated by Europeans, and eventually those tribes that had fought with and for the victor found their lands taken over by whites as European immigration to the new world increased.

After the wars the British government realized the necessity for native allies on the frontier, so the government issued the Royal proclamation of 1763, which outlined plans for permanent Indian territory west of the Alleghenies. The proclamation forbade private individuals or organizations to take or buy tribal lands, but because the authorities could not police the frontier indefinitely against the stream of settlers moving south and west, the proclamation was a failure.

Indian resistance

In 1776 when the colonies rebelled the Indians were again divided and weakened. Those tribes that had fought for the British lost their lands and the new United States signed treaties with the south-eastern nations, forcing them to cede lands already seized by whites, but recognizing and guaranteeing their title to lands remaining. This "nation to nation" relationship was reaffirmed by the US Congress in October 1988 on the 200th anniversary of the Constitution.

In 1828 Andrew Jackson, an avowed Indian hater, was elected president. He was of the opinion that all tribes east of the Mississippi river should be moved, by force if necessary, west of the Mississippi. Jackson's policy had the greatest effect on the "Five Civilized Tribes"; the Creeks, Chickasaws, Cherokees and Choctaws of Mississippi, Alabama and Georgia, and the Seminoles of Florida which had been ceded to the USA from Spain in 1821. These tribes were living peacefully with their non-Indian neighbours and had embraced the European social educational and political systems. In 1830, when president Jackson's Indian Removal Act became law, the tribes were removed one by one to land in present day Oklahoma. The Cherokees, under the leadership of chief John Ross, fought back through the federal courts which in 1832 upheld their case in a decision that said that they were independent political communities that retained their individual rights. Jackson's reply was that John Marshall (Supreme Court Justice) had made his decision so now let him enforce it. Later that year the Georgia government held a lottery and much of the Cherokee's land was distributed to the winners.

Some of the Cherokees resisted and continued to live a marginal existence in the area, but they were eventually moved by force to modern Oklahoma. In this move 4,000 Cherokee died and the journey became known as the "trail of tears". A small group of Cherokees however managed to escape and hid in the Carolina mountains as well as a large part of the Seminoles who held out in the Florida swamps. After seven years of fighting the army gave up and left the Indians alone but, despite this small victory, 1832 marked the end of armed resistance east of the Mississippi.

This pattern was followed throughout much of

the 1800s. As new territory in the west was granted statehood, lands which had been promised to Indians in perpetuity was gradually taken away and the Indians herded onto reservations in areas that were not yet given statehood or had not yet been found to be economically profitable for the whites. When Indian land was not given freely it was taken by deceit or force, and sometimes whole populations were wiped out in the process. By 1880 in California the Indian population fell from an estimated pre-European level of 350,000 to 20,000.

The only successful resistance effort came from the plains region which was home to the tribes who, since the middle of the eighteenth century, had adopted the horse and gun from the Europeans. These tribes, the Sioux, Cheyenne and Comanche among them, had established a warrior ethic and developed great military skill to protect their hunting territories from encroachment by whites. Sporadic fighting continued in this region until the 1880s when small bands of Apaches, who had continued to hold out in the south-west, were finally subdued. By the end of the century the Indians were completely dependent on their conquerors, and the population was down to one tenth of its pre-European level due to disease and warfare.

The General Allotment Act was passed in 1887. Also known as the Dawes Act after the Senator who initiated the proposal, it was an honest attempt by some to transform Indian society by assimilation. Indians were each given a plot of land, approximately 160 acres, in trust until the Indian owner was thought competent enough to hold the land in fee simple. The economic effect of the Act was that, by 1890, 17.4 million acres of Indian land which had been retained after the wars of the 1880s were now part of the public domain and eventually more than 90 million acres of Indian land no longer belonged to them.

The social effects of the Act were even greater. Tribes were broken up when tribal lands were lost and the social structure of the tribes was threatened. The old system of communal property which was vital to Indian social and traditional survival was destroyed and the Indians were left feeling discontented and hopeless. Young Indians were deprived of their traditions and did not get the skills necessary to survive in the white world. As a result they found themselves caught between two worlds neither of which they were equipped to deal with.

Twentieth century developments

The Meriam Report, published in 1928, described the Indians as destitute and the housing, sanitation and health conditions of the Indians as deplorable. In 1933, when Franklin Roosevelt became president, the direction of Indian policy was changed. The Reorganization Act of 1934 was accepted by 191 tribes and became law. It re-established the sovereignty of Indian tribes and tribal governments were given the authority to draw up constitutions and to assume judicial and fiscal control over the reservations. Allotment of tribal lands was halted, two million dollars was allotted for Indian land acquisition and a 10 million dollar loan fund was established so that economic enterprises could be undertaken by the Indians themselves. Religious freedoms were extended, educational programmes were re-evaluated and the O'Malley Act of 1934 gave the BIA authority to make contracts with federal, state and local agencies for specific Indian programmes.

Despite the war and the depression the Indian New Deal achieved good results. Indian beef-cattle holdings increased by 105% and their yield of animal products over 20 times. Indians became good credit risks, for of the $12 million that had been loaned to Indians only $3627 had been cancelled as uncollectable. However there were those who argued that the Indians should be more rapidly absorbed into mainstream America, and during the 1950s when Dillon S. Meyer (who had been in charge of Japanese internment during the Second World War), became the Commissioner of Indian Affairs, the new official policy toward the Indians changed. The policy was embodied in the House Concurrent Report (HRC) 108, which was adopted by Congress in 1953 and stated that the Indians should be freed as soon as possible from all federal supervision and responsibility; thus they would be forced to assimilate into white society. Another similar bill was passed extending the authority of states to enact similar legislation.

Some Indian groups fought against termination, arguing that supervision should continue for a period of time so that the tribes could prepare themselves for termination. However, by 1960, 61 Indian tribes and bands had been terminated. Termination was also followed by a policy of withdrawal which meant that development projects were discontinued, loan funds were frozen and federal services ceased. In 1944 the National Congress of American Indians had been formed, to represent every recognized tribe in the country. By 1960 they, along with the new Indian leaders who had fought in World War II and the Korean war, and were more aware of how white society functioned, managed to stop the termination policy and it has never actually been resumed.

The original function of the Bureau of Indian Affairs (BIA) was to hold the lands in trust for the tribes. Because of its structure the BIA has over the years become unresponsive to the plight of the Indians and very bureaucratic. The head of the bureau is the Assistant Secretary for Indian Affairs, who has ultimate control over the various Indian nations' constitutions, the composition of their governments, their power to make contracts, the disposition of their property and the funding and implementation of most programmes that affect them. The BIA has authority to veto decisions made by the tribal Councils. The policies of the Bureau are decided by the Congressional Committee on Interior and Insular Affairs and by the Indian section of the Bureau of the Budget, which is subject to changing political fashions in the country. The BIA also has a position in the Department of the Interior which is under the management of the Assistant Secretary for Public Land Management.

The Bureau has at times been negligent or has abused its function and authority. One example of the many abuses by the BIA concerns the land rights of the 3,650 Cheyenne people living in their original homeland of eastern Montana on 433,434 acres of land that is rich in coal. Between 1966 and 1971 the BIA drew up leases with energy companies which were economically unfavourable to the tribe, without any protective clauses to protect either the land or the Cheyenne population. After six years of legal battles, the leases were finally revoked by act of Congress in 1980. Although several mineral companies received compensation the Cheyenne did not.

Indian organizations

The 1960s saw an increase in Indian political activity. In 1961 the Chicago American Indian Conference was held and representatives of 90 tribes set out the goals of the Indian community. They wanted to retain their Indian culture and special relationship with the Federal government but they also proposed improving government programmes so that one day Indians would be self-sufficient.

The same year the National Indian Youth Council (NIYC) was founded by 10 college-educated Indians. The NIYC was a more radical group whose leaders were impatient with the BIA. They wanted a clear definition of Indian culture and Indian rights and their first focus of attention was on the north-west states and native fishing rights. They staged sit-ins and fish-ins and demanded recognition of the rights guaranteed to the Indians in treaties made with them by the Federal government. When the BIA was slow to act the NIYC decided to use force if necessary to resist state action and a series of confrontations followed. The efforts were successful and the government eventually did file charges against the state governments on behalf of the Indians.

Other more radical Indian groups also followed.

One was the American Indian Movement (AIM), which consisted mainly of urban Indians. They used confrontations and demonstrations to draw attention to the problems of native Americans. In 1972 they and a number of other groups organized a march on Washington known as the "Trail of Broken Treaties" to present a list of grievances and a 20-point programme to stress the treaty rights of the tribes. The Indians were not able to meet with officials and the 20-point programme, which was formulated by a number of representatives from different groups around the country, was never considered. This was partly due to the fault of AIM itself who were perceived by the public as destructive because of damage done to the BIA building which the marchers occupied for six days when they found out that officials would not meet with them. In addition members of the Tribal Chairman's Association which was formed to counteract the more radical elements of groups like AIM held a press conference denouncing the demonstrators.

During the 1960s legal aid organizations were also set up to help the Indians fight for their rights in the courts. One of the most important of these organizations was the Native American Rights Fund (NARF). The NARF encouraged non-recognized Indian groups such as some Eastern Indian groups to present claims for their land. The government eventually settled claims with many of the tribes. One such example is the Passamquoddy and Penobscott Indians of Maine, who received 300,000 acres of undeveloped land and $27.5 million. The Indians went on to invest their money and land into small businesses that have provided jobs for Indians as well as non-Indians in the area.

American Indian organizations have forged international links with other oppressed indigenous peoples. In response to their attempts to be awarded UN representation as a sovereign nation the UN Working Group on Indigenous Populations Working Grants was established in 1982.

Social and economic position

Indians tend to be very poor. Most still live on reservations where work is scarce. In 1985 half of the Indian workforce had no work while in some areas unemployment was as high as 75%. There are housing shortages on the reservations and 55% of homes are sub-standard. The Indian population has a greater incidence of communicable diseases and fatal infectious illnesses. Over the years a welfare society has developed. Many Indian people are depressed, lacking in initiative, self assurance and not able to live successfully in their own culture or the white culture. These symptoms usually manifest themselves in violence, delinquency drunkenness and despair. Suicide and accidents are the single biggest cause of Indian deaths. The suicide rate is twice the national average and most of the accidents are related to alcohol and drug abuse. Crimes of violence are 10 times more frequent on reservations than among the population as a whole.

The Indians were forced to part with 64% of the land which they retained at the end of the Indian Wars of the 1880s and today less than 53 million acres, mostly in the mid-west and the south-west, belongs to them. These areas tend to have severe water shortages and limited economic potential. The Indian population has increased five-fold over the past century and the land base which has remained constant is unable to sustain them. The BIA estimated that 75% of the land is suitable only for the least intensive grazing, the least most profitable form of agriculture, while 10% of the land has viable resources of oil, gas and minerals. Twenty-five per cent of all remaining Indian lands is in the hands of non-Indian owners because of legal entanglements.

In 1964 the Economic Opportunity Act was passed, and Indians gained access to funds not controlled by the BIA. Although the budget for the Indians was small the results were good as Indians planned and implemented programmes. For example in Washington state the Lummis, who were one of the poorest tribes, were able to establish a successful fish-farming business based on Indian cultural traditions. Because of these successes more money was eventually channelled to Indian communities.

In 1970 President Nixon outlined various proposed administrative reforms. Although many of his proposals were never followed, the sacred Blue Lake of Taos Pueblo which the Indians had been trying to recover since 1906 was returned to them, the composition of the Congressional Sub-Committee of Indian Affairs was changed so that it was more responsive to Indian needs and Louis Bruce, a business man of Indian ancestry became Commissioner of the BIA. Later in the 1970s legislation was passed to allow some Indian tribes to take responsibility for running most or all of their federal programmes.

In 1975 25 Indian tribes in the north-west joined together to form the Council of Energy Resource Tribes, which is modelled on OPEC. In addition many other tribes have been taking advantage of legislation such as the Indian Tax Status Act of 1980 to enter into enterprises that can attract money from outside the reservation. Indeed these and other types of legislation have allowed Indians to become more self-reliant. Although reservations that follow a policy of economic and industrial expansion have a higher percentage of social breakdown, other legislative measures, like the Indian Religious Freedom Act, may help to offset

these developments by allowing the Indians to retain their traditions and culture. The Act, which was passed during the 1970s, gives the same degree of protection to Indian faiths that is given to other religious faiths in the USA. This has also meant that there could be greater protection for Indian burial places and sacred sites.

Government aid to the Indians and Indian programmes has continued to increase despite budget cuts during the Reagan administration. Despite this there has been little improvement in the economic circumstances of the Indians. They are still unable to support themselves on their own land, therefore economic dependence on the government continues. The increase in government funding has meant increased involvement in the lives of the Indians. The BIA and other federal agencies now provide more than half the jobs for Indians and 60% of the Indian's personal income. These figures are higher in reservation communities where there are no significant alternative sources of employment and wealth.

In 1979 the largest Indian land settlement in American history was awarded to Sioux Indians when they won a court case against the USA which had been going on for almost a century. The Indians were awarded $105 million dollars for the illegal seizure of the Black Hills in 1880. The Indians refused to accept the money and wanted the land instead, for it represented more than just an economic opportunity. They saw it as a chance once again to be reunited as one nation in their traditional homeland. In 1985, the Senator of New Jersey introduced a bill whereby the federally owned land, including some of the most important Indian burial sites, would be returned to them. There are a number of other land claims pending, such as those of the Western Shoshone in Nevada and the Yurok, Karok and Tolawa in the north-west. A highly controversial case has been the partition of disputed land between members of the Hopi and Dine (Navajo) peoples.

In the early 1970s the Indian Education Act was passed. This allowed the Indian communities to run their own schools and to emphasize their own cultures and histories. This was then put under the Department of Health Education and Welfare. The head of the Indian Education Office was given the rank of Assistant Secretary and therefore had direct access to the White House. In addition the Tribally Controlled Community Colleges Act was also established and is today a very successful programme. It gives the tribal government authority to establish centres for further education where members are able to return to college and learn more about their own history and culture while receiving qualifications. This was an important step for American Indians whose school drop-out rate is between 45% and 62% and who do not always have the skill or the capital required to undertake enterprises that would make the best use of their lands and resources.

However, the Indians have been able to make advances legally, politically, educationally and, when given the opportunity, they have also been successful economically.

(See also *Indians and Metis of Canada; Hawaiians, Indigenous; Inuits*)

Asian-Americans

Alternative names: **Asian-Pacific-Americans, various specific names e.g. Chinese-Americans, Korean-Americans etc.**
Location: **all-USA, concentration on west coast**
Population: **about 6.5 million**
% of population: **2.7%**
Religion: **various**
Language: **English, various Asian languages**

"Asian-American" and more recently "Asian-Pacific-American" are the generic terms used to describe the various communities within the USA which have their ethnic origins in Asia. Apart from their immigrant Asian origins and a common experience of discrimination (which however does vary considerably in time, place and intensity between communities) the various communities differ in language, religion, culture and their experiences in the USA.

Some Asian-American communities have long been established in the USA, especially Chinese and Japanese immigrants, many of whom came at the end of the nineteenth and beginnings of the twentieth centuries, mainly as manual labourers to the west coast and Hawaii. But the repeal of racially biased immigration legislation in 1965, together with a large-scale intake of Indo-Chinese refugees from 1975, significantly altered both the numbers and ethnic profile of Asian-Americans. According to the 1980 census 21% of Asian-Americans were of Chinese origin, 20% were Filipino, 15% Japanese, 12% Vietnamese, 11% Korean, 10% Asian-Indian and the remainder from elsewhere in Asia. Over the past decade the proportions have altered and the largest group is now Filipino rather than Chinese while the numbers of Vietnamese and Koreans are greater than those of Japanese.

Collectively Asian-Americans are the fastest growing group of the American population. Forty per cent of the USA's annual intake of 600,000 immigrants comes from Asia and Pacific island countries. Half of all Indo-Chinese refugees are in the USA and there are continuing refugee resettlement and family reunion programmes which will result in an intake of over 30,000 per year for several more years. Although Asian-Americans are found throughout the USA, half the Asian-

American population today lives in California or Hawaii.

Asian-Americans are often described as a "model minority" — educated, hard working, unassertive. Asian-Americans do appear to have some of these characteristics. The 1980 census found that Asian-American families had a median income of $23,600 compared to $20,800 for white families. This figure reflected higher Asian levels of education and professional qualifications and higher household work participation rates. Both indigenous Asian communities and immigrants are more likely to have had a graduate education than other groups and to encourage their children to do well educationally.

Yet these figures also hide disparities. Chinese-Americans, Japanese-Americans and Asian-Indian-Americans do better than average in education and income; Korean-Americans and Filipino-Americans also do better than average but not so well as the other three groups; while the Indo-Chinese have generally done poorly. Korean-Americans have tended to work in small family businesses, often inner-city grocery stores, but the next generation is likely to be more oriented towards the professions. Filipino-American immigrants, despite an education in English and experience of American culture, tend to be employed in manual and service jobs. In both the Korean and Filipino communities, women outnumber men, which is a factor in their lower average earnings.

The first group of Vietnamese refugees in 1975 have generally done well educationally and in business. Later refugees, mostly farmers, fishermen and small traders, have lacked the language, skills and capital to reach the same levels. Probably the worst off are the smaller communities of Hmong (Hill Tribe people) from Laos and Cambodian refugees.

Asian-Americans face varying levels of discrimination. There have been sporadic violent attacks on different groups, particularly from economically depressed whites or blacks who see low-wage unskilled Asians as economic competition. On a different level there is alleged to be a "glass ceiling" which limits the earnings and promotion opportunities of Asian-Americans in large companies. While Asian-Americans have done well in professions such as medicine, engineering or computing, there are few in the top echelons of management or government. Most recently there have been allegations that some universities and colleges are attempting to limit their intakes of Asian students.

(See also *Japanese-Americans*)

Black Americans

Alternative names: **African Americans**
Location: **throughout USA**
Population: **approximately 27 million**
% of population: **11.3%**
Religion: **various**
Language: **English**

There are approximately 27 million Black Americans living in the United States. They make up the largest non-white minority group. The majority are descended from the large slave populations who were imported into North America between the seventeenth and nineteenth centuries. They therefore share a common experience of discrimination, which despite the removal of legal barriers to full equality, continues in part today. Although Black Americans were formerly concentrated in the southern states, today they can be found throughout the USA, especially in the large cities of the eastern seaboard, mid-west and south.

Slavery

Black people have a history in America that goes back to the time of the founding of the original 13 colonies. When the British landed at Jamestown in Virginia in 1619 there were an estimated 23 black men and women among their passengers. There is evidence that at the beginning of the seventeenth century black people enjoyed a position of equal status with whites and were not slaves but indentured servants. A 1651 report gives evidence of an Anthony Johnson, a free black, living in Virginia who received a grant of 250 acres of land and imported five servants.

In documents from the period, blacks who arrived in the colonies were listed as Negroes and described as servants, not slaves. It is unclear as to the exact time that slavery became instituted but by 1641 Massachusetts gave statutory recognition to slavery and other states followed suit. Whether for economic reasons, or because black people were not under the protection of any recognized government or because blacks like other servants could not escape and blend readily into the predominantly white society, slavery in the USA became associated with the black race. In Virginia in the 1660s statutes were passed that made black people slaves for life and forbade intermarriage between whites and blacks, which in itself suggests that it was practised. Similar statutes were adopted by all of the 13 colonies.

Even at this stage blacks as well as whites protested against the institution of slavery but nonetheless it lasted for more than two more centuries in the USA. One of the earliest groups to protest were the Quakers in Germantown Pennsylvania who made a formal protest denouncing slavery as early as 1688. The period of the early 1700s is also filled with reports of slave revolts from New York to South Carolina and there are records in Massachusetts of slaves petitioning the legislature for their freedom. Eight such petitions were filed during the Revolutionary War.

Despite this fact, however, many blacks, slave and free alike, fought in the Revolutionary War for the colonies while others fought for the British. Crispus Attucks, an ex-slave, was the first to die for the cause of American independence in 1770 at the Boston Massacre which is regarded as the beginning of the war for independence. However in 1787 when the US Constitution was approved in Philadelphia it contained three clauses protecting the institution of slavery: blacks were given the status of property and considered to be three-fifths of a person.

Vermont abolished slavery in 1777 and by 1804 all the northern colonies had passed similar legislation. However in the south where slave labour was needed on the enormous plantations the system continued well into the mid-nineteenth century. In the states where slavery was practised blacks could be sold away from family members. Although many converted to Christianity, in these states slave marriages were not encouraged or sanctioned by any church though procreation was encouraged to ensure an additional supply of labour, and laws were passed prohibiting the education of slaves: some states going so far as to prohibit the education of free blacks as well.

During this period many blacks escaped to safety in the north and Canada via the underground railroad, a network of houses and churches staffed by individuals who offered shelter and safety to the slaves. Such acts prompted the passage in 1793 by the US Congress of the Fugitive Slave Law which made it a criminal offence to harbour runaway slaves. By the beginning of the nineteenth century most northern states passed similar laws. In 1807 Congress banned the importation of slaves but not slavery itself. The riots and protests against slavery continued and in 1854, 2,000 troops were needed to escort Anthony Burns, a fugitive slave, through the streets of Boston to return him to the south.

In 1863 as the Civil War between the northern (Union) and southern (Confederate) states escalated, the Emancipation Proclamation was signed by President Lincoln and the slaves in the confederate states, except for certain areas in Louisiana and West Virginia, were freed. The proclamation also did not apply to the slaves in the border states. Again when asked to fight for their country blacks responded, as they had during the Revolutionary War and the war of 1812. As many as 185,000 black soldiers fought in the Union Army during the Civil War and as many as 29,000 in the Union Navy.

Reconstruction

The period following the Civil War was known as Reconstruction. During this period black people finally received the protection of the 13th, 14th, and 15th Amendments to the US Constitution that guaranteed them the right of freedom, the right of full citizenship and the right to vote. They made use of their new-found political power to elect government officials and political leaders. Black Americans were elected to congressional posts and attended schools, and intermarriage between the races increased. The first Civil Rights Act was passed in 1875. It provided for access to public facilities and accommodation without regard to race, colour or previous condition of servitude. The Act gave federal authorities the right to protect the constitutional rights of blacks when states failed to do so. That same year there were eight blacks in Congress; one senator and seven Congressmen.

However, there were white Americans who did not want equality for blacks and had already slowly started to take away the rights that blacks thought had been guaranteed. States began to put conditions on a person's right to vote. There were poll taxes that blacks could not afford; literacy tests that blacks who were not educated could not read; "grandfather clauses" which restricted the right to vote to those whose grandfathers had been free persons. These laws restricted but did not stop black voters so fear and intimidation were also used. This was also the beginnings of white supremacist groups like the Ku Klux Klan who used terror and intimidation to stop blacks from participating in the political process and to keep them in a subordinate condition. In 1883 there were 53 reported lynchings of black men; in 1886, 74; and in 1897, 123. From 1883 to 1952 there were reported lynchings every year.

"Jim Crow" also emerged during this period. Essentially based on racist ideology the Jim Crow system and laws came to represent a doctrine described as "separate but equal". In 1883 when the Civil Rights Act was deemed unconstitutional and in 1896 when the Supreme Court upheld the separate but equal doctrine in *Plessy v. Ferguson* the Jim Crow system was firmly in place and would remain secure well into the middle of the twentieth century. Those blacks who immigrated to the north found that they faced the same discrimination and where the discrimination was not legal in the form of ordinances *de facto* segregation had virtually the same effect.

Black organizations

The period between the end of Reconstruction and the Civil Rights Movement of the 1960s seem deceptively calm. Blacks seemed to have become complacent and to accept the inequality in the USA despite the fact that these rights were guaranteed in the Constitution. It was during this period, however, that the legal, political, economical and educational foundations were being laid and organizations being formed that would later be used in the 1960s to attain civil rights for blacks. During this time when blacks found that they were not welcome at white institutions black colleges and universities became very popular. Black fraternities and sororities emerged and the United Negro College Fund was incorporated in 1944.

The legal foundations were also being laid as the Supreme Court slowly eroded the oppressive laws and practices of the southern as well as the northern states. One such example came as early as 1915 when the Supreme Court in the case of *Guinn v. United States* held that grandfather clauses in the Oklahoma and Maryland constitutions violated the

15th Amendment. This was also followed by similar decisions such as the decisions in *Buchanan v. Warley* in which the Court struck down a Kentucky ordinance requiring separate black and white residential areas. The NAACP Legal Defence and Educational Fund was incorporated in 1939 with Thurgood Marshall as director. He would later become the first black US Supreme Court Justice. In 1946 the US Supreme Court banned segregation in interstate bus travel.

The beginnings of the civil disobedience movement was also present during this period and political organizations that would be influential during the Civil Rights movement of the 1960s were formed. The National Association for the Advancement of Coloured People (NAACP) was formed in 1901. This was followed by the formation of the National Urban League in 1911. In 1942 blacks and whites organized the Congress of Race Equality in Chicago and some of its members staged a sit-in. This organization would later play a major role during the 1960s Civil Rights movement. A march on Washington was planned to protest discrimination in the armed forces but was called off after President Roosevelt met with black leaders and issued Executive Order 8802, forbidding racial and religious discrimination in war industries and government training programmes. The first black congressman was elected from the east coast, Adam Clayton Powell, in 1944. In 1947 the NAACP drew up a petition on racism and presented it to the United Nations.

Blacks were also emerging in other areas. The early part of the century saw blacks involved in the arts, entertainment and sports and gaining wide acclaim and acceptance by whites. In 1938 when a black artist Marian Anderson could not perform in Constitutional Hall an estimated 75,000 black and white supporters attended an outdoor concert at the Lincoln Monument in Washington D.C. This was the time of the Harlem renaissance. Jesse Owens, a black athlete, won four gold medals at the 1936 Olympic Games. The armed forces were desegregated in 1948. In 1950 Gwendolyn Brooks, a black poet, was awarded the Pulitzer Prize and in 1952 the Tuskegee Institute reported that there were no lynchings that year for the first time in 71 years.

The Civil Rights Movement

The Civil Rights Movement which had begun unofficially years earlier finally resulted in major gains for blacks educationally, socially, politically,

legally and economically during the 1960s. Modelled after the teachings of Gandhi, Black Americans and white supporters led by Dr Martin Luther King Jr were able to gain legal and political advances in their struggle for equality through nonviolent protest and civil disobedience. Dr King was first recognized when he organized the year-long Montgomery, Alabama, bus boycott during 1955. The blacks in the city boycotted the buses to protest the arrest of Rosa Parks, a black woman who refused to give up her seat to a white man and move to the rear of the bus.[1]

The Civil Rights Movement was composed of various different groups like the Student Nonviolent Coordinating Committee (SNCC) founded in 1960 and other already established groups like the NAACP and CORE. It was characterized by sit-ins which blacks and white supporters sat-in at white-only establishments and refused to move. Civil Rights activists also participated in "Freedom Rides" to reinforce desegregation, and instituted voter registration drives all over the south to ensure that black voters would be represented.

However, the 1960s also saw strong opposition from whites who did not want desegregation and did not believe in equal rights for blacks. Lynchings began again as white opposition increased, riots and protests became more frequent, symbolized most vividly in Alabama in 1963 as nonviolent marchers were attacked by police with fire hoses and dogs. In the south there were numerous bombings and killings and some civil rights activists and supporters lost their lives.

Opposition to civil rights implementation was not confined to the south though this was the area in which the most violent protests occurred. Civil Rights leaders, activists and students were also fighting to end *de facto* segregation in the north as well. At schools and universities throughout the north students staged walkouts and protests to draw attention to such segregation. In 1963 in one of the largest civil rights demonstrations in history more than 250,000 Americans participated in the March on Washington. Among the supporters were people from every walk of life including religious leaders from the Protestant, Catholic, and Jewish faiths.

Other organizations and movements grew out of the Civil Rights Movement. A strong sense of nationalism was beginning and it manifested itself in the Nation of Islam whose members established temples throughout the north and recruited many followers. Among their most influential and prominent leaders was Malcolm X. Other organizations

---

[1]Dr King was later awarded the Nobel Prize for Peace for his non-violent efforts against racist practices. He was assassinated in Memphis, Tennessee, in 1968. In 1986 a public holiday was instituted to commemorate his work — the first time a Black American has been so remembered.

also emerged as more and more blacks became frustrated by the seemingly long road to equality. The Black Power movement was formed in 1966 by Stokely Carmichael of SNCC and Floyd McKissick of CORE. Their strategy was based on black control of institutions, organizations, resources and the formation of black political parties. The Black Panther party was formed in 1966. These years saw black anger and frustration in the ghettos of the big northern and western cities finally boil over into massive riots in which lives were lost and property destroyed.

By the end of the 1960s blacks had attained very significant advances. The Supreme Court which had for a long time appeared to be working alone in safeguarding the rights guaranteed to blacks in the US Constitution was now being supported by both the legislative and judicial branches of government. In 1964 the Civil Rights Act was passed which outlawed discrimination in public facilities and was followed a year later by the Voting Rights Act which enabled blacks to participate fully in state and federal elections. For the first time since Reconstruction there was once again a black senator in Congress, Edward Brooks of Massachusetts. In 1965 President Johnson also issued an Executive Order requiring all federal contractors to have affirmative action programmes and implemented compliance by loss of contracts and other penalties. In addition an anti-poverty campaign was launched and equal employment opportunity laws were also passed.

Political developments

The effect of the 1960s is that blacks have managed to do relatively well in local and regional politics. While in the past many Black Americans gave their allegiance to the Republican Party because of its association with Lincoln, today they are overwhelmingly Democrat Party voters. There are approximately 6,000 black elected officials. In more and more cities blacks are competing for mayoral positions as is currently happening in Chicago and New York, while in Atlanta, Georgia there has been a black mayor for more than 16 years. However, blacks do not seem to fare as well on the national level (at the present there are no black senators) but recent events seem to suggest that this may be changing. In the 1988 presidential elections Jesse Jackson, a black candidate, placed a healthy second in the Democrat leadership race, and Ron Brown the lawyer who chaired Jackson's campaign later became chairman of the Democratic Party, the highest position ever gained by a black person in one of the main parties in the American political system.

Recent Supreme Court decisions however threaten to undo the 25 years of Civil Rights advances made by black Americans. The court by its recent decisions has been chipping away at the affirmative action programmes which require that blacks be given equal opportunities in employment. In June of 1989 the Court in a five-to-four decision said that white employees had the right to challenge affirmative action programmes for minorities. This case was brought by white firemen of Birmingham, Alabama, who challenged the fire department's new affirmative action programme. Before the affirmative action programme was introduced there were 42 black firemen out of 453 in Birmingham and none of them were ranked lieutenant, captain or battalion chief. The action was brought by firemen when the city promoted its first black lieutenant.

This was the third such decision made by the Supreme Court in 1989 which could have detrimental effects on Black Americans. The first of these decisions came in January 1989 when the court held unconstitutional a Virginia scheme which set aside 30% of public works contracts for minority-owned companies and contractors. The second decision came in June 1989 when the Supreme Court reversed an 18-year precedent regarding employment discrimination. The new decision said that in employment discrimination cases the burden of proof is now on the plaintiff. In previous cases when statistical evidence could be produced to suggest discrimination it was up to the company to disprove that this was not its policy.

Education

Most of the predominantly black colleges were established after the Civil War in the south. There were six such institutions in Atlanta alone, among them Spellman and Morehouse colleges and Howard University was also established in Washington D.C. At first, black colleges remained popular, because access to white institutions of higher education was limited since desegregation was practised institutionally or socially, but even today black institutions remain a viable source of black education in America.

In 1954 in the Supreme Court decision of *Brown v. Topeka Board of Education* the Supreme Court held that racial segregation in public schools was unconstitutional, and separate facilities were inherently unequal. This reversed the earlier separate but equal Supreme Court decision handed down in *Plessy v. Ferguson* in 1896. One of the most poignant examples of the struggle of blacks' fight for higher education and of the opposition of white Americans was the scene outside Little Rock Central High School in Little Rock, Arkansas, as nine black children tried to gain entrance and were stopped by the National Guard who were sent there by the Governor to block their entry. Later President Kennedy sent in paratroopers to ensure the safety of black children attempting to enter schools in the south where the separate but equal doctrine, though declared unconstitutional by the Supreme Court, was still being followed.

In order to desegregate schools "bussing" was used in both the north and the south. White and black children were sent to schools outside their immediate neighbourhoods. White children left the public schools to attend private schools. Bussing led to riots and protests and was later abandoned but the damage was already done. In some urban areas today public schools remain almost entirely black or white. With the declining prestige of the public school educational system and the financial inability of the majority of black families to send their children to private schools, black children once again face the prospect of inadequate education.

During the 1960s blacks not only fought for and won equal opportunities in education but also sought and attained curriculum provisions. They wanted courses that provided information on black American history as well as contributions made by black Americans. The effects of this aspect of the black American struggle can be seen most influentially at the university and college level where black studies classes are usually offered.

However, recent developments in the trends of the number of black students attending educational institutions are disturbing. During the 1980s the number of black males attending institutions of higher education has decreased significantly. 1988 statistics showed that one out of every three black children entering high school will drop out. Some leaders blame this trend on the Reagan administration which increasingly replaced college grants with loans and the apparent attitude of colleges which seem aggressively to recruit only those black students with athletic ability. Still others blame the problem on the drug-dominated societies of the urban areas in which most black Americans live.

Economic and social developments

The events of the 1960s, including affirmative action programmes, have helped a number of blacks economically. The federal government through equal opportunity laws and a commitment by businesses to recruit and retain minorities has given Black Americans a chance to improve their economic position. The number of middle-class blacks has risen significantly. This is in keeping with the overall prosperity of the past two decades. The overall poverty rate has fallen and during the

Reagan administration the unemployment rate declined by almost 3%.

However the number of poor black families has increased and continues to do so, even in cities like Atlanta whose overall economic success has allowed a strong black middle class to emerge. Approximately one third of the Black American population live at or below the poverty level, and even where employment rates are relatively high the problem still exists. According to the federal Equal Employment Opportunity Commission, even though blacks have an employment rate of 66% in 11 southern states, they hold jobs in the lowest-paying category. Real income for blacks has decreased by 20% over the past 10 years and in 1988 the average income for black families was 60% of that for whites. In 1980, 13% of America's black male population was classified as "inactive", i.e. not employed and not at school. Of black American children, 45.8% grow up in poverty. With the recent Supreme Court decisions and recent educational policies regarding college grants and loans many black leaders are beginning to fear that the traditional route to the middle class for the next generation of blacks has been greatly narrowed.

The life expectancy rate for blacks is lower than that for whites. In 1985 according to a report issued by the National Center for Health Statistics the life expectancy for blacks, which was 69.5 years, fell to 69.4, while that for whites increased to 75.4 years. Infant mortality is more than double that of whites and accounts for a large part of the difference in the expectancy figures.

In urban centres where blacks are concentrated schools are short of money, housing is bad and social services are poor. In these surroundings drug dealing and violence are common events. A system of poverty seems to have emerged that is passed down from generation to generation. During the 1980s the big cities have seen an increase in the number of gangs and gang-related deaths. The members of these gangs and the victims of their crimes are usually black teenage males. The problem has been linked to the illegal selling of drugs. Drugs remain a problem especially for young urban blacks who can earn hundreds of dollars daily when involved in the trafficking of illegal substances such as crack, a cheap cocaine mixture. Crack wars are now a major cause of death for America's young black male population. In Washington D.C., a city of barely 750,000, there were an estimated 308 murders in 1988. Most of the victims were black males 15 years or under.

Another troubling development is the increase in the number of black-on-black crimes and which are now higher than the overall American crime rate which itself is very high. The Bureau of Justice estimates that every one in 133 Americans will be the victim of homicide, but the figures for black males is one in 21. In addition there is a one in 10 chance that a black urban male will be the victim or perpetrator of a homicide, which is the leading cause of death for black males aged 15–34. While 83% of all Americans will be the victim of an attempted or completed crime, the rate for black males is 92%. In 1985 blacks accounted for 47% of those arrested for violent crimes and 62% of those arrested for robbery. Of the black victims of robbery 90% were robbed by other blacks. In Washington D.C. the murder rate has risen by 40% since 1987 and most victims and perpetrators are young black men. Black males now make up more than 40% of America's prison population and in some cities they account for more than 60% of the prison population, an alarming statistic given the fact that blacks make up less than 12% of the population. Recent surveys have shown that discrimination also exists within the judicial system, with, for example, blacks more likely to be given the death penalty in states where it exists than are whites convicted of the same crimes.

Current issues

Some black organizations supported by a growing number of black leaders argue that blacks should be paid reparation as compensation for slavery just as the Japanese-Americans were paid for the period during World War II when they were interned in government camps. They argue that this money can be given to black organizations to enable them to develop institutions and services that could aid the descendants of slaves in America on economic, educational and political levels. So far the question, although an important one, has not been addressed in the political arena in a substantive way.

Another recent development concerns a name change for Black Americans. Some prominent Black Americans, Jesse Jackson among them, have been arguing that Black Americans should cease to be called black and should be referred to as African-Americans. This may seem like a minute point but socially and culturally this has a great deal of significance. What blacks call themselves has been of great importance to them ever since emancipation. A name change has accompanied every change in self-awareness and political activity. During the days of slavery blacks were given their name and identity by their masters who could change their name at any time. When blacks were emancipated they rejected the name negro and began to use the term coloured. During the 1960s when it became beautiful to be black the term was once again changed to reflect the changing black perception of themselves. At a time when poverty is high, drug abuse is increasing, family disruption is prevalent in most black urban communities and the number of racially motivated attacks on minorities has increased, the time may be right for a name change and a new sense of pride and reaffirmation of goals and ideals for Black/African-Americans.

French Canadians

Alternative names: **"Quebecois" (in Quebec), Arcadians (in eastern states)**
Location: **80% in Quebec, remainder throughout Canada**
Population: **6–6.5 million**
% of population: **25%; 80% of Quebec population**
Religion: **Catholic**
Language: **French-Canadian[1]**

The French Canadians are the descendants of the French settlers who came to settle along the St Lawrence River and eastern seaboard from the early seventeenth century. They formed, and continue as, a distinctive linguistic and cultural group within Canada which has resisted assimilation into the Anglo-Protestant Canadian mainstream (although this itself is today far more diffuse after large-scale Eastern European and non-European migration) and seeks greater communal autonomy and linguistic protection. French-Canadians form about one quarter of the Canadian population and 80% live in the province of Quebec with smaller communities elsewhere.

The colonial period

French settlers came to Canada from 1608 in the wake of French trading companies. They settled on

[1]French Canadian as distinguished from standard French.

the banks of the St Lawrence River, founding small rural parishes, where the Catholic Church played a dominant role in cultural and social life. The settlers were of homogenous social origins and formed a strongly integrated society on the basis of common values, institutions, values and religion. By the time of the British conquest in 1760 the French settlements were already different in many ways from their origins in France, more conservative, more religious and with influences from the Indian peoples that surrounded them.

The British conquest removed French administrative structures and made the French Canadians a minority group. In 1763 the British attempted to enforce an assimilationist policy whereby the Catholic religion was not recognized, French Canadians were excluded from the administration and were made to swear allegiance to the British crown. However in 1774 this policy was reversed as the British needed French Canadian support against the American Revolution. The Quebec Act of 1774 restored the power of the Catholic Church and allowed the use of civil French laws which have continued in Quebec to this date. However the loss of the American colonies meant that loyalists settled in Canada, which both disrupted the cultural homogeneity of the French settlements and brought liberal ideas. The Constitutional Act of 1791 divided the colony into Upper and Lower Canada, where English and French Canadians respectively predominated, the first increasingly commercial and trade oriented, the second overwhelmingly rural.

Difficult economic conditions and political discontent produced the French Canadian rebellion of 1837-38. The rebellion was put down after two brief military campaigns but an enquiry for the British government by Lord Durham found "two nations at war within one state". He recommended the political union of the two provinces in order to assimilate the French (whom he considered to be inferior). The Union Act of 1840 gave equal representation to both Lower and Upper Canada, although the French were at this stage the majority of the population, and did not recognize the use of the French language in the Assembly. British immigration was encouraged and only a decade later the French were the minority population. The French response to these developments took two complementary forms. Politically they endeavoured to gain some rights within the system and eventually obtained recognition of the French language, participation in the system of political patronage and some compensation for losses suffered during the rebellion. Socially they became more conservative and inward looking, upholding the Catholic faith, the French language and a number of traditions and customs.

Federation

The need for economic unity brought further constitutional change in the British North American Act of 1867 which united four provinces (Ontario — formerly Upper Canada, New Brunswick, Nova Scotia, and Quebec — formerly Lower Canada) into a federation. While the federal government controlled economic and foreign affairs, the provinces were given socio-cultural areas, education, cultural and civil rights. The new constitution guaranteed certain language rights to the francophone minority such as the right to use French in Parliament and the federal courts, as well as in courts in Quebec. Within Quebec itself civil French law was recognized and upheld and the French language had equal status to English in official matters. There was no mention of the linguistic rights of Francophone minorities residing outside Quebec. Certain rights based on religion (e.g. Catholic and Protestant schools) were recognized but this did not stop the passing of legislation unfavourable to French speakers outside Quebec as happened in Ontario and Manitoba.

French Canadians found themselves increasingly disadvantaged. Preference in immigration to immigrants from the British Isles and northern Europe and the addition of new western provinces to the federation meant that the proportion of French Canadians in the population dropped, despite their high birthrates. Political decisions in foreign affairs which supported Britain alienated French Canadians and provoked serious political crises within Canada. The most radical changes came from within Quebec as the rural-based society began to change into an urban and industrial one. In 1900 Quebecois society was 60% rural but by 1931 it had become 63% urban, most notably in Montreal and Quebec City. The church lost some of its influence and a new class of nationalist and radical intellectuals and trade unionists emerged. There was growing resentment not just at English-speaking Canadians but at economic domination by Canadian and US firms.

The "Quiet Revolution" in the 1960s

In the early 1960s a new group of intellectuals who rejected the traditional French Canadian culture and isolation took power in Quebec. They rejected the idea of conserving a rural society but instead wished to build an industrial, pluralist and French society. They looked to neighbouring Ontario and the USA as economic models and of a Quebecois society for Quebecois rather than a separate French Canadian society. One of the first sectors to be affected was education, where the state took over from the church and made the system more democratic and accessible. Similar reforms took place with regard to health and welfare. The state, which had previously been non-interventionist, began to intervene in the economy creating state companies and greatly increasing the numbers working in the civil service. Instead of leaving the federal government to establish modernization programmes the state government took this responsibility onto itself and withdrew from some federal programmes. It built up direct contacts with France and Francophone countries and attempted to build up an international profile for itself, brought to world attention in President de Gaulle's visit of 1968 when he proclaimed "Long live a Free Quebec". From the middle of the 1960s the movement for a "Quiet Revolution" began to lose momentum as economic difficulties and labour unrest increased, and the anglophone upper and middle classes resented the changes that were being made to increase the power of both the state and the French speakers. The "quiet revolution" ushered in an era of artistic and literary flowering in French-speaking Canada.

In October 1970 a political crisis developed as the result of the abduction of the British Consul and the violent murder of the Labour Minister of Quebec, by Quebec separatists from the Front de Libération de Québec (FLQ). The kidnappers demanded a ransom, safe passage and the publication of an FLQ manifesto. Following unsuccessful negotiations, the Canadian government invoked at the request of the Quebec government the 1914 War Measures Act providing for emergency powers and several hundred political suspects were arrested, although most were soon released. Despite the fact that most Quebecois did not support the methods of the FLQ, there was some sympathy for their aims of independence. This was reflected in the surprise victory of the Parti Québécois (PQ), under the leadership of René Levesque, in Quebec in 1976. The PQ did not support complete separation as such but had as its aim to achieve political sovereignty in economic association with Canada.

The language question

The 1960s and 1970s saw profound social changes in Quebec. The birthrate, once among the highest in the world, dropped to become the lowest in Canada. With a high birthrate French Canadians were able to maintain their share of the Quebecois population even though there were extensive immigration both from English speakers and non-

English speaking immigrants. This would not have mattered greatly if there had been significant recruitment of French speakers from other sectors of the population. But few English speakers wished to learn French and most immigrants preferred to have their children educated in English which they saw as more advantageous for employment.[2] The more immigrants tended to become anglophones the more isolated and hostile French Canadians became. Some of this feeling resulted in provincial legislation to protect the French language. This process had actually begun in 1963 with the Royal Commission on Bilingualism and Biculturalism established by the federal government. One of its main recommendations was the establishment of bilingual districts in places where the minority language is spoken by at least 10% of the local population, and the use of both official languages in government services, schools and courts. The studies of the Royal Commission showed disparities in income, education and employment between French and English speakers in Quebec with the French speakers greatly disadvantaged.

In 1968 the provincial government established a commission into the French language and the means of promoting it in Quebec. At the end of 1972 the Commission produced its report in which it confirmed the observations made by the Royal Commission. It recommended that French be made the official language of Quebec and that measures be taken to increase the use of French in the workplace and in education. However it supported the use of persuasion rather than constraint in the use of French. In 1974 the provincial government adopted a new and controversial language law which made French the official language and restricted for the first time the right of parents to choose the language in which children could be educated. Further measures were implemented by the PQ government which in 1977 adopted a "Charter of the French language" which made French the official language of Quebec, to be used in government administration, in government contracts and collective bargaining agreements, and in nursery, primary and secondary schools. This new language policy created great antagonism among those who were opposed to it, most notably Anglophones and immigrants. However it did appear to create conditions favourable to French speakers and the 1981 census showed that the numbers of Quebec residents whose first language was English dropped in five years from 800,000 to 706,000 — about 11% of the population.

---

[2]The present Quebec government has attempted to overcome this by paying families larger amounts for third or subsequent children and recruiting French-speaking immigrants from France, Lebanon and Haiti. Haitians now comprise the largest numbers of French-speaking immigrants; they are reported to have faced racial discrimination from some French Canadians.

Political status

Two political and constitutional developments at the beginning of the 1980s have laid the basis for present developments in Quebec. One was the referendum defeat of a proposal for Quebec sovereignty in May 1980 and the other the repatriation of the Canadian Constitution in 1982. The referendum, sponsored by the PQ, asked voters to choose between the present status and a form of "sovereignty-association" which was widely seen as a step towards separation and Quebec independence. Sixty per cent voted against the option, including 52% of the French-speaking population and 95% of non-French speakers. The result was a blow for PQ, which however accepted the result and which, despite divisions and the formation of a pro-independence group within the PQ, voted in January 1985, to drop its long-term goal of independence. The PQ lost office in the Quebec elections of 1985 winning only 23 of the 122 seats to the Liberal Party's (LP) 99. In September 1988 under a new leader it again adopted a pro-independence policy. By this time it had lost much of its former support and trailed well behind the ruling LP in the opinion polls.

The 1982 repatriation of the British North America Act of 1867 and the adoption of a new Canadian Constitution also produced conflicts between Quebec and the federal government. Quebec was concerned that the powers given to the central government would override specific laws concerning language protection and promote greater centralization. Therefore, alone of the 10 Canadian provinces, Quebec refused to accede to the Constitution and agreement to do so only came well after the LP victory of 1985 when the federal government, in an agreement known as the Meech Lake accord, recognized Quebec's distinctive identity and culture and its powers to protect the French language. To date however Quebec has not yet signed the Constitution.

A further crisis over language policy developed in late 1988, when the Canadian Supreme Court ruled that part of the 1977 French Language Charter, which dealt with provisions for French language only on commercial and public signs, was invalid as it ignored the fundamental rights of non-French speakers. The Quebec government announced that it would compromise on some aspects but would not abandon its French language policy. The issue provoked divisions in both the province and the government with three English-speaking cabinet ministers resigning. Mass rallies were held and there were threats of violence from both French- and English-speaking extremists.

French speakers outside Quebec

There are about one million French-Canadians in provinces other than Quebec. None of these groups comprise a majority, most are relatively small and probably declining in numbers, as urbanization increases and isolated French-speaking communities become rarer.

The eastern state of New Brunswick has the highest proportion outside Quebec. One third of its population of 700,000 are French speaking, mainly concentrated in the north and north-east. French speakers here are known as "Arcadians"[3] as are communities in the other maritime states. New Brunswick has special legislation to protect the French language and it is given official status as a language of education. Arcadians have formed an Arcadian political party which urges that a separate Arcadian province be created from French-speaking areas in New Brunswick; it won 10% of the vote in the 1979 provincial elections. Arcadians are concentrated in forestry and fishing sectors and are the poorest section of the New Brunswick population.

The largest non-Quebecois French minority is found in Ontario where there may be half-a-million people of French origin. But not all speak French fluently and the numbers appear to be dropping. There are no official guarantees for the protection of French speakers and although French is recognized as a language of education it is not given as an automatic right. In Manitoba French Canadians once formed a majority of the population; today they are about 6% of the population and only two-thirds of these speak fluent French. In 1980 a Supreme Court ruling overturned the previous English-language-only policy of the Manitoba government; further favourable rulings followed. However most of the population of Manitoba appears to be against recognition of French as an official language and in 1984 an attempt to make both English and French official languages failed.

(See also *Mexican Americans*)

---

[3]The Arcadians refused to swear allegiance to the British crown in 1755. The British authorities rounded them up, destroyed their farms and deported them to American colonies. Many later returned to Canada while others became the "Cajuns" — French speakers in Louisiana.

Hawaiians, Indigenous

Alternative names: "Native Hawaiians"
Location: Hawaii
Population: 180,000 with 50% or greater Hawaiian ancestry
% of population: 18% of Hawaiian population
Religion: Christian, indigenous religious practices
Language: English, Hawaiian languages

Indigenous Hawaiians are the descendants of the original Polynesian inhabitants of the Hawaiian Islands, a group of islands in the eastern Pacific. Formerly an independent kingdom and later a US territory, from 1959 Hawaii became the 50th US state. Today two groups are recognized under US law. "Native Hawaiians" are those with over 50% Hawaiian blood while "Hawaiians" have less than 50% Hawaiian blood or cannot prove their exact descent. The two groups are roughly equal in size and together total about 180,000 of the one million strong mixed immigrant population.

Polynesian peoples have lived in the Hawaiian islands for thousands of years. Although they were skilful navigators and traded with other Pacific peoples they were relatively isolated. European contacts began from the eighteenth century, when explorers and missionaries came to the islands. Hawaiian society was complex and hierarchical in many respects with traditional chiefs, royal lineages and a ruling monarch. From 1779 to 1893 the kingdom of Hawaii was recognized as a sovereign nation, entering into treaties and conventions with many governments.

Despite its independence Hawaii was placed under considerable pressure from foreign contacts. Christian missionaries arrived from 1820 and established a strong influence in religious and secular life. Land ownership was codified into an Anglo-American system where it could be sold in fee simple, in contrast to the Hawaiian system where it was not owned in the western sense but allocated by the *moi*, the ruling chief of each island. Since Hawaiians did not understand the new land laws, they did not register their title, and thus large areas passed under the control of foreign individuals and corporations. Because many Hawaiians refused to work on the new sugar plantations at the low wages offered, workers from Asia were imported. The "missionary party", an alliance of missionary offspring and business, became the most powerful force in the islands.

US annexation

It was these groups who urged that Hawaii should have closer links with the USA, either by Treaties or Reciprocity or, preferably, by annexation. This was both to secure markets for plantation produce and to gain Pearl Harbor as a US naval base. The Hawaiian monarch, King David Kalakaua, opposed these plans, but in 1887, under force of arms and threat of death to himself, his family and supporters, he signed what became known as the "Bayonet Constitution". This constitution stripped him of power and gave control of the House of Nobles to the missionary party. Pearl Harbor was handed over to the US and the Reciprocity Treaty was extended. Kalakaua died in 1891 and was succeeded by his sister Liliuokalani, who was shortly after petitioned by two-thirds of Hawaiian voters (this included settlers as well as Hawaiians) to restore the old system of government. By January 1893 she had completed the draft of a new constitution and stated . . . "I shall firmly endeavour to preserve the autonomy and absolute independence of this Kingdom".

Those who favoured annexation, who were now joined by John L. Stevens, the American Minister Plenipotentiary who had control over the American military based in Hawaii, launched a military takeover and established a "provisional government". Liliuokalani was forced to surrender her authority but did so to the US government rather than the "provisional government". President Harrison was willing to legalize annexation but the incoming President Grover Cleveland refused to do so and authorized an investigation into the circumstances of the military action. The investigation found that "the lawful government of Hawaii was overthrown" as a result of a conspiracy involving US forces. Cleveland refused to forward the Treaty to the Senate but the members of the provisional government refused to yield their power and US forces continued to remain in Hawaii. The provisional government announced the convening of a Constitutional Convention for the "Republic of Hawaii". Only those who renounced their loyalty to Queen Liliuokalani and who passed other tests could vote; in the event only 20% of eligible electors did so. The "Republic of Hawaii" was established on July 4, 1894.

It lasted for only four years for when William McKinley succeeded to the US presidency in 1898 the provisional government ceded "absolutely and without reserve to the USA all rights of sovereignty of whatsoever kind in and over the Hawaiian Islands". McKinley then obtained a joint resolution for the annexation from both Houses of Congress. The Organic Act of April 30, 1900 established a territorial government and declared all citizens of the Republic of Hawaii as automatically American citizens.

This period from 1900 saw an increase in the total population as many settlers came from the mainland USA and Asia to work on the plantations, a tightening of US economic control and the development of Pearl Harbor as an important military base. Hawaiians became a small and unprivileged minority group. In US-run schools children were forbidden to speak native languages, while traditional religious practices, dancing, music and healing practices were discouraged and parents were encouraged to give children English rather than Hawaiian names.

US statehood

Most native Hawaiians welcomed statehood in 1959 as they saw it as a means of gaining equal treatment with other Americans. Yet "Native Hawaiians" and "Hawaiians" remain massively disadvantaged economically and socially. Most Hawaiians today are city-dwelling wage labourers, concentrated in low-wage service sectors, with high levels of unemployment and underemployment. Few have direct access to land. Land Trusts were established during the period of direct US control and were later transferred to the Hawaiian state government, for benefit of Hawaiians, but only a small amount of this land has been transferred to Hawaiians while some areas have been leased to industry, agriculture and the US military. Hawaiians were found by a US Senate Select Committee on Indian Affairs to have lower life expectancy, higher levels of disease, higher rates of social

problems and limited availability to social services than other Americans.

In the 1970s a Hawaiian "nationalist" movement has emerged focusing on many of the issues that have engaged other colonized indigenous peoples; land rights, language, cultural and religious practices, discrimination. In 1976 religious claims were first brought against the federal government for respect for Hawaiian sacred sites, including burial areas. In response state legislation created an Office of Hawaiian Affairs to recognize Hawaiians and their concerns as identical to those of Native Americans. However at the federal level Hawaiians do not have the same "nation to nation" relationship as implied in treaty agreements with indigenous American Indian communities, since no treaties were signed at the time of the US annexation.

There have been attempts by Indigenous Hawaiians to recreate a Hawaiian identity. There has been a revival of interest in relearning the Hawaiian languages, which few Hawaiians today speak fluently, and in learning traditional arts such as chanting, weaving, feather *leis* and the *hula*. Traditional religious practices, such as *pele*, or the spirit of the volcano, which were once forbidden and are now guaranteed under the Hawaiian state Constitution (Article 12, Section 7) have been retaught to a new generation. Campaigns have been launched around the protection of land, especially sacred sites, from desecration by the military, energy interests or the tourist industry. For example the Protect *Kaho'olawe'Ohana* movement has organized since 1976 to stop the US and other military forces from shelling the sacred island of Kaho'olawe in military exercises; Indigenous Hawaiians joined environmental groups to protest the building of a geothermal energy-producing facility at Kilauea Volcano, Big Island, and in 1987 protests took place against the exhumation of a traditional burial site to build a hotel.

Indians and Metis of Canada

Alternative names: **Various tribal names**
Location: **throughout Canada**
Population: **625,000–1.2 million**
% of population: **2.5%–4.75%**
Religion: **Christianity, various Indian beliefs**
Language: **English, Indian languages**

The Indians are survivors of small aboriginal societies, most of whose land was colonized by Europeans, and who have been unable either to retain fully their traditional way of life or to adapt successfully to the alien social structure of their colonizers. The Metis are peoples of Indian and Euro-

pean descent who are not always recognized as Indians. Indians and Metis are divided not only by tribe and language group but by artificial legal classifications.

Indians are classified legally as either Status or non-Status Indians. Status Indians are native people defined as Indian under the Indian Act of 1880 and are the direct responsibility of the federal government. They number about 326,000, are registered as part of an Indian band and live or are entitled to live on a reserve. Some 573 bands have the use of 2,243 reserves with a total area of just over six million acres, but 30% of Status Indians now live away from reserves. They have some privileges, such as exemption from certain taxes, but their freedom is heavily restricted in other areas; for example their land, education and economic enterprises are controlled by the administration. Approximately half of the Status Indians are Treaty Indians; their ancestors signed treaties with the government which surrendered lands in exchange for reserves and certain services.

Status Indians may renounce their special legal standing, receive their share of the band's resources and give up their right to a home on the reserve to live as ordinary Canadian citizens. This process is known as "enfranchisement" and this decision is not only irrevocable but applies to their descendants as well as to their immediate family. Indian status may also be lost or gained through marriage. Because of this and other peculiar legal distinctions set forth in the Indian Act it can sometimes happen that a full blooded Indian has no Indian status, while persons without any native ancestry can belong to a band and live on a reserve.

There are probably about 300,000 non-Status Indians, individuals of native ancestry who have given up or lost their Indian status because of legal distinctions and are therefore not recognized as Indian. Most are Metis, of mixed white/Indian descent, but many have more Indian blood than some of the status group. Often shunned by both Indian and white society, most have not totally been absorbed into the mainstream of Canadian society and continue to follow a traditional way of life, though they have none of the privileges of Indians under the law and are therefore often poorer than their status relatives.

The numbers of Metis are the most difficult to estimate. The last Canadian census indicated that 90,000 people identified themselves as Metis but Metis organizations have claimed numbers up to 850,000. The position of Metis is the most ambiguous of all the indigenous groups but it may be that a new sense of pride in their heritage is increasing the numbers of Metis who wish to be so identified. Metis mainly live in the western provinces of Manitoba, Saskatchewan and Alberta.

Background and history

"Indian" is a term that encompasses a wide range of peoples. In pre-European times the Indians probably numbered between 200,000 and 300,000

peoples living throughout the area which is now Canada. They were divided among 50 distinct societies with their own cultural characteristics and dialects or languages. There were 10 different language families, six in the area west of the Rocky mountains and four over the rest of the country. The social and economic structure of each band depended on the region in which they lived, but all had oral traditions, taboos played an important role in society, and their religion was animistic based on an idea of a spirit world parallel to their own with powerful supernatural beings who influenced their lives.

The forest area, which stretched from the Atlantic coast to the Rockies, was inhabited by Indians belonging to the Algonkian and Athapaskan language families. They depended on hunting large animals like caribou and moose, supplemented by smaller mammals, wild plants and fish. They had a migratory existence living in temporary shelter and following the seasonal movement of game. They had no strong system of leadership and depended on co-operation and a strong sense of mutual responsibility. This type of social and political structure was followed by Indians who lived just below the arctic tundra region as well as by the Siouan speaking people who lived in the prairie region south of the forest area.

West of the Rockies was the Pacific coast region with its more temperate climate and abundance of wildlife. The Indians in this area depended partly on food gathering and hunting but primarily on fishing. They lived in permanent village communities and had a comparatively high population density. They were organized into hierarchical chiefdoms and a person's status and place in the group was determined by birth and wealth.

East of the forest region in what is now southern Quebec and stretching south across the modern US/Canadian border lived the Iroquian speaking people. They were the most northerly of a series of hunting tribes that stretched along the Atlantic seaboard of what is now the USA. They were warlike and constantly fought among themselves, lived in permanent villages, had an agricultural economy, and their societal structure was matrilineal. Women owned the houses and land and did most of the cultivation of crops while the men defended the settlements and did some hunting to supplement the agricultural economy. Though men held offices as leaders and decision makers they were appointed to these offices by women. During the sixteenth century the Indians of this area formed three confederacies. Only one survived, the League of Five Nations, and until 200 years ago it remained a major political force.

In 1608 when the first permanent white settlement was established in Quebec as an economic venture to exploit the possibilities of the fur trade, the Indians helped the early settlers to survive and trade was established between the two groups. The Indians traded furs and provided guides in exchange for military assistance which they used against their traditional enemies. Over time the Indians lost the art of making their own weapons and relied entirely on those of the whites. Migratory bands who were hunters for use were transformed into hunters for trade and thus social structures were radically changed. Between the sixteenth and the nineteenth centuries there was intensive European colonial expansion. In the early stages of colonization the Indian was vital to European survival so the tribe was able to retain much of their land and independence. Three important factors shaped the lives of the Indians in the early stages of colonization; the economic considerations of the fur traders, the religious considerations of the missionaries and the military considerations of the French and English who were at war over control of the colony. It was with these considerations in mind that the Proclamation of 1763 was issued by the British. Firm boundaries were drawn between Indian territory and colonial lands and Indians had legal title to the lands which they occupied, on which no white settlements were allowed. These rights could only be extinguished by a treaty with the crown.

By the middle of the nineteenth century Europeans had become well enough established to dispense with the assistance and co-operation of the native people. With the end of the French/English hostilities, the rebellion of the American colonies and the defeat of the British in 1783, expansion began in earnest. The main objective of the whites became settlement and new policies were introduced. During the 1850s and 1860s treaties were entered into with the Indians in which land was exchanged for services. After all of Britain's North American possessions except Newfoundland had passed to Canada the Indian Act of 1880 was passed, which deprived the Indians of most of their lands and isolated them from white society.

The Indian Act was one of a series of Acts that were passed during the last 30 years of the nineteenth century. These Acts placed restrictions on the Indians and gave the government absolute power to organize their lives. Indians were removed to small reserves where they could pose no threat to white settlement, and could be shielded from unscrupulous drink pedlars and other undesirable products of white society. The Indians lost control over virtually every aspect of their lives. The Minister of Indian Affairs had responsibility for the band's resources, including land and livestock, ultimate authority over medical services, and employment; could dismiss the chief

and council if he chose and could countermand any of their decisions.

Indians adjusted differently depending on their culture and history. The maritime Indians, with their long history of friendly relations with the French, and the west coast Indians, with their hierarchical systems of government, found it easier to deal with the new policies of the whites than did the forest Indians, who found it hard to understand the political and legal institutions of the Europeans and could not adjust to materialistic and competitive values. The Metis under Louis Riel declared an independent republic at Batoche in Saskatchewan, demanding basic rights. The government sent in mounted police and army units to arrest the leaders and return the Indians forcibly to reserves. By 1901 the Indian population had been reduced to approximately one third of its pre-European level.

Political developments

During the 1920s and 1930s Canadian Indians made attempts to form native associations but these were hampered by suspicion and inexperience. Many Indians served in the Canadian armed forces during World War II, some with distinction. This experience brought members of the white and Indian communities together and highlighted the problems and the differences between their conditions. As a result in the late 1940s the Senate established a committee to reconsider the Indian Act. For the first time Indians were consulted before changes were implemented and a new Indian Act was passed in 1951 which gave the band councils greater autonomy and eased certain legal restrictions. The government also reconsidered its educational responsibilities, health services were improved and expenditures on Indians increased. Although the government was spending more money on the Indians the main beneficiary of the increased budget was not the Indians but the expanded government departments. This accentuated the problems of inefficiency and unresponsiveness and hampered the implementation of urgently needed projects.

The 1960s brought change in native attitudes and saw increased political and social activity by Indians as well as cultural awareness and pride. The National Indian Council was formed during the early 1960s. It was the first nationwide organization of its kind and represented both Status and non-Status Indians. In 1967 the organization dissolved and eventually became two new organizations: the Native Council of Canada, which represented non-Status Indians, and the National Indian Brotherhood (NIB), which represented Status Indians. This new generation of Indian leaders was articulate and better educated that their predecessors. They understood the nature of white institutions. They focused on land and treaty rights, socio-economic development and education, but sought to attain these changes without renouncing their Indianness. In 1966 Indian administration was moved to the newly formed Department of Indian Affairs and Northern Development, and in 1969 the White Paper document was issued. Indian leaders had not been consulted before the proposal was put forth and their organizations joined together to denounce the proposal which they saw as an attempt to abolish their few remaining rights. Their efforts were successful and the document was later abandoned.

Land rights

The most controversial issue remains land rights. Among Status Indians 50% are Treaty Indians. These treaties were signed "for as long as the sun shall shine" to there is legal recognition of their land rights. The Non-Treaty Indians however have had to pressure the government for any agreements on aboriginal rights. They argued that the Proclamation of 1763, which had never been repealed, stated and confirmed the official policy of aboriginal land title. If true they would have a claim for more than half of Canada and their leaders are seeking settlements based on recognition of this claim.

In the 1970s the Indians gathered legal support for their demand for recognition of their aboriginal rights and in 1973, in British Columbia, the Nishga tribe made such a claim in court. Although they lost the case in a four-to-three decision of the Supreme Court of Canada the head of the Department of Indian Affairs issued a policy statement that the government would observe the spirit of treaties as well as the letter.

With the oil crisis of the early 1970s the government tried harder to settle claims with the Indians so that areas could be opened up for development. In 1975 the first comprehensive land claims settlement agreement was signed between the federal government, the provincial government of Quebec, and the Cree Indians and Inuits of the James Bay area. The agreement gave the Cree and the Inuit exclusive use of 5,408 square miles, exclusive hunting, fishing and trapping rights in an additional 60,000 square miles and a certain amount of power to influence the nature of development. Over a period of time the native peoples will also receive $225 million as compensation for their extinguished aboriginal title.

In other areas of Canada however solutions have not been readily available. The Nishga Indians who have been demanding recognition of their land rights as early as the 1900s have been continually impeded by the provincial government of British Columbia. After demonstrations, boycotts and protests, the provincial government finally arranged for a meeting with the Minister of Indian Affairs and the Nishga tribal government. In addition, agreements in the Northwest Territories have been slow to materialize because of the split that has occurred among the Indians themselves.

Land struggles, some of them involving the use of force by the government, have continued throughout Canada. Some Indian nations have straddled the US/Canadian border and have continued to travel and trade across the border without restrictions. An attempt to tax the internal trade of the Haudenoshaunee Mohawk people at Kahnawake, Quebec, by the Canadian government in June 1988 led to a number of arrests. In Alberta the Lubicon Lake Cree people, who had been offered a reserve by the federal government almost half a century before but had never received it, blockaded 90 square kilometres of their traditional land in October 1988 and declared a sovereign nation with rights and legislation. They were especially angered by the fact that the land had been used extensively for oil drilling, ruining the traditional fishing and hunting economy, yet the Lubicon had never received any compensation or royalties. After six days of blockade and many arrests, the Alberta Premier agreed to negotiate with the Lubicon Lake chief and the Lubicon were promised a reserve. However there were many problems with the federal government on the question of third party rights and financial subsidies and the issue resulted in protracted legal proceedings. There are also threats to the peoples of the West Coast, such as the Haida, where extensive logging has destroyed forests.

The publication in 1986 of "Living Treaties: Lasting Agreements", the final report of the Task Force on comprehensive claims (areas of Canada where the government has never made any settlement over land) is a landmark in official understanding of comprehensive claims and should, if implemented, mark a major advance for Indian groups in isolated areas such as NWT, Yukon, British Columbia, Labrador and mainland Newfoundland.

Constitutional changes

Native rights were recognized and protected under the Royal Proclamation of 1763 and later the British North America Act of 1867. From the late 1970s there were efforts by the Liberal Party government of Pierre Trudeau to "patriate" the Canadian Constitution, in part prompted by separatist pressure from Quebec. This aroused fears in Indian, Metis and Inuit communities who had noted Trudeau's 1969 proposals to end the special status of Indian communities. Indigenous groups began a process of publicizing and lobbying, not only in Canada but in the UK, the ex-colonial power and holder of the Constitution. Trudeau initially promised to give "a high priority to the involvement of Indian, Inuit and Metis representatives in the process of constitutional reform" but only at a special conference to be convened after the patriation had been completed and the basic structures of the new arrangements completed. The Indians had proposed that a clause stating "The Aboriginal rights and treaty rights of the Aboriginal peoples of Canada are hereby confirmed and recognized" and this was approved in an all-party agreement in the Canadian House of Commons in February 1981. Several provincial governments, however, refused to support the patriation plan unless this commitment was withdrawn, and as a result it was unanimously repudiated by the Prime Minister and 10 provincial ministers in November 1981. Subsequently a compromise was reached whereby the Canadian Constitution would contain the phrase: "The existing Aboriginal and treaty rights of the Aboriginal peoples of Canada are hereby recognized and affirmed", but this is less strong than the original proposal and there are fears that it could be used to limit the rights of native peoples.

Other fears were that aboriginal constitutional rights could be altered by majority vote. Since Indians and Metis are a minority in every state, they wished to entrench aboriginal rights to be invulnerable to popular pressures. They also wished to extend indigenous rights. In 1981 a last-minute amendment ensured that further talks on the constitution would continue between the federal and provincial governments and Indian groups. In 1984 the Constitution was amended to give constitutional protection to rights contained in existing or future land claims agreements and to guarantee that the constitutional rights of native people would not be altered without their participation.

Canada's federal structure has proved to be a major difficulty for native peoples. Some Indian groups, such as the Assembly of First Nations, representing Indians who are registered and recognized under federal legislation, has expressed fears that dealing with provincial governments could lead to compromises on their rights. Provinces have strongly resisted any attempts by either the federal government or Indian groups to restrict their autonomy. To date Quebec has not signed the 1982 Constitution and fears giving any sign that it recognizes indigenous rights as a federal sphere. Certainly the federal government appears to give greater weight to the views of the powerful provincial governments rather than the powerless Indians. In March 1987 a conference which could have lead to self-government for indigenous peoples ended in failure after three states — British Columbia, Alberta and Saskatchewan — vetoed a constitutional amendment and Quebec boycotted the meeting entirely. One month later the Lake Meech Accord between federal and provincial leaders recognized some minority rights for English and French speakers.

Social and educational developments

Reserves have been in effect for a hundred years and continue to shape the lives of native people. Reserves separate whites and Indians and tend to be small and isolated. They offer few opportunities because they have limited potential as farmland and are too small for the Indians to live by the traditional pursuits of hunting and trapping while their remoteness and small populations make them unattractive to industry. In law the reserves do not belong to the Indians but to the government whose duty it is to exploit the resources for the benefit of the Indians. If Indians want to initiate economic enterprises of their own they are hampered by lack of capital and obstructed by the administrative restrictions which surround every area of their life.

Among Canadians as a whole in 1982 unemployment was 8.6% while among Indians it was 60%. In 1969 the average income of a Canadian family was $8,874 while 88% of all Indian families made less than $3,000 and about 50% made less than $1,000, including welfare payments. The differentials continue today. Eighty-eight per cent of Indians live in sub-standard housing as against 11% of Canadians as a whole. The Indian infant mortality rate is more than twice that for Canadians, and Indians are ten times more likely to suffer from tuberculosis. Their life-span is less than other Canadians and their suicide rate is seven that of non-Indians. Alcoholism has reached epidemic proportions and there is widespread delinquency, so while Indians make up only 3% of the population, at any one time they make up between 30% to 60% of the inmates in jails, usually serving short sentences for petty crimes like drunkenness and vagrancy. Many are there because they cannot afford to pay a fine. These problems are a common pattern among Canada's Indians, although the Indians in the north who follow a more traditional hunting life style have fewer problems of delinquency, maladjustment and social collapse than tribes which have come under stronger pressure to conform to the white Canadian norm.

In the 1950s the government took greater control of the reserve schools to ensure that standards were maintained and to integrate Indian children into white schools. The academic performance of most Indian children remained poor for the educational system was designed to meet the needs of white children and did not take into consideration the unique cultural and social problems faced by native children. In the 1960s, 61% of Indian children dropped out of school before grade six, 97% before grade 12, and only 150 were enrolled in full-time courses at university level.

The opposition to the White Paper Document of 1969 had strengthened the Indian organizations and forced them to focus on exactly what they wanted. The Indians' educational objectives were put forth in an NIB paper in 1972 and presented to the Minister of Indian Affairs. The government committed itself to implementing the proposal. Among other things, the proposal suggested that there be more parental responsibility and local control, that authority for reserve schools should be transferred to the bands, that Indians should be represented on provincial school boards, and that traditional values and culture should be encouraged. However, by the 1980s there was little improvement. While 88% of all Canadian children completed high school only 6% of Indian children did so.

(See also *American Indians; Inuits*)

Inuits

Alternative names: **Eskimo, various tribal names**
Location: **Greenland, Alaska, Canada, Siberia (USSR)**
Population: **approximately: 45,000, 30,000, 25,000, 1,500 respectively**
% of population: **85% of Greenland's population; tiny minorities in USA, Canada, USSR**
Religion: **Christianity, Inuit beliefs**
Language: **Kalatadisu, Inupiaq; Inupiak, Yupik; Inuktitut**

Inuits are the indigenous people of Siberia, Alaska, Canada and Greenland. In the circumpolar world there are approximately 100,000 Inuit: 1,500 in Siberia, 30,000 in Alaska, 25,000 in Canada and 42,000 in Greenland. Their languages are of the Eskaleut language family: Yupik in Siberia and south-west Alaska and Inupiaq from north Alaska right across to Greenland. Both languages have common origins but are mutually unintelligible.

Before contact with Europeans the Inuits lived as semi-nomadic hunters, moving from camp to camp to follow game. Camps were usually made up of several related families. They depended on game, mostly marine mammals and occasionally on caribou and fish for their food and clothing. The important social unit was the family. Although they had no written language they had a rich oral tradition. The underlying themes of their tribal social and legal structure were collective responsibility and loyalty. Their government was a flexible system based on consensus.

GREENLAND

Greenland is the world's largest island with an area of over 2 million square kilometres, although only 15% of this is ice-free. It has a population of 53,000 of which more than 45,000 are Inuits. Before the late eighteenth century, when Denmark began to trade with the Inuits, the people depended on a natural economy of seal hunting which supplied all of their needs. Today there remain only a few Inuit families living in the north-west and east of the island who are largely self-sufficient.

The beginning of trade with Denmark in the eighteenth century led to severe food shortages and Denmark undertook measures to protect not only its own economic interests but also to shield the Inuits from further exploitation and contact with the industrial world. This policy remained in effect until after World War II when the Greenlanders declared to the United Nations that they wished to remain attached to Denmark, but that the isolationism, colonialism and trade monopoly must end.

In 1953 Greenland became a Danish county with a provincial council and with direct representation of two members in the *Folketing* in Copenhagen. It gained self-rule in 1979 and today the Inuit majority exercises democratic control through the electoral system. Greenland's parliament, the *Landsting*, with 17 members, is responsible for industry, taxation, education, and cultural affairs, but matters of defence, foreign policy, the courts and police still remain in the hands of Denmark, and Greenlanders remain Danish citizens. However, there have been moves towards decolonization and in 1985 the *Landsting* exercised its rights of veto and Greenland withdrew its membership from the European Economic Community. The elections of

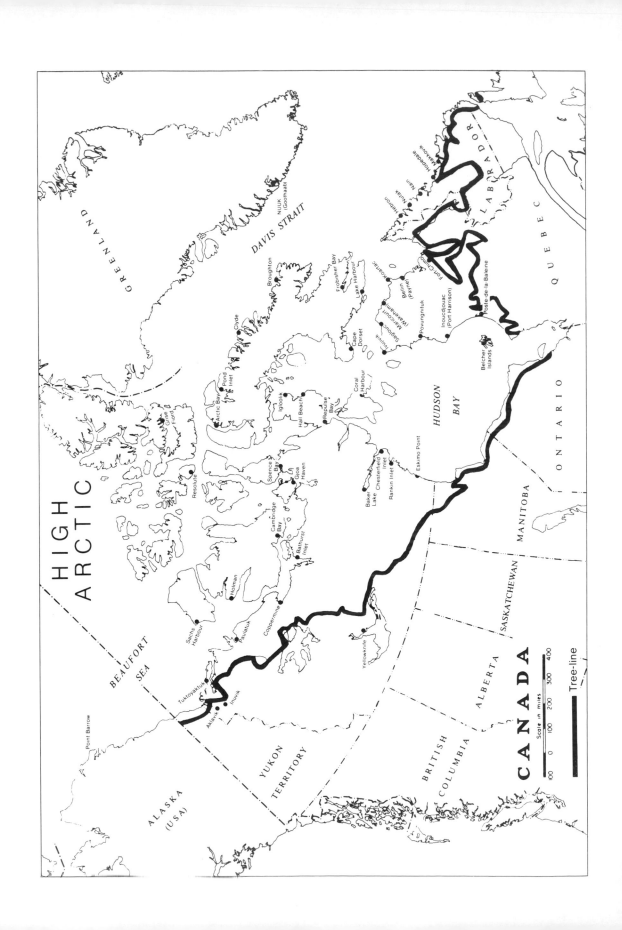

1987 affirmed the position of the Siamut and Inuit Ataquatigiit parties under Prime Minister Jonathan Motzfeldt.

Following the political reforms of 1953 attempts were made to improve the living conditions of the Inuits, and in 1956 an educational system similar to the one in Denmark was introduced. Both Inuit and Danish are taught at the primary and secondary level and the younger generation of Inuits is bilingual. However there is no university in Greenland and Inuit students wishing to pursue higher education normally study at Danish institutions. A continuing problem is the situation of the Inuit who were relocated in 1953 to make way for the US air base at Thule (Qanaq), who have never received compensation. They have presented their demands to a Review Committee of the Danish Parliament which was due to report before the end of 1989 but to date does not appear to have begun substantive work to review the case.

ALASKA

Alaska was part of the Russian empire from the mid-eighteenth century to the nineteenth century and was purchased by the US from Russia in 1867. It became the 49th and largest US state in 1959 and today it is the largest source of US oil. Alaska has an estimated population of 382,000, of which fewer than one eighth is native to the state. Although Alaska has extensive fur, salmon and forestry industries, participation in these industries by the indigenous peoples is minimal. In addition energy which is abundant in Alaska is expensive for rural villages.

The Inuit, Aleuts and Indians are the indigenous peoples of Alaska. The Inuit, who number 30,000, are the largest of the three groups. The tribes derive their names from geography and economy of the regions where they live, e.g. South Alaskan (salmon). Prior to contact with whites the Inuit lived in skin tents in the summer and sod or drift wood houses in winter. A semi-nomadic people, most lived and hunted in the inlets and coast of Arctic Alaska while some lived further inland and hunted caribou to survive. Of the estimated 3,000 caribou hunters only 50 remain.

Aleuts and Indians

The Aleuts are native to the Aleut islands in the Bering Sea. These bleak frostless lands are prone to high winds and deep fog. The Aleuts call themselves "unangan" which means "people". They were a self-sufficient race whose economy was based on hunting a variety of animals including seals, sea-lions and whales. They lived in semi-subterranean houses built up and roofed with sod and buried their dead in the numerous volcanic caves about the islands. The Aleut language is of the same family as the Inuit, but both are mutually unintelligible. When education was formalized in Alaska in the 1880s a Cyrillic alphabet had already been designed for the Aleuts some 50 years earlier. Today there are less than 4,000 Aleuts, 300 of whom live on the Commander Islands which remain attached to the Soviet Union.

In 1942 during the Japanese attack on the islands many Aleuts were removed to the mainland. In 1988 the US Congress agreed that survivors of the removal should be compensated up to $12,000 per person. The whaling conservation efforts have also affected the Aleut economy as much of their livelihood depends on the limited annual catch. They have argued at the International Whaling Commission that their catch should not be subsumed into an annual US quota but should be calculated separately.

The Indians have a hierarchical culture similar to some other Pacific Coast Indians. The root of their language is Na Dene, of which the largest group is Athabascan to which most sub-groups in Alaska belong. The Tlingit inhabit the southern coast of Alaska and originally stretched down into California. Theirs was an agricultural and fishing economy and they had a caste system with a slave class as well as a monotheistic faith supported by lesser spirits.

The Tinneh live further inland along the Yukon River and its tributaries. Their economy was based on hunting and salmon fishing. They are more assimilated than the Tlingit but their participation in the thriving salmon industry is still minimal.

Land rights

From the 1880s to 1890s prospectors arrived in Alaska seeking gold, copper and silver, but most migration took place after 1950. There was a surge of immigration when oil was discovered in 1968. This led to the formation of the Native Land Claims Movement (NLCM). The Alaskan oil pipeline proposal elicited a strong outcry from ecological conservationists and the NLCM was able to lay claims for recognition and compensation.

In 1971 the US Congress passed the Alaskan Native Claims Settlement Act (ANSCA). The Act extinguished aboriginal land titles in Alaska, and mandated that modern profit-making corporations be established to administer and manage the cash and land award totalling $962.5 million and approximately 44 million acres of land. Individual and tribal entities received relatively small amounts of money and no land. Instead all indigenous persons of more than one quarter native blood born before December 18, 1971 received shares in these newly formed co-operations.

The provisions of ANSCA have been criticized

by indigenous activists. Those born after 1971 have no legal interest either directly or indirectly in the land except by inheritance. In 1991 shares can be legally sold to outsiders which will most probably lead to corporate takeover and large tracts of Alaskan wilderness being opened up for mineral and other development. The land-holding corporations also face the threat of bankruptcy in which case a corporation's assets, including land, could be attached by creditors. In addition, 20 years after the establishment of ANSCA lands, even undeveloped lands may be taxed by the state. Rural villages will most likely fail to meet these tax obligations and the land could pass to the state. ANSCA also extinguished subsistence rights of hunting and fishing and today state and federal laws often restrict subsistence activities, which many native communities still rely on in order to survive. Forced acceptance of the profit motive and the attendant requirements of individualism and competition may undermine long-standing cultural values which operate to minimize conflict. The establishment of new corporate institutions with a hierarchical organization of technicians, managers and executive decision-makers has replaced traditional leadership patterns that bonded natives into cohesive groups.

Native dissatisfaction with the ANSCA resulted in the amendments passed by the US Congress (Public Law 100-241 1988) in February 1988. These amendments resolved the questions of extending stock restrictions in order to restrict the likelihood of outside takeovers, allowed stock to be issued to those born after 1971 and to those who had missed out in the original settlement, and extended protection against taxation on undeveloped land. However the corporate system itself remained in place and there is likely to be increasing pressure on developed native lands. The amendments to the ANSCA were supported or accepted by the statewide umbrella organization, the Alaska Federation of Natives, but were vigorously opposed by the Alaska Native Coalition which withdrew from the AFN in 1987 on this issue.

CANADA

The Canadian Arctic was first granted to the Hudson's Bay Company, the most important commercial interest in the fur trade. In 1870 it was given by the company to the Canadian government, which renamed the area the Northwest Territories (NWT). With this annexation the Inuit became Canadian citizens.

American and Scottish whalers were the first Europeans to have a substantial economic interest in the north and thus had a substantial effect on the Inuit who lived along the coast. In less than a decade they were successful in almost wiping out several whale populations. During their stay the Inuit, who were knowledgeable about the water and the whales in the area, were pressed into service on the European and American ships, and were paid in wages. Trade was practised and some whites took Inuit wives.

When the economic value of the whale hunt declined, the fur trade, which had been the economic foundation of Canada, slowly turned northwards as traders increasingly searched for new sources of fur. During the nineteenth century trade was established between the Inuit and the Canadians. The Inuit abandoned traditional hunting ways, in which trapping was unimportant, in order to get the furs to barter for trade goods. As they began to depend more and more on trade items such as guns, old hunting techniques were no longer used. In 1940 when the fur industry collapsed and most of the posts closed, the Inuits were unable to return to their original way of life so they subsisted precariously in a mixed economy: some hunting, some trapping, occasional work for wages with the white people and trading for such staple goods as guns, flour and tea.

The 1950s brought widespread starvation and death to the Inuit as a result of the epidemics which swept through their camps in the 1940s and the change of animal migration patterns in the 1950s. The government which had in the past left the welfare and education of the Northwest Territories to the missionaries and traders began to move groups away from their camps to places where they could be properly administered. They moved the Inuit from their semi-nomadic camps of about three families to settlements of 50 families or more. The government then embarked on creating housing, schools, improving health care and setting up local Eskimo Councils to encourage the growth of community government. The efforts proved successful and from 1941 to 1971 the infant mortality and death rate among the Inuit dropped.

White men came later to the western Arctic than to the east coast. The whaling industry brought alcohol and diseases which decimated the Inuit. By 1910 the population of 2,000 Mackenzie Inuit had been reduced to about 130. Because of the abundance of certain types of furs, the west remained affluent even during the 1930s and 1940s which were so disastrous for Inuit in other areas. The fur industry in this area gave way eventually to oil and gas development.

Labrador and Quebec

Areas like Labrador were always more appealing to white men because the climate and topography were more familiar to settlers and it was easier to make a living from fishing and whaling in these areas. Therefore the impact on these communities in these areas was considerably greater. Labrador was colonized in 1770 by Moravian missionaries. The Moravians traded with the Inuits but kept goods like liquor out of the territory. By the 1800s white settlers had begun to move into the territory and by 1900 they were an important element. However, both whites and Inuits respected each other and both lived from the resources of the land and had similar economic systems. The Inuit of Labrador remained under British rule until 1949, at which time they joined the confederation as part of Newfoundland.

In Quebec the provincial government did not take up its responsibility for the Inuit in its area until 1963. It had won a court battle which classified the Inuits in that area as Indian, and therefore the responsibility of the federal government. Thus in the Northwest Territories the Inuit were an entirely federal responsibility while in Quebec and Labrador responsibility for the Inuit was divided between the province and the federal government. This arrangement led at times to tensions and different standards being applied to the Inuit depending on the area in which they lived.

The Newfoundland government was reluctant to consider the question of aboriginal rights and refused to admit that the native people could have special status even after 1973, when the federal government had admitted that these rights existed. The provincial government of Quebec came into direct conflict with Inuits in the 1970s when it called for sovereignty for Quebec and came close to demanding outright separation from Canada. It passed a bill to restrict the use of English and the Inuit, who had been educated in English, protested.

The Innu are the original inhabitants of the Quebec-Labrador peninsula. Today there are approximately 9,000 living in Labrador. In September 1988 many were arrested for participating in sit-ins which were staged to protest the refusal of the government to negotiate their land claims. They assert that they never gave up their land to the government nor did they permit their territory to be used by NATO airforces for low-level flying, which seriously disrupts the wildlife, especially caribou, on which the Innu economy depends. In April 1989 the courts found the Innu not guilty. However the NATO flights and the protests continue.

Political and legal developments

In 1960, when native people were finally given the right to vote in federal elections, the Inuits were already wards of the federal government. They could no longer return to their old way of life because they were now too dependant, and their right to hunt freely was slowly eroded by the restrictive quotas set by the government on the hunting of some animals. In 1967 the government of the Northwest Territories in Yellowknife was established under the authority of the federal Department of Indian Affairs and Northern Development, which was responsible for all Inuit and Indian affairs. This new government took over the administration of some federal services and immediately concentrated on the development of local government.

When oil was discovered in Alaska in 1968 this led to a rush of speculation in Canada. As a result, the Inuit of the Beaufort Sea area where exploration had been stimulated formed in 1969 a political organization called the Committee for Original People's Entitlement (COPE). It was the first organization of its kind in the Arctic. Its purpose was to defend the rights of the Inuit before they were swamped in the rush of development. In 1971 The Tapirisat of Canada (ITC), a national organization with essentially the same purpose, was also formed.

The same year that COPE was formed a government policy document White Paper was issued. It refused to recognize aboriginal rights. It argued that native people had no special rights which entitled them to anything different from other Canadians. That same year the Nishga Indians brought the government of British Columbia to court and the case reached the Supreme Court of Canada. Though the case was dismissed on a technicality it forced the government to re-evaluate its position on aboriginal rights and it committed itself to settling outstanding claims. COPE and the ITC formulated proposals which stated that their rights had never been surrendered by conquest or by treaty and that they were entitled to compensation of various kinds. The proposal was ratified at a general assembly representing all the Inuit in the NWT in November 1975 and finally presented to the Canadian Government for negotiation in February of 1976.

The Cree and the Inuit of James Bay are the beneficiaries of the first major modern land claims agreement negotiated by the Canadian Government. In April 1971 the James Bay hydro-electric project was announced. The project would generate 30% of Canada's power by damming all the major rivers flowing into James Bay from the eastern side. The land in the area would be flooded, yet the provincial government had not consulted the Inuit who lived in the eastern area, and had done little research into the environmental effects of such a scheme. The Cree and the Inuit in the area attempted to stop the project. They were unsuccessful politically, but they were able to gain an injunction from the court. Eight days later the injunction was overturned on appeal; however the government became worried that future work could be suspended so negotiations took place and an agreement was reached a year later in 1974. This agreement freed the land for development by exchanging native rights for a package of benefits, which included $C90 million in cash, title to 5,250 square miles of hunting grounds, exclusive hunting and fishing rights on a further 60,000 square miles, and various social programmes that carried a perpetual governmental responsibility. Some Inuit communities could not be consulted by their representatives and became upset that their aboriginal rights had been given up in exchange for the benefit package. They rejected the agreement and they are now lobbying to have their rights restored to them.

After the agreement, there was a feeling in the government that the Inuit peoples were rich and therefore no longer needed to have programmes and services to which they were still in fact entitled. Health care standards dropped after the signing of the agreement and are only now recovering. Also the $225 million cash payment to be shared between the Cree and Inuit was to be paid out in instalments until 1977 which made the actual value much lower because of inflation. The Inuit eventually took grievances about the agreement to a committee of the Canadian Parliament in March 1981 and gave evidence which so embarrassed the federal government that it immediately ordered a review of its responsibilities in the implementation of the agreement. In February 1982 the review committee agreed that there was a serious problem. The government committed some funds to improve its performance and agreed to honour the spirit of the agreement in a more constructive way.

COPE and the ITC also proposed that the NWT be divided and administered under two different governments. They argued that a natural division existed along the treeline which ran from the Mackenzie Delta diagonally to the NWT Manitoba border and separated the tundra land of the Inuit from the forest of the Dene (Indians). They also argued that the regions had two different climates and geography and the peoples had different cultures. They proposed not only the division but a new government in the eastern territory which would be called Nanavut. The proposed area of Nanavut has a 75% Inuit population and the Inuit hope that this will ensure that the new government would be representative of the Inuits. They also proposed that participation in Canadian elections be limited to those with residence of three years. This would limit the ability of the north's large transient white population, who stayed an average of only two years, to exercise undue influence in the north.

This remains the most controversial aspect of the proposal. In 1979 a native majority was elected to the NWT government. They established a Unity Committee which held hearings across the North to evaluate the need for division. Sixty per cent of the Inuit population wanted the NWT to be divided. The Council and the native groups, now working closely together, carried the results to Ottawa and in November 1982 the Minister of Indian and Northern Affairs announced that, subject to certain conditions, the NWT would be divided. However, to date this division has not been carried out.

Education and social developments

At the end of the nineteenth century missionaries transported a syllabic writing system to the eastern Arctic, and the native population was at the time more literate than most of the white men who arrived in the north. The missionaries trained teachers, and up to 1949 when Labrador joined Canada all schools in the area were taught in Inuktitut. In 1974 the ITC set up the Inuit Language Commission which proposed a dual orthography so that roman and syllabic systems could be used interchangeably. At an international level, Inuit have expressed hope that a pan-Inuit writing system and language would be developed.

The government did not start to build schools in the NWT until the 1940s. Before then it had left this responsibility to the missionary groups. In 1944, 80% of Inuit children were not taught in schools, which used curricula from the south and did not teach in the native languages. In 1967 after the NWT government was established in Yellowknife, individuals in the Department of Education began to push for native language and Inuit culture to be included in the curriculum. In 1972 the first Inuit teacher graduated and the Inuit cultural programme was set up in some schools. After the native peoples gained control of the NWT Council in 1979 a committee was elected to make a systematic evaluation of education. The committee recommended that control of education be decentralized, that the government support the use of native languages in the schools through programmes of training for native teachers, that there be development of relevant curricula in the native languages and that the system of adult education be vastly improved. Inuit children are now taught in Inuktitut through to grade three, and since 1980 a teacher education programme in Forbisher Bay has been training Inuit teachers. Thirty-seven of the 359 teachers in Inuit schools have graduated from the programme. The number of Inuit students going on to post-secondary education has jumped from 16 in 1978-79 to 154 in 1983-84.

In 1975 the ITC proposed the Inukshuk project

to make Inuktitut TV programmes available. After a six-month experiment which proved successful the Inuit Broadcasting Corporation (IBC) was formed. The IBC now produced five half-hours of Inuktitut programming including current affairs cultural programmes and sports, out of five production centres across the north. With government funding of over one million dollars a year the IBC is helping to draw together the scattered Canadian Inuit communities into a political and cultural force.

In spite of government efforts to involve them in wage labour the Inuit have stubbornly refused to give up their feeling for the land and for the land-based renewable resources economy. The marketing of Inuit crafts have been successful, yet the government has done very little to organize and support hunting and trapping which are fundamental to a successful land-based way of life. The Inuits insist that it is possible to create a local and regional economy based on products of the hunt, which would allow the hunters greater self-sufficiency, and they are now urging the government to consider ways to support the land-based economy in a systematic way.

Trapping is the only source of income for most native people and to the Inuit seal hunting is truly a subsistence activity as compared to the commercial seal-pup harvests in other parts of Canada. The Inuits disagree with the commercial culling methods, and feel victimized by the European seal skin ban. The economic consequences of the ban have been drastic and have forced some Inuit to give up hunting. They continue to lobby the European Parliament for an exemption to the ban, but without success.

CONCLUSION

Despite their scattered numbers and division between a four different governments, Inuit communities face many common problems. School dropout, teenage psychosis, suicide and alcoholism have been high. A large part of the problem came from removing children from traditional village life, where values of non-aggression and non-competitiveness contrast with the white image of educational and business success. Even in Greenland with its Inuit majority the destruction of the old ways of hunting and fishing and their replacement by small towns also gave way to boredom and drinking. Alcoholism remains a problem as does suicide. The suicide rates in Greenland, generally among young people, are four times the rate in Denmark which itself has one of the highest suicide levels in the world. In Alaska alcoholism in native communities is held responsible for high levels of suicides, murders, rapes, child abuse and fatal accidents. But alcoholism itself is a symptom of the hopelessness and alienation of a people wrenched away from their traditional beliefs and way of life.

Despoilation of the environment is another common factor. Formerly inaccessible areas are being opened to mining and hydro-electric power. Oil companies provide 85% of the state revenue of Alaska. An Alaskan oil spill from a tanker in Prince William Sound, Alaska, in early 1989 polluted large areas of sea and shore. The "Greenhouse effect" may yet produce further changes in the environment with serious consequences for the Inuit.

Inuit from all states have created a common forum in the Inuit Circumpolar Conference (ICC) which was established in Barrow Alaska in 1977 by Inuit from Alaska, Canada and Greenland, to address concerns about oil and gas developments in Alaska and Canada. In 1981 the ICC was successful in postponing hearings on the proposed Arctic Pilot Project (APP), a proposal to ship liquefied natural gas from the Canadian high Arctic to Southern Canada. In 1983 it was granted Non-Governmental Organization (NGO) status at the United Nations.

(See also *Saami* in **Western Europe and Scandinavia**)

Japanese-Americans

Alternative names: "Issei", "Nisei", "Sansei" (First, second, third generation Japanese Americans respectively)
Location: **mainly west coast USA and Hawaii**
Population: **about 700,000 (1980)**
% of population: **0.3%**
Religion: **various**
Language: **Japanese, English**

Japanese-Americans are the descendants of Japanese immigrants to the USA. They are the second largest group of Japanese outside Japan, after the one million strong Japanese community in Brazil. They are distinctive among US minority groups in that one of the two major communities, that in the West Coast states, was collectively interned as punishment during World War II,[1] a detention which is now widely recognized as being unjust and unnecessary.

The majority of Japanese settlers came to the USA between 1900 and 1924, where they settled in two main areas. One community settled in the Hawaii, where at the outbreak of war in 1941 they numbered about 158,000 — about 27% of the population and an important skilled labour force. During the war about 2,000 were taken into custody on the mainland but the vast majority remained free. It was argued by the administrators of the islands that they were too important to the economy to intern.

During the war there were no acts of sabotage by Japanese-Americans in Hawaii and Nisei troops served with distinction in combat with the US forces. Today there are about 260,000 Japanese-Americans in Hawaii, some of whom have intermarried with peoples from other ethnic backgrounds.

Japanese settlers on the west coast of the USA initially faced institutionalized discrimination. Some states banned intermarriage and Japanese settlers could not obtain US citizenship and were thus unable to own farm land or practise in many professions. Despite discrimination, a combination of hard work, community solidarity and educational achievement meant that by 1940 the Japanese-American community had achieved modest prosperity.

The Japanese-American communities of the western states were subject to a internment order — Executive Order 9066 of February 19, 1942 — removing them from a "restricted military zone" in parts of the four states of Washington, Oregon, California and Arizona. The internment began in early 1942 and the camps were not closed down until early 1946, although most detainees were released from 1945. The internment order was supposedly for security reasons although no sabotage or attempted sabotage by Japanese-Americans took place on the Pacific coast and it was alleged that some groups saw the Japanese as an economic threat. The internment order covered all Japanese whatever their legal status, whether aliens, resident immigrants or American born citizens. A total of 110,000 to 120,000 people were interned in camps in the interior of the USA, about two-thirds of whom were US citizens and most of the remainder permanent residents of the USA. The internment order was challenged and initially upheld by the Supreme Court but in December 1944 the court found it to be unconstitutional. Conditions in the camps were often harsh and although camp inmates were encouraged to leave the camps for work and study in other states, anti-Japanese prejudice made this difficult. Some camp inmates were drafted for military service and fought in Europe.

The fight for redress and compensation by Japanese-Americans with regard to internment has continued since the war and gained new impetus in the 1980s. In 1948 Congress enacted the Evacuation Claims Act which gave some compensation to victims; in 1952 Japanese Issei (and foreigners) were able to obtain citizenship; in 1956 California's alien land laws were repealed; in 1976 Executive Order 9066 was rescinded; in 1983 a Congressional-backed Commission of Enquiry held public hearings and recommended monetary compensation for victims; while also in 1983 new court cases concerning internment were filed, in part based on new research into wartime archives.

Redress is being sought along three specific lines. Firstly, the three persons who lost their Supreme Court cases in 1943 and 1944 are applying for a writ of coram nobis to quash their original convictions. Secondly, a group of Japanese-Americans are engaged in a class action against the USA to seek economic compensation totalling approximately $24 billion to the victims or their relatives.

---

[1]Italian and German-Americans resident on the Eastern seaboard were given individual loyalty hearings but not interned en masse.

In 1984 this suit was dismissed by a District Court but was later challenged in the Supreme Court. Thirdly, a group of Japanese-Americans is attempting to gain compensation by means of Congressional legislation and is claiming a total of $20,000 per person for each of the 60,000 surviving internees — about $1.25 billion in all. This strategy appears to have been the most successful as in August 1988 the House of Representatives and the Senate approved the legislation while President Reagan indicated that he would sign it.

Japanese-Americans are today regarded as one of the most successful American minority groups. They have higher than average income, educational levels and professional qualifications — factors which are sometimes ascribed to cultural as well as economic factors. But in many ways the Japanese-American community, now largely third and fourth generation, has lost some of its distinctiveness. Most Japanese-Americans live in non-Japanese-American neighbourhoods and have friendships and professional ties that cross ethnic lines. Marriage outside the community is increasingly common. Approximately 60% of the Sansei now marry non-Japanese-Americans. Few Sansei speak Japanese and the numbers are likely to decline further unless Japanese immigration to the USA (currently about 4,000 annually) increases greatly. Despite impressive qualifications, few Japanese-Americans have reached the highest levels of management. They have however fared well in electoral terms and were recently represented by three Japanese-American Senators and one member of the House of Representatives.

(See also *Asian-Americans; Japanese-Canadians*)

Japanese-Canadians

Location: **mainly west coast of Canada**
Religion: **various**
Language: **Japanese, English**

Japanese-Canadians are the descendants of immigrants from Japan, most of whom settled on the Pacific seaboard of Canada in the early twentieth century. Like Japanese-Americans they were interned and deported en masse from certain areas during World War II.

In 1942, 22,000 Japanese-Canadians were removed from the west coast and "relocated" to "exclusion centres". This was supposedly for reasons of national security although the then Prime Minister disclosed to the House of Commons in 1944 that "no person of Japanese race born in Canada has been charged with any act of sabotage or disloyalty during the years of war". Japanese-Canadian property was impounded and sold at low prices by the government in 1943 and the costs of internment deducted from the proceeds. The camps were not emptied until 1947 and Japanese-Canadians were not allowed to return to the west coast until 1949. Some Japanese-Canadians were deported and exiled after the war.

The Bird Commission awarded Japanese-Canadians compensation of $1.3m for 1,400 claims. This amount is widely regarded as inadequate but to date no further compensation is forthcoming for the estimated 12,000 survivors of the relocation. Although later governments have expressed regret for the actions against the community, to date there has been no formal apology by the government. Today Japanese-Canadians are asking for an assessment of losses and compensation, a formal apology and constitutional safeguards (including a review of the War Measures Act) to ensure that similar actions cannot take place in the future.

(See also *Japanese-Americans*)

Mexican Americans

Alternative names: **Hispanics, Chicanos**
Location: **all USA, especially south-western states**
Population: **12.1 million**
% of population: **5% of total US population**
Religion: **Catholic**
Language: **Spanish, English**

Mexican Americans can be divided into two main groups; those who have lived in the south-west of the USA for several centuries and more recent immigrants from Mexico. Numbers are not always easy to determine.[1] According to the 1980 census there were approximately 12.1 million people of Mexican heritage in the USA, and another 7.3 million who were of different Hispanic ancestry.[2] Because more recent Mexican immigrants frequently live in the USA without legal status these figures are probably considerably higher. Mexican Americans are the largest group of people of Hispanic or latin heritage in the USA and one of the fastest growing minority groups.

Most Mexican Americans live in the five south-western states of California (34% of all Hispanics), Texas (21%), New Mexico, Arizona and Oklahoma, but there are large populations in cities throughout the country. In New Mexico one third of the population is Hispanic, in both Texas and California over one quarter, and Los Angeles has the world's third largest group of urban Mexicans, after Mexico City and Guadalahara. Both indigenous and immigrant Mexican Americans have high birthrates and this, coupled with continuing legal and illegal migration, will ensure that their numbers and proportion of the population will increase.

The colonial period

Mexican Americans are the descendants of the Mestizo, generally considered to be peoples of mixed or Spanish and Indian blood. However there were Jews among the original conquistadors; other ethnic groups included Arabs and Moors, an estimated one quarter of a million Africans brought to Mexico as slaves and thousands of Chinese who had come to Mexico on the Spanish galleons of the Manilla trade. They all contributed to the making of the Mestizo.

When the Spaniards entered the capital of the Aztec empire, which is now present day Mexico City, they were astonished to find a city as magnificent as Constantinople and Rome. The native Indians welcomed the Spaniards whom they believed to be the messengers of the Gods as foretold by their legends. Unions between Spaniard men and native women resulted in the growth of a racially diverse population. There was also religious diversity. By the 1550s there were 300 Jews in Mexico City, one quarter of the Spanish population, and later Jewish converts. These Jews were persecuted by the Holy Inquisition and most fled northwards towards present-day New Mexico which encompassed the land from the north of Mexico to present-day San Antonio in Texas. They, along with others who settled on the mountain slopes of desert valleys in the south-west of the USA, were not Spanish settlers but Mestizo and Indians who more often survived the rigors of the wilderness. These early settlers were outcasts and the royal officials of Mexico city referred to them as neither Spanish or Mexican but as barbaric Indians.

These Mexicans farmed as the Indians had, using dry farming and little water. Their farms and mountain villages were small. Ranching was more profitable and soon prospered. Eventually the land on the frontier was given to the settlers by royal decree and later by the Mexican government after its independence from Spain in 1821. There were at least 1,715 of these land grants which covered the entire south-west from present-day California to Texas and encompassed millions of acres, which today are some of the richest agricultural and most expensive urban lands in the USA. Life on the frontier depended on co-operation so the land grants and deeds for irrigation and pasture were given as communal property. Over time the land became as sacred to the settlers as it had to the original Indian inhabitants.

In the Rio Grande Valley of Texas the almost three million cattle on the ranches were the most sought after spoils of the Mexican American War and these herds were the beginning of the present-day livestock industry in the American West. The

---

[1]Until the 1960s Mexican Americans were not counted in the government census because they were listed as "white" and not as a separate minority group.
[2]Puerto Ricans, Cubans, Spanish, Central or South American.

original cowboy was the Mexican or Indian *vaquero* and much of what is today recognized as (American) Western culture was adopted from the Mexican Americans.

Incorporation into the USA

In 1845 the USA annexed Texas and gained control over the remainder of the south-west in the Mexican-American War of 1846-1848. In the Treaty of Guadalupe Hidalgo in February 1848 Mexico renounced claims to Texas, recognized the Rio Grande frontier and, in return for 15 million dollars, ceded New Mexico and California. Since the Land Grants were officially decreed they were recognized in the Treaty of Guadalupe Hidalgo which declared ". . . In the said territories property of every kind now belonging to the Mexicans shall be respected . . .", a stand later upheld by the US Supreme Court. Despite this 80% of the lands were lost to the heirs of the Land Grants. In New Mexico an order was issued in English that unless land grants were re-registered in the capital they would be confiscated. Since few of the Mexicans could read English most did not obey this order and their land was confiscated. The same process was followed in California, Texas, Colorado and Arizona.

The gold rush of 1849 brought new immigrants to California and the south-west. However the majority of the rural population was Spanish-speaking and almost all Mexican Americans lived in rural areas in isolated and self-reliant communities — a situation which was to continue until well into the twentieth century. In California and New Mexico where state constitutions were of necessity written in both Spanish and English, Spanish remained the first language of the majority of the population until the twentieth century.

By 1930 half of the Mexican American population was basically rural but at the end of World War II there was an exodus to the cities. The villagers tried to hang on to their traditions and communal cultures and created for themselves a city within a city, the *barrio*, which although integrated into the larger city remains separated by the distinct culture, language and identity of its inhabitants. Along with their customs they brought their traditional rivalries which made it hard for them to come together as a political force.

Before World War I Mexicans began to cross the border into America. They were usually refugees seeking to escape the revolutions and counter-revolutions that were taking place in Mexico. After World War II there was a flood of illegal immigration across the Mexican American border and these illegal immigrants came to be know by the derisive term of "wetback". By 1970 they were estimated to number between seven and nine million.

These illegal immigrants generally worked in the fields without protection of the law and were usually underpaid and abused.

Political developments

Following World War II some Mexican Americans made unsuccessful efforts to reclaim the land that had been granted to them in the Treaty of Guadalupe Hidalgo. In the 1960s the *Alianza Federal de Los Pueblos Libres* (The Federal Alliance of Free City States) was organized to re-establish the legality of the Land Grants. The *Allianza*, which was formed by Reies Tijerina, gained notoriety when they raided a Courthouse in New Mexico and elected their own Land Grant officials and also issued a proclamation announcing that ". . . the USA had no title for New Mexico — all trespassers must get out. All Spanish and Indian pueblos are free forever". When these earlier efforts proved unsuccessful Tijerina lobbied Congress to appoint a federal commission to investigate the Land Claims but although a number of bills have been introduced, to date, no lands have been returned. If their claim is ever recognized the Mexican Americans would be entitled to some of the wealthiest land in the nation. Convinced that only international pressure would bring about adherence to their claim and the terms of the Treaty of Guadalupe Hidalgo, Tijerina and the Land Grant heirs sought the aid of the then Mexican president Luis Echeverria who agreed to take the matter to the United Nations. However the present political and economic situation in Mexico makes it highly unlikely that Mexican pressure would succeed.

As farms and ranches became more profitable in the south-west, land syndicates were formed which employed large numbers of *campesinos* (farm labourers). Illegal immigrants became an important part of the workforce, but without either political representation or legal knowledge were usually forced to work long hours at rates of pay below the legal minimum. During the mid-1960s the National Farm Workers Union was organized by Caesar Chavez. The struggles of Mexican American workers in the fruit and vegetable farms of California in particular, and the imaginative public and union boycott tactics used, brought the plight of these workers to nationwide attention.

During the 1960s the chicano movement was born. *Chicano*, a word that is an insult to Mexican Americans, took on new meaning as the students in the *barrios* of California cities began to popularize the word as a symbol of defiance in the schools where the speaking of Spanish was forbidden. The Chicanos, as they were soon to be called, established themselves as a new political movement and the *barrios* which had in the past been divided began to come together. Hundreds of political and social groups were established in the *barrios* where there had been previously only a few. These groups wanted to change the stereotype of the Mexican American as well as to improve their economic and social positions within the country.

National as well as local organizations were established to accomplish these goals. Some would eventually be supported by government agencies and for the first time Mexican Americans were represented in high office on the national level by Grace Olivarez who became head of the Community Services Administration and Lionel Castillo who was appointed the Commissioner of Immigration. Increased Mexican-American participation in elections in the south-west resulted in the election of Raul Castro as Governor of Arizona and Jerry Apodaca as Governor of New Mexico but their administrations were marked by scandal and loss of popular support.

Despite growing political awareness in the sixties however, in 1976 when nearly five million Spanish-speaking Americans were eligible to vote, 60% of them Mexican Americans, less than 40% actually did vote. In California where in 1976 the Mexican Americans made up almost 16% of the population they held only 2% of elected offices while nation-wide they held only 3.4% of government jobs and in the Congress there were only four Mexican American representatives. But there were signs of change. By the end of the 1970s registration drives managed to bring in 300,000 Mexican American voters in California and 160,000 in Texas. In the south-west where racism against Mexican Americans is strongest new political participation is significant and they could emerge as a major political force.

Yet there are also problems. In California only one in four Hispanics voted in 1986. Perhaps one third of the total were ineligible to vote as illegal immigrants. There are claims that local and state constituencies are deliberately drawn to exclude Mexican Americans and other minority groups from power. In September 1988 the Justice Department filed a suit against Los Angeles County claiming that voting districts have been designed deliberately to exclude Mexican Americans, none of whom have ever held elected office in the county. (The same was true for blacks and Asian-Americans.) Two-thirds of the Hispanic vote goes to the Democrat Party. However, compared to black Americans, as a community, Hispanics are politically quiescent at a national level. In August 1988 President Reagan nominated Lauro Cavazos as the Secretary on Education, the first Hispanic in the US Cabinet.

Economic and social developments

The 1960s saw a rise in the number of middle-class Mexican Americans. They left the *barrios* and began to assimilate into American culture creating a gap between themselves and the people in the *barrios* where life had remained the same. In 1980, the *barrios* people were usually poorer than those outside, the average income was only two-thirds of the national average, more than one fifth of the people lived below the poverty level, there was lack of education and job skills were poor. This has changed little over the past decade. Rates of disease, malnutrition, crime, poor housing, are all higher in Mexican American communities than white areas of American cities. Mexican Americans on average receive fewer years of schooling than most other sectors of the population although less so than in the past.

The language question

By the 1970s an established programme of bilingual education, introduced by federal legislation, permitted the teaching of Spanish and English in schools. While some Mexican-Americans saw this as an important recognition of the role of Spanish, others including the Council of Mexican American Educators in the Federal Office of Education saw it as a deception. They claimed that it authorized the use of Spanish to teach English and not for its own sake. If it succeeds it eliminates itself and if it fails it defeats itself. What these authorities want is truly bilingual education and a system that recognizes and preserves Mexican-American language and culture. They want not only to teach English to Spanish-speaking people but to teach Spanish to English-speaking people, a mutual recognition and respect they say does not now exist.

The Voting Rights Act makes bilingual ballots mandatory where non-English speakers are concentrated in significant numbers. It is possible in many areas to use Spanish in court proceedings. Spanish is widely spoken and Spanish is used in commercial signs, press and other media. Yet California, the state with the largest Mexican-American population, has an official-English law and other states are following this lead. Access to education and employment provides a strong incentive to be fluent in English; according to a recent study 95% of Mexican-born Americans speak English and the majority of second-generation Mexican-Americans speak only English.

(See also *French Canadians; Puerto Ricans*)

Puerto Ricans

Alternative names: **"Boricuas"**
Location: **Island of Puerto Rico, Caribbean, and USA**
Population: **approximately 3.3 million in Puerto Rico, 2 million in USA**
% of population: **together 2.2% of US population**
Religion: **Roman Catholic**
Language: **Spanish, English**

Puerto Ricans are the inhabitants of the Caribbean island of Puerto Rico and are the descendants of the various peoples who have inhabited the island over the last 500 years — principally Spanish settlers, African slaves, immigrants from Europe and Asia, in addition to indigenous Indians, most of whom appear to have been wiped out by Spanish colonizers. The predominant influence is that of Spain, who ruled the island for over 400 years, although today Puerto Rico is a "Commonwealth" in a "Free Associated State" (Estado Libre Asociado) status with the USA, and its people are US Citizens, although they do not vote as Puerto Ricans in Congressional elections.

The island of Puerto Rico, home of the Taino Indians, was "discovered" by Christopher Columbus in 1493 on his second voyage to the Americas. Spanish colonization began in 1508 and Indians were conscripted by settlers under the *encomienda* system, a thinly disguised form of slavery, to work the land. Spanish rule was so harsh that despite Indian resistance and some reforms of the *encomienda* system, most of the Indian population was wiped out within 10 years and from 1519 the Spanish began the importation of African slaves, a practice which continued for several centuries, until slavery was abolished in 1873. Spanish rule continued with variations for four centuries until 1897 when after much agitation Puerto Rico was granted a Charter of Autonomy in November 1897. Despite promising beginnings the autonomous government had little chance to prove itself as the USA, following a policy of "manifest destiny" in the Caribbean, invaded the island in July 1898. In December Spain formally ceded Puerto Rico (together with the Philippines and Guam) to the USA.

Spanish rule had resulted in a deeply divided and unequal society. There was a tiny educated elite and middle class and, of a population of almost one million people, 300,000 blacks and mulattoes were the poorest. Literacy was only 17%, land ownership was concentrated in a small section of the population and there were few roads or transport facilities.

US political rule

Initially the USA established military rule but this was not viable in the long term. The Foraker Act of 1900 created a body called "the people of Puerto Rico"[1] who were neither American citizens nor citizens of an independent nation. The USA appointed the Governor, the majority of the Executive Council and had a Congressional veto over the indigenous House of Delegates. The system fuelled local resentment and pro-independence feeling grew. The situation was changed by the Jones-Shafroth Act of 1917 which proclaimed American citizenship for Puerto Ricans. This citizenship was automatically granted, unless Puerto Ricans signed a document refusing it. Local pro-independence leaders saw the conferring of US citizenship as taking away the natural right to choose citizenship. Under the Jones-Shafroth Act Puerto Rico was allowed more self-government with the election of a local Senate but the American government retained the power of veto over legislation.

Puerto Rico gained mixed benefits from US rule. Improvements were evident in public health, education and infrastructure but the economy became dominated by absentee US corporations. The depression of the 1930s resulted in an economic collapse, with high unemployment and soaring inflation. A militant Nationalist Party was formed and there was a series of confrontations between Nationalists and local police. Reformist liberals formed the Popular Democratic Party led by Luis Munoz Marín, later to become the dominant political figure in the island's history. In the 1940 elections the Popular Democrats won power under the slogan *Pan, Tierra y Libertad* ("Bread, Land and Liberty") and did not put forward specific plans for Puerto Rico's future political status.

The Popular Democrats under Munoz Marín

---

[1] The island's name was changed by Washington to "Porto Rico" and remained as such until 1932, when a joint Congressional resolution, approved by President Hoover, restored the original name. The name change created great resentment by Puerto Ricans.

and later Robert Sanchez Vilella, remained in power for 28 years until 1968.

During this time there were further constitutional changes in the status of Puerto Rico. In 1946 the first indigenous Puerto Rican governor was appointed and in 1948 the first gubernatorial elections were held and Munoz Marín became the island's first elected leader. In 1950 the US President signed Public Law 600 which allowed Puerto Ricans to draft their own constitution under the "Commonwealth" *Estado Libre Asociado* (Free Associated State) form of government. Shortly after the US advised the UN that Puerto Rico was a "self-governing territory". In 1967, 60% of voters in a plebiscite on the status of the island voted to retain Commonwealth status.

Puerto Rican politics

There have been three main strands in Puerto Rican political life coalescing around the three perceived options for Puerto Rico's political status. These are the retention of the present Commonwealth status, perhaps with modifications, complete independence, and full statehood and integration in the USA.

In electoral terms those who wish to retain Commonwealth status have been the most consistently successful. The Popular Democrats remained in power for 28 years until 1968, when a split allowed the pro-statehood New Progressive Party into power. The Popular Democrats under Rafael Hernández Colón regained power in 1972, with 50% of the vote. In 1976 the New Progressives under Carlos Romero Barceló gained power with 48.3% of the vote compared to 45.3% for the Popular Democrats. In 1980 Romero Barceló was reelected as Governor but with a margin of only 3,000 votes while the Popular Democrats gained control of the legislature. In 1984 the Popular Democrats under Hernández Colón again won the governorship and the legislature.

The Popular Democrats hope to gain more autonomy for Puerto Rico under the present Commonwealth status but they know that this depends in large part on a convincing defeat of the pro-statehood party, coupled with the victory of a Democrat President in the US. In general Republicans tend to favour the statehood option and both Presidents Ford and Reagan made statements in support of Puerto Rican statehood, although in practice there was no change to the status quo nor does such change appear likely in the future. However in the 1970s and early 1980s Puerto Rico received "statelike" treatment in most federal aid programmes, notably that of Food Stamps. In 1982 the Congress took Puerto Rico out of the Food Stamp programme and substituted a reduced block grant to run its own smaller nutritional programme.

The option of full independence has been one which has gained emotional support but little electoral success. For example in the 1967 plebiscite only 0.6% voted for complete independence and in the 1976 elections two pro-independence parties gained only 6.4% of the vote. Pro-independence activists have sometimes used violent methods for their cause and some have been tried and jailed. They have sought UN intervention and have received support from the UN Committee on Decolonization but — due to resistance on the part of the USA — have been unable to have the topic debated at the General Assembly. Opposition to the ideal of full independence is especially strong on economic grounds as it would remove the US trade, aid and citizenship links. A referendum, offering a choice between increased autonomy within Commonwealth status, full statehood or independence, is expected to take place in 1991.

Social and economic factors

Puerto Rico is poor by the standards of the mainland USA but its average income is above that of most independent Caribbean island states. In 1982 unemployment had reached 24% and 60% of the island's families remained below the US poverty line. Fifty-six per cent of the population was eligible for food stamps and in 1981-82 the island received $875 m in food stamps — 10% of the US total, although the Puerto Rican population is only 2% of the US population. Only massive infusions of federal grants, payments and loans, were able to lower the differentials somewhat, accounting for $4 billion a year of the gross national product of $11.7 billion. Some critics have argued that over-dependence on the US for subsidies has crippled the economy and work ethic, while supporters of the present status say that these subsidies have encouraged industries to set up in Puerto Rico, where wage levels are lower than the mainland but initial setting up costs are higher.

Puerto Rican immigration to the USA

Large-scale Puerto Rican migration to the USA began after World War II, when a combination of economic boom conditions in the USA, depressed conditions in Puerto Rico and the development of cheap air travel between the two resulted in a quadrupling of the Puerto Rican population in the USA between 1940 and 1950 to 310,000. During the next decade migration accelerated so that by 1960 there were 887,000 Puerto Ricans in the USA, including 272,000 US-born Puerto Ricans. In the 1970s migration slowed to around 20,000 a year as economic recession reduced the opportunities available; even so by 1970 the Puerto Rican population had grown to 1.3 million. In 1980 it had reached just over two million, a 41% increase, evenly split between island and US-born Puerto Ricans. Return migration is also an important factor with US-born Puerto Ricans returning to work or retire on Puerto Rico.

Puerto Ricans had initially concentrated in New York and 82% of the migrants resided in New York City in 1952. By 1980 the population was far more dispersed with only 49% in New York and large concentrations in New Jersey, Illinois, Florida, California and Pennsylvania. However in New York Puerto Ricans are still 10% of the population and 25% of the school population. Initially the migrants were unskilled or semi-skilled workers but today there is a broader spectrum of skills including professionals and graduates, who cannot find work on the island.

Puerto Ricans are part of the growing communities of Hispanic origin in the USA and are the largest Hispanic community in the north-east. Family income is the lowest for any racial or ethnic group in the US apart from native American Indians. One reason is that the Puerto Rican population is predominantly a young one — nearly half the population is still of school age. Other factors have to do with language — the first language of the Puerto Rican population is Spanish — residence, education and discrimination.

Most Puerto Ricans (75% in 1980) live in inner-city areas and are thus both urban and poor. Few own their own homes and many lack their own transportation which limits job opportunities. Families are larger than the US average. Significant gains have been made in access to education although Puerto Ricans, starting from a low level, are still less likely to finish high school or college than most Americans. Island-born children are more likely to have educational problems than US-born ones. Mother tongue, bilingual and bi-cultural educational programmes are improving access for many, who formerly would have been alienated by language problems.

According to the 1980 census Puerto Ricans had an unemployment rate of 11.7% compared to 8.9% for all Spanish origin persons and 6.6% for all Americans. However the true, unrecorded unemployment rate is much higher. Most Puerto Ricans work in manufacturing, transport, clerical and service industries, where they tend to earn salaries at the bottom of the scale. There are however growing numbers in the professional and managerial categories.

Puerto Ricans also face problems of discrimination although this problem is recognized and official attempts are being made to tackle it. For example in the early 1970s when Puerto Ricans were 10% of New York's population they held only 6% of the jobs in the city administration, including only 3% of administrators and 2% of professional jobs, and were only 1.8% of the police force. Similar figures were reported from other cities. In 1976 a US Employment Opportunity Commission reported discrimination in trade unions and apprenticeships.

Puerto Ricans in the USA have the right to vote in federal and state elections but voting participation is low, in contrast to the regular 80% participation levels recorded in Puerto Rico itself. In 1980 there was only one Puerto Rican Congressman, representing the South Bronx district of New York, where there is a heavy concentration of Puerto Ricans.[2] In an effort to increase electoral strength and representation on issues affecting Puerto Rico the National Puerto Rican Coalition was formed in the late 1970s.

(See also *Mexican Americans*)

[2]Puerto Rico's Resident Commissioner has a voice but no vote in the House of Representatives, although he can vote in the various committees to which he belongs.

Further References

The Inuit of Canada, MRG Report No. 60, 1983

Canada's Indians, MRG Report No. 21, 1982

French Canada in Crisis, MRG Report No. 44, 1982

The Original Americans: US Indians, MRG Report No. 31, 1986

The Mexican Americans, MRG Report No. 39, 1979

Puerto Ricans in the US, MRG Report No. 58, 1983

Haitian Refugees in the US, MRG Report No. 52, 1986

SOUTH AND CENTRAL AMERICA

The minorities question in South and Central America is dominated by the case of the Amerindians, though there are many other important issues. The Spanish, Portuguese, British, French and Dutch colonization of the area destroyed the indigenous empires, and reduced the peoples to powerlessness through conquest, annihilation, enslavement, assimilation, evangelization, and social and political domination. The States of Latin America do not reflect native power, but the power of the colonizers and immigrants from Europe. The indigenous peoples do not have the same residue of treaties and agreements with the invading powers as exists in North America.

The starting point for the current renaissance of Indian organizations and action for justice is not therefore the implementation of historic agreements but basic human rights. Contemporary involvement in ecological issues has also helped to focus interest on the survival of forest-dwelling Indians whose non-destructive relationship to their environment is qualitatively different from that of the new peoples. Most Amerindians, however, are now peasant agriculturalists or survivors at the margins of society at some remove from centres of power. Concern for the maintenance of authentic cultures must, therefore, be matched by concern for the social and economic condition of indigenous groups and their participation in the social order.

Besides the Amerindians, the situation of South Americans of African descent is also negative in terms of discrimination and social deprivation. Descendants of slaves (Brazil was the last major nation to abolish the slave trade) find that colour counts against them: "blackness" can still indicate social inferiority despite the reality of racial mixing and the vivid cultural contributions made by imported peoples. The overall "melting-pot" philosophy favoured in the regions does not necessarily operate to secure justice and equality, even for those whose desire is to be integrated into the mainstream of society.

The reports carry over to other issues related to this "melting-pot" — the Welsh of Patagonia and the Falklands/Malvinas. Current social and political structures in Latin America are on the whole intolerant of expressions of non-Latin cultural specifics. Minorities are expected to become assimilated, to speak Spanish or Portuguese, and assume the identity of their host cultures.

Instruments on Minority Rights

The record of State participation in general human rights instruments is good. Most States are also parties to the American Convention on Human Rights and the ILO's Convention on Indigenous and Tribal Populations (see *Appendix 2.1*). A notable omission is the refusal of Brazil to become a party to either International Covenant on Human Rights, though it is a party to the International Convention on the Elimination of all Forms of Racial Discrimination (see *Appendix 2.2*). How much this means in practice is not clear, since Chile is a party to these instruments, despite a very poor record on human rights.

Latin American States played a prominent part in the drafting of the Universal Declaration of Human Rights. During the drafting, Government representatives gave expression to a view on minorities which has been maintained with great consistency until the present day: that there is no need for special or targeted rights for minorities; general human rights on a non-discriminatory basis were sufficient. Further, many Latin American States deny that they have minorities. Article 27 of the International Covenant on Civil and Political Rights opens with the phrase "in those States in which ethnic, religious or linguistic minorities exist . . .". This was suggested by Chile to the Human Rights Commission, and, according to its representative, the Article was neither general in scope nor universal in application — it did not pertain to Chile. The representative of Brazil put the matter succinctly: "Brazil and the other American States did not recognize the existence of minorities on the American continent." For a minority to exist "a group of people must have been transferred 'en bloc' without a chance to express their will freely, to a State with a population most of whom differed from them in race, language or religion. Thus, groups which had been gradually and deliberately formed by immigrants within a country could not be considered minorities". So individuals who might well be treated as a collective with its own rights in European constitutions are instead guaranteed a full range of civil, political, economic and social rights. As noted above, assimilation of minorities is the general policy followed in Latin America. Thus, Article 2 of Mexico's *Ley General de Población* describes Mexican priorities as "fusion of the nation's ethnic groups, assimilation of foreigners and the preparation of indigenous groups for incorporation in national life through an improvement in their physical, economic and social conditions". The States, for example, will usually designate an official language, lack of fluency in which may disbar from voting in national elections.

However, a distinction must be made between "new" immigrants and indigenous groups. A number of States have made important modifications to their legal systems in recent years to recognize, perhaps for the first time, the indigenous peoples' contribution to culture and society. Peru's decree law 21156 (1976) provides: "Quechua is recognized as an official language of the Republic on the same footing as Spanish." Important modifications in the area of indigenous status have also been made recently by States such as Argentina, Brazil, Guatemala, Nicaragua and Panama. The most extensive concession to the indigenous groups has been made by Nicaragua. The Constitution declares that "the people of Nicaragua are multi-ethnic and are an integral part of the Central American nation" (Article 8); and "Spanish is the official language of the State. The languages of the [indigenous] communities of the Atlantic Coast shall also have official use in the cases established by law" (Article 11). Further, "the communities of the Atlantic Coast are an indivisible part of the Nicaraguan people, enjoy the same rights and have the same obligations as all Nicaraguans . . . [they] . . . have the right to preserve and develop their cultural identities within the framework of the national unity, to be granted their own forms of social organization, and to administer their local affairs according to their traditions".

The State recognizes communal forms of land ownership of the communities of the Atlantic Coast. Equally, it recognizes their "enjoyment, use and benefit of the waters and forests of the communal lands" (Article 89). Article 90 strikes a very positive note on the cultural contribution of the indigenous people: "The communities of the Atlantic Coast have the right to the free expression and preservation of their language, art and culture. The development of their culture and their values enriches the national culture . . . ." Article 181 promises that the State will implement, through law, autonomous government in the regions inhabited by the communities of the Atlantic Coast for the exercise of their rights. The autonomy law has been promulgated (see *Appendix 2.3*). These developments open a gap between the treatment accorded to the newest (immigrants) and oldest strata (the indigenous) in Latin American society; neither exercise political hegemony but the uniqueness of the latter group is slowly being recognized after centuries of oppression and neglect.

Treatment of minorities

The general standard of human rights in Latin America has been low in recent years, partly because of the retreat of democracy and the rise of military and authoritarian governments. In a general climate of oppression, minorities of various kinds are the first to suffer in terms of their economic and social levels, as well as in civil and political rights. The restoration of democracy which has taken place in Argentina, Bolivia, Brazil, Uruguay and other States may do much to ameliorate these conditions. The existence of democratic governments and written constitutions is an essential preliminary to further action. The implementation of guarantees of non-discrimination and equality can then be translated into reality.

On the other hand, appropriate policies for indigenous groups must be devised. The ILO's Convention of Indigenous and Tribal Populations has been widely supported by governments because it is a convention on the protection and integration of indigenous populations. The concept of integration can easily become a policy of assimilation, with a concomitant lack of respect for the authenticity of indigenous culture. Anthropology has gradually purged its vocabulary of notions of the "primitive", the "undeveloped", the "inferior", and moved towards the replacement of hierarchical assumptions about cultures by understanding and appreciation of the diverse cultural responses to their environment evolved by human groups. Law and policy require similar adaptations. The recognition of the indigenous contribution in some States is welcome, but not all States participate. International developments may assist policy-makers: the ILO has produced a revised Convention on the Indigenous with the overall aim of reducing the stress on integration and increasing the element of participation by indigenous peoples in decisions about their future. The United Nations is moving towards a Universal Declaration of Indigenous Rights (see *Appendix 2.4*) which will incorporate concepts of the authentic identity and status of indigenous peoples and "ethnodevelopment": the right of the peoples to develop along freely chosen lines within the larger family of the State.

For all that, there is always opposition and resistance to challenges to the power and privilege of dominant groups. The indigenous peoples form an authentic Fourth World, an underclass with a fragile power to repel external pressures. Five centuries of oppression and marginalization have destroyed much of their unique civilizations. The task of saving them some place in a developing continent is itself a major one.

Afro-Brazilians

Alternative names: **"people of colour", various specific terms**
Location: **throughout Brazil, especially in Bahia province**
Population: **13-57 million**
% of population: **10%-44%**
Religion: **Catholic, indigenous African beliefs**
Language: **Portuguese**

The Afro-Brazilians are the descendants of the African slaves who were brought to Brazil by the Portuguese colonizers and who today comprise one of the largest groups of people of African descent in the world, larger in fact than in many African countries. According to the 1980 census 44% of the population are *preto* or *pardo* (black or coloured). Yet it is difficult to define the meaning of the term "black" in the Brazilian context. Some 20 different shades of colour are recognized by Brazilians, ranging from white to black. The term "people of colour" covers almost all groups who are recognizably non-white while "mulatto" signifies a mixed race group which is neither black nor white. There are probably about 10% of the population who are recognizably black or distinctly dark and considerably more who have some African ancestry.

These factors make it particularly difficult to draw conclusions concerning legal, political, social and economic rights. Although Brazil prides itself on being a racial democracy there exists strong pressure to aspire to "whiteness", Afro-Brazilians are almost completely unrepresented in any area of decision-making in the country's administration or commerce.

West African slaves were imported by Portuguese colonists from around 1530 to work the sugar cane plantations. Slavery continued until 1888, 66 years after Brazil had obtained independence from Portugal. It is estimated that during those years some 3.65 million men, women and children were imported, of whom about 1.2 million were sent to the province of Bahia. Salavador Bahia has become the most African of Brazilian cities and even today many aspects of African influence are present. Other provinces and states to which slaves were sent include Rio de Janeiro, Minas Gerais, São Paulo, Pernambuco, Rio Grande do Sol and Parana.

The blackness of the population is believed to have been diminished by significant, often subsidized, European migration between 1850 and 1900, and the tendency for marriages and unions to involve the mixing of races. The Portuguese are often considered to be less bigoted than their Anglo-Saxon counterparts and an ecclesiastical belief in the possibility of slaves possessing souls, and therefore human rights, became recognized in law. In theory, slaves were allowed to buy their freedom and even take out complaints against their masters. In practice however many of these rights did not exist.

There exists in Brazil today the potential to create a genuinely racially egalitarian society. The 1951 Alfonso Arinos Law made discrimination based on race or colour in public establishments, education and employment a criminal offence punishable by a jail term or fine, and Brazil is a signatory to the Convention on the Elimination of All-Racial

Discrimination. Yet at present blacks, almost without exception, find themselves outside the mainstream of political decision-making and it seems that the only areas where they can achieve prominence are in entertainment and football.

In any case Brazil is a highly stratified society within which upward mobility is difficult for the working class and poor. Decision-making is in the hands of a tiny elite, which used to comprise the landowners but now includes members drawn from industry, the armed forces, the intelligentsia and church. Furthermore from 1964 to 1985 the country was ruled by a military elite and political parties were forced to operate within a narrow spectrum. The introduction of democracy has not however brought greater equality and recent "economic restructuring" has severely affected the poorest groups.

The distinction between theory and practice is very important in an assessment of the Afro-Brazilian position because there are no legal impediments to his or her advancement in society. The claim that "people of colour" are not discriminated against is only valid if the broadest definition of that term is applied and it is not true for Africans and dark mulattoes. It seems that the social, economic and political structures are such that, by their very nature, they act against the interests of the Afro-Brazilian. The result is that the few blacks who make the leap to "whiteness" tend to perpetuate the myth that Brazilian society is egalitarian. With the abolition of slavery no measures were put in place to give the ex-slave a position where he could take advantage of the competition he would encounter in a rapidly expanding economy. Thus he was handicapped from the start and a series of ultimately self-reinforcing myths were perpetuated about blacks. A popular saying has it that: "In Brazil there is no racism; the negro knows his place." In a society which denies the presence of discrimination, racism surfaces in more subtle guises. The term *boa aparentica* —

good appearance — is a typical example of how, in advertisements for housing, employment or education, blacks can be discriminated against with total impunity.

The latest census figures confirm that Afro-Brazilians fare worse than whites in terms of their education, health, employment and earnings (even when they are doing the same job as whites) while their infant mortality and life expectancy rates are lower. In the 1985 Congress there were only three black members of a total of 548 while in the Catholic Church out of 12,000 priests only 20 were black and of 340 bishops only six were black.

While Afro-Brazilians have been encouraged to believe that they are the most fortunate of all the blacks in the Americas, especially in comparison with those of the USA, political action on a small scale has continued since the 1930s. A group formed to unite "people of colour", *A Frenta Negra Brasileira* — The Black Brazilian Front — proposed improving political, social and economic conditions for all blacks and mulattoes. The group gained considerable support but was suspended following a *coup d'etat*. When the ban was finally lifted the group emerged without its political programme emphasizing instead cultural and recreational activities.

In 1978 the first racial demonstration in living memory took place in São Paulo. Five thousand people took part in the event which was organized by the Unified Black Movement Against Racial Discrimination. But incidents like this tend to be sporadic, symptomatic perhaps of a general disregard for the issues raised by race in Brazil. 1988 was the centenary of the abolition of slavery in Brazil and Afro-Brazilians used the occasion to again draw attention to their disadvantaged position in Brazilian society, even though official celebrations ignored the descendants of the slaves and their contribution to Brazil.

(See also *Afro-Cubans*)

Afro-Cubans

Alternative names: **Cuban-Africans**
Location: **throughout Cuba, especially Oriente province**
Population: **3-4 million (est.)**
% of population: **30%-40% (est.)**
Religion: **Catholicism, African beliefs**
Language: **Spanish**

Post-revolutionary Cuba claims to be the most racially harmonious society in Latin America. Even before the revolution of 1959, the island was regarded by many as a model in racial harmony. However, scant records and a paucity of systematic studies both pre- and post-revolution make accurate assessment of these claims almost impossible. As in Brazil, there are few pure blacks or pure whites — most Cubans find themselves somewhere between the two extremes. As a result, the social order of the country can quite legitimately be viewed in terms of social class. Another problem is the polarization of commentators on the subject. Facts are distorted or omitted to further political argument, leaving little room for consensus of opinion.

Blacks first arrived in Cuba as slaves to work the plantations about 450 years ago. They played a prominent role in the war of independence from Spain between 1895 and 1898, constituting the bulk of the rank-and-file (though not officers) but failed to achieve equality after the subsequent victory. After attaining liberty from slavery in 1886 the struggle for racial equality was fought within the prevailing political structures and through existing political parties. The Constitution of 1901 guaranteed formal equality of all races. By 1908 an organization which later became the *Partido de los Independientes de Color* was formed. The Morua Amendments to the Electoral Reform Law of 1910 effectively closed the door to parties organized along racial lines and led the *Independientes* to take up arms. The war of 1912, often belittlingly referred to as *la querrita del 12* ("the little war of 12") saw the death of thousands of blacks, both rebels and civilians, in direct war actions and in race riots and massacres.

The *Independientes* were more or less erradicated by the war and its aftermath, and no other political organization of blacks emerged before the revolution of 1959. The so-called 50% law, passed after the 1933 radical uprising, established that all employers must employ at least 50% Cuban natives. Although this did not materially alter discrimination against blacks, it did improve their employment situation. Batista, a mulatto, by rebelling with rank-and-file against the army, effectively eliminated the army's elite and paved the way for blacks to enter all ranks of the armed forces.

While the Constitutional Convention of 1940 produced a document which established full equality for all Cubans, the administration was slow to enact complementary legislation. However, there is some evidence to suggest that in the lead-up to the 1959 revolution, the position of the Afro-Cuban was improving, if not with respect to their fellow country people, then at least in absolute terms. It seems, also, that during the later part of Batista's rule, there was a concerted effort to divert black attention from the gathering revolutionary movement — which was portrayed as mainly for the benefit of whites. The effort was only partly successful. When revolutionary forces entered the streets of Havana in 1959, blacks were represented at all levels, from officials to privates.

Since the revolution, it is true to say that, whatever the incidence of racial prejudice, actual discrimination has been eliminated. No-one is barred access to jobs, education or social facilities of any kind for reasons of skin colour. Blacks, as the lowest pre-revolutionary social order, have perhaps gained most. Early redistributive measures — the two Agrarian Reform Laws and the Urban Law, amongst others — improved the status of Afro-Cubans. Castro was at great pains to address racial prejudice in Cuban society, but has been criticized by some commentators for not introducing elements of "positive discrimination". Although 30% to 40% of the population are of African descent, this figure is not reflected in the top echelons of the country's power structure. However, the second echelon reveals many Afro-Cubans in relative positions of power, though no formal study has been made to verify the extent of black participation in Cuban government.

Before 1959, while discrimination was officially illegal, prejudice was rife. Public schools, which suffered from shortages of resources, were integrated, while private schools were almost exclusively white. Some 30% of high school students attended private schools before the revolution. By 1961, the private school system had disappeared and a more integrated system had taken its place. While the revolutionary government has taken measures to equalize access to health care, developing a public health system with the emphasis on prevention, some commentators conclude that racial inequality in public health remains a feature of Cuban life. Other changes since the revolution occurred in the housing sector. While no housing discrimination existed pre-revolution, Afro-Cubans tended to live in more dilapidated areas. But the revolution brought an immediate 50% reduction in rents and eventually ownership of houses for occupiers. As a result, the rate of black home ownership is high. But 30 years after the Revolution many Cubans, both black and white, may well have higher expectations and ambitions than the present system can offer.

(See also *Afro-Brazilians*)

Amerindians of South America

Alternative name: **over 100 separate peoples (see map)**
Location: **throughout South America**
Population: **total 20.5 million**
% of population: **from over 50% (Bolivia, Peru) to less than 1% (e.g. Brazil 0.17%)**
Religion: **indigenous beliefs, Catholic, Protestant**
Language: **various**

The Amerindians are the original peoples of the South American continent, who from the time of the first European invasion 500 years ago and the continuous settlement since, have had their populations decimated by a combination of warfare and disease. More than 20 million Amerindians have died — a figure equal to that of the original pre-European population. Amerindians are found throughout South America; they are not a homogenous group and are divided into many peoples — increasingly referred to as "nations". The two major divisions are between those of the Andean highlands and of the tropical lowlands which contain the Amazon and Orinoco River basins. The rights of indigenous people centre on the principle of self-determination and especially land rights.

History

The first Amerindians crossed the frozen Bering Straits about 30,000 years ago and between 15,000 and 20,000 years ago began to spread throughout the highlands and lowlands of South America. Agricultural settlements began to appear around 5,000 years ago. The most famous quasi-state organization — there were several — was the Quichua-speaking Incas who held power between present-day Equador in the north and northern Chile and Argentina in the south. The continent contained a broad spectrum of socio-economic and cultural patterns.

Soon after Colombus' arrival on American soil, Spain and Portugal had agreed to divide the uncharted world amongst themselves. The colonists were eager to exploit trade in wood and sugar, which soon brought them into conflict with the indigenous peoples. Labour shortages caused colonists to seek indigenous slaves which produced resistance in the form of hostilities that lasted throughout the century. To complicate matters, French and Dutch interests in the continent fought Portuguese hegemony — and exploited Indian resistance to their own ends. Meanwhile Jesuit missionaries tried to bring Indians into *reducions*, where they were killed in their hundreds of thousands by diseases such as dysentry, influenza and smallpox. Settlers looking for more land were also responsible for countless deaths among Amerindians. On the Pacific coast, the Spanish did not bother setting up trading relations, but proceeded to milk the Andean area for minerals.

By 1750 the continent was under Iberian rule, although many areas defied the invaders. Portugal expelled the Jesuits in 1759 and Spain followed nine years later. The French Bourbon dynasty, which had control of the Spanish throne began to liberalize practices in Peru, mainly as a means of combating British interests in the area. However, Britain eventually gained economic predominance in South America, Andean Indian resistance in Quichua and Aymara, though solidly backed, was put down. Even today several

Amerindians of South America

Panama
Panama City

Venezuela
Carácas

Georgetown
Paramaribo

Guyana
Surinam
French Guiana
Cayenne

Bogotá

Colombia

Ecuador
Quito

Peru

Lima

Bolivia
La Paz

Brazil
Brasília

Chile
Santiago

Paraguay
Asunción

Argentina

Uruguay
Buenos Aires
Montevideo

Pacific Ocean

Atlantic Ocean

Falklands
(Malvinas)

**List of
indigenous peoples
shown on the map**

Venezuela
1   Wayuu (Guajiro)
2   Yukpa
3   Paujanos
4   Barí
5   Warao
6   Piaroa
7   Piaroa
8   Pemon
9   Akwayo
10 Panare
11 Ye'cuana
12 Yanomami

Columbia
13 Paez
14 Guanbiano
15 Cuna
16 Emberá
1   Wayuu (Guajiro)
17 Guahibo (Cuiva)

Ecuador
18 Quichua
19 Shuar
20 Waorani
21 Cofán
22 Secoya
23 Siona
24 Zaparo
25 Otavalo
26 Colorados
    Pinchada
27 Cayapa

Peru
28 Aguaruna
29 Quechua
30 Aymara
31 Huambisa
32 Harakmbut
33 Ashaninka (Campa)
34 Yanesha
    (Amuesha)
35 Amarakaeri
36 Shipibo

Bolivia
37 Chiriguanos
38 Aymara
39 Toromonas
40 Jora
41 Chimanes
42 Mojos
43 Movima
44 Chiquitanos
45 Guarayos
46 Mataco
47 Ayoreo

Chile
48 Aymara
49 Mapuche
50 Yamana
51 Qawasqar

Argentina
52 Kollas
53 Tobas
54 Mataco
55 Guarani
56 Mapuche
57 Tehuelches
58 Selk'nam
59 Chiriguano
60 Mocovi
61 Mbya Guarani
62 Onu

Paraguay
63 Toba-Maskoy
64 Ayoreo
65 Mataco
66 Mbaya
67 Aché
68 Ava-Chiripá

Brazil
69 Urueu-wau-wau
70 Yanomami
71 Cinta Larga
72 Xavante
73 Pataxo-Ha-Ha-Hae
74 Kaingang
75 Arara
76 Parakana
77 Kreen Akarore
78 Txukahame
79 Waimiri-Atroari
80 Nambikwara
81 Xokleng
82 Guarani
83 Asurini
84 Surui
85 Gavioe
86 Tukano
87 Baniwa
88 Maku
89 Karajá
90 Tubarao
91 Arua
92 Zoró
93 Tapirapá

French Guiana
94 Arawak
95 Galibi
96 Palikur
97 Emerillon
98 Oyampi
99 Wayana

Guyana
100 Akawaio
101 Patamona
102 Arekuna Makusi
103 Waiwai

Surinam
104 Trio
105 Wayana
106 Akuriyo
107 Arawak
108 Carib

0   200   400   600   800 Statute Miles

0   200 400 600 800 1000 1200 Kilometres

Amerindians of South America

movements take their names from the resistance movements of the 1770s. American-born Creoles proved more successful with their independence drive and out of this movement 17 republics had been created by 1825. For the Amerindians, independence did not provide emancipation, Brazil did not gain Republic status until 1889. After independence many Europeans migrated to South America and took over Indian land.

Wars between the Republics in the nineteenth century had further devastating effects on the Amerindians. The War of the Pacific, won by Chile, was fought over nitrate resources. The victorious Chilean army was then used to decimate the Mapuche people. When the army invaded Peru, resistance against occupation was largely Indian, Other wars included the War of the Triple Alliance — between Paraguay and Brazil, Argentina and Uruguay, and the Chaco War, fought between Bolivia and Paraguay. The new Republics were unable to maintain their liberal stances and power fell into the hands of personal leaders — the *caudillos* — who, with their own armies set about the destruction of peoples such as the Mapuche.

Through the nineteenth and twentieth centuries various economic booms such as in rubber, oil and coffee have resulted in the often ruthless exploitation of Amerindians. The best documented case took place in Putumayo river region of Peru, where rubber exploitation led to deaths of 40,000 Indians between 1886 and 1919. The end of World War I brought an end to British supremacy in South America. Between 1919 and 1929 US foreign investment in Andean countries rose from US $10 million to $316 million. Rapid industrialization brought many Indians to the cities. Out of these masses grew organizations which challenged the powers of the oligarchies who backed the *caudillos*. Writers such as Gonzalez Prado and Mariategui advocated nationalism coupled with indigenous social and philosophical ideals. The world economic crisis of the 1930s brought a wave of populist and nationalist feelings. In this climate the Indian Protection Service (SPI), formed in Brazil in 1910, and the Mexican model were employed to contact Indian groups and protect them until they were ready for integration.

In the 20 years following World War II industrial expansion increased the demand for foreign capital. Costs rose and the industrial boom declined causing several South American countries to fall into the hands of military dictatorships. International banks began to look for clients to whom they could lend money — a trend which increased with the oil crisis of the

1970s. In Brazil, mining, agriculture, pastoralism and forest exploitation increased invasions of Indian territory while powerful interests within the renamed state organ for Indian protection — the National Indian Foundation (FUNAI) — worked to facilitate the government's development plans. Currently external debt of South American countries exceeds US $250 billion, a factor which has aided the demise of the powers of the military dictatorships.

Land rights

During the past 30 years all Andean countries have recognized some form of agrarian reform, often with disastrous results for Indians. In 1952 the Bolivian Reform, which divided communal land into thousands of individual allotments, resulted in the destruction of many communities. Chile brought in similar legislation in 1979 which reduced Mapuche communities from 2,066 to 655. Peru, in contrast, brought in reforms which emphasized communality, but problems with lack of credit, a weak infrastructure and the machinations of ex-landlords have limited their effects. However the recent decline of military power has seen, at best, a slow return of land to the indigenous population. Generally, the return to democracy has done little to benefit the Amerindians.

The Amerindians are unanimous in their demands for the recognition of their territorial rights. A symbiotic relationship between the highland peoples of the *quichua* — from the relatively fertile lower mountain slopes, and the *puna* — from the higher mountain areas, has helped to maintain a complementary link between the social groups of both zones. The Maoist liberation movement, *Sendero Luminoso*, tried to break these ties in 1982–83 to create "self-sufficiency" and made many enemies as a result. Peoples of these regions tend to live in stable communities based on herding and the agricultural cycle. The lowlands are divided between *varzea* — the fertile flood plains — and *terra firma* where land is not particularly productive. The inhabitants of *terra firma* have traditionally been more migratory, relying on hunting and fishing more than horticultural production. Dualism is a primary feature of Andean thinking, linking the spiritual world with the human environment. The consequences of encroachment on indigenous lands have severely disrupted traditional life in lowland South America. Between 10% and 25% of all indigenous people live in urban areas, while only about 10% of Indian land is recognized as such. A current messianic movement known as *Israelitas* which is spreading through the Peruvian highlands, is largely in response to the havoc wreaked by *Sendero Luminoso* and the Peruvian armed forces.

Throughout the twentieth century the political and economic influence of the USA has increased in South America. Apart from receiving, on average, 30%–40% of each country's exports, the USA invests millions of dollars in development and support aid through the US Agency for International Development — USAID — which is accountable to the State department, the World Bank and the Inter-American Development Bank — IDB. While with one hand, USAID supports many indigenous organizations, with its other, it joins the multilateral banks in projects which threaten indigenous people's very existence. Multinational companies operate throughout South America specializing in extractive, agricultural, pastoral or energy concerns. State debts arising from these investments cut down on progressive policies towards indigenous peoples.

The Christian Church in South America often works in favour of indigenous peoples, but the proselytizing nature of their work is also counter-productive. The division between Catholic and Protestant churches is divisive and confusing and as a result, some people abandon their traditional beliefs, while others ignore missionary work altogether. Catholic missionaries work on a congregational basis where they attract Indians to live on mission stations which in many ways resemble the old Jesuit *reducions*. Economic power is concentrated in the missions which are usually based on Iberian farming communities containing feudalistic elements.

Economic and religious intervention in Amerindian societies can take two forms. The anti-indigenous form destroys life, land and culture, whereas the more fashionable approach now is the indigenist way which softens the blow of heavy-handed integration. However, the end result is the same — the initiative for change and self-development is taken out of the hands of indigenous peoples who are paternalistically guided onto the "right path".

Since the European invasion, indigenous communities throughout the continent have co-operated to resist the occupation of their territories. This has taken three forms: avoiding conflict by moving to another area; using the weapons of the occupiers — a political means; or force. Religious movements such as the *Israelitas*, mentioned above, and *Loma Santa* have employed these three strategies in attempts to gain self-determination and indigenous rights. Many groups now exist which cross national boundaries. Their organizations work at community, regional, national and international levels and their strategies, primarily non-violent, embrace Indianism, which follows strict ethnic lines, or entryism, which involves groups in the politics of their country.

Venezuela

There are about 150,000 indigenous people in Venezuela, divided into some 30 language groups. The country is divided into 20 states and two territories, each with its own autonomous assembly.

Under the *Ley de Misiones*, a law passed in 1915, the Catholic Church was given responsibility for the conversion and integration of indigenous peoples. In 1948 the National Indigenist Commission was founded and in 1952 its technical arm, the Central Office of Indigenous Affairs — OCAI, was formed. A decree in 1959 gave the commission powers to work independently of the Church, but in practice this did not happen until the late 1960s. Recently OCAI has been transferred to the Ministry of Education and Internal Affairs, diminishing its already limited powers. At present, the government seems reluctant to take any major initiative on the indigenous question.

Most groups, such as the Bari, Wayuu, Yukpas, Paujanos, Piaroa, Pemon and Akwayo, suffer from a similar problem of colonists taking away their lands. The Warao and Karinas, in the north-east, are affected by oil exploration.

Colombia

There are about 300,000 indigenous peoples in Colombia dividing into more than 60 nations.

The central government has been a democracy since 1958. The country shares many legislative similarities to Venezuela — three-quarters of the indigenous-owned land is in the hands of missionaries. The Division of Indigenous Affairs (DAI) was set up in 1960. It has an inspection service, advisory body and eight commissions. Its effect on indigenous rights has been minimal. INCORA, the Colombian Institute of Agrarian Reform, set up reserve lands for Indians, but pressure from non-Indian landowners has minimized its effect.

In the Cauca region, 200,000 Paez and Guambiano Indians have had large tracts of land taken from them, but under CRIC — the Indigenous Regional Council, they have to some extent peacefully re-occupied their land. North of Cauca, in the rainforests, groups such as the Cuna and Embera have managed to retain their cultural identity in spite of having their land reduced from 10,000 hectares to 2,000 hectares. To the east, the Wayuu (Guajiro) have had 50,000 ha of their land leased to mining and tourist industries. In eastern Colombia the Guahibo have, since 1975, been demanding a reserved area from the government.

Ecuador

Nearly three million indigenous peoples live in the highlands. Most numerous are the Quichua-speaking groups and the Shuar. The lowlands are home to the smaller nations — the Wrarani, Cofan, Secoyas, Siona and Zaparos.

After a decade of largely military dictatorships, the country has had democracy since 1979. There is no legislation specifically for the indigenous peoples. Forced labour was abolished in 1964 and the *haciendas* were expropriated. These moves had little effect on the distribution of land and the Institute for Agrarian Reform and Colonization (IERAC) has been slow to implement changes, which, in any case, concentrate on individual land ownership, which the Indians reject as divisive. Shortages of land in the highlands have increased migration to the cities and groups such as the Cayapas and Colorados have retreated into the forest to escape encroachment. Between 10% and 15% of the Ecuadorian Amazon was destroyed during the first oil boom and colonization is still a major problem for the Indians. Violence erupted between the Shuar and colonists — a pattern which has been repeated throughout the Amazon.

Peru

The Quichua and Aymara peoples of the highlands of Peru constitute about half the total population — some nine million people in all. The Peruvian Amazon contains about 60 nations with a population of around 100,000.

Peru contains 25 departments operating under a democratic constitution which came into effect in 1980. A radical military dictatorship set up a co-operative land system in 1968 which served to break down the *hacienda* system, but most of the benefits were lost with changes in government and the disbandonment of the pro-Indian SINAMOS organization. Land rights in the forest are more or less ignored by the government and, although in the early 1970s some communities received titles, the process allowing this was slowed down after 1978.

The most serious violations of human rights among the indigenous peoples of South America are taking place in the highlands of Peru. Fighting between government forces and *Sendero Luminoso* has apparently caused the death or disappearance of 7,000 Indians. Indians suspected of supporting *Sendero* have been imprisoned and tortured. *Sendero* itself has destroyed traditional exchange patterns with its ideology. In the lowlands massive forest exploitation is taking place displacing groups such as the Aguaruna, Huambisa and Harakmbut.

Bolivia

The highlands of Bolivia are occupied by some three million Quichua and one million Aymara speaking peoples, while the lowlands are divided amongst about 30 nations totalling 150,000 people.

Bolivia is divided into nine departments and its governments shift between democracy and dictatorship. While agriculture and tin mining are officially Bolivia's main economies, unofficially, cocaine has surpassed these. When the present MNR government came to power in 1954 land reforms broke the *hacienda* system and gave land to 170,000 families. Based on individual titles, the law had the effect of dissipating the highland communities. Lowland communities are now trying to ensure that their titles are communal.

Allegations of torture of Indians, especially those belonging to Indianist movements, are widespread and many Indians have been killed in riots and attempted coups. It seems that in the past 10 years, four groups have died out — the Simonianos, Toromonas, Bororo and Jora, while others — the Chimanes, Mojos and Movima — are under threat.

Chile

About 15,000 Aymara people live in the north of Chile, some one million Mapuche live south of Santiago and yet further south live various nomadic peoples.

Chile is divided into 13 regions under the central government. While the Mapuche have borne the brunt of Chilean legislation, being forced into reserves and agricultural work, the Allende government began to restore land to them. These efforts were reversed by the Pinochet regime which called for the "division of the reserves and the liquidation of Indian communities". In 1978 a group of Regional Mapuche Councils was formed comprising Mapuche who were willing to work with the government. The Aymara and other indigenous groups are also affected by legislation aimed at the Mapuche. Since 1986 there has been a severe escalation of oppression of the Mapuche. A further threat for the Bio-Bio Mapuche is the hydro-electric project which will flood vast tracts of their land.

Argentina

There are 16 indigenous nations in Argentina consisting of nearly 350,000 people, living mainly in the north near the borders with Bolivia and Paraguay. Further south are some 36,000 Mapuche. The main criticism of the Argentinian government is that they break up Indian land and that their development policies are paternalistic. The State has a current National Plan for Indigenist Policy which promotes community development, supports culture, land and economic regeneration. Colonization is the main problem facing most Indians in the state. The Mapuche, divided by an arbitary border from their kin in Chile, seek free access.

Paraguay

There are 17 indigenous nations in Paraguay with a total population thought to be as high as 80,000. Most were once nomadic but have been forced to settle. The country has an eastern and a western province divided into 14 and 15 departments respectively. While the law recognizes indigenous communities, it also allows Indians to be forcibly resettled and makes no provision for enforcement of the law. The same can be said for the labour law.

The last 30 years have seen more land taken from the Indians than at any other time. This country, notorious for its "manhunts" in the past, is still allegedly host to "manhunters" in the form of the New Tribes Mission, who have been accused of hunting the Ayoreo people. Deforestation, particularly in the east, is another problem facing indigenous peoples.

Brazil

There are 225 indigenous nations in Brazil making a total of over 225,000 people. The nations live in a wide variety of environments, but most inhabit the Amazon and central regions of the country. Brazil is a federal republic with 23 states and three federal territories. Under a 1967 law, the government has sub-surface rights to indigenous land, can relocate Indians and also lease land to third parties. Since 1983 two Presidential Decrees have further eroded

Indian rights. Since the "economic miracle" of 1968 enormous expansion has led to repeated violations of indigenous rights.

Road building has brought dislocation and disease and hydro-electric projects threaten to flood the land of 35 nations. Mining and colonization are also serious threats. Threats to the rain forest by extensive logging have recently focused international attention onto the situation of indigenous peoples in Brazil, most notably at Altamira in February 1989, when 500 Indians met with officials from the World Bank, the government and international media. Earlier in June 1988 Indian groups had succeeded in modifying the section on Indians in the new Brazilian Constitution.

Guyana

Coastal Amerindians in Guyana are largely acculturated but in the interior there are the Arawak-speaking Wapisiana and the Carib-speaking Akawaio, Patamona, Arekuna Makusi and Waiwai — in all about 45,000 Indians. The Hinterland Department of the Ministry of Regional Development deals with Indian affairs. The Amerindian act of 1978 allows for titling of land to individuals and communities, with several exceptions.

Suriname

There are about 8,000 Amerindians in Suriname and several "Bush Negroes" — communities derived from runaway slaves of the eighteenth century. In the interior live the Trio, Wayana and Akuriyo, while Arawaks and Caribs inhabit the coast. The indigenous population has no special legislation and, while some villages have titles to land, all ownership rights belong to the government. The civil war which has been waged in Suriname since 1986, and in which the Amerindians have remained neutral, finally began to affect them. Reports indicate that Indians, mainly Arawaks, Caribs and Wayanas, have been relocated by government and guerrilla forces.

French Guiana

There are 4,500 indigenous people in French Guiana — on the coast live the Arawak, Galibi and Palikur, while inland are the Emerillon, Oyampi and Wayana. "Bush Negroes" also live in the interior. The country is still a French colony and administered by a Commissioner. Under the Inini Statute indigenous people could live as they liked, but in 1969 the Statute was abolished and the people abruptly brought under French socio-cultural rule. Traditional land rights are not recognized, leaving Indians open to invasion from a possible 30,000 French colonists and Brazilian gold prospectors.

Indians organizing

Indian resistance has taken many forms, guerrilla warfare or insurrection (often against hopeless odds), religious movements and, most commonly, indigenous political organizations. These have a long history starting from the sixteenth century; however from the 1970s new indigenous organizations have, for the first time, been able to transcend national and state barriers and to challenge repressive governments. These movements can be Indianist, i.e. wholly-Indian in membership and values, or syndicalist, joining together with non-Indians, most notably in political parties and trade unions. An Indian women's movement has also developed which emphasizes the relationship between colonization and the exploitation of women. International solidarity has been sought with other oppressed indigenous peoples and various Amerindian groups have worked through such UN bodies as the UN Working Group on Indigenous Populations and the International Labour Organization. Indians have joined together with human rights groups and, more recently, the international environment movement to fight for land rights and the protection of their land, rivers and forests. Such actions are important in the fight to save Indian peoples and their unique cultures from the death and destruction which continues to face them.

(See also *Caribs of Dominica; Maya of Guatemala; Mexico's Indians; Miskito Indians of Nicaragua*)

Caribs of Dominica

Alternative names: **Kwaib, Callinago**
Location: **Dominica, Windward Islands**
Population: **2,500 (70 "pure Carib")**
% of population: **3%**
Religion: **Christian**
Language: **French creole, English**

The Caribs (also called Callinago or Kwaib), are an indigenous minority of the island of Dominica, an independent state in the Eastern Caribbean. They are unique in being the last surviving Amerindian community in the Caribbean,[1] even though most of the Caribs are of mixed racial background. Of the total Carib population of about 2,500 only about 70 are "pure Carib", a further 300 are largely Carib while the remainder are of mixed Carib and African ancestry.

The Caribs were originally a branch of the Galibi Indians of Guyana who arrived in the Caribbean Islands around 1200 AD. The Carib men conquered the Arawaks and took local Arawak women, a fact reflected, until the early twentieth century, in their language; men spoke Carib, women Arawak. Society was matrilocal, even today this practice is fairly common. Columbus landed on Dominica in 1493 but the Spanish and other Europeans were kept at bay for 200 years while the other Callinago and Arawak peoples were exterminated by the colonizers. Ownership of the island was disputed throughout the eighteenth century by France and England but it was finally captured by the English in 1759 who allowed the French settlers to remain and sold the remaining cultivable land to English settlers.

The Caribs were driven north to the least accessible land and were allotted 134 acres without title by Queen Charlotte. By the end of the eighteenth century, 15,000 slaves had been imported from Africa to work the settlers' land. By 1903, when the British administrator gave the Caribs their present reserve (again without title), the population had dwindled. There are disputes as to the intended boundaries of the reserve and Caribs allege that areas which were intended to be incorporated have been wrongly withheld from its territory. In 1930 police raided

[1]Clusters of population with some Amerindian features have been noted in Guadeloupe and St Vincent, where the Caribs, along with those of Dominica, had signed a treaty with the French in 1660 stating that the two islands would not be colonized but would remain non-aliened Carib territory.

the reserve and two Caribs were killed and others injured.

It was not until November 1978 when Dominica achieved independence that Carib people were granted legal title to 3,700 acres of territory but this was after several years of deadlock with the government over an issue where Carib customary law conflicted with Dominican law. Under Carib law a Carib man may bring a non-Carib woman to live with him on Carib land but a Carib women with a non-Carib husband did not have the same entitlement. This, the Caribs argued, was the only way to protect the racial integrity of the Caribs. However the predominantly black Dominican government maintained that this could not be tolerated under the Dominican constitution and that it would prevent future "integration" of the Caribs with other Dominicans. Behind this dispute lay the increasing pressure on land in the island.

(See also *Miskito Indians of Nicaragua*)

The Caribs have always elected a chief whose duty it is to act in their interest. Prestige apart he enjoys no special privileges and acts together with a Council of five men. During the run-up to independence it was the Chief who negotiated with the Dominican government on the land issue. Traditionally the Caribs have been self-sufficient hunters and sailors but more recently they have devoted themselves to crafts and the production of goods for exchange, fishing, basket weaving and canoe-making. Some work as agricultural labourers on plantations outside the reserve. Apart from its natural beauty, the Caribs are the major tourist attraction on Dominica but they are also the most marginalized section of the population. Illiteracy and population density are higher than for the majority and in 1982 the only electricity on the reserve was connected to the local police station.

East Indians of the Caribbean

Alternative names: **Indo-Caribbeans, Hindustanis**
Location: **Caribbean island and rim countries**
Population: **Trinidad 460,000; Guyana 400,000; Suriname 147,000**
% of population: **Trinidad 40%; Guyana 51%; Suriname 37%**
Religion: **Hindu, Muslim, Christian**
Language: **"Hindustani" (local dialect of Hindi/Urdu), English or Dutch**

The "East Indians" of the Caribbean and Caribbean rim countries are the descendants of immigrants from the Indian sub-continent. Despite their name they are no relation to the indigenous aboriginal "Indians" who inhabit or formerly inhabited the area. The East Indians are, along with Black Afro-Caribbeans ("West Indians"), one of the two major ethnic groups in Trinidad and Tobago, Guyana and Suriname. There are also East Indian communities in Jamaica (one estimate for 1980 gives the East Indian population as 50,000), Grenada and the French islands of Martinique and Guadeloupe.

Indians were first brought to the Caribbean from the mid-1840s to work on white-owned sugar plantations as indentured labour to replace newly freed African slaves. The majority of immigrants were young men; later disturbances on the plantations forced the authorities to try

and correct the imbalance. Indenture was usually for five years and the labourer was subject to restricting and paternalistic regulations which were sometimes described as "a new system of slavery". After an initial number of years it was possible for the labourer to return to India but since many were offered land in order to entice them to stay near the estates, most stayed in their new country.

The racial tensions and stereotypes of later years were formed during the colonial period. Indians worked for less than Africans and were regarded as cheap and malleable labour. There were differences of culture between the Hindu and Muslim Indians and the Christian Africans. While the Africans, who were more likely to be literate in English, filled the jobs in the urban and commercial sectors, Indians were most likely to remain labourers and small farmers.

Trinidad and Tobago[1]

The East Indians of Trinidad and Tobago comprise around 40% of the total population; the remainder is mainly of African descent, with other groups of Chinese, Portuguese and Whites. Most East Indians are Hindus, divided into three main sects, most notably the Maha Sabha. About 15% are Muslims, mainly merchants and urban dwellers, and a small group are Christians, who are predominantly professionals and businessmen. Hindus are much more likely to be small farmers. Trinidad and Tobago became independent in 1962 and is a member of the Commonwealth.

From the mid-1950s politics was dominated by the People's National Movement (PNM) led by Eric Williams. Most Indians saw this as a black nationalist movement and attempted to build Indian parties to counter this, not very successfully. However economic problems and the growth of a "Black Power" movement among Africans led to increasingly authoritarian government which to some extent helped to overcome overt clashes between ethnic groups.

Trinidad, although a small island of a little over 5,000 square kilometres, has rich agricultural land and considerable oil reserves. During the nineteenth and early twentieth century both Indians and Africans worked in agriculture — the Indians in sugar, both on plantations and their own small plots, and the Africans in cocoa. When the market for cocoa collapsed in the 1920s the Africans moved into the oil, manufacturing, construction and service industries. Africans still dominate these sectors while Indians have done well in agriculture, the professions and small commercial enterprises. Indians are however under-represented in government service and economic sectors directly under government influence. The relative lack of economic competition between the two groups has meant that although racial divisions are evident they rarely emerge as overt tensions. In addition, oil income helped to make Trinidad one of the richest states in the Caribbean and Latin America throughout the 1970s.

The collapse of oil prices in the 1980s harmed both groups economically (*per capita* income fell by one third) and in 1986 the umbrella opposition party, the National Alliance for Reconstruction (NAR), decisively defeated the PNM after it had held power for 30 years. The NAR claimed to be a genuine multiracial party; however by 1989 it had split partly on racial and partly on political grounds, three Indian ministers had been sacked and a new Indian-based party had been formed.

Guyana

The East Indians of Guyana comprise slightly over 50% of the total population while the other main group is of African descent with much smaller groups of Portuguese and Chinese. There is also a small Amerindian community in the interior of the country. Most East Indians are Hindus with smaller groups of Muslims and Christians. Guyana, formerly the colony of British Guiana, became independent in 1966 and is a member of the Commonwealth.

Land shortage and competition for the small amount of land on the alluvial coastal strip, shaped the relationship between the two major ethnic groups in British Guiana. Africans bitterly resented the Indian indentured labour in the plantations and the economic competition that followed. Indians also established small rice farms. Africans worked in the bauxite industry and mining, while minor retailing was dominated by the Portuguese and Chinese. Africans dominated the civil service and police where Indians were, and continue to be, under-represented. As Indians moved into the towns from rural areas, areas of conflict were sharpened. There was widespread rioting and racial violence between East Indians and Africans in 1962-64, in which over 150 died. Indians had initially missed out on educational opportunities, as children were needed in the plantation labour force and they feared the effects of missionary-run schools. They later started establishing their own schools and participated more proportionately in government-run schools. After the value of Western educational qualifications became clear many Indians educated their children outside the country, and as a result Indians are today slightly over-represented in the professions of law and medicine.

The ethnic divide laid the basis for the main divisions with Guyanese politics, although these divisions were consistently exploited by the UK and later the USA, and the ruling party which has become consistently more authoritarian. However in the postwar period the two groups

[1] In 1987 the NAR government acknowledged the right of Tobago, the much smaller island to the north-east of Trinidad, to full internal self-government under the terms of an act passed in 1980. There were some indications that the islanders might push for further autonomy or even independence.

appeared united against colonial domination with the formation of the pro-independence socialist party the People's Progressive Party (PPP) with an Indian, Cheddi Jagan, as leader and an Afro-Guyanese, L.F.S. Burnham, as party chairman. The PPP won the first limited elections held under adult suffrage in 1953 but the then Governor, claiming that the PPP was communist, suspended the constitution and revoked adult suffrage, which was not reinstated until 1957. The effect of the suspension was to remove the unity between Afro- and Indian-Guyanese and split the PPP on racial lines. In 1955 Burnham left the PPP to found the mainly Afro-Guyanese-supported People's National Congress (PNC).

The PPP was returned to power in 1957 and 1961, committed to socialist policies. There was widespread opposition to an attempted financial reform in 1962, which placed extra taxes on the middle class and foreign companies. The opposition to the PPP came from the business community, urban residents and the PNC and was backed by the USA, fearing another Cuba in the region. However the PNP survived in government until 1964, when the UK government abolished the "first-past-the-post" electoral system to one of proportional representation. After the 1964 elections the PPP was unable to obtain an absolute majority and was replaced as the governing party by the PNC in coalition with the business-dominated United Force Party.

The PNC has continued to dominate Guyanese politics since independence, winning every election overwhelmingly. There have been well-documented allegations of continued vote-rigging and deliberate exclusion of potential political opponents, including East Indians, from suffrage, at every election to date. Guyana, now solely ruled by the PNC, became an independent "Co-operative-Republic" in 1970 and instituted a new constitution in 1980, which made constitutional change dependent upon a two-thirds majority in Parliament rather than on a referendum. The PNC government has since been increasingly authoritarian and right-wing. The bauxite and sugar companies which dominated the economy were nationalized; however chronic mismanagement and world economic depression has devastated the Guyanese economy, further — adding to racial tensions. By the mid-1980s Guyana had the second lowest income *per capita* in the Caribbean, after Haiti.

In the early 1980s there was the emergence of Afro-Guyanese opposition to the government with the formation of the "new left" Working People's Alliance (WPA), which in 1986 joined with the PPP and other parties in the opposition Patriotic Coalition for Democracy. However most Afro-Guyanese appear to give their support to the PNC,[2] led by President Hoyte after the death of President Burnham in 1985, perhaps because it is still a source of employment in an increasingly depressed economy. However, large numbers of Guyanese of all groups have left the country. Of the total population of 800,000, 100,000 live abroad and in recent years increasing numbers have sought political asylum in Canada. Human rights violations and racial tensions continue; there have been many reports of deliberate police harassment of Indians and the failure of police and government to act against Afro-Guyanese gangs who terrorize Indian communities.

Suriname

The East Indians of Suriname, known locally as Hindustanis, comprise around 37% of the population of just under 400,000. At the time of independence in 1975 they were probably around half of the population; however large-scale emigration to the Netherlands has lowered their numbers considerably. The other ethnic groups are Afro-Surinamese, known locally as Creoles, Javanese (descendants of immigrants/indentured labourers from the then Dutch East Indies), Maroons (also known as bush-negroes), Chinese, Amerindians and small groups of Middle Eastern or European descent.

Indians first came to Suriname after the abolition of slavery in 1863. The Dutch had established control over the coastal areas in the years after 1667 and attempted to establish a plantation economy by the importation of African slaves. The Africans suffered greatly under slavery and many fled into the jungles of the interior. After slavery was abolished there was an agreement between the UK and the Netherlands for the importation of sub-continental Indians as contract labourers; 34,300 came in the years between 1873 and 1916. A similar number of Javanese were also imported slightly later. Both groups stayed, the Indians often becoming small independent rice farmers, traders and businessmen. Some Creoles also became small farmers while many others settled in the capital city of Paramaribo

---

[2]Of course the true level of support is impossible to state because of persistent electoral irregularities. Both the UK Parliamentary Human Rights Group and Americas Watch have testified to the use of fraudulent practices.

or worked in mining, forestry, industry or public administration. Indians only started entering this last area after 1950.

Until the introduction of universal adult suffrage in 1949, Suriname (called until independence, Surinam) had been ruled by a small wealthy group, mainly European and a few Creoles. Internal autonomy came in 1954 with an Electoral Act based on racially demarcated constituencies. Economic, cultural and linguistic factors already divided the ethnic groups, the Electoral Act encouraged continued ethnic divisions into political organization. Two main parties emerged — the United Reform Party (VHP) and the National Party of Suriname (NPS) — respectively Hindustani and Creole. After 19 years of shared or single-party rule the Party of the National Republic (PNR) won power in 1973 and announced it would seek independence by 1975. The other ethnic groups were generally not in favour of independence as they feared Creole domination (as had happened in Guyana) and the leader of the VHP, J. Lachmon, put forward a plan for phased independence.

The Netherlands government supported plans for Suriname's independence which was set for November 25, 1975. The Surimanese were, until independence, Dutch citizens and able to move freely between Suriname and the Netherlands. High unemployment in Suriname had caused many people to emigrate but the numbers rose greatly in the two years before independence to 150,000 — about one third of the population. Many of these were Hindustanis and from this time their share in the population began to drop. Those Surinamese who resided in Holland at the time of independence remained Dutch citizens,

those in Suriname became Surinamese citizens.[3] The Dutch government also agreed to give 3.2 billion Dutch guilders ($US 4.7 billion) as development aid in the next 10 years.

To a large extent the fears expressed before independence of Creole domination have been fulfilled but, unlike Guyana, the East Indian population has not been the chief target of repression. This is partly because their numbers have dropped because of emigration, partly because of the greater ethnic diversity and also because the worst violations have taken place in a counter-insurgency war in the jungles of the interior with the Maroons and Amerindians as the main victims. In 1980 a military coup overthrew the PNR government of Henck Aaron and there followed over the next seven years, until elections for a new National Assembly in late 1987, a number of attempted coups and killings of political opponents. The elections were contested by a coalition party called the Front for Democracy and Development (FDD), which consisted of the NPS, VNR and the KTPI which represented the Javanese population. It won the elections overwhelmingly by 40 seats to a combined opposition total of 11. The National Assembly elected Mr Ramsewk Shankar, a Hindustani, as President and Mr Henck Arron as Vice President. J. Lachmon became Speaker of the National Assembly. To date the FDD government has survived and has initiated peace talks with rebel forces. However the military still appears to have considerable influence and it is difficult to evaluate the long-term viability of a civilian and multi-racial government in Suriname.

(See also *Indian Fijians* in **Oceania**)

---

[3]In practice the division has not been as rigid as might appear. Suriname citizens can still enter the Netherlands, although with restrictions, and family reunion and resettlement are relatively easy.

Maroons of Suriname

Alternative names: **Bush negroes**
Location: **interior and east Suriname**
Population: **40,000**
% of population: **10%**
Religion: **indigenous beliefs**
Language: **Dutch creole**

The Maroons, also known locally as bush ne-groes, are the descendants of African slaves who fled slavery to found a separate and distinct society in the interior jungles. They form about 10% of the total population of Suriname but are, with the Amerindians, the poorest and most marginal sector of society. During the mid-1980s they became the chief victims in a counter-insurgency war fought between government and rebels.

Although the Dutch acquired the area of Suriname from the English in 1667, it was not until 1686 that they effectively controlled the coastal area, in the process driving the indigenous Amerindians deep into the interior. The Dutch then imported African slaves to work a plantation economy based on sugar, cocoa and coffee. From the late seventeenth century over 300,000 Africans were captured and transported to Suriname to a form of slavery which was especially harsh even by the standards of the age. Large numbers of slaves managed to escape to the central jungles where they joined earlier colonies of escapees. There they built a unique Afro-American culture and society with its social and political systems based on their original homelands of west Africa and which was self-sufficient through hunting and agriculture. They used the jungles as a base in their continuing guerrilla war for freedom and in 1760, after several unsuccessful military campaigns by the Dutch, Maroons signed the Treaty of Ouca with the plantation owners of the coast, which guaranteed their autonomy. They thus became the first peoples of the Americas to gain independence from colonial control.

For over two centuries the Maroons have retained their distinctive identity based on their West African origins and desire for isolation. Traditional social organization is strong. They are organized in six main groups, with tribal leaders called *Granmans*, village leaders called Captains and priests who communicate with forest-dwelling spirits. After the abolition of slavery in 1863 they continued to live in their own communities and distinguished themselves from the former slaves, the Creoles. They visited and communicated with the outside world but on their own terms. International borders, until recently, have meant little; one group of Maroons, the Aluku (also called Boni) live in French Guiana and there have been constant contacts between Maroons in both countries. Until the recent conflict most Maroons continued to live in the eastern interior areas; some have moved to work as labourers in Paramaribo or in bauxite settlements. But all keep contact with the tribe and village. Some of those living in the villages receive salaries and recognition from the government because of their roles within the tribal governments.

After independence in 1975 Suriname was governed as a parliamentary democracy until its overthrow by a military coup in 1980 led by Sergeant (later Lt. Col.) Desi Bourterse. Meanwhile discontent among the Maroons had grown, partly from resentment of the domination by the Creole military and partly because of plans to remove them from the jungles and settle them in towns. Traditional treaty rights allowing for political, cultural and religious freedoms were ignored and the government tried to impose "people's committees" in their place. It has also been reported that Bourterse made derogatory remarks against Maroons, threatening to kill and bomb them.

A small group of men, many of whom were Maroons, and led by a former bodyguard of Bourterse, Roony Brunswijk, formed the "Junglecommand", a poorly equipped guerrilla group of about 100 men. In July 1986 it attacked three government military posts and followed this with a series of victories and by the end of the year it was in command of most of eastern Suriname. The government forces retaliated and in the ensuing months the Maroons were the main victims of a series of government massacres, individual murders, attacks, detentions and harassments. Food supplies were also disrupted. As a result from late 1986 over 10,000 Maroons and Amerindians fled to French Guiana while others left for a precarious safety in Paramaribo.

The refugees placed serious strains on the infrastructure of French Guiana (total population about 90,000 including illegal immigrants) and its already strained relations with Suriname.

The French government would not recognize the Maroons as refugees under the 1951 Geneva Convention but described them as "displaced persons". They did however provide them with food, shelter and medical care, which was supplemented by relief agencies, while in late 1988 UNHCR was allowed to open a local office to assist the refugees. UNHCR was also allowed to open an office in Paramaribo.

At the beginning of 1988 democratic parliamentary government was restored in Suriname. Both the new government and the Junglecommand indicated their desire for a cease-fire and a negotiated peace, along with the voluntary return of all refugees. A church group acted as an intermediary and in June 1988 the two groups signed a document known as the Protocols of St Jean in which specific proposals were made to withdraw troops and demilitarize certain areas. The proposals were not implemented, perhaps because of opposition from the Surinamese military, and in August 1988 the army began further operations against the Junglecommand. These failed and an uneasy stalemate followed.

A further attempt at conciliation occurred in June 1989 when representatives of the parliament and Junglecommand met and agreed on a programme to terminate hostilities. The Portal Agreement provided for, among other things, the lifting of the state of emergency in the eastern region, the safe return of refugees and the providing of financial, material and administrative aid for Maroon and Amerindian communities. An appendix also detailed further demands of the Junglecommand which related to the minority rights of the Maroons, such as the withdrawal of all armed forces from Maroon traditional territory, the incorporation of the Junglecommand into the civil, police and economic reconstruction forces, and the decentralization of Suriname into autonomous regions. However, to date, the agreement has to be implemented and there are doubts as to the commitment of both the Surinamese Army and some factions of the Junglecommand to comply with its provisions. In addition refugees are reluctant to return while the Surinamese army occupies the eastern regions.

(See also *Afro-Brazilians; Afro-Cubans; East Indians of the Caribbean*)

Maya of Guatemala

Name: **Mayan Indians**
Alternative names: **various ethnic groups: Achi, Aguacateco, Cakchiquel, Chorti, Chuj, Itza, Ixil, Jacalteco, Kanjobal, Kekchi, Man, Maya-Mopan, Pocoman, Pokomchi, Quiche, Rabinal Achi, Sacapulteco, Sipacapense, Tacaneco, Tzutujil, Uspanteco**
Location: **The Highlands of Guatemala; also Mexico, Belize**
Population: **3-5.6 million**
% of population: **38%–70%**
Religion: **Indigenous beliefs, Catholic, Protestant**
Language: **various Indian languages including Quiche, Mam, Cakchiquel, Kekchi**

The Maya are the indigenous people of Guatemala and refer to themselves as the "natural" people. They are the pure-blooded descendents of the Mayan architects of the "lost" jungle cities of Central America and are speakers of 22 Mayan languages. Most live in the western Altiplano (highlands) but they inter-mix in many areas with *ladinos*, people of mixed Indian and Spanish descent. It is not always easy to define an Indian but the crucial factors are language and culture rather than biology. Indians hold traditional Indian values which are woven into a code from which there is little individual deviation, are subsistence farmers and have an attachment to their land which is spiritual,

and an all-pervading sense of the magical and supernatural.

The problem of definition means that there have been widely differing estimates of the total numbers of Indians in Guatemala. The 1981 census puts it at 38% but independent estimates range up to 70%. According to Guatemalan government censuses, the proportion of indigenous people in the national population has declined from 78% in 1774 to 43% in 1964, but these figures are widely distrusted and the census officials admit that there is a 12% error margin. Another reason why the proportion has dropped has to do with increasing "ladinoization" and assimilatory pressures but even if the proportion is decreasing, over the years the numbers of Indians have increased.

The Maya were conquered by the Spanish conquistadors in the early sixteenth century but the potential culture shock was cushioned by the fact that for the majority of Indians the Spanish hierarchy took the place of the Mayan lords and priests. The symbols of the Catholic religion had parallels with Mayan beliefs and were adopted by the Maya who used them to maintain an adapted but still very Indian way of life. The Indians were parcelled out with Spanish *encomiendas* (land grants) as virtual slaves and herded into *congregaciones* (settlements). Submission to the patron became a way of survival against overwhelming odds. Independence in 1821 did not greatly change the Indian situation except for removing some of the regulations on the treatment of Indian labour and communal lands, which were often expropriated and given over to new cash crops such as coffee.

These factors resulted in increasing loss of Indian land to *ladino* landowners, a factor which continues today. Land has been divided into smaller and smaller plots. The reforming government of President Arevalo which attempted to redistribute land and encourage political and labour organization among Indians was overthrown in 1954 by a right-wing coup. Afraid of communist influence, the Catholic Church launched *Acción Católica*, a lay catechist movement designed to re-establish Catholic orthodoxy among the Maya. It achieved notable success but even more successful were the Protestants who in the last 15 years have converted at least 20% of the population. The Catholics won favour and acceptance by showing respect for indigenous culture and helped reform some destructive practices and encouraged education and literacy, and their influence was generally a radical one. The Protestants also organized education and campaigned against alcohol but their impact was a generally conservative one, especially the small fundamentalist American-based sects, who preached obedience to authority.

In the 1960s and 1970s important changes were taking place in traditional Indian life. Population pressure meant larger numbers of small farms and many Indians migrated to the coast to work on coffee plantations in terrible conditions. The market economy became more important, co-operatives, established during the Arbenz period, taught new skills and techniques. All of these factors lead to a new awareness among Indians that they had rights; there was an increasing demand for health care and education and new forms of political organization.

These factors were intensified by the February 1976 earthquake which killed 27,000 people (overwhelmingly Indians) and made a million people homeless.

Political repression in Guatemala grew, especially during the regime of President Arana Osorio in 1970–73. From 1972 guerrilla armies began to organize among Indians, previously considered poor revolutionary material, and resulted in the emergence of the Guerrilla Army of the Poor (EGP) in Ixcan, the Organization of the People in Arms (ORPA) in the Sierra Madre mountains and the Rebel Armed Forces (FAR) in the northern jungles of Petan and Alta Veraz. Indians joined the new guerrilla forces, especially the EGP's Local Clandestine Committees and Local Irregular Forces, in response to the army occupations of Indian towns and villages, and kidnappings, murders and "disappearances". Attacks on Indian communities combined with the elimination of Indian community leaders convinced many that the government was waging an ethnic genocide and cultural annihilation of Mayan peoples. Many Maya felt that joining the guerrillas was their only hope of survival. Non-rural Indians organized into unions, slumdwellers' committees and community groups and the formation of both the National Committee of Trade Union Unity (CNUS) and the Peasant Unity Committee expressed some of these aspirations.

Greatly intensified repression began after March 1982 when General Garcia was forced to resign and was replaced by General Rios Montt who launched a massive counter-insurgency campaign against the guerillas' base in the countryside. "Plan Victoria 82" ruthlessly hunted down Indian "subversives", homes were burnt and villages destroyed. Perhaps 10,000 Indians were killed. Over 700,000 civilians, largely Indians, were recruited into civilian militias, forced to fight in the front line against the guerrillas. Many families were left destitute as their men were taken by the army and they were deprived of their land and herded into so-called "model villages" controlled by the army. Over 200,000 Maya fled as refugees to Mexico, Honduras, Belize, the USA and elsewhere. Many others became displaced persons in Guatemala City or in remote jungle areas outside army control; perhaps half-a-million Maya were internal refugees within Guatemala. The total impact of this and later campaigns has been devastating for the Maya and can be described as genocidal; the most sustained attempt to destroy them and their way of life since the Spanish conquest.

Guatemala's appalling human rights record

drew international criticism and this may have been one factor in the restoration of civilian government in 1982 when the Christian Democrat Vinicio Cerezo became President. But the power of the military still remained intact in the countryside. Councils of Development became the main method of control, and projects, model villages and civilian patrols remained under tight military control. At first it did appear that there was a fall in the number of human rights abuses but by 1987 there was again a significant increase in killings and "disappearances". Indigenous peoples joined with *ladinos* in monitoring and campaigning on human rights issues — most notably in the Mutual Support Group (GAM) where of the 1,000 members, 850 were Indian women. In 1958 came the Council of Ethnic Communities (CERJ) — "*Runujel Junam*" (meaning "everyone is equal" in Quiche). Just as significant has been the formation of the National Association of Peasants for Land (ANC) which demonstrated for land reform and by 1989 had 15,000 members. Four Indians won seats in the constituent elections in July 1984, one of them being the first elected representative of an all-Indian party.

Within Guatemala, Indians remain at the very bottom of all socio-economic indices. Life expectancy for an Indian is 16 years lower than for a *ladino*. Indigenous infant mortality rates are as high as 134 per 1,000 compared to a national average of 80 per 1,000, while 82% of children under

five suffer from malnutrition. The government does provide health posts and medical centres in rural areas but there is an almost total lack of materials and staff. Only 19% of indigenous people are literate compared to 50% of *ladinos*, and in any case most education is in Spanish rather than indigenous languages. Real incomes have fallen precipitously in the last decade and 43% of the Guatemalan population live below the official poverty line. Ethnic discrimination is very basic; Indians are often equated with animals or sub-humans. Such racism is made even more insidious by state proclamations of equality and concern for its Indian citizens. Mayan culture is appropriated and exploited for national symbolism and tourism.

Mayan Indians are still under threat in Guatemala. At the end of 1987 the army launched an "End of the Year Offensive" which continued until well into 1988 and killed many Indians, displaced 7,000 more and forced 3,000 others hiding in the mountains to surrender to the military. Yet despite the overwhelming odds against them in the past they have managed to adapt and survive while retaining the basis of their beliefs and attachment to the land. As one of the largest Indian nations in the Americas and one of the few indigenous peoples anywhere in the world still to constitute a majority within a state, sheer numbers should ensure their physical survival. But their cultural survival still remains in the balance.

(See also *Amerindians of South America; Mexico's Indians; Miskito Indians of Nicaragua*)

Mexico's Indians

Alternative names: **Various, including Nahautl, Maya, Zapotec**
Location: **Mexico, central and southern states**
Population: **5.7 million**
% of population: **8.5%**
Religion: **Catholic, indigenous Indian beliefs (sometimes mixed together)**
Language: **Nahautl, Maya, Zapotec plus some 30 other languages**

Indians, the descendants of the indigenous peoples of Mexico, represent ethnic groups with varying levels of social and cultural development. Most live in the central and southern states of Mexico. Although the lot of Mexico's Indians is generally better than that of most Latin American Indians, they still tend to find themselves at the bottom of the social order of the mixed Mexican population, where

approximately 60% are *Mestizos*, i.e. of mixed Spanish-Indian descent.

Prior to the arrival of the first Spanish conquerors in 1519, Mexico had seen 2,000 years of Indian civilization which had produced, among other things, the magnificent architecture of the Yucatan peninsula. The latest, and relative newcomers to power, were the Aztecs. Thanks to their bloodthirsty religious rituals, other groups encountered by the Spanish proved more than willing to participate in their overthrow.

For the next 300 years "New Spain" was the most important part of the Spanish Empire and some 200,000 white settlers moved there. Strenuous efforts were made to eradicate the native culture and institutions, while the Spanish allowed, and even encouraged, development at local level, thus widening the social differences already apparent at the time of Aztec domination.

The population, thought to be as high as 20 million at the time of the conquest, was decimated through disease and, a century later, had fallen to about two million. Another factor was the destruction of the socio-economic structures, particularly the introduction of mining and cattle ranching. *Economiendas* were established to provide labour, but were replaced after 1550 by a system of forced wage labour. Voluntary labour was finally introduced but under this system Indians, tricked into debt-bondage, became virtual slaves under the *hacienda* system. The Indians did receive some legal protection, but after independence in 1821, they lost their special rights as liberal political thought was dominant. After the revolution of 1910–20 which left Mexico in chaos, Indian rights were ignored. With the presidency of Lazaro Cardenas (1936–40), Indians were encouraged to become "Mexican". The Independent Department of Native Affairs was established in 1946 and placed under the Ministry of Education. As a result, Indian children were taught Spanish; brigades of Native Improvement were set up and legal support centres were established.

At Patzcuaro, at the first Inter-American Indigenista Congress in 1940, the Inter-American Indigenist Institution (III), based in Mexico City, was set up. It conducted medical research and socio-anthropological projects in Indian areas. It functions as a semi-governmental institution with autonomous status. Co-ordination centres were created such as the National Indigenist Institution (INI). There are now some 50 of these centres, controlled by anthropologists, which are seen as more advanced than other Latin American countries, in regard to both consistency and realism.

Relationships between the Indians and the Spanish and *Mestizo* (mixed race) population is, and historically has always been, based on commerce. What little land is owned by Indians is often too poor to support them, so most must seek waged labour in a market where they are regarded as inferior both by Spanish and *Mestizo* employers. Their work is usually menial, they tend to be cheated in shops, forced to sell their goods at cheap prices and are generally treated with a lack of respect.

Indians still live in over-crowded, often substandard housing, and few children spend much time at school, although by law they are required to do so. They are needed at home to work for their parents. Where basic needs are met, Indians have proved highly receptive to literacy and modern technology providing, it seems, that their social customs and symbolic values are not destroyed. The INI makes no direct attempt to secure the latter, but simply aims to improve health, communications, education and agriculture in order to incorporate Indians into a pluralistic society, rather than trying to make them conform.

Social change and mobility are only possible for most Indians by ceasing to be Indian. This can be achieved by moving to cities, learning Spanish, or by marrying *Mestizos*. Many of the poorest city dwellers and illegal immigrants working as cheap labour in the USA are the Indians of yesterday. They have ceased to be part of Mexico's Indian population and have become part of Mexico's burgeoning poor. Many *Mestizos* in Indian areas resent what they regard as the government's treatment of Indians as a privileged underclass, partly because it reduces their own chances of exploiting them, and partly because many *Mestizos* are themselves poor and feel ignored.

As with many poor *Mestizos*, Indians suffer from land shortage which has forced many to act as low-paid agricultural labourers. There have been many reports of human rights violations against Indian communities, especially in the southern states of Oaxaca and Chiapas, where Amnesty International has documented political killings, detention, "disappearances" and torture of Indians fighting for land rights.

(See also *Maya of Guatemala; Miskito Indians of Nicaragua*)

Miskito Indians of Nicaragua

Location: **Atlantic seaboard of Nicaragua, Mosquita.**
Population: **75,000-130,000**
% of population: **less than 5%**
Religion: **Moravian**
Language: **Creole, English, indigenous languages**

The Miskito Indians of Nicaragua live mainly on the north-east coast of the country, paying scant regard to the established Honduran border, on the other side of which as many as 40,000 Miskitos may live. They have played an important role in the international indigenous movement of the 1980s and have, with the advent of counter-revolutionary movements, been in conflict with the revolutionary Sandinista government which came to power in 1979. Their chief aim is one of self-determination. No formal census of the Miskitos has ever been taken, as a result of which population figures tend to be misrepresented by both sides. There are also other smaller indigenous groups in the area; the Suma, Rama and Garifunos.

During the seventeenth and eighteenth centuries the western Caribbean formed a front between the competing Spanish and British forces. The effects on the native Miskito population was profound as they became party to, as well as victims of, the long-term European and, later, American battle for the region. A British protectorate was formed over Mosquita between 1824 and 1860, but during the 1860s and 1870s American interests, relying on the Monroe Doctrine, supported the unification of a Nicaraguan state in order to allow greater American access to the region. In 1860 the Treaty of Managua gave Nicaragua sovereignty over the "Mosquito Reserve", while excluding nearly all the traditional Miskito areas — allowing them to fall under Nicaraguan rule — a state of affairs that could not have arisen had the Miskitos had a say.

The Moravian Church began missionary work in 1849 at the invitation of the Miskito King, a move initiated by Britain. Although the church was democratic in character, its effect on the cultural, social and economic structures of the Miskitos was profound. Once the process of conversion began (the Moravian missionaries apparently enjoyed no success for some 30 years), Christianity came to define social status. However, the acceptance of Christian values also seems to have made the Miskitos more susceptible to exploitation and the Moravians acted as mediators between them and the outside world — a state of affairs that continues to the present.

In 1894 the Mosquito Reserve was dissolved — "reincorporated" into the Nicaraguan state — which led to a local uprising that was eventually quelled by the US Marines. However the Atlantic Coast was never fully integrated into the state and tended to be exploited for its natural resources and labour. The national war of liberation from 1927 to 1933 offered the Miskitos an opportunity to shrug off American domination of their region and the nationalist leader, Augusto César Sandino, found strong allies on the Atlantic Coast. The assassination of Sandino by Anastacio Somoza saw the installation of a dictatorship which lasted until 1979. It is often thought that the Miskitos and others on the Atlantic coast were not particularly oppressed during the Somocista era, and that they are therefore a sort of fifth column in the post-revolutionary Sandinista state, but it is doubtful that many would wish to see the return of dictatorship. It is also believed that more research into the Somocista era would reveal a greater level of repression than is generally agreed. During the 1960s the Miskitos began organizing defence against territorial encroachment from the regime. This culminated in the formation in 1972 of the Alliance for Progress of Miskitos and Sumus (ALPROMISU).

The Sandinista National Liberation Front (FSLN) took power in July 1979 after a bitter guerrilla struggle and large-scale loss of life. The new government undoubtedly had good intentions towards the Atlantic Coast, though it seems very little study had been made of the indigenous question. Many of the programmes initiated were unrelated and often antagonistic to, the realities of the Atlantic Coast. Yet rights were recognized and, as a result, MISURASATA (Miskito, Sumo, Rama, and Sandinistas United), was formed. Among other things, it carried out literacy programmes. In 1980, a Ministry for the Atlantic coast was formed — INNICA. The Minister appointed to head it was not from the region and he spoke only Spanish; nor was MISURASATA consulted. INNICA was dissolved in 1982, but its research institute, CIDCA, which was similarly criticized, remained.

The reasons why Miskitos took up arms against the Sandinista government in 1981–82 was hotly debated. Following the exit from Nicaragua to Honduras of many of the MISURASATA leaders and their followers, counter-revolutionary forces attacked Miskito villages, causing the inhabitants to flee in all directions. 40,000 Miskitos took refuge in Honduras, by this time generally agreed to be under the influence of the Reagan administration, where they were accepted in refugee camps. Many were converted to the cause of the "Contra" counter-revolutionaries, who were fighting a covert war against the Sandinistas. The Nicaraguan government then made the controversial decision to evacuate the villages on the Honduran border. While tensions, fanned by international media coverage, ran high, by the end of 1983 it became clear to the Nicaraguan government that the vast majority of people from the region who had been implicated, had been manipulated or were simply aiding family members. At this point, the government declared an amnesty for most Miskitos imprisoned or in exile.

The leader of MISURASATA, Brooklyn Riviera, took advantage of the Nicaraguan government's offer of talks in late 1984. He insisted on negotiating the terms of autonomy, but the Nicaraguan government refused to deal solely with MISURASATA, arguing that it did not represent all the Miskitos, or the other Indian groups. In spite of the slow pace of negotiations, many Miskitos returned from exile and began the process of reconstruction. Security concerns were overwhelmed by more pressing problems, such as the lack of food in the area. The process of repatriation was almost stopped by a US grant of $300,000 to armed Miskitos in Honduras for the purpose of attacking Nicaraguan security forces, but the cease-fire agreements held.

The autonomy law, passed in 1987, is an attempt to balance national unity with the multi-ethnic character of the country. It provides that three specific areas fundamental to the indigenous population's demands lie within the control of the autonomous governments; promotion of cultures and languages, land, water, and forests. The administrative structure divides the Atlantic coast into two regional governments with administrative capitals at Puerto Cabezas and Bluefields. The Miskitos would prefer one autonomous government to two, but the government contends that the present structure takes account of transport and communication difficulties. Other problems are the means of election, which provides no built-in ethnic balance; the one-year residency qualification required to stand for office; and a perceived lack of effective power by Miskitos.

The autonomous regions are now in place and their future depends at least in part on political and economic developments outside the region, such as the ending of US support for Contra rebels and an improvement in the rapidly deteriorating Nicaraguan economy. In October 1988 the Atlantic Coast suffered a further setback as a result of massive devastation by Hurricane Joan.

(See also *Maya of Guatemala; Mexico's Indians*)

Welsh of Patagonia

Location: **Patagonia, southern Argentina**
Population: **about 10,000**
% of population: **0.03% of Argentine population**
Religion: **Non-conformist Protestant**
Language: **Welsh, Spanish**

The first Welsh settlement in Patagonia was established in the Lower Chubut Valley in 1865 as a result of emigration — mainly by non-conformists — from Wales and North America. Terms for the settlement were negotiated with the Argentine government, who saw the settlement as an opportunity to consolidate their claim to the area. By the middle of the 1880s all agricultural land in the Lower Chubut Valley had been claimed and a new settlement — Cwn Hyfryd — was established 600 km west in the Andes. Immigration ceased in 1914, by which time some 3,000 immigrants had entered the two settlements.

During the first 50 years, differing views of political autonomy caused a degree of conflict with the national authorities. Welsh attempts to gain local administrative control through numerical superiority were regarded with suspicion. Conflict over the question of language led to an attempt at secession at the turn of the century and, although the move failed, the Argentine government was prompted to encourage non-Welsh settlement in the region.

Welsh farming was organized as a co-operative society to which all farmers belonged. The society was responsible for marketing produce and extended loans to individual farmers. By 1914, the society's 17 branches effectively dominated the regional economy, but a combination of international depression and a series of poor harvests resulted in the society's liquidation in 1930. In the 1930s and 1940s large amounts of land were bought by non-Welsh. Since 1958 when Chubut achieved provincial status, taxation incentives have brought many non-Welsh enterprises from Buenos Aires. This resulted in profound changes within the agricultural community — still largely Welsh — and brought it into direct competition with the better located and better financed agriculture of the Rio Negro.

The social and cultural life of the Welsh centred on the 17 non-conformist Chapels which continued to teach the Welsh language. The Chapels also administered a community medical insurance with the British Hospital at Buenos Aires, but the creation of a state medical scheme by the Peron government ended the need for such insurance and Chapel membership rapidly decreased. This, and the demise of other organizations, such as the co-operative society, the irrigation society and the railway company, all of which demanded from their employees a knowledge of Welsh, along with the Argentine government's elimination of the teaching of Welsh in schools, had a debilitating effect on the maintenance of the language. Welshness became associated with low socio-economic status and there developed a tendency for the younger generation to reject the language.

However ethnic discrimination against the Welsh is minimal, and while their socio-economic status may have declined, together with the relative importance of agriculture in Argentina, they are not regarded as low as others, such as the Chileans. The Welsh do however lack economic control except in the agricultural sector. As they are no longer seen as a political or cultural threat, token support is extended to some of their activities, such as an annual Eisteddfod. Their main dissatisfaction stems from their inability to give their children Welsh names, having instead to choose from an official list of Christian names.

Further References

The Position of Blacks in Brazilian and Cuban Society, MRG Report No. 7, 1979

East Indians of Trinidad and Guyana, MRG Report No. 13, 1979

The Amerindians of South America, MRG Report No. 15, 1987

The Maya of Guatemala, MRG Report No. 62, 1989

The Miskito Indians of Nicaragua, MRG Report No. 79, 1988

WESTERN EUROPE AND SCANDINAVIA

The history of minority questions is intimately associated with political and social developments on the continent of Europe. From the time of the Reformation, religious groups have been the subject of protective treaties. The first examples involved the protection of some groups of Christians from others. Territorial change sometimes resulted in the transfer of groups of one religious confession to territory ruled by a ruler of a different confession. The agreement between transferor and transferee would specify that religious conformity would not be demanded and the group could continue to worship according to its custom. Rulers also made unilateral declarations of religious tolerance towards their subjects. In the nineteenth century, attention shifted from religion to nationality as the doctrine of the nation-state took hold. Race or nationality became the badge of difference and motive for oppression, and various national or international mechanisms of protection were engaged. The incidence of minorities was recognized to only a limited degree under the system of protection of minorities devised by the League of Nations (see Introduction to Eastern Europe): Austria and Finland came under the aegis of the League but not other Western states. A policy of Italianization could therefore be followed by Fascist Italy without attracting significant international condemnation. The assumption was that the Western European states had reached such a standard of civilization that their humanitarian standards were beyond the reach of criticism — unlike the hapless states of Eastern Europe who could not be trusted to respect human rights.

Nazi treatment of the Jews and other groups changed this perception. On the continent of Europe, the response involved both the entrenchment of universal human rights and special measures of protection for particular groups. The protection of the rights of minorities in Europe is attempted through a variety of general and specific international instruments and general and specific constitutional provisions. Postwar Europe has also seen a rise in minority consciousness and the development of local and transnational groupings to promote popular awareness and articulate grievances. The slow though not painless growth of states always claimed its victims. Minorities have reacted to threats to their existence and identity as discrete groups and have refused to merge or be submerged in the social whole whose boundary is the state. The development of supranational organizations like the European Communities has appeared to some as heralding the demise of the nation-state and this too has increased awareness of the cultural and spiritual potential of a specific identity within the larger complex.

The minorities reviewed are basically of three kinds. The smaller linguistic and cultural groups in Europe are numerous and very self-conscious. They make demands for recognition on the part of states and are recognized in many cases. Europe also contains minorities belonging to the category of indigenous peoples and their treatment may be instructively compared with that elsewhere. The Roma or Gypsy population represent a third category by which European pretensions may be judged. They are scattered over the various states and are subjected to different legal and social regimes, but frequent injustice. Their freedom of movement, an inherent component of their culture, is difficult to accommodate within the settled territoriality of the nation-state.

Instruments on Minority Rights

The European Convention on Human Rights and Fundamental Freedom does not contain an article providing positive rights to minorities; instead, there is a basic provision on non-discrimination in Article 14: "The enjoyment of the rights and freedoms . . . in this Convention shall be secured without discrimination on any ground such as sex, race, colour, language, religion, political or other opinion, national or social origin, association with a national minority, property, birth or other status." Attempts to insert a more specific article in the Convention were not successful. The non-binding but influential Helsinki Final Act outlines a specific but weak article on minorities in its "Declaration on Principles": "The participating States on whose territories national minorities exist will respect the right of persons belonging to such minorities to equality before the law, will afford them the full opportunity for the actual enjoyment of human rights and fundamental freedoms and will, in this manner, protect their legitimate interests in this sphere." The opening qualification on the "existence" of minorities is unhelpful, since it could function as an invitation to states to deny their presence in the state. Also, the protection of minorities is confined to "national" groups, which is perhaps even more uncertain in meaning than "ethnic" or "racial", but may imply some narrowing of scope. The limited obligations represented in the Final Act are considerably strengthened by the 1988 Concluding Document of the Vienna Conference on Security and Co-operation in Europe (see *Appendix 3.1*) which places emphasis on effective implementation of rights including freedom of religion and the rights of national minorities. Despite weakness in the documents, it is instructive nonetheless that Western Europe has overlapping international instruments on minorities — in addition to the general international treaties on human rights on which the record of European acceptance is commendable.

Additionally, some minority groups are the beneficiaries of specific treaties and arrangements in the manner of the nineteenth and previous centuries. These exist in relation to South Tyrol (Austria/Italy), Danes in Germany and Germans in Denmark (Denmark/Germany), Croats and Slovenes in Austria (Austrian State Treaty), Northern Ireland (Anglo-Irish Agreement), and the Aaland Islanders of Finland (Finland/Sweden). Forms of linguistic and cultural autonomy and rights of representation on behalf of minorities are provided by the treaties which in general reflect the interests of kin-states of the minorities in question. Such treaties are not specific to Europe (see, for example, Introduction to South Asia), but are characteristic. They may make a contribution to the stabilization of some situations but have had only limited success in defusing conflict (see South Tyrol and Northern Ireland).

Besides treaty guarantees on minorities, Western Europe displays a range of constitutional arrangements to incorporate minorities into the life of nations. Linguistic, cultural and political autonomy within essentially unitary states, federalism, specific regimes for language speakers in education and public life short of autonomy, laws forbidding discrimination, are all represented. Some arrangements test the fabric of a coherent, integrated state. The new Constitution of Belgium (finally effective in 1989) divides the nation into the autonomous regions of Flanders, Wallonia and Brussels: the basis of the division is linguistic, between Dutch- and French-speaking groups, with the capital Brussels as the third, bilingual autonomous zone. The whole intention of the division into language communities is to maintain cultural distinctiveness even at the expense of individual choice. The territorial principle is dominant: the rights of the individual do not altogether depend on preferences but on geographic location. The effect of a complicated bifurcation of rights is that each linguistic community is treated as a corporate entity with its own rights. Effects reach from the level of government to the level of the individual. The case of Switzerland is another extreme example of coping with linguistic particularism. The 25 cantons have different cultural and religious characteristics, but even these have minorities within their borders, and cultural sovereignty reaches down to the village level. This paradigm of the importance of local identity in state organization does not always remove disaffection: the Jurassien separatists of the 1960s and '70s fought a public campaign to free themselves from the canton of Bern, adopting the tested techniques of liberation movements in the wider world.

Spain and Italy, two states with centralist traditions, have attempted to combine national unity with a commitment to a high degree of linguistic/cultural autonomy for particular groups. The Spanish Constitution of 1978 expresses the view that: "The Constitution is based on the indissoluble unity of the Spanish nation, the common and indivisible country of all Spaniards, and recognizes and guarantees the right to self-government of nationalities and regions of which it is composed and solidarity amongst them all." Article 3(3) expresses a theorem which many have tried to argue in relation to minorities: that they help to consolidate rather than threaten the nation: "The wealth of the different language variations of Spain is a cultural heritage which shall be the object of special respect and protection." Self-governing communities in Spain, including the Basque country (Euskadi) and Catalonia, exercise a broad range of functions within their territorial bases, including linguistic and cultural rights. The elaboration of these rights rests on specific autonomy statutes. Italy is in concept a unitary state with substantial devolution. Article 5 of the Constitution describes a "Republic . . . one and indivisible . . .". It is nonetheless a Republic which recognizes and promotes local autonomy. Article 116 recognizes regional autonomy in accordance with special statutes for Sardinia, Trentino-Alto Adige, Friuli-Venezia-Giulia, Val D'Aosta and Sicily. The background is a general Rights of Man constitution. Ethnic identity in Italy is sometimes as important as membership of the wider Italian community: in the South Tyrol, identity governs which school a child attends, access to employment in public administration, housing, and the qualifications of candidates for elections.

Treatment of minorities

Whatever the limits of local control for particular minorities, the recognition of a group by the state is an important step towards recognition of cultural pluralism. Many groups do not, however, benefit from such initiatives. France is a state which has maintained a centralist tradition largely intact to the detriment of groups such as the Bretons whose identity would be better recognized in almost any other European state. Recognition of the Saami in the north of Europe is a state-dependent variable. Territorial concentration of minorities is an important preliminary to recognition — witness the precarious position of sometimes nomadic Roma.

Constitutional developments and experiments have proceeded apace especially since World War II. It is not inconceivable that further constitutional innovations will address the problems of groups outside the purview of the contemporary developments. Many of Europe's minorities remain under threat. Processes of assimilation pose constant questions on how the integrity of cultures can be maintained. In the main, assimilation has been abandoned as official state policy, but smaller groups may be unable to command the resources necessary for the preservation of language and culture. Larger groups may have larger ambitions, and display extremes of militancy. At one end of the spectrum, the politics of ETA and the IRA challenges the state in the name of self-determination. It is not clear if their activities "colour" perceptions of the legitimacy of minorities' grievances in general, but there is always that danger. The contemporary European experience displays some of the virtues of accommodation between state and minority, and some of its limitations.

Aaland Islanders

Location: **The Gulfs of Bothnia and Finland**
Population: **21,700 Swedish speakers**
% of population: **95% of Aaland Island population**
Religion: **Protestant**
Language: **Swedish**

The Aaland (Aland) Islanders are the Swedish-speaking inhabitants of the Finnish islands of Aaland. Ceded with the rest of Finland to Russia in 1809 the Islands were returned to Finland by the League of Nations in 1921, despite calls by the Islanders for reunification with Sweden. The Finnish government undertook to respect and preserve the Swedish language, culture and traditions of the Islanders and the Swedish government agreed to withdraw its claim to sovereignty over the Islands.

Under the Autonomy Act of 1952 the Islands collectively are a province of Finland with a single-chamber parliament of 27 members, and administration is controlled by a seven-member Provincial Executive Council. Members of the Council are appointed by the parliament but the chairman (also Governor of the Islands) must be approved by the Finnish government, and all laws issued by the Islands' parliament must be ratified by the President of the Republic. The provincial parliament determines the Islands' budget and has legislative power over matters pertaining to education, electoral law, taxation, housing, agriculture and fisheries, commerce and industry, health and hos-

pital services. The Swedish character of the Islands is preserved through regulations on language, education, regional citizenship and the acquisition of property on the Islands. Swedish is the official language of the Islands, although a Finn may use his language before the courts; it is also the medium of education. Aaland regional citizenship is conferred upon citizens who have spent five years in residence on the islands and only those with regional citizenship can acquire land or vote in communal and provincial elections. These and other provisions have made the Aaland Islands a model worldwide for the treatment of minority groups by a host nation.

The Aaland Islanders form part of a much larger Swedish community in Finland which in 1982 totalled 305,000, or 6.3% of a total population of 4.85 million. Most Swedish speakers live in the coastal areas of south and south-western Finland where 44 communes are totally Swedish-speaking. Swedish, along with Finnish, is a national language of Finland, and although there is no special provision for the maintenance of Swedish as on the Aaland Islands, institutional arrangements ensure its continued use in education and the media, whilst close economic and cultural ties between Finland and Sweden ensure the role of Swedish as a language of everyday communication. About 75% of Swedish speakers vote for the Swedish Peoples' Party which has representation in the Finnish Parliament.

(See also *Saami of Lapland*)

Alsatians

Location: **Alsace-Lorraine, north-east France**
Population: **1.55 million (Alsace); 300,000-400,000 (Thionese Lorraine)**
% of Population: **Alsatian speakers : 75% of Alsace population; 50% of Thionese Lorraine population**
Religion: **Catholic**
Language: **Alsatian dialect of German, German, French**

The Alsatians are the inhabitants of the region of Alsace and part of Lorraine on France's border with Germany and Switzerland, which has changed hands between France and Germany five times in the last 250 years. The Alsatians have a strong German tradition. The oldest known poem in the German language was written in Alsace, German humanism flourished there and leaders of the German peasant revolt of 1525 came from the region.

Alsace first became French under the Treaty of Westphalia but continued to enjoy a high degree of autonomy. After 1789, however, the region was brought into line with other departments. Most links with Germany were severed and a decree was passed that anyone who could not speak official French would be shot. Alsace was annexed to Germany after the Franco-Prussian war in 1871 and reverted to France after the Treaty of Versailles. In 1940 it was taken over by Germany and at that time Alsatians suffered violence and discrimination at the hands of the Nazis. German was to be learned within two years by all citizens and all notices and official signs were to be in German. After World War II Alsace once again became a French province and the teaching of German was forbidden. The number of French-speakers increased greatly and only 20% of Alsatians now read and write in Alsatian German, which has no official recognition; however, Alsatian continues to be used in everyday life and family situations, more commonly among older people, rural dwellers and the working class than among younger professionals.

German is taught in elementary and secondary schools as a separate subject. On the other hand, French predominates in the social and official life of the region and it is the language of public administration. Only some older people today lack any competency in French and large numbers of people are effectively bilingual, a process assisted by press, radio and television from Germany and Switzerland.

Although the Alsatian dialect is gradually being forgotten there has been a revival of interest amongst Alsatians and courses in Alsatian literature and history are now taught in people's education colleges. Alsatian newspapers have also been started with the aim of preserving the culture of Alsace. The *Mouvement Regionaliste d'Alsace-Lorraine* campaigns for a decentralized France within a federal Europe and for both French and German to be the official languages of Alsace. Alsatians have also called for a greater say in the economic affairs of Alsace, a region heavily involved with the German iron, steel and coal industries because of its location. It is felt by some that the interests of large — often multi-national — industries sometimes supersede those of the people of Alsace. A growing number of young Alsatians cross the border daily to work in Germany and Switzerland for considerably higher wages than in France. Increasing calls for the government to take a more responsible approach to the region's economy have not as yet met with much success and Alsace continues to lag behind other regions of France economically.

(See also *Bretons*)

Azoreans

Location: **Atlantic Ocean, 1,300–1,800 km west of Portugal**
Population: **350,000**
% of population: **3.5% of Portuguese population**
Religion: **Catholic**
Language: **Portuguese**

The Azoreans inhabit the nine Azores islands in the Atlantic Ocean. The islands were discovered by Europeans in 1351 and settled by Portuguese in the fifteenth century. Spanish immigration followed, as did African, British and Flemish immigrants. The Azores are administratively part of Portugal, not a colony, and are thus a part of Europe. The majority of Azoreans are peasant farmers working for large landowners and lack of job opportunities has caused a steady stream of emigration — mostly to Canada and the United States — and a resultant decrease in population. The Azores occupy a strategic position in the Atlantic Ocean, with a major base established on one of the islands.

With the overthrow of dictatorship in Portugal in 1974, the Azoreans, only 2% of whom voted communist in the elections of 1975, demanded independence. In this demand they were encouraged by the fact that Lisbon was now relinquishing its African colonies. The call for independence was led by the Azorean Liberation Front (FLA) which carried out a series of attacks on Communist Party offices throughout the islands, forcing their closure. Civil governors of the islands and communists holding posts in the farming co-operatives were also forced to resign, and internal administration was surrendered by the Portuguese government to six islanders chosen by the Socialist and Popular Democratic parties. The FLA announced the formation of a provisional government and continued bombing attacks, but the level of support given to the FLA was uncertain as its only base was on the main island of San Miguel where it maintained strong links with wealthy landowners. There were allegations that separatists had links with right-wingers in the USA and elsewhere, backed by Azoreans living in the USA who wished to destabilize the islands politically and bring about a breakaway from Portugal and either independence or US statehood.

The 1976 Constitution granted a measure of autonomy to the Azores and, as in Madeira, this has helped to defuse tensions, although many Azoreans are still critical of rule from Lisbon. The islands are poor and have little appeal for tourists and remittances from Azoreans in the USA remain a major source of income.

(See also *Madeira*)

Basques

Alternative names: **Euskera, Vascos**
Location: **Basque provinces of north-west Spain; also the French Department of Pyrénées-Atlantiques**
Population: **2.2 million, 50% Basque speakers**
% of population: **5.5% of Spanish population**
Religion: **Catholic**
Language: **Basque (Eskuara)**

The Basques are the inhabitants of the region on both sides of the western Pyrenees, although the vast majority live on the southern (Spanish) side. They are physically distinct from neighbouring peoples although still of Mediterranean stock, and their language, which has many dialects, is isolated from other Indo-European languages although it has some similarities with Magyar and Finnic.

The Franco era

The Basque country was not invaded by Moors and so became an asylum for fugitive Christians during the Islamic conquests. It is a strongly Catholic region and the saints Ignatius Loyola and Francis Xavier were Basques. Basques have never seen themselves as either Spanish or French and have consistently maintained a tradition of independence, which has been assisted by the mountainous terrain of the Basque country. Basques were granted *fueros* — ancient rights which guaranteed a large measure of self-rule. When Spain centralized its political system during the nineteenth century the existing provinces of Vizcaya, Guipuzcoa, Navarra and Alava were retained but with their constitutions much weakened.

During the Spanish Civil War the Basques sided with the Republicans (although Navarre which is only partly inhabited by Basques was Nationalist) and as a consequence the Basque country was subject to especially vicious treatment by the Nationalist forces, including the bombing of the ancient Basque capital of Guernica by the Germans. With the victory of Franco's forces a process of revenge began — over 21,000 people were estimated to have died, many thousands more were imprisoned or fled into exile and all vestiges of the ancient constitutions and independent status were removed.

The Basque Country is a relatively wealthy industrialized region, industry having been established by an upper class financial elite with ready access to central government. The working class was, and remains, largely composed of unassimilated immigrants and reaction against both groups has contributed to the development of nationalist feeling. During General Franco's rule regional nationalist sentiment was officially repressed. The use of Basque outside the home was forbidden and cultural and educational activities specifically Basque in nature were similarly banned. From the 1950s onward this repressive policy was relaxed somewhat. Special part-time schools for the teaching of Basque language and culture provided for over 33,000 pupils, some of them the children of immigrant families who by now made up over 50% of the Basque working class.

Basque nationalism

In 1954 the militant organization *Euskad Ta Azkatasurra* (ETA) (Basque Homeland and Freedom) was formed. ETA was a hierarchically-structured organization dedicated to the overthrow of Franco's dictatorship. Although at its height ETA had only about 1,000 members its impact was enormous, and it was responsible for an unprecedented degree of terrorist activity including bank robberies, kidnappings and assassinations. The government countered this activity by using strong police tactics in the Basque region. Illegal searches, arrests, detention and brutality towards prisoners were commonplace, and in certain cases military courts were used to try offenders.

Following the death of Franco in 1975 Basques joined together in protests against police action in their region and demanded complete independence from Spain. In the 1977 elections over 75% of the Basque electorate supported parties committed to regional self-government, either socialist parties or avowedly nationalist parties such as the *Partido Nacioalista Vasco* (PNV). Terrorist activity continued, and it was partly due to ETA-inspired violence that Suarez's premiership came to an end in 1981; however, popular support for ETA dropped markedly when liberal democracy and regional government became a reality in Spain and many ETA members became active in the conventional political arena, although a new generation of militant nationalists emerged to support ETA.

As with the other three major regions the Basque country has been given a considerable amount of local autonomy through a regional parliament instituted in 1979, in the "Statute of Guernica". The initial referendum on the new Spanish constitution had been boycotted by a majority of Basques and of those who voted, over one quarter voted against it. However in the referendum on the Statute over 60% of the Basque electorate voted and of these over 80% voted in favour. There is a Basque police force (also created by the Statute of Guernica), the Basque language is used in administration and in education and the Basque flag and symbols used widely. In the Basque parliament in the elections of 1980 and 1984 the PNV became the largest party and also the government; however an internal split in 1986 and regional elections meant that they lost power to the local Socialist parties who became the largest regional party and later formed a coalition with one faction of the PNV (the other forming a new party, the *Eusko Alkartasuna* (EA)). An important factor in Basque politics was the emergence of *Herri Batasuna* (HB) (United People), a militant separatist party, with links with ETA. In the regional elections of 1986 it gained over 17% of the vote. Explicitly Basque nationalist parties held 13 seats in the federal Congress of Deputies in the elections of 1986.

Regional autonomy appears to have satisfied the aspirations of most Basques. Basque nationalist terrorism has continued, however, with a series of bombings, mainly against police and army personnel. Civilians have also been killed and some indiscriminate civilian killings have produced demonstrations against terrorism. Basque terrorist activity continues to remain one of the major threats to the stability of the Spanish government, which has dealt with the continuing threat by on the one hand encouraging ETA activists to abandon their position and return to mainstream Basque life, and on the other by enacting harsh anti-terrorist legislation. This double policy has so far been largely successful but there has been criticism of the anti-terrorist legislation which is thought by many to be too severe. In November 1983 the Congress of Deputies approved new anti-terrorist measures in the Basque region, including the detention of suspects without trial for up to two-and-a-half years. There have been some attempts to negotiate with ETA officials, some of whom live in exile, but to date this has not been successful in bringing about a political settlement.

During the Franco era the French government took little part in containing terrorist activities, but the presence of exiled ETA members in France and concern with the perhaps 200,000 Basques living on French territory has since caused the authorities to act closely with the Spanish government and France now denies sanctuary to those wanted by the Spanish authorities. In the 1980s it began to deport ETA activists to Spain or elsewhere.

Although terrorism is declining in Spain the Basques continue to feel a sense of grievance against the government. Whereas during the 1970s the provinces of Vizcaya and Guipuzcoa were the two richest in Spain, by 1981 they had fallen to seventh and sixth positions. This loss of wealth is due in part to political instability caused by ETA's terrorist activities but it also indicates the problems created by the economic recession and the need for a restructuring of industry in the region, especially the heavy industries of ship-building and steel.

The Basques in France

There are no official statistics on the numbers of Basque speakers in France. During the Franco era many Basque and other Spanish exiles fled to France but many of these have since returned to Spain. In addition some French Basques no longer speak the language, which has no official recognition, although some educational courses are conducted in Basque and there is a small Basque press. One estimate gives 80,000 Basque speakers in France, about 40% of the present population of the Department of Pyrénées-Atlantique.

(See also *Catalans; Galicians*)

Belgium: Flemings, Walloons and Germans

Location: **Flemings: Flanders, northern Belgium; Walloons: Wallonia, southern Belgium; Germans: close to borders of Germany and Luxembourg**
Population: **Flemings: 5.5 million (pop. of Flanders); Walloons (French speakers): 4 million; Germans: 100,000**
% of population: **Flemings: 57%; Walloons (French speakers): 42%; Germans: 1%**
Religion: **Flemings: Catholic; Walloons: Catholic**
Language: **Flemings: Dutch, Flemish dialects; Walloons: French dialects; Germans: German dialects**

Belgium is one of Western Europe's newest states founded only in 1830 and is a multilingual plural state. Its history has been shaped by the conflicts, consensus and compromises reached between its two principal peoples, the Flemings and the Walloons. The Flemings are the Dutch-speaking inhabitants of the region known as Flanders in northern Belgium. They are of Teutonic stock, but their history has been inextricably bound up with that of their southern neighbours, the latin Walloons who are French-speaking. Today the Flemings are the majority population but the Walloons are still a large minority, whose previous dominance and language cannot be ignored. There is also a much smaller minority group of indigenous German speakers.

History

The territory of the modern kingdom of Belgium has been subject to many different political regimes. The language frontier between Germanic north-west Europe and Gallic north-west Europe was established by the fifth century and by the tenth century present-day Belgium was part of the "middle kingdom" of Lotharingia. Part of this kingdom was the region later known as Flanders and by the eleventh century the Counts of Flanders held most of present-day Belgium, the Netherlands and north-west France. Bruges, Ghent and Ypres were three of the largest towns in northern Europe and there was an influx of people from the countryside into the towns, leading to the abolition of serfdom in Flanders during the thirteenth century, much earlier than in the rest of Europe. In the fifteenth century Burgundy was united with Flanders in what became known as the "Low Countries" or the "Burgundian Circle" and there followed a period of flourishing Flemish trade and culture. Antwerp emerged as a major port, and became an

BELGIUM
THE LINGUISTIC AREAS

⊙ National capital
⊙ Provincial capital
― Provincial frontiers

▦ Dutch language region
▦ French language region
▦ German language region
▦ Bi-lingual district (French - Dutch)
▦ Dutch speaking area with protected French-speaking minority
▦ French speaking area with protected Dutch-speaking minority
▦ French speaking area with protected German speaking minority
▦ German speaking area with protected French-speaking minority

0   20   40 M

Source: Carpress

important centre of trade in glass, tapestries, diamonds and lace. This period also produced the great exponents of the Flemish school of painting, Jan van Eyck and, later, Rubens.

The "Burgundian circle" gradually declined from the mid-sixteenth century when it came under the rule of the Spanish-born Philip II who had little understanding of the people of the region. The "revolt of the Netherlands" which began in 1580 lasted until the recognition of the northern part of the Low Countries as the Dutch Republic in 1648. Flanders and Brabant remained subject to Spain. In the second half of the seventeenth century what is sometimes referred to as the Flemish region of France[1] — a region including Dunkirk, Douai and Lille — was taken by Louis XIV. The people of Flanders and Brabant were now divided from the Dutch who spoke almost the same language: by the nineteenth century Dutch had developed into a sophisticated language with uniform grammar and syntax whereas Flemish had become fragmented into a number of dialects. The changes were also crippling economically for Flanders, and Antwerp was unable to survive the huge taxes levied by the Dutch on goods passing in and out of the Flemish city. In 1713 the Spanish provinces were transferred to Austria as the Austrian Netherlands. French was now becoming a common language of the elite and when the country was captured by France in 1794 French was increasingly used. In 1815 Flanders was united with Holland, but differences of language, culture and historic feeling between the Dutch and Flemish led to a "Belgian" rebellion. The European Powers intervened and in 1830 Belgium was recognized as an independent kingdom under Leopold of Saxe-Coburg. It was later guaranteed neutrality in perpetuity by the five great powers.

The constitution of 1831 endorsed freedom of religion, of expression and of association, and limited the powers of the monarchy; however it failed to achieve a sense of national unity among Belgians. While no specific commitment to the French language was made in the constitution, in practice French became the sole language of law, politics, the administration and the army. During World War I the neutrality of Belgium was violated by Germany which invaded in 1914 and occupied the territory until 1918. There was a second invasion in 1940 but after the liberation of 1945 Belgium made a remarkable economic recovery and formed with the Netherlands and Luxembourg the economic union known as the Benelux.

Flanders and the Flemish movement

Present-day Flanders has a strong sense of national identity. Leaders of the early Flemish movement were literary figures whose dual objective was to promote the use of the Flemish language and maintain interest in Flemish culture. It was not until the predominantly Flemish Catholic Party came to power at the end of the nineteenth century however that Flemish grievances were clearly voiced. The vast majority of Belgium's senior civil servants were French-speaking Walloons; French was used exclusively in public life and Dutch was not generally taught in primary schools despite the laws passed to encourage teaching in Dutch. Although Flemings did not want French to become the language of Flanders it was difficult for them to choose which of the three or four different Flemish dialects to promote and Dutch was at first not favoured. In 1896 it was decided that Dutch would be the language of Flanders and Flemish became standardized as Dutch.

Many of the Fleming's grievances were rapidly redressed once they had been voiced, but by the 1930s 75% of army officers and over 80% of diplomats were still French-speakers. In World War II, as in World War I, Germany exploited Flemish nationalism by treating Flemish language and culture with respect and creating Dutch-speaking faculties at universities in occupied Brussels. Their tactics were successful in many cases and thousands of Belgians were later found guilty of collaboration at postwar trials. In 1954 a number of small groups amalgamated to form the *Volksunie* party which had much influence in the 1960s, but by far the dominant party in Flanders was the Social Christian Party (CVP).

The Walloons

The word "walloon" or "wallonia" was used by early Germanic tribes of central Europe to refer to Celtic peoples. It was also used in the fifteenth century to describe soldiers from the Low Countries. The word was first used to refer specifically to French-speaking southern Belgium in the mid-nineteenth century when it became clear to Francophones that the growth of the Flemish movement was becoming a threat to French ascendancy. Early Walloon societies such as the Walloon Union were formed in Flanders. Their members stressed that French should remain the principal language of Belgium although they accepted the use of both French and Flemish in the two communities. At the

[1]This area, known as Westhoek, contains the city of Dunkirk and areas to the west of the Belgian border. Dunkirk and other urban areas are now mainly French-speaking but residents of country areas continue to use Flemish. Probably about 100,000 of the 350,000 residents of the area are Flemish-speakers. Flemish in France has no official status although a limited amount of education is conducted in Flemish.

turn of the century Walloon nationalism became increasingly associated with Socialism, a situation which was to be repeated during the economic crisis of the 1950s and 1960s. Walloons were divided into those who advocated fusion with France and the federalists. At the end of World War II many were hostile towards the Flemings, many of whom had collaborated with Germany. At the Walloon national congress of 1945, 486 of the 1,048 Walloon delegates voted for union with France and 391 for federalism. After a second debate the majority voted for Walloon "autonomy" within a federal Belgium.

Wallonia, which had been one of the first European regions to be industrialized, suffered an economic decline after the war, due mainly to the collapse of the coal and iron-ore mining industries. A decision by the Swedish to build a huge steel strip mill in Flanders rather than Wallonia caused considerable protest on the part of the *Mouvement Populaire Wallon*. Between 1956 and 1976, 66% of foreign investment went to Flanders, 27% to Wallonia and 7% to the Brussels region, and by 1974 the *per capita* income of Flemings had exceeded that of Walloons whose birthrate was now declining. By 1957 Walloons made up an estimated 28% of the Belgian population.

Initially the two major Walloon parties were the Walloon regionalist party, now known as the *Front Wallon*, and the *Rassemblement Wallon* (RW). After the 1968 elections the two parties merged to form a joint parliamentary group. A split within the RW party in 1976 resulted in RW parliamentary representation being cut by two-thirds. The *Front Démocratique des Francophones* (FDF) has now emerged as the most influential party in the city of Brussels.

The tri-regional solution

Although by the 1960s Flanders was growing in prosperity, Flemings resented the increasing "gallicization" of Brussels, largely as a result of the growing number of European Communities officials residing there. As a direct result of Flemish pressure the language laws of 1962–63 were passed. The language frontier between Flanders and Wallonia was fixed by law, with the region of Mouscron-Comines or Walloon Flanders being transferred to the Walloon province of Hainaut and the Fourons region becoming part of Flemish Limburg. The city of Brussels was restricted to 19 communes and so the surrounding countryside was protected from further expansion by the largely French-speaking city.

Constitutional changes enacted between 1967 and 1971 introduced profound changes in Belgium's governmental structure. Article 32 *bis* of the constitution provided for the division into Dutch- and French-speaking groups of all members of the national parliament and for them to exercise as members of two cultural councils legislative authority in cultural matters over citizens in their respective cultural communities. Belgium was divided into four linguistic territories: the unilingual Dutch, French and German territories and the bilingual territory of Brussels-Capital (new Article 3 *bis*). According to Article 107 *quater* Belgium comprised three regions: the Walloon region, the Flemish region and the Brussels region. Regional institutions were set up to deal with regional matters but the precise nature of such matters remained unresolved.

This proved to be a great problem in efforts to achieve a lasting consensus and stable government. An effort was made in 1974 to set up Regional Councils but this did not obtain the necessary two-thirds majority in Parliament. After an unsuccessful attempt to develop a Pacte Communautaire — an elaborate five-tier government structure which would satisfy the aspirations of both Dutch and Flemish speakers — the Social Christian (*Front Démocratique des Francophones* — FDF) Socialist alliance collapsed in 1980. An interim government and elections followed and after a short-lived Social Christian-Socialist-FDF coalition, a Social Christian-Liberal-Socialist alliance was formed led by Wilfred Martens and the government continued to implement plans for the devolution of Flanders and Wallonia.

The constitutional reform of the 1980s

The attempt to create a workable consensus lead to further changes of the Constitution in 1980. Henceforth at the federal level there were three communities (Flemish, French and German-speaking) and three regions (Flemish, Brussels and Walloon). The subjects of the communities are dependent upon linguistic affiliation while those of the regions on geographic area. Thus Flanders consists of both the Flemish community and the Flemish region; Wallonia consists only of the Walloon region, although this greatly overlaps the French-speaking community. As yet there is no definite solution for Brussels-Capital and the Brussels region continues to function within the national government. The structures are detailed and elaborate but they are seriously flawed by a lack of clarity in the law, the incomplete character of the reform and the lack of financial independence by the new community and regional bodies. A series of central government powers were due to be transferred to the three regions on January 1st, 1989 but because of disputes — largely over financing — the transfer was delayed.

The elections of 1981 and 1985 resulted in a continuous decline of the linguistic parties. After the elections of 1985 the RW disappeared, the FDF was considerably weakened and the *Volksunie* lost seats. Linguistic parties always had only a minority following although they played a disproportionate role in policy-making; today there appears to be a swing back to mainstream parties. In 1986 a linguistic crisis developed over the status of the tiny rural district of Fourons/Voeren close to the Dutch border, a majority French-speaking area in a Dutch-speaking district. A maverick French-speaking mayor refused to take a competency test in Dutch and as a result was dismissed as mayor. The issue was a factor in toppling two coalitions but was finally settled by early 1989 when the mayor agreed to step down in return for political concessions.

The German-speaking minority

There are about 100,000 German speakers in Belgium, living in a discontinuous area along the frontier with Germany and Luxembourg. Some have been part of Belgium from the early nineteenth century, others since German areas were annexed to Belgium in 1920. Various varieties of German are spoken and there is no linguistic unity as such. Only in "Neu-Belgien", the cantons of Eupen-Sankt-Vith, are German-speakers a majority. German is one of the recognized linguistic regions and three cultural communities of Belgium and theoretically has equal linguistic and cultural rights with Dutch and French speakers; in practice, given the relatively small size of the community, inevitably there are inequalities; although the proximity of neighbouring Germany means that there is much linguistic and cultural stimulation via German publications and media. There is a German–Belgian radio station and a newspaper. In Neu-Belgien it is necessary to know German in order to work in local administration and the use of German has long been allowed in local courts.

The future

There have been many predictions that Belgium, founded as a largely artificial state, would collapse with its constituent peoples going different ways. There have been frequent political and constitutional crises and a constant reworking of the relationships between the centre and the regions, the Flemings and the Walloons, Brussels and the rest of the country. Yet the state has survived each crisis and will most probably continue to do so. The two major communities are relatively balanced in numbers — certainly one cannot completely block the aspirations of the other — and proportional representation is used in all elections. Neither major community has expressed a wish to join with another country, either the Netherlands or France, and neither of these states has intervened on behalf of linguistic rights in Belgium. There has been an attempt always to resolve problems within a Belgium state — albeit a devolved one. Explicitly linguistic parties have only ever claimed the following of a minority of either community. Apart from an occasional fracas, communal violence is unknown. Intermarriage between members of the two communities has been common. Belgium's economic position as a trading nation and the headquarters of the European Communities has encouraged the development of multilingualism within the country.

Bretons

Location: **Breton peninsula, western France**
Population: **2.5 million; 500,000 Breton speakers**
% of population: **4.5% of French population; 20% of Breton population are Breton speakers**
Religion: **Catholic**
Language: **French, Breton (mainly in western areas)**

The Bretons are the inhabitants of Brittany, an area deeply influenced by the Celtic settlers from Britain (hence the name Brittany) who arrived from the fourth century AD, fleeing from Saxon expansionism. The language Breton is close to both the Welsh and the now extinct Cornish language and has affinities with other Celtic languages. Breton speakers are now a minority within Brittany and are probably about 20% of the population of the peninsula.

The Breton kingdoms retained their independence for many centuries but after a successful military campaign they were annexed to France by treaty in 1532. However they were able to retain a parliament and administrative autonomy. This autonomy was destroyed in the French Revolution when the National Assembly abolished the special rights and privileges of the provinces in favour of equal rights for all areas; Brittany then became, as did the rest of France, divided into government departments administered from the centre. An uprising against the revolutionary forces resulted in a scorched earth policy and thousands of deaths. Since that time Brittany has remained part of France, currently consisting of five departments with a population of about 2.5 million. In 1956 four of these departments were formed into one of the country's 22 regions for the purpose of economic planning. In 1974 a regional assembly was established, which was elected indirectly and had powers over the region's budget.

French domination also brought with it the French language. In 1539 the Ordinance of Villiers-Cotterets required that French be used exclusively for law, contracts and all official acts and this was further emphasized after the Revolution. Nevertheless the isolation of Brittany meant that the Breton language continued in use by the peasantry well into the nineteenth and early twentieth centuries, along with a strong and distinctive Celtic tradition. But since that time there has been a strong cultural assimilation and language shift towards French. In 1886 there were an estimated 1.3 million Breton speakers in western Brittany, but by 1974 this number had halved to about 665,000; about 44% of the population of western Brittany. Only about half of this number spoke Breton on a daily basis, mostly older people. In the eastern half of Brittany French is the everyday language. One of the main reasons for the decline of the language was the deliberate policy of educating all children in French and suppression of the use of Breton in schools.

Not surprisingly there has been a movement to restore the use of the Breton language. This has achieved some success and Breton is now taught in some schools and colleges, although it is still sub-servient to French. There are evening classes, summer schools and correspondence courses, dozens of small Breton language publications and some radio and TV programmes in Breton. Yet it is reported that government clerks may refuse to issue birth certificates to parents who wish to give their children certain Breton names. There has also been a series of political movements aimed at achieving independence for Brittany, either within the French federal system, notably the *Comité d'étude et de liaison des intérêts Bretons* (CELIB) and more radical political parties such as the *Strollard ar Vro* (SAV) (the Breton Party) and left-wing groups. Terrorist organizations such as the *Armée Républicaine Bretonne* (ARB) and the *Front Libération de la Bretagne* (FLB) have been responsible for a number of bombings.

Few Bretons today see independence as a realistic option and the only Breton political party which has done well in electoral terms is the *Union Démocratique Bretonne* (UDB), which has performed well in local elections, and which seeks a popularly elected Breton Assembly. Although many Bretons may sympathize with the aims of the bombers, few agree with their methods. While successive French governments have promised to respect the rights of linguistic minorities this has made little real impact and the Breton language will probably continue to decline as an everyday tongue. However young Breton intellectuals, often living in Paris or elsewhere, seem determined not to let the language die. Economic factors continue to discriminate against Brittany, which in the mid-1970s was one of the poorest areas of France and was developing at a slower rate than the rest of the economy. High unemployment, low wages and emigration seem likely to continue.

(See also *Alsatians; Welsh*)

Catalans

Location: **Catalonia, region of north-east Spain**
Population: **5.7 million, 80% Catalan speakers**
% of population: **14.5% of Spanish population**
Religion: **Catholic**
Language: **Catalan, Spanish, some French speakers**

The Catalans are the native inhabitants of the former principality of Catalonia which was once a commercially flourishing and independent political entity and is now divided into the provinces of Barcelona, Tarragona, Lerida and Gerona. The Cata-lans, a mixture of Pyrenean and Mediterranean peoples, speak the Catalan dialect which has a greater affinity with Provençal than Spanish, and French influence in Catalonia has been consistently strong. There are also Catalan speakers outside

Catalonia — in the Balearic Islands and the area around Valencia in Spain; in France, Andorra and Sardinia.

The Franco era

Catalans have long been fiercely regionalistic and they repeatedly took part in Carlist and Republican revolts, the last of which, in 1932, resulted in Catalonia being made an autonomous region within the Spanish state. The widely-spoken local language and common culture were important factors in the shaping of a sense of national identity, and a literary revival in the nineteenth century inspired Catalan intellectuals and middle-class groups to lead a Catalan nationalist movement. Catalonia was, and remains, a prosperous region within Spain. Industry has thrived and Catalans enjoyed a disproportionate share of the country's industrial wealth, due largely to the activities of a local entrepreneurial class. The increasing centralization of government was particularly resented by this politically aware group, especially as state bureaucracy was far less efficient than local government bodies. The regional aspirations of the Catalans and Basques were seen as a threat to Spanish unity by "nationalistic" political forces, led by General Franco, and Catalans supported the defeated Republican forces in the Civil War of the 1930s.

Under the Franco regime Catalans suffered severe political and cultural repression. The Catalonian autonomous government was abolished and its leader extradited from Vichy France and shot. Regional-based parties were banned. Catalonia's share of government funding dropped steadily and Catalan businessmen were actively discouraged from investing surplus capital within Catalonia. The use of Catalan outside the home was banned as were street and shop signs in Catalan. Any expression of Catalan culture was forbidden and teachers were expected to demonstrate "political reliability" or face dismissal or compulsory transfer to other regions. During the 1950s there was some relaxation of policy and the everyday unofficial use of Catalan was once again permitted as were some folk festivals. Large numbers of immigrants from other, poorer, Spanish regions moved into Catalonia, however, particularly in the 1960s, until well over 50% of its unskilled or semi-skilled workforce was not Catalan.

During the 1950s Catalans were among the leaders of nationwide resistance to Franco's rule. In this they were supported by a large group of Catalan and Basque clergy who were mostly moderate Socialists or Christian Democrats and who tended to support the regional cause. Unlike the Basques, however, the Catalans only rarely resorted to violent methods of protest. Due to their well-estab-lished cultural and economic identity they were a self-confident community able to resolve local conflict through co-operation rather than confrontation.

The post-Franco era

With the death in 1975 of General Franco the Catalan people entered a new phase. Continuing demands for regional autonomy were supported by massive strike action to which the government was slow to respond, partly due to its fear of regionalism, a fear exacerbated by the disruptive actions of ETA, the Basque terrorist group. In 1977, at the first elections to be held in the post-Franco era, an alliance of explicitly pro-Catalan parties secured 10 seats in the lower house of the new Parliament and Catalan leaders were able to present a relatively united front to the central government in the unofficial *Assemblea de Catalunya* (formed in the last years of the Franco regime). Catalonia (along with the Basque country, Andalucia and Galicia) was one of four regions granted a higher degree of autonomy than others. There have been Catalan complaints of official tardiness in implementation of regional reforms.

The attempted military coup of 1982 was a sharp reminder of unresolved problems as government attempted its remodelling process but in 1982 power was democratically passed to an elected Socialist government and the backlog of social and administrative reform is gradually being dealt with. It appears that the repressive measures used against Catalans during the Franco regime have been finally abandoned. The Catalan language and culture is now visible and encouraged by the regional government and non-Catalan immigrants have also learnt Catalan, thus confirming its position as a viable language. Spain's entry into the EC in 1986 also gave Catalonia — which has traditionally looked northwards rather than to Madrid — hopes for continued regional autonomy and economic integration within Europe.

Catalans in France

Catalan-speaking lands, known as Catalonia-Nord (corresponding to the department of Pyrénées-Orientales), were annexed to the French crown in the Treaty of the Pyrenees in 1659. Today probably 200,000 out of a total of 300,000 inhabitants speak Catalan in the 4,000 square kilometres of Catalonia-Nord. As with other minority languages in France there is no official legal recognition of Catalan although it is possible for some education to be given in Catalan and various groups work for the promotion and maintenance of the Catalan language. However the main impetus for its continued use is the active Catalan language and culture in Spain. Catalonia-Nord has severe economic prob-lems of historic underdevelopment, diminishing land use and high unemployment.

(See also *Basques; Galicians*)

Ceuta and Melilla

Location: **northern coast of Morocco**
Population: **Ceuta: 65,000, Melilla: 53,000**
% of population: **Ceuta: 80% Spanish, 20% Moroccan; Melilla: 66% Spanish, 34% Moroccan**
Religion: **Catholic, Muslim**
Language: **Spanish, Arabic**

Ceuta and Melilla are two small Spanish-ruled enclaves on the north coast of Morocco, the last remainder of Spain's 600-year-old African empire. Administratively they are part of the autonomous government of Andalucia. Ethnically they are a mixture of Spaniards, Muslims with Spanish nationality, and Moroccans, who reside there legally or illegally.

The continued existence of the two enclaves has been an issue of contention between Spain and Morocco. Morocco claimed them and brought the issue before the UN Decolonization Committee in 1975 and compared Spain's presence to the British in Gibraltar. However in 1986 the Moroccan monarch stated that a solution must come through "dialogue and persuasion".

There has been politically motivated violence and ethnic disturbances in both Ceuta and Melilla over the past decade. The majority of resident Spaniards are opposed to change while many Moroccans wish for union with Morocco. Some Muslims feel that there should be special provisions to protect their religious, language and cultural rights within Spain. The Socialist government has attempted to raise the living standards and grant permanent status and equal rights to Muslims living in Ceuta and Melilla. A new Spanish Aliens law was introduced in 1985 and it was announced that all Muslims who applied for residence permits would obtain Spanish nationality within 10 years, while those whose papers were not in order would be expelled. There are economic reasons why many Muslims wish the enclaves to remain Spanish. Both the cities are free ports attracting tourists from the mainland. However with the removal of border controls within the European Communities in 1992 their present status may be problematic.

(See also *Gibraltarians*)

Corsicans

Location: **French island in western Mediterranean**
Population: **112,000 (1978)**
% of population: **between 50%-65%**
Religion: **Catholic**
Language: **Dialect of Italian**

The Corsicans are the Italian dialect-speaking inhabitants of the island of Corsica which was ruled by various Italian states for 1,300 years before being bought by France in 1768 after a brief period of independence. In 1900 the population was native Corsican but there are now substantial Sardinian, Moroccan, French Algerian and French com-munities on the island, and over 400,000 Corsicans have now emigrated in search of work. Today more Corsicans live and work in mainland France than in Corsica, and there is some uncertainty over the proportion of Corsicans in the population; although 50% is a commonly quoted figure the 1975 census gave 64% with a further 13% of mixed Corsican-French parentage.

Corsica's economy is heavily dependent on viticulture and tourism. The industries are not controlled by Corsicans and the traditional Corsican hostelries have largely been replaced by hotel chains. The vineyards are now almost completely owned by non-Corsicans as a result of a scheme to resettle Algerian *colons* on agricultural land with low mortgages not available to Corsicans. Whereas in 1960 90% of the workforce was Corsican, by 1978 the figure had dropped to only 30% and there were plans for the import of more non-Corsicans to expand the tourist industry.

Protest movements have grown since the 1960s and several groups are legally recognized, of which *Union pour la Corse* (UPC) was the most important political party. Other, illegal, organizations, notably the *Front National de la Corse* (FLNC), have been chiefly responsible for the growth of violence which resulted in hundreds of bomb explosions each year, mainly directed against foreign-owned property. Whilst various French governments have condemned all violent attempts at separatism some concessions have been made, notably the establishment of a cheaper transport system to the mainland and the provision of cheaper agricultural land to Corsican farmers. Corsican protest groups have demanded the removal of the three foreign legion posts on the island, the expulsion of the *colons* and the re-distribution of land, and more Corsican involvement in the tourist industry.

During the 1970s separatist violence grew but the government of Giscard d'Estaing refused to grant special status to the island although it promised

more funds with which to overcome economic inequalities. The Socialist government after its election in 1981 promised a special statute for Corsica which would give it more autonomy than was granted to other regions and would include a popularly elected regional assembly controlling land transactions, employment and broadcasting. Demands for compulsory bilingualism and the reservation of jobs for Corsicans were rejected, however. The Assembly was first elected in August 1982 since when there have been several elections due to the absence of a stable majority. There have been many problems in its operation but nevertheless it does appear to have defused some of the tensions and a 1983 poll showed that 93% of Corsicans wanted the island to remain French whilst only 4% said that it should become independent. (In the elections only 10% of Corsicans voted for separatist parties.) Terrorist groups continued to operate, but they lost much public sympathy when they altered their policy in favour of attacking people rather than property. In 1983 the FLNC was banned after the killing of a French immigrant and it is since reported to be relying for support partially on criminal "protection money". There have also been terrorist attacks by pro-French immigrant groups, and the tourist industry has suffered as a result of the bombings.

Corsica's problems remain those of any isolated area with a narrow economic base. The unemployment rate is 10% higher than the national average and the area is heavily dependent on pension and welfare payments.

Croats of Austria

Location: **Burgenland, eastern Austria**
Population: **26,100 total; 18,800 in Burgenland**
% of population: **7% of Burgenland population**
Religion: **Catholic**
Language: **Croat dialect**

Croats have lived in Burgenland, a province along Austria's border with Hungary since the mid-fifteenth century. The area formerly belonged to Hungary but after World War I became part of Austria. In addition to the 18,800 speakers recorded in Burgenland, several thousand Croat speakers live in the Vienna area. Burgenland also has a Magyar (Hungarian) speaking minority of 4,000.

Along with the Slovenes the Croats are the subject of both Article 7 of the Austrian State Treaty of 1955 and the Ethnic Groups Act of 1976. However there has been less controversy concerning the Croat situation, possibly because of its position bordering Hungary rather than Yugoslavia. The 1937 School Act governs teaching in settlements with a Croat majority but the lack of Croat textbooks is a problem. There is a formal right to use the Croat language in courts and administration but as 90% of the Burgenland population speaks only German this is difficult to practise. The Croatian Cultural Society has been a focus of culture, education and political activity.

(See also *Slovenes of Austria*)

Danes of West Germany

Location: **Schleswig-Holstein, Germany's border with Denmark**
Population: **60,000-70,000 (1980)**
% of population: **8.5% of population of Schleswig-Holstein**
Religion: **Protestant**
Language: **Danish (dialect)**

The Danish minority in West Germany is concentrated in the region of Schleswig-Holstein which was part of Denmark until 1863. In that year the direct male line of Denmark died out and the duchies of Schleswig and Holstein were claimed by both Germany and Denmark. A series of diplomatic manoeuvres and the Austro-Prussian War of 1866 were followed by the annexation of the duchies by Prussia. In 1920 a referendum in North and Central Schleswig resulted in the restoration of North Schleswig to Denmark while Central Schleswig remained a part of Germany.

Since 1920 the Danish minority in Germany has fluctuated in size, and the loyalties of the Danes were particularly called into question during World War II when many crossed into Denmark and others began calling for minority rights. The situation in Schleswig-Holstein became more serious when over one million refugees and expelled persons from East Germany entered the region after the war, doubling the resident population and altering the ethnic balance in favour of the Germans. Although some refugees were moved into other regions the majority remained in Schleswig-Holstein, which lacked the economic and financial resources to deal with them. A declaration of

minority rights was negotiated in 1949. Under this declaration, known as the Kiel Declaration, Danish schools were funded by government and a committee was established to deal with Danish grievances. From 1947 the Danish minority was represented in the Kiel Land Parliament but the decline in Danish votes and a 5% exclusion clause in Schleswig-Holstein election law caused the Danes to lose their parliamentary representation.

In 1954 renewed negotiations in Kiel, Bonn and Copenhagen led to the provision by Federal government of funds for a large land improvement programme in the region and a reciprocal agreement between West Germany and Denmark over existing minority problems on both sides of the border. Although no internationally legally binding agreement was signed, both countries submitted unilateral — but almost identical — declarations to their respective parliaments for approval and both are politically binding. The 5% exclusion clause was removed in Schleswig-Holstein and Danish parliamentary representation was re-established. Co-operation between the two countries has resulted in a successful relationship between the minority and majority populations in this now comparatively wealthy border region.

(See also *Germans of Denmark*)

Faroe Islanders

Alternative names: **Faroese, Foroyar, Faeroerne**
Location: **Faroe Islands, North Atlantic, 1,300 km from Denmark**
Population: **45,750**
% of population: **0.9% of Danish population**
Religion: **Lutheran**
Language: **Faronese (Foroyskt)**

The Faroe Islanders are the inhabitants of the Faroe Islands, one of the 14 *Amt* (counties) of Denmark. Their isolated position in the North Atlantic Ocean, midway between the Shetland Islands (UK) and Iceland, and their distinct cultural and linguistic characteristics, give them the status of a minority.

The Faroe Islanders claim descent from Viking

settlers of the eighth and ninth centuries. At one stage they were part of Norway (and are in fact geographically closer to Norway than Denmark) but when Denmark ceded Norway to Sweden in 1814 the Faroe Islands, along with Iceland and Greenland, remained with Denmark. At first Norwegian law continued to operate in the Faroes but this was abolished along with the local parliament, the *Logting* (said to be the oldest parliamentary body in Europe) and the Faroes became a Danish county. The *Logting* was later reconstituted and in 1948 The Home Rule Act, supplemented by further measures in 1975, granted the *Logting* legislative powers including the control of the economy and withdrawal from the EC. Some members of the *Logting* are directly elected while other seats are distributed to parties by a system of proportional representation. There are six main parties, supporting policies which range from independence to greater local autonomy to greater integration with Denmark. The *Logting* sends two representatives to the Danish parliament.

To a large extent the Faroese have maintained their separateness as a linguistic and cultural group. The Faroese language is related to both Icelandic and rural Norwegian and has the same official status in the islands as Danish. It is the main means of communication within the islands and is used in the Parliament, local radio, churches and cultural activities. There are six newspapers and over 100 books a year produced in Faroese. Education is in Faroese although all children are obliged to learn Danish. Danish government policy is sympathetic to aspirations for the development of Faroese culture.

A threat might come from the small population and the narrow economic base of the islands, which are overwhelmingly dependent on deep sea fishing, encouraged by grants from the central government. While this has produced a relatively high level of income and secure way of life, there is little employment for educated professional people, who generally receive higher education on the Danish mainland and find employment there. Yet the population has continued to grow, considerable investment has been made in communications within the islands and with other countries and a tourist industry is being developed. The Faroese Islanders are noted for their energy and self-reliance and as such have been able to protect their culture and language more than most small European minorities.

(See also *Germans of Denmark*; *Inuits* (of Greenland) in **North America**)

Frisians

Name: **Frisians; West, North, East**
Location: **Netherlands, Federal Republic of Germany**
Population: **total about 700,000**
% of population: **Netherlands about 4%**
Religion: **mainly Reformed Church**
Language: **Frisian dialects, Dutch, German**

Frisian-language speakers comprise a linguistic and cultural minority group of northern Europe and are today divided into three distinct groups; the Western Frisians of the northern Netherlands and the Northern and East Frisians of the German Federal Republic. Frisian is a language of the West Germanic family but the three Frisian-speaking groups today speak different dialects of Frisian which are not always mutually intelligible, for example the dialect of the North Frisians is unintelligible outside their own community to all but a few educated speakers of West Frisian. Despite the official recognition given to West Frisian, Frisian today is in general a language in decline.

The West Frisians

The West Frisians are based in the province of Friesland in the north of the Netherlands. It includes the islands of Texel, Vlieland, Terschelling, Ameland, Schiermonnikoog and Rottum. Of the 550,000 inhabitants, about 400,000 are Frisian language speakers with probably another 300,000 living outside the province. As a language West Frisian is more like English than Dutch in many respects but many town dwellers speak "town Frisian", a mixed dialect of Dutch and Frisian dating back to the seventeenth century.

Friesland, previously semi-independent and later part of the Hapsburg Empire, joined the United Republic of the Netherlands in 1648. It was, and remains, one of the poorer areas of the country, leading to large-scale emigration to North America in the nineteenth century. Despite this, in the seventeenth century a Frisian language movement was born and this continued into the nineteenth century. In the early twentieth century the Frisian Movement expressed identity mainly in literary terms and this laid the basis for modern West Frisian identity. In 1938 the Fryske Academy was established and pioneered the teaching of Frisian in schools.

Friesland is unique among the eleven provinces of the Netherlands in having its own language which is allowed restricted use in courts of law. Frisian has been recognized as a medium of educational instruction since 1955 and in 1975 the Dutch government accepted a proposal that it be used in primary schooling and be made a compulsory study subject. The language is also studied at colleges and five universities elsewhere in the Netherlands. Frisian is spoken to some extent in the provincial council and bilingual signs are permitted. There is a modest Frisian weekly and monthly press.

However other factors mitigate against the use of Frisian. There is no Frisian TV service and only a small radio programme daily. Most Frisians speak Dutch for business purposes and use Frisian in the home. The province has lost much of its agricultural base and has little industry, and there is high emigration among young people, while non-Frisian speakers holiday or retire there.

The North Frisians

The North Frisians live in the *land* of Schleswig-Holstein in the Federal Republic of Germany in an area known as the Kreis of Nord Friesland. In 1970 it had a total population of 154,000 of which about 60,000 were said to consider themselves Frisians. However only a minority speak Frisian and the numbers have dwindled steadily from 19,300 in 1890 to 15,000 in 1928 and 10,000 in 1968.

It is questionable whether the North Frisians can be regarded as a national minority in the same way as the West Frisians are since the language has been virtually abandoned in favour of local German dialects and there has been continuous intermarriage between Frisians, Germans and Danes for centuries. German has been used in schooling since the introduction of state education in the nineteenth century while during the Nazi period use of the Frisian language was forbidden. Today some classes in primary and secondary education are conducted in Frisian. The North Frisians have no special legal position as a minority group, unlike the Danish minority. Economic conditions are poor and emigration levels are high; while tourism is welcomed for economic reasons, it has further undermined the Frisian character of the area.

The East Frisians

The speakers of East Frisian in the late 1970s comprised about 11,000 people in Saterland in the Federal Republic of Germany, south of the town of Emden. Although geographically they are relatively close to West Frisian speakers they are seen as having collaborated with the Nazi regime and this partly explains the lack of close regular contact between the different groups. Like the North Frisians they have no special legal position as a minority group.

Friulians

Location: **North-east Italy**
Population: **600,000**
% of population: **1% of Italian population**
Religion: **Catholic**
Language: **Friulian, also Venetian dialects of Italian**

The Friulians live in the region of Friuli-Venezia-Giulia along Italy's border with Austria and Yugoslavia. The Friulian language, like Romantsch and Ladin, is a member of the Rhaeto-Romanche family. Earliest books in the language date from 1150 and Friulian was used in law and government from the fourteenth century. It is now spoken by about 600,000 of the 800,000 inhabitants of Friuli. There is also a small community in the parish of Sauris in the Carnic Alps whose population amounts to less than one thousand and whose members speak Friulian in addition to an ancient German dialect, High German and Italian.

Known in Roman times as Patria Fori Julii, Friuli was a sovereign state throughout the Middle Ages. It was occupied by Napoleon in 1797 and

came under Austrian rule between 1814 and 1866, when it became part of a reunited Italy. The region is economically rather backward. Farming and stock-raising are the principal occupations and there is some light industry and a hydro-electric installation.

Today the Venetian dialects of Italian are being increasingly used in the towns and also in the southern parts of Friuli. Friulian has only been taught in some schools since the 1970s and has not been used by the Church since World War II. There is a monthly newspaper which is published by *Int Furlane*, a society dedicated to promoting the Friulian language; two daily newspapers each carry one page of Friulian and there are 40 hours per week of Friulian-language radio broadcasts and a bilingual

TV channel. Many Friulians feel that the regional government has done little to encourage the use of Friulian, however, apart from introducing it to the curriculum of the Theological Seminary at Udine, and the great majority of those attending Friulian language classes attend voluntary classes.

In 1963 Friuli-Venezia-Giulia was made the fourth region of Italy but Trieste, which is outside the Friulian-speaking area, was made the regional capital. It has been often felt by Friulians that their area should not have been incorporated into the new region. There have been calls for an adjustment in the Regional Statute to make Friuli an autonomous administrative unit, for the re-introduction of Friulian language teaching in schools and for the creation of a university at Udine.

(See also *Ladins, Romantsch speakers of Switzerland*)

Gaelic speakers of Scotland

Name: **Gaels**
Location: **Throughout Scotland, particularly northern highlands and western islands**
Population: **79,307 bilingual (Gaelic/English) speakers**
% of population: **1.64% (bilingual)**
Religion: **Protestant, Catholic**
Language: **Gadhelic (Gaelic), English**

Scottish Gaels are found throughout the country but the largest concentration is in the Western Isles Region where in 1981 79.5% were Gaelic-speaking, and in Skye and Lochalsh, 53.6%; while smaller but significant minorities are found in the sparsely populated areas of Sutherland and Argyll. Significant numbers are also found in the major towns and cities but in most Scottish communities Gaelic speakers are in a tiny minority.

Gaelic was the dominant language in Scotland between the ninth and thirteenth centuries but gradually declined thereafter, a process assisted by a certain amount of active repression. The Statute of Iona (1609), for example, sought to direct chiefly families towards English schooling for their children; during the eighteenth and nineteenth centuries Gaelic was either regarded as an anachronism to be eradicated or an irrelevance to be disregarded. The crushing of the Jacobite rising of 1745, the enforced clearances of the Highland peasants to make way for sheep and the subsequent emigration of thousands of Gaelic speakers in the eighteenth and nineteenth centuries[1], brought about a severe reduction in the number of Gaelic speakers in the central highlands, leaving only the coastal areas of the Highlands and Islands Gaelic-speaking. The Gaelic cause was promoted in 1891 with the founding of The Highland Association which has acted as a pressure group helping among other things to re-establish Gaelic in the educational system.

The political climate for the maintenance of the Gaelic language is better now than it has been for several hundred years. Whilst Gaelic is not used in courts or in public business there has been a resurgence of interest in the language, partly an outcome of the growing mood of nationalism in Scotland, and official attitudes are no longer actively repressive. The Western Isles Region now has an official bilingual policy which is being gradually and selectively implemented in schools and in business. The Education (Scotland) Act 1980 specifies an obligation on the education authorities to make provision at all stages for Gaelic in Gaelic-speaking areas. The Scottish National Party has a comprehensive Gaelic policy. Gaelic is well established on radio and is also featured on television, and a Gaelic Repertory Theatre Company has been formed. The Scottish Gaelic Texts Society, founded in the 1930s, has published a series of Gaelic publications, and the government has provided funds for further publications. Gaelic continues to have a strong base in the Free Church and Free Presbyterian Church.

Yet it appears that although the new interest in Gaelic language and culture will continue, the narrowing economic base in the Highlands and Islands, the drift southwards and the deaths of the last of the monoglot Gaelic speakers, will make it difficult for numbers to expand and for the language to survive outside the outer islands.

(See also *Welsh*)

[1]Some set up Gaelic speaking communities in Canada, in Nova Scotia, Cape Breton and Prince Edward Island, which survive today.

Galicians

Alternative names: **Gallegos**
Location: **North-western Spain**
Population: **3 million approx.**
% of population: **7.2% of Spanish population**
Relgion: **Catholic**
Language: **Gallegan (Gallego), Spanish**

The Galicians are the inhabitants of the remote north-western region of Spain, bordering northern Portugal. This region has been occupied by Celts, Phoenicians, Greeks and Suevis and provided a bastion against the Roman invasion. It later became a haven for Spaniards fleeing Moorish domination, and has long enjoyed a distinctive history, language and culture. The Galicians are a Celtic minority and share certain cultural traits with other Celtic peoples. Like the Scots, Irish and Bretons the Galicians use bagpipes, for example, and the school of lyric poetry, which once greatly influenced Spanish literature, has strong links with the Celtic tradition. The city of Santiago de Compostella has been a centre of pilgrimage since the ninth century.

Economically Galicia is one of the poorest regions in Spain. Communications were poor until recently, agriculture is bedevilled by over-division of the land and unemployment is high. The majority of men are obliged to emigrate for part of their lives and emigration has become a tradition, leaving many women to do work traditionally assigned to men. From the late 1960s extensive road-building linking Galicia with the rest of Spain has ended some of the region's social and cultural isolation however and during the 1970s and 1980s there have been an increasing number of migrants returning to Galicia. Tourism has increased and there has been a boom in property prices in the coastal areas.

Unlike other Spanish regions, Galicia has experienced little political unrest. There is an autonomous government of Galicia, established under the 1978 constitution, but there have been few moves towards true autonomy. There is a separatist party and small separatist groups have committed violent acts, but in general politics in the region follow a strongly conservative tradition. A campaign to have Gallegan reinstated as a respected language rather than a regional dialect has not as yet been accepted by the authorities.

(See also *Basques; Catalans*)

Germans of Denmark

Location: **North Schleswig, Danish border with West Germany**
Population: **15,000-20,000 (1980)**
% of population: **6%-8% of North Schleswig**
Religion: **Protestant**
Language: **German**

The division of the border region of Schleswig in 1920 left North Schleswig in Denmark with a small German minority. The German occupation of Denmark during World War II and the activities of members of that minority discredited the minority as a whole in Danish eyes. Collaborators were brought to trial, schools closed and property confiscated.

Fearful that a treaty or agreement regarding the German minority might be abused by the German government if it were binding under international law the Danish government stressed that there was no need for the German community to be granted minority rights since they were sufficiently protected as Danish citizens. The government also refused to discuss the treatment of the German minority or formally to recognize the border. Germans were able to elect a representative to the Danish parliament in 1953 however, and the community was granted the right to maintain private secondary schools. As with Danish speakers in Germany the German speakers of Denmark were protected by the unilateral declarations adopted by both parliaments in 1955. Since the 1960s there has been a thawing in the Danish attitude towards the Germans. In 1964 a decline in votes caused the German minority to lose its parliamentary representation but a substitute consultative committee was established in order that everyday problems might be discussed. By co-operating with the Centre Democrats, a Danish party, the German community was once again able to return a German MP to Copenhagen between 1973 and 1979.

The position of the German minority in Denmark is now secure. Substantial subsidies and improved relations between Denmark and West Germany have ensured that the community enjoys a reasonably high standard of living and that it retains its cultural identity, and German is a compulsory subject in all Danish schools.

(See also *Danes of West Germany*)

Gibraltarians

Alternative names: **"Llanitos"**
Location: **Rock of Gibraltar, peninsula at southernmost point of Spain**
Population: **20,000 of total population of 29,200**
% of population: **68%**
Religion: **Catholic**
Language: **English, Spanish, "Llanito" ("Yanito")**

The Gibraltarians are the permanent residents of the Rock of Gibraltar, under UK sovereignty for over two centuries. Its population derives from a mixture of peoples — Catalans, Spaniards, Genoese, Portuguese, Maltese and British. Most Gibraltarians read and speak English and Spanish although a local dialect, *Llanito*, is also spoken. Their nationality is British although they are not entitled to automatic residence in the UK.

The Rock was seized by the British from the Spanish in 1704 and confirmed as a British possession ". . . for ever . . ." in 1713 by the Treaty of Utrecht. Gibraltar became a crown colony in 1830 and remained an important British naval and military base thereafter. It was granted a greater measure of self-government in 1964 and a new constitution in 1969 giving it a House of Assembly. Spain had brought the Gibraltar question before the UN in 1963 and 1964 and had imposed restrictions on passage between Gibraltar and Spain from 1966. At a referendum held in the colony in September 1967 Gibraltarians voted overwhelmingly (12,762 to 44) to retain association with the UK. Spain closed the frontier with Gibraltar in June 1969; despite improved relations with the UK after the death of Franco it remained closed until February 1985.

Several developments since 1985 have given indications that both Spain and the UK are attempting to find a new status for Gibraltar. The 1981 Immigration Act gave Gibraltarians (along with Hong Kong) British dependent territory status and "British Overseas" passports which in effect deprived them of the automatic right of abode in the UK. Economically the reopening of the border has resulted in increased ties of work, trade and tourism between Gibraltarians and Spaniards. The announcement by the UK in early 1989 that it would withdraw the garrison presently based in Gibraltar would eventually also result in a loss of jobs and greater interdependence with the mainland.

In March 1987, after two decades of Conservative government in Gibraltar, the Socialists gained power under Joe Bossano with eventual independence for Gibraltar as a goal. It was felt that the removal of border controls and further moves towards unity within the European Communities after 1992 might make previous Spanish claims for sovereignty redundant. In February 1989 the Spanish Foreign Minister suggested that Gibraltar might become a European Hong Kong, with Spain gaining control over the territory but with the people retaining their existing rights, laws and customs. However the UK Foreign Secretary assured Gibraltarians that there would be no change in Gibraltar's status against their wishes.

(See also *Ceuta and Melilla*)

Greeks, Croatians and Albanians of Italy

Location: **Southern Italy**
Population: **Greeks: 7,500–15,000; Croatians: 2000–3000; Albanians (Tosko): 80,000 speakers**
% of population: **0.17% total**
Religion: **Greek Orthodox (Greek); Catholic (Croatian, Albanian)**
Language: **Community languages, plus Italian**

The Greeks, Croats and Albanians of southern Italy are tiny minorities not enumerated on the official census and virtually ignored by the Italian state. It is hard to estimate the numbers involved and the communities are often no more than small villages where only the older generation retains its own language as mother tongue.

Greeks

Speakers of the Italiot dialect of Greek are descendants of Byzantine invaders who entered Italy between the sixth and tenth centuries. Today they are found around Salento in Puglia and in the east of Reggio Calabria. Although there has been a renewed interest in Greek culture since 1955 the Italiot Greek is no longer used in schools or churches and the younger generation speaks only Italian.

Croatians

Croatian speakers are found only in three villages in Molise in southern Italy. They are the descendants of refugees who escaped the Turkish invasions of present-day Croatia during the fifteenth and sixteenth centuries and their language is an archaic form of that spoken along the border between the Yugoslav Republic of Croatia and Bosnia. During the last 30 years there has been a revival of interest in Croatian culture and the Primate of the Catholic Church in Yugoslavia conducted mass in Croatian in 1967. The Italian branch of the International Association for the Defence of Threatened Languages and Cultures has encouraged the renewal of

contacts with Croatia. Free Croatian–Italian grammars have been distributed among the villagers and at one stage there was a bilingual journal; despite these moves the Croatian language is the smallest minority language in Italy and is unlikely to survive in view of the small numbers involved.

Albanians

The Albanians (Arbereshe) are more numerous than the two other small minorities and may number up to one quarter of a million in total. They are descended from mercenaries used by King Alfonso of Naples in the fifteenth century and from those who fled the Turkish conquest of Albania. They live scattered throughout the poor farming regions of Calabria, Abruzzo, Basilicate, Molise, Campania, Puglia and Sicily and there are substantial settlements in big Italian cities. However only about one third of those of Albanian descent are believed to have a working knowledge of Albanian as an everyday language although almost all speak Italian also. There is an Institute of Albanian Studies at Palermo and the Albanian language can be studied at the universities of Rome and Naples but it is not taught in schools and has no official status. Several Albanian speakers have held prominent positions in Italy's political and religious life and there have been a number of notable Italian writers of Albanian descent. There are a number of languages and cultural societies which act to protect and promote the Albanian language in Italy. In recent years it has been possible for Albanian speakers to visit Albania and to renew cultural and linguistic ties with that country.

(See also *Sardinians*)

Jurassians of Switzerland

Location: **north-west of Berne canton**
Population: **67,000**
% of population: **about 1%**
Religion: **67% Catholic, 33% protestant**
Language: **French**

The Jurassians are a French-speaking people who were for nine centuries citizens of the autonomous Prince Bishopric of the Holy Roman Empire, and then briefly French subjects. The Jura, a mountainous wooded region, comprising seven districts which together constitute a distinct geographical area, was joined to the mainly German-speaking Swiss canton of Berne as a result of the Congress of Vienna in 1815. Berne grew to become an exceptionally large canton of the 24 then in existence, with about one million inhabitants, almost 15% of the Swiss population.

Because of the degree of decentralization and direct democracy within the cantons of Switzerland, French was preserved as the main language of local administration and education; nevertheless the 1950s and 1960s saw a rise in militancy within the Jurassian community. Particularly strong was the *Rassemblement Jurassien*, a non-party movement formed in 1948 with the aim of creating a separate canton of Jura. The movement gained much support and demonstrations were given widespread publicity. Although the mainly Catholic Jurassians seemed to have few obvious grievances, their language and religion being respected by the German-speaking Protestants, many felt the need to have their own small powerful canton.[1] A Commission appointed in 1968 found the demand to be reasonable but also found the situation to be much complicated by the actions of unionist movements based in the three southern districts. It was recommended that if 20% of the electorate of any district so demanded a second referendum would

be carried out to decide the future of that district, and a third referendum would be needed in border communes.

In 1970 self-determination was granted to the Jura as a whole and in 1974 the separatist vote gained a small majority in the Jura. The following year the three southern districts opted out of the new canton although over one third of electors voted for staying in. A third referendum in border communes resulted in eight southern communes joining the new canton and one northern district opting out. A major issue was which citizens qualified for a vote on the matter, almost half the citizens of the southern districts originating in German-speaking areas.

The new canton of Jura had at its inception a population of about 67,000 and it was admitted to the Swiss federation on January 1, 1979. The arrangement satisfied the majority of Jurassians but some felt that the Jura, for nine centuries a single territorial unit, had been split into two by those who had opted to remain in Berne canton, largely French-speaking Protestants and German-speaking immigrants, and at the time of separation Berne had a French-speaking minority of 32,000 people or 4.8% of the population. There have been as a result clashes between extremists on both sides. The Jurassian movement has been unusual in the Swiss context, not because of the wish to form a new political unit or divide an existing one, or because of the issue of minorities as such, but because of its (occasional) resort to violence.

[1]Cantons are represented by two members in the Council of States and in proportion to their population in the National Council, although all have at least one member.

Ladins of Italy

Location: **mainly Bolanzo province of Italy**
Population: **35,000 (est.)**
% of population: **4% of Bolzano province**
Religion: **Catholic**
Language: **Ladin**

The Ladins are a small minority whose language is a dialect of the Rhaeto-Romanche family of languages. The majority of Ladins live in northern Italy, mainly in the Valle Gardena and the Valle Badia. They have for centuries maintained political allegiance to Austria and to the German-speaking minority of South Tyrol. In 1810 they appealed unsuccessfully to prevent their annexation by Italy and throughout the nineteenth century they resisted all attempts to assimilate them.

Until World War I Ladin was taught in primary schools, but from 1921 under Mussolini this practice was banned as was the word Ladin. In 1939 the governments of Germany and Italy reached an agreement on evacuation under which some 2,000 Ladins left the South Tyrol for Austria in order to escape deportation to other parts of Italy. A Statute of Autonomy passed in 1948 once more allowed the teaching of Ladin during the first year at primary level in Trentino, but not in the provinces of Trento and Belluno, where there is still no provision for the teaching of Ladin despite a campaign led by the Ladin media and intellectuals.

Calls for the unification of all Ladin-speakers in the Dolomite Alps within a single administrative unit are unlikely to achieve their aim as the Ladins themselves are a diverse group living amidst Italian and German speakers. Ladins continue to identify their cause with that of the German speakers of South Tyrol; most are politically and socially conservative and give their support to the *Südtiroler Volkspartei.*

(See also *Friulians; Romantsch speakers of Switzerland*)

Madeirans

Location: **Atlantic Ocean, 850 km from Portugal and 580 km from Morocco**
Population: **300,000**
% of population: **2.5% of Portuguese population**
Religion: **Catholic**
Language: **Portuguese**

The Madeirans live on the two densely populated Madeira islands in the Atlantic ocean. They are Portuguese citizens and ethnically they are closely related to the population of the Iberian peninsula. As in the Azores, long-standing grievances against the Portuguese government during the period of dictatorship have led to a high rate of emigration — the majority going to Venezuela — and the island's population declined by 6% in the 1960s.

The overthrow of dictatorship in Portugal in 1974 resulted in independence demands in the Madeiras. Members of the Madeira Archipelago Liberation Front (FLAMA) carried out bomb attacks and attempted to remove the civil governor, and several other separatist groups were also formed, but after the islands were granted local autonomy in 1976 the centralist Social Democratic Party under President Joao Haodim gained power and has won three successive elections. The party continues to press for greater autonomy however, especially in fiscal, tax and exchange controls.

Autonomy and political stability has brought economic growth and an improved standard of living to Madeira. Electricity and water have been brought to remote areas, the infant mortality rate has fallen by half, educational facilities have improved and emigration has dropped. Under an agreement with Lisbon, 6% of EC regional aid funds granted to Portugal go to Madeira. The economy remains largely dependent on tourism and agriculture but there are hopes for diversification.

(See also *Azoreans*)

Northern Ireland

Alternative names: **Ulster**
Location: **north-eastern area of Ireland**
Population: **1,482,000 (1981); Protestants 1,067,500; Catholics 414,500**
% of population: **Protestants: 72%; Catholics: 28%**
Religion: **Protestant (50% Presbyterians); Catholic**
Language: **English**

The six counties of the province of Northern Ireland, often referred to as Ulster[1], are part of the United Kingdom and have existed as a separate political entity since the 1921 Treaty which partitioned Ireland (the Treaty came into effect on January 1, 1922) into the Irish Free State[2] and Northern Ireland. For over three hundred years there has been a troubled relationship between the two major religious communities, the majority Protestants and the minority Catholics; a problem which dates back to the British colonization of the region in the seventeenth century.

History

The English crown had an uneasy dominance over parts of Ireland from the eleventh century. Eager to prevent rebellion against their rule in the seventeenth century they offered grants of land, previously seized from the Irish, to any who were willing to maintain forces to suppress such rebellions. Thousands of Scots and English migrated to the region and accepted the land grants in the so-called Protestant Plantation. Most settled in the north-eastern counties where they gradually came to be in the majority. Differences of origin and religion combined with the circumstances of entry, caused enmity between the two communities. Cromwell's brutal 1649 military campaign in Ireland further alienated Catholics and entrenched Protestant ascendancy. Many Irish Catholics supported the Catholic "Jacobite" claim to the crown and the Protestant William of Orange decisively defeated Catholic forces at the Battle of the Boyne in 1690. These events, most especially the actions of the Protestant apprentice boys of Derry (Londonderry), are still relived in the myths and present struggles of Catholics and Protestants today.

In 1801 an Act of Settlement made Ireland part of the United Kingdom. Disastrous famines in the mid-nineteenth century resulted in large-scale emigration and depopulation. However industries such as textiles and ship-building were also established primarily in the north in Belfast and Londonderry. From the mid-nineteenth century there were demands for Home Rule (autonomy) for Ireland. There were several attempts by parliament to implement such a measure in 1886, 1893 and finally in 1912. This aroused great opposition in Protestant-dominated Ulster which did not wish to be dominated by Catholic Dublin and an armed Ulster Volunteer Force was ready to resist its imposition. When the bill had its third reading in 1914 Ireland seemed on the brink of civil war. Home rule was not put into operation because of World War I and in 1916 an armed uprising, known as the Easter Uprising, was suppressed by British troops. After this *Sinn Fein* and Irish Republican Army troops conducted a guerrilla war against the British which ended only with the 1921 Treaty and agreed partition of Ireland between a Free State in the south (about 75% of the territory of the island) and the six provinces of Antrim, Down, Armagh, Londonderry, Tyrone and Fermanagh which became Northern Ireland. In the south many would not accept the partition and as a result a civil war was fought which eventually resulted in a victory for the supporters of partition.

In the north a separate Northern Ireland Parliament was established, which was effectively dominated for almost 50 years by a small group of Protestants. The communities tended to remain apart each with their own religious affiliation and way of life but there was little overt violence between them. However the majority Protestants were in a position of advantage in housing and employment while Catholics were not only discriminated against in public housing and industrial employment but were often prevented from voting in elections, thus entrenching the Protestant political dominance. The relative proportions between the communities — about three to one in favour of the Protestants — changed little, for although Catholics had a higher birth rate, their poverty also meant that they migrated in greater numbers.

"The Troubles"

The educational reforms of the 1940s created better educational standards and spawned a new gen-

---

[1]Ulster was one of the four historic provinces of Ireland and was larger than the present area of Northern Ireland.
[2]From 1936 Eire and from 1949 the Republic of Ireland.

Atlantic Ocean

Kintyre

Ireland

Derry
Londonderry

Antrim
● Ballymena

L. Neagh

BELFAST ◉

Tyrone
● Omagh

Enniskillen
Fermanagh

Armagh
● Armagh

Down
Downpatrick ●

Irish Sea

☐ Protestant majority
▨ R.Catholic majority

Northern Ireland

eration of Catholics dissatisfied with second-class status and prepared to take part in the running of the province. However it was not until the late 1960s that clashes broke out when growing — and at first mainly peaceful — civil rights agitation culminated in serious rioting in Londonderry in October 1968 and the militancy of the Catholics caused a similar militant backlash among some Protestants. In August 1969, 90 houses in the Catholic Falls Road area of Belfast were destroyed by Protestants and the British Army was called in to restore order. Some reforms of the franchise, the police and local government (all of which had favoured Protestants) were attempted by the Northern Ireland government but it appeared too late to stem the rising tide of violence and in any case they were badly received by the Protestants.

The number of violent incidents in the province increased dramatically after the arrival of British troops. At first the troops were welcomed by the Catholic population but later they became bitterly opposed. The most serious incident was "bloody Sunday" in January 1972 when 13 Catholic demonstrators were shot dead by British troops. Many Catholics, especially in working-class areas of Belfast and Londonderry, supported paramilitary groups such as the Irish Republican Army (IRA) which began a campaign of terror within the province which reached a peak after the introduction of internment without trial in August 1971. Terrorist attacks spread to mainland Britain and were at first aimed at military targets but later became indiscriminate. Bombs exploded in pubs, hotels and cars and in 1974 a series of civilian bombings, resulting in large-scale loss of life, outraged opinion in the UK and Ireland. In response to these bombings the UK government introduced the Prevention of Terrorism Act (PTA) of 1974, which gave special powers for terrorist suspects to be held by police for longer than normal periods without charge. The PTA has been renewed by successive UK governments. There have been continued terrorist attacks since in both Northern Ireland, especially on police stations and military installations, and on the UK mainland, including the deaths of Conservative Party politician Airey

Neave and Earl Mountbatten in 1979 together with an attempt to assassinate members of the UK Cabinet at Brighton in 1984.

Internment without trial ended in 1975. During the period of internment there had been allegations by the Irish government and others of maltreatment of suspects by the military and police during interrogation sessions and the Dublin government had complained to the European Commission on Human Rights, which in 1978 ruled that interrogation methods were not torture but "cruel and inhuman treatment". Since that time Amnesty International has reported that reports of ill-treatment have dropped considerably, although it has continued to express concern over practices such as strip-searching of prisoners and a possible "shoot to kill" policy by elements in the Royal Ulster Constabulary (RUC). Special category status was introduced to deal with the large numbers of extra prisoners — both Unionist and Republicans — during the troubles. Although this was not an official political status its partial withdrawal in 1976 caused demonstrations by the Nationalists and the prisoners themselves. Its complete withdrawal in 1980 led to protests by Republican prisoners in the "H-Block" prison culminated in a hunger strike by prisoners which resulted in the deaths of 10 prisoners before the strike was called off. Those who died included Bobby Sands, who had been elected to the Parliament at Westminster during his internment. Amnesty International has also expressed concern about the widespread use of "Diplock Courts", introduced during the 1970s, which have no juries and are presided over by a senior judge, and the "supergrass" trials which took place between 1983 and 1985.

Changes in governmental structures

It became obvious very early in the Troubles that the governmental structure in Northern Ireland would always give a majority to the Protestants and that they would use it to block further advancement for the Catholics. Attempts to reform Stormont (the Northern Irish parliament) failed primarily to intransigence by Protestants, and in March 1972 Stormont was suspended for one year by the Westminster government and ruled directly from London by William Whitelaw as Secretary of State for Northern Ireland. The change was welcomed by most Catholic opposition leaders but was opposed by most Protestants, who organized a two-day general strike which disrupted the Northern Ireland economy. There were attempts over the next year to create an alternative structure but while these initially appeared promising, they soon collapsed amid unprecedented violence in mid-

1972, while a referendum, the Border Poll conducted in March 1973, was boycotted by the Catholic community. In May 1973 a Northern Ireland Assembly Bill was enacted, providing for an election on June 28 with an executive, drawn from members from both communities to be appointed by the Secretary of State for Northern Ireland. Although the elections did take place the executive was not appointed until December and consisted of members from the Unionist Party, the main Protestant group, the Social Democratic Labour Party (SDLP), the main Catholic party and the much smaller Alliance Party, a non-communal centralist group. In that month a Tripartite (UK, Northern Ireland, Republic of Ireland) Conference held at Sunningdale established an Anglo-Irish Commission on Law Enforcement, but when the Assembly met in January 1974 there were violent scenes and the Unionist Party split and withdrew from the power-sharing executive, which finally collapsed after a strike by Protestant workers in April 1974.

There have been other attempts to create direct government in Northern Ireland. In late 1974 a Constitutional Convention discussion paper was published which featured a deliberate non-Executive body. The election and first meeting of the convention took place in April 1975 but the Ulster United Unionist Council declared its opposition to any form of power sharing. The Atkins Constitutional Conference opened without the Official Unionists in January 1980 but it adjourned in March and the two-option devolution proposals put forward were rejected by all parties. Elections to a Northern Ireland Assembly, set up under the Northern Ireland Bill of 1982, were held in October 1982 but the Assembly failed to function as members of the SDLP and *Sinn Fein* (the legal political party of the Provisional Irish Republican Army) refused to take their seats. Other parties temporarily withdrew from it and the Assembly was dissolved in 1986. The major reason for the failure of these institutions has been the refusal of major Protestant parties to accept meaningful sharing of power with Catholic-dominated organizations, although the Protestants appear to be neither as united or as powerful as in the past and several attempts at successful strike action by Protestant organizations have failed.

The Anglo-Irish Agreement

The Anglo-Irish Agreement, also known as the Hillsborough Accord, specified that an Inter-Governmental Conference concerned with Northern Ireland and the relationship between the two parts of Ireland be established, and that representatives of both the UK and the Republic of Ireland meet on a regular basis to put forward views on the future of Northern Ireland. The Agreement explicitly accepted that a change in the status of Northern Ireland could only come about with the consent of the majority of the population of the province, that for the moment the majority did not wish to change their status, but if in the future the majority wished to join a united Ireland both parliaments (i.e. UK and Ireland) would enact legislation to enable this to take place. It also recognized for the first time a clear-cut advisory role for the Irish government in the affairs of the north. The Agreement was formally recognized by the UK and Irish governments in November 1985.

Immediate opposition to the Agreement came from the Ulster Unionists who denounced it as giving a foreign government the right to interfere in the province's affairs. Unionist MPs at Westminster resigned in protest; in January 1986 most were re-elected but on smaller turnouts. Attempts to organize strikes and other protests have generally been regarded as an irritant but not as a serious obstacle to its implementation. The SDLP and Alliance Party have generally supported the agreement as have, in practice, the main British and Irish Parties. Nationalists such as *Sinn Fein* have denounced the Agreement as perpetuating British occupation of Northern Ireland; however they also admit that the Agreement came about in part because of the strength of nationalist feeling. There have since been several meetings of the Inter-Governmental Conference and, despite disagreements and disappointments on both sides, to date it has survived.

Group perceptions and politics

The position of the Protestants in Ulster is fraught with tension: they are the ruling majority but they feel themselves to be a besieged minority, since south of the border the Protestants form less than 5% of the population. Protestants are aware that the British government saw Irish unity as the ultimate objective in 1921 and fear that the Anglo-Irish agreement of 1985 leads the same way. They are distrustful of the British and the chief concern of erstwhile Ulster governments has been the preservation of the border with the Irish (Catholic) republic. They are fearful of Catholics who they see as wishing to destroy the basis of the Northern-Irish state and reunite with the rest of Ireland and of being dictated to by the strictures of the Roman Catholic Church. Thus the Protestants have developed a siege-mentality.

The Catholics, on the other hand, feel with justification that they are discriminated against. They are the poorer community, historically the under-

dogs. The Catholic unemployment rate is high, averaging 35% in 1988, and in some areas much higher; the amount of low cost housing is inadequate for their needs and they play little part in the administration of the province. Most of Northern Ireland's wealth is found in the eastern counties and in the city of Belfast where the greater part of the population (mostly Protestants) live. Catholics feel a sense of bitterness that the western (and mostly Catholic) counties of Londonderry. Tyrone and Fermanagh remain largely poor and underdeveloped. The alarming unemployment rate contributes markedly to a sense of frustration among Catholic men and this in turn finds expression in high levels of political violence.

The two communities live in fear of each other and look for support to the British government and the Irish government respectively; meanwhile extremist politicians on both sides exploit these fears to gain support for their policies. Ian Paisley commands an emotional response from Protestants of all classes and has succeeded in gaining election as a Democratic Unionist at Westminster and as a Member of the European Parliament at Strasbourg. Gerry Adams, the leader of *Sinn Fein*, makes a similar appeal to Catholics and has also been elected as a Westminster MP although he refuses to accept his seat. The SDLP is a mainly Catholic-supported party which pursues a peaceful solution while of necessity tolerating the Catholic community's ambivalent attitude to political violence. The RUC and the part-time local Ulster Defence Regiment (UDR) are paramilitary groups formed to control security, but charges of Protestant partisanship have been directed at both and there are very few Catholics in either.

A major obstacle to a rapprochement between the two communities has been the segregation of schools along a religious divide. Until recently Catholic and Protestant children did not meet in schools. The situation has been seriously aggravated by increasing segregation on new estates, some of which are in themselves highly alienating (such as the Divis Flats in Belfast, now in the process of being demolished); a segregation which governments have been obliged to impose after attempts at integrated living failed. Segregation is especially apparent in working-class areas of Belfast (such as the Catholic Falls Road and the Protestant Shankill Road) and Derry (such as the Catholic Bogside and the Protestant Waterside). Working places are also segregated, despite the efforts of the government's Fair Employment Agency, and as a result Catholics and Protestants rarely meet and mutual fear and distrust is intensified and perpetuated. A new move to integrate schooling has proved popular but the numbers of pupils attending these schools is still very small.

The present situation

Northern Ireland has, with the Basque country, been the longest running and most violent conflict in postwar western Europe. According to the Irish Information Partnership there were 2,170 conflict-related deaths in the province between 1969 and 1987, of which 1507 were committed by the IRA and other armed Republican groups and 663 by Loyalist armed groups. Over 300 deaths were caused by the army and police and there were further deaths as a result of civilians being caught in crossfire. Although British troops were sent into Northern Ireland as a supposedly temporary measure, 20 years later 10,000 are still stationed there, although most routine security work is now handled by the 13,000-strong RUC and the 6,000-strong

UDR. More than 12,000 people have been charged with terrorist offences and the present prison population stands at 2,000. The already disadvantaged economy has been further hit by political violence and economic recession.

However, despite the continuing conflict, some observers have seen signs of progress in the implementation of the Anglo-Irish Agreement, the working together of different political parties and factions in local government, the emergence of a growing middle class across denominational lines and the normalization of life in many areas. Churches, trade unions and peace groups have been working to achieve greater tolerance between the two communities and there are some hopes that further integration within the European communities might have far-reaching effects.

(See also *Protestants of Eire*)

Protestants of Eire

Location: **Mostly Dublin and throughout Donegal, Cavan, Monaghan and Leitrim, bordering N. Ireland**
Population: **115,400**
% of population: **3% of Eire's population; 9% of Dublin's population**
Religion: **Various Protestant denominations**
Language: **English**

The Protestant population of Eire, or the Republic of Ireland, is a small and diminishing minority. In the mid-nineteenth century, when British rule was at its height, Protestants were in the ascendancy in the island and numbered over 800,000. Those who remain are mostly living along the border with Northern Ireland although a small number live elsewhere in the Republic, notably in County Cork.

The Protestants of Eire retain an influence out of proportion to their numbers. Although they are not an identifiable political force, 6.5% are company directors, managers or company secretaries compared with less than 1% of Catholics, and about one fifth of farmers working over 200 acres are Protestant; they are greatly under-represented in the senior ranks of the civil service, however, and very few have entered parliament although there have been two Protestant presidents, Dr Douglas Hyde and Erskine Childers. A small number of those living close to the border are members of Orange Lodges and reject the republican state, but the majority play little part in politics.

Article 44 of the constitution, which was repealed in 1972, declared that the Catholic Church as the guardian of the faith of the great

majority of citizens had a special position in the state. In various areas the law of the state has been interpreted according to Catholic doctrine and applies equally to Catholic and Protestant. Laws concerning divorce, contraception, blasphemy and censorship all affect Protestants. A Catholic must obtain a special dispensation in order to marry a non-Catholic, and the children of mixed Protestant–Catholic marriages have by law to be raised in the Catholic faith. In 1961 it was estimated that one third of Protestant men marrying in that year and one fifth of Protestant women married a Catholic partner, and this trend is having a major impact on the Protestant population of the Republic. As the numbers of mixed marriages is rising steadily there is a steady decline in the number of Protestants as a result of this ruling by the Church. There has been much debate in the Republic about the provisions relating to the Church and some minor changes have been introduced although these have met with considerable opposition. Some contraceptives are now available, for example.

Protestants in Eire are declining numerically and they seem more willing to assimilate now than has previously been the case. There is little or no economic discrimination against them as individuals and as they are less and less perceived as a threatening community by the Catholic majority

(See also *Northern Ireland*)

they are under less political pressure than in the past.

Roma in Western Europe

Name: **Roma, Romany**
Alternative names: **Gypsies, Manush, Sinti, Travellers, Tsiganes, Zingari**
Location: **Throughout Western Europe**
Population: **over 1.5 million (est.)**
% of population: **0.45%**
Religion: **Christian, Muslim**
Language: **Romany**

The Roma or Gypsies are a nomadic and semi-nomadic people whose ancestors left North India over 1,000 years ago and who are now scattered throughout the world. Considered suspect and inferior by Europeans because of their Eastern origins and foreign tongue, the Roma have for centuries been subjected to prejudice and in some cases direct exploitation. In addition to the nomadic and unsettled Roma there are some 70,000 migrant workers in France, West Germany and Italy, most of whom come from Yugoslavia, Turkey and Spain. Change of location is usually a result of economic considerations or official pressure rather than an inherently nomadic way of life. Their distinctive way of life has meant that Romany society is insular in character and centres around the extended family group.

Based on available census figures and previous estimates (taking into account the high birthrate among Roma) and including associated sedentary and nomadic groups, the following figures give the number of Roma and their percentage of the population by country in 1986: Spain — 745,000 (1.95%); France — 260,000 (0.47%); Italy — 120,000 (0.21%); Portugal — 105,000 (1.5%); UK — 90,000 (0.16%); West Germany — 84,000 (0.14%); Netherlands — 40,000 (0.28%); Switzerland — 35,000 (0.54%); Belgium — 20,000 (0.2%); Austria — 19,000 (0.01%); Eire — 18,000 (0.53%); Sweden — 15,000 (0.18%); Finland — 8,000 (0.16%); Norway — 5,000 (0.12%); Denmark — 4,500 (0.09%).

Between 1935 and 1945 at least 400,000 Roma are known to have died at the hands of Nazis. Despite their treatment few received adequate compensation from the West German government, and anti-Roma prejudice has not abated. In almost every country the Roma are prevented from travelling freely and the majority are stateless. The Council of Europe set out proposals for improving the rights of the Romany people in 1969. These proposals included the construction of well-equipped caravan sites and permanent housing in colder climates, the provision of schooling for Romany children, the establishment of national bodies to deal with Romany issues and the granting of citizenship to stateless people wherever possible. Whilst some countries have done much to implement these proposals the majority have made little effort to further the Romany cause.

France

In France there has been a recent upsurge in the number of Romany groups. In 1983 the *Office National des Affaires Tsiganes* was created to advise government on policy towards the Roma; however there is still legal discrimination against this minority. Roma are required to carry a travel permit and their movements are limited to specific places of residence. Under the same law, passed in 1969, anyone who cannot prove unbroken residence in one place for three years is disenfranchised. In addition to the nomadic Roma there are more than 100,000 semi-sedentary Roma living for the most part in the notorious bidonvilles or slums.

Romany children must be registered at school wherever they stop but although the authorities claim that a high proportion are being educated the majority are illiterate. Government circulars have been issued to district authorities urging the setting up of caravan sites but not all authorities comply. However, 30 caravan sites have been established since 1970 and two housing settlements have been built at Grasse and Marseilles. In 1972 door-to-door sales were banned thus removing one source of income for the travelling Manush and this may have contributed to the rise in begging and a growing rate of delinquency.

Belgium

From January 1975 Roma have been able to acquire Belgian citizenship. Government policy has provided for the provision of serviced camping sites for several years and in 1978 the first legal caravan park was opened in Ostend, but so far few local councils have responded positively to government directives and at least 20% have passed by-laws against the parking of caravans and camping. These by-laws make registration of residence — necessary in order to qualify for full citizenship — almost impossible, and prevent Romany children, who make up 60% of the community, from attending school with any regularity. The infant mortality rate is 20% higher than the national average, a situation not helped by residence on municipal refuse tips and unhealthy wasteland.

West Germany

The plight of West German Roma has changed radically since the 1981 Gottingen congress which focused government attention on their problems. A meeting with Chancellor Schmidt brought belated recognition of Roma persecution and genocide by the Nazis, and the Central Council of German Sinti and Roma has received financial support for pursuing individual casework and other matters. "Criminal" records inherited from the Nazi regime and used by regional police bureaux have been destroyed. The Central Council has also sought compensation from German companies for Romany survivors of the Nazi forced-labour programme, of whom about 15,000 are still alive. So far the claims have not been accepted and there is still prejudice against Roma. In 1984 a group of Yugoslav-born Roma who had settled in Darmstadt in 1979 were evicted and driven out of town, their houses and workshops bulldozed and destroyed.

Italy

In Italy Italian-born Sinti and foreign Roma are constantly harassed. They are discouraged from camping and established quarters are frequently broken up. In towns they face particular hostility and frequently live in squalid conditions on the outskirts of towns. A recent survey found that over 70% of families had lost one or more children through illness, often of a respiratory nature. Life expectancy is short and less than 3% of Roma and Sinti live beyond 60 years. Begging — especially by Yugoslavian gypsy children — has become a major problem and children caught begging have been forcibly removed from their parents and given up for adoption.

The voluntary organization *Opera Nomadi* has attempted to mediate between local authorities and Roma to provide education for Roma children, but although some 60 special classes have been set up, tens of thousands remain outside the schooling system. Activist groups are calling for the modification of housing laws to include caravan sites. They are also demanding financial assistance to those towns willing to give permanent shelter to Roma, and recognition of Roma as a linguistic minority, which should improve their constitutional status.

Spain

Spain has the largest Roma population in Western Europe. There are about 600,000 Roma and also 150,000 Quinquis who lead a similar nomadic lifestyle. An Interministerial Commission has found that the average life expectancy of a Rom is 43 years; half the Roma working population is unemployed; 80% of Roma adults have never been to school; and only 50% of Roma children are receiving schooling. Local authorities have been encouraged to provide housing for Roma, most of whom are living in shacks on the outskirts of cities. Some municipal authorities have responded positively but the population as a whole has reacted unfavourably and there has been violence directed against the Roma. In Zaragossa there was serious rioting for almost a week as a result of an announcement by the municipal authorities that 36 Roma families were to be temporarily housed on part of a housing project. In Segovia province a mob of several hundred led by the local mayor forced a family to leave their home which was then bulldozed.

Some advances have been made: a Roma member of the Spanish parliament (*Cortes*), Juan de Dios Ramirez, has successfully campaigned for the removal of anti-gypsy legislation enforced during the Franco era, and by 1981 there were 124 government-subsidized centres for Romany children attended by some 4,000 pupils. Whilst these reception classes are much needed, another 100,000 Romany children are still without schooling of any kind.

The Netherlands

The Netherlands has taken a lead in the provision of well-serviced caravan parks for indigenous nomadic families, although policy towards stateless and foreign Roma remains strict. Implementation of the 1968 Caravan Sites Act has involved the setting up of large trailer-home parks and small family units. Some of the larger centres are equipped with social activity buildings, and over 70 special schools, adult education classes and kindergartens have been established. The Netherlands is seen by

Roma as an example to be emulated in its efforts to accommodate its Roma population.

Britain

Very few of the nomadic and semi-nomadic peoples of Britain are actually Roma. The majority are of Irish extraction and are known as Travellers. The position of Travellers in Britain is poor and steadily deteriorating. The 1959 Highways Act, which legislated against roadside camping, and the general policy of "moving on" adopted by local authorities has meant that at least 5,000 children are receiving no education and a further 20,000 are receiving inadequate education. In 1984 a report by the Save the Children Fund stated that the infant mortality rate amongst Travellers is 15 times higher than the national average. Under a ruling of the High Court in 1985 county authorities are obliged to provide sites for Travellers but there is much popular opposition to such sites and there have been cases of caravans being removed from official sites. The Department of the Environment has advocated the provision of a chain of 10 stopping places with up to 40 pitches each for some 250 families, and the building of 60 small sites for a further 300 families, but it will be hard to implement these proposals.

Eire (Ireland)

The Traveller population has doubled in Eire in the last 20 years. Forced evictions and hostility have continued despite the government urging of immediate provision of sites. In 1980 a Supreme Court ruling stated that before evicting families local authorities must offer a suitable alternative site. Over 630 families are now living in the Dublin area alone, most of them on illegal sites from which they are frequently moved on. Less than half the children of these Travellers are receiving education of any sort; infant mortality is three times the national average, and life expectancy is half the national average. There are several self-help

(For Greece, see *Roma* in **Eastern Europe**)

groups but widespread prejudice remains a barrier to real change.

Sweden

The Swedish government has shown generosity in accepting into the country hundreds of Roma expelled from Poland. These Roma are being treated as refugees because they left Poland carrying only exit permits, and they have been assisted to find jobs and housing in Sweden. Many Finnish Roma have also entered the country in recent years. Despite government policy the public attitude to Roma is one of ill-will which has on occasion expressed itself in violence. The Finnish Roma have formed their own association in Stockholm and many have been housed in municipal apartments and housing estates. Romany is taught in several special schools and there are Roma teachers and social workers. Although Romany immigrants have received government assistance the needs of the older nomadic Tattare have not as yet been recognized.

Switzerland

The 35,000 Swiss Roma have fared better in recent years than in the past when there was a long-standing policy of forcibly removing children from their parents. Under this scheme, started in 1926, some 700 children were housed in orphanages and juvenile detention centres. The scheme was abandoned in 1973 after individual dossiers were passed to the press, and the government is now attempting to repair some of the damage is has caused by reuniting children with their parents. Local authorities are now beginning to set up caravan sites although there is still harassment of nomadic families. An annual cultural festival organized by the Romany association has strengthened a sense of unity among the Roma. The International Romany Union's UN office is based in Berne and this has assisted their cause politically and socially.

Romantsch speakers of Switzerland

Alternative names: **also spelt Romansh, Romanche**
Location: **Graubunden/Grisons canton**
Population: **about 50,000 speakers**
% of population: **0.8% of Swiss population**
Religion: **Catholic**
Language: **Romantsch/Swiss German**

Romantsch-speakers are the smallest linguistic minority in Switzerland, comprising about 50,000 speakers or less than 1% of the population. Switzerland as a state is characterized by linguistic diversity and a federated and decentralized administrative system. There are four national languages: German (more accurately Swiss–German) spoken as a first language by about 70% of the population, French by just under 20%, Italian by 10%, and Romantsch.

Romantsch is a Rhaeto-Romanche language derived from Latin and which has affinities with Ladin and Friulian. All the Romantsch language communities are contained in the tri-lingual canton of Graubunden/Grisons (Grischun in Romanche) in the east of Switzerland. The language has had official recognition since 1938 and was given further federal protection in 1983 when the federal parliament passed a law for the protection of the Rhaeto-Romanche language and culture. Federal funds are channelled through a local body and a chair in Romantsch literature has been established at Zurich University. Unlike the other three languages it does not appear on state or official documents, regulations or monuments.

The number of Romantsch speakers has declined this century, mainly for economic reasons, since Romantsch speakers lived in high, economically poor, valleys and emigrated to the lowlands for work. Tourism has promoted the use of Swiss–German and today Romantsch speakers comprise fewer than 50% of the population in their own territory; many of these do not speak the language regularly. A further problem is posed by the language itself, as Romantsch has three main written forms and seven spoken dialects. Attempts are presently being made to evolve a standard language (*Romantsch grischun*) with an extended vocabulary.

(See also *Friulians; Ladins of Italy*)

Saami

Alternative names: **also spelt Sami, Same, Somi, also called Lapps**
Location: **Norway, Sweden, Finland, USSR**
Population: **Total: 60,000: Norway 40,000, Sweden 15,000, Finland 4000, Soviet Union 1500-2000 (est. 1971)**
% of population: **Norway 1%, Sweden 0.2%, Finland 0.08%**
Religion: **Protestant**
Language: **Saami, Norwegian, Swedish, Finnish**

The Saami, more widely known to outsiders as Lapps (a name which they consider as derogatory), are the indigenous people of the region in northernmost Europe known as Lapland, the major part of which falls within the Arctic Circle. By tradition they are a nomadic people, living by hunting, fishing and reindeer-herding, but many have taken to farming in the twentieth century. Demographic statistics are largely lacking but the figures given indicate a considerably higher number of Saami than had previously been thought.

The origins of the Saami are unknown. Various hypotheses have claimed them to be amongst other things Mongoloid, Finnish, and the survivors of a root race for both Mongoloid and Caucasian races. The Saami language belongs to the western division of the Finno-Ugric branch of the Uralric family. There are a number of major dialects, not always mutually intelligible, which can be divided into three groups: Eastern, Central and Southern Saami. There have been Saami–Finnish relations for at least 2,000 years and Saami contains many words borrowed from the Finnish; although Norwegian and Swedish are increasingly used in the northern regions it is still possible to find areas in which the population is trilingual, speaking Saami, Finnish and Norwegian or Swedish.

History and background

Saami once lived throughout Fenno-Scandia as hunters and fishermen as well as reindeer herders. Raiders and traders from the south entered Saami-land searching for food and furs; later the traders were licensed by the monarchical governments to the south who began to claim the Saami lands, and non-Saami settlers slowly pushed Saamis to the far north. National borders were not fixed and Saamis migrated through different spheres of influence. When the Norwegian–Swedish border in the north was specified in 1751, Saami traditional grazing rights were guaranteed in a codicil to the boundary agreement. The dissolution of the Swedish–Norwegian union in 1905 restricted Saami grazing rights in Norway and some Saami were relocated further south. Efforts were made in the interwar period by the various countries to improve the poor living standards of the Saami. The borders were closed during World War II and much of Norwe-gian Lapland was destroyed by retreating German troops.

Christian missionary activity, which began in the eleventh century, has had a major impact on the lives of the Saami and has caused the near-eradica-tion of their earlier Shamanistic practices. The major transition to Christianity occurred in the 1600s and the Church played an important role in Saami education and in facilitating colonial admin-istration. The eastern Saami are strongly influ-enced by the Greek Orthodox Church and else-where a puritanical fundamentalist movement founded by Lars Levi Laestadius has a strong fol-lowing.

Sweden

The Swedish Supreme Court has recognized Saami immemorial land rights in principle, but in practice these rights are ignored and the government does not recognize general Saami ownership of land. The issue of damage by Saami reindeer to settlers' property has been a dominating theme in herding law and herding and farming systems have con-sequently been separated as much as possible. An area of some 24,000 square kilometres has been divided into 52 districts which are designated as herding land, although only about 137,000 square kilometres are usable pastureland. There is a limit on the number of reindeer permitted in each dis-trict based on the number of reindeer needed to support a normal family and the need to avoid over-grazing. At present between 300 and 500 rein-deer per family are thought to be appropriate.

Saami who give up herding are obliged to leave the herding districts.

Reindeer herding has been seriously threatened by the proliferation of extractive industries and by tourism. The growth of the timber, mining and hydro-electric industries has brought an increas-ingly large population to the north and the Saami have become a major tourist attraction. Nowhere in Sweden do Saami form a majority of the popula-tion and consequently they do not have a strong voice politically. Swedish Saami political and cul-tural organizations such as the Confederation of Swedish Saami (LSS) receive financial aid from the Saami Fund which comprises money received in compensation for lands taken from the Saami for non-herding purposes.

Norway

The Department of Agriculture administers rein-deer herding in Norway, but each region has its own local administration, and reindeer-herding Saami are represented at both local and central levels of administration. In Norway non-Saami can only practise herding outside designated areas. As in Sweden there is conflict between Saami and industry over the loss of important pasturage. The combined resistance of the Saami and conser-vationists to the construction of the Alta hydro-electric dam was a significant factor in altering gov-ernment policy. As the largest Saami group and the most militant, Norwegian Saami have been active in campaigning both inside and outside Norway. There are several Saami political organizations of which the Confederation of Norwegian Reindeer Herders (NRL) is perhaps the most influential, dealing with economic, social educational and cul-tural issues and promoting the herders' cause against extractive industries which endanger the grazing lands.

A report by the Norwegian Saami Rights Com-mission presented in 1985 led to the establishment of a Norwegian Saami parliament and in 1987 a new paragraph was added to the report to the effect that Saami language and culture should be safeguarded. Since 1971 the Culture Board of Nor-way has promoted Saami literary activity and there is now a Saami publishing company.

Finland

The herding areas of Finland are divided into 56 districts. Each district has a communal treasury to which members pay according to their reindeer stock. Each district is a member of the central organization which is responsible for Saami admin-istration, development and research. Non-Saami are permitted to own and herd reindeer provided they live within the herding area. Herders may earn the main part of their income from sources other than herding, unlike Saami in Sweden.

The Finnish Saami Parliament had its first meeting in 1976. It is concerned with Saami rights and development and may also present cases to the different authorities. The parliament has 20 representatives and there are elections every fourth year. There is also a Saami Delegation which prepares government recommendations regarding the Saami and monitors the development of Saami economic conditions.

The USSR

There are many different reindeer-herding peoples in the Soviet Union, of whom the Saami are just one group. At the time of the Russian Revolution these peoples were assessed to be at a "pre-capitalist" stage of development and were encouraged to develop socialistic cultural values whilst at the same time continuing their national form of culture. Reindeer ownership was collectivized although some small-scale private ownership still exists. All reindeer-herding farms are worked collectively: the state owns the reindeer and the workers are paid by the state. Reindeer-herding is not considered to be merely a traditional life-style permitted by government. It is vital to the northern economy and it has been estimated that 77%, or 2,400,000, of the world's tame reindeer are found in the Soviet Union. Reindeer-herders are highly paid and well-provided with schooling, housing and social facilities. Cultural contact with the Saami of the Fenno-Scandian countries has increased recently.

Effects of nuclear fallout

The Saami have been profoundly affected by nuclear fallout from the Chernobyl disaster of 1986. In Norway the concentration of Cesium 134 and 137 rose to 10 times the limit set by Nordic governments. The absorption properties of the lichen and the grazing habits of the reindeer have meant that reindeer herders in certain areas have a continuing problem and thousands of reindeer have been confiscated, their meat declared unfit for human consumption. In some areas new methods have been used to decontaminate the reindeer with a certain degree of success and families have been forced to change their eating habits. In those areas worse hit by the disaster the effects seem likely to continue for many years, forcing more Saami out of the herding areas and thus reducing the size of the Saami herding community, already a small minority within the Saami population.

The Chernobyl disaster brought new impetus to Saami co-operation within the region and outside. This process had started well before 1986. Through the Nordic Saami Council the Saami of Sweden, Norway and Finland became members of the World Council of Indigenous Peoples (WCIO) in 1975. Saami have also testified at the UN Working group on Indigenous Populations in Geneva.

(See also *Inuits* in **North America**; *Native peoples of the North and Siberia* in **USSR**)

Sardinians

Location: **Italian island in western Mediterranean**
Population: **1,586,000 (1981)**
Percentage of population: **2.7% of Italian population**
Religion: **Catholic**
Language: **Sardinian, Italian, Catalan**

The Sardinians are the indigenous inhabitants of Sardinia, a large island in the western Mediterranean which has been an autonomous region of Italy with a Special Statute since 1948. Historically it is considered to be the most isolated area within the Italian federation.

Sardinia has been ruled by Pisa, Aragon, Castile (Spain) and Piedmont, and the language of each ruling power has contributed to the romance language spoken by the island's people. There are several varieties of the Sardinian language, most notably "Campidanese" in the south and "Logudorese" in the north, along with "Nuorese/Barbaricino" in the central mountains and "Gallurese" and "Sassarese" in Gallura. Two other languages are also present; Catalan in the city of Alghero and "Tabarchino" in Carloforto and Calasetta. Castillian was used by officials and educators up to 1764 when the Pietmontese made Italian the official language.

The Sardinian language, unlike some other minority languages in Italy, does not enjoy any official recognition. Nevertheless it does appear to be widely diffused among the population. There are varying estimates as to the numbers of speakers but one estimate from the 1970s indicates that perhaps

1.2 million of the 1.6 million population speak Sardinian, most strongly in rural areas and much less in cities where it is confined to the domestic setting. Probably about 450,000 people speak Logudorese and about 600,000 Campidanese. Non-Sardinian immigrants from other areas of Italy only rarely know the language.

The immediate focus of most Sardinian cultural and political movements is to gain the same status for Sardinian as the other recognized minority languages. In 1977/78 and 1983 proposals were put forward in favour of Sardinian/Italian bilinguism but as yet this has not been recognized. Several movement exist, on both a political and academic level, for the protection and promotion of Sardinian. A major problem remains the lack of a unified Sardinian language and scholars are working on a common orthography. Education is almost entirely in Italian but in the 1980s Sardinian was introduced on an experimental basis as a separate subject in elementary and secondary schools.

There have been a number of movements aimed at gaining either greater autonomy or political independence for Sardinia. The oldest of these is the *Partito Sardo di Azione* (Sardinian Action Party) founded in 1921, which supports the ideal of an independent state, possibly in a European Mediterranean Federation. During the 1970s and 1980s many movements and associations (both on the right and the left) aiming at independence emerged. Sardinia is a relatively poor region compared to northern Italy and emigration has been high, but although economically backward and industrially undeveloped, Sardinia is not as poor or deprived as many areas in the south of Italy. Tourism has emerged as a major industry and there has been some conflict between the needs of tourists and locals.

(See also *Corsicans*; *Greeks, Croatians and Albanians of Italy*)

Slovenes of Austria

Location: **southern parts of Carinthia**
Population: **18,800 (1981 census)**
% of population: **2.7% of Carinthian population**
Religion: **Catholic**
Language: **Slovene and its dialects**

Slovenes have been living in Carinthia, Austria's border region with Yugoslavia and Italy, since the sixth century. In 1335 the province came into the possession of Austria and after World War I the south-western corner of the region was ceded to Italy and the south-eastern corner to Yugoslavia, with the inhabitants of the Klagenfurt district voting to remain within Austria rather than join with Yugoslavia. As a result of this redistribution of territory about 400,000 Slovenes remained in Italy and 90,000 in Austria. The Slovenes should be distinguished from a group of Slavs who speak dialects known collectively as Windisch, which are of Slavonic base but make use of numerous German words. The term Windisch was originally used by Germans to describe all Slavonic peoples in their territory and was synonymous with Slovene until the late nineteenth century.

During World War II Carinthia was the only province in Austria to put up armed resistance against Germany. Many Slovene farmers were deported to Germany, others escaped to fight with Tito's partisans against Hitler and others joined right-wing groups.

Article 7 of the State Treaty of May 1955 provided for the protection of the Slovene and other minorities and since that time Slovenes have been granted the right to educate their children in their mother-tongue at state schools and to use Slovene in courts of law and for all official purposes within the province. Discrimination against Slovenes on linguistic grounds is prohibited. Despite these provisions a clause recommending that all place-name signs should be bilingual was not adequately implemented and this caused a great deal of friction between Slovenes and the German-speaking majority. Bombings and other acts of violence were perpetrated by activist groups from both communities. Whilst German activists called for the complete assimilation of the Slovene-speakers into the German linguistic and cultural sphere a small group of Slovene activists were demanding a Slovene Carinthia, preferably linked to Yugoslavia and including the Windisch minority. The Windisch tend to ally themselves more to the German speakers, however, and refuse to be included in the Slavonic ethnic group.

In 1972 legislation was passed to hasten the erection of bilingual place-name signs, but many were torn down by German language nationalists. In

1976 the Austrian government held a controversial language census in an attempt to determine the numbers of speakers of each language. Many Slovene speakers boycotted the census, however, and the government later conceded that the attempt had been a failure. The 1976 Ethnic Groups Act further recognized the rights of non-German-speaking Austrians, and Slovenes today have a thriving cultural life and little cause for dissatisfaction. There are monolingual and bilingual schools, two weekly newspapers, daily radio broadcasts, a cultural centre and two cultural bodies, one Catholic and one Marxist. All parishes

in the officially Slovene-speaking areas have Slovene-speaking priests and Slovene is used in church affairs and in the courts in those regions. The number of Slovenes calling for unification with Yugoslavia is tiny and many are now following the Windisch path to assimilation with German-speakers, especially in the tourist areas. In 1987 the Austrian parliament made a decision to end bilingual education in primary schools and to separate German and Slovenes into different areas. This decision has caused anxiety within the Slovene community.

(See also *Croats of Austria*; *Slovenes of Italy*)

Slovenes of Italy

Location: **Trieste, Friuli-Venezia Giulia**
Population: **52,000**
Percentage of population: **0.1% of Italian population**
Religion: **Catholic**
Language: **Slovene, Italian**

The Slovene speakers of Italy are largely those which remained inside the borders of the Italian republic in the region of Trieste after World War II. This area has had a chequered political history and from the end of the war until a final settlement in 1975 was the subject of a dispute between Italy and Yugoslavia. In addition there are some small indigenous communities of Slovene speakers, descendents of earlier waves of immigrants.

The area in and around the port city of Trieste had been under Austrian control from the fourteenth century until after World War I when it was awarded to Italy in 1920 under the Treaty of Rapallo. At the end of World War II Trieste and its surrounding hinterland was claimed by Yugoslavia, partially on the grounds that it was inhabited by Slovene and Croat speakers. In fact the area was ethnically mixed although Trieste City itself was mainly Italian. Since agreement between Italy and Yugoslavia was not possible, the southern area was placed under Yugoslavian administration while the northern area, including Trieste, remained under an Allied (US and UK) military administration, and was divided into two zones. In 1947 it became a Free Territory of Trieste under UN Security Council administration, although in practice it remained under Allied military administration. Continuing friction between the Italian and Yugoslav governments and the Allied powers led to a memorandum of understanding between the Italian, Yugoslav, British and US governments

(known as the London Memorandum of 5 October 1954) which in effect gave the city of Trieste and the northern zone to Italy, while the southern zone was awarded to Yugoslavia. Among the provisions of the Memorandum was a special statute on the rights of the population of the areas to be transferred, including the rights to use their own language and the use of bilingual street names and other public inscriptions in districts where ethnic minorities constituted at least one quarter of the population. The memorandum, which was a *de facto* agreement, was superseded by a *de jure* agreement in the Treaty of Osimo signed on October 1, 1975, and which came into force on April 3, 1977. This Treaty reaffirmed the minority rights of the 1954 agreement.

In addition to the Treaty of Osimo the Italian government has passed a number of laws concerning the language rights of the Slovene minority. In addition in 1963 Trieste became capital of the newly created special-statute region of the Friuli-Venezia Giulia.

According to official Italian government figures Slovene speakers totalled 52,000 out of a total of 632,000 people in the 32 communes where Slovene speakers reside. However other estimates give a figure of over 100,000. Slovene speakers are almost always bilingual as few non-Slovenes know the language. In addition the Slovene spoken in Italian areas is in many ways rather archaic and it has at least six main dialects. During the interwar period the Italian government laid down various restrictions on the language, which has affected its present development.

The province of Trieste has the best provisions for Slovene speakers, mainly because of the effects of the laws and the Treaty, the existence of Trieste as a free port and the proximity of Yugoslavia.

(See also *Friulians*; *Slovenes of Austria*)

There are various types of Slovene and bilingual schools, Slovene is allowed to be used in local courts and on some official documents. There are well established Slovene cultural organizations, numerous papers and periodicals, some of which receive finance from the regional administration, and Slovene language radio programmes.

South Tyroleans

Location: **North Italian province of Bolzano or South Tyrol**
Population: **280,000 (1981)**
% of population: **66% in Bolzano province; 0.5% of total Italian population**
Religion: **Catholic**
Language: **German**

The German-speaking population of South Tyrol, on Italy's border with Austria, is a close-knit ethnically homogeneous farming community who for 14 centuries were a part of the German-speaking world. Italy entered World War I on the side of Britain and France on the understanding that in the event of victory it would be granted South Tyrol, this took place in 1919. Following the Fascist seizure of power in 1922 there was outright oppression of the South Tyroleans. The use of the German language was forbidden in public life and German-speaking officials were replaced by Italians. Schools were Italianized as were personal names, and employment in local factories was reserved for Italians, forcing Germans back to the land for their livelihood whilst the urban centres became increasingly Italianized.

In June 1939 an agreement was signed by Germany and Italy whereby the entire population of the South Tyrol was given the choice of transference to the German Reich, keeping their ethnic identity but losing their homeland, or complete assimilation into the Italian population, with the prospect of deportation to other parts of Italy. Under intense pressure the majority opted for transference to the Reich and some 75,000 had been transferred when war intervened. A third of these later returned to Italy.

Under the terms of the Paris Peace Conference Agreement of 1946, parity between German and Italian was to be restored, German was again to be taught in primary and secondary schools and German forms of surnames were once more permitted. Regional autonomy was granted but it covered not only the South Tyrol but the entire region of Trentino-Alto Adige, in which Italians were in the majority. As a result true autonomy according

to the terms of the Paris Agreement was not implemented in South Tyrol. There was increasing immigration of Italians into the region and many thousands of German speakers migrated to Switzerland, Austria and West Germany. Whereas in 1910 some 97% of the population was German-speaking the percentage had dropped to 62% by 1961, and the main towns of South Tyrol had gradually become almost completely Italianized. Resentment at government failure to implement the Paris Agreement expressed itself through the actions of the *Südtiroler Volkspartei* (SVP) and extremist organizations which were responsible for a number of terrorist attacks.

In 1969 the Italian government agreed to alter the Statute of Autonomy to lessen its pro-Italian bias, and the 1972 Statute granted the region full powers in matters other than currency, taxes, foreign affairs and defence, and the province was to receive a share of central finance proportionate to its population and territory within the Italian state. German now has full official status with Italian and all official documents, signs and announcements must be in both languages. The 1972 Autonomy Statute has greatly eased tensions and improved the position of the German speakers. The numbers of Italians in the province declined and there was an economic boom, especially in the tourist sector; nevertheless some tension persists. The majority of the specific reforms promised in 1969 have been implemented but some remain outstanding. The tourist industry has expanded so rapidly that Italian temporary workers fill job vacancies. Extremist groups have continued to commit terrorist acts, mainly bombings of Italian property; there were 139 such attacks in the decade 1978-1988. Most German speakers continue to support the SVP which dominated the provincial government and negotiated with the central government for increased linguistic rights. In 1988 the Italian parliament was due to vote on a package of further linguistic rights for German speakers, a move backed by the Austrian government.

(See also *Friulians*; *Ladins*)

Welsh

Alternative names: **Cymru**
Location: **mountainous western region of UK**
Population: **2,645,000, of which 503,549 (18.9%) are Welsh speakers**
% of population: **4.5% of UK population (Welsh speakers less than 1%)**
Religion: **Various Protestant denominations**
Language: **Welsh, English**

The Welsh are the descendants of the British branch of Celtic-speaking peoples, who once lived throughout Britain, but who were forced to retreat into the more remote mountainous areas by successive waves of invaders, and who today survive in Wales and Brittany. Wales is one of the four components of the United Kingdom (with England, Scotland and Northern Ireland) but is subject to the same legal and administrative processes as England.

Until the defeat of the last Welsh Prince, Llywelyn ap Gruffudd, in 1282, when Wales became subject to English rule, Welsh was the predominant language of all of Wales and was used in law, administration and government and had a rich bardic literature. Under the Tudor monarchs of the sixteenth century Wales became more firmly part of the English state particularly after the Acts of Union of 1536 and 1542, which established English as the language of government. On the other hand the position of the Welsh language was strengthened after the translation of the Bible and Book of Common Prayer, which established Welsh as the main language of religious life for the next three centuries.

The industrial revolution, which brought many thousands of English-speaking workers to the new industries of south Wales, and the Education Acts of 1870 and 1889, further weakened the position of Welsh. Education was in English and children were punished for speaking in Welsh. Despite the efforts of Welsh exiles in London and elsewhere to rediscover and promote Welsh language and culture, the number of Welsh speakers has continued to decline through the twentieth century. From a total of 929,000 in 1900, 50% of the then population, it declined to 503,500 or 18.9% in 1981. Of these the vast majority were bilingual with only 21,283 recorded as solely Welsh speakers. Most Welsh speakers were concentrated in the north and centre of Wales with the greatest concentrations in Gwynedd, Clwyd, Dyfed and Powys.

The decline in numbers in part reflects economic and social factors of declining industry, high unemployment and emigration, a greatly reduced role for Welsh religious observance, especially in the chapels, and increased exposure to English through radio, TV and tourism. However the language probably has a stronger legal position today than in the past. No longer are school children punished for using Welsh; Welsh education and bilingual Welsh–English education are common, although not practised in the majority of Welsh schools, and a Welsh pre-school movement has been funded by the Welsh office. Welsh is increasingly taught in areas where Welsh is no longer a majority language, such as Pontypridd in the south, where 20% of children now attend Welsh-language schools. Radio Cymru was established in 1978 and Sianel Pedwar Cymru (TV) in 1982. The 1967 Welsh Language Act recognizes that Welsh is of "equal validity" with English in government and administration within Wales and this provision has been used by local councils in the north of Wales, where documentation and correspondence is translated into Welsh/English as a matter of course. These councils require employees to demonstrate a Welsh language requirement but this has provoked resentment among some English speakers and the Commission for Racial Equality has ruled in favour of the right of a monoglot English speaker to be appointed to a position if they held a superior professional qualification to a Welsh/English speaker.

Wales retains its constitutional status within the UK although there have been some efforts to give it more autonomy. A major cause of Welsh resentment was removed with the disestablishment of the Anglican church in Wales in 1914 although this did not become operative until 1920 (most Welsh have followed non-conformist Protestant denominations). A referendum held in Wales in March 1979 to devolve some executive (not legislative) powers to a Welsh Assembly was defeated by a vote of four to one against the concept. There is a Welsh nationalist party, *Plaid Cymru*, which has gained a measure of support, especially in the north, and which currently has three seats in the parliament at Westminster. There are also a number of dissident Welsh nationalist groups who have sometimes resorted to violence, overwhelmingly against English-owned property, to press their demands for further language protection, political autonomy or independence. Although most Welsh neither speak the language, nor support demands for autonomy, there is a general wish to overcome Welsh economic disadvantages and a strong feeling of possessing a distinct identity and culture.

(See also *Bretons*; *Gaelic speakers of Scotland*)

Further References

The Two Irelands, MRG Report No. 2, 1984

The Basques and Catalans, MRG Report No. 9 1987

The Flemings and Walloons of Belgium, MRG report No. 46, 1980

Co-existence in some plural European societies, MRG Report No. 72, 1986

EASTERN EUROPE
(including Greece but not including European USSR)

Eastern Europe, including the Balkans, has long been associated with upheavals relating to minorities, lending the term "balkanization" to the vocabulary of politics. The sustained attack by European Powers on the subject territories of the Ottoman Empire advanced the peoples of the region to a troubled independence deriving in part from the emergence of States of considerable ethnic and religious complexity. The new States were not trusted by the powers to deal with their minorities and were subjected to various regimes designed to ensure regional stability. The nineteenth century Great Power practice of recognition of these States conditional on fair treatment of minorities was followed in the twentieth century by a broad surveillance by the League of Nations and post-World War II treaties on human rights. All the States, except Greece, now fall into the Communist orbit, but with considerable degrees of diversity and dependence on the USSR.

The emergence of socialism does not appear to have lessened ethnic tensions in the region. On the contrary, Eastern Europe is a cauldron of discontent where levels of dissonance between the States and their minorities are severe. One problem derives from the existence of conglomerate States such as Yugoslavia: the Serb-Croat-Slovene State created after World War I attempted to weld together disparate nationalities in a State which has demonstrated both stability and instability in its short history. The nationalities have recently reasserted themselves in forcible terms and the state structure appears fragile. Another type of minority is represented by the Hungarians in Romania: ethnicity is divided since the cession of Transylvania to Romania from Hungary in 1919; Hungary remains an active kin-state. Neighbourly relations between socialist Hungary and socialist Romania are under strain in consequence of assimilationist policies pursued by the Government of President Ceausescu. A third type of minority is represented by Turkish or Turkicized groups in which religious and ethnic elements are difficult to separate. The Roma are a fourth presence in Eastern Europe, long established, numerous and culturally distinct from their neighbours. The political, ethnic and social mix of Eastern Europe lends distinctiveness to its involvement with minorities: wider lessons can possibly be learned on conditions for the viability of multi-cultural States, and the application of Marxist principles to nationalist issues.

Instruments on Minority Rights

The Eastern European States abstained from voting on the Universal Declaration of Human Rights, a position which has since been "redeemed" by participation in the Helsinki process (see introduction to section on Western Europe and Scandinavia) and ratification of specific treaties on human rights. Albania has remained outside these general developments, though it has become a party to the Convention on the Prevention and Punishment of the Crime of Genocide which recognizes the right to existence of "national, ethnical, racial or religious groups" (Article II). Greece is not a party to the International Covenant on Civil and Political Rights with its crucial Article 27 on minority rights, but is a party to the Covenant on Economic, Social and Cultural Rights and to the International Convention on the Elimination of All Forms of Racial Discrimination.

Besides the general contemporary instruments, the regions of Eastern Europe retain certain "traces" from the League of Nations period when all of the States in this group were party to treaties on minorities (these treaties also contained general provisions for the benefit of all the inhabitants or nationals of the States, but only the minorities' provisions were "internationalized"). For example, both Greece and Turkey have invoked the provisions of the Treaty of Lausanne 1923 (see *Appendix 4.1*), Section III of which deals with protection of minorities, accusing each other of violation of its provisions regarding non-Muslim and Muslim minorities respectively. Bilateral arrangements for dealing with minorities issues may still have some plausibility in a region where minority-related inter-State disputes continue: the Protocol of February 1988 between Turkey and Bulgaria providing for negotiations to settle the question of the Turkish minority in Bulgaria is a case in point.

The absence of a specific regional instrument for the promotion and protection of human rights, such as the European Convention on Human Rights, means that particular stress must be laid on legal provisions to protect minorities in state constitutions, and on developments at the United Nations and through the Helsinki process. There has been noticeable United Nations interest in developments in Bulgaria, Greece, Romania and Yugoslavia. The Vienna Conference (see introduction to Western Europe and Scandinavia) recognized the need for States to improve their CSCE commitments: they will (a) exchange information and respond to requests for information and to representations made to them by other participating States on human rights questions: (b) hold bilateral meetings with any other participating State that so requests on human rights questions: (c) enable any participating State to bring the attention of the other States, any questions pertaining to human rights.

It is difficult to be sanguine about the relevance and effectiveness of the various constitutional provisions in the light of such pressing violations of minority rights as are apparent in cases such as Romania. The Romanian Constitution recognizes the right of the "co-inhabiting nationalities" living alongside the Romanian people to enjoy their culture. The cultures of the co-inhabiting nationalities are declared to be a component part of the culture of the country as a whole. Other articles provide rights for all as the basis of equality and non-discrimination; free use of native language and books, newspapers and education at all levels in these languages, and institutional use of local languages in the relevant regions. The problem is not one of concept, but of implementation of such provisions, though respect for local language is not consistently expressed in the constitution: for example, judicial proceedings are conducted in Romanian, ensuring its use in areas populated by people of non-Romanian nationality. The Bulgarian Constitution of 1971 (see *Appendix 4.2*) also refers to principles of equality and non-discrimination, as well as to the entitlement of citizens of non-Bulgarian extraction to study their own language in addition to the compulsory study of Bulgarian. Article 35(4) provides that: "The propagation of hate or humiliation of man because of race, national or religious application is forbidden and shall be punished." Citizens are also guaranteed freedom of conscience and creed, freedom of speech, assembly, etc. — the standard formulations of civil and political rights. All of this, and a series of agreements from the period of the League of Nations involving Bulgaria and Turkey, is difficult to equate with the intense policies of Bulgarization pursued by the present regime, primarily affecting Turks, but also other minorities. Bulgaria adopts the expedient at the United Nations and other international fora of denying the existence of various minorities or allowing them only a narrow, partial "existence" by claiming, for example, that there is no Turkish minority in Bulgaria, but only a Muslim minority of Bulgarians who adopted Islam under Ottoman rule.

Treatment of minorities

Eastern Europe retains its historic "status" as a region of fragile relations between states and ethnic or religious groups. The historical effects of Ottoman occupation are still manifest in treatment accorded to Turkish/Islamic groups. "Balkanization" is still a threat. States of complex ethnic construction such as Yugoslavia exhibit fissiparous tendencies as nationalities assert themselves and instances of ethnic repression persist. The treatment of minorities is often closely correlated with general standards of human rights. This is particularly true in the case of Romania where a repressive and totalitarian regime functions as such to all its citizens. The Hungarian minority is singled out for the most intense campaign of assimilation because its economically and culturally independent characteristics threaten the unified, homogenous model of development of Romania favoured by the present regime. These remarks apply, with variations as appropriate, to Bulgaria, though in this case the ethnic issue is crucial; the present repression appears to have been triggered by Government concern at, among other things, the rising Turkish birthrate. This is also a case where, from the Government's point of view, repression may have backfired, since the resulting exodus of Turks to Turkey has deprived Bulgaria of vital agricultural and industrial skills.

Romania's independent economic status appears to make it less vulnerable than Bulgaria to international pressure to curb human rights abuses. In general the prognosis for treatment of minorities is very unclear. It appears rather extraordinary to report policies of forced assimilation, cultural genocide and mass migration of populations in Europe in the late twentieth century. Such policies operate in a region in which they are potentially quite destabilizing. However, the more "benign" model of minority integration represented (in general) by Yugoslavia is undergoing great stress. The result of the Yugoslavian experiment holds great significance for all minorities in the region. But its long-term success is by no means assured.

Greeks of Albania

Location: **South in the districts of Korce and Gjirokaster**
Population: **Officially 50,000: probably 200,000**
% of population: **2%-7.5%**
Religion: **Eastern Orthodox Christian**
Language: **Greek**

The Greeks are the largest minority in Albania and predominantly live in the southern regions of the country. The minority's identity derives mainly from its adherence to the Greek Orthodox Church and the use of the Greek language and names. The post-war communist government has attempted to eradicate religious practices; it has forbidden the use of "foreign" and religious names; and reportedly it has discouraged the use of the Greek language in public places. There are also allegations that the authorities have moved Albanians into Greek majority areas and moved Greeks out thus dispersing the Greek community. Albania is a highly centralized state and the Albanian Party of Labour (the Communist Party) is the sole authorised political party and rigorously controls political, cultural and economic life. Many of the above measures are also applied to the entire Albanian population and as such are not explicitly aimed at the Greek or other minorities.

Although no recent statistics for ethnic minorities have been published in Albania, the Greek minority is officially recognized by the authorities. Greek language schools have existed in Albania since the sixteenth century. In 1922 the Albanian government reported that 36 Greek schools existed in southern Albania. The number of such schools today is unknown. If a village is comprised of Greek minority residents then the village may obtain a Greek language school and other privileges. However minority status is reportedly granted only to wholly Greek villages and once two or three Albanian families arrive, the village loses that status and some reports indicate that there has been a decrease in the number of Greek schools in recent years. Greek children attending Greek language schools are taught in Greek during the first four years, subsequent Greek instruction being only as a foreign language.

Religion was officially attacked after World War II when the communists took power and in 1967 Albania was officially proclaimed "the first atheist state in the world" and all forms of organized religious activity were banned. Some 630 major Orthodox Churches were razed to the ground and an equal number converted to other uses.

In 1975 the government ordered name-changes for "citizens who have inappropriate names and offensive surnames from a political, ideological, and moral standpoint". According to refugees this order did not affect Muslim names although Greeks with religious names were reportedly obliged to change them. Decree No 225, also in 1975, ordered changing geographical place names with religious connotations, and this decree was also apparently applied to some non-religious Greek town names as well.

Although there is no direct evidence of legal prohibitions against the use of Greek in public many refugees have reported *de facto* restrictions in certain settings. A non-Greek escapee said that in his village none of the minorities, Macedonian, Italian or Greek, were allowed to speak their own languages outside their homes. Some schools allegedly forbid children to speak Greek to each other and Greeks in internal exile, a widely used punishment, are reported to be forbidden to speak Greek outside their homes. Further reported restrictions on the use of Greek are when visiting prisoners in Albanian prisons and during military service.

Enver Hoxha who effectively ruled the country since the end of 1944, died in April 1985. His successor, Ramiz Alia, may be easing the government's harsh policies. For example visitors in 1988 report extensive restoration of churches and mosques as cultural relics and tourist sites. Albania has also opened its borders to allow Greek nationals to visit relatives in Albania and some Albanians are now allowed to travel to Greece. Numbers have increased steadily: in 1984, 87 Albanians travelled to Greece; in 1985, 301; and in 1986, 535. In 1985, 1,265 Greeks travelled to Albania and in 1987 the figure was over 6,000. Cultural exchanges are also occurring between the two countries.

Hungarians of Czechoslovakia

Alternative names: **Magyars**
Location: **Slovakia**
Population: **590,000**
% of population: **3.8%**
Religion: **Catholic and Protestant**
Language: **Hungarian**

The Hungarians of Czechoslovakia live predominantly in Slovakia, the eastern portion of present-day Czechoslovakia, where they constitute just over 11% of the population. They are descended from the Magyars, known today as the Hungarians, who invaded the Danube basin at the end of the seventh century and made Slovakia part of the Kingdom of Hungary which was later incorporated into the Hapsburg Empire. The defeat of the Hapsburg Empire in World War I and the subsequent 1920 Treaty of Trianon left over one million Hungarians in the new state of Czechoslovakia.

After a harsh period immediately following World War II, conditions for the Hungarian minority improved somewhat during the 1950s and 1960s. The liberalization movement known as the Prague Spring of 1968 resulted in significant improvements in the rights of the Hungarian minority and despite the Soviet-led invasion of August 1968 which crushed this movement, the National Assembly passed the Nationalities Law on 27 October, 1968. This law which is still in operation states that the minorities (the Hungarian minority is the largest, other minorities recognized by the law are: the Germans who reside almost exclusively in the Czech lands and number some 56,000; the Poles numbering some 70,000 also residing in the Czech lands; and the Ukrainian or Ruthenian minority numbering some 48,000 mostly in Slovakia) are represented in proportion to their numbers in representative bodies and other elected organs, and can receive instruction in their own languages and use their languages for official purposes in their own areas as well as having access to the press and media.

Despite these legal guarantees there are frequent complaints of declining educational provisions for Hungarians and the number of Hungarian-language elementary schools has declined from 609 in 1950 to about 280 at the present with only 30 secondary schools and one higher educational institution, a teachers' training college. According to the Slovak Minister of Education, at the end of the 1970s some 48,000 children studied in Hungarian-language classes while in 1987 the figure was over 50,000. In Eastern and Central Slovakia 50% of Hungarian children attend Hungarian-language schools, while in Western Slovakia the figure is 80%. However only 5-6% of Hungarians in Slovakia apply or gain entry to polytechnics or university and 40-45% of the Hungarian primary and secondary school teachers will retire in Slovakia in the next decade.

The main cultural body for Hungarians is The Cultural Association of Hungarian Working People of Czechoslovakia (CSEMADOK) which has 92,000 members. After the Prague Spring, CSEMADOK was expelled from the National Front, an umbrella body controlled by the authorities, due to having pursued political activities, and was put under direct control of the Slovak Minister of Culture until 1987 when it regained some measure of autonomy. The leading campaigner for Hungarian minority rights within Czechoslovakia is however Miklos Duray, a leader of the Hungarian youth movement during the Prague Spring and spokesman for the unofficial Committee for the Protection of Hungarian Minority Rights, who has frequently been subject to official harassment on account of his activities. Duray led a successful campaign against a proposed measure in November 1983 to curb Hungarian language classes and following this campaign he was arrested and detained for one year before being released following international protest.

(See also *Hungarians of Romania; Slovaks of Czechoslovakia*)

Hungarians of Romania

Alternative names: **Magyars, Szeklers**
Location: **Predominantly Transylvania**
Population: **1.7-2 million**
% of population: **8-10%**
Religion: **Catholic, Calvinist, Unitarian**
Language: **Hungarian**

The Hungarians of Romania live overwhelmingly in Transylvania, the western third of the country, although Bucharest is thought to have some 200,000 Hungarians and there are others in other settlements in the Regat (the old Romanian provinces of Moldavia and Wallachia). There are also long-established Hungarian settlements on the eastern foothills of the Carpathians, particularly around Bacau.

The population of Transylvania is extremely complex. About three-fifths of its total population of seven million is Romanian. The bulk of the rest is Hungarian. There is a German minority which has declined in recent years from perhaps 400,000 due to the ethnic Germans being allowed to emigrate to West Germany at a reported price of DM 6000 per head paid by the West German government (over 14,000 emigrated in 1984 alone), and smaller minorities of Serbs, Ukrainians and other much smaller groups of Slovaks, Czechs, Bulgarians and others. There are also an unspecified number of Roma (Gypsies). Many of the settlements are nationally mixed and there are comparatively few communes which do not contain a minority population of at least one nationality. All urban settlements are mixed and the dynamics of urbanization have ensured that the composition of several towns has undergone changes over the last 40 years.

The census of 1977 gave 1,705,810 Hungarians and a further 1,604 Szeklers out of a total population of 21,559,416. Hungarian sources however assert that there some two million Hungarians in Romania. The Szeklers (*Secui* in Romanian) are an ethnographically distinct part of the minority living predominantly in the counties of Covasna, Harghita and Mures. In the 1977 census, respondents could return their nationality as "Szekler" but most of the 600,000-700,000 Szeklers declared themselves to be Hungarians. The Szeklers speak Hungarian, in fact Hungarian intellectuals in both Romania and Hungary agree that the Szeklers speak the purest and most attractive form of Hungarian. Historically they were settled in the Carpathian bend as guardians of the eastern marches of the Kingdom of Hungary and enjoyed some

special privileges. The majority of the Szeklers are Calvinist or Unitarian by religion.

Religion

Roman Catholics in Transylvania are almost entirely Hungarians and Germans — in the case of the Germans it is the Schwaben of the Banat who are Catholic. All members of the Calvinist Church are Hungarian just as virtually all Lutherans are Saxon Germans. The Unitarians are Hungarian. The Romanians are overwhelmingly Orthodox although other Free Church communities like the Baptists have attracted large numbers of Romanians in recent years.

Historically, Transylvania was the scene of the first post-Reformation experiment in religious toleration. The Edict of Turda in 1568 recognized the mixed religious character of the province and marked an acceptance of it at a time when religious wars were at their height elsewhere in Europe. By this edict, the four "recognized" religions were Roman Catholic, Calvinist, Lutheran and Unitarian. The Orthodox Church, to which the majority of Romanian believers adhere, was merely "tolerated". This unusual religious dispensation has meant that religious adherence has come to be identified with national and cultural loyalties, that Churches have tended to be regarded as national institutions which have helped to underpin national cultures and that attacks on religious life have been interpreted in national as much as religious terms.

History

The central problem of the history of Transylvania is that there are separate Romanian and Hungarian histories, both firmly articulated and neither compatible with each other. Both claim the area as having ensured the survival of the respective nations and their separate existence over the centuries and neither seem able to accept that it should be part of the other's state territory, although Hungarian leaders have in recent times repeatedly denied any claim on Romanian territory.

The Romanian variant of Transylvania's history is the theory of Daco-Roman continuity which is that the Dacians, the original inhabitants of Romania, were conquered by the Roman Empire in the first and second centuries AD. This was followed by a rapid fusion of Dacian and Latin culture resulting in the birth of Romanian national culture. After the withdrawal of the Roman legions, the Dacians, or more properly the Daco-Romans, withdrew to their Transylvanian mountain fastnesses and remained there conserving their Latin language and culture despite waves of foreign invaders including the Hungarians. The Hungarian version however is that when the Hungarian conquest of the central Danube basin took place at the end of the ninth century, Transylvania was only sparsely occupied by Slavonic tribes. The Hungarian Kingdom slowly extended its power over the region settling Szeklers and Saxon (German) colonists to strengthen its economic development. The Romanian population is accounted for by immigration of Romanian shepherds practising transhumance who crossed the Carpathian passes from the thirteenth century onwards and were given the right to settle there by the Hungarian rulers. For the Hungarians, Transylvania is regarded as the entity which guaranteed the historic continuity of the Hungarian state and ensured its survival despite the submergence of the Kingdom either through Ottoman or Hapsburg conquest.

The mixed character of Transylvania was recognized very early by the so-called Union of Three Nations (1437, reaffirmed in 1542). The three nations, properly nations who represented the nobility and in no way correspond to nations in the modern sense, were the Magyars, the Saxons and the Szeklers. After the destruction of the medieval Kingdom of Hungary by the Ottoman Empire after the Battle of Mohacs in 1526, Transylvania retained a precarious autonomy between the Hapsburgs and the Ottomans. At times it acted as an independent state and, in this capacity, signed the Treaty of Westphalia in 1648 which ended the devastating Thirty Years' War. The different nature of Transylvania was recognized after the expulsion of the Turks by its separate incorporation into the Hapsburg domains as a Principality apart from Hungary proper. In 1848-9, the Transylvanian *diet*, controlled by the Hungarian nobility, opted for union with Hungary despite hostility from both the Romanians and the Saxons. This union was implemented after the 1867 *Ausgleich* (compromise) and thereafter the Hungarians promoted a policy of rapid Magyarization which was ineffective in the countryside and only partly so in the towns. This policy was resented by all the minorities and they all turned against the

Hungarians of Romania

Hungarian state in 1918. The Treaty of Trianon in 1920 gave the historic Transylvania together with other Romanian inhabited lands (Banat, Crisana, Maramues) to Romania despite the large numbers of Hungarians living there. In 1940, after the forced cessation of Bessarabia to the USSR, Hungary claimed Transylvania and a somewhat reluctant Germany and Italy agreed that Hungary could annex northern Transylvania, about two-fifths of the territories lost in 1918 and with a Hungarian majority. Southern Transylvania remained part of Romania.

After Romania's change of sides in the war in August 1944, Transylvania was rapidly overrun by the Soviet and Romanian armies but the local Soviet commanders decided to establish what was a *de facto* autonomous communist state of Northern Transylvania under joint Hungarian-Romanian MADOSZ administration

until March 1945, since when Romanian sovereignty over Transylvania has been complete.

Post-war developments

Immediately after the return of northern Transylvania to the Romanian administration in 1945, a process of re-Romanianization was undertaken with the creation of new Romanian institutions and the elimination or downgrading of Hungarian ones. The spirit of co-operation of the MADOSZ period was ended and both the left and the right used the minority question as an instrument of political mobilization. The right used anti-Hungarian propaganda as a nationalist lever, whilst the left courted support of the Hungarians and offered it guarantees for its national and cultural existence. In fact the bulk of the Hungarians, particularly the left-leaning intelligentsia, supported the left believing that

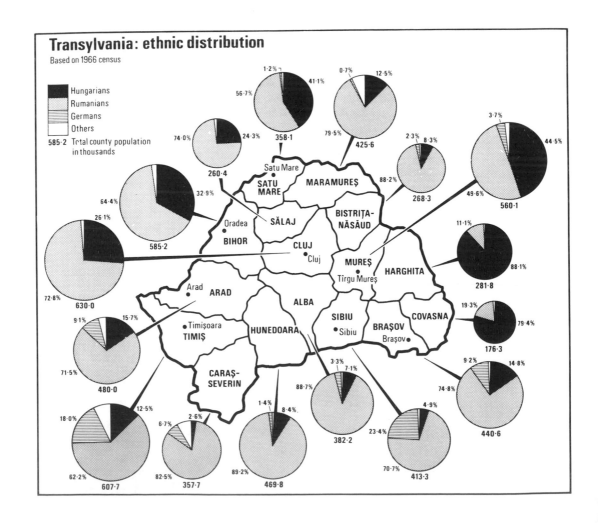

Transylvania: ethnic distribution

Based on 1966 census

■ Hungarians
▨ Rumanians
▤ Germans
☐ Others

585·2 Total county population in thousands

for the first time in the history of Transylvania a form of coexistence between Hungarians and Romanians would be possible. This phase ended with the consolidation of power by Gheorghe Gheorghiu-Dej after 1949. Following the Rajk trials in Hungary, Dej moved against the Hungarian People's Alliance and had many of its leaders arrested — probably as much a move against an autonomous political organization as an anti-Hungarian one. The power struggle culminated in the elimination of the "Moscovites" from the Romanian leadership, among them the Hungarian Vasile Luca (Laszlo Luka in Hungarian). The Magyarophile Romanian Prime Minister Petru Groza, whom many Hungarians saw as a guarantor of their rights, also lost his post around this time. The ensuing Stalinist terror affected Romanian intellectuals as well as Hungarian ones but the arrests and deportations was a harder blow for the minority given the difference in their respective sizes.

At the same time, the Romanian government established the Hungarian Autonomous Province, consisting of the Szekler counties, based on the Soviet model of autonomous territorial organization — a good illustration of the two-fold nature of Romanian policy, that of accompanying internal repression with external concessions. In January 1953 Dej declared that the national question had been solved for good in Romania and henceforth the authorities rejected any public discussion of the problem on the grounds that to do so would be chauvinism. The facade quality of the apparent concessions was shown by the fact that the Hungarian Autonomous Province was autonomous in name only. Its organization differed in no way from the other 16 provinces and it was never given a statute. On the other hand, its existence was used as a pretext for not opening Hungarian cultural facilities elsewhere, with the result that it acquired the reputation of being a Hungarian ghetto. The Hungarian People's Alliance was dissolved at this time and with it disappeared the last collective institution charged with protecting Hungarian interests. This had the result that in practice minority rights became enforceable only individually and not collectively, which made them void for all practical purposes. Simultaneously, the minority's links with Hungary were being severed — subscriptions to Hungarian journals were banned, newspapers were no longer sold in public, travel to Hungary was made almost impossible — this in a situation where there was hardly a family in Transylvania without relatives or friends in Hungary. Thus the pressure to force Hungarian culture and Hungarian life into private had

already begun by the mid-1950s. Hungarians were furthermore dismissed from all important nationwide institutions (The Ministry of Interior, Foreign Ministry, officer corps) except where the facade had to be maintained e.g. the Politburo or Central Committee of the party.

It should be added that during this period, the Hungarians were by no means the worst affected among the nationalities. The Serbian minority was expelled *en masse* from the Banat to the Baragan plain and was constrained to live in appalling conditions; the Germans had been stripped of their property and many deported to the USSR as "prisoners-of-war"; and there was a strong anti-Semitic campaign disguised as anti-Zionism. Also the Romanian majority of all social classes suffered from the excesses of the Stalinist period and police terror.

The next major event was the Hungarian Revolution of 1956 which enjoyed support from Romanians as well as Hungarians in Romania. There were joint Hungarian-Romanian student demonstrations in Cluj and elsewhere. These were followed by a wave of arrests and culminated in the liquidation of the separate Hungarian educational network, above all, the Bolyai University at Cluj which was technically merged with the Romanian-language Babes University in 1959. The elimination of the secondary school network followed with the unification of Hungarian and Romanian schools and the creation of Hungarian-language sections enabling better supervision by the authorities. The principle of unification of Hungarian and Romanian institutions was extended to include houses of culture, theatres, folklore groups etc. The Hungarian Autonomous Province was reorganized in 1960 in such a way as to lose its overwhelmingly Hungarian character by the detaching of purely Hungarian-inhabited territories and the adding of purely Romanian ones. It was renamed the Mures-Hungarian Autonomous Province. When it was abolished completely eight years later, the authorities promised initially that the entire Szeklerland would be united into a single, strong Hungarian county; in fact the area was split three ways with the creation of two weak Hungarian counties (Covasna and Harghita) and a mixed Hungarian-Romanian one (Mures).

The next turning point was 1968. At this stage there was considerable dissatisfaction among the minority and the Romanian leadership felt that this could give the USSR a pretext for intervention in Hungarian affairs in the aftermath of the invasion of Czechoslavkia. Thereafter, Romania's policy towards the minority became more subtle by making concessions, as far as possible in areas of secondary importance, and then subsequently withdrawing them. The setting up of the Council of Workers of Hungarian nationality (CWHN) was a typical example in that it was in practice entirely without powers and its recommendations, when it made any, were ignored. In 1967-8 the publication network was reorganized and several new Hungarian-language newspapers were launched — one for each county with a substantial number of Hungarian inhabitants. In 1974, using paper shortage as the pretext, both Romanian and Hungarian newspapers were cut in size and circulation; the Romanian ones were later restored to their original size and print, the Hungarian ones were not.

In the administration, there appears to be general agreement that the number of Hungarians is kept up to the proportion of Hungarians in the general population. Hungarian representation in the higher party organs like the Central Committee, in local party committees, and in the Grand National Assembly or the People's Councils is maintained at the proclaimed level. However these are largely facade institutions with no real powers and Hungarians are often entirely excluded from real policy-making organs like the local party bureaux. Thus in the mid-1970s there were no Hungarians on the party bureaux in the counties of Timis, Arad and Maramures, all of which contain sizeable Hungarian populations. The alternative is to appoint "facade" Hungarians, individuals who have in effect accepted Romanianization and are seen so by the Hungarians. Reportedly the number of Hungarian policemen in Transylvania is minimal.

From the mid-1970s onwards, a growing number of Hungarian intellectuals came to feel that the situation was less and less tenable. Additionally international action, notably the Helsinki Summit Final Act, specifically drew attention to nationality rights and the concept of "human rights", and additional leverage was provided due to the state's supposed independent foreign policy and its contingent dependence on Western approval. The result was an increase in the amount of information on the Hungarian minority in Transylvania and consequent pressure on the Romanian leadership to account for its treatment of the minority. In 1977 Karol Kiraly, a member of the Hungarian minority and previous Central Committee member, sent three letters to high-ranking party members in which he claimed that the Hungarian minority was being forcibly assimilated and discriminated against in the fields of culture, education and employment. His protest was reportedly supported by Ion Ghoerghe Maurer, a former Prime Minister of Romania, and seven prominent officials belonging to the Hungarian minority. In the early 1980s an unofficial Hungarian language publication *Ellenpontok* (Counterpoints) appeared briefly which similarly claimed an official policy of assimilation against the Hungarians. The editors were arrested and pressured into emigrating to Hungary.

Education and culture

The main grievances of the Hungarian minority concern education and culture. The Hungarians in Transylvania had a long tradition of a high level of education — notably through the religious schools — and a well-educated intelligentsia and qualified skilled working class. Immediately after the war, the full education network, taking in nursery, primary, secondary and university levels was organized. Hungarian language schools were opened throughout Transylvania where there was a substantial Hungarian population and even in the Regat — in the Hungarian inhabited areas of Moldavia — there were 72 Hungarian-language schools in 1958 (there were none by the mid-1970s). In the aftermath of 1956 however, a decision was taken to dismantle this in two general stages. First, Hungarian schools were merged with Romanian ones and functioned as "sections"; and subsequently the two sections were *de facto* merged, so that in practical terms it became a privilege to receive an education in Hungarian. As a result, university education in Hungarian shrank drastically. Internal regulations on minimum numbers of students needed to establish study groups in a particular subject and judicial use of the admission system have allowed the authorities at times to keep to below the minimum the number of Hungarian students which would have allowed the formation of Hungarian-language study groups.

Similar policies have been followed regarding primary and secondary education. Law No. 278/1973 stipulates that at primary level there must be a minimum of 25 applicants every year before a minority language instruction class can be opened for that year. At secondary level the minimum number is 36. By contrast there is no restriction on Romanian pupils. For a while parents attempted to resolve the problem of shortages in numbers by bussing children to the nearest village where a Hungarian school still existed but this was banned on the pretext of insufficient petrol. Parallel with the closing down of Hungarian-language classes has been the declining numbers of Hungarian teachers with many sent to non-Hungarian parts of Romania, as are many who do succeed in completing an education in Hungarian thus severing their links with the minority.

In terms of cultural provisions, Hungarian complaints concentrate on the shortages of materials and increasing control of Hungarian institutions by non-Hungarian speaking Romanians. For example, after the merger of the Hungarian theatre at Tirgu Mures, a new director was appointed who knew no Hungarian and meetings of the Hungarian section of the Cluj branch of the Romanian Writers Union have to be held in Romanian due to the presence of monoglot Romanian writers. Shortages of paper are regularly used to curtail Hungarian publishing activities. Recently Hungarian language publications have been required to refer to the country's place names in Romanian. Hungarian first names without Romanian equivalents have also been banned.

Hungarians also see President Ceausescu's avowed policy of "systemization" — whereby it is planned to destroy half of Romania's 13,000 or so villages by the year 2000 and re-house the inhabitants in "agro-industrial towns" — as a measure aimed at eradicating Hungarian culture in Transylvania and elsewhere in Romania. It appears that the policy is not specifically aimed at the Hungarian or any other minority and applies equally to Romanian villages. It seems that Ceausescu is attempting to eradicate all vestiges of pre-socialist national culture in his attempt to create the new "socialist Romanian citizen". However this measure if carried through will certainly adversely affect the Hungarian (as well as other) minority's cultural heritage owing to the present continuing survival of traditional Hungarian values and way of life in the villages. Uprooting these villages will inevitably aid assimilation.

Relations with Hungary

On a number of occasions in the past, the USSR has tacitly encouraged the Hungarian party to express criticism of the Romanian party in international communist terms — criticism that was automatically translated by public opinion in both states as criticism in national terms, i.e. focused on Transylvania. In May 1977, the Romanian government agreed to hold bilateral discussions with Hungary on the problem of the minority. A joint communiqué was issued in which the Hungarian minority in Romania and the Romanian minority in Hungary (some 25,000) were declared to be bridges between the two nations. Cultural contacts were agreed and a Hungarian consulate would be (re-)opened in Cluj.

Despite this meeting, the entire question of cultural links between the Hungarian minority and the Hungarian state remained highly sensitive and has become more so. Most Hungarian publications, including the Hungarian party's daily paper are banned and copies confiscated at the border. A regulation introduced in 1974 by the Romanian authorities forbade foreign tourists overnight stays in private houses, the only exception being relationships in the first degree (parent, sibling). This regulation has been strictly enforced in Transylvania and prevents Hungarians from Hungary from staying with relatives or friends. Tension between the two countries over Romania's treatment of the minority has increased and become progressively more open after Janos Kadar's departure as leader of the Hungarian party and the progressive liberalization in Hungary which, as well as allowing Hungarian citizens far greater access to consumer outlets in marked contrast to the situation in Romania, has allowed Hungarian public opinion to raise the issue of the minority ever more vocally. The Hungarian authorities have raised the issue at a number of international forums. The Romanians have responded with accusations of Hungarian irredentism and have closed the Hungarian consulates in Bucharest and Cluj.

Refugees

In the last two years, an unprecedented situation has occurred with thousands of Hungarians from Romania fleeing to Hungary and applying for asylum there. In 1988, 13,400 refugees were legally accepted and granted temporary residence permits by the Hungarian authorities. Around 12,700 of these remain in Hungary, the rest having left for the West or returned (a very small number) to Romania. Of these refugees the overwhelming majority were Hungarians with only some 8% being ethnic Romanians. The number of Hungarians from Romania in Hungary was over 25,000 by August 1989 with many unregistered. In the summer of 1989 some 300 refugees were arriving each week from Romania to Hungary of which approximately 27% (a far higher proportion than before reflecting the general feeling of dissatisfaction with the Romanian regime among the Romanian as well as the

Hungarian and other minority populations) were Romanian. The status of the refugees in Hungary is under debate. At present they cannot ask for members of their families to join them. In 1988 1,650 were returned to Romania but the number for 1989 is far lower with only 29 being sent back by July. About half the refugees are skilled workers with agricultural workers accounting for only 2% of the total which would indicate that

the "systemization" is not a major reason for the exodus. In an attempt to prevent this outflow, the Romanian authorities started to build a fence along the Hungarian/Romanian border in 1988 — by mid-June 1989 some 78 kilometres out of a projected 300 had been completed. However on 24 June for no apparent reason part of the fence began to be dismantled.

(see also *Hungarians of Czechoslovakia; Yugoslavia*)

Macedonians of Bulgaria

Location: **South-west of Bulgaria in the Pirin region**
Population: **250,000 (est.)**
% of population: **2.75%**
Religion: **Eastern Orthodox Christian**
Language: **Macedonian, Bulgarian**

The Macedonians (a Slavic people, not to be confused with the subjects of Phillip of Macedon in antiquity) live in the south-western regions of Bulgaria. Successive censuses have given conflicting figures for the numbers of Macedonians in Bulgaria. The results of the 1946 Bulgarian census concerning the Macedonian population were never made public by the Bulgarian authorities. However, Yugoslav sources claim that 252,908 people declared themselves as Macedonians in that census. The census of 1956 recorded 187,789 Macedonians, over 95% of whom lived in the Pirin region where they made up 63.8% of the population. However, in the 1965 census the number of people declaring themselves as Macedonian had dropped to only 8,750 and in the district of Blagoevgrad which previously had the highest percentage of Macedonians the percentage was less than 1%.

Bulgaria has traditionally claimed that the Macedonians (including those living in Yugoslavia and Greece) are ethnic Bulgarians. However immediately after World War II when Georgi Dimitrov, both of whose parents were from Macedonia, was leader, the Bulgarian Communist Party (BCP) fully recognized a separate Macedonian nationality and allowed extensive contact between Pirin Macedonia and the newly formed Macedonian Republic in post-war Yugoslavia. Following his death and the break between Yugoslavia and the USSR, Bulgarian unease at this recognition

became more apparent and the Bulgarians were prepared only to admit that the process of nationality for the Macedonians began in 1918. Later the date was changed to 1944 and at the April plenum of the BCP in 1956 when Todor Zhivkov cemented his power, it appears that it was decided to no longer recognize a separate Macedonian nationality. Since then the Bulgarian authorities and those of the Socialist Republic of Macedonia in the post-war Yugoslav federation have engaged in mutual polemics over the history and language[1] of the Macedonians.

Throughout the early 1960s the Bulgarian authorities, when renewing the compulsory personal identity cards, allegedly issued cards stating that the holder was Bulgarian by ethnicity to those who had previously held cards stating that they were Macedonian. Also from the early 1960s, there have reportedly been a number of political trials of people accused of activity based on Macedonian nationalism. For example, a group of inhabitants of Blagoevgrad were tried in 1962 by the District Court of Blagoevgrad on charges of creating a group whose aims were the secession of Pirin Macedonia from the People's Republic of Bulgaria and in 1964 four people from Blagoevgrad were reportedly tried for writing "We are Macedonians" and "Long live the Macedonian nation" on a restaurant wall. Since the introduction of the latest Criminal Code in 1968, most of those accused of propagating such "anti-democratic and nationalist ideology" have

---

[1]The Macedonian language was only codified after the Second World War and shares nearly all the distinct characteristics which separate Bulgarian from the other Slav languages.

been charged under Articles 108 and 109 which deal respectively with "anti-state agitation and propaganda" and with forming or leading and membership of an illegal group. Article 39 (1) of the People's Militia Law of 1976 (amended on August 12, 1983) also allows administrative punishment (that is without trial), which has reportedly been used to forcibly resettle members of the Macedonian ethnic minority in other areas of the country. According to Yugoslav sources, whole families were forced to move from the Pirin region to other regions in the north because of their affirmation of a Macedonian ethnicity distinct from Bulgarian. At the same time as this repression, the Bulgarian authorities have concentrated resources into the Pirin region, the health resort of Sandanski being a notable example, apparently so as to lessen any possible attraction from neighbouring Yugoslavia.

(See also *Yugoslavia; Macedonians of Greece*)

Macedonians of Greece

Alternative names: **Slavophone Hellenes, Bulgarians**
Location: **In the north of the country in Aegean Macedonia**
Population: **No reliable estimates; large diaspora in Eastern Europe, Canada and Australia**
Religion: **Eastern Orthodox Christian**
Language: **Macedonian, Bulgarian, Greek**

The Macedonians are a Slavic people who live in Macedonia, an area in the Balkan peninsula which is today divided between Greece, Yugoslavia and Bulgaria. The Greek authorities have from the outset of the modern Greek state consistently denied the existence of the Slav Macedonians as a separate people from the Greeks and instead officially referred to them as Slavophone Greeks while the Bulgarians claimed them to be Bulgarians — in common speech the Greek population referred to them as Bulgarians and the notion of them as a separate people, the Macedonians, only really came later in this century, especially after the World War II and the founding of the Socialist Republic of Macedonia in neighbouring Yugoslavia.

The Balkan Wars of 1912-13 and after

Assessing population figures is problematic due to the tendency to exaggerate the number of the Greek or Slav populations depending on which side is making the assessment — the Greeks, the Bulgarians or the Yugoslavs. One of the most detailed assessments is a Yugoslav one, just before the Balkan Wars of 1912 (which saw the liberation of the areas from Ottoman rule). Using Bulgarian and Greek sources, it estimates that there were in Aegean Macedonia: 326,426 Macedonians; 40,921 Muslim Macedonians (Pomaks); 289,973 Turks; 4,240 Christian Turks; 2,112 Cherkez (Mongols); 240,019 Greeks; 13,753 Muslim Greeks; 5,584 Muslim Albanians; 3,291 Christian Albanians;

45,457 Vlachs; 3,500 Muslim Vlachs; 59,596 Jews; 29,803 Gypsies; and 8,100 others making a total of 1,073,549 inhabitants.

However, from 1913 to 1926 there were large-scale changes in the population structure due to ethnic migrations. During and immediately after the Balkan Wars about 15,000 Slavs left the new Greek territories for Bulgaria while many Greeks from Thrace, Pirin and Vardar Macedonia moved to be under Greek rule. More significant was the Greek–Bulgarian convention of November 27, 1919 which allowed voluntary population exchange in which some 25,000 Greeks left Bulgaria for Greece and between 52,000 and 72,000, depending on which estimate is used, Slavs left Greece for Bulgaria, mostly from Eastern Aegean Macedonia which from then onwards remained virtually Slav free. Most Slavs living west of the Vardar river, especially bordering on Yugoslavia, chose to remain. Greece was obliged to protect its Slav minorities and these obligations were further stipulated in the Treaty of Sèvres in 1920 with educational rights and guarantees for the use of their mother tongue for official purposes. In September 1924 Greece and Bulgaria signed a protocol known as the Kalfov-Politis Agreement which placed the "Bulgarian" minority in Greece under the protection of the League of Nations which prompted the Yugoslavs to renounce the Greek–Serbian treaty of 1913 in protest. On January 15, 1925 Greece announced that they would not follow the protocol and henceforth treated the Slavs as Greeks. In 1926 the Greek government ordered in decree No 332 of November 1926 that all Slavonic names of towns, villages, rivers and mountains should be replaced by Greek ones.

Up until the Balkan Wars there were in Aegean Macedonia under the control of the Exarchate Church (the Eastern Orthodox Christian Church founded in 1870 which used the Slav vernacular in place of the previously used Greek language) 19 primary schools in towns and 186 in villages with 320 teachers catering for 12,895 pupils in Bulgarian. In addition there were four Serbian schools and some 200 or so other Slav primary schools supported by village communities. All these Slavonic schools were closed and the inventories destroyed while in the Slavonic churches the icons were repainted with Greek names.

Population exchanges

Larger population exchanges took place between Greece and Turkey following the Greco-Turkish war of 1920-22. The peace treaty of July 1924 stipulated that the Greek and Turkish populations of Turkey and Greece respectively were to be exchanged, except for the Greeks of Istanbul and the Turks of Western Thrace. Again, as so often in the Balkans, religion was the criterion used to define "Greek" or "Turk" which resulted in many non-Turkish Muslims (Slavs and Greeks) emigrating to Turkey and conversely Turkish-speaking Christians to Greece. In this exchange some 390,000 Muslims (mostly Turks) emigrated to Turkey and over 1,200,000 Greeks left Turkey of whom some 540,000 settled in Aegean Macedonia along with about 100,000 more Greek refugees who had come before 1920. Thus there was an influx of over 600,000 Greek refugees into Aegean Macedonia while the Turkish and Pomak population outside of Western Thrace mostly emigrated. The official Greek census of 1928 recorded 1,237,000 Greeks; 82,000 Slavophones; and 93,000 others although this census almost certainly exaggerated the number of Greeks.

The position of the Macedonian minority worsened in the period 1936-41 under the Metaxas regime which viewed the minority as a danger to Greece's security and large numbers (Yugoslav sources allege over 5,000) Macedonians were interned from the border regions with Yugoslavia, and night schools were opened to teach adult Macedonians the Greek language. The repression was further stepped up after the beginning of the Greco-Italian war in October 1940, despite the numbers of Macedonians fighting loyally in Greece's armies,

with, according to Yugoslav sources, some 1,600 Macedonians interned on the islands of Thasos and Kefallinia (Cephalonia).

After the defeat of Greece by the Axis powers in 1941, Bulgaria occupied the eastern portion of Greek Aegean Macedonia, excepting Salonika which was occupied by the Germans, and a small part of the western portion. The remainder was under the Italians. In the portions under Bulgarian rule the Bulgarians imported settlers from Bulgaria and acted such that even a German report of the time described the Bulgarian occupation as "a regime of terror which can only be described as 'Balkan' ". In Kavalla alone over 700 shops and enterprises were expropriated and large numbers of Greeks expelled or deprived of their right to work by a licence system that banned the practice of a trade or profession without permission from the occupying authorities. The Bulgarians acted with such ruthlessness that the Greek population, many of whom were previously emigrés from Turkey and who were understandably hostile to being once more ruled by a foreign power, became bitterly anti-Bulgarian. Thus Bulgaria, in the brief period when she finally controlled some of the areas in Aegean Macedonia she always claimed, succeeded in alienating the populations under its control in Aegean Macedonia while losing influence to the Yugoslavs in Western Aegean Macedonia.

The Greek Civil War 1943-49

Another product of the brutal Bulgarian rule was that the Greek population became more violently opposed than ever to the idea of a "United Macedonia", incorporating the areas of Macedonia in Yugoslavia and Bulgaria as well as in Greece, which, up until the change of line of the Comintern in the mid-1930s to Popular Fronts following Hitler's rise to power, had been the Greek Communist Party's (KKE) policy. This line, which was always unpopular with rank and file Greeks, was resumed by the Communist-controlled resistance movement The National Liberation Front, EAM, and its military wing, ELAS, and in 1943 EAM-ELAS tried to organize resistance in Aegean Macedonia. Tito's aide Vukmanovic-Tempo, who was very successful in Yugoslav Vardar Macedonia, set up SNOF, the Slav National Liberation Front, which comprised Macedonian Slav Partisan units allied to ELAS but this provoked prolonged resistance from non-Communist Greeks especially from a movement called "The Protectors of Northern

Greece" (YVE), and relations between ELAS and SNOF were strained.

The Greek Civil War which began in earnest in late 1946 (after a brief "First Round" and "Second Round" in 1943-4) between the Communist controlled ELAS and non-Communists supported by Britain and later the USA, saw the exodus of many Slavs and Greek Communist Party members fleeing to Yugoslavia. The last round of the civil war which lasted until 1949 saw SNOF reformed as NOF (National Liberation Front) and up to 40% of the Communist forces comprising of Macedonians. However the struggle at the top of the KKE between Nikos Zachariades and Markos Vafiadis, who had close links with Tito which even survived the initial Stalin-Tito break of 1948, which ended in Markos' retirement due to "ill-health" in January 1949, was followed by an attempt by the KKE to set up an anti-Tito NOF but by now the war was virtually lost for the Communists and only gestures remained. On 1 March 1949 "Free Greece", the communist radio station, broadcasted a declaration of an Independent United Macedonia which was not recognized by the USSR or its allies and only caused alarm in the rank and file of the KKE. On July 1949, Tito closed the Yugoslav-Greek frontier.

The post-war period

During the World War II and the ensuing civil war the Slavs of Aegean Macedonia had enjoyed language rights such as education in Slavonic which had been denied them before except for the brief appearance of a Slavonic primer, *Abecedar*, in September 1925. In the period after the civil war the Macedonians were, not surprisingly, seen as potentially disloyal to the Greek state and steps were taken to try and remove such "undesirable aliens" from the sensitive border regions with Yugoslavia. In 1953 decree no. 2536 was enacted to colonize the northern territories "with new colonists with healthy national consciousness" — the anti-Macedonian element in this law was evident by the exclusion of the Turks in Western Thrace from such measures. In this period it was forbidden for Macedonians to use the Slavonic forms for their names and henceforth only Greek forms could be used for official purposes — a measure with obvious parallels to recent Bulgarian measures against its minorities. In the early part of 1954 the Papagos government resolved to remove all Macedonians from official posts in Aegean Macedonia. In the border regions with Yugoslavia peasants were

not allowed to move from their villages and in 1959 in the villages around Lerin, Kostur and Kajlari, the inhabitants were asked to confirm publicly in front of officials that they did not speak Macedonian. Such measures led to many emigrating to Australia or Canada.

Since the civil war, the official denial of a Macedonian minority in Greece has remained constant regardless of the government in power and the military dictatorship of 1967-74 saw a worsening of the minority situation with many Macedonians interned or imprisoned. The return to democracy in Greece saw an improvement with the abandonment of official terror. However the education system and the lack of job opportunities for those who declared themselves to be Macedonian in any branch of the state bureaucracy have greatly aided assimilation into the Greek majority and the Greek authorities have apparently been successful in achieving this aim. It is noticeable that Macedonian nationalism appears much stronger in emigrés from Aegean Macedonia, not merely in Yugoslavia but also Australia or Canada, than in the area itself. The massive dilution of the Macedonian population by emigration on the one hand and influx of Greeks on the other combined with the experience of the civil war has made the aim of some kind of Macedonian state incorporating Aegean Macedonia merely a dream shared by few.

Successive Greek governments have continued to show hostility to any idea of Macedonian nationalism within Greece or without, both in relation to the Socialist Republic of Macedonia in Yugoslavia and the large numbers of Macedonians who fled Greece in the civil war. The property of these refugees was confiscated by the Greek government by Decree 2536/53 which also deprived them of their Greek citizenship. The Greek government later enacted a law so that the property would be returned to refugees who are "Greek by birth" — i.e. to those who renounce their Macedonian identity and adopt Greek names. Greece also has consistently denied entry visas to these refugees except in a few cases to attend funerals etc. but even then with difficulty.

After Andreas Papandreou and his Greek Socialist party PASOK came to power in Greece in 1981, Skopje's Kiril i Metodija University was taken off the list of foreign academic institutions whose degrees are recognized by Greece as the instruction at the university was in a language, Macedonian, not "internationally recognized". Greece has repeatedly refused Yugoslavia's initiatives to bilaterally abolish visas and while Serbs, Croats or other Yugoslav nationals have few problems, special proof is reportedly needed from Macedonian entry visa applicants that they were not born in Aegean Macedonia. Papandreou himself has explicitly denied the existence of a Macedonian minority in Greece and stated that he would not accept any dialogue on this matter. The fall of the PASOK government in June 1989 has not at the time of writing resulted in any significant change.

(See also *Yugoslavia; Macedonians of Bulgaria*)

Pomaks of Bulgaria

Alternative names: **Bulgarian Muslims, Bulgarian Mohammedans**
Location: **mainly in the south in the Rhodope mountains around Smolyan**
Population: **150,000 (est.)**
% of population: **1.7%**
Religion: **Muslim**
Language: **Bulgarian**

The Bulgarian Muslims, usually called by the term "Pomaks", are a religious minority. They are Slav Bulgarians who speak Bulgarian as their mother tongue but whose religion and customs are Islamic. They are estimated to number in excess of 150,000 and live in compact settlements in the mountainous regions of the Rhodope mountains in south-western and southern Bulgaria.

Since 1948 the Bulgarian authorities have made repeated attempts to induce the Pomaks to change their names, renounce their faith and become integrated into the socialist Bulgarian state. In the period 1971 to 1973 the authorities pursued a concerted campaign to force the Pomaks to change their names by obliging them to choose new ones from a list of "official" Bulgarian names. The Pomaks were obliged to hand in their old identity papers and receive new ones made out in new Bulgarian names. Some Pomaks, mostly old people but some young ones as well, refused but, without new identity papers, no pensions, state salary or money from a bank account could be drawn.

There were a number of instances of violent resistance. For example, in 1971 there were riots in Pazardzhik in which two Communist Party functionaries were reportedly killed. The authorities reacted by arresting large numbers of people. Two Pomaks were condemned to death and two others sentenced to 15 years' imprisonment. A group of Pomaks travelled to Sofia and protested against these measures but were stopped near the town of Samakov by the militia and in a violent clash two Pomaks were shot dead and 50 wounded. There were also reported violent clashes in Barutin and around Devin. Intensive military operations were carried out in May 1972 in Blagoevgrad and surrounding districts against the Pomaks which resulted in many deaths of Pomaks who resisted the forced assimilation. In March 1973 security forces supported by border guards again entered several villages in Blagoevgrad district and went from house to house with prepared lists of Bulgarian names from which the Pomak inhabitants were obliged to select new names. In the violent resistance which ensued at least eight people were reported to have died, including one army officer, and a number of people wounded. Large numbers of Pomaks were arrested, 20 from the village of Kornitsa alone, and sentenced to three to 15 years' imprisonment. About 100 Pomaks were also deported to other areas in Bulgaria.

In prison the Pomaks suffered particularly harsh treatment. If they failed to use or respond to the Bulgarian name assigned to them by the authorities they risked being deprived of their right to visits from their families. In 1975 Amnesty International was informed that about 500 Pomaks were serving prison sentences in Belene prison camp and the same organization reported that in 1977 there were 40 to 50 Pomaks held in Stara Zagora Prison, many kept in solitary confinement with reduced rations for periods longer than the maximum 14 days allowed by Bulgarian penal law. Former prisoners from Stara Zagora Prison have alleged that Pomaks have been placed for as long as three days in a special concrete cell, "one metre square", which has a curved floor often covered with water. In winter the water freezes, and prisoners put in this cell have suffered from kidney diseases and pneumonia.

Demonstrations were reported to have taken place on August 15, 1989 by Pomaks protesting at the authorities' apparent refusal to issue passports to people living in the predominantly Pomak area around Gotse Delcher — a new pass-port law was to be implemented in September 1989 and over 300,000 ethnic Turks emigrated to Turkey in 1989. Protests reportedly occurred in over a dozen villages including Hvostyane, Kornitsa, Lazhinista, Breznitsa, Dabnitsa and Blatska. Security forces sealed off at least six villages with unconfirmed reports of some deaths of protesters.

(See also *Turks of Bulgaria*)

Roma in Eastern Europe

Alternative names: **Gypsies, Tsigani**
Location: **throughout Eastern Europe**
Population: **3-3.5 million (est.)**
% of population: **2-2.5%**
Religion: **Christian, Muslim**
Language: **Romanes, various languages**

Roma originated from North India. From the fifth century onwards, Roma filtered into the Persian and later Arab empires of the Middle East, early groups of them reaching Byzantium in the tenth century. Their attachment to established religions, whether Hindu, Muslim or Christian, appears to have been a matter of convenience rather than conviction. In the Balkans where Ottoman rule lasted longest in Europe, especially Bulgaria, the majority are Muslim while in areas which historically have been under Christian control they are Christian by persuasion.

Traditionally independent and the product of migration and adaption, the Roma have in all countries remained predominantly outside the various systems in operation, be they feudal, capitalist or socialist, by becoming horse-dealers, smiths, musicians and more recently scavengers. The Roma have historically been persecuted and/or discriminated against in all countries of Eastern Europe and have suffered from racism. During the Second World War when Eastern Europe fell under the domination of the Nazis, genocide was used against the Roma and some half a million are believed to have died.

Based on available census figures and previous estimates (taking into account the high birth rate among Roma) and including associated seden-tary and nomadic groups, the following figures give the number of Roma and their percentage of the population by country in 1986: Yugo-slavia — 850,000 (3.7%); Romania — 760,000 (3.35%); Hungary — 560,000 (5.21%); Bulgaria — 475,000 (5.3%); Czechoslovakia — 410,000 (2.66%); Greece — 140,000 (1.4%); Albania — 80,000 (2.75%); Poland — 70,000 (0.19%) and East Germany — 2,500 (0.01%).

The socialist countries of Eastern Europe have applied pressure to stop travelling Roma, and settled Roma are encouraged to assimilate. However the move after 1981 of the head-quarters of the International Romani Union (IRU) from Switzerland to Yugoslavia and the emergence in Yugoslavia of a full emancipation movement with outlets to television, radio and press has brought the position of Roma in Eastern Europe more to the fore. While Bulgaria and also Czechoslovakia continue heavy-handed assimila-tion policies, such policies have been defeated recently in Hungary and are on the defensive elsewhere. Only Yugoslavia (and the USSR) have recognized Roma as a nationality.

Poland

Poland was the first post-war socialist state to try and integrate nomadic Roma voluntarily, but later adopted coercive methods. According to official figures 25% gave up the road during the early phase responding to offers of housing and employment. A negative attitude to Roma remains among the population at large and there have been several serious attacks on Roma since 1981. Additionally many hundreds of Roma have been expelled from Poland and not allowed to re-enter. However Roma in Tarnowie have formed a Romani Cultural Society and were permitted to send representatives to the 3rd World Romani Congress.

Hungary

Although in 1979 the Communist Party decided that Roma did not warrant national minority status, they were allowed to organize on a national basis and *Orszagos Ciganytanacs* was founded which superseded the consultative *Ciganyszovetseg* set up in 1974 which in turn had superseded a similar body functioning between 1958 and 1960. The new National Romani Council has however broader representation and influence than its predecessors. A second organization, the Rom Cultural Association was set up in May 1986 which links some 200 local clubs and 40 dance ensembles.

The Hungarian authorities are among the few in Europe who admit the true number of Roma. Fewer than 15% have skilled jobs and less than 5% of those are employed in the professions. Life expectancy for Roma remains 15 years lower than the average. Many Roma live in the east of the country, especially in Nograd region. Some 70,000 live in Budapest, many in self-made squatter settlements on the outskirts. Although half the 2,100 Rom settlements are situated near larger Hungarian villages, a proportion of the children are not attending school. Discrimination plays some part in this as the birth-rate among Roma has increased by 13% while the general population has a zero growth rate and many elementary schools are reluctant to allow the large intake. Two schools have experimented with the use of Romanes but its introduction has not yet been generally accepted.

Romania

Although one of the largest national minorities in Romania, Roma are also the most deprived. Many are still travelling (official figures say 10% are on the road at any one time) and while there are no special laws against nomadism, such as those passed in Bulgaria, travelling Roma meet much intolerance. Horse-trading has been prohibited but many Roma follow other traditional trades such as spoon and sieve making, and coppersmithing. A number of Roma own small fairground shows.

In 1985 the first Rom organization *Phralipe* (Brotherhood) for almost 50 years was established with official permission. It held a cultural festival at Bistritza Monastery on the occasion of the annual Rom pilgrimage to this Eastern Orthodox shrine and it is planned to repeat the festival every year. A number of small scale cultural gatherings have also been planned. However Romania is a highly centralized state and the government is pursuing a policy of attempted homogenization of the population to create a "socialist Romanian nation". There have also been reports of Roma expelled from Romania into Hungary.

Bulgaria

While Bulgaria has made a determined effort to raise the living standards and educational opportunities of the large Romani minority, the authorities have been equally firm in denying Roma the right to preserve their own identity and culture through the formation of socio-political organizations with only a few local music ensembles allowed at present. In the period 1953-4 there was an operation to settle the nomadic Roma, often in the northern plain below the Danube, and in the case of the majority Muslim Roma to change their names. At least 20,000 families have received plots of land and low-interest loans to build their own houses and numerous settlements have been created on collective farms. However an overall policy of assimilation of the country's minorities has resulted in a further name-changing campaign in the late 1970s, and restrictions on the practice of Islamic religious ceremonies which accompanied the crackdown against the country's Turkish minority in 1984-5 have also adversely affected Muslim Roma.

Despite this assimilation policy, the large settled communities such as the 45,000 Roma in Sliven, and the quarters in Sofia, Varna and Plovdiv remain strongholds of Romani social life and the assimilation policies appear to have had little impact. Small-scale discrimination against Roma continues in everyday life.

Czechoslovakia

The situation of Roma in Czechoslovakia has declined in recent years. The two Romani unions, in the Czech-lands and in Slovakia, were disbanded in 1973 after just three years of existence when they had mobilized over 20,000 members. At the same time the authorities decided that Roma were to be denied nationality status and plans for the introduction of Romanes into schools were dropped. In the past 20 years villages and urban quarters have been forcibly dispersed and the inhabitants moved to other parts of the country in an attempt to reduce concentrations of Roma which had reached 20% in some locations. At the same time Roma have migrated from backward Slovakia into the more developed Czech-lands and there are probably some 150,000 Roma living in Bohemia and Moravia today. Everywhere unemployment remains high and only one child in six completes the upper grades of elementary school in Slovakia.

A controversial policy of inducing Roma women who have had two children to undergo sterilization as an act of "socialist humanity" has been in operation since the late 1970s and some, including the IRU representative at the United Nations in Geneva, Dr Jan Cibula, himself a founder member of the Slovak Romani Union, now resident in Switzerland, have alleged that this is a policy of compulsory sterilization which is both unwarranted and unconstitutional.

Yugoslavia

Yugoslavia has the largest Rom population in Europe which also has important links with emigrant Rom groups in France, Germany, the United States, Australia and elsewhere. Since 1981, the 850,000 Roma in Yugoslavia have "nationality status" on equal footing with other national minorities like the Albanians, Turks or Hungarians. Since 1983 Romanes has been used in state schools. At least 10 primary schools are using the Romani language as the teaching medium for the first four grades, and the number will rapidly rise once more Rom teachers can be trained. The breakthrough occurred in the Albanian populated region of Kosovo, where Muslim Roma have had a hard time making their voice heard in the past. Pristina television station in Kosovo now has a weekly programme in Romanes and Belgrade radio is broadcasting regularly in the language as are the smaller stations of Nis and Tetovo. Publications are still rare but there are several full length books which have been issued as well as a new grammar and dictionary.

The bigger communities in Belgrade, Nis, Suto Orizari (Skopje) and other towns have had their own cultural and social associations for many years. The Belgrade *Drustva Rom* was founded in 1930 and Skopje's *Phralipe* (Brotherhood) in 1948. Today there are some 60 such local associations, linked in Serbia by the Romani Union, presided over by Sait Balic who is also president of the IRU. An annual festival has been held for the past 15 years, and several national and international events have also been held. In 1986 the IRU co-sponsored the International Symposium on the Romani Language and History in Sarajevo. Perhaps the most significant feature is the Romani town of Suto Orizari outside Skopje, comprising some 35,000 inhabitants, with its own elected council and M.P. This town enjoys a higher standard of living than many Macedonian villages.

Despite these advances, the majority of Roma continue to live well below the economic average and there is discrimination in the work place and in the streets. Only a few hundred Roma have benefitted from university education and entered the professions. Half the wage earners are industrial workers and 20% are farmers — many owning their land. The rest are self-employed artisans and small traders. Nomadism has dwindled although it is still present.

The granting of nationality status in 1981 resulted in a significant increase in the number of Roma declaring themselves as such although there was resistance to their recognition as a nationality. For example, Macedonia had designated Roma as an "ethnic group" (lower in the hierarchy of recognized peoples), which appeared to violate the federal constitution with the intention of depriving them of nationality rights.

Greece

The lack of statistics available for ethnic minorities and the official Greek position of classifying as Greeks all those who use Greek in everyday language — even if it is not their mother-tongue — especially if they are of Orthodox faith again makes assessing the numbers of Roma and other minorities very hard. Estimates from official Greek sources give the figure for Roma as far lower than outside observers who estimate the number at 140,000 of whom 45,000 are nomadic Muslims. Many Muslim Roma live in Macedonia and Western Thrace where there is a community of them, numbering 1,500-2,000, in Komotini alone. Although Greece is a member of the Council of Europe, its 1969 recommendations on Roma have yet to be implemented. The Panhellenic Romani Association has held council elections in Thessaloniki and Athens since at least 1980 and about 50 houses have been built for Roma in Serrai.

Muslim Roma have in practice only been accepted as Greek citizens after baptism and admission to the Orthodox Church, and the Bishop of Florina in Aegean Macedonia has continued to lead a church mission to convert Muslim Roma to Orthodoxy. This controversial activity has drawn attention to the critical situation of Muslim Roma who lack citizenship and thus basic civil rights. A law passed in 1979 designed to enable them to obtain identity cards has had little apparent effect due to most lacking birth-certificates. The Ministry of Education is looking at the educational needs of the Muslim

Roma population but travelling Roma are still faced with the 1976 law making camping illegal outside of organized sites — virtually all of which are for tourists and banned to Roma. Roma, as is so common elsewhere, are at the bottom of the social order.

(See also *Roma in Western Europe* in **Western Europe and Scandinavia;** *Roma in the USSR* in **USSR;** *Roma in Turkey* in **Middle East and North Africa**)

Slovaks of Czechoslovakia

Location: **Mainly in Slovakia**
Population: **4.8 million**
% of population: **31.3%**
Religion: **Mainly Catholic**
Language: **Slovak**

The Slovaks are a Slavonic people living mainly in Slovakia, the eastern portion of present day Czechoslovakia, where they constitute over 85% of the population. Slovaks lived in Slovakia long before the Magyars, known today as the Hungarians, invaded the Danube basin at the end of the seventh century and made Slovakia part of the Kingdom of Hungary. The area was later incorporated into the Hapsburg Empire. Latin was the official language of Hungary until 1793 after which Hungarian became the official language. At about the same time Slovak was first codified by the Slovak scholar Bernolak. The rights of minorities, Slovaks, Croats and Serbs, within Hungary and the Hapsburg Empire became one of the central issues in the nineteenth and early twentieth century.

During the revolutionary year of 1848 there was a Slovak insurrection against the Magyars and Ludovit Stur proclaimed a short-lived independence for Slovakia. After 1867 when the Magyars gained considerable autonomy within the Hapsburg empire the position of the Slovaks deteriorated. Despite the submission of the Slovak memorandum of 1861 by Stefan Marko Daxner which called for minority rights for Slovaks, the authorities in Hungary pursued a concerted policy of Magyarization. The *Matica Slovenska*, the only Slovak cultural institution was closed as were three Slovak high schools. All Slovak primary schools were later abolished and Slovaks were officially referred to as "Slovak-speaking Magyars". The results of this assimilation policy were that in 1918 only a handful were able to write in orthographical Slovak and the numbers of Slovaks had declined dramatically. Almost all secondary school pupils considered themselves to be Magyar rather than Slovak and total assimilation seemed probable with only the Catholic and Lutheran clergy, due to their economic independence, in a position to defend Slovak national interests. Among them was Andrej Hlinka who founded the Slovak People's Party in 1905 to fight in the Hungarian Parliament for Slovak rights.

The defeat of the Hapsburg Empire, the Russian Revolution, and the ensuing confused situation in central Europe immediately after World War I allowed the proclamation of a short-lived Slovakian Soviet Republic in July 1919 which lasted three weeks. The 1920 Treaty of Trianon allowed the formation of Czecho-slovakia which was to be a federated union of Czechs and Slovaks. However the Czechs dominated the new state from the outset and while the position of Slovaks in the new state was considerably better than before, there was still discontent. The Slovak People's Party continued its fight for national rights and although it was the strongest party in Slovakia it was always outvoted by the combined votes of the Czech or Czechoslovak orientated parties. The collapse of Czechoslovakia following the Munich agreement with Nazi Germany led in March 1939 to the setting up, under Nazi suzerainty, of the "Slovak Republic" under the clerical-fascist leadership of the Slovak People's Party now led by Jozef Tiso who had succeeded Hlinka. The Slovak republic strengthened national consciousness and saw the creation of Slovak faculties and the founding of the Slovak Academy of Arts and Science.

The defeat of Nazi Germany saw the end of the Slovak republic and the recreation of Czecho-slovakia except for the loss of Sub-Carpathian Ukraine to the USSR. The Agreement of Kosice in 1945 granted some self-government to Slovakia. The Communist Party, which was to rule after 1948, was initially in favour of a distinct Slovak identity and autonomy and the 1948 Constitution provided for organs of Slovak self-government. However this was soon replaced by centralization and the Slovaks again fell under greater Czech domination than before 1939. A campaign against Slovak nationalism in the 1950s saw the execution of Vladimir Clementis and the imprisonment of Gustav Husak and other leading Slovak communists and the subordination of the Slovak party to Prague. The 1960 Constitution openly articulated extreme centralism and reduced even further Slovak self-government.

After 1963 there was a resurgence of Slovak cultural nationalism and some limited improvements. One of the main strands of the reform movement, which blossomed in the "Prague Spring" of 1968, was the question of national equality. In Slovakia this was, according to opinion polls, more important than the issue of democratization. (In the Czech-lands however democracy was the main issue with national equality only in seventh place.) Husak, now rehabilitated, became deputy Prime Minister in charge of constitutional reform. The Soviet-led invasion of August 1968 and the ensuing occupation saw the gradual dismantling of the liberalization measures introduced during the Prague Spring under the leadership of Alexander Dubcek. There was however no reversion to the previous subordination of the Slovaks vis-à-vis the Czechs. On October 28, 1969, the constitutional law on federation was adopted by the National Assembly and Czechoslovakia was divided into two federal states and Slovak statehood restored in the form of the Slovak Socialist Republic. Husak replaced Dubcek as de facto leader of Czechoslovakia. Although the new arrangement, which remains to the present, does not grant full parity nor a complete ban on majoritization, there are substantial safeguards against the Czechs using their numerical strength to outvote Slovaks and the Slovaks are assured a powerful position in enactment of all-state legislation within the framework of the communist system.

(See also *Hungarians of Czechoslovakia*)

Sorbs of East Germany

Alternative name: **Wends**
Location: **Lusatia in the German Democratic Republic (DDR)**
Population: **70,000 (est.)**
% of population: **0.4%**
Religion: **Catholic**
Language: **Sorb, German**

The Sorbs, formerly known as Wends, are the indigenous inhabitants of Lusatia (German: Lausitz) — a region situated about 80 kilometres to the south-east of Berlin on the borders with Poland and Czechoslovakia. They are the survivors of the Slavonic tribes which once occupied most of the territory between the Elbe and the Oder and are related to the Poles and Czechs. Despite their small numbers, never more than a few hundred thousand, and lacking political status since the eleventh century, they have been a clearly recognizable ethnic group throughout their history.

Invaded by Germans, Poles and Czechs, they survived the religious conflicts of the Reformation. Divided between Saxony and Prussia by the Congress of Vienna in 1815, and ravaged by the Napoleonic Wars, the Sorbs failed to develop the same degree of national consciousness as most other Slavonic peoples and remained a largely rural population throughout the first half of the nineteenth century. A major event in their history was the opening in 1904 of the *Serbski Dom,* the headquarters and library of the *Macica Serbska,* Lusatia's principal cultural organization, which soon became the principal symbol of national pride.

After World War I, during which many Sorbs had served and died in great numbers, many believed that the defeat of Germany meant independence for all minorities who had been under Prussian control. However despite Czech demands for Sorbian independence at the 1919 Peace Conference, the Sorbs were not mentioned in the final treaties. Under the Weimar Republic every opportunity was taken to strengthen the German elements in Lusatia. With the rise of Hitler, the minority's institutions were closed down and, in 1935, publications in Sorb were banned. Only Catholic publications were allowed due to the Nazi Concordat with the Vatican. The contents of the *Macica Serbska* were confiscated and private Sorbian books seized and burnt. Many intellectuals and public figures were arrested and some sent to concentration camps. During World War II, there were plans to transplant the entire community but the Germans were defeated at Stalingrad before they could be implemented.

In the wake of the Soviet advance, a Sorbian National Council was set up in Prague demanding political independence for Lusatia, a seat in the United Nations, Sorb language schools and land reform. The first Sorb newspaper was published in 1946 and the first Sorb-language secondary school opened in the following year.

The government of the German Democratic Republic (DDR), since 1948, has clearly done a great deal to protect the identity of the minority: the principle of the "Law for the Protection of the Sorbian Population's Right", passed on March 23 of that year, providing for instruction in Sorb, has not been fundamentally changed. There are many schools with Sorb as the language of instruction at all levels, and a course in the language and history of Lusatia at Karl Marx University in Leipzig. The constitution of the DDR (Article 11, October 7, 1949, and Article 40, April 6, 1968) states that the Sorbs' development must not be hindered but encouraged in every possible way and these guarantees exist *de jure* and *de facto*. Sorb is specifically authorized in local government, in law and in all official documents, while Sorbs can again use their original names which were banned under the Nazis. The State Council has one statutory Sorbian member, while there are four Sorbian deputies in the *Volkskammer*, nine

in the Council of Dresden and 18 in Cottbus. The Ministry of the Interior has a special department for Sorbian affairs.

Sorbian culture has continued to flourish with many books in Sorbian published. There is also a professional theatre company and a daily newspaper in Sorb, as well as a variety of magazines. The language is rarely heard on television but some 25 hours a week are broadcast on radio. The *Domowina* sponsors concerts, films, plays and folk evenings, sporting events, exhibitions and festivals.

However, a gradual assimilation is taking place and numbers have declined from 166,000 in 1868 to about 70,000 according to official DDR figures (West German sources give a lower figure). The language is much better preserved in country areas than in towns, especially in Upper Lusatia. Bautzen, a town with about 45,000 inhabitants, now has only a thousand Sorb-speakers and most of its other areas are linguistically mixed. Many of the Germans expelled after the war from territories beyond the Oder-Neisse line and from the Sudetenland were re-settled in Lusatia with profound effects on the linguistic composition of the area. German workers continue to be attracted there by the development of brown coal resources. The highest concentration of Sorbs is around Kamenz, still a predominately Catholic village. In central areas the process of Germanization is complete: where the language survives at all in these parts it is usually spoken by the old. How long the remaining Sorb speakers will be able to preserve their identity is a matter for speculation.

Turks of Bulgaria

Location: **Mainly the north-east, and the south around Kardzhali**
Population: **900,000 (est.)**
% of population: **10%**
Religion: **Muslim**
Language: **Turkish**

Ethnic Turks have lived in Bulgaria since the time of the Ottoman Turkish conquest in the fourteenth Century. After the collapse of Ottoman rule in the late nineteenth Century and the emergence of the modern Bulgarian state there were successive waves of emigration, mostly to Turkey, but many Turks remained. They live mostly in compact communities in the south of the country in the Arda river basin and in the

north-east in the Dobrudzha region. They also live in scattered communities in the central and eastern Stara Planina (the Balkan Mountains) and in the Rhodope mountains.

Until the most recent campaign to assimilate them in late 1984 and early 1985, the ethnic Turks were officially recognized as a "national minority" along with certain other minorities. However, even this recognition was circumscribed by a general reservation about the very idea of minorities in Bulgaria and the 1971 Constitution, unlike the 1947 Constitution, makes no specific references to ethnic minorities but rather refers to "citizens of non-Bulgarian origin" (Article 45). Since 1985 the only recognized minorities in Bulgaria with their own minority organizations are the small number of Jews and the Armenians.

The 1965 census recorded 746,755 ethnic Turks, an increase of approximately 90,000 on the 1956 figure. Since then there have been no official figures for the total numbers of members of ethnic minorities in Bulgaria and in 1975 the section recording nationality on personal identity cards was reportedly removed. Although 900,000 or 10% of the Bulgarian population is a commonly accepted figure, some observers believe that there may be up to 1.5 million. In 1989 with mass immigration to Turkey, these numbers would have again changed.

Emigration

At various times since the end of World War II Bulgaria and Turkey have reached agreement over the emigration of Turks from Bulgaria to Turkey. The largest number of such emigrants left Bulgaria in the period 1949-1951. In August 1950 the Bulgarian Government announced that a total of 250,000 Turks had applied to leave. The Turkish Government, on the other hand, said it was unable to receive such a huge mass of people within such a short time and in November 1950 closed its border with Bulgaria because of "illegal crossing of borders". Two months later an agreement was reached by both governments that only those Turks who were in possession of a Turkish entry visa would be allowed to leave. Despite this agreement Bulgaria continued to evict Turks so that in November 1951 Turkey again closed its border. According to the Turkish authorities, Bulgaria had forged Turkish entry visas in order to rid itself of as many Turks as possible. However, some 155,000 left Bulgaria for Turkey in this period.

In 1968 a further agreement was reached which allowed the departure of close relatives of those who had left in the period 1944-1951. This agreement expired on November 30, 1978. The last official Bulgarian figure for those who emigrated under this agreement was 52,392 up to August 1977; however Turkish sources state that some 130,000 left in total in this period. Following the expiry of this agreement all emigration except for a few individual cases was stopped and during the assimilation campaign of 1984-85, the authorities

denied the existence of ethnic Turks in Bulgaria claiming that the Turks were in fact descendants of Slav Bulgarians forcibly islamicized under the period of Ottoman rule, and as such there was no need for any further emigration agreements. Continuing opposition against this policy from the ethnic Turkish population and changes in the strict regulations concerning freedom of movement of Bulgarian citizens to other countries resulted in a drastic change of policy in May 1989 with over 300,000 Turks emigrating to Turkey by late August 1989 alone.

Official policies

After the end of World War II, the Bulgarian Communist Party (BCP) took power in Bulgaria and has retained control over the country till the present day. In line with Marxist-Leninist theory, the first Constitution of the People's Republic of Bulgaria, adopted on December 4, 1947, contained provision for minority groups. For example, Article 71 stated that although the study of Bulgarian was obligatory in schools, "National minorities have a right to be educated in their vernacular, and to develop their vernacular, and to develop their national culture". A Turkish language department at Sofia University was established as well as a number of Turkish language publications and schooling in Turkish.

Yet Turkish language schools were later merged with Bulgarian schools and by the early 1970s the teaching of Turkish in Bulgarian schools had ceased. The Department of Turkish at Sofia University which reportedly attracted large numbers of students, of whom 70% were estimated to be ethnic Turks, stopped admitting students. In 1974 the whole department was shut down and replaced by a department for Arabic studies with a new staff and only a few students — mostly apparently children of diplomatic staff stationed in Arab countries. If the aim of this was to prevent the formation of a Turkish intelligentsia which might lead a movement in the future for minority rights this may have been counter-productive as ethnic Turks were forced to pursue other subjects which had better job prospects.

After 1951 the Bulgarian government and BCP made attempts to integrate Turks into the state and party apparatus and large numbers were admitted into the BCP. However, there was constant criticism in official publications about their lack of party discipline and socialist consciousness. In 1971, the BCP programme which is still in force, stated that "the citizens of our country of different national origins will come ever closer together". By the mid-1970s the use of the term "unified Bulgarian socialist nation" became common parlance in official publications and speeches. In a speech of March 1985, Stanko Todorov, the then Chairman of the National Assembly, categorically stated that Bulgaria was a "one-nation state" and that in the "Bulgarian nation there are no parts of any other peoples and nations".

Ethnic Turks are reportedly unable to join the police force or make their career in the army and ethnic Turk conscripts serve in unarmed units engaged in national construction, for example building work after a couple of weeks rudimentary training with substitute weapons. The inference is that the Bulgarian authorities do not trust the ethnic Turks enough to train them properly in the army.

Both the Pomaks (islamicized Slavs) and the ethnic Turks (with the exception of the Gagauz, estimated to number a few thousand, who profess the Eastern Orthodox Christian faith and live near Varna in the north) are Muslim. As religion was until this century more important than language in differentiating between different groups the Pomaks tended to feel greater affinity with the Turks than with Christian Bulgarians. Religious observance is higher among ethnic Turks than among Slav Bulgarians. Adherence to the Islamic faith was and is seen by the authorities as being a key factor inhibiting loyalty to the communist government and there have been many official attacks against the penetration of Islamic influence into the country and against Islamic religious customs like fasting during the month of Ramadan and the circumcision of male infants.

Population growth

The growth rate of the Bulgarian population has been consistently decreasing in recent years. In 1980 the natural growth rate — that is the rate measured by the difference between the number of births and the number of deaths — was 3.6 per 1000, the lowest since records began. In 1981 it dropped to 2.8, in 1982 it dropped again to 2.7 and in 1984 it was again down to 2.4. There have been a number of articles on this decline in the official press in recent years. The growth rates for the minorities — especially the ethnic Turks, the Pomaks, and the Gypsies — has been considerably higher than that for the majority of the population. Additionally there has been a continuous drift from rural areas to towns and cities although this

drift is not so marked for the minorities. Due to their high birth rate, the Turks are estimated to be some 15-20% of the work force and were, before the mass emigration of May-June 1989, becoming increasingly dominant in the important tobacco growing areas in the south and the wheat growing areas in the north-east. The authorities have admitted that the mass emigration of 1989 has caused considerable economic upheaval.

Assimilation policies

Ethnic Turks and Pomaks have often deliberately or otherwise been confused with each other and ethnic Turks were in many cases subjected to the same pressures as the Pomaks (who were forcibly assimilated in the 1970s), especially where they inhabited the same village communities, to induce them to exchange their Muslim names for Bulgarian ones and, in effect, to renounce their religion and ethnic identity. This confusion between ethnic Turks and Pomaks has been deliberately used by the Bulgarian authorities since the name-changing campaign of 1984/5.

In late 1984 and early 1985 the Bulgarian authorities, in line with the declared policy of making Bulgaria a "unified socialist nation", conducted a countrywide campaign to forcibly assimilate the entire Turkish minority. Tanks and troops surrounded Turkish villages and the inhabitants were forced, often literally at gunpoint, to change their names from Turkish/Islamic ones to those deemed more "Bulgarian" — e.g. Emine Ibrahimova became Elizaveta Ignatova. The speaking of Turkish was banned on pain of a fine or worse, many mosques were shut and Islamic practices like circumcision of male children were proscribed on pain of prison sentences both for the parents and those performing the operation. There were large scale demonstrations against this policy by ethnic Turks, especially in the south of the country where the campaign began and the authorities responded with force. Hundreds were arrested and imprisoned and many killed during the campaign. Since then the authorities have denied the existence of the minority claiming instead that they are descendants of Bulgarians forcibly islamicized under the Ottomans (i.e. Pomaks) who have "requested" new names as part of a "voluntary" and "spontaneous" "rebirth" process.

The events of 1989

Following the brutal repression during the name-changing campaign of 1984-5 the situation was one of small scale sporadic protest arising out of a largely passive albeit sullen acceptance of the status quo by the ethnic Turkish population. This radically changed in early 1989 with the mass participation in various unofficial protest groups and large-scale protest action on a country-wide basis.

Mass protest began again in May 1989 with hunger strikes by ethnic Turks in Silistra, Shumen and Razgrad and some other villages in the north-east. The numbers on hunger-strike rose from 30 to approximately 200 by mid-May to over 1,000 by mid-June, and there were corresponding peaceful demonstrations in support by hundreds of ethnic Turks, mostly women and children, in Silistra and Shumen on May 14-15. More hunger-strikers publicized their actions via foreign radio stations and mass demonstrations occurred in late May throughout the north-east and in the south of the country where ethnic Turks predominate. The authorities responded with force and many (reportedly the number was as high as 60) demonstrators were killed. Most deaths were from gunshot wounds after troops opened fire on protesting crowds or some from injuries received from beatings which were widespread and indiscriminate throughout all ethnic Turkish regions in the north-east and south. Following the mass demonstrations involving thousands of participants, most affected areas were quickly put under martial law with troops and tanks and fire-engines (water-cannon was widely used as crowd control) installed. In the southern regions, especially in Dzhebel, the authorities began widespread beatings, going from house to house and indiscriminately beating the inhabitants. Similarly those caught in the streets faced arbitrary beatings.

On May 23, 1989, the authorities issued a statement admitting that demonstrations had occurred but claimed that they were caused by misapprehension about the soon-to-be-introduced new passport law, and incitement from foreign radio stations and "extremists". Three people were admitted to have died but the authorities maintained that one had died from heart-failure while the other two had died from ricocheting bullets fired as warning shots. On 15 June in a statement to the Ambassadors of countries participating in the CSCE process at the conference held in Paris, Deputy Foreign Minister Ivan Ganev gave a detailed list of demonstrations and "disorders" which had taken place in Bulgaria between May 20-27 which had resulted in, he said, seven deaths and 28 people wounded. He denied that the demonstrations were peaceful and that anybody had been expelled from Bulgaria. He extensively blamed the activities of the Turkish secret services in fomenting trouble among "Bulgarian Muslims" — i.e. ethnic Turks.

Mass expulsions and emigration in 1989

In tandem with the policy of attempted intimidation through force the authorities embarked on a policy of expelling activists from Bulgaria. All the initial Turkish leaders of the mass protests were expelled by early June and the expulsions soon grew into a flood. Some 500 had been expelled by June 7 but the number had risen to 14,000 by June 14 and there were thousands arriving each day. By early July the figure had exceeded 100,000 with official indications of 250,000 more to come — 250,000 had arrived by early August 1989. The sheer size of the numbers involved indicate that while the first to be expelled were activists, many of whom did not want to leave but left due to the threat of imprisonment or other threats to them or their families, the authorities apparently seem to be allowing large numbers to emigrate. Many ethnic Turks have decided that the policy of forced assimilation and the attendant official repression is such that there is no future for them in Bulgaria and despite having to give up, in many cases, a settled life of financial security have opted for a new life in Turkey. Many, especially those expelled in or before May and early June were given only a few hours notice and were not allowed to take more than a small bag and no money. All were obliged to leave houses and other valuables behind although some were informed by the authorities that if they returned within five years they could reclaim their property. Again, the most recent refugees have been able to leave with, in some cases more possessions, (cars, water-heaters etc) although the valuables left behind remain considerable. By late August over 300,000 had left and the Turkish authorities closed the border. There were also, at the time of writing, reports of Bulgarian security forces entering ethnic Turkish areas in Bulgaria with the aim of stemming the flood of refugees.

(See also *Pomaks of Bulgaria; Turks of Western Thrace; Yugoslavia*)

Turks of Western Thrace

Location: **Western Thrace in Greece**
Population: **100,000-120,000** (est.)
% of population: **1%-2%**
Religion: **Muslim**
Language: **Turkish**

The Turks of Western Thrace are a remnant from the Ottoman empire which ruled the area until its liberation in the early part of the twentieth century. Assessing the number of Turks, and other minorities, in Greece is problematic. The census of 1928 recorded 191,000 Turks while the 1951 census recorded 180,000 Turks of whom 92,000 were Muslims and 87,000 were Orthodox.

While some Turks live on the Greek islands neighbouring Turkey, most live in Western Thrace. The Pomaks, Muslim Slavs and a small number of Muslim Greeks, tend to live also in Western Thrace in villages in the southern Rhodope and due to the official reticence to give figures for ethnic minorities, only for religious ones, it is hard to separate them from the Turks; however the villages near the Bulgarian border in all three provinces of Western Thrace are predominantly Pomak. Many Pomaks also live in Komotini and Xanthi and some also live in Dhidhimotikhon. Official Greek sources tend to claim that the Turks are Pomaks or Muslim Greeks while conversely the Turks claim the Pomaks as Turks. Estimates from the Information Office at the Greek embassy in London based on the 1981 census figures give a total of 110,000 people belonging to religious minorities of whom some 60,000 are Turkish-speaking Muslims; 30,000 Pomaks; and 20,000 Athingani (descendants of Christian heretics expelled from Asia Minor during Byzantine rule) or Gypsies. However, Turkish-Muslim sources from Western Thrace claim a total of 100-120,000 Turkish-speaking Muslims in Western Thrace and most observers estimate between 100,000 and 120,000 Muslims out of a total of some 360,000 in Western Thrace recorded in the census of 1971. Of the other minorities there are small populations of Gagauz, Christian Turkish-speaking people, for example around the city of Alexandroupolis, and Sarakatsani, Greek-speaking transhumants, especially in the village of Palladion.

Turkey is Greece's traditional enemy, despite being a NATO pact partner, and, similarly to Bulgaria, Greece fears Turkish expansion. Much of Western Thrace is a restricted area due to reasons of national security. These areas are the border areas with Bulgaria where many Turks and Pomaks live and in these militarized areas large portions of land has been expropriated from Pomaks and Turks and the inhabitants of these areas are severely restricted in their freedom of movement to a 30 kilometre radius of their residence. Decree 1366/1938 which forbids foreign nationals to buy land near border areas is still operational and it is claimed that this decree is used against ethnic Turks and Pomaks even though they are Greek citizens.

In the exchange of populations following the Greco-Turkish war of 1920-22 some 60,000 Greek refugees from Asia Minor were allowed, in contravention to the Treaty of Lausanne, to settle in Western Thrace and under steady administrative and economic pressure from the Greek authorities a gradual migration of Muslims to Turkey ensued; this is particularly noticeable in the previously Muslim province of Ebros where the population now is Greek Orthodox. The Second World War and the civil war saw a rise in the number of such emigrés and some 20,000 left for Turkey in the period 1939-51 while emigration continues to the present day.

The deterioration of relations with Turkey over the developing situation in Cyprus saw a corresponding deterioration of the situation of the Turkish minority in Western Thrace with increased pressure to induce emigration. Under the military dictatorship of 1967-74 the situation worsened. Members of the Turkish-minority community boards, elected under provision of Decree 2345/1920, were dismissed and replaced by non-elected people, appointed by government agencies, prepared to act contrary to the interests of the Muslim community. In this period Greeks, including many Sarakatsani, were given financial inducement to move into Western Thrace to dilute the Muslim Turkish-speaking population.

Despite the return to democracy in 1974 the trend continued, aided by Greek reaction to the Turkish invasion of Cyprus. There has been no return to the former democratic practices as stipulated in Decree 2345/1920 and when the Mufti of Komotini died on July 2, 1985 he was replaced by a government appointee. When the new Mufti resigned almost immediately due to community protests he was replaced six months later by another appointee without consultation. Since 1977 all the place-names in Komotini were changed from Turkish forms to Greek forms and henceforth it was forbidden to use the old names for official purposes, apparently on pain of fine or even imprisonment. Mention of the Turkish name in parenthesis after the Greek names is also forbidden.

Over a long period there have been growing complaints by Muslims, Turks and Pomaks, that they, unlike Greek Orthodox Christians, cannot buy real estate, except for a few select people who co-operate with the authorities, neither can they negotiate loans or credits; building construction for Turkish houses has been withheld for many years resulting in the Turks being forced to live in backward conditions; neither is permission to build or restore mosques forthcoming; Muslims have been particularly affected by expropriation of land for public use without adequate compensation, and the re-allocation of land in Western Thrace which began in 1967 has resulted in their receiving inferior land in exchange; Muslims are virtually excluded from the state bureaucracy and hindered in business matters by difficulties in obtaining business and driving licences and even subject to punitive levies; despite constitutional guarantees, Turks who leave Greece, even for a temporary period, have been denied re-entry under Article 19 of the Greek Nationality Law which states "A person who is of foreign origin leaving Greek territories without the intention of returning may be deprived of Greek citizenship", and obtaining normal five-year passports is difficult for many Turks. Additionally it is alleged that the authorities are attempting to disperse the minority by moving unemployed Turks and Pomaks to other areas, where once registered they are unable to return to Western Thrace, and are pressured under pain of dismissal to change their names to Greek ones.

In the vital field of education the Greek authorities have steadily increased teaching in Greek at the expense of Turkish. From the 1960s onwards religious teachers from the Arab world have progressively been reduced while the employment of teachers from Turkey to Turkish schools in Western Thrace has been stopped. Since 1968 only graduates from a special academy in Thessaloniki can be qualified to teach in Turkish schools. This academy takes much of its intake from Greek secondary schools and,

its critics claim, relies on an outdated religious curriculum deliberately to create an incompetent Hellenized education system in Western Thrace isolated from the mainstream of modern Turkish culture.

The situation has deteriorated with the authorities introducing an entrance exam for the two Turkish minority schools in Komotini and Xanthi — there are some 300 Turkish primary schools — and a directorate from the government in March 1981 stipulating that graduate examinations from Turkish secondary and high schools have to be in Greek. The implementation of this law in 1985 with in some cases merely a few months' notice was extremely hard on the students. The result of these measures has been a dramatic decline in secondary school students in Turkish schools from 227 in Xanthi and 305 in Komotini in 1983–4, to 85 and 42 respectively in 1986–7. Greek history books portray Turks in crude stereotypes and while Turkish pupils are allowed some books from Turkey there have been inexplicable delays resulting in long outdated textbooks having to be used.

The authorities have also prohibited the use of the adjective "Turkish" in titles denoting associations etc., and the Turkish Teachers Association in Western Thrace was closed by order of Komotini court on March 20, 1986, a decision upheld by the Athens High Court on July 28, 1986.

Over a long period there have been many individual complaints by ethnic Turks at the deteriorating position of the minority in Western Thrace. Such protests are apparently gathering force. In the summer of 1988 there was a large-scale demonstration by Turks in Komotini which was followed by two bomb explosions — one in the central mosque and one in a cemetery of a neighbourhood mosque. Nobody was injured in these attacks which Turks see as an act of provocation by the Greeks against the Turkish minority. Additionally there have been a number of appeals by Turks in Western Thrace to outside bodies like the UN and Council of Europe. On June 18, 1989 Sadik Ahmet, who had been arrested in August 1988 and sentenced to two and a half years' imprisonment after he had petitioned the Council of Europe detailing many of the complaints listed above, stood for Parliament as an independent Turkish candidate and was elected with some 32% of the vote illustrating the support for him among the Turkish population.

(See also *Turks of Bulgaria*)

Vlachs

Alternative names: **Aromani, Cincari, Karakachani, Koutsovlachs**
Location: **Greece, Yugoslavia, Albania and Bulgaria**
Population: **Not possible to estimate reliably**
Religion: **Eastern Orthodox Christian**
Language: **Aromanian**

The Vlachs are a latin-speaking people — they speak a distinctive form of Romanian — living south of Danube in Albania, Bulgaria, Yugoslavia (predominantly in Serbia and Vardar Macedonia) and primarily in Greece. They are an historically old people who ante-date the more modern arrivals to the Balkan Peninsula like the Slavs and Turks. Perhaps because of this they, unlike other minorities, do not appear to live in particularly concentrated areas, with the exception of the "Vlach capital" Aminciu (Metsovon) in the Pindus mountains at the headlands of the five rivers of the Pindus range in Greece.

Assessing their numbers is difficult and compounded by a lack of separatist current among Vlachs which has resulted in their apparent peaceful assimilation into majority ethnic groups. In this the shared religious faith of Eastern Orthodoxy has been an important factor. The Vlachs in Yugoslavia live in Serbia and especially Macedonia and around Bitola, Resen and Krusevo. There are Vlach societies in Bitola and Skopje and these societies have pointed to the lack of language rights for Vlachs in schools and in religious matters — e.g. the appeal in February 1988 by the *Pitu Guli* Cultural Association in Skopje to the Foreign Ministers of Yugoslavia, Albania, Bulgaria, Greece, Romania and Turkey who were meeting in Belgrade — but with little apparent effect. Successive censuses has shown a gradual decline in their numbers.

In Bulgaria the Vlachs have been subjected to the same "Bulgarization" process as the country's other minorities (excepting the small number of Jews and Armenians) and it appears that the assimilatory pressures are such that the language will soon die out. There is very little information available on the situation of Vlachs in Albania.

Vlachs in Greece

In Greece where the largest community lives, the censuses of 1935 and 1951 recorded 19,703 and 39,855 Vlachs respectively although the classification as Greek of all those who use Greek as "language of daily use" has tended to

greatly underestimate the number of minorities like the Vlachs who tend to be hellenophile and are almost entirely Orthodox Christian by religion (hence Greek Orthodox). The number of Vlachs in subsequent censuses has not been recorded. Some emigré Vlach sources claim an exaggerated figure of 600,000 in Greece.

Vlachs tend to live in mountainous regions especially in the Pindus mountains. The area north-west of Polikastrion has a population of Meglen Vlachs who speak a Slav language as their mother-tongue. The Vlachs are similar to the Sarakatsani — Greek-speaking transhumant shepherds — but less mobile and are seasonally nomadic as shepherds in the mountains while pursuing other fields of employment like medicine, law, taxi-driving etc.

Traditionally the Vlachs have held an important position in inland Greece and under Ottoman domination they, due to their traditional occupations of shepherding and transport of goods by caravan, tended to control overland trade in the Greek provinces of the Ottoman empire while the Greeks controlled the sea trade. Many Vlachs identified themselves with Greeks, due to having received Greek education in Greek schools, and took a leading role in the struggle for Greek independence. However some, influenced by the Romanian national movement and the close similarities between their languages, attempted to have church services and schooling in their vernacular — a move which was strongly resisted by the Greek Orthodox hierarchy. This latter strand of Vlach distinctness from Greeks was soon patronized by the new Romanian state leading to the creation of Romanian churches and schools in Macedonia, which was then still part of the Ottoman empire, funded by the Romanian state. In these schools children were taught Aromanian in the lower grades and then later Romanian, as it was a recognized literary language. By 1912 the Romanian state was subsidizing over 30 such schools in Macedonia. The savage internecine warfare in Macedonia from the 1890s to 1914 by rival armed bands of Serbs, Bulgarians and Greeks as the new national states competed for the decaying Ottoman empire was especially hard on the Vlachs who for the most part could not defend themselves well and there were massacres of Vlachs with churches and villages burnt by Greek nationalists. This bleak period finished after the settlement of the Balkan Wars and even in 1913 the Greek Prime Minister Venizelos signed an agreement with the Romanians to officially allow Romanian schools for Vlachs in the Greek state. The Vlach nationalist movement continued under Romanian tutelage but never recovered from the violence late in the nineteenth century.

The rise of fascism in Italy and Romania led to attempts, especially during the Italian occupation of parts of Greece during the Second World War, to harness the Vlachs to the fascist cause and an autonomous "Principality of the Pindus" was even declared by an extremist named Alcibiades Diamandi of Samarina consisting of Epirus, Macedonia and all of Thessaly with Diamandi as Prince and a compatriot as head of the "Roman Legion" — an army of Vlach fascists. After the end of World War II the new Romanian state chose not to carry on financing the schools and churches in Greece.

The majority of Vlachs who saw themselves as distinct from Greeks tended to emigrate with the result that separatist feeling is much stronger in the diaspora than in the homeland. There is no apparent nationalist or separatist feeling among the Vlachs of Greece despite the occasional hostility towards them from the more nationalistic sections of Greek society usually manifested in objecting to the use of the Vlach language — it is frequently used in public places in Metsovon and elsewhere. Such pressure has in the past tended to intimidate Vlachs living in the cities in mixed communities from speaking their own language and under the dictatorship of the Colonels from 1967 to 1974 Vlachs were even threatened with imprisonment for speaking Aromanian. However since the 1980s the

situation has improved as the Greek government apparently recognizes that the Vlachs, unlike the Turks or Macedonians constitute no threat, real or potential, to the Greek state and many "Vlach Cultural Societies" have come into existence and since 1984 there has been a huge annual festival for all Vlach villages of Greece. Despite this improvement the Greeks are still very wary of acknowledging any minorities and hold to the position that the Vlachs are Greeks who speak an unusual dialect. When Vlach activists in Germany contacted the European Community's Bureau of Lesser Known Languages which resulted in the European Community enquiring of Greece the position of the Vlachs there was a strong reaction within Greece, involving leading Vlachs like Evangelos Averoff, against this outside intervention and a corresponding criticism of the burgeoning local cultural efforts. This has led to a severe limitation of activities along previous lines by Vlachs in Greece.

Among the large numbers of Vlachs who emigrated during the course of the century there is some pro-Romanian feeling (due to linguistic and cultural similarities) and conversely some anti-Greek or anti-Yugoslav feeling. These emigrés have formed Vlach associations in a number of places, France, USA, West Germany etc, and have held two international Vlach congresses in West Germany in September 1985 in Mannheim, and in August 1988 in Freiburg. A central question at these conferences has been the lack of a defined Vlach language (there is however a Vlach-Romanian dictionary) and Vlachs from Greece pressed for the use of the Greek alphabet so as not to antagonize the Greek authorities. However the other participants preferred the more obvious choice of the Latin alphabet — the antagonism between "Panhellenes" and "Superromani", often becoming a struggle between Vlachs in Greece and those in the diaspora, is a constant factor in Vlach issues.

Yugoslavia

Location: **south-eastern Europe**
Population: **22.4 million (1981)**
% of population: **Serbs 36.3%, Croats 20%, Slovenes 8%, Muslims 9%, Montenegrins 2.6%, Macedonians 6%, Albanians 7.7%, and 17 other recognized ethnic minorities**
Religion: **various**
Language: **various**

Of all the countries in Europe, the Socialist Federal Republic of Yugoslavia is the least homogeneous. It is a multi-national federation with a three-tier system of national rights as follows: (i) the "Nations of Yugoslavia", each with a national home based in one of the republics — this an important point in denying the Albanians republican status in Kosovo as their national home is outside Yugoslavia (see below). There are six officially recognized "Nations of Yugoslavia": Croats, Macedonians, Montenegrins, Muslims (an ethnic category recognized as a nation since the 1971 census), Serbs and Slovenes; (ii) the "Nationalities of Yugoslavia" which are legally allowed a variety of language and cultural rights. There are 18 ethnic minorities — the largest being the Albanians and the Hungarians concentrated in Kosovo and the Vojvodina respectively — of which 10 are officially recognized as "Nationalities of Yugoslavia": Albanians, Bulgarians, Czechs, Gypsies, Italians, Hungarians, Romanians, Ruthenians, Slovaks and Turks; and (iii) "other Nationalities and Ethnic Groups", which are the remaining ethnic groups: Austrians, Greeks, Jews, Germans, Poles, Russians, Ukrainians, Vlachs and others including those who classify themselves as "Yugoslavs".

History

Yugoslavia came into existence in December 1918 as the Kingdom of Serbs, Croats and Slovenes at the end of World War I. It united the former Austro-Hungarian territories of Slovenia, Croatia-Slavonia, the Vojvodina, Dalmatia and Bosnia-Hercegovina, and the kingdoms of Montenegro and Serbia (including territories corresponding approximately to present-day Macedonia and Kosovo).

In 1941, during World War I, Yugoslavia was invaded by the Axis powers. The following years saw fierce resistance to the occupying forces accompanied by bitter civil war. At the end of the war, in which military and political ascendancy had been gained by the communist-led resistance movement (the Partisans) under Marshal Tito, the king was deposed and the

Federal People's Republic of Yugoslavia was proclaimed in January 1946.

The Socialist Federal Republic of Yugoslavia (SFRJ), as the country was renamed in 1963, is a federal state comprising six constituent republics: Bosnia-Hercegovina (of which the capital is Sarajevo); Croatia (Zagreb); Macedonia (Skopje); Montenegro (Titograd); Slovenia (Ljubljana) and Serbia (Belgrade) — which incorporates the two "autonomous provinces" of the Vojvodina (Novi Sad) and Kosovo (Pristina). The federal capital is Belgrade. Succeeding constitutions have been carefully worded so that while the right "to self-determination, including the right to secession" of each of the "Nations of Yugoslavia", is mentioned, it is asserted that these nations "on the basis of their will freely expressed" during World War II have united. This means that constitutionally the nations have made a binding decision and the right of secession no longer applies.

Religion and the state are separate under the constitution; the main Christian denominations are the Serbian and Macedonian Orthodox Churches with an estimated eight million adherents, and the Roman Catholic Church with some six million adherents, mainly Croats and Slovenes. There is also a large Muslim community, believed to number about four million, including ethnic Slavs in Bosnia-Hercegovina, most Albanians and the Turkish minority. There are over 30 other, often very small, religious communities, mostly Protestant.

Until very recently the League of Communists of Yugoslavia (SKJ) was the sole authorized political party. It controlled political life through its domination of key "socio-political organizations" especially the Socialist Alliance of Working People of Yugoslavia (SSRNJ). However in the last year or so the beginnings of political pluralism have become evident especially in Slovenia, where a more liberal climate prevails, with non-communist groups entering the SSRNJ, and the issue is widely discussed elsewhere. Despite this the SKJ remains at the present the dominant political force in the country. Since the death of President Tito (who was

President of the Republic, President of the SKJ and Commander-in-Chief of the Armed Forces), the SKJ has been headed by a 23-member collective leadership, the Presidium of the Central Committee, the presidency of which rotates annually. The functions of the head of state are exercised by a nine-member collegial body, the Presidency of the SFRJ, comprising representatives of each republic and autonomous province and *ex officio* the president of the SKJ Presidium. The presidency of this body rotates annually also. In all the main legislative bodies as in other federal bodies the principle of equal representation of all republics and proportional representation of provinces prevails. Thus the Yugoslav federation is based on the principle of national equality not ethnic proportionality and each republic practises internally a policy of national quotas — for example the current head of the Croatian party is a Serb. Each republic and autonomous province, in addition to its own assembly, has its own governmental apparatus and judiciary.

The Serbs

The largest single Yugoslav national group, although still a minority, are the Serbs. According to the 1981 census there were 8,140,507 Serbs in Yugoslavia or 36.3% of the total population of 22,427,585. Serbs live mainly in the republic of Serbia, where they make up 85.4% of the population without taking into consideration the autonomous provinces of Kosovo and Vojvodina where they constituted 13.2% and 54.4% respectively in 1981, and also in the republic of Bosnia-Hercegovina where they constituted 32% of the population. Serbs settled in the Balkan Peninsula in the seventh century. By the twelfth century the Serbs established their own state which reached the height of its power in the fourteenth century based in the present-day territory of Kosovo which, although now populated overwhelmingly by Albanians, remains emotionally part of the Serbian heartland.

From the mid-fifteenth century until the early 1800s Serbia was occupied by the Ottoman Turks and large numbers of Serbs migrated northwards to the Vojvodina, then part of the Kingdom of Hungary in the Hapsburg empire, to escape Ottoman domination. The Vojvodina was a mosaic of 10 ethnic groups due to the desire of the Hapsburg Empire to settle different national groups there to create a bulwark against the Ottomans. After a series of bloody uprisings, Serbia was granted autonomy

within the Ottoman empire in 1815 and in 1878 it became formally independent. After the Balkan Wars of 1912-3, Serbia expanded its territory. Following the assassination of Austrian Archduke Franz Ferdinand in Sarajevo in June 1914, Serbia defied an Austrian ultimatum and was attacked by the central powers, triggering off World War I. After great loss of life Serbia emerged as one of the victors when the new map of Europe was drawn up after the war.

Their experience of independence and heritage as well as being the largest group allowed the Serbs to dominate the new kingdom which became known as Yugoslavia. This led to considerable tension, especially with the Croats and after World War II there was a constant effort to limit Serbian dominance of the new state especially after the fall in 1966 of Alexander Rankovic, a Serb, vice-president of Yugoslavia and chief of the powerful state security police, leading eventually to the constitution of 1974 which truly made Yugoslavia a federation and, according to some observers, even a confederation.

However, in the past two years, especially as a result of the situation regarding the Albanians in Kosovo [see below] there has been a Serbian backlash against what many Serbs see as discriminatory measures in the Yugoslav federation which adversely affect them, most notably the powers granted to the autonomous provinces under the 1974 constitution despite their ostensibly being part of the Serbian Republic. Also many Serbs regard the distinction between Serbs and Montenegrins as artificial. The leadership of the League of Communists of Serbia, appealing to this resurgent national sentiment, has committed itself to reasserting Serbian control over the autonomous provinces and also Montenegro and in 1988 there were mass demonstrations and rallies throughout Serbia and in certain other parts of the country in support of these aims. A result of this pressure has been the unprecedented downfall of party leaderships opposed to Serbian aspirations in the autonomous provinces and in the republic of Montenegro.

The Croats

The Croats are the second largest national grouping in Yugoslavia. In 1981 they numbered 4,428,043 or just under 20% of the population. Croats live mainly in Croatia and Bosnia-Hercegovina. They make up 70% of the population of the republic of Croatia — Serbs make up 11% and "Yugoslavs" [see below] make up some 8%. Croats also make up just over 18% of the population of Bosnia–Hercegovina. Like the Serbs, the Croats settled in present-day Yugoslavia in the seventh century but an independent Croat state lasted only until 1102. From then onwards Croatia belonged first to the Kingdom of Hungary and then to the Hapsburg Empire. The Croats are overwhelmingly Catholic and use the Latin alphabet, as opposed to the Serbs who are Orthodox and who use cyrillic script. Both speak Serbo-Croat although some claim that Croatian is a separate language to Serbian. As mentioned above relations between Serbs and Croats were strained in the post-1918 state and the *Ustasha*, a Croatian separatist and pro-fascist underground movement was founded in the early 1930s. During World War II, an "Independent State of Croatia" (incorporating Bosnia-Hercegovina) was established under Axis protection. It was administered by the *Ustasha*, who, under Ante Pavelic, persecuted and killed Jews, Serbs, Romanies and Croatian opponents of the regime. Memories of this infamous period live on, compounded by reprisals against Croats by Serb partisan units.

Croatia, which includes most of the Dalmatian coast, the main tourist attraction, is responsible for some 50% of the country's foreign trade and is the major foreign currency earner. This has been a source of constant tension with Croats resenting having to share this revenue with the other republics and a feeling that Croats are once more the victims of Serb domination. Some small groups, especially in the large Croat diaspora (see below) call for an independent Croatia. Croatian nationalism has always been viewed with official hostility, however the late 1960s saw the growth of an increasingly assertive nationalism in Croatia which was supported by both members and non-members of the Croatian League of Communists. This "mass movement", as it came to be called, was abruptly curbed in December 1971 by the arrest of its leading members and a purge of the Croatian League of Communists which in turn was followed by a purge of reformers in the Serbian party apparatus as the government tried to avoid the stigma of vendetta against any single national group as well as reaffirming control.

The Slovenes

The Slovenes account for just under 8% of the population and live predominantly in the republic of Slovenia in the north-west of the country. Slovenia is the most homogenous of the republics with Slovenes accounting for some 90%

of the population. Slovenia, along with Croatia belonged to the Hapsburg Empire until 1918 and culturally the Slovenes look more to Western Europe than do their compatriots. The Slovene language, although Slavic, differs considerably from Serbo-Croat and the Catholic Church is firmly entrenched. Slovenia is the most developed part of the country and has the highest *per capita* income. The economic gap between Slovenia and the more backward southern regions, especially Kosovo, Macedonia and Montenegro, continues to expand and Slovenia has come to rely on migrant labour from the poorer Yugoslav republics which in recent years has on occasions resulted in ethnic tension between Slovenes and their "guest-workers". While the Yugoslav federation has proved a convenient market for Slovenian goods there is a current of feeling in Slovenia which resents Slovenia paying a large amount into the federal budget to help develop the poorer southern regions. Slovenia has for many years been by far the most liberal of the republics with a good human rights record which has contrasted greatly with other areas. The resurgent Serbian nationalism led by Slobodan Milosevic (see above) and the continuing economic and political crisis which grips the country have in the past year fuelled separatist tendencies. On September 27, 1989, the Slovene Assembly overwhelmingly endorsed amendments to the Republic's Constitution which explicitly allows the Republic to secede.

The Muslims

The term Muslim in Yugoslavia is used to describe descendants of Slavs who converted to Islam under the period of Ottoman rule. Since 1971 they have been officially recognized as a distinct "Yugoslav Nation" who make up about 9% of the population, mostly in Bosnia-Hercegovina where they are the largest single group constituting 39% of the population. They also constitute some 13.4% of Montenegro's small population.

Although the overwhelming majority of Muslims speak Serbo-Croat there are some 40,000 or so Macedonian-speaking Muslims, often called Pomaks. These are descendants of Macedonians as opposed to Serbs or Croats who converted during the Ottoman period and their inclusion in the term is something of an anomaly (see below). It should be stressed that the term "Muslim" does not refer to the Albanian, largely Muslim, or Turkish, wholly Muslim, minorities.

The area of Bosnia-Hercegovina was the scene of many of the worst atrocities committed during the civil war in World War II and the ethnic mix of Orthodox Serbs, Catholic Croats and Muslim Slavs has historically been an explosive one with both Serbia and Croatia claiming the territory for their own. In addition immediately after the war an organization called "Young Muslims" was set up ostensibly to protect Muslims in Bosnia from alleged ill-treatment by the communist partisans. The Yugoslav authorities outlawed this group which they described as a terrorist one. In a way the republic of Bosnia-Hercegovina, which was created specifically to find some form of *modus vivendi* for the three main groups, well portrays the ethnic tangle in Yugoslavia as it is here that the three main religions meet head on. In the Balkans religion has historically been one of the main differentiators between different peoples. In the light of this and the tendency for both Serbs and Croats to claim the Muslim Slavs of Bosnia as their own, the separate "Muslim" category was introduced. The ethnic tangle and competing rivalries has resulted in Bosnia being somewhat notorious in the matter of human rights with individuals from all three ethnic groups persecuted for any manifestation of nationalism not sanctioned by the party. Despite religious freedom guaranteed under the constitution religious practice, with its close correlation with a particular national standpoint, has often been viewed with official distrust especially Roman Catholicism due to its centre of authority being outside the country. This has especially been so in Bosnia-Hercegovina and in Croatia. Also any form of Islamic fundamentalism has been severely treated as being a party to a conspiracy to make Bosnia-Hercegovina an "ethnically pure Islamic Republic".

The Montenegrins

The republic of Montenegro lies in the south of the country on the northern borders of Albania. It is extremely mountainous with a total population of only 584,310. The Montenegrins number 579,043 or some 2.6% of the population. The majority live in Montenegro where they constitute 68% of the population with the remainder largely made up of Muslims (13.4%) and Albanians (6.5%). The Montenegrins speak Serbo-Croat and are Orthodox and have been traditional allies of the Serbs with some alleging that they are in fact Serbs; a constant feature of Austro-Hungarian policy, which saw the emergent Serbian state as a rival for Bosnia in the late nineteenth century, was to prevent the independent Serbian and Montenegrin states from uniting. The area has been plagued by wars and raids and even during the Ottoman occupation parts of Montenegro were so inaccessible as to escape Ottoman control. Montenegrins have traditionally made good soldiers and their territory proved extremely suitable for the partisan struggle. A result of this is that Montenegrins have a far higher number in the army officer corps than their percentage in the population would suggest. The resurgent Serbian nationalism of the last two years has had profound effects in Montenegro with the replacement of the republic's leadership with those more in tune with the current Serbian leadership (see above).

The Macedonians

The "Macedonian Question" has historically been one of the most contentious in Europe. In 1981 there were 1,341,598 Macedonians or 6% of the population, the overwhelming majority of whom lived in the republic of Macedonia where they constituted 67% of the population — Albanians (19.8%) and Turks (4.5%) being the main minorities (see below). The Slavs of Macedonia began to settle in the area by the sixth century, and Slavs and Proto-Bulgarians, a Turkic people, combined to form the first Bulgarian state. By the end of the thirteenth century the Serbs had established hegemony over much of the Balkans and Serbian penetration into Macedonia occurred. The Ottoman Turks then invaded and the area was the last to be freed from Ottoman control in the Balkan Wars of 1912–3.

In the preceding decades it had been claimed by Serbia, Bulgaria and Greece — all of whom considered the inhabitants to belong to their respective nationalities. Additionally there was an indigenous organization, the Internal Macedonian Revolutionary Organization (IMRO), which was split between those who wanted to unite with Bulgaria and those who wanted a united independent Macedonia comprising the present-day republic and areas in Greece and Bulgaria. The overall result of all these competing rivalries in Macedonia was disastrous for the actual population, which by most accounts was most sympathetic to one of the wings of IMRO, with the peasants being subjected to repeated visits by armed gangs from the IMRO factions, Serbs, Bulgarians and Greeks as well as the Ottoman authorities until the Balkan Wars when the Ottoman empire was finally driven out of Macedonia and the whole area partitioned between Serbia, Greece and Bulgaria.

Since then the portion now in Yugoslavia —

Vardar Macedonia — has, except during the two World Wars when for a sizeable period most of it was occupied by Bulgaria — belonged firstly to Serbia and then after World War I to what became Yugoslavia. In line with Serbian claims that the Macedonians were in fact Southern Serbs, the Church was put under the control of the Serbian Patriarchate and Serbian, the official language, became compulsory both in schools and public life. This policy alienated the population and spread pro-Bulgarian feeling.

During World War II, Bulgaria, allied to Nazi Germany, occupied most of Vardar Macedonia, and although Hitler did not allow Bulgaria to formally annex the territories they occupied both in Yugoslavia and Greece, the Bulgarian government acted as if they had. Bulgarian officials were sent in, teachers were replaced by Bulgarian ones. However the overbearing attitude of many Bulgarians soon alienated the population.

The Yugoslav Communist Party's attitude to the Macedonian question underwent successive changes until during World War II when under Tito's leadership the Partisans resolved to create a Macedonian republic within a new federal Yugoslavia. This republic was seen as providing a bridge between Yugoslavia and Bulgaria which would be united in a Balkan federation which might also include Albania which was also under communist control after the war, and Greece where there was a civil war between the communists and non-communists for control. The Bulgarian leader, Georgi Dimitrov both of whose parents were from Macedonia, was receptive to Tito's plans of uniting Vardar Macedonia in Yugoslavia with Pirin Macedonia in Bulgaria but his death in July 1949 and the break between Tito and Stalin over Tito's ambitions made the Yugoslav-Bulgarian co-operation a short-lived affair. Henceforth relations between the new Macedonian republic and Bulgaria would be strained and this situation has lasted till the present.

In the new republic of Macedonia the new authorities quickly set about consolidating their position. The new nation needed a written language and initially the spoken dialect of northern Macedonia was chosen as the basis for the Macedonian language but this was deemed as too close to Serbian and the dialects of Bitola-Veles became the norm. These dialects were closer to the Bulgarian literary language but as the Bulgarian was based upon the eastern Bulgarian dialects it allowed enough differentiation for the Yugoslavs to claim that it was a language distinct from Bulgarian — a point which Bulgaria has

bitterly disputed ever since. The alphabet was accepted on May 3, 1945, the orthography on June 7, 1945 and the first primer in the new language appeared by 1946 which year also saw the founding of a Macedonian Department of the Faculty of Philosophy in Skopje. A grammar of the Macedonian Literary Language appeared in 1952 and the Institute for the Macedonian Language "Krste P. Misirkov" was founded in 1953. Since the end of World War II the new republic has used the full weight of the education system and the bureaucracy to make the new language common parlance. In addition to the new language the new republic needed a history and the new school textbooks quickly reflected this need by tracing the Macedonian nation back through history.

Religion was another important tool for the new authorities and the freeing of the Orthodox church in Yugoslav Macedonia from Serbian control with the autocephalous Macedonian Orthodox Church and the revival of the ancient archbishopric of Ohrid in 1958 was an important step along the path to nationhood — a rare occurrence of atheist state co-operation with organized religion. This move was resisted by the Serbian Orthodox Church as was the final declaration of the autocephalous status of the Macedonian Church on July 18, 1967. The Serbian Orthodox Church, along with the other Orthodox Churches, remains firm in its refusal to recognize the Macedonian Church. Relations between the Macedonian Orthodox Church and the authorities in Yugoslav Macedonia have continued to be good aided by a common front against the threat of Albanian nationalism and the attendant growth of Islam (see below).

Thus the authorities have overcome the residual pro-Bulgarian feeling among much of the population and apparently have been successful in building a distinct national consciousness based on the available differences between Macedonia and Bulgaria proper. The change from the pre-war situation of unrecognized minority status and attempted assimilation by Serbia to the current one where the Macedonians are the majority people in their own republic with considerable autonomy within Yugoslavia's federation/confederation has obvious attractions. The authorities have also been aided by the comparative lack of attraction for its population of Bulgaria, which remained within the Soviet block, in comparison to the new Yugoslavia. However the current desperate economic, political and social situation in Yugoslavia and the national question of the Albanians within Yugoslavia which threatens the new republic probably more than any of the other republics including Serbia [see below], as well as Bulgaria's continuing ambitions make the future still problematic for the Macedonian republic.

The Albanians

The largest "Nationality of Yugoslavia" is the Albanian one with just over 1.7 million or 7.7% of the total population. The Albanians, who claim descent from the ancient Illyrians, live mainly in Kosovo, where they now constitute over 85% of the population, and in compact communities in Western Macedonia bordering on Albania where they constitute some 19.8% of the population. Kosovo, which for centuries has been inhabited by a mixed population occupies a major place in the national consciousness of both the Serbs and the Albanians. It has become the focus of competing claims and ethnic conflict. For the Serbs it is the heartland of the medieval Serbian kingdom where many of the greatest monuments of the (Christian) Serbian Orthodox Church are located. For the majority ethnic Albanian population (predominately Muslim but with some Roman Catholics) it was in Kosovo that the Albanian national revival began with the founding of the League of Prizren in 1878.

Post-war Yugoslavia saw major improvements in the status of ethnic Albanians in Yugoslavia. For the first time they were recognized as a distinct national group; their language was recognized as one of Yugoslavia's official languages and Albanians gained the right to education in the vernacular. These gains were however undermined by repressive policies for which Alexander Rankovic, a Serb and head of the state security police has been held responsible. After his downfall in 1966 Serbs and Montenegrins lost their dominance in the Kosovo political and administrative apparatus and Albanian dissatisfaction was allowed to come out in the open with large-scale demonstrations in November 1968 calling for Kosovo to be granted republican status. To grant such a republic is officially seen as being merely the first stage towards the unification of Kosovo province, and other regions inhabited by ethnic Albanians especially in Macedonia, with neighbouring Albania, an aim explicitly formulated by a minority of Albanian nationalists. The constitution of 1974 compromised and made Kosovo an autonomous province within the Serbian republic with, *de facto* if not *de jure,* many of the powers of a republic within the Yugoslav federation. At the same time Kosovo experienced significant demographic changes due to the extremely high natural birth rate among the Albanians and the emigration of Serbs and Montenegrins (over 30,000 reportedly left the province between 1971 and 1981).

Though naturally rich in resources, Kosovo is economically one of the most backward regions in Yugoslavia and economic problems have exacerbated growing nationalist unrest. The setting up of an Albanian university in Pristina, the capital of Kosovo, in 1968 and the huge number of Albanian students who enrol there, in part due to the acute unemployment problem in Kosovo, helped create a large Albanian intelligentsia with little outlet in terms of job opportunities for them. This dangerous situation helped to fuel nationalist discontent on the part of the Albanians which exploded in 1981 with massive demonstrations, calling again for Kosovo to become a republic, which needed the army to restore order and in which many died — according to official sources nine or 11 people died and several hundred wounded but unofficial sources estimated far higher casualty figures and the Central Committee of the League of Communists of Serbia was reportedly told that over 300 people had died in the course of the demonstrations. Since then over 7,000 Albanians, mostly young men (students, teachers and even school children), have been arrested and imprisoned in Kosovo for nationalist activity with many receiving prison sentences of six years or more.

These events further soured ethnic relations and since 1981 Serbs and Montenegrins have continued to emigrate in large numbers complaining of physical attacks and intimidation by ethnic Albanians who are now also beginning to dominate demographically in some southern areas of Serbia proper. These reports are hard to assess. Official statistics however do not support Serb allegations of "genocide". In November 1988 due to pressure from Serbia (see above) Azem Vllasi, an ethnic Albanian and former Kosovo party leader, resigned from the Kosovo politburo. This sparked off mass demonstrations by ethnic Albanians and a general strike in Kosovo in protest at this and at the constitutional changes limiting the province's autonomy which the Serbian leadership was pushing through. In February 1989 troops were sent into Kosovo and when the changes were passed in March there were clashes between Albanian demonstrators and troops in which at least 24 people were killed and hundreds arrested and detained. Following these disturbances up to 2,000 Albanian workers were jailed for up to 60 days or fined, sacked or disciplined for taking industrial action and there has been a widespread purge of party organizations and journalists and teachers with an unknown number of school students expelled from schools.

Albanians also make up just under 20% of the population of the republic of Macedonia and there have been similar if smaller-scale nationalist manifestations by Albanians in Macedonia over the years. The authorities there have reacted with, if anything, even greater severity in terms of penal sentencing than the authorities in Kosovo. Should a proposed seventh republic comprising the Albanian dominated areas of Western Macedonia as well as Kosovo occur this would severely truncate the Macedonian republic and almost certainly revive Bulgarian (and even Greek and Serb) claims to the remaining rump. Thus the growth of Albanian nationalism in Macedonia could prove fatal not only to the territorial integrity of the republic but even to the very existence of the Macedonian nation.

As a result, despite many constitutional and educational guarantees there has been an escalation of anti-Albanian policies in Macedonia. These include: a ban on certain names deemed to be overtly nationalistic; a ban on the sale of property in the western part of the republic to prevent Albanians buying out Macedonians and creating "ethnically pure territories"; an amendment to the law on religious teaching to prohibit the attendance of organized religious instruction by young people up to the age of 15. This last measure is to counter the rise of Islam which is seen in Macedonia, as opposed to Kosovo, as a tool of Albanian nationalism with alleged pressure of assimilation being put on Muslim non-Albanians (Turks and Pomaks) by the Albanians. To counter this the authorities have also encouraged Pomaks, who are Slav Macedonian by descent, to declare themselves as such and have helped them with official organizations. A result has been a dramatic increase in the number of declared "Muslims" (Pomaks) in Macedonia from 1,248 in 1971 to 39,555 in 1981. Additionally it was reported that a package of administrative measures would be introduced to try and "stop aggressive demographic expansion" of the Albanians. However the most explosive issue in Macedonia has been the enforcing of a law on secondary school education which has resulted in the closure of classes of Albanian pupils and compelled many to attend mixed classes with instruction in Macedonian. This resulted in demonstrations by pupils in Gostivar and Kumanovo in late 1988.

Inter-marriage between Albanians and other groups especially Slavs is rare and the Albanian problem remains the most explosive single issue of the Yugoslav national question.

The Turks

The Turks, remnants from the long Ottoman occupation, numbered 101,291 in the 1981 census of which the majority, 86,691, lived in Macedonia where they constituted 4% of the population. Assessing the number of minorities like the Turks and other Islamic minorities in the republic of Macedonia is somewhat problematic. The census of 1948 gave 95,940 Turks while that of 1953 recorded 203,938 and by the next census seven years later the number was only 131,481. Immediately after World War II the Turks had been seen as suspect due to friendship between Turkey and the West and as a result many Turks declared themselves to be Albanians in the 1948 census. However by 1953, following the break by Yugoslavia with the Cominform, the Albanians were now seen as being suspect and so now many Albanians declared themselves to be Turks — of the 203,938 in the 1953 census, 32,392 gave Macedonian as their native tongue and 27,086 gave Albanian, and the number of declared Albanians fell from 179,389 in 1948 to 165,524 in 1953. The period following 1953 saw extensive emigration to Turkey of large numbers of Yugoslavia's Turkish minority — some 80,000 according to figures from Yugoslavia's statistical yearbooks or over 150,000 according to some Turkish sources. However some of these emigrants were unable to speak any Turkish and were in fact Muslim Albanians who fearing for their position in post-war communist Yugoslavia claimed to be Turks so as to take advantage of the permitted emigration.

In the 1971 census there were 108,552 Turks and by the census of 1981 their numbers had apparently dropped to 86,690. Such a decline is more surprising given the high-birth rate of the Turks in Yugoslavia which would have been expected to result in an increase of some 20,000 in the period 1971-1981 instead of a decrease of over 20,000. It appears that many who previously declared themselves to be Turks now call themselves Muslims (see above) while others now declare themselves to be Albanians or Gypsies (see *Roma in Eastern Europe* entry). The Macedonian authorities, worried at the rise of Albanian nationalism, assert that many Turks have been Albanianized under pressure.

Similar to the Albanians, the Turks, a recognized nationality of Yugoslavia, have been allowed educational and cultural rights from the outset of the post-war government. There are also television and radio programmes and a newspaper, *Birlik,* as well as various cultural organizations and similar.

The Hungarians, Slovaks, Romanians, and Ruthenians

The Hungarians, a residue from the Austro-Hungarian Empire, numbered 426,867 in 1981 and live predominantly in the Vojvodina, generally in the vicinity of the border with Hungary, where they constitute just under 19% of the population. The handling of this and other minorities in the province by the Yugoslav government since World War II has been highly creditable. Because of its diversified ethnic composition, the Vojvodina was made into an autonomous province within the Serbian republic, similarly to Kosovo (see above). Serbs make up the majority in the Vojvodina (54.5%) and the other minorities are Croats (5.4%), and the majority of Yugoslavia's small populations of Slovaks (80,334 in Yugoslavia — 69,549 in the Vojvodina), Romanians (54,955-47,289), and Ruthenians (23,286-19,305). To satisfy the various national traditions there are five official languages in the province: Serbo-Croat; Hungarian; Slovak; Romanian and Ruthenian. Hungarians have about 200 elementary schools, a daily newspaper, and the provincial radio station broadcasts regularly in Hungarian. There are few signs of Hungarian dissatisfaction. However, as noted above, in 1988 resurgent Serbian nationalism led to a downfall of the Vojvodina party leadership opposed to Serb aspirations and greater control over the province by Serbia and this may lead to dissatisfaction in the province which, unlike Kosovo, has in the past proved successful as a bridge between Yugoslavia and her neighbours.

Others including those declaring themselves as "Yugoslavs"

The situation regarding the Roma (Gypsies) and the Vlachs in Yugoslavia is covered in other entries (see *Roma* and *Vlachs*). Among the remaining minorities in Yugoslavia's ethnic mosaic there are Bulgarians (as opposed to Macedonians — see above) numbering 36,189 mostly in the republic of Serbia bordering on Bulgaria, and small numbers of Czechs (19,624) and Italians (15,132) mostly in Croatia. Since the census of 1961 there has been a separate category for those who wish to classify themselves as "Yugoslavs" as opposed to other classifications

(Serb, Croat etc). The number of people doing so has dramatically increased in the last census. In 1971 the figure fell to 273,077 from 317,124 in 1961, but in 1981 the figure was 1,219,024 or some 5.4% of the population perhaps reflecting a turning away by a significant proportion of the population from the perennial national question which has become so tense in recent years compounded by the present economic difficulties. The spread of these "Yugoslavs" however is not uniform and their numbers are significantly very small in Macedonia and Kosovo (0.2% and 0.7% respectively) where the Albanian national question is most acute, and small in Slovenia (1.3%). The biggest increases have come in Bosnia-Hercegovina (where the percentage in 1981 was 7.9%), Croatia (8.2%), Serbia proper (4.7%), and the Vojvodina (8.2%).

Yugoslav emigrés

The exact number of Yugoslav emigrés is very hard to calculate. Official figures in 1979 stated that there were 400,000 Yugoslav emigrants in Turkey, over 300,000 in Australia, a similar number in Canada, and about 200,000 in South America, although others give far higher numbers. Many have retained their national identity and cultural separateness.

The Yugoslav emigré scene is extremely complicated — in 1976 official Yugoslav sources stated that there were 230 emigré organizations hostile to the government of which 127 were Croat ones, 78 Serb, 11 Slovene, nine Albanian; six Macedonian and six Muslim. The largest emigré national group are the Croats and the largest emigré organization, the Croatian National Council (HNV), claims to represent a potential of three million Croats in the diaspora. There are also large numbers of migrant workers from all over Yugoslavia in Western Europe, especially in West Germany, although this number has declined from a high of over one million in the 1970s due to the economic situation and the rise in unemployment in Western Europe. There are a large number of emigré organizations which are overwhelmingly based on national (Serb, Croat, Albanian etc) lines.

The largest and perhaps the most consistently hostile of the emigré groups to the current authorities are the Croats although Albanian groups since the clampdown in 1981 (see above) have lately become as, if not more, hostile. There have been a number of terrorist attacks on Yugoslav representatives abroad. The HNV was founded in Toronto Canada in the early 1970s and is an umbrella organization similar to the pre-war Croatian Peasant Party with a moderate wing and more radical factions. It aims at an independent Croatia through pacific and legalistic means. The Yugoslav authorities brand it as a terrorist organization with strong links to the *Ustasha* fascist period (see above). While there are offshoots of Ustasha in the HNV, mostly in Argentina but also in FRG, the acts of terrorism in the past 20 years have been performed by smaller, more militant Croat groups in France, FRG, USA, Sweden, UK, Canada, Paraguay, Venezuela and Australia. Additionally there are claims that the Yugoslav secret service (SDS) has been responsible for some terrorist acts, especially the assassination of known Yugoslav opposition activists, Croats and Albanians, abroad.

Both Croat and the Albanian emigré groups have actively pursued attempts to set up contacts within Yugoslavia and the authorities inevitably respond harshly. In the past extreme Croat groups have attempted violent action within Yugoslavia although such actions have apparently decreased in recent years. However the continuing tension in Kosovo and the apparent failure by Albanians there to achieve republican status for Kosovo by peaceful means has led to a more aggressive stance from the emigrés.

The Albanian opposition groups tend to be either "Marxist-Leninist" in ideology often looking to Albania as a model, or "monarchist" looking to the anti-communist resistance in Albania during World War II, the *Balli Kombetar*, and the former royal family of Albania. These monarchists are especially strong in Turkey where many Muslim Albanians emigrated during the 1950s. Similarly many of the Serbian opposition emigré groups are royalists with loyalties to the pre-war Yugoslav/Serbian monarchy and the

Chetniks — the Serbian based anti-communist resistance movement in World War II. There is a community of interest between emigré Croats and emigré Albanians as both are hostile to what they deem "Great Serb chauvinism" and neither claim territory belonging to each other.

There are large Macedonian communities especially in Australia. A minority calls for a united independent Macedonia including parts of present day Bulgaria and Greece. The majority however are not at odds with the Yugoslav authorities — a reflection of the fact that while frustrated nationalism is the main driving force behind the actions of many other Yugoslav emigré groups, the Macedonians have for the first time in recent history been granted some say in their own affairs by the Yugoslav government. The setting up of the autocephalous Macedonian Church in 1967 (see above) has been especially significant with the corresponding founding of churches among the Macedonian emigré communities. There is a small "Free Slovenia" movement based in Argentina and a very small number of Montenegrins who hope for the return of the Montenegrin royalty. Montenegrins were also numerous in the ranks of "the Cominformists" — those who supported the Comintern (Soviet) line in 1948 at the time of the Tito–Stalin break — and some remain active in exile. There are also some active Muslim emigrés whose main political organization is the "Bosnia-Hercegovina Muslims Association" which calls for Yugoslavia to be a "confederation of free and independent countries". Finally there are many emigré groups which are seen as friendly by the Yugoslav authorities and have been set up under their aegis to serve both guest workers and emigrés.

(See also *Macedonians of Bulgaria; Macedonians of Greece; Roma in Eastern Europe; Vlachs*)

Further References

The Hungarians of Romania, MRG Report No. 37, 1978

Minorities in the Balkans, MRG Report No. 82, 1989

Roma: Europe's Gypsies, MRG Report No. 14, 1987

USSR

The USSR is unique among the "regions" comprehended by this directory, in that the "region" is constituted by only one State. However, the scale and complexity of the USSR, with 15 Union Republics, Autonomous Soviet Socialist Republics and Autonomous Regions, a population approaching 300 million, an
enormous geographical spread of nationalities and minority groups, makes it appropriate to consider the
whole unit separately. The scale of ethnic complexity resembles an Empire. The tendency of the structure
of the USSR is to accommodate particular nationalities/ethnic groups in an appropriate republic or region,
though these are also inhabited, almost inevitably, by various other ethnic minority groups. The Russians
undoubtedly represent the most prominent ethnic group in the USSR, though the population balance is
changing in favour of other groups, most notably non-European peoples.

While it is impossible to adopt too "reductionist" an approach to an organization of such intricacy, the
principal types of minority may be tentatively summarized. The Baltic States — Estonia, Latvia and
Lithuania — are Republics which recently enjoyed an independent statehood. This was destroyed through
the machinations of Hitler and Stalin, though a number of Western states, including the USA, recognize
only the *de facto* incorporation of the Republics into the USSR, and not their incorporation *de jure* . The
Baltic States themselves were subjected to the League of Nations regime for the protection of minorities,
as an aspect of their emergent statehood. The Estonian laws on cultural autonomy were widely admired.
Statehood was consolidated, but proved to be short-lived.

The Baltic people represent an economically advanced region within the USSR with a very clear sense
of national identity, different to that of Russians and other peoples within the USSR. The Muslims of the
USSR represent another, more widespread, antidote to the secular orthodoxy of the USSR. They are
concentrated in Central Asia and are mainly Sunni in affiliation. They are a growing minority and have
sometimes been influenced by contemporary movements of a fundamentalist nature within Islam. Religious groups as a whole function as a specific type of minority within the USSR. Religion can provide a
transcendental and (in some cases) transnational challenge to a State such as the USSR which explicitly
bases itself on a materialistic, atheist philosophy in which religion is seen as a relic of the superstitious
practices of a pre-revolutionary age. Whatever guarantees of religious freedom may exist in the USSR, all
religious organizations have been, to a greater or lesser extent, curtailed.

A third category of minority is constituted by deported groups such as the Crimean Tatars and the Volga
Germans. Mass deportations have been a feature of Stalinist totalitarianism. The excuse in the above cases
was that of collaboration with the Nazis. Whatever other human rights violations may be practised against
such groups, the continuing structural violation is severance from their homeland, and repatriation is the
principal demand.

The USSR has claimed in the past to have "solved" the nationalities problem; under current conditions
the ideal of rapprochement of nationalities seems further away than ever. This ideal was sullied by the
methods used to achieve it, and many groups throughout the USSR harbour deep historical resentments.
Perestroika now has an ethnic dimension: group demands for a self-determination and autonomy have
been invested with tremendous force by recent political changes. Mutations of political structure and practice may follow from the new ethnic consciousness in the USSR; the capacity of the system to adapt to
change will be tested to the full.

Instruments on Minority Rights

Despite the initial hesitations over post-UN Charter developments in human rights, the USSR has signed
and ratified all the major treaties relevant to minorities — in strong contrast to the USA which has been
unwilling to undertake such commitments. On the other hand, the USSR interprets the process of

implementation of treaties in its own manner, exhibiting a preference for national over international procedures. Resistance to international scrutiny of its human rights performance has been maintained, but is gradually eroding: the Helsinki process (see Introduction to Eastern Europe) is particularly significant in this respect. Another significant move is the acceptance by the USSR in 1989 of the compulsory jurisdiction of the World Court in disputes over important human rights treaties.

The 1977 Constitution of the USSR makes various commitments to its citizens, and ethnic/national issues are addressed (see *Appendix* 5.1). Article 36 provides that "citizens of the USSR of different races and nationalities have equal rights". The Article describes a policy for nationalities: the exercise of these rights "is ensured by a policy of all-round development and drawing together of all the nations and nationalities of the USSR". Article 72 provides the startling right of each Union Republic "freely to secede from the USSR". Of course, as both Lenin and Stalin warned, the granting of a right is one thing, its exercise is another, and the exercise of self-determination may be counter-revolutionary. There is, however, sufficient in the Constitution for the various nationalities to draw inspiration from, and great potential for friction between, the State and Republics: for example, a corollary to "all-round development" is provided by Article 19, whereby the State "shall promote the intensification of the social homogeneity of society; the eradication of differences . . . between town and countryside, intellectual and physical labour and the all-round development", etc. In this context, the way to achieve development is by homogeneity rather than respect for difference.

The Constitution contains a full range of rights and duties for individual citizens, including "classic" freedoms such as freedom of conscience. Article 4 is crucial: "The Soviet Union and all its agencies shall operate on the basis of socialist legality and ensure the protection of the legal order, and the rights and freedoms of the citizens." Article 34 states that "Citizens in the USSR shall be equal before the law irrespective of origins, social and property status, racial and national affiliation, sex, education, language, attitude towards religion, type and nature of occupation, place of residence and other circumstances. The equality of citizens of the USSR shall be ensured in all areas of economic, political, social and cultural life".

Besides the Constitution of the USSR, there are separate constitutions, along specific patterns, for Union Republics and Autonomous Republics, and a great deal of sub-constitutional legislation dealing with human rights and nationality issues. These evince widespread respect for local language use in official and educational matters. Set against this to some degree are the Rules of the Communist Party of the Soviet Union: a Party Member shall be "an active conductor of the ideas of socialist internationalism and Soviet patriotism [and shall] . . . wage a struggle against survivals of nationalism and chauvinism . . .". However, the Communist Party organizations are required to follow the principle of friendship and fraternity of all peoples of the USSR. In the legislation as a whole there is a tension between centralization and devolution, homogeneity and heterogeneity of culture, respect for local characteristics and a concern for "progress" that is difficult to resolve.

Treatment of minorities

The individual profiles of groups largely speak for themselves on the impact of ideology and legislation on minorities. Like Yugoslavia, the USSR represents a notable structural experiment for the accommodation of national differences within a single framework. Like Yugoslavia, the constituent elements are newly assertive, to an unprecedented degree. The USSR carries the heavier burdens of complexity, and a history of injustice to peoples from the heavy hand of totalitarian rule. Grave injustices are still perpetuated. There is some way to go before constitutional freedoms are a reality for citizens. Human rights, rather than purity of ideology, set contemporary standards for the well-being of minorities and all Soviet citizens. It is to be hoped that ethnic ferment in the USSR will not create a backlash, stifling the implementation of rights and freedoms purchased at such cost to human life.

Armenians

Alternative names: **Khai**
Location: **Armenia (Caucasus, south-west USSR), other parts of USSR, Turkey, Middle East, N. America, W. Europe, Australia**
Population: **4.2 million (USSR census 1979), 4.5 million (est. 1989), approx 1.8 million living in diaspora**
% of population: **1.6% (1979 and est. 1989)**
Religion: **Gregorian Christianity (Apostolic)**
Language: **Armenian (which has its own distinctive alphabet)**

The Armenians share with the Jews one of the most tragic histories of persecution, oppression and diaspora while displaying a rare tenacity for survival and a high degree of national self-awareness. Indeed, the events in the twentieth century that bring to mind the Armenians: the massacres of 1915, terrorism in the 1970s-1980s, the bloody ethnic clashes with Azerbaidjanis (1988/9) and the earthquake (1988) are all tinged with tragedy.

History and background

The Armenians understandably take great pride in their history, for not only was Armenia a great power at the time of Julius Caesar (first century BC), but also it is the oldest extant Christian nation in the world, having been converted by St Gregory in 301 AD. (The Armenian Church developed independently of both Constantinople and Rome and is therefore neither Catholic nor Orthodox.) An important part of the early Byzantine Empire, Armenia was invaded by the Turks in 1064 (the beginning of nearly a millennium of strife between the two peoples). Some Armenians migrated to Cilicia (on the Mediterranean Sea) and others to the Crimea (on the Black Sea) but by the fifteenth century Armenia had been swallowed up by the Ottoman Empire. In the early nineteenth century Eastern Armenia (now Soviet Armenia, just 10% of historical Greater Armenia) was incorporated into the Russian Empire. In the late nineteenth century Armenians formed armed irredentist groups that engaged in terroristic activity. Such activities provoked savage reaction from the Turkish authorities culminating in the 1894-96 massacres (in which it is claimed up to 300,000 Armenians perished) and 1915 massacres (in which up to one-and-a-half million Armenians died) and Turkish Armenia was virtually cleared of its native population. The Armenians' sense of grievance at the world's indifference to this national tragedy has passed from generation to generation to this day.

The defeat of the Turks in World War I and the collapse of the Russian Empire in 1917 allowed one of the Armenian irredentist groups — the *Dashnaks* (Union) — to proclaim an independent Armenian state in 1918. However, the Red Army established Soviet power in November 1920 and this was finally consolidated in 1921. In order to check local nationalism in the region Armenia, Azerbaidjan and Georgia were merged into the Transcaucasian Socialist Federative Soviet Republic, which joined the USSR in 1922. Only in 1936 was the Armenian SSR to emerge as a separate entity. To this day it remains the only Armenian state in the world and thus, in spite of political differences, it retains a special place in the affections of Armenians in the diaspora. By this time the formerly Armenian territory of Nakhichevan (the population of which was overwhelmingly Azerbaidjani) had been attached to Azerbaidjan, as had the Nagorno-Karabakh region (which, although on Azerbaidjani territory was populated mainly by Armenians). The failure of Stalin to wrest back from Turkey the area surrounding Mount Ararat adjoining Armenia was a source of bitter resentment after World War II. From the war there has been a steady stream of Armenian immigrants from Turkey, Iran and Lebanon, causing the Republic's population to rise by 22% between 1970 and 1979. More recently there has been a reverse flow, mainly to North America (more than 6,000 left in 1980 alone) and the population rose by only a further 8% between 1979 and 1989.

Armenians in the diaspora have taken advantage of the relaxed atmosphere of *glasnost* to increase links with Soviet Armenians and the international response to the Armenian earthquake in December 1988 played a major role in advancing better East–West relations.

Constitution and law

In theory the Armenian Soviet Socialist Republic (population 3.3 million in 1989) is a sovereign state that has freely joined the USSR federation. In reality it has been hitherto a mere constituent part of the USSR, which controls its foreign affairs, military formations, economic and commercial relations in a highly centralized fashion. Although the Soviet Constitution of 1977 allows for Armenia to elect its own legislative (Supreme Soviet), executive (Council of Ministers), and judiciary (Supreme Court), control is effectively exercised by the cen-

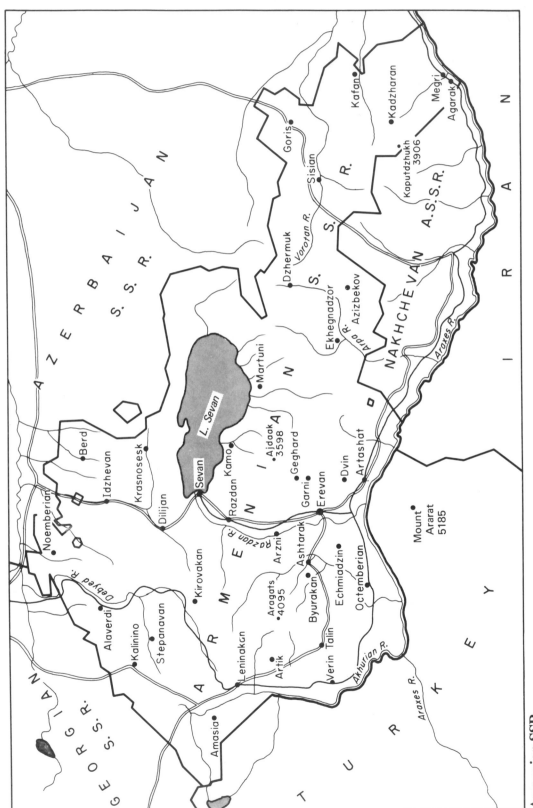

Armenian SSR

tralized and Russian-dominated Communist Party of the Soviet Union (CPSU). As part of the USSR federation, Armenia elects 11 deputies to the Council of Nationalities and three to the Council of the Union in the 542 member Supreme Soviet of the USSR.

The Constitution also allows each Union Republic to secede from the USSR, but the primacy of All-Union legislation effectively invalidates this right. Similarly, the constitutional provision that all citizens of the USSR of different races and nationalities have equal rights has been severely compromised by the domination in the USSR of Slavic (essentially Russian) political, economic and social norms. It could be argued that the Armenians' assertive national consciousness and high levels of education have mitigated the effects of these policies, they being the only nationality other than the Russians to have schools teaching in their own language outside of their native republic.

Recent developments in political, economic and social rights

Although the Nagorno-Karabakh crisis and the Armenian earthquake disaster have dominated the headlines of late, the movement for national self-assertion in Armenia has developed on a far broader front, encompassing ecological, emigration, religious, and national issues. For example, just before the crisis erupted in Nagorno-Karabakh in February 1988, there were demonstrations in the capital, Yerevan, against the pollution of Lake Sevan, nuclear power plants in the Republic and the effluence from a synthetic rubber factory. At the same time relations with Moscow were soured when *Pravda* (presumably with the backing of the Politburo) launched an attack on corruption among the Armenian Communist Party leadership.

Armenians are well-placed to co-ordinate policies aimed at national self-determination, for they constitute nearly 90% of the Republic's population (2.7 million or 66% of all Armenians, 1979), with almost a million more (22.5%) in neighbouring Georgia and Azerbaidjan. More significantly, the Republic has by far the lowest number of Russians (70,000 or 2.3%) in any of the Union Republics (the next lowest is 350,000 in Turkmenistan) and Armenian is firmly established as the main language (only Armenia and Georgia of the Union Republics have retained their distinctive scripts).

The deep-seated grievances against the Turks (and, after the Susha massacres in Nagorno-Karabakh in 1920, the Azerbaidjanis) surfaced following the Sumgait ethnic clashes of February 1988 when 26 Armenians and eight Azerbaidjanis were killed (although it is claimed that hundreds of Armenians died, some in the most grisly cir-

cumstances). Massive demonstrations in Moscow and Stepanakert (capital of Nagorno-Karabakh) in March spread to Yerevan in April when the airport was closed. In May the Karabakh Committee was reactivated to press for the return of the enclave to Armenia, but its leaders were subjected to repressions by the central authorities. In June 1988 the Armenian Supreme Soviet voted for the incorporation of the enclave (re-named the Artsakh Autonomous Republic) into Armenia, but the Azerbaidjan Supreme Soviet reversed this and Moscow ruled the Armenian action unconstitutional. Tension remained high throughout the summer and in September the area was put under military control and closed to outsiders. More clashes occurred in November, taking the death toll to over 100 and causing more than 100,000 refugees in each direction as Armenians fled Azerbaidjan and Nakhichevan and Azerbaidjanis quit Armenia and Karabakh.

The terrible earthquake that hit the Leninakan area in December 1988 (with the loss of 25,000 lives) temporarily stopped the violence. The tremendous international response to this tragedy and the genuine gratitude expressed by the Soviet people in general and the Armenians in particular assisted the improvement in relations between East and West.

However, the decision in January 1989 to place the enclave under direct Moscow rule sparked off demonstrations and strikes in Azerbaidjan and a policy of non-compliance in Armenia. The following month saw massive demonstrations in Armenia on the anniversary of the Sumgait clashes. Violence flared again in July 1989, when two Azerbaidjanis were killed in Nagorno-Karabakh and throughout August 1989 there were strikes and nationalist demonstrations in Baku.

In what was regarded by the Armenian community as a positive development, in June 1989 the Turkish government opened the archives of the Ottoman Empire, a move it is hoped that will lead to the full facts of the Armenian massacre being brought to light.

Given the build-up of ethnic, nationalist, economic and cultural grievances in this part of the world, the prospects for a peaceful resolution of the Nagorno-Karabakh question do not look bright. The Soviet authorities are caught between the two factions and cannot easily satisfy one without alienating the other.

Migration and diaspora

The Armenian diaspora began effectively in 387 AD when the Romans and Persians carved up Armenia, became a flood in the eleventh century and reached its zenith during the years of the Turkish massacres. The Armenians have not always been fortunate in choosing their places of exile; Beirut, Tehran and Cyprus all having substantial Armenian communities. Many from these regions migrated to Soviet Armenia in the 1970s and were probably amongst those who remigrated to North America in the 1980s.

It is North America that contains the largest Armenian community outside the homeland, estimated at some half-a-million. The American Armenian community was particularly active in organizing relief aid for the victims of the earthquake. On the other hand, the activities of ASALA and other Armenian groups adopting terroristic tactics against Turkish targets in the USA and elsewhere have not been welcomed by all Armenians (although they did oblige Turkey to pull out of the Los Angeles Olympics in 1984 for fear of terrorist attacks on its athletes).

France also has a large Armenian community numbering some quarter of a million and there are still sizeable communities in Turkey, Iran, Syria, Lebanon and Cyprus.

Minorities in Armenia

With 90% of the population of the Republic Armenians, there are fewer minority people in Armenia than in any other Union Republic. Apart from the small numbers of Azerbaidjanis and Russians (see above) there are 51,000 Kurds (1.7%) and 6,000 Assyrians (0.2%).

(See also *Armenians of Turkey and the Middle East* in **Middle East and North Africa**; *Azerbaidjanis*)

Azerbaidjanis

Alternative names: **Azeris, Azeri Tatars, Azeri Turks**
Location: **Azerbaidjan (Caucasus, south-west USSR), other parts of USSR, Iran, Iraq**
Population: **5.5 million (USSR census 1979), 6.4 million (est. 1989), 13 million (est.) in Iran**
% of population: **2.1% (1979), 2.2% (est. 1989)**
Religion: **Muslim: Shi'ite (75%); Sunni (25%)**
Language: **Azerbaidjani**

The Azerbaidjanis until recently did not attract anything like as much attention as their less numerous neighbours in the Caucasus — the Armenians and Georgians. Recent events in Iran (which has a substantial Azerbaidjani minority) and, in particular, Nagorno-Karabakh (the predominantly Armenian enclave within Azerbaidjan) has thrust this little-known nation into the limelight. One of the earliest nations now occupying the USSR to become Muslim they are not closely linked to the other Turkic Muslim peoples of Soviet Central Asia. However, in both the Slavic–Turkic ethnic and Christian–Muslim religious divides, the Azerbaidjanis identify with the Uzbeks and Tatars.

History and background

Many great civilizations (Median, Persian, Sassanid) and conquerors (Alexander the Great and Timur the Lame) have succeeded one another on Azerbaidjani soil. From the sixteenth century it has been the object of a tussle between Iran, Turkey and Russia. Although Peter the Great's navy occupied the capital — Baku — in 1723 it was not until 1828 that Azerbaidjan came under Russian control. The oil reserves in and around the Caspian Sea ensured the rapid development of Baku as a major industrial centre and the Azerbaidjanis, who had long become a sedentary population, became the most advanced Muslim people in that part of the Empire. As a result, by the time of the 1917 revolutions there were in Azerbaidjan groups seeking a workers' state (Baku Commune) or a national republic (the *Musavet* or Equality party). Soviet power was eventually established in 1920 and in 1922 Azerbaidjan joined the USSR as part of the Transcaucasian Federation. In 1936 the Azerbaidjan Soviet Socialist Republic was formed with jurisdiction over both the Nakhichevan Autonomous Republic (a predominantly Azerbaidjani enclave surrounded by Iran and Armenia) and Nagorno-Karabakh (an Armenian enclave on Azerbaidjani territory), the two areas at the heart of the present ethnic crisis in the region.

Constitution and law

In theory the Azerbaidjan Soviet Socialist Republic (population 7 million in 1989) is a sovereign state that has freely joined the USSR federation. In reality the USSR hitherto has controlled its foreign affairs, military formations, economic and commercial relations in a highly centralized fashion. Although the Soviet Constitution of 1977 allows

Azerbaidjan to elect its own legislative (Supreme Soviet), executive (Council of Ministers) and judiciary (Supreme Court), control is effectively exercised by the centralized and Russian-dominated Communist Party of the Soviet Union (CPSU) through its Republican branch. As part of the USSR, Azerbaidjan elects 11 deputies to the Council of Nationalities and five to the Council of the Union in the 542-member USSR Supreme Soviet (elections every five years).

The Constitution also allows each Union Republic to secede from the USSR, but the primacy of All-Union legislation effectively invalidates this right. Similarly, the constitutional provision that all citizens of the USSR of different races and nationalities have equal rights has been severely compromised by the domination in the USSR of Slavic (essentially Russian) political, economic and social norms.

Recent developments in political, economic and social rights

Although the clashes with Armenians over Nagorno-Karabakh have dominated recent developments, they have served as a catalyst for a more general resurgence of Azerbaidjani nationalism aimed as much against the Russians as the Armenians. National consciousness is fostered both by the concentration of Azerbaidjanis (86% of whom live in their native republic, a further 4.7% in Georgia and 2.9% in Armenia, 1979) and by the current strength of the Azerbaidjan language vis-à-vis Russian (97.9% of Azerbaidjanis normally use their native language, whereas only 1.8% recognize Russian as their first language and only 29.5% speak it well).

The traditional Azerbaidjani–Armenian hostility broke out anew in February 1988, following radio reports of Azerbaidjani casualties during ethnic clashes in Armenia. In serious disturbances in the oil town of Sumgait (north of Baku), 34 were reported killed (26 Armenians and eight Azerbaidjanis) although Armenian sources put their casualties in hundreds. This brought tension in Nagorno-Karabakh (75% Armenian but Azerbaidjani-run since 1923) to boiling point and massive demonstrations, strikes and political agitation throughout

(See also *Armenians*; *Other Muslim Peoples*)

the summer of 1988 sought to have the region transferred to Armenia.

In November 1988 trouble broke out again when an Azerbaidjani convicted for murdering an Armenian in the Sumgait riots was sentenced to death. Widespread ethnic clashes led to 70 deaths and a two-way exodus of Azerbaidjanis fleeing Armenia and Armenians quitting Azerbaidjan and Nakhichevan. Demonstrations in Baku lasted for 18 days into December demanding economic sovereignty for the Republic. The Armenian earthquake of December 1988 temporarily stemmed the tide but there was profound discontent at the decision in January 1989 to place Nagorno-Karabakh under direct control of Moscow. In July 1989 two Azerbaidjanis were killed in the enclave and August saw massive demonstrations and strikes in Baku organized by the Azerbaidjan Popular Front (a movement led mainly by intellectuals) who demanded the recall of their deputies from the Soviet parliament and the restoration of Azerbaidjani control over Nagorno-Karabakh. With over 100 dead in communal clashes already and no obvious resolution to the problem, the situation remains extremely tense.

A further source of conflict is the fact that, whereas the Georgians and Armenians are represented in the Communist Party of the Soviet Union on a par with or better than their proportion of the Soviet population, the Azerbaidjanis (with 293,000 or 1.6%, 1982) are under-represented and have less than their share of senior posts in political, economic and military hierarchies.

Minorities in Azerbaidjan

In 1979 Azerbaidjanis constituted 78% of the population of the Republic, which had three significant minority groups: equal numbers of Armenians and Russians (475,000 or 7.9%) and Daghestani people (205,000 or 3.4%, mostly Shi'ite Lezghins). As a result of substantially higher Azerbaidjani birthrates and the deterioration in inter-ethnic relations recently, it is anticipated that the proportion of Armenians and Russians will fall significantly.

There is also a small minority of Tats (9,000 or 0.1% 1979) or Mountain Jews, an Iranian people converted to Judaism.

Byelorussians

Alternative names: **White Russians**
Location: **Byelorussia (western USSR), other parts of USSR, Poland, North America, Western Europe**
Population: **9.5 million (USSR census 1979), 10.1 million (est. 1989)**
% of population: **3.6% (1979), 3.5% (est. 1989)**
Religion: **Christianity (Orthodox and Catholic)**
Language: **Byelorussian, Russian**

The Byelorussians are the least numerous of the three East Slavic nations of the USSR. Together with the Russians and Ukrainians they constitute 72.2% of the Soviet population (1979). For the most part sharing with the Ukrainians a proximity in ethnic, linguistic, religious and cultural relations to the Russians, the Byelorussians have attracted even less attention as a national minority than their southern neighbours. This despite having a population comparable to that of Hungary and occupying a land the size of England and Scotland. Paradoxically, although sharing with the Ukrainians the right to full membership of the United Nations, of all the major nations in the USSR the Byelorussians are in the greatest danger of losing their distinctive identity.

History and background

The Byelorussians trace their ancestry to the unified Russian state of Kiev Rus (ninth to eleventh centuries) and inherited in common with the Russians and Ukrainians Orthodox Christianity, Old Church Slavonic and the Cyrillic alphabet. With the decline of Kievan Rus and the Mongol–Tatar invasion of the thirteenth century, Byelorussia was dominated by Lithuania and Poland until the partitions of the latter in the eighteenth century brought incorporation into the Russian Empire. Following the collapse of Empire and the revolutions of 1917 an independent state was established briefly in 1918 until the establishment of Soviet power on January 1, 1919. Under the Treaty of Riga (1921) Western Byelorussia was ceded to Poland (reclaimed in 1939) and in 1922 the remainder joined the USSR as a constituent Republic. Having suffered under Stalin in the 1930s, the greatest trial for the Byelorussians was the German occupation during World War II, in which the Republic lost 2.2 million people despite heroic partisan resistance. Since the war assimilation to Soviet Russian culture continued and it is only recently that manifestations of Byelorussian national consciousness have become frequent.

Constitution and law

In theory the Byelorussian Soviet Socialist Republic (population 10.2 million in 1989) is a sovereign state that has freely joined the USSR federation. It is a full member of the United Nations. In reality, Byelorussia has hitherto been a constituent part of the USSR, which controls its foreign affairs, economic, military and commercial relations in a highly-centralized fashion. Although the Soviet Constitution of 1977 provides for Byelorussia to elect its own legislative (Supreme Soviet), executive (Council of Ministers) and judiciary (Supreme Court) control is exercised effectively by the centralized and Russian-dominated Communist Party of the Soviet Union (CPSU) through its Republican branch. As part of the USSR federation Byelorussia elects 11 deputies to the Council of Nationalities and 10 to the Council of the Union in the 542-member Supreme Soviet of the USSR (elections every five years). The Constitution also allows each Union Republic to secede from the USSR but the primacy of All-Union legislation effectively prescribes this right. Similarly, the constitutional assertion that all citizens of the USSR of different races and nationalities have equal rights has been severely compromised by the domination of Slavic (essentially Russian) political, cultural and economic norms.

Recent developments in political, economic and social rights

Because the Byelorussians are considered the most junior partner of the East Slavic ethnic bloc that has dominated the USSR since its formation, they tend to identify — and be identified — with the Russians. As is the case with the Ukrainians, those Byelorussians that accept the pre-eminence of Soviet Russian culture can rise to the very top of Soviet society (Andrei Gromyko, the late President of the USSR, was from Byelorussia), while those who stress Byelorussian autonomy tend to be accused of "bourgeois nationalism". In the crucial Slavic–Turkic ethnic divide that is emerging in the USSR the Byelorussians are perceived as belonging to the former. Indeed, 98% of the Republic's population are Slavs (the highest proportion among Soviet republics). A low birthrate and a high degree of assimilation has allowed the Byelorussians to be overtaken as the third most numerous Soviet nation by the Uzbeks (who thus have grounds for claiming Byelorussia's seat in the UN).

Despite this, the Byelorussians have been experiencing something of a nationalist revival of late. This is due partly to developments in neighbouring Poland and the Baltic republics, the widespread dissatisfaction with ecological issues following the Chernobyl nuclear accident of April 1986 across the border in the Ukraine (106,000 Byelorussians had to be evacuated from their homes), and the failure of local Communist Party officials to implement the policies of *glasnost* and *perestroika*. Such was the resistance of local Party leaders that the founding congress of the Byelorussian Popular Front in June 1989 had to be held in neighbouring Lithuania. The forceful repression of mass demonstrations, such as that organized by the Byelorussian branch of the anti-Stalinist Memorial association in Minsk (February 1989), rebounded on the authorities when several leading Party figures failed to be elected in the March 1989 elections to the USSR Congress of Peoples' Deputies.

However, it is the language issue that is central to Byelorussian national awareness. In 1979, only 74.2% of Byelorussians considered Byelorussian their native language (the lowest percentage for any Union Republic). Russian was rapidly replacing the native language in schools, particularly in tertiary education, and Byelorussians enjoyed only 0.8 books in their native language *per capita* per year (1982) compared to an average for the USSR of 6.8. Byelorussian, it was claimed, was to be heard only in the countryside and the Republican Writers' Union. It is anticipated that the status of Byelorussian will become a major issue in the run-up to the forthcoming elections to the Byelorussian Supreme Soviet.

Migration and diaspora

In 1979, 80% of all Soviet Byelorussians lived in their native Republic. They are to be found, however, in all parts of the USSR with large concentrations in the RSFSR (1.05 million or 11%) and the Ukrainian SSR (406,000 or 4.3%). Thus, over 95% of Byelorussians live in the three Slavic republics. Outside their native republic Byelorussians tend to use facilities (schools and periodicals) provided for the Russian population, often rationalizing that Russian is the lingua franca of all Soviet peoples, not just the Russians. With 668,000 (3.8% 1982) members of the CPSU, the Byelorussians are slightly over represented and this is reflected in the senior positions they hold in political, economic and military hierarchies (the more numerous Uzbeks had only 411,000 members or 2.3%).

Minorities in Byelorussia

The three major national minorities in Byelorussia according to the 1979 census were all Slavic: the Russians (1.1 million or 12%); Poles (403,000 or 4.2%) and Ukrainians (231,000 or 2.4%). Apart from the Catholic Poles (mainly in Western Byelorussia) who have complained of religious discrimination, these groups appeared to live harmoniously. The only other significant national minority are the Jews (135,000 or 1.4%), although numbers have been greatly reduced (through assimilation, war losses and emigration) since the times when Byelorussia was part of the Pale of Settlement (1815-1917) and supported large Yiddish-speaking Jewish communities. It is anticipated that there will be strong opposition from the non-native population should moves be made to make Byelorussian the official language of the Republic.

Deported Nationalities

Names: **Volga Germans, Crimean Tatars, Meskhetian Turks, Koreans, Greeks, Kurds**
Location: **Central Asia, Kazakhstan, Western Siberia and other parts of USSR**
Population: **(estimated 1989) 2 million Volga Germans, 400,000 Koreans, 400,000 Greeks, 200,000 Crimean Tatars, 116,000 Kurds and 60,000 Meskhetian Turks (totals for USSR)**
% of population: **1.2% (est. 1989)**
Religion: **Christianity (Lutheran: Volga Germans, Orthodox: Greeks); Muslim (Crimean Tatars, Meskhetians, Kurds); Buddhist (Koreans)**
Languages: **German, Crimean Tatar, Korean, Greek, Turkish, Kurdish**

The deportation of entire nationalities by Stalin prior to, during and after World War II remains one of the darkest pages of the history of Soviet national policies. Although all of the national groups accused of "collaboration with the enemy" have since been cleared of such charges, the

nationalities listed here have not been able as yet to return to their traditional homelands (as were the Balkars, Chechens, Ingush, Karachai and Kalmyks after their reprieve in the 1950s). Although only the Crimean Tatars and the Volga Germans had their own distinct territorial formation prior to deporta-

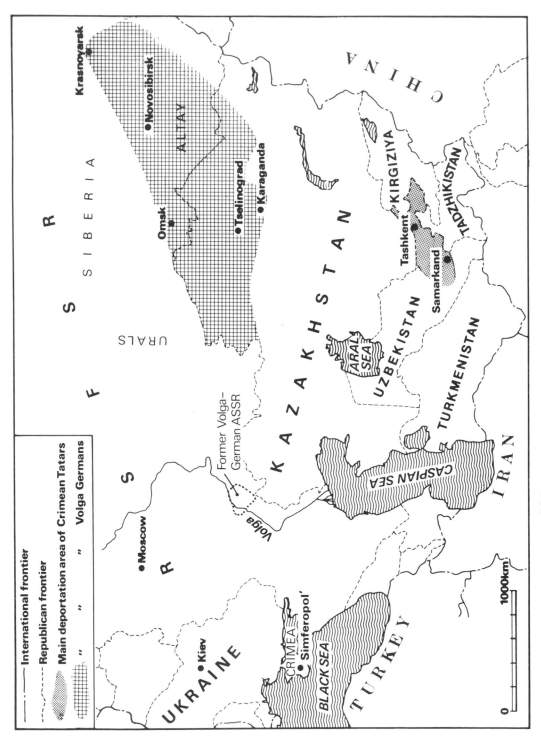

Deported Nationalities of the USSR

Legend:
- International frontier
- " " Republican frontier
- " " Main deportation area of Crimean Tatars
- Volga Germans

Map labels:
Krasnoyarsk
Novosibirsk
ALTAY
SIBERIA
Omsk
Tselinograd
Karaganda
URALS
U S S R
KAZAKHSTAN
CHINA
KIRGIZIYA
Tashkent
Samarkand
TADZHIKISTAN
ARAL SEA
UZBEKISTAN
TURKMENISTAN
Former Volga–German ASSR
Volga
Moscow
CASPIAN SEA
IRAN
UKRAINE
Kiev
CRIMEA
Simferopol'
BLACK SEA
TURKEY
1000km
0

tion, the Greeks, Koreans, Kurds and Turks all had traditional areas of residence. Only the Greeks (who have traditionally inhabited the Crimea and Black Sea coast in the Ukraine and Georgia) and the Kurds (concentrated in Armenia and Georgia) have been allowed back to their homelands in any numbers, although neither has any autonomous rights to self-determination. Apart from the Koreans (who were deported from the Far East) all of the above groups settled traditionally in the Crimea and the Caucasus.

History and background

Although only the Kurds and Meskhetian Turks may strictly be categorized as indigenous to their homelands, all of the other groups (with the exception of the Koreans who settled in the Vladivostok area only from the 1860s) have a long history of settlement. Thus, there have been Greek settlements along the Black Sea coast since before Russian history began and the Tatars entered Crimea in the thirteenth century (where they established a semi-autonomous khanate from the fifteenth century until its incorporation by Russia in 1783). Small groups of migrant Germans had settled in Russia from the sixteenth century but it was Catherine the Great's decree in 1763, opening up the empty steppe land along the Volga to German farmers, that started large-scale migration.

The Germans (from Volynia in the north-west Ukraine) were the first to suffer deportation in 1915, during World War I, but a decree of the following year expelling the Volga Germans was eventually rescinded by the Bolsheviks (Lenin was himself part-German).

In the early decades of Soviet rule, the Crimean Tatars, Koreans and Volga Germans all experienced a relative "golden age", their communities all serving as examples of national minority progress and autonomy. The Volga German Workers' Commune (from 1924 the Volga German Autonomous Republic) was established in 1918 and the Crimean ASSR was formed in 1921 (even though Tatars made up only 25% of the Republic's population). Purges of "bourgeois nationalists", the collectivization campaign and, finally, the Stalin purges in 1936-38 brought this era of autonomy to an end.

The first to suffer were the Koreans; during the height of the Soviet–Japanese tension over Manchuria in 1937, *Pravda* published an article entitled "Foreign Espionage in the Soviet Far East", which accused the Koreans of collaborating with the Japanese. The Koreans were subsequently deported en masse to Uzbekistan and Kazakhstan, where, with 163,000 and 92,000 respectively (1979), they continue to form sizeable minorities.

The Volga Germans were the next to go, following Hitler's attack on the USSR in June 1941. From August 1941 to March 1942 some 800,000 Soviet Germans were deported from European Russia to Siberia, the Altai and Kazakhstan; and the Volga German ASSR was abolished.

The mass deportations of Soviet nationalities commenced with the Red Army's liberation of areas in the Crimea and Caucasus formerly under Nazi control. In 1943-44, the Crimean Tatars, along with the Balkars, Chechens, Ingush, Karachai and Kalmyks were all deported to Uzbekistan, Kazakhstan, the Urals and Siberia for alleged "collaboration". It is estimated that more than 100,000 Crimean Tatars alone died in transit or as a result of famine in their new areas of settlement (where they also had to contend with the hostility of the local population).

In November 1944, the deportation to the arid steppes of Uzbekistan and Kazakhstan was ordered of the Meskhetian Turks, together with other Muslim groups occupying the Soviet–Turkish border (Kurds, Turkmen, Karapapakh Azeris and Khemshili Armenians), not because of collaboration with the Nazis (who failed to penetrate this far south) but "for their own safety". Up to 30,000 of the 200,000 deported are claimed to have perished en route.

Finally, in 1949 (as part of Stalin's anti-Tito drive) thousands of Greeks, including many refugees from the Greek Civil War, were deported from the border zones in Georgia and the Ukraine and sent into the interior.

With the death of Stalin in 1953, the deportation policy was reviewed and by 1956 renounced. However, the Meskhetians, Crimean Tatars and Volga Germans were not allowed to resettle their former homelands as, it was claimed, all had "taken root" in their new areas of residence. Even after the rehabilitation decrees (for the Germans in 1964, the Tatars in 1967 — the Meskhetians had never been accused of collaboration), this remained the official line. Since then, all three deported groups have mounted highly publicized campaigns for resettlement.

Constitution and law

Lacking any territorial formation of their own, the above groups lack even the theoretical autonomy granted to the Union and Autonomous Republics. At 1.9 million (1979) the German population was the 13th largest nationality in the USSR and represented the biggest nation not to have its own autonomous territory (compare the one million Estonians). In terms of population the Volga Germans, Crimean Tatars, Greeks and Koreans might all expect their own autonomous republics, while the Kurds and Meskhetians might seek autonomous regions.

Recent developments in political, economic and social rights

Although attention has been focused on the re-settlement campaigns by Crimean Tatars, Volga Germans and Meskhetian Turks, there have been developments among the other deported nationalities. Among them, only the Koreans appear to have more or less adapted to their area of exile and there has thus far been little evidence of a co-ordinated movement requesting resettlement in the Far East. The Kurds are more concerned with irredentist campaigns with their compatriots in Iran, Iraq, Syria and Turkey and the Greeks have recently (July 1989) formed an All-Union Society of Soviet Greeks to represent their interests, thus following the earlier example of the German "Renaissance" society that published its manifesto in the spring of 1989. This latter society unites viewpoints ranging from the re-establishment of the Volga German homeland to the formation of a "fifth" German state (after West Germany, East Germany, Austria and Switzerland).

Following the rapprochement between the West German and Soviet governments in the early 1970s, Germans became the second largest minority (after the Jews) amongst Soviet emigrants (55,000 left in the 1970s alone). With the cooling off in relations following the Soviet invasion of Afghanistan in 1979 these numbers fell sharply (to a mere 460 in 1985). Since 1987, the general improvement in human rights in the Soviet Union and progress in East–West detente have been accompanied by a further surge in German emigration.

Although both the Crimean Tatars and the Meskhetian Turks have communities of compatriots in Turkey, the emphasis of their campaign has been much less on emigration. Due to the efforts of Aleksei Kosterin and Piotr Grigorenko, the Crimean Tatars have been a *cause célèbre* amongst

Soviet human rights activists since 1968, and the resurgence of militant Islam has made their plight even more sensitive to the Soviet authorities. On May 18, 1988 (the 44th anniversary of their expulsion from their homeland), up to 25,000 Crimean Tatars demonstrated in 22 Soviet villages and towns and, in June 1988, demonstrations spread to Moscow. A Soviet Government commission under the then Soviet President Andrei Gromyko delivered its report in June 1988 and reiterated the right of Crimean Tatars to settle in the Crimea, have their own schools in Uzbekistan etc. However, the commission concluded that "there are no grounds for establishing Crimean autonomy". With only some 15,000 Tatars in a Crimean population that has now reached 2.5 million, it is most unlikely that this policy will be reversed. It is equally predictable, however, that the Crimean Tatars will continue to mount a co-ordinated and high-profile campaign for a restoration of their rights.

The far less numerous Meskhetian Turks really only came to the attention of the world's media following the ethnic clashes in the Fergana region of Uzbekistan in June 1989. Tension between the Turkish and Uzbek communities erupted into bloody clashes that left 105 dead and 1,011 injured. More than 16,000 Meskhetians had to be evacuated to Central Russia. Closely identified with their co-religionists — the Azerbaidjanis (with whom they are counted in Soviet census returns) — the Meskhetians are not welcome presently in the Georgian Republic (where their home region of Meskhet-Dzhavakheti lies), due to the exacerbation of Georgian–Abkhazian relations (particularly after the Sukhumi clashes of July 1989) and the high tension between Christians (Armenians) and Muslims (Azerbaidjanis) in the Caucasus.

The promised review of the CPSU's national policy certainly will address the fate of the deported nationalities but, apart from ensuring their equal rights in language, education and cultural life, there would appear to be little prospect of demands for full territorial autonomy to be met.

(See also *Georgians*; *Kazakhs*; *Other Muslim Peoples*; *Tatars*; *Uzbeks*)

Estonians, Latvians, Lithuanians of the Soviet Baltic Republics

Location: **Baltic Coast of USSR**
Population: **Estonians; 1.0 million; Latvians: 1.4 million; Lithuanians: 2.9 million (1979)**
% of population: **Estonians: 0.4%; Latvians: 0.5%; Lithuanians: 1.1%**
Religion: **Christian (Estonians and Latvians mainly Protestant, Lithuanians mainly Roman Catholic)**
Languages: **Estonian, Latvian and Lithuanian**

It is only as a result of events in the twentieth century that it has become appropriate to speak of Estonia, Latvia and Lithuania as a distinct group of countries. Ethnically the Latvians and Lithuanians are related to each other but not to the Estonians, and historically Estonia and Latvia have had similar experiences while Lithuanian history followed a completely different course until the end of the eighteenth century. All three countries experienced a brief period of independence between 1918 and 1940, a period of great importance in the national consciousness of the Baltic peoples. In June 1940 they were forcibly — and according to international law, illegally — incorporated into the Soviet Union, after Hitler and Stalin together assigned the area to the Soviet "sphere of interest", in two secret protocols to the Molotov-Ribbentrop Treaty of Non-Aggression of 1939. After a very turbulent period during the war, which included two further invasions by Germany and the Soviet Union respectively, the countries suffered a further period of terror under Stalin. Since these years the Baltic States have existed as republics within the Soviet Union, administered by its highly centralized political and economic system. During this period extensive immigration of Russian workers for Soviet heavy industry has taken place in Estonia and Latvia, and to a lesser extent in Lithuania. The nationality problem, denied by the Soviet authorities until very recently, has resurfaced dramatically since 1987. The Baltic peoples are demanding not just minority rights but a democratic right of national self-determination manifested in some form of economic and political autonomy or even independence. This has aroused fears in Moscow of the disintegration of the Soviet Union, and fears among the Baltic Russian communities of minority status. Tensions are growing rapidly, with both Baltic and Russian communities now perceiving themselves as threatened minorities.

History

Before 1918 only Lithuania had ever enjoyed a period of independence, in the great Polish–Lithuanian State (1569-1795). Otherwise all three countries have been under the influence of one or other of the great regional powers, Germany and

Russia. In the nineteenth and early twentieth centuries, during which the countries were contained within the Russian Empire, national consciousness developed and later demands for autonomy within the empire. In 1915-1920 the region was the site of intense struggles by both German and Russian forces to establish their influence in this highly strategic region. In the midst of the turmoil all three Baltic countries declared their independence, but following the defeat of Germany in the west in November 1918 and the withdrawal of German forces, the three fledgling nations were submitted to a return of Russian (Bolshevik) forces. After a war of liberation, the whole region was finally cleared of foreign forces by the start of 1920 and each country signed peace treaties with the Soviet Union granting mutual security on favourable terms for both sides.

During the inter-war period both Germany and the Soviet Union were consolidating their power, while the nation-states of Europe, including the Baltic States, remained internally weak and externally divided. In the secret protocols to the Molotov-Ribbentrop Treaty of Non-Aggression in 1939 the region between the two great powers was divided into spheres of influence — the Baltic States fell to the Soviet Union. Eventually on June 17, 1940, Soviet troops entered and rapidly consolidated their power by means of highly irregular elections, sweeping changes in the administrative apparatus and the transfer of real power into the hands of Soviet officials. There followed "a period of terror", with a total of about 150,000 deaths and deportations in the three countries, in an attempt to liquidate national cohesion.

Upon the outbreak of war, revolt against the Soviet system broke out in all three states, which contributed much to the rapid advance of the Nazi armies in the summer of 1941. But the Germans too resorted to tactics of terror, and the region suffered extermination of Jews on a massive scale (about 250,000 died).

The Soviets returned in 1944 and gradually re-established order and maintained it by use of force. Collectivization of agriculture was achieved through mass deportations of farming communities, numbers being counted in hundreds of thousands. Forced industrialization, on the other hand, was a means of bringing in huge numbers of

Russian workers. The educated elites fled to the West in large numbers. In Lithuania the Roman Catholic Church suffered particularly, through its intimate association with national consciousness and its widespread popular support. Guerrilla resistance was put down by overwhelming force and massive deportations were used to quell areas of active resistance. Stalinism succeeded in reducing the Baltic peoples to submission, although the national consciousness was never destroyed, as has been illustrated very dramatically in the years since Mikhail Gorbachev took office.

Legal and constitutional position

Lenin had believed that "class" was a greater force than "nation"; with an end to the exploitative relationship between nations, attachment to the nation would gradually and naturally give way to "proletarian internationalism". Lenin predicted that after an initial flourishing of national culture, nations would experience a drawing together (*sblizhenie*) and eventual merging (*sliyanie*). Stalin developed the concept that only the proletariat, whose sole voice was the Communist Party, has the right to national self-determination: the highly centralized Communist Party would therefore express the will of all working people for unity, and would undertake the task of political socialization through education, propaganda, the media etc. The Soviet constitutions have, therefore, been based on the principle of "national in form, socialist in content": republics retain the right of national self-determination through the right to secede, while the highly centralized Party would guarantee the socialist content and therefore unity. The current Constitution of 1977 reads (Article 27): "The USSR is an integral, federal, multinational state formed on the principle of socialist federalism as a result of the free self-determination of nations and the voluntary association of equal Soviet Socialist Republics." The stated right to national self-determination is effectively negated by the principle of "socialist federalism", which guarantees unity and the integral nature of the federation.

The Soviet Communist Party has based the legitimacy of the incorporation of the Baltic States into the Soviet Union on the claim that the Baltic nations joined voluntarily through the elections of July 1940 (this is why it was so important for the Soviet Union to stage-manage what had the appearance of a democratic process). The official Soviet line has been that Soviet support in overthrowing fascism was granted in response to spontaneous uprisings of the working people, under the leadership of the Communist Party. In reality, the Communists had only a negligible following at that time.

Civil and political rights

In Lithuania and Estonia human rights activity has been greater in proportion to the population than anywhere else in the USSR, and national concerns predominate. There has always been a tension between "ethno-federalism" and a unitary state, and the authorities in Moscow have had constantly to "encourage" the natural developments predicted by Lenin. This was especially the case under Kruschev, who favoured Lenin's idea of merging and promoted the concept of the "new Soviet person" and of cultural unification at a higher level.

Until the incontrovertible evidence of the period since 1987, the national problem was consistently denied, and the expression of nationalist sentiments in the Baltic countries invariably led to repression. In Lithuania the Roman Catholic Church has suffered particular persecution, acting as a clear locus of national consciousness (in much the same way as in Poland), and vigorously defending human and religious rights.

Language concerns. The 1977 Constitution guarantees "the possibility to use one's native language and the languages of other peoples of the USSR" (article 36), and "the opportunity to attend a school where teaching is in the native language". At the same time, the Russian language has constantly been promoted; the 1977 Constitution of the Soviet Union refers to the "Soviet people" with Russian as a "common language", and in line with this new emphasis, the Brezhnev regime published a decree in October 1978 to encourage the use of Russian as the language of "communication", "friendship" and "brotherhood". The teaching of Russian was increased substantially, from kindergarten upwards and on television, and in the 1980s the number of Russian teachers has increased by many thousands. Fluency in Russian is needed for higher education and beyond. The State monopoly of publishing has resulted in a large preponderance of publications in the Russian language.

Demographic concerns. The following population ratios illustrate the demographic situation, comparing figures for national populations before incorporation into the Soviet Union with figures for 1980: *Estonia* 1939, 92%; 1980, 64.5%; *Latvia* 1939, 77%; 1980, 54%; *Lithuania* 1939, 76%; 1980, 80%. The national Estonian and Lithuanian populations have seen an almost zero growth rate in the last half century. The total population, however, has been increasing through immigration of non-nationals.

Over-industrialization of Estonia and Latvia without due concern for local labour conditions has been the cause of labour shortages, necessitating immigration, mainly of Russians. The large military presence in the highly strategic Baltic region has also led to an influx of Russians. The Russian communities are mostly blue-collar and military workers, forming close-knit urban groups. The lack of integration is exacerbated by the fact that the Estonians and Latvians consider themselves in some ways culturally superior to the immigrant Russians who mostly take less skilled jobs.

Baltic nationals have accused the central authorities of deliberate assimilation policies; of the various different nationalities, it is the Russians that have been given special facilities, such as schools and priority housing. Whether deliberate policy or not, the net result is similar, and until very recently the Soviet authorities have shown little willingness to take precautionary measures against such trends.

Economic and social rights

The Baltic region is the most productive of the Soviet Union, and the standard of living is higher than the Soviet average. Agriculture is strong in all three republics compared to the rest of the Soviet Union, and Estonia and Latvia also have a strong industrial base. It would be wrong to speak of a deliberate policy of economic exploitation of the Baltic countries by the central authorities in Moscow. The problems are due rather more to the functioning of the system itself. Like the rest of the Soviet economy, the Baltic economies suffer from the problems of centralization; the greatest economic power lies with the all-union economic ministries based in Moscow — republican ministries remain weak. (Under Krushchev an attempt was made at regional decentralization but this was aborted in the 1960s after complete failure.) Centralization has caused informational overload at the centre in Moscow, and this prevents the central planners from knowing in detail what needs doing in each enterprise in the Baltic area, and what can be done most efficiently. There are also cultural and linguistic barriers, and a natural tendency for the centre to act according to its own interests.

Of particular concern to the Baltic peoples has been the severe industrial pollution, especially around the main cities. Environmental problems have become an issue of national sovereignty because the heavy industries responsible for most of the pollution were mostly installed by the Soviet authorities and are run from Moscow. Territorial control agencies lack the power to stop the powerful central industrial lobbies. Popular environmental protest has grown to huge proportions in the past few years, and some policy changes have been effected as a result.

The people of Estonia and Latvia consider themselves harder workers and better wealth creators than the Russians, and they have a sense that they are being dragged back by their amalgamation with more backward regions of the Soviet Union. It is impossible to say how the Baltic economies would have fared if independent; it is possible, however, to compare them with the Finnish economy. The Baltic and Finnish economies were in a comparable condition at the end of the war, and it is clear that the Finns now enjoy a higher standard of living. There have recently been shortages of food in Estonia, milk and meat in particular, giving rise to considerable resentment being expressed in the press and in the numerous recent demonstrations.

As for participation in politics, the highly centralized Communist Party, directed from Moscow, has been completely dominated by Russians, as have State institutions, especially the military and the interior. Important Party posts within the Baltic countries, for example the persons responsible for cadre selection, have also been Russians. Nevertheless, the lower echelons of the Party and State apparatus within the Baltic countries have had to be staffed by Baltic peoples, and these have shown a persistent, though discreet, tendency to further national interests. In the current climate, this interest has expressed itself openly even at the highest levels, and the federal structure of both Party and State, only nominal in the past, has taken on real significance.

Emigré communities

Baltic emigré communities are well organized and tightly knit. There are various organizations representing the interests of their respective countries. There is a US based umbrella group called the "Baltic World Council", and in the UK there is an active "Baltic Council". For many years the Soviet authorities have suppressed the idea of a national identity and culture transcending geographical boundaries, but in recent years, particularly since 1987, cultural ties with the emigré communities have grown very much stronger.

Other minority groups in the Baltic region

Other minorities within the individual Baltic countries (mostly nationals from other Baltic countries, Germans, Jews and Poles) have even fewer national and cultural rights. These communities are small and are very prone to the Russian influence.

Recent events

The situation in the Baltic countries has changed dramatically in the two years 1988 to 1989. Gorbachev has been seeking to create a new foundation for his legitimacy in public consent. The ethos of "glasnost" and democratization that has followed has suddenly given the Baltic peoples a chance at last to express their national grievances, and Baltic society has mobilized on a massive scale. This has manifested itself most dramatically in enormous demonstrations which have taken place on all national anniversaries (1989 and 1990 are the 50th anniversaries of all the events leading up to the Soviet occupation). New associations have been formed, most important of which are People's Fronts in all three countries (called *"Sajudis"* in Lithuania). Also important are more radical organizations calling for complete independence, and a burgeoning environmental movement. In 1989 the People's Fronts began holding joint assemblies to co-ordinate their positions.

The central demand of the Baltic peoples is for sovereignty. Some see this in the form of sovereignty within a Soviet federation, others as independence outside the USSR. There is a trend towards more radical demands as time goes on. The demands for sovereignty cover issues such as the economy, immigration regulations, citizenship and language, foreign policy, control over the military, and independent representation at the United Nations. The debate on the true events of 1939 and 1940 has been one of the most central; on it rests the entire legitimacy of the present order.

The republican Communist Parties, predominantly made up of Baltic nationals, and newly dependent on public opinion as a result of Gorbachev's policies (especially the advent of multi-party elections), have gone a long way in responding to the national demands. The Estonian Party has gone furthest in this direction, maintaining good relations with the Estonian People's Front. Their main problem, however, is their simultaneous dependence on the Party in Moscow; the problem increases as popular demands and Moscow's requirements diverge. There is pressure on the Party in Lithuania, for example, to sever its ties with the Party in Moscow in the run-up to regional elections in the autumn of 1989. The republican Supreme Soviets (parliaments) have been enacting increasingly radical legislation. This has included, for example, declarations of sovereignty, laws enhancing economic autonomy, immigration restrictions, language laws, legalization of national flags, citizenship laws, changing the clocks to Finnish and Swedish time, and especially, the right to veto Soviet legislation if seen to contradict national interests.

The Baltic area, given its comparatively strong economy, could be Gorbachev's best hope of making a success of economic reform; at the same time the nationality issue makes any attempt at decentralization highly risky. Moscow has granted a very considerable degree of autonomy (including a declaration that the republics could undertake any economic reform they wanted in 1990 without consulting Moscow), but such measures only seem to increase the appetite for more. In the summer of 1989 Moscow began to indicate strongly that it was losing patience; at the time of writing tensions are high as fears of a confrontation grow. The central authorities are beginning to have a very real fear of the complete disintegration of the Soviet Union.

The other main problem is that of the Russians living in the Baltic areas. Not all Russians are against more autonomy, since many stand to gain from it, but Russian movements, made up mainly of workers, have developed in all three countries. New legislation in Estonia in August 1989 restricting the franchise brought about a 10-day strike by Russians. A situation is developing where all the major communities in the Baltic area are perceiving themselves as beleaguered minorities. There is a further danger that the fears of the Russian communities in the Baltic countries will coincide with fears of the (mainly Russian) authorities in Moscow of a complete disintegration of the Soviet Union.

Ethnic Religious Minorities

JEWS

Location: **throughout USSR, concentrated in European cities**
Population: **1.8 million (USSR census 1979); total worldwide population estimated at 15 million (6 million USA, 3 million Israel, 1975)**
% of population: **0.7% (1979)**
Religion: **Judaism**
Language: **Russian, Yiddish, Hebrew**

The Soviet Jews have become synonymous with the human rights' movement in the USSR over the past 20 years and thus have been a major factor in East–West relations. Highly organized and supported by influential Jewish communities in the United States, Europe and, of course, Israel as well as human rights' organizations throughout the world, the Soviet Jews until recently dominated Western media coverage of Soviet minorities. The advent of the Gorbachev era of *glasnost*, with improved East–West relations, progress on human rights and increased Jewish emigration, combined with the widespread manifestations of national self-determination by peoples far more numerous than the Jews, have radically altered that situation.

History and background of Jewish migration and diaspora in Russia/USSR

The Turkic Khazars practised Judaism in their khanate (on the Lower Volga to the Sea of Azov) from the seventh to tenth centuries, and Vladimir, Grand Prince of Kiev Rus, considered converting to Judaism before finally choosing Greek Orthodox Christianity. Jews, however, only became a significant national minority in Russia with the expansion of the Empire westwards and the partition of Poland (late eighteenth century). True, there already existed a tradition of anti-semitism amongst the Eastern Slavic peoples, manifested notably in the massacre of some 100,000 Jews by the Ukrainian leader Bogdan Khmelnitsky in the mid-seventeenth century. This found physical expression from 1815 until 1917 when most of the five million Jews of the Russian Empire were confined to the Pale of Settlement (located in present-day Poland, Ukraine, Byelorussia and Moldavia). A series of pogroms and deportations from 1871 to 1906 engendered waves of emigration — two million emigrated mainly to the United States between 1880 and 1914 — and attracted the attention and condemnation of the world community. Such repressions also gave rise in the Russian Empire to socialist and Zionist groups, the latter seeking initially an independent Jewish state within the Russian framework, and the former an internationalist, secular solution to discrimination. Thus the Jewish Bund (formed 1897) was the forerunner of the Russian Social Democratic and Labour Party and Jews figured prominently in both the Bolshevik (Trotsky, Zinoviev) and Menshevik (Martov) wings. Although the Marxist–Leninists that came to power in 1917 did not recognize the Jews as a separate nationality, it was not until Stalin had consolidated himself in power that anti-semitic policies became apparent. Initially overshadowed by Nazi atrocities in World War II (which claimed a total of six million Jewish lives), they became most conspicuous in the last years of Stalin's life. Thus, cultural autonomy, including the use of Yiddish and Hebrew, was abolished and strict quotas were set for the entry of Jews into higher educational establishments.

Some of these measures were relaxed after Stalin's death, but the formation of the state of Israel (1948) and, especially, Israel's victory over the USSR's Arab allies in the 1967 war led to the Soviet authorities adopting policies ensuring that overt manifestations of Jewish self-determination (including the right to emigrate to Israel) would be suppressed. Although Jewish emigration from the USSR rose from 229 in 1968 to 51,300 in 1979, use of the word "refusenik" (applied to those Jews refused permission to emigrate) became so widespread that it entered the English language.

At the same time, the high degree of urbanization (98%), assimilation, knowledge of Russian (83.3% claim it as their first language, 1979) and levels of education amongst Soviet Jews have allowed many Jews who have accepted the Soviet norms of life to form a mobilized diaspora and rise to the top of their professions (for example, Jews represent 1.4% of all members of the CPSU but only 0.7% of the population, 1982).

Constitution and law

The only territorial autonomy afforded the near two million Soviet Jews (it is estimated that some 10–15% hide their national identity for various reasons) is the Jewish Autonomous Region, established in 1934 in the Far East of the country on the border with China. However, as less than 1% of Soviet Jews live in the region (in which they constitute just 5.4% of the population) this cannot be regarded as a proper homeland, although the region does elect two deputies to the Council of Nationalities in the USSR Supreme Soviet. It has been suggested that, had a Jewish region been established within the old Pale of Settlement, it might have been more successful, but as the entire area of the Pale came under Nazi control in World War II, this seems doubtful. Since the formation of Israel, Jewish self-determination has been directed more at emigration than at establishing autonomy within the USSR.

Recent developments in political, economic and social rights

The loss of 2.5 million Soviet Jews during World War II, the emigration of a further 250,000 between 1968 and 1980, and the Russification of yet others through mixed marriage and assimilation, combined with the decline of Yiddish, Hebrew and organized Judaism, has had a devastating effect on Jewish culture in the USSR. Despite 90% of Soviet Jews being Ashkenasi, who might be expected to speak Yiddish, in fact only 14.2% of Soviet Jews in 1979 claimed it as their first language (and only a further 5.4% as their second tongue). This compares to 90.7% of Byelorussian Jews who spoke Yiddish in 1926. Hebrew, the language of

Jewish theology, has fared equally badly. Joseph Begun, who led the movement to legalize the teaching of Hebrew in the Soviet Union, was imprisoned for "anti-Soviet agitation and propaganda" in 1983 and released only five years later, just one of the many Jews to fall foul of the Soviet authorities. Significantly, the number of synagogues has fallen from approximately 5,000 in 1917 to less than 100 now.

However, the situation has taken a turn for the better since the 1960s (particularly since the notorious publication in 1964 of T.K. Kichko's anti-semitic tract "Judaism without Embellishment" which was condemned by Western communist parties). Admittedly, the unprecedently high rates of Jewish emigration ended with the sharp deterioration of East–West relations following the Soviet invasion of Afghanistan, the non-ratification of the SALT II agreement by the US Congress and its passing of the Jackson–Vanick Amendment that linked the granting of the USSR favoured-nation trading status to Soviet emigration policies (1979). By 1983 the number of Jewish emigrants had fallen to 1,315 and the polarization of attitudes was manifested in that year by the formation of eminent pro-regime

(See also *Byelorussians*; *Moldavians*; *Ukrainians*)

Jews in the USSR of an Anti-Zionist Committee.

The Gorbachev reforms, however, appear to have eased restrictions on emigration, released Jewish political prisoners, re-established the validity of Judaism as a faith and Hebrew as a language and even led to a rapprochement with Israel (which shares the Soviet Union's concern that a large proportion of Soviet Jews emigrate not to Israel but to the United States). In August of 1989, a Zionists' Union was established in Moscow. Nonetheless, there remain complaints about the treatment of thousands of "refuseniks" and a worrying by-product of *glasnost* has been the emergence of *Pamyat* (Memory), a Russian nationalist organization with more than a hint of anti-semitism.

Jewish minorities

In 1979, there were an estimated 22,000 Tats (an Iranian people living in the Caucasus, also known as the Mountain Jews), a majority of whom profess Judaism (the remainder are Muslims). Their population has decreased from 29,000 in 1926. In addition there are some 200,000 Oriental Jews living in the Caucasus and Soviet Central Asia.

BUDDHISTS

Names: **Buryats, Kalmyks, Tuvinians**
Location: **Lower Volga region (Kalmyks), south-eastern USSR (Buryats, Tuvinians); also in Mongolia and China**
Population: **Buryats: 353,000 (USSR census 1979), 400,000 (est. 1989); Kalmyks; 147,000 (1979), 160,000 (est. 1989): Tuvinians: 166,000 (1979), 190,000 (est. 1989)**
% of population: **0.25% (1979), 0.26% (est. 1989)**
Religion: **Buddhist, Orthodox Christianity and Shamanism (minorities)**
Language: **Buryat, Kalmyk (both Mongol languages), Tuvinian (Turkic), Mongolian**

The Buddhist peoples of the USSR have not attracted anything like the attention paid to the much more numerous Soviet Muslims. In essence, however, the two groups share many of the same problems and aspirations. Certainly, the Buryats, Kalmyks and Tuvinians would tend to identify with the Uzbeks, Tatars and Azerbaidjanis in the key Slavic–Non Slavic ethnic divide.

History and background

The Buryats and Kalmyks are Mongol peoples sharing a common ancestry with the tribes that destroyed the first Russian state — Kievan Rus — in the thirteenth century. The Tuvinians are a Turkic people that fell under the Mongol yoke at about

the same time. Buryatia had been colonized by the Russians as early as the mid-seventeenth century, about the same time as the nomadic Kalmyks settled in the Lower Volga. The Kalmyks, too, were incorporated into the Russian Empire in the eighteenth century, at which time Catherine the Great encouraged substantial German immigration to the steppes along the Lower Volga to discourage Kalmyk expansion. The Tuvinians were under Manchurian rule until briefly becoming a Russian protectorate in 1914. The building of the Trans-Siberian Railway at the turn of the nineteenth to twentieth centuries accelerated the process of Westernization and Russification. After the October Revolution and Civil War, Eastern Buryatia was occupied by Japanese and American troops and from 1920-22 formed part of the Far Eastern Republic. Tuva was proclaimed an independent people's republic in 1921 (although, in effect a Soviet vassal state); a status it retained until being incorporated into the USSR in 1944 as an Autonomous Republic within the RSFSR. The Kalmyk Autonomous Region was established in 1923 and became an Autonomous Republic in 1935.

The leading figure in Soviet Buddhism in the post-Revolutionary years was Lama Agvan Dordzhiev, who developed the notion that Buddhist modernism was compatible with communism. However, in the 1930s with rising tension in Manchuria, Stalin accused Soviet Buddhists of collaboration and subjected them to severe repressions. In 1943, the entire Kalmyk people was deported to Central Asia and Siberia, being allowed to return only in 1957. Two Buddhist monasteries were reopened in Chita (Eastern Siberia) and Ivolginsk (Buryatia) at the end of World War II but by 1978 it was claimed that the number of lamas had decreased from 10,000 prior to the Revolution to 40. In 1950 a Buddhist Central Council of the USSR was established in Ivolginsk.

Constitution and law

All three Buddhist peoples in the Soviet Union (the Koreans are also nominally Buddhist, but appear to have few organized facilities to practise their religion) have their own Autonomous Republic which, in theory, gives each nationality the right to elect its own legislative, executive and judiciary. However, only the Tuvinians are the majority

nation within its own republic (60% — 36% Russians, 1979); the Kalmyks constitute 40.5% (Russians 42%) and the Buryats a mere 22.3% (Russians 70%). Each republic elects four deputies to the Council of Nationalities in the USSR Supreme Soviet. In addition Buryats are the indigenous people in the Aginski-Buryat and Ust-Ordynsky Buryat Autonomous Areas (one deputy each).

Recent developments in political, economic and social rights

Until very recently the Buddhist peoples of the USSR had not been as vocal nor as militant as their Muslim compatriots, and the process of secularization and Russification appeared to be proceeding apace, particularly in the towns. However, the visit in 1979 of the Dalai Lama to the *datsan* (monastery) in Ivolginsk, was witnessed, reportedly, by "thousands of believers". The recent upsurge of nationalist activity in the Soviet Union appears to have affected thus far only the Buryats among the Buddhist peoples, there being reports of nationalist disturbances in Ulan Ude (capital of Buryatia) in August 1989. However, one suspects that the Kalmyks (who still harbour deep resentment at their treatment under Stalin) and the Tuvinians (with their links to Mongolia and recent history of, albeit nominal, independence) may assert themselves in the near future. Moreover, bearing in mind that the ecology movement in the USSR started with protests at the pollution of Lake Baikal (which is virtually surrounded by Buryat territory), environmental issues may well become the rallying factor for nationalist sentiments in Buryatia.

Georgians

Alternative names: **Kartveli**
Location: **Georgia (Caucasus, south-west USSR), other parts of USSR**
Population: **3.6 million (USSR census 1979), 3.9 million (est. 1989)**
% of population: **1.4% (1979 and est. 1989)**
Religion: **Orthodox Christianity, Muslim (minority)**
Language: **Georgian (which has its own distinctive alphabet)**

The Georgians represent one of the oldest and most developed civilizations on Soviet territory. Long renowned for their hospitality, wine and politicians (from Stalin to Shevardnadze), they have recently been in the headlines for the civil and ethnic strife that has erupted within their borders. Passionately attached to their fertile, mountainous land (a higher proportion of Georgians live within their own Union Republic than any other national-

ity in the USSR — 96.1% in 1979), the Georgians hitherto had seemed satisfied to live within a larger federation. However, the decline of their traditional enemies, the Turks and Persians, the deteriorating economic situation in the USSR, and the increase in ethnic conflicts in the neighbouring republics of Armenia and Azerbaidjan, have led to unprecedented mass demonstrations for national self-determination.

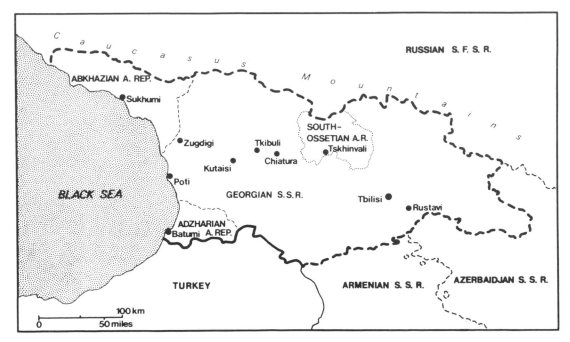

Georgian SSR

History and background

Georgia was known to the ancient Greeks as Colchis, the land in which Jason and the Argonauts sought the Golden Fleece. Christianity reached Georgia in the fourth century and the Church became autocephalous in the eleventh century, electing its own Catholicos-Patriarch. Caught between the might of Turkey, Persia and Byzantium, Georgia was frequently ravaged by invaders. However, for a brief period in the eleventh and twelfth centuries in the reigns of King David and Queen Tamara, Georgia experienced a renaissance. During Tamara's reign Shota Rustaveli wrote the Georgian epic poem "The Knight in the Panther's Skin", thus initiating a long tradition of literary and artistic excellence amongst Georgians.

Following Tamara's death in 1212, Georgia's fortunes plunged and the land was invaded by the Persians and Mongols and, subsequently, by the Ottoman Turks. Seeking protection from the Turks, Georgia appealed for help from Russia, but by 1809 it had been incorporated fully into the Russian Empire. Having used Georgia as a base for military operations against Daghestan, Persia and Turkey in the first half of the nineteenth century, Russia proceeded to repress manifestations of Georgian independence until the 1917 revolutions. During and after the revolutions Georgia became a bastion of the Menshevik wing of the Social Democrats, who led an independent government from 1918 until 1921, when Soviet power was established after the Red Army had occupied the territory.

In 1922 Georgia formed part of the Transcaucasian Socialist Federative Soviet Republic which joined the USSR, and became a full Union Republic only in 1936. Despite the fact that Stalin, a Georgian, succeeded Lenin as Party leader, Georgia suffered greatly from the purges of the 1930s. Indeed, another Georgian, its Party secretary, Beria, was to become Commissar of Stalin's dreaded secret police, the NKVD. After the deaths of both Stalin and Beria in 1953, Georgia was controlled for nearly 20 years by V. Mzhvananadze and his so-called "Georgian Mafia" (during which time there were demonstrations against Moscow's de-Stalinization campaigns, especially that of 1956). His replacement as Party secretary in 1972, Shevardnadze, initiated a drive against crime and corruption that won him some popularity in the Republic, but set off a series of arson and bomb attacks in the Georgian capital, Tbilisi (in 1973 the Opera House was burned and in 1976 the government headquarters were bombed). Since then the overriding issue for most Georgians has been the Russification of the Republic, and mass demonstrations headed off attempts to downgrade the status of the Georgian language in 1978. In 1981 there were further demonstrations in Tbilisi against Russification. Even on the sports field, the success of the Dynamo Tbilisi soccer team against its

Russian and Ukrainian rivals has been accompanied by mass manifestations of national jubilation.

Constitution and law

In theory the Georgian Soviet Socialist Republic (population 5.45 million in 1989) is a sovereign state that has freely joined the USSR federation. In reality it hitherto has been a constituent part of the USSR, which controls its foreign affairs, military, economic and social relations in a highly centralized fashion. Although the Soviet Constitution of 1977 allows for Georgia to elect its own legislative (Supreme Soviet), executive (Council of Ministers) and judiciary (Supreme Court), control is effectively exercised by the centralized and Russian-dominated Communist Party of the Soviet Union (CPSU) through its Republican branch. As part of the USSR federation, Georgia elects 11 deputies to the Council of Nationalities and five to the Council of the Union in the 542-member Supreme Soviet of the USSR (elections every five years).

The Constitution also allows for each Union Republic to secede from the USSR, but the primacy of All-Union legislation effectively invalidates this right. Similarly, the constitutional provision that all citizens of the USSR of different races and nationalities are equal has been severely compromised by the dominance in the USSR of Slavic (essentially Russian) political, economic and cultural norms. The Georgians have been more successful than most nations in the USSR, however, in resisting the implementation of Russification policies.

Recent developments in political, economic and social rights

Although recent press reports on Georgia have highlighted the twin problems of Georgians as a minority vis-à-vis the Russians, and Georgian relations with their own national minority — the Muslim Abkhazians — there have been manifestations of discontent over a far wider range in recent years.

For example, after four Georgians were sentenced to death in 1984 for trying unsuccessfully to hijack a plane to the West, 3,000 Georgians including many prominent figures in the arts signed a protest petition. In October 1987, the Ilya Chavchavadze Society was formed (named after a leading Georgian Menshevik who was assassinated by the Bolsheviks in 1907) to promote the cause of independence, along with the more moderate Shota Rustaveli Society (that seeks merely autonomy) and the even more radical Georgian National Democratic Party. In September 1988 there was a mass demonstration against a planned hydroelectric dam in the Republic. The following month there was communal violence in Marneuli (in the south-east of Georgia where about quarter of a million Azerbaidjanis live) after an Azerbaidjani was accused of raping a Georgian girl.

Massive protest demonstrations were held in November 1988 against proposed changes in the Soviet Constitution and the Republican Supreme Soviet formally rejected the proposals. Further nationalist demonstrations occurred in February 1989 to mark the anniversary of Georgia's loss of independence in 1921.

However, it was the situation in Abkhazia that led to nationalist feelings boiling over in the spring of 1989. Abkhazia (which had been a separate republic from 1921 to 1931) sought to withdraw from Georgia and, in March 1989, it proclaimed its intention to do so. The local Party leader was sacked, but 10,000 Georgians gathered in Lenin Square, Tbilisi on the night of April 8-9 to protest at the situation. The local authorities lost control of the situation and Ministry of Interior troops armed with shovels and poison-gas were sent in to disperse the crowd. There were 20 deaths, including 12 women, and five leaders of informal nationalist groups were arrested. Despite a thorough investigation by the Soviet authorities in Moscow and the dismissal of leading Party officials, anti-Russian feeling in the Republic continues to run high.

More nationalist demonstrations occurred in July 1989, this time in Sukhumi, the Black Sea resort that is capital of Abkhazia. Plans were announced to open a branch of Tbilisi University there, despite the strong objections of the Abkhazians (who constitute just 20% of the population of their autonomous republic and are very sensitive to Georgian domination). In the ensuing ethnic clashes 14 were killed. Thus the situation in Abkhazia and Georgia as a whole remains extremely tense.

Minorities in Georgia

Despite the fact that 96% of Georgians live in Georgia, they constitute only 68.8% of the Republic's population (1979). There are sizeable minorities of Armenians (448,000 or 9%); Russians (372,000 or 7.4%); and Azerbaidjanis (256,000 or 5.1%). There are also 160,500 Ossetians (3.2%) — living mostly in the South Ossetian Autonomous Republic; 85,000 Abkhazians (1.7%) living in the Abkhazian ASSR; 95,000 Greeks (1.9%); and 26,000 Kurds (0.5%).

In addition to the Azerbaidjanis and Kurds, many of the 300,000 Georgians living in the Adzharian ASSR are Shi'ite Muslims (there is no Adzharian people; it was the part of Georgia closest to Turkey and, therefore, the region in which Muslim influence was strongest). Furthermore, up to 200,000 Meskhetian Turks (also Shi'ite Muslims) formerly inhabited Meskhet-Dzhavakheti, Georgia's border region with Turkey, until deported by Stalin in 1944 to Uzbekistan. The Georgians are resisting their return for fear of more ethnic unrest, pointing to the deterioration in relations between the Georgians and the Sunni Muslim Abkhazians (a proportion of the Ossetians are also Sunni Muslims).

(See also *Deported Nationalities; Other Muslim Peoples*)

Finally, there is a small community of 28,000 Georgian Jews, many of whom have emigrated in recent years, and even smaller groups of Mingrelians, Svanetians and Laz (all ethnically related to the Georgians).

In short, the national situation in Georgia is a microcosm of the situation throughout the USSR, with smaller peoples anxious to take advantage of the policy of *glasnost* in order to reduce the influence of their more numerous neighbours.

Kazakhs

Alternative names: **Kirghiz (until 1925)**
Location: **Kazakhstan (Central Asia), other parts of the USSR, China, Mongolia, Afghanistan**
Population: **6.6 million (USSR census 1979), 8 million (est. 1989)**
% of population: **2.5% (1979), 2.8% (est. 1989)**
Religion: **Sunni Muslim**
Language: **Kazakh**

The Kazakhs have the dubious distinction of being the only nationality in the USSR to constitute a minority in its native Union Republic (although demographic trends and a heightened sensitivity to European migration may soon redress this). The second largest Soviet Republic (after the RSFSR) it covers an area almost the size of Western Europe. Despite having the most Europeanized and secularized of the Muslim elites in Central Asia, the Kazakhs are experiencing a revival of Islamic awareness.

History and background

A mixture of Turkic and Mongol peoples, the Kazakhs led a nomadic existence until recent times. From the late fifteenth century they were organized into three great *zhuz* (hordes): the Greater, Middle and Lesser Hordes. The latter two hordes came under Russian protection as early as the 1730s, but the Greater Horde was not incorporated into the Empire until the 1860s. After some fierce resistance from local nationalists, Cossacks and White Army detachments, Soviet power was finally established in 1920, and the Kirghiz Autonomous Republic was admitted to the RSFSR. In 1925 it was renamed as the Kazakh ASSR (the people now known as Kirghiz were then called the Karakirghiz) and in 1936 it became the Kazakh Soviet Socialist Republic.

In the 1930s the still largely nomadic Kazakhs were subjected to a brutal campaign of sedentariza-

tion. Nonetheless, elements of their tribal organization appear to have survived and many Kazakhs still identify first with their horde, then their tribe and only then with a nationality.

The area of Central Asia with the longest exposure to Russian colonization, Kazakhstan has long been recognized as an area of strategic importance. It has been the site of some of the Soviet Union's most grandiose industrial (Turkestan–Siberian Railroad in the 1920s) and agricultural (the Virgin Lands scheme of the 1950s) projects, as well as the launch pad for the Soviet space programme (Baikonur) and the dumping-ground for deported nationalities (notably the Volga Germans and Koreans).

Constitution and law

In theory the Kazakh Soviet Socialist Republic (population 16.5 million in 1989) is a sovereign state that has freely joined the USSR federation. In reality Kazakhstan hitherto has been a constituent part of the USSR, which controls its foreign affairs, military formations, economic and commercial relations in a highly centralized fashion. Although the Soviet Constitution of 1977 allows Kazakhstan to elect its own legislative (Supreme Soviet), executive (Council of Ministers) and judiciary (Supreme Court), control is exercised by the centralized and Russian-dominated Communist Party of the Soviet Union (CPSU). As part of the USSR federation, Kazakhstan elects 11 deputies to the Council of

Nationalities and 14 to the Council of the Union in the 542-member Supreme Soviet of the USSR (every five years).

The Constitution also allows each Union Republic to secede from the USSR, but the primacy of All-Union legislation effectively renders this right invalid. Similarly, the constitutional provision that all citizens of the USSR of different races and nationalities have equal rights has been severely compromised by the domination in the USSR of Slavic (essentially Russian) political, cultural and economic norms.

Recent developments in political, economic and social rights

The most obvious benefit to the Kazakhs of Soviet power has been the spread of literacy. This has risen amongst the population in the nine to 49 age range from 8.1% in 1897 to 99.8% in 1979. However, there is little evidence of the long-advocated "drawing together" of Kazakh and Russian peoples. According to the 1979 census, only 131,000 (2%) of Kazakhs recognized Russian as their native language, although a further 52.3% claimed to speak it well. In contrast, only 353 out of the six million Russians in Kazakhstan (0.01%) named Kazakh as their native language and a mere 40,000 (0.66%) could speak it proficiently.

Although the Kazakhs have shown a greater propensity than their Turkic neighbours to migrate to Russia (500,000 or 7.9%), fully 91.9% of Kazakhs live in their native republic or Central Asia. Moreover, essentially all Kazakhs are Muslims and, together with their co-religionists of other Turkic nationalities, certainly already constitute a majority within the Republic. (The 1989 census will most probably reveal that the Kazakhs have overtaken the Russians as the most numerous nationality in Kazakhstan.)

The secularization of the Kazakh elite is reflected in the fact that there are almost as many Kazakhs (344,000 1982) in the CPSU as the far more numerous Uzbeks (411,000) although, at 1.9% of the overall membership, the Kazakhs are still under-represented. One of their number, Dinmukhamed Kunaev, served in the CPSU Politburo from 1972 until 1986 and his replacement by a Russian, Gennady Kolbin, sparked off ethnic violence in the capital, Alma Ata. Since then several senior Kazakh Party and state officials have been removed for corruption. In June 1989 there were serious clashes between Kazakhs and migrants from the Caucasus in the oil town of Novy Uzen on the Mangyshlak Peninsula, which resulted in five deaths and 50 injuries.

Minorities in Kazakhstan

Even if the Kazakhs have finally overtaken the Russians as the largest nationality in the Republic, Kazakhstan still has the biggest Russian population (6 million in 1979) outside the RSFSR and the Ukraine. The Russians tend to be concentrated in the Northern, Eastern and Central Regions, while the Kazakhs predominate in the South and West. Any attempts by the indigenous population to make Kazakh the official language of the Republic would clearly be resisted by the Russians who would claim that it is the lingua franca of all Soviet peoples.

The third largest national group in Kazakhstan are the Germans of whom there are 900,000 (6.1% 1979). The vast majority of these are Volga Germans deported from their autonomous republic in 1941 and still seeking to return to their homeland or, increasingly, to emigrate to West Germany. Another deported nationality in the Republic are the Koreans (92,000 or 0.6%) originally from the Soviet Far East.

There are also small minorities of Turkic Uigurs (148,000 or 1%) and Tibetan Dungans (22,500 or 0.2%) who have migrated from neighbouring China.

Moldavians

Alternative names: **Romanians, Bessarabians**
Location: **Moldavia (south-west USSR), other parts of USSR, Romania**
Population: **3 million (USSR census 1979) 3.3 million (est. 1989)**
% of population: **1.1% (1979 and est. 1989)**
Religion: **Orthodox Christianity**
Language: **Moldavian (a dialect of Romanian), Russian**

The Moldavians have no recent history as an independent nation and many consider themselves to be Romanian to whom they certainly are closely related ethnically, culturally and linguistically. They represent something of an anomaly among Soviet republics, belonging to neither the Slav,

Baltic, Central Asian nor Caucasian geographical groupings. The only major Latin minority within the USSR, the Moldavians are especially sensitive to Russification policies as recent events in the Republic have demonstrated.

History and background

Since losing its independence in the sixteenth century, Moldavia has been dominated in turn by the Ottoman Turks, the Russian Empire, Romania and the USSR. Its strategic position on the Dniester and Prut rivers along the Black Sea coast made it the centuries-long object of struggle between the Turks and the Russians, until the latter won control in 1812. Although Soviet power was declared throughout Moldavia after the October Revolution in 1917, Bessarabia was lost to Romania during the Civil War. In 1924 the remaining part of Moldavia was proclaimed an autonomous republic within the Ukrainian SSR. On the seizure of Bessarabia in 1940, the Moldavian Soviet Socialist Republic was formed. Overrun by Axis troops in World War II, Moldavia was liberated by the Red Army in 1944. Since the war there has been substantial Russian and Ukrainian immigration into the Republic. Although it has the highest population density of any Union Republic in the USSR, its population is the most rural (59% in 1981) in European Russia.

Constitution and law

In theory the Moldavian Soviet Socialist Republic (population 4.3 million in 1989) is a sovereign state that has freely acceded to the USSR federation. In reality Moldavia has hitherto been merely a constituent part of the USSR, which controls its foreign affairs, military formations, economic and commercial relations in a highly centralized fashion. Although the Soviet Constitution of 1977 provides for Moldavia to elect its own legislative (Supreme Soviet), executive (Council of Ministers) and judiciary (Supreme Court), control is effected by the centralized and Russian-dominated Communist Party of the Soviet Union (CPSU) through its Republican branch in Moldavia. As part of the USSR federation, Moldavia elects 11 deputies to the Council of Nationalities and four to the Council of the Union in the 542-member Supreme Soviet of the USSR (at five-yearly intervals).

The Constitution also allows each Union Republic to secede from the USSR, but the primacy of All-Union legislation effectively invalidates this right. Similarly, the constitutional provision that all citizens of the USSR of different races and nationalities have equal rights has been severely compromised by the domination in the USSR of Slavic (essentially Russian) political, cultural and economic norms.

Recent developments in political, economic and social rights

With 95% of Soviet Moldavians living in the Moldavian SSR and neighbouring regions of the Ukraine and 96.5% using Moldavian as their native tongue (1979), the language issue has figured prominently in Moldavian movements for self-determination. The two main points at issue are the status of Moldavian as the official language of the Republic (in which Moldavians represent 64% of the population, 1979) and the replacement of the Cyrillic script (introduced in 1940 to distinguish it from Romanian) with the Latin alphabet (which is used in the Baltic republics). In the summer of 1988 a Moldavian Democratic Movement for Perestroika held demonstrations on this issue in spite of resistance from local Party authorities (led by Semyon Grossu, one of the few survivors from the Brezhnev era). Early in 1989 the Moldavian authorities conceded that these issues should be addressed in a forthcoming language law and mass demonstrations in March and August 1989 reflected impatience with what was perceived as foot-dragging by the authorities. The publication of the secret protocols of the Nazi–Soviet Pact of 1939 (under which the USSR occupied Bessarabia) has fuelled further nationalist sentiments. The forthcoming elections to the Moldavian Supreme Soviet are likely to bring these conflicts to a head.

Minorities in Moldavia

Even by Soviet standards Moldavia represents quite a hotch-potch of nationalities. It is the only Union Republic in which Ukrainian immigrants (561,000 or 14.2%, 1979) outnumber Russians (506,000 or 12.8%); it has the largest Turkic nation in the USSR — the 138,000 Orthodox Christian Gagauzi — not to have its own territorial formation; and has the highest percentage of Soviet Jews (80,000 or 2%) in its population (from 1815 to 1917 Moldavia formed part of the Jewish Pale of Settlement and its capital — Kishinev — had a thriving Yiddish-speaking Jewish community). Lacking educational and cultural facilities in their own language, Ukrainians are subject to Russification in Moldavia so both Slavic groups are set to fight hard on the language issue.

Native Peoples of the North and Siberia

Names: **(i) Karelians, Komi (Zyrians), Komi-Permyaks, Saami (Lapps); (ii) Maris (Cheremiss), Mordvinians, Udmurts (Votyaks), Chuvash; (iii) Mansi, Khanti (Ostyak), Yakuts (Saka), Altais, Dolgans, Khakass, Evenks (Tungus), Eveni; (iv) Nanai, Ul'chi, Udegei, Inuit (Eskimos), Chukchi, Koryaks, Nivkhs; (i) and (iii) Nentsi (Samoyeds)**
Location: **(i) Northern European (ii) Central (iii) Siberian (iv) Far Eastern regions of USSR**
Population: **4.5 million (USSR census 1979), 5 million (est. 1989), ranging from 1,500 Inuit to 1.75 million Chuvash and 1.2 million Mordvinians**
% of population: **1.7% (1979 and est. 1989)**
Religion: **Orthodox Christianity, Shamanism, some Muslims**
Language: **each of the above nationalities has its own language in the following groups: a) Finnic (Karelian, Saami, Mordvinian, Mari, Udmurt, Komi); Ugric (Khanti, Mansi); Samoyed (Nentsi); b) Turkic (Chuvash, Yakuts, Altais, Khakass, Dolgans); c) Paleoasiatic (Chukchi, Koryaki, Nivkhs); d) Tungusic (Evenks, Eveni, Nanai, Ul'chi, Udegei)**

History and background

These groups represent indigenous populations occupying the territory over which the Russian state has spread since the twelfth century. Thus, the thickly forested areas populated by such Finnic peoples as the Karelians (who were a part of Kiev Rus), the Mordvinians, Udmurts, Mari and Komi, were among the first to be colonized by the Russians; while the Chuvash (a Turkic people probably descended from the Volga Bulgars) had become Russian subjects and Christians by 1551. A similar fate awaited the Turkic Yakuts and related Dolgans by the seventeenth century and, eventually, the groups in Manchuria, the Far North and East of the country. It is customary to distinguish between these larger groups of long-colonized peoples and the smaller, nomadic "peoples of the north" (who in 1979 had a total population of just 158,000, ranging from the 30,000 Nentsi, 27,300 Evenks and 21,000 Khanties to an estimated 97 Aleuts living off the coast of Kamchatka).

Although the older colonized peoples have long been sedentary and have largely assimilated to Russian norms of life (especially the Karelians, Mordvinians, Komis, Maris, Udmurts and Chuvash), this is not the case with the smaller peoples, despite great efforts to stamp out Shamanism and the old nomadic way of life.

In many of the territories, immigrant Russians far outnumber the local population, especially in Karelia (where the Karelians accounted for just 11% of the population in 1979, whereas the Russians formed 70%), Komi (Komis 24.5%, Russians 55%) and Udmurtia (Udmurts 31.7%, Russians 57.4%). Most of the indigenous populations are rural, speak Russian (e.g. 83% of Chuvash) and their own language (82% Chuvash). All use the Cyrillic script, although only the Chuvash have

always done so, the Latin script having been widespread in the 1920s and 30s.

Constitution and law

The following peoples have their own autonomous republics (and thus are theoretically able to elect their own legislative, executive and judicial organs and send four deputies each to the Council of Nationalities in the USSR Supreme Soviet): Karelia (population 1.1 million in 1989 — from 1940 until 1956 it was a Union Republic); Komi (population 1.26 million); Mari (population 0.75 million); Mordovia (population 0.96 million — a fall of 3% in the period 1979-1989); Udmurtia (population 1.6 million); Chuvashia (population 1.33 million); and Yakutia (population 1.1 million for a territory more than five times the size of France). The Altai (Gorno-Altai, population 192,000) and Khakass (population 569,000) in the far south of Siberia both have their own autonomous regions (which do not form states or governments and send only two deputies each to the Council of Nationalities) and the following have their own autonomous areas (which each send one deputy): Komi-Permyaks (population 159,000): Koryaks (population 39,000): Nenets (population 55,000); Dolgan-Nenets (population 55,000); Khanti-Mansi (population 269,000): Chukchi (population 158,000), Evenki (population 24,000) and Yamalo-Nenets (population 487,000). In most of these areas Russians outnumber the indigenous populations.

Recent developments in political, economic and social rights

The high degree of assimilation and long exposure to Russian culture has diluted the sense of national consciousness in the older colonized areas, although the heavily outnumbered Karelians understandably relate to the neighbouring and nationalist minded Finns and Estonians. The indigenous population growth tends to be small (in the case of Mordovia and Komi-Permyak it is actually falling) except in areas of rapid industrial development. Thus the formerly most sparsely populated areas of the USSR (e.g. Yakutia, 0.3 persons per square kilometre 1979) and the Evenki Autonomous Area (0.03 persons) have both experienced significant population growth (29% and 55% respectively) in the last decade. The combined effect of industrial development (a high proportion of the USSR's resources in energy and precious metals lie in these areas, and in 1974 construction commenced on the Baikal-Amur Railway through the region in order to exploit this wealth), environmental degradation and cultural assimilation has had a negative effect on the lives of the indigenous peoples, a fact that was first admitted by a Soviet representative to the International Labour Office in Geneva in June 1989.

In August 1989 the draft programme of the CPSU's National Policy advocated the convening of a Congress of Representatives of the Native Peoples of the North, Siberia and the Far East and the formation of an Association to safeguard their interests.

As most of the territory lies in border zones or areas of strategic importance, travel tends to be severely restricted in and out of these regions. A recent breakthrough in this respect was the reunion between Soviet and American Yupik Eskimos in Chukotka in June 1988 (it is worth noting that hitherto had a Soviet Eskimo wished to travel legally the four miles from Big Diomede Island in the USSR to Little Diomede Island in the USA in the Bering Strait, s/he would have had to go round the world to do it). Although sensitive to the aboriginal tribes' traditional way of life, the Soviet authorities have tried hard to Europeanize the indigenous peoples by means of education in boarding schools, sedentarization programmes and repeated attacks on vestiges of Shamanism (a word which in the 1930s was synonymous with *kulak*). However, for the most part, the aboriginal peoples have been encouraged merely to modernize their traditional occupations (trapping, fishing, reindeer herding etc.) rather than join the industrial workforce, and have thus kept somewhat apart from the migrant Russians. (In the Stalinist era there was a vast network of labour camps — the Gulag Archipelago — in this area; now workers are lured from the "European mainland" by higher wages.) Nonetheless, it seems likely that the reassessment of the Soviet nationalities' policy has occurred just in time to save some of the smaller peoples (and possibly the larger ones too) from extinction as distinctive national groups.

Other Muslim Peoples

Names: **(i) Tadjiks, Turkmen, Kirghiz, Karakalpaks; (ii) Bashkirs; (iii) Chechens, Ossetians, Avars, Lezghins, Kabardins, Dargins, Kurds, Abkhazians, Ingush, Adygeis, Kumyks, Karachais**
Location: **(i) Central Asian (ii) Central (iii) Caucasian regions of USSR; China (Kirghiz and Tadjiks); Afghanistan (Kirghiz, Tadjiks and Turkmen); Iran (Turkmen, Kurds); Iraq (Kurds); Turkey (Kurds); Syria (Kurds)**
Population: **about 13 million (1979), est. 15-16 million (1989)**
% of population; **5% (1979), est. 5.5% (1989)**
Religion: **Sunni Muslim, Shi'ite Muslim (Lezghins, Kurds). Many Ossetians are Orthodox Christian**
Language: **each of the nations named above has its own language**

Together with the Uzbeks, Kazakhs, Tatars and Azerbaidjanis, this group represented nearly 44 million people (17% of the population) in 1979 and probably accounts for nearly 53 million (18.4%) in 1989. It is estimated that by 2000, Muslims will constitute one quarter of the Soviet population, provide one third of Soviet Army recruits and one half of all Soviet births. With the worldwide resurgence of Islam, the Iranian Revolution and the Afghan War, the Soviet Union's rapidly growing Muslim population has become a key political, economic and social factor.

History and background

Most Soviet Muslims are Turkic peoples, but the Tadjiks, Ossetians and Kurds are Iranian and the Daghestani peoples (Avars, Lezghins, Dargins etc.), Abkhazians, Chechens and Kabardins are Indo-European, as are the Muslim Georgians and Gypsies.

The overwhelming majority of Soviet Muslims are Sunni Hanafis, except for Daghestan (where the majority are Sunni Shafe'is), Azerbaidjan (75% of the Azerbaidjanis are Shi'ite, as are the

Lezghins, Kurds and Meskhetian Turks) and Gorno-Badakhstan (where the Pamir Tadjiks are Ismaelis). This is reflected in the structure of the official Muslim organizations recognized by the Soviet State. Thus the four spiritual directorates serve Central Asia and Kazakhstan (based in Tashkent, Sunni Hanafi); Europe and Siberia (based in Ufa, Bashkiria — Sunni Hanafi); Northern Caucasus and Daghestan (Makhachkala, Daghestan — Sunni Shafe'i) and Transcausasia (Baku, Azerbaidjan — Shi'ite). However, the unofficial side of Soviet Islam — the *Sufi* brotherhoods based on secret *Tariqa* (Path to God) societies — is very widespread and is particularly strong in the Northern Caucasus.

Given the ethnic, linguistic and geographical diversity of Soviet Muslims there would appear to be little prospect of a cohesive Pan-Islamic movement flourishing in the USSR. However, there is a common resentment at the repression of Islamic customs and at the dominance of Slavic cultural norms. Morover, in Central Asia, the concept of the Muslim *Umma* (commonwealth or community) is still strong.

Constitution and law

The three largest of the smaller Muslim nations: the Tadjiks (estimated in 1989 at 3.9 million or 1.4% of Soviet population); Turkmen 2.6 million or 0.9%) and Kirghiz (2.3 million or 0.8%) all have their own Union Republics (population 1989: 5.1 million, 3.5 million and 4.3 million respectively). As such each elects 11 deputies to the Council of Nationalities and three to the Council of the Union in the 542 member Supreme Soviet of the USSR (every five years). In addition they nominally have the right to secede from the USSR federation.

The next largest grouping are the peoples of Daghestan (Avars, Lezghins, Dargins, Kumyks), who in 1989 had an estimated combined total of 1.8 million or 0.6% of the Soviet population. They reside in the Daghestan Autonomous Republic (part of the RSFSR), where they constitute an overwhelming majority. The estimated 1.4 million Baskhkirs (0.5%) also have an Autonomous Republic within the RSFSR but account for only 24% (1979) of the population (Russians 40%, Tatars 24%). The estimated 840,000 (0.3%) Chechens share with the less numerous Ingush (200,000) the Chechen-Ingush Autonomous Republic in the RSFSR and the 360,000 Kabardins (0.1%) share with the 75,000 Balkars the Kabardin-Balkar ASSR. The 400,000 Karakalpaks (0.15%) and the 100,000 Abkhazians (0.03%) have their own autonomous republics within Uzbekistan and Georgia respectively. All these territorial formations elect four deputies to the Council of Nationalities and a varying number (depending on population density) to the Council of the Union in the USSR Supreme Soviet.

The Ossetians (estimated at 570,000 or 0.3%) are divided between the North Ossetian ASSR in the RSFSR (four deputies to the Council of Nationalities) and the South Ossetian Autonomous Region in Georgia (two deputies). Other groups having autonomous regions in the RSFSR are the 150,000 (0.05%) Adygeis and the 150,000 Karachais (who share the Karachai-Circassian AR with the 50,000 Circassians). The Karachais, Balkars, Chechens and Ingush were all deported during World War II but allowed to return home in the 1950s — the Crimean Tatars and Meskhetian Turks are still in exile.

In addition the estimated 200,000 Pamir Tadjiks have their own Gorno-Badakhstan Autonomous Region in Tadjikistan, about 300,000 Georgians (a large proportion of whom are Shi'ite Muslim) live in the Adzharian ASSR in Georgia, and approximately half of the 200,000 Roma Gypsy (Romani) population of the USSR is Muslim.

Recent developments in political, economic and social rights

Most of the groups listed have hitherto been relatively untouched by the ethnic violence that has erupted recently in Central Asia and the Caucasus. However, there were nationalist riots in Tadjikistan in December 1988 and Turkmenia in May 1989. In Tadjikistan in July 1989 security forces shot dead two rioters in ethnic clashes between Kirghiz and Tadjiks, and Lezghins were involved in bloody clashes with Kazakhs in Novy Uzen (Kazakhstan) in June 1989. In July 1989 11 people were killed in clashes between Muslim Abkhazians and Orthodox Christian Georgians after plans were announced to open a branch of Tbilisi University in the Abkhazian capital, Sukhumi. Given the proximity of other flashpoints in Armenia, Azerbaidjan and Uzbekistan the potential for outbursts of nationalism among these groups is apparent.

(See also *Azerbaidjanis*; *Deported Nationalities*; *Kazakhs*; *Tatars*; *Uzbeks*)

Roma in the USSR

Alternative names: **Gypsies**
Location: **throughout USSR**
Population: **209,000 (1979) (unofficial est. 500,000)**
% of population: **0.1%**
Religion: **Muslim: 50%; Christian: 50%**
Language: **Romani, various Soviet languages**

Roma in the USSR are part of the much wider Roma community, and like elsewhere in Eastern Europe and Western Europe, have faced official assimilation policies and prejudice. According to the 1979 census they numbered 209,000 while other (unofficial) estimates placed their true numbers at over half a million. In the past ethnic origin was frequently denied (for example the number of Roma registering their nationality declined by 33% between 1959 and 1969) but this seems now to be changing and the figure rose by 20% during the census taken in 1979. Almost half the Roma live within the RSFSR while large communities exist in the Ukraine and Moldavia. The Luli, who are related to the Roma of Europe, live in the Asian Republics.

Roma are officially recognized as a national minority of Indian origin. As in many states in Eastern Europe nomadism was made illegal in the postwar period and the vast majority of Roma are now settled. Some groups however manage to travel in the summer months and have found a valuable economic niche as seasonal workers on collective farms. In recent years they have experienced a revival in their national culture through the Moscow Romani theatre and music ensembles and there are publications in the Romani language. After many years during which it was not possible to form a national association or to participate in the international Romani movement, there have been recent initiatives to allow more cultural autonomy and international contacts.

(See also *Roma* in **Western Europe and Scandinavia**, *Roma* in **Eastern Europe** and *Roma in Turkey* in **Middle East and North Africa**)

Tatars

Alternative names: **Volga Tatars (Kazan, Astrakhan, Kasymov and Mishari), Crimean Tatars, Siberian Tatars, Lithuanian Tatars, Kryashen**
Location: **Tataria (West Central USSR); other parts of USSR (especially Central Asia, Kazakhstan, south-west Siberia), Eastern Europe, Turkey, China**
Population: **6.3 million (USSR census 1979), 6.7 million (est. 1989)**
% of population: **2.4% (1979), 2.3% (est. 1989)**
Religion: **Sunni Muslim, Orthodox Christianity (minority)**
Language: **Tatar, Crimean Tatar, Russian**

The Tatars are by far the largest national minority in the USSR not to have its own Union Republic, being the sixth largest grouping in the USSR (thus being more numerous than nine peoples having their own SSR). In practice, all Union Republics share borders with foreign countries whereas Tataria (on the Middle Volga) is surrounded by Russian territory and could not secede from the USSR. Moreover, only 26% of Tatars live in the Tatar Autonomous Republic where they constitute under half of the population, the other 74% being dispersed throughout the USSR.

In fact, it is wrong to refer to a single Tatar people for the various groups on the Volga, in the Crimea, Siberia and Lithuania, have developed quite separately since the fourteenth century and retain only the most tenuous of links with one another. To add to the confusion, all Turkic peoples in European Russia until recently were referred to as Tatars (for example, many Armenians still call the Azerbaidjanis Azeri Tatars).

History and background

All Tatars in the USSR are remnants of the Golden Horde, the Turkic tribes led by the Mongols under Batu Khan that subjugated Russia from 1237 in an empire that stretched from the Polish to the Chinese borders and from the Black Sea to Siberia. The ending of the Mongol–Tatar yoke in 1480 and the fall of the two great Tatar khanates of Kazan (1552) and Astrakhan (1556) to Ivan IV reversed 300 years of oppression, although the separate Crimean Khanate retained a measure of independence until 1783.

Empress Catherine II regarded Islam (to which the Tatars had been converted in the fourteenth century) a reasonable religion and much better suited than Orthodox Christianity to the task of civilizing her Asian realms. The Volga Tatars were to become the undisputed leaders of Russian Islam and from then on played a crucial role in the development of the Empire's more backward regions. This led to the emergence of a prosperous Tatar merchant class, a high rate of urbanization and assimilation and a mobilized diaspora throughout the Empire. After fierce fighting in the Russian Civil War, Soviet power was finally consolidated in Tataria and the Tatar Autonomous Soviet Socialist Republic was formed in 1920.

Constitution and law

The Tatar Autonomous Soviet Socialist Republic (population 3.6 million in 1989) is a constituent part of the RSFSR, which belongs to the USSR federation. In theory, the Soviet Constitution of 1977 allows Tataria to elect its own legislative (Supreme Soviet), executive (Council of Ministers) and judiciary (Supreme Court). However, in practice, control is exercised through the centralized and Russian-dominated Communist Party of the Soviet Union through its Republican branch. As an autonomous republic, Tataria elects four deputies to the Council of Nationalities (whereas Estonia as a Union Republic elects 11) and has a tiny proportion (usually two or three) of the 146 deputies elected in the RSFSR to the Council of the Union in the 542-member Supreme Soviet of the USSR. The constitutional provision that all citizens of the USSR of different races and nationalities are equal is severely compromised by the domination of Slavic (essentially Russian) political, economic and social norms. Thus, the 74% of Tatars that live outside Tataria do not have the same provision, in terms of schools and publications in their native language, as the Russians (although the latter would argue that Russian is the lingua franca of all Soviet peoples).

Recent developments in political, economic and social rights

The Volga Tatars are one of the three main "target" groups of Soviet Muslims (the others being the Uzbeks and Azerbaidjanis).[1] They domi-
nate the European and Siberian spiritual directorate (one of four in the USSR) based at Ufa, in the neighbouring republic of Bashkiria. In August 1989 they celebrated in this city the 1,100 years since the conversion of the Volga Bulgars to Islam.

Dispersed throughout Central Asia, Siberia and the Lower Volga, the Tatars are highly urbanized. As a result they have a much lower birthrate than other Muslim nations in the USSR (between 1970 and 1979 it was 6.5%, the same as the Russians). The high degree of assimilation is shown by the fact that 69% of Tatars are fluent in Russian (compared with 49.8% Ukrainians and 26.7% Georgians) and 82% speak it well (compared with 49.3% Uzbeks and 25.4% Turkmen). The Tatars' apparent readiness to accept Russian culture has been rewarded in that they have the highest *per capita* membership of the CPSU amongst all major Turkic groups (2% of the Party in 1982). By contrast, the 150,000 Siberian Tatars (descendants of the so-called White Horde and also called the Tobolsk, Chulimsk and Barabas Tatars) are predominantly rural, culturally isolated and shamanistic.

Having been instrumental in spreading Islam throughout the Russian Empire (even among the predominantly Christian Mordvinians, Udmurts and Chuvash), the Tatars have been overtaken numerically and in influence by the Uzbeks. The lack of unified homeland has hampered the Tatars in articulating demands for autonomy and self-determination, although the resurgence of Islam has had a considerable impact. Ecological issues have also been a source of discontent and in 1989 there were mass demonstrations on the banks of the Kama River in Tataria to protest at the construction of a nuclear power station at Kamskiye Polyany.

Migration and diaspora

Surprisingly, the Tatars constitute the second largest nationality in the RSFSR (five million or 3.6% in 1979) concentrated mostly in Tataria (1.6 million or 26%) and Bashkiria (940,000 or 15%). A further 1.2 million (18.3%) reside in Kazakhstan and Central Asia and there are small communities in Azerbaidjan (31,000), Lithuania (5,000) and every major city in the USSR.

Tatar minorities

The long exposure to Slavic culture inevitably led to a proportion of Tatars becoming Orthodox Christians. It is estimated that about quarter of a million (4%) Tatars are Kryashens (or Christian Tatars).

(See also *Deported Nationalities*; *Other Muslim Peoples*)

[1]Target groups are those with which other groups tend to identify and look to for initiatives.

Ukrainians

Alternative names: **Little or Lesser Russians (to 1917): Ruthenians (historical): Cossacks (historical): khokhols (slang)**
Location: **Ukraine (south-west USSR), other parts of USSR, Eastern Europe, North America, Western Europe, South America, Australia**
Population: **42.3 million (USSR census 1979), 44 million (est. 1989), 3 million abroad**
% of population: **16.2% (1979), 15.3% (est. 1989)**
Religion: **Christianity (Orthodox and "Uniate" Catholic)**
Language: **Ukrainian, Russian**

The Ukrainians constitute the second largest nation in the USSR after the 145 million Russians (known prior to 1917 as the Great or Greater Russians). As such they are the largest national minority in Europe and, arguably, the world. Occupying a land the size of France with a population greater than that of Poland, the Ukrainians have failed in recent history to achieve genuine and lasting independent statehood. For more than 300 years they have been dominated by their fellow Eastern Slavs and, for the most part, co-religionists — the Russians. Indeed, the very name Ukraine means "at the border" in Russian.

History and background

The Ukrainians, in common with the Byelorussians and Russians, trace their ancestry to the unified state of Kievan Rus, which flourished from the ninth to twelfth centuries and was destroyed by the Mongol–Tatar invasion in the thirteenth century. Thus, the adoption of Orthodox Christianity in 988, the use of Old Church Slavonic and its Cyrillic script were common to all three East Slavic nations. However, the disintegration of Kiev Rus led to a separate development for the Ukraine until its controversial union with Russia in 1654. In this intervening period the main Western influences came from Poland and Lithuania, culminating in 1596 with a part of the Ukrainian Orthodox clergy acknowledging the primacy of Rome while retaining the Eastern Rite, thus forming the "Uniate" Church. At the same time many Orthodox Ukrainians fled to the no man's land of the South Ukrainian steppes where they set up the semi-autonomous Cossack communities that were to dominate Ukrainian political life until their suppression in the eighteenth century (and final destruction in the 1930s).

The autocratic nature of the Russian Empire precluded lasting manifestations of Ukrainian self-determination and the process of Russification proceeded apace, particularly in the rapidly-growing industrial centres. Thus, the nineteenth century Ukrainian writer, Nikolai Gogol, achieved fame by writing in Russian rather than his native Ukrainian, whereas his compatriot, the poet Taras Shevchenko, provoked hostile reaction from the Tsarist authorities with the nationalist sentiments of his work. When the Empire finally broke up in 1917 there were short-lived attempts to establish an independent Ukrainian state but, by 1920, Soviet power had been established throughout the Ukraine (although Western Ukraine was ceded to Poland until 1939). Stalin's policies (collectivization leading to the famine of 1933, the purges etc.) hit the Ukrainians with particular ferocity and doubts over their loyalty in World War II — in which it is estimated the Ukraine lost 5.5 million people, including nearly one million Jews — increased pressure on so-called Ukrainian "bourgeois nationalism".

The post-Stalinist "thaw" in the 1950s to 1960s and the current era of *glasnost* have seen revivals of Ukrainian national consciousness. Of particular note in the earlier period were the accounts of Ukrainian dissident trials compiled by Vyacheslav Chornovil and the critique "Internationalism or Russification" by the literary critic Ivan Dzyuba. Despite harassment and repression in the 1970s, particularly after the relatively tolerant Ukrainian Communist Party leader, Shelest, was replaced in 1972 by Shcherbitsky, Ukrainians continued to play a key role in dissident political, literary and religious activities.

Constitution and law

In theory the Ukrainian Soviet Socialist Republic (population 51.7 million in 1989) is a sovereign state and has full membership of the United Nations. In reality the Ukraine has hitherto been little more than a constituent part of the USSR, which controls its foreign affairs, economic, military and commercial relations in a highly centralized fashion. Although the Soviet Constitution of 1977 provides for the Ukraine to elect its own legislative (Supreme Soviet), executive (Council of Ministers) and judiciary (Supreme Court), power resides effectively in the centralized and Russian-dominated Communist Party of the Soviet Union through its Republican branch in the Ukraine.

Ukrainian SSR

However, the forthcoming elections to the Ukrainian Supreme Soviet promise to end this monopoly. As part of the USSR, the Ukraine also elects 11 Deputies to the Council of Nationalities and 52 to the Council of the Union in the 542-member Supreme Soviet of the USSR (every five years).

The Constitution also allows each Union Republic to secede from the USSR but the primacy of All-Union legislation over that of a constituent Republic effectively invalidates this.

Similarly, the constitutional assertion that all citizens of the USSR of different races and nationalities have equal rights has been severely compromised by the domination in the USSR of Slavic (essentially Russian) political, cultural and economic norms.

Recent developments in political, economic and social rights

Even in the current unprecedented wave of national unrest in the USSR, the Ukrainians hitherto have remained relatively quiet. To some extent this is due to the special relationship between the Ukrainians and Russians, a relationship which until very recently was pivotal in ensur-

ing harmonious national policies in the USSR. However, the rapid growth of the Soviet Muslim population has brought to the forefront long-standing and deep-seated contradictions between the Eastern Slavs and Turkic peoples of the USSR. In this fundamental ethnic divide the Ukrainians and Byelorussians tend to identify — and be identified — with the Russians. In practical terms this means that a Ukrainian who accepts the pre-eminence of Russian culture will suffer little real discrimination and may reach the very highest position in the political, state and military hierarchies (for example, Nikolai Podgorny became President of the USSR). Those Ukrainians who actively resist assimilation may not expect to be rewarded with similar tolerance or upward mobility.

The impact of Russification is more apparent among Ukrainians living outside of their native Republic, there being no Ukrainian-language schools or periodicals for the 5.8 million Ukrainians in other Republics. They, naturally, tend to share the facilities accorded to the Russians, who are very well provided for in this respect. As a result, only 69% of Ukrainians living outside their Republic considered Ukrainian their native language compared with 89% in the Ukraine (1979). Even within the Ukraine, however, the language is sometimes overshadowed by Russian, Ukrainians enjoying on average only 2.2 books *per capita* per annum in their native language compared with a USSR average of 6.8 (1982).

It is hard to escape the conclusion that, had the Soviet Union consisted only of Eastern Slavs, the long-advocated "drawing together" of peoples to form a single Soviet people might, in time, have occurred. However, it is precisely the policies of assimilation that have been applied by the Russians to their junior partners — the Ukrainians and Byelorussians — that have aroused such resentment and opposition when directed at non-Slavic minorities. Thus, although the movement for complete independence is not as strong as in the Baltic republics, Ukrainians are also demanding economic and cultural autonomy and genuinely equal rights in language, education, religion etc.

The Chernobyl nuclear accident on Ukrainian soil in April 1986 was a major turning point in national relations in the USSR, focusing attention on dissatisfaction with economic, social and environmental policies, while at the same time imbuing the policy of *glasnost* with important new content. As a result, many of the Ukrainians' long-standing grievances have recently resurfaced. These include the status of the Uniate Church, the future of the Ukrainian language, the anti-Ukrainian excesses of Stalin and the popular demand for genuine civil liberties. Thus the legality of the notorious Synod of Lvov, which in 1946 abolished the Uniate Church, has been challenged, Uniate bishops have commenced to preach more openly (most notably at the public mass in the summer of 1988 held to celebrate the millennium of Christianity in Russia), Pope John Paul II has agreed to serve as Chairman of the Synod of Uniate Bishops and there have been sharp exchanges in the Soviet press between representatives of the Orthodox Church, who still strongly oppose reconstituting the Uniate Church, and journalists claiming that there are four million Uniate Catholics in the Ukraine. On the other hand, the defiant visionary Josyf Terelya (now in exile in Canada) has been replaced as Chairman of the Central Committee of Ukrainian Uniate Catholics by the more conciliatory Ivan Gell.

Among the popular organizations that have emerged recently are an environmental movement — Green World — formed in the wake of the Chernobyl disaster by writer Oles Honchar; a Popular Movement for *Perestroika* (*Narodni Ruch*) which, since November 1988, has drawn members mainly from the cultural and technical intelligentsia and skilled workers in mass campaigns for economic autonomy and political pluralism (and was particularly effective in the March 1989 elections to the Congress of People's Deputies in stopping the election of several leading Party and state officials who stood unopposed); the Ukrainian Language Society active since January 1989 under the leadership of writer Dmitry Pavlichko; and the anti-Stalinist Memorial Association formed early in 1989 in protest at what is perceived as the continuing cover-up of Stalin's crimes in the Ukraine. A particular bone of contention is the monument in Bikovnya Forest, near Kiev, which the Soviet authorities recognize as a site of Nazi atrocities but which Memorial claims was a place where Stalin's secret police — the NKVD — executed up to 150,000 Ukrainians.

Repeatedly in 1989 these organizations were able to engender mass demonstrations in the Ukraine against the inflexible attitude of the Shcherbitsky leadership. However, it was the strike of the Donbas coalminers, in the Ukraine's industrial heartland, that posed the strongest challenge to the regime in July 1989. That strike was called off after the personal intervention of President Gorbachev who would appear to have retained the support of many of the protesters. This raises the question as to whether most Ukrainians would be satisfied with merely a return to the relatively relaxed era of Ukrainization in 1920-1930 prior to Stalin's reversal of that policy or whether they would like to follow the path of Poland towards a pluralistic democratic state. To some extent there exists a geographical divide, with the West Ukrainians (who were under Polish rule from 1921-1939) tending to be the more radical. However, the Soviet authorities too appear split — between the "conservatives" in Kiev and the "reformers" in Moscow, the latter being aware that, however the situation develops with smaller nationalities in the USSR, the future of the federation depends to a great extent on the Ukrainians.

Migration and diaspora

Apart from the estimated three million Ukrainians living abroad who maintain their native cultural, religious and linguistic traditions, there are large concentrations of Ukrainians in most Soviet republics. Indeed in Moldavia (1979) the 561,000 Ukrainians (14.2%) outnumber the 506,000 Russians (12.8%). However, the largest concentrations are in the RSFSR (3.66 million or 8.6% of all Soviet Ukrainians) and Kazakhstan (898,000 or 2.1%). Only the 36.5 million Ukrainians (1979) living in their native Republic, where they constitute 73.6% of the population, have access to Ukrainian schools (although it is claimed that only 16% of schools in the Republic teach in Ukrainian).

Significantly, Ukrainians account for 16% (2.8 million 1982) of all members of the CPSU (i.e. roughly on a par with their proportion of the Soviet population).

Minorities in the Ukraine

The Ukraine has no autonomous national formations within its borders but there are about 80 nationalities living in the Republic. Moveover, until 1940 the Moldavian Autonomous Soviet Socialist Republic (ASSR) was part of the Ukraine as, since 1954, has been the Crimea (formerly the territory of the Crimean Tatar ASSR until the expulsion to Central Asia of the Tatars in 1944). In addition, semi-autonomous Cossack communities existed along the Don and Dnieper rivers until the collectivization drive of the 1930s (with the subsequent famine of 1933 which decimated the local peasantry). Territorial acquisitions in World War II (Western Ukraine, Bessarabia, Northern Bukovina and Transcarpathia) led to further influxes of other nationalities and continued Russian immigration means that there are now more than 11 million (21%) Russians living in the Ukraine out of a total of 13.5m non-Ukrainians (27%). Should there be any moves to make Ukrainian the official language of the Republic, there is sure to be stiff opposition from the Russian minority who would claim that Russian is the language of the Soviet peoples, not just its largest nationality.

Being part of the Jewish Pale of Settlement from 1815 to 1917, the Ukraine has long had a large Jewish population and, although it had shrunk (by assimilation, emigration and war casualties) to 634,000 by 1979, this represented one third of all Soviet Jews and the third largest national group in the Ukraine. There are long-standing charges of anti-semitism levelled at Ukrainian authorities, culminating in the Khmelnitsky massacres of the mid-seventeenth century and the pogroms of the late-nineteenth to early-twentieth centuries.

It is to be hoped, therefore, that any moves towards Ukrainian self-determination will be accompanied by increased tolerance towards the minorities living within the Republic.

Uzbeks

Alternative names: **Turkestanis**
Location: **Uzbekistan (Central Asia, USSR), other parts of USSR, Afghanistan, China**
Population: **12.5 million (USSR Census 1979), 16 million (est. 1989)**
% of population: **4.8% (1979), 5.6% (est. 1989)**
Religion: **Sunni Muslim**
Language: **Uzbek**

The Uzbeks are the most numerous of the non-Slavic nations of the USSR and thus constitute, in the opinion of many, the largest of the classically "colonized" peoples of the Soviet Union. Even more importantly, in the light of recent events, they are by far the largest of the three main "target" groups of Soviet Muslims (the others being the Volga Tatars and Azerbaidjanis).[1] Probably the most religious of all the Central Asian Muslims, Uzbek relations with the Soviet Slavs are rapidly becoming the most critical of all ethnic relationships in the USSR.

History and background

The Uzbeks probably get their name from the Tatar khan Uzbek who converted the Golden Horde to the Muslim faith in the fourteenth century. They occupy a land with a rich history of civilization stretching back to the eighth century BC. Originally a nomadic tribe, they became sedentary some 300 years ago, coming under Russian influence only in the 1860s. Although Soviet power was proclaimed throughout Turkestan after the 1917 revolutions, Basmach nationalists fought the Red Army until they were finally eliminated in 1933. In 1924 the Soviet authorities split up Turkestan along national lines and the Uzbek Soviet Socialist Republic was admitted into the USSR. Uzbekistan has since become the chief producer of Soviet cotton, but the economic and ecological effects of reliance on this monoculture have become a source of friction in recent years. Periodic campaigns aimed at eroding the influence of Islam appear to have had little effect on the Uzbeks who have continued with their faith within the limits laid down by successive Soviet regimes and have taken advantage of the recent relaxation of attitudes towards religion in the Gorbachev era. One of the four main spiritual directorates of Soviet Islam (for Central Asia and Kazakhstan) is located in Tashkent, the capital of Uzbekistan, as are two *madrasahs*

[1] Target groups are those with which other groups tend to identify and look to for initiatives. Thus Central Asian Muslims look to the Uzbeks as a model.

(seminaries) and the publication "Muslims of the Soviet East". In 1966 an earthquake virtually destroyed the capital, Tashkent, which has since been rebuilt as a modern Europeanized city. On the other hand, the ancient cities of Bukhara and Samarkand have retained much of their Oriental character. Similarly, although key elements of Muslim culture have been suppressed, the traditional tea house (*chaikhana*) and skull-caps (*tubiteika*) are much in evidence.

Constitution and law

In theory the Uzbek Soviet Socialist Republic (population 20 million in 1989) is a sovereign state that has freely joined the USSR federation. In reality, Uzbekistan has been hitherto a constituent part of the USSR, which controls its foreign affairs, military formations, economic and commercial relations in a highly centralized fashion. Although the Soviet Constitution of 1977 provides for Uzbekistan electing its own legislative (Supreme Soviet), executive (Council of Ministers) and judiciary (Supreme Court); control is exercised by the centralized and Russian-dominated Communist Party of the Soviet Union (CPSU) through its Republican branch. As part of the USSR federation Uzbekistan elects 11 deputies to the Council of Nationalities (the Chairman of which Rafik Nishanov is an Uzbek) and 14 to the Council of the Union in the 542 member Supreme Soviet of the USSR (at five-yearly intervals).

The Constitution also allows each Union Republic to secede from the USSR, but the primacy of All-Union legislation effectively invalidates this right. Similarly, the constitutional provision that all citizens of the USSR of different races and nationalities have equal rights has been severely compromised by the domination in the USSR of Slavic (essentially Russian) political, cultural and economic norms.

Recent developments in political, economic and social rights

One of the undisputed benefits of Soviet power in Uzbekistan has been the spread of literacy, which has grown in the age-group nine to 49 from 3.6% in 1897 to 99.9% in 1979. This has not been accompanied by the anticipated "drawing together" of the Uzbek and Russian peoples. Thus, in 1979, only 0.63% of Uzbeks (78,000) considered Russian their native tongue, although a further 49.3% claimed a good knowledge of it. Moreover, the Uzbeks have shown little inclination to migrate, 99.3% of all Uzbeks living in Central Asia and Kazakhstan and only 72,000 (0.58%) in the RSFSR. Given the high Uzbek birthrate (29% in 1970-79) compared to that of the RSFSR (6%) this is likely to precipitate unemployment in Uzbekistan (already estimated at half a million people) and a shortage of labour in the new industrial areas of the Russian North. This lack of integration is reflected in the fact that Uzbeks constitute 5.6% of the population but, in 1982, represented just 2.3% (411,000) of the CPSU membership. This accounts for the relatively few Uzbeks in leading positions in political, economic and military hierarchies.

This situation was exacerbated during the Brezhnev era (1964-82) when Uzbek Party and state leaders became enmeshed in corruption rings, the exposure of which under Gorbachev has given rise to some national friction.

However, the central bone of contention for Uzbeks remains the Soviet authorities' attitude to Islam. Although they represent only 68.7% of the population of Uzbekistan, the Uzbeks have been remarkably successful in retaining their homogenity and cultural integrity. Despite the presence of 1.66 million Russians (10.8%, 1979) residing in the large cities of Uzbekistan, fully 84.1% of the population are Muslim. Sixty-five years after the partition of Turkmenistan, the concept of *Dar-ul-Islam* (Land of Religion) remains strong in Central Asia. The closure of mosques (from 26,279 throughout the Russian Empire in 1912 to 450 in 1976), the banning of the *hadj* (pilgrimage to Mecca), the replacement of Arabic script (in which the Koran is written) first by Latin in the 1920s and then by Cyrillic in the 1940s and restrictions on Muslim publications and religious practices appear until recently to have been accepted with passive resignation and few persistent demands for autonomy or self-determination.

However, the worldwide resurgence of Islam, the Iranian Revolution and, especially, the Afghan War, have raised the aspirations of the Uzbek Muslims. At the same time Slav immigration and the utilization of Uzbekistan and neighbouring Kazakhstan as a dumping-ground for deported nationalities, together with rising discontent at the economic and ecological state of the Republic, have created grievances which have resulted in disturbances, most notably the ethnic clashes between Uzbeks and Meskhetian Turks in the Fergana Valley (May and June 1989), which resulted in 105 deaths and 1,011 injuries. There is evidence that, although these clashes were between two Muslim groups, anti-Russian feeling was running high amongst the rioters. Nationalist sentiments gave rise in 1988 to the *Birlik* (Unity) movement. Given the numerical superiority of the Uzbeks in Turkestan, there is understandable concern amongst neighbouring Turkic peoples at their growing dominance in the region and complaints have been raised at assimilation policies promoted in

Uzbekistan. However, if the Pan-Turkic movement is to be revived it is likely to be led by the Uzbeks.

Minorities in Uzbekistan

Although the largest minority in Uzbekistan, only 465 out of 1.66 million Russians in the Republic (0.03%) consider Uzbek their native language and a mere 97,652 (5.9%) speak it well. Moreover, although there is a degree of intermarriage, it is still relatively rare for a Russian man to marry an Uzbek woman. Europeans still constitute the majority of the population of Tashkent, which with 1.8 million inhabitants is the fourth largest city in the USSR and the most Europeanized part of Central Asia.

However, the best known minorities in Uzbekistan are the Crimean Tatars and Meskhetian Turks, nationalities deported in 1944 and seeking a return to their homelands since. Less well-known are the 163,000 Koreans (deported in the 1930s from the Soviet Far East).

In addition there is a total of 649,000 Tatars (the 1979 census did not distinguish between the ethnically-diverse Volga and Crimean Tatars) and nearly 300,000 Karakalpaks, a formerly nomadic people closely related to the Kazakhs, who have had their own Autonomous Republic in Western Uzbekistan since 1925.

(See also *Deported Nationalities*; *Other Muslim Peoples*)

Further References

Religious Minorities in the Soviet Union, MRG Report No. 1, 1984

The Crimean Tatars, Volga Germans and Meskhetians: Soviet treatment of some national minorities, MRG Report No. 6, 1980

The Armenians, MRG Report No. 32, 1987

The Ukrainians and Georgians, Report No. 50, 1981

MIDDLE EAST AND NORTH AFRICA

Among many issues, that of the treatment of minorities figures prominently in the turbulent politics of the Middle East. The States of the region are immensely varied in their political structures and orientation, their origins, their ethnic and religious composition. As a corollary, the minorities under consideration exhibit a variety of demands and aspirations. Properly considered, some "minorities" are not minorities at all: thus the Palestinians are *de facto* a minority in Israel, Lebanon, Jordan and other host-States, but in the eyes of the international community, and *de jure* from the point of international law, they constitute a people with a right to self-determination. The fact that the right will inevitably have to be exercised with regard to the rights of other States and peoples in the region (principally Israel) does not negate their entitlement. The exercise of this self-determination will require major political and territorial realignments. This is a feature of the doctrine of which many States are fearful in terms of setting precedents which may work against them. While the Palestinians have established a special case, others have not.

The Kurds constitute a clear example of the kind of minority whose ambitions work against the State system and the inscription of its rules in international law. If the Kurds were to be recognized as holding the right of self-determination, this would, if translated into the vocabulary of independence, subtract from the territorial integrity of Iran, Iraq, Turkey, and, to a lesser extent, Syria. The Kurds, along with the Armenians, made a breakthrough in their ambitions to rule themselves at the Paris Peace Conference following World War I, securing a conditional promise of independence from Turkey in the Treaty of Sèvres. The collapse of the Ottoman Empire and the rise of the Turkish State destroyed this ambition, and the subsequent Treaty of Lausanne did not refer to the Kurds by name. Their treatment since then demonstrates that even a tenuous independence is preferable to permanent minority status in sternly nationalist States such as Turkey and Iraq.

Other minorities include the myriad religious groups, often of millennial antiquity, in this region which is the cradle of the great monotheistic religions of Judaism, Christianity and Islam. The general Islamicization following Arab expansion in the seventh and subsequent centuries AD resulted in unique systems of accommodation between Islamic polities and non-Islamic "Peoples of the Book", and by extension Zoroastrians, Hindus, Buddhists and adherents of other scriptural religions. The Ottoman *Millet* system gave Christians and Jews protected status within the Empire. Remnants of this system still exist, for example in Israel, giving a particular community dimension to the treatment of minority groups. However, the tolerance accorded to other religions was not always manifested, and the contemporary rise of Islamic fundamentalism in States such as Iran has created grave problems for minority religions, including those related to, but outside mainstream Islam. The Baha'is, Alawis, and Assyrians are among those groups which have suffered religious intolerance to varying degrees. The position of the Baha'is in Iran is particularly serious. Iran tries to deflect international criticism of its treatment of this group by denying that Baha'ism constitutes a religion: rather, it is described as a product of the colonial era, and can thus be aligned with all the other evils of colonialism as deserving of elimination. Denial of the existence of a religious minority parallels claims made by governments in many States that they have no minorities (see introduction to South and Central America). The first, minimal requirement of an effective international supervision of minority rights must be a means of establishing that the groups "exist". Regrettably, there is as yet no legally binding definition of what constitutes a minority.

The retreat of the Ottomans, the rise of Arab nationalism, the emergence of Arab Socialism, intolerance and continued interference by the powers in the region produce many other minority issues. Lebanon and Cyprus have fragmented under a combination of internal and external pressures. Christianity, Judaism and Islam can appear to be mutually irreconcilable. The eruption of Israel on the international scene has brought a new dimension of conflict. Rival groups use terror as a weapon in their struggles. The Middle East has occupied the centre of the world stage in recent decades and will do so for some time to come. Tolerance, rapprochement, stability and a consistent structure of rights for individuals, peoples and minorities appear to be distant prospects.

Instruments on Minority Rights

There is no general "Islamic" treaty on human rights comparable to regional instruments in Europe and the Americas. States profess difficulties with some aspects of contemporary human rights instruments such as the Universal Declaration. Saudi Arabia abstained on the vote for this instrument, arguing that it proclaimed freedom to change one's religion, a "freedom" not permitted to Muslims. Iran has also stated that any conflict between the Quran and human rights must be resolved in favour of the former. Islamic scholars who debate the relationship between Islam and human rights are not of one mind, but the relative lack of Islamic participation in the drafting of the Universal Declaration is still capable of exciting adverse comment. Despite this, Iran is a party to the UN Covenants on Human Rights and other instruments such as the Genocide Convention. The record of other States in the region is generally good in terms of ratification of instruments. Turkey is one exception: it has not ratified the UN Covenants nor the Convention against Racial Discrimination. Turkey is, however, a party to the European Convention on Human Rights and, in that context, has accepted the right of individuals to petition the Council of Europe at Strasbourg regarding human rights violations. Saudi Arabia has the least number of ratifications of human rights treaties: of the major relevant treaties, only the Genocide Convention has attracted its support. Israel has signed but not ratified the UN Covenants, but is a party to the Convention against Racial Discrimination. The independence of Cyprus was secured by specific international treaties containing guarantees for the Greek and Turkish communities. The principles of this "communalism" were embodied in the complex Constitution of Cyprus 1960. In this case, the attempt to secure minority representation in the State through particular agreements proved ineffective.

In terms of constitutional law, there is a considerable variety of minority-related regimes, both negative and positive. Privilege for particular peoples may flow from such as Israel's Declaration of Independence in 1944: a guiding principle of State policy is ". . .the natural right of the Jewish people to be master of its own fate, like all other nations, in its own sovereign State. . . The State of Israel will be open for Jewish immigration and for the ingathering of the exiles. . .". On the other hand, the Declaration promises to ". . .foster the development of the country for the benefit of all its inhabitants. . .". Religious communities in Israel enjoy recognition and considerable autonomy; religious laws of the communities govern their members in matters of personal status. Broad forms of autonomy may also be found in such as the Autonomy Law of 1974 for the Kurds in Iraq. Some instruction on relative treatment of groups may be gained from comparison of the legal regimes to which a dispersed group such as the Kurds are subjected. Whatever the defects of implementation, the regime in Iraq is at least potentially better than that in Turkey. The preamble to the 1982 Constitution of Turkey recites that ". . .no protection shall be afforded to thoughts or opinions contrary to Turkish national interests, the principle of the existence of Turkey as an indivisible entity. . . Turkish historical and moral values, or the nationalism, principles, reforms and modernism of Atatürk. . .". The Constitution devotes itself to secularizing, modernizing and homogenizing the population of Turkey. Article 26 of the Constitution provides that "no language prohibited by law shall be used in the expression and dissemination of thought". This genre of stipulation is so rare in modern constitutions as to call for comment or at least some indication as to what is addressed. The prohibited language appears to be Kurdish so that the target is, unsurprisingly, a minority group. It is an interesting speculation for the future to assess the compatibility of this provision with provisions in the European Convention on Human Rights on freedom of expression.

Treatment of minorities

The complex politics of the Middle East do not allow for ready generalizations about minorities. States both maintain traditions of tolerance and commit atrocities. Fierce passions of a religious or nationalist nature can displace structures of law and rights. The Kurdish Autonomy Law has not saved Iraq from allegations of genocide. The religiously inspired revolution in Iran created enormous problems for human rights, and some minorities were singled out for singularly oppressive treatment.

The disintegrating State of Lebanon allows inter-minority conflicts to run virtually unchecked. Traditional, established religious communities need continued vigilance in unsympathetic States. The Israeli treatment of Palestinians stems in part from the siege mentality displayed by that State, the fear of being submerged in a sea of hostility. Jews in turn may suffer privations in States beyond Israel: anti-Zionism may become anti-Semitism. Perhaps what is most required is some degree of stability. Before structures designed to promote civil and social justice can operate, a degree of order is required. A binding statement of human rights for the region would assist — though the North African States may be parties to the African Charter on Human and Peoples' Rights, and Turkey and Cyprus adhere to the European Convention. In the same way as Africa has adapted the basic philosophy of human rights to its own history and traditions, so may the Islamic States in the fullness of time.

Alawis of Syria

Location: **Latakia province, north-western Syria**
Population: **800,000 (est.)**
% of population: **11%**
Religion: **heterodox branch of Shi'a Islam**
Language: **Arabic**

The Alawis are a religious sect inhabiting the underdeveloped and densely settled mountainous region of Jabal Alawi of Latakia province in Syria. Their origins are unclear but they are a splinter group of the Shi'a branch of Islam who view themselves as Shi'ite Muslims, although the majority Sunni population consider them to be religious heretics. Like the Druzes, they believe in the transmigration of the soul and they also follow several eclectic practices which place them at the fringes of Islam.

Since the traditional Islamic state was theocratic, the Alawis were thought of as political as well as religious dissidents and were pronounced in the fourteenth century to be "more infidel than the Jews or Christians". In order to protect itself from discrimination by other Syrians the Alawi community sought refuge in a remote mountainous region where they remained fiercely independent from central government until well into the twentieth century despite administrative reforms introduced during the nineteenth century.

French rule was extended to the region between World Wars I and II and the Alawis were granted a degree of autonomy, but little was done to alleviate the cumulative effects of discrimination. Approximately 61% of Alawis were reported to have trachoma, a much higher percentage than among other Syrian communities. Malnutrition and high infant mortality rates were accompanied by poor educational facilities. As a result of poverty and poor opportunities many Alawis emigrated, most to the cities of Lebanon where they took the lowest paid and least desirable jobs and were subject to further discrimination.

In post-independent Syria the lowly position of the Alawis caused them to be attracted by the socialist secularist Ba'ath party. Over the past forty years they have become increasingly involved in the party and by the early 1960s some had taken leading positions within both the Ba'ath party and the armed forces, and when in 1963 a military coup brought the Ba'athists to power the Alawis were suddenly playing a leading role in national politics.

Between 1966 and 1976, 27% of all members of the Regional Command of the party and 21% of all cabinet ministers were Alawis, and ministers from Latakia province held 35 of the 59 portfolios. It was estimated that 18 of the top 25 command positions in the armed forces were held by Alawis. President Assad is himself an Alawi. Clearly in view of the general attitude towards the Alawis this situation is potentially explosive, and several prominent Alawis were assassinated in the late 1970s. Attempts by the Ba'athist regime to convince the Sunni majority that Alawi doctrine and practices are fully Islamic have not been entirely successful.

The 1980s have seen several attempts to overthrow Alawi dominance, principally by Sunnis from such groups as the Muslim Brotherhood. In 1979 over 50 military cadets, mainly Alawis, were killed, there were riots in Aleppo in 1980 and an attempted military coup in 1982 was led by the air force, the branch of the military where the officers are principally Sunni Muslims. The Assad regime is highly repressive and thousands of people have been jailed, including some Alawis. It has been reported that despite Alawi dominance in the army and security forces, those who have remained in the villages of Latakia have been economically neglected.

Armenians of Turkey and the Middle East

Location: **Istanbul, Lebanon, Iran and other Middle Eastern countries**
Population: **Total 350,000-400,000 (est.)**
% of population: **Lebanon 5%; elsewhere much smaller**
Religion: **Armenian Apostolic Church and other Christian churches**
Language: **Armenian**

The Armenians are a distinctive people whose traditional homeland lies in eastern Anatolia straddling present day Turkey and the USSR. They have faced a series of genocidal massacres, most notably in 1895 and 1915, which has reduced them to a small minority in Turkey and scattered them throughout the Near East, western Europe and elsewhere. The core of the Armenian community today is in Soviet Armenia.

The Armenians are descended from ancient tribes who inhabited Eastern Anatolia for thousands of years and who from about 600 BC intermingled with an invading people called "Hayasa" from central Anatolia and adopted an Indo-European language. At the time of Julius Caesar the Armenians ruled a great independent kingdom, although this was later conquered by the Romans. Armenians became Christians from the third century AD, making them the oldest Christian nation, and the Armenian church proved of vital importance in preserving Armenian unity in the following centuries, which saw domination by the Byzantines, Seljuks and Ottomans. Throughout these centuries Armenians were deported or emigrated in great numbers, often establishing themselves in trade and banking.

Armenians in the Ottoman Empire

Within the Ottoman Empire Armenians were organized into their own *millet* or semi-autonomous community, with the Armenian Patriarch of Constantinople at its head. In the mid-nineteenth century there were probably about 2.5 million Armenians in Turkey but they faced strong pressure from the neighbouring Kurds and later Muslims who had fled from Russian domination. Armenian nationalist sentiment grew during the nineteenth century; few however sought independence but rather administrative reforms and cultural and religious freedoms. After the disappointment of the Treaty of Berlin of 1878 (which promised protection to the Armenians by western powers but failed to give it) Armenian self-defence groups and armed revolutionary societies were formed and the first Armenian uprising, the Samsun rising of 1894, was suppressed with considerable ferocity by Ottoman troops. This led to a series of massacres of Armenians in the 1890s in which perhaps 300,000 Armenians died.

The Young Turk revolution of 1908 at first promised new reforms, but within a year there was a further massacre in which 30,000 Armenians were killed. The ideology of the ruling triumvirate was now pan-Turkism (or pan-Turanianism) which had as its goal the uniting of all Turkic peoples and the Turkicizing of the minorities. During World War I and despite the fact that 250,000 Armenian men were conscripted and fought loyally in the armies of the Ottoman Empire, the Turkish Ottoman government turned on the Armenians and from April 1915 began a series of systematic and genocidal massacres. In towns and villages in Turkish Armenia and Asia Minor the entire Armenian population was ordered out, the men shot and the women and children forced to walk southwards in huge convoys into the deserts of northern Syria; a journey in which most perished. The survivors were herded into large open-air concentration camps in Ottoman Syria where they were tortured and killed. The killing continued well into 1916 and beyond. The present Turkish government still refuses to concede either the scale of the killings or that it was a deliberate policy — despite evidence for both — maintaining that it was a civil war between armed bands. The number of Armenians killed was probably in the region of 1.5 million with another half a million refugees. From a population which had been over 2 million, 100,000 Armenians remained in Turkey.

Independent Armenia 1918-20

On May 28, 1918 an independent Armenian nation was declared after victories by Armenian commanders in the vacuum left following the Soviet withdrawal from the Caucasus in 1917 and the defeat of the Ottomans. Thanks to initial British support the territory of independent Armenia grew considerably and included not only present-day Soviet Armenia but Kars and Ardahan in present day Turkey. Economic conditions were catastrophic, there was famine and privation in the winter of 1918-19, although there was a recognizable improvement by early 1920. But it was meaningful support from the great powers which was crucial, and this was not forthcoming. Although President Wilson of the USA delineated and gave legal recognition to an independent Armenia, none of the powers were prepared to back it by arms, especially in the face of a revived Turkey under Kemal Atatürk who reached an understanding with the USSR. Turks invaded Kars, the Soviets closed in from Azerbaijan and proclaimed a Soviet republic in Erevan (to which the independent Armenian government decided peacefully to accede) and the arrangement between the two was confirmed in the Treaty of Kars (October 1921). Independent Armenia ceased to exist. (For Soviet Armenia see **USSR**.)

Armenians in Turkey

After the war there were relatively few Armenians left within Turkey. In the early years of the State when Turkey was fighting to establish itself they, along with other minority groups, suffered badly; however for most of the inter-war years Armenians were able to live relatively unmolested lives, although mainly in Istanbul and a few other cities. Those who attempted to return and claim lands and properties were often attacked by local mobs. In 1939 a further 15,000 Armenians left the Alexandretta district of Syria which had been ceded to Turkey, and Armenians suffered from discriminatory taxes imposed on non-Muslim minorities during World War II. The main protection for all non-Muslim minorities in Turkey was the Treaty of Lausanne of July 1923, signed by a number of European and other powers and guaranteed by the League of Nations, most specifically Articles 38-44, which guaranteed the life, liberty, freedom of movement, religious tolerance, education and customs of the minorities by the Turkish state. Yet the provisions of this Treaty, which is still valid,[1] have not in general been fulfilled by the Turkish government.

According to the Turkish census of 1960 there were 52,756 Armenian speakers in Turkey, the majority of whom (37,700) were in Istanbul. Today these numbers are probably smaller. Most Armenians have been able to live reasonably well, provided they kept a low profile and abstained from political activities. There were however riots against them (and the small Greek minority) in 1955, financial and property restrictions on the church, and educational restriction on community schools in the 1970s and onwards, and official harassment in the early 1980s in response to isolated incidents of Armenian terrorism (from Armenian groups outside Turkey). In addition scholars have protested against government neglect, destruction or misrepresentation of Armenian cultural monuments in Eastern Turkey. The Turkish government continues to deny charges of genocide of Armenians in 1915 although in 1989 it announced that it would open historical archives to scholars. It also continues to deny any Armenian historical presence and in December 1986 the publisher of a Turkish version of the Encyclopedia Britannica was facing prosecution because it contained an article on an Armenian state in Anatolia in the eleventh century.

Iran

Armenians have lived in Persia from the early seventeenth century, when Shah Abbas deported thousands from the plain of Ararat to his capital at Isfahan where they founded a colony at New Julfa. However most of Iran's 180,000 Armenians now live in Tehran where the community has several churches and cultural institutions, including a newspaper. Before the overthrow of the Shah, Tehran Armenians owned many prosperous business concerns, including breweries. Current economic and political upheavals have proved serious to Armenian business interests and many have subsequently left Iran. Nevertheless the Armenian community is a recognized religious minority and thus has been accorded some protection by the authorities.

---

[1] in international law, since the UN has been proved to be the legitimate successor to the League of Nations in the case of Namibia.

Lebanon

After the massacres of 1915 Lebanon was the centre of the Armenian world (with Soviet Armenia). The Catholicos of the Great House of Cilicia, the Patriarch of the Armenian Catholics, and the President of the Union of Armenian Evangelical Churches in the Middle East have their headquarters in the Beirut area. The Armenian population of perhaps 175,000 (in the mid-1980s) constitutes 5% of the Lebanese population and are the seventh largest community. The majority live in Beirut and its suburbs. Before the outbreak of the civil war there were 60 Armenian schools, 20 Armenian churches and a dozen magazines and newspapers based there. There were three major Armenian political parties — the nationalist Dashnaks, the more conservative Ramgavars and the progressive Hunchaks. Armenians played an important role in the Lebanese business world.

The civil war has been disastrous for the Armenian community, even though it has sought to maintain a neutral stance. However by the end of 1986 an estimated 1,000 Armenians had been killed and many thousands wounded. The murderous 1989 bombardment and subsequent exodus from Beirut was only the final chapter in the flight of the Armenian community from the Lebanon often to sanctuary organized by the Armenian diaspora around the world. Large numbers are now trying to re-establish themselves in Nicosia, which will probably inherit the central role of Beirut.

Elsewhere in the Middle East (for Armenians in the USSR, see **USSR**)

The Armenian community in Cyprus suffered in the Turkish invasion of 1974 during which an Armenian High School was hit by a Turkish bomb. Armenians in the northern sector have been turned out of their homes and shops and Armenian churches and monuments destroyed by Turkish troops or settlers. There are smaller Armenian communities in Egypt, Jordan, Syria, Israel and Iraq.

Baha'is of Iran

Location: **Tehran, Shiraz and elsewhere**
Population: **150,000-300,000**
% of population: **0.4%-0.7%**
Religion: **Baha'i**
Language: **Farsi**

The Baha'is are a religious minority whose numbers worldwide probably exceed three million. Baha'ism is a modern religion, founded in the mid-nineteenth century in southern Iran as an offshoot of Shia Islam.

Baha'is believe in a completely transcendent and unknowable God, manifestation of whose divine essence is revealed to believers in the form of prophets or messengers who appear through the ages. Membership of the faith is not automatic at birth but must be taken consciously once a child reaches maturity. Baha'is believe in the unity of man and religion and in universal education, sexual equality and world peace. They are opposed to all forms of prejudice and must not belong to any political party. There is no priesthood among Baha'is but there is an administrative hierarchy with considerable authority. The Baha'ullah, second Missionary manifestation of God, was exiled to Palestine by the Persian authorities long before the state of Israel was created, and the Baha'i World Centre is now in Haifa in Israel, a fact which has frequently been held against them by Islamic governments. Missionary activity has carried Baha'ism to many parts of the world, including North America, India, South-East Asia and Africa.

Persecution in Iran

Prejudice against the Baha'is has been very strong in Iran, especially by the present fundamentalist Islamic government in power since 1979. Baha'is have been accused not only of being heretics but also of co-operating actively with the Shah's regime and of being opposed to the present regime. They have been suspected of achieving success because of their membership of what is perceived as an elitist and semi-secret society (similar to that of freemasonry), and they are believed to be agents of Zionism. Baha'is are also accused of being morally corrupt.

Persecution of Baha'is has occurred since the founding of the faith and at least 3,000 Baha'is are believed to have died between 1848-52. The first half of the twentieth century was relatively peaceful although the Baha'is were always treated as second class citizens. Following a coup in 1955 there were an increasing number of attacks on Baha'i property, and public broadcasts denouncing Baha'i practices, including during the latter years of the Pahlavi reign, a time of relative liberalization, Baha'is were denied many of the rights enjoyed by others.

Since the victory in 1979 of Islamic fundamentalists under the leadership of Ayatollah Khomeini the position of the Baha'is has deteriorated dramatically. Within Iran the Baha'is are denied recognition as a religious minority. The Constitution of the Islamic Republic provides official recognition to four religions: Islam (including Sunni Islam), Christianity, Judaism and Zoroastrianism. All civil rights stem from the Constitution and many aspects of personal status and law are governed by religious law; thus the Baha'is are faced with having to choose between denying their faith or breaking the law.

Since 1979 that the Baha'is have been officially persecuted because of their religious beliefs is beyond doubt and by March 1985, 195 Baha'is (almost all of whom were actively involved in the administration of the Baha'i community) were known to have been killed by the administration. There has been confiscation of property, including all property belonging to Baha'is collectively, looting and arson. The House of Bab, the most holy Baha'i shrine in Iran, was also destroyed in September 1979. In August 1983 the government formally announced a ban on all the administrative and community activities of the Baha'i faith and declared membership in a Baha'i administrative institution to be a criminal offence. Although the Baha'is immediately disbanded the institutions, arrests followed and by mid-1985 there were reported to have been over 700 Baha'is being held without

charge in Iranian prisons. Torture has reportedly been systematically applied and deaths while in custody have increased. In 1983 there was a mass execution in Shiraz of 17 Baha'is including seven women and three teenage girls who were hanged for refusing to recant their faith.

Economic pressure has also been imposed with the aim, it would seem, of rendering the Baha'i community bankrupt. Education has been restricted and Baha'is are not permitted to open their own schools, unlike other religious minorities. In 1982 all Baha'i government employees — including doctors, nurses and teachers — were dismissed from their jobs. Baha'is are no longer eligible for new identity cards unless they profess membership of one of the four official religions. In addition to being denied civil rights the Baha'is have been subject to vilification through the state-controlled media.

International reaction to the persecution of Iran's Baha'i citizens has been expressed through the Council of Europe since 1981 and the UN Commission of Human Rights; however the Iranian government continues to deny that religious persecution is taking place but charges the Baha'i community with being a politically-motivated, Western-backed, pro-Zionist organization.

Although reliable information is not always available it appears that the level of persecution of the Baha'i community has fallen somewhat since the mid-1980s. While summary arrest and detention continues, the numbers detained have dropped and in June 1987, 200 Baha'is were reported to have been in detention, solely because of their faith. The numbers of Baha'is killed or executed by mobs has also fallen. Economic pressure and harassment continues, religious freedom is denied and Baha'is were unable to obtain passports and exit permits unless they recanted their faith.

(See also *Ahmadis of Pakistan* in **South Asia**)

Beduin of Israel

Alternative names: **various tribal names**
Location: **Negev desert, Galilee**
Population: **probably 130,000**
% of population: **3% of Israel's population, 15% of Israel's Arab population**
Religion: **Muslim**
Language: **Arabic**

Many nations in the Middle East and North Africa have Beduin populations — pastoral nomads who inhabit desert areas stretching from Iran to Western Sahara. At one stage they were a substantial part of the population but today are a minority in every country.

The Beduin Arabs of Israel are no longer nomads and they are part of the Palestinian Arab minority, which comprises 18% of the population of Israel within its 1967 borders. 15% of this group are Beduin who are classified as a separate minority group by the Israeli government, along with the Druzes and Circassians. Beduin Arabs in Israel are divided into two main groups — the smaller of about 40,000 lives in the Galilee and the larger of about 90,000 lives in the Negev desert. Both communities are tribally organized into common descent groups of widely varying size although the importance of these groups has diminished in the context of the modern state.

History

Beduin tribes first entered Palestine in the fifth century AD but little is known about them in the following centuries. During the centuries of Ottoman rule Beduin tribes controlled the Negev and were established in the Galilee. The Ottomans halted Beduin raids on settled villages and by the second half of the nineteenth century the Beduin economy had become a mixed pastoral and agricultural one. Most land in the Negev was not registered in accordance with the law and was characterized as "mawat" or dead land. Under the British authorities who ruled Palestine from 1917 to 1948 land registration was completed everywhere except in the Negev. However Beduin ownership and use of the land was recognized by the authorities and also by the Jewish organizations who bought some Beduin land around Beersheba. Beduin however remained very poor and wage labour played an increasing role in their life.

During the 1948 Arab-Israeli war most of the Beduin Arab population fled or were expelled. In the Negev numbers fell from an estimated 65,000-95,000 to about 13,000 and Galilee

Beduin, already a much smaller community, were also reduced. The Beduin who remained were confined to various closed military areas and in the Negev into one "reservation" east of Beersheba. Eleven of the 19 remaining tribes were forcibly removed from their lands and although they were assured that they would later be able to return, this was never permitted and most still live on the land where they were relocated at the time.

Israeli rule

The Arabs of the Negev suffered the harshest rule under military government. The reason given for this was security but the real reasons were concerned with the expropriation of land and houses and the resettlement and employment of the large numbers of Jewish immigrants who were now entering Israel. Military government was not lifted until 1966 and the Negev Beduin, who had been very isolated in the closed areas, found out that most of their lands had been registered in the name of the State under a 1953 law which confiscated the land of "absentees" — even if they were refugees or had been earlier removed from the land by the State. This also happened in the case of the Galilee Beduin, although most of their lands had been registered.

Although there were promises of a land settlement from 1966 and throughout the 1970s the Beduin filed land claims, no claims have been settled and it is not possible for Beduin to prove ownership of land in court. However it is relatively easy for the Beduin to prove ownership for the purposes of compensation and title to much Beduin land has passed into the hands of the State in this manner. Further land was expropriated to construct the Tal-al-Malah air base constructed in the area of the former Beduin reserve. The Negev Land Acquisition (Peace Treaty with Egypt) Bill which became law in 1980, eventually resulted in the evacuation of 700 Beduin families from the base area and the expropriation of their land at inadequate rates of compensation.

The government has also attempted to settle Beduin in concentrated urban settlements although this is very different to the preferred Beduin way of life of small tribal concentrations living in hamlets near their lands. In the Galilee about 85% of Beduin live in government settlements and in the Negev about 45%. Others in the Negev live in two large unplanned villages for which the government has promised infrastructure and legal status and various smaller, illegal hamlets. Buildings in areas other than government settlements are regarded as illegal and those who live in or construct buildings without a licence are liable to have them demolished and risk a fine or jail sentence. This process has placed great pressure on Beduin to move into government settlements although the government has claimed that the provision of government services in the settlements encourages people to move there and services such as electricity and paved roads are denied to illegal settlements.

Discrimination

There have been many allegations of brutality by Beduin and others of the activities of the "Green Patrol", a force operated by the Nature Reserves Authority and which deals almost exclusively with Beduin. Beduin Arabs, like other Arabs in Israel, do not receive equal access to water quotas and are subject to restrictions on leases of agricultural and grazing land and

herd restrictions. The government settlements for Beduin do not have the same funding or facilities as Jewish Israeli settlements and there are longer periods before elections are allowed to the local councils. A survey in one settlement found that Beduin disliked the relatively high population density and would prefer to give up town life. Employment in the settlements is low because there is no industry and Beduin therefore must seek employment outside them — mainly low paying jobs in Jewish Israeli development towns. In areas of education and health Beduin are also disadvantaged.

Beduin are generally perceived by Jewish Israelis as being "loyal Arabs" and therefore different from other Palestinians. However Palestinians in the Occupied Territories also often see Beduin this way and have the impression that all Beduin serve in the military. In fact both these views are misleading: although some Beduin do serve in the military, often those are from a small number of tribes, or do so for financial reasons. Beduin see themselves as Palestinians although they are in general resigned to being Israeli citizens. In the past Beduin have tended to be seen as passive but today there are Beduin organizations working for change and greater awareness in the social and cultural field. Both Beduin communities have undergone radical social change over the past 40 years from largely traditional societies under the control of sheikhs to ones in which younger educated men play the most important role.

Berbers

Alternative names: **Kabylian (Algeria)**
Location: **North African coastal plains and adjoining mountain ranges**
Population: **Morocco 6 million; Algeria 3.6-5 million**
% of population: **Morocco 40%, Algeria 15-20%**
Religion: **Islam**
Language: **Berber, Arabic**

The Berbers are the indigenous inhabitants of the North African littoral, isolated from the rest of Africa by the Sahara desert. They are the descendants of the Capsian culture of prehistoric North Africa but have been subject to much racial admixture over centuries of invasion. From the mid seventh century waves of Arab migration into the region brought cultural changes and introduced Islam, which the Berbers willingly accepted, although the character of North Africa remained Berber.

Although rural Berber life remained largely

unchanged by Arab influence those living in the cities found their language, tribal law and oral literary traditions being replaced by Arabic traditions. Forced back into the mountain regions by the city-based sultanates, the Berbers refused to recognize central authority or to pay taxes.

The French, who occupied North Africa from 1839 when they took Algeria, recognized the differences between the Arabs and the largely mountain-dwelling Berbers and subjected the two sectors to different regimes of administration, encouraging the expression of Berber culture and using Berber recruits in the French army. In the major Berber areas Berber-speakers constituted between 60% and 100% of the population. The Berbers reacted to the distinction made by the French by rapidly adopting Arabic language and customs, although they also took advantage of their new economic and commercial opportunities, and many migrated annually to work for French farmers or moved into the cities and formed urban enclaves.

Morocco

Because of its mountainous terrain, its distance from the centre of the Arabic speaking world and its traditionally-based monarchy and structure as a "Sovereign Moslem State", Morocco is the State with the highest proportion of Berber speakers; possibly 40% of its 20 million population. The major area of Berber concentrations are the Rif, Middle Atlas, High Atlas and Anti-Atlas. During the colonial period the French tried to foster Berber language and culture and used the Berber areas as a recruiting ground for the French army. The Berbers played an important part in the fighting during the independence struggle — the Moroccan Army of Liberation was formed in the Rif in 1953/4.

After independence the Berbers were well represented in the army and police force but much less so in government. They very often felt isolated from central government as their patrons under the French lost their influence and Berber tribal groups suffered accordingly. In the first three years of independence there were two major tribal uprisings and constant rural agitation against Istiqlal, the urban nationalist group which had led the independence struggle. The uprisings were crushed by the army but those involved were not necessarily severely punished and the monarchy used the uprisings as an excuse to curb the political power of Istiqlal and increase the power of the monarchy. Berber resentment was formalized — with encouragement from the monarchy — in the formation of an explicitly Berber-based political party in 1958. In 1973 there was a Berber tribal revolt near Gwilmima in the Atlas which was severely crushed.

The main causes of Berber resentment appear to be local grievances, such as economic deprivation and the feeling that the central government is ignoring their problems, rather than a Berber consciousness as such. There have been similar resentments among Arabic speakers in rural areas and cities. The Berber language, already divided into several different forms which are not always mutually intelligible, is reduced in importance by constant migration to cities where Arabic is an essential means of communication and where Berber social structures are eroded.

Algeria

The Berber-speaking population of Algeria may comprise up to one quarter of the population of 24 million[1] and is concentrated in the mainly mountainous areas of Kabyle, Chaouia, the Mzab and the Sahara. About half of the Berber-speaking population comes from the area of Kabyle and it is this area, and its language, which has played the most important Berber role in modern Algeria. During the colonial period the French administration attempted to shield the Berbers from "contamination" from Arabic language and culture, and recruited Kabyles into the French army and into posts in the colonial administration. Nevertheless Kabyle and Chaouia played a vital role in the War of Independence against the French.

At independence in 1962 Arabic became the sole national language of Algeria, both as a rejection of colonialism and a means of unifying the nation by the ruling Front National de Libération (FLN). Linguistic and cultural expressions of Berber were not allowed and this created resentment among Berber speakers, as did attempts to increase the numbers of Arabic speakers in the administration. In September 1963, Dr Ait Ahmad, a Kabyle leader of the resistance to the French, led a revolt against the government. The revolt was crushed and Ait was arrested and sentenced to death, although he later fled into exile in France where he formed the Front des Forces Socialistes (FLS). The 1976 National Charter emphasized the theme of national unity. Despite attempts to promote Arabic, French continued to be used in some areas of official work and further attempts were made to enforce literary Arabic as the language of government.

Berber resistance to the imposition of literary Arabic has taken several forms. Although the government has feared Berber separatism there appears to be little support for separatism as such and more for a greater recognition of Berber identity and rights for Berber speakers within a more democratic and pluralist Algerian state. There have been a number of Berber opposi-

[1] Estimates of numbers and proportions vary widely but most seem to lie in the region of 15%-20% of the population.

tion movements both in France and Algeria, often with socialist sympathies. However the most enduring form of Berber opposition has come from broader based cultural movements. Through the 1970s Berber musicians and poets used a modernized form of traditional Berber music to implicitly criticize the Algerian regime. Although popular demand eventually forced the government to allow such music in the media, singers and groups were not allowed to perform in the Kabyle.

In March 1980 the government banned a lecture on ancient Kabyle poetry by a lecturer at Tizi Ouzou university in Kabyle. Demonstrations and strikes throughout the Kabyle and other Berber areas, and by Berber students at Algiers, Tizi Ouzou and other universities followed, and were met by violence by government troops. In the repression over 30 people died, several hundred were injured and many Berber activists, including intellectuals and musicians, were arrested. The government later announced that a Chair of Kabyle Studies would be restored at Algiers University (it had previously been abolished) and another created at Tizi Ouzou. However the Arabization programme would continue.

The Berber Cultural Movement and other Berber organizations have generally supported the ideal of Algeria as a bilingual state, with recognition given to both Berber languages and colloquial Arabic, which is in fact the language of the majority of the population, rather than literary Arabic. They also stress the fusion of Berber and Arabic cultures which has taken place in Algeria. As a result they have often allied themselves with non-Berbers who wish to achieve a more democratic and pluralist government. In 1985 there were further arrests and imprisonment of Berber activists.

The spontaneous nationwide protests of October 1988, in which Berbers participated in Algiers and in the Kabyle, forced the Algerian leadership into support for constitutional change, including ending the one-party system. In July 1989 a new political parties law was passed by the National Assembly which allowed for groups independent of the FLN to apply for registration and to compete in national elections. Among those which applied were the FLS and the Rally for Culture and Democracy, a Berber organization. The new law however prohibits groups "based exclusively on a particular religion, language, region, sex or race" and states that parties must use only the Arabic language in their official communiqués.

Tunisia

The Berber speaking minority in Tunisia is very much smaller in both numbers and as a proportion of the population than in either Morocco or Algeria and lives mainly in isolated pockets. The government claims that they have been integrated into Arab-Muslim culture and do not constitute an autonomous localized minority of specific character. Because of this it is difficult to evaluate the Berber situation, but they do not appear to have faced the same problems or developed the same opposition to government as in the other countries.

Copts of Egypt

Alternative names: **Orthodox Coptic Christians**
Location: **Egypt**
Population: **6 million plus**
% of population: **probably 12-15%**
Religion: **Coptic or Church of Egypt**
Language: **Arabic, Coptic (religious language)**

The Copts are a relatively small but sometimes influential religious minority, members of a Church believed to have been founded by St Mark the Evangelist. Egypt became part of the Byzantine Empire in AD 395 and the Egyptian Church was separated from the Christian community in AD 451. Copts adhere to a Monophysite doctrine which holds that Christ was both God and Man and that both natures were united in Christ, implying perfect rather than imperfect union.

There are also Coptic communities in Sudan (approximately 100,000), and various Middle Eastern countries, the USA and some western European countries. Canada and Australia also have small Coptic communities.

In the seventh century Egypt fell to Arab Muslims and an uprising in 830 left Christians in a minority in Egypt for the first time. From the ninth century onward the Copts were persecuted by their Muslim rulers, in turn Arab, Circassian and Ottoman. Churches were destroyed, books burnt and elders imprisoned or put to death. By the time the British had taken Egypt in 1882 the Copts had been reduced to only some 10% of the total population. Many government servants were Copts, however, since they had been found to be better educated than the Muslims.

Freedom of worship is restricted in Egypt today by a law retained from 1856 which severely limits the freedom to build churches. Hospitals built and administered by the different Christian denominations have been confiscated as have some schools and church lands. Christians are considered to be infidels and although a Christian who converts to Islam is not considered apostate, a Muslim who converts to Christianity is.

Copts are drafted in proportionately higher numbers than Muslims into the armed forces but never attain senior positions; in 1977 only two of the cabinet's 55 ministers were Copts. Military and police colleges restrict Christian admission and Christians are not accepted into the departments of gynaecology or obstetrics in medical schools. Despite their reluctance to admit Coptic students into Egyptian colleges the authorities have so far refused to allow the establishment of a Christian university.

For Egypt's Copts the greatest threats have come from the increasing influence and power of Islamic fundamentalists, such as the Muslim Brotherhood. These groups have also posed a threat to the governments of Nasser, Sadat (who was assassinated by extremists within the army) and Mubarak, and there have been periodic mass arrests of followers of the Muslim Brotherhood. Therefore many Copts see their best course as a politically quiescent one, attempting to work quietly within their own community and without provoking the government to act against them.

The most serious crisis came in June 1981 when, after Muslim-Coptic riots in Cairo had left 20 dead, President Sadat initiated a clampdown on both Copts and Muslim extremists. The Coptic Pope Shenouda III was stripped of his authority and exiled to a desert monastery and 125 Coptic clergy and lay activists were arrested. Three Coptic associations were banned and Coptic publications closed down. Apparently many Copts welcomed the arrests as they feared that Coptic militants were likely to antagonize Islamic extremists into further acts of violence. Pope Shenouda was released and allowed to resume his religious duties in early 1985. Since that time relations between the Copts and the government are reported to have been better, although the Coptic church has kept a low profile.

It is difficult to gain information about the present position of the Coptic community. Even the population figures are a matter of guesswork as official figures underestimate their numbers while some "Coptic nationalists" claim up to one quarter of the population as Copts. Copts share many of the same characteristics as other Egyptians; there are poor rural Coptic villagers, unskilled labourers in city slums, migrants to Gulf States, an educated middle class and some in a position of power, such as the three Christian ministers in the government in 1988. Sections of both Muslim and Coptic communities practise female circumcision. The Upper Egypt Christian Association was one of the pioneers of education in Egypt and still has many Muslims in its schools.

In addition to the Orthodox Coptic confession there are other Christian communities such as the Catholic Copts, who number around 150,000, and about 200,000 Protestants. In the case of intermarriage between these confessions the Coptic Church insists on the non-Coptic partner being rebaptised according to Coptic rites, and there is a ban on shared communnion.

Cyprus

Location: **Largest island of eastern Mediterranean**
Population: **Total 657,000; Greek-Cypriots 510,000 (est.), Turkish-Cypriots 140,000 (est.)**
% of population: **Greek-Cypriots 78%, Turkish-Cypriots 18%**
Religion: **Greek Orthodox, Sunni Muslim**
Language: **Greek, Turkish, English**

The island of Cyprus lies 80 kilometres from the Turkish coastline and 800 kilometres from the Greek mainland. The population, given as 556,000 at the last reliable census at independence in 1960, is 78% Greek and 18% Turkish, with small Armenian, Maronite and British communities. The island is 9,251 square kilometres in size, 225 kilometres long and 94 kilometres wide at its widest point.

Mycenaean Greeks are known to have colonized Cyprus in the second millennium BC and the island passed under the authority of Assyria, Greece, and Rome. In 1570-1 the Turks took Cyprus from the Venetians, and Muslims settled throughout the island. The Turks maintained control over the territory until 1878, when it was ceded to Britain for administrative purposes; the British formally annexed it in 1914, making it a Crown Colony.

The pursuit of Enosis

From the early nineteenth century Greek-Cypriots had favoured union with Greece, a concept known as Enosis. In this they were inspired by events in Crete and other Greek-speaking islands, which had thrown off Ottoman domination to become part of independent Greece. The British had acceded to demands for Enosis when they relinquished the Ionian islands including Corfu, but they opposed the call for the merging of Cyprus with Greece since Cyprus formed part of their strategic line to the Middle and Far East; another reason for British opposition to Enosis was the delicate position *vis-à-vis* the two communities on the island. Relations between Greeks and Turks were tense throughout the region and Britain did not want to provoke a civil war. On the mainland, conflicts between the Greeks and Turks in Asian Turkey had resulted in 1923 in a massive and compulsory exchange of populations, eliminating the Greeks from Asia and allowing them to remain only in Istanbul and two islands of Turkey whilst the Turks were expelled from Crete and most other Greek territory.

Cyprus was not involved in the population exchanges, having been annexed by Britain, and Turkey renounced all claims to sovereignty over the island as part of the 1923 agreement; nevertheless Greek-Cypriots continued to call for Enosis and demonstrations continued sporadically. In 1931 Government House was burnt to the ground, and in 1955 attacks on government buildings and residences were organized and carried out by EOKA (The National Organization of Cyprus Fighters), led by Colonel Giorgios Grivas, who had led an extreme right-wing guerrilla group during the Axis occupation of Greece.

Self-government

In 1956, as EOKA attacks intensified, the British prepared proposals on self-government under British sovereignty. Opposition to the proposals

— on the grounds that it wasn't Enosis — was led by Michael Mouskos, recently appointed Archbishop Makarios, and Colonel Grivas. The Turkish government favoured partition, one of the options considered by Britain. Violence between the two communities escalated in 1958 and for the first time Archbishop Makarios indicated that he would accept independence for Cyprus rather than union with Greece. Direct talks between Greece, Turkey and Britain resulted in February 1959 in an agreement comprised of three treaties and a Constitution. The Treaty of Establishment declared Cyprus a sovereign republic with the exception of two British bases. The Treaty of Alliance between Cyprus, Greece and Turkey included provision for Greek and Turkish troops to be stationed on the island, and the Treaty of Guarantee gave the three outside states the right to act singly or collectively to maintain the status of the island. The Constitution provided for the election of a Greek Cypriot President and a Turkish Cypriot Vice-President, each with a veto power, and there was to be a House of Representatives and two communal chambers, one Greek and the other Turkish. The public services were to employ people on a 70:30 Greek-Turkish ratio. The agreement came into effect on August 16, 1960, with Cyprus being admitted to the Commonwealth in March 1961. Archbishop Makarios was declared the first President of Cyprus and Dr Kutchuk Vice-President.

The 1960s were marked by a series of crises. In November 1963 Makarios proposed 13 amendments to the constitution, amendments which had the effect of removing distinctions of nationality and both streamlining the administration and resolving the conflict in the Greek favour. The Turkish government rejected the proposals and the tension erupted into violence in which the Greeks launched a paramilitary attack on Turks in Nicosia and Larnaca, taking 700 hostages. In 1964 there were widescale killings on both sides, and villages were looted or destroyed as 20,000 Turks fled their villages in the south. An uneasy truce was declared and the British, Turkish and Greek forces already on the island were formed into a temporary peace-keeping force. Various attempts at a solution failed, rejected by one side or the other, and the Turks were by now settling in enclaves. In 1967 Grivas led an attack against Turkish Cypriots at Kophinou. The Turkish government demanded Grivas' immediate return to Greece in addition to the withdrawal of Greek troops illegally based on the island. Greece, now ruled by a military junta, capitulated to the Turkish demands, a decision which contributed to Makarios' change of view regarding the desirability of Enosis.

The crisis of 1974

Makarios' decision to give up the pursuit of Enosis led to deteriorating relations between Cyprus and the Greek junta and to the fomenting of a new internal opposition to Makarios from supporters of Grivas and Enosis. There were two assassination attempts on Makarios in 1970 and 1974. Following the latter attack, which had been authorized by the Greek government, Makarios escaped to Akrotiri and was replaced by Nicos Sampson, former EOKA terrorist and leader of the 1963 attack on the Turks of Omorphita. The Turkish government, deeply offended by this appointment, called for Sampson's immediate removal, and when no prompt reaction was forthcoming Turkish troops landed in Cyprus and advanced southward, reportedly looting property and murdering indiscriminately. Despite mediation by the British and the establishment of a UN ceasefire on July 22, massive Turkish troop reinforcements were shipped into the island. A narrow corridor between Kyrenia and Nicosia held by the Turks was extended, until 36% of the island was under Turkish control, a situation which continues today.

Cyprus is today divided into two ethnic zones by a barrier — known as the Green Line — which runs for 180 kilometres right across the island and through the capital Nicosia. 180,000 people are refugees on one or other side of the divide, and there are now fewer than 1000 Greeks living in the north and about 130 Turks in the south, both groups regularly receiving supplies from the UN. Reports of Turkish atrocities were widespread and many of the 1,619 Greeks missing are believed to have been taken to the Turkish mainland and presumably killed. Evidence of retaliatory massacres by the Greeks has also been found. The great majority of Greek refugees have now been rehoused in new estates, although they still hope to return eventually to their homes in the north. The Turkish sector, under the leadership of Rauf Denktaş, contained most of the country's cargo-holding capacity in the port of Famagusta, most of the tourist industry — with 65% of existing hotel accommodation and 87% of hotels under construction — 50% of agricultural exports including 75% of citrus fruits, and nearly 50% of the country's industrial production.

Community perceptions and politics

The Greeks dealt with the disastrous loss of revenue by embarking on a huge building boom, concentrating particularly on Limassol. Whereas they began by indiscriminately erecting buildings, they now carefully plan all building schemes. Since the Greek-Cypriot government, under the leadership of Spyros Kyprianou and later George Vassiliou, is almost universally acknowledged as the government of the island (the northern government being recognized only by Turkey) the Greek community has been able to rely on the EC and World Bank for financial assistance, and they have been greatly helped by the collapse of Beirut as the economic, financial and servicing centre of the Middle East, a role which Greek Cyprus looks set to assume. Recognized as the government of Cyprus, the Greek-Cypriot government has the advantage of representing the island at international conferences where it is able to influence the decision-making process of other countries regarding Cyprus. Ships have been discouraged from putting in at the northern port of Famagusta, the export of citrus fruits from the north has been curtailed and Turkish Cypriot stamps have been declared illegal and invalid. The Greeks see this influence as being their only answer to the illegal occupation of over one third of their country by the Turkish army and the theft of their assets.

The Turkish Cypriots undoubtedly feel more secure living as a separate community and have enthusiastically embraced the opportunity offered by the wealth of the north. There is a lively system of multi-party politics and the November 1983 declaration of independence as the Republic of North Cyprus was very popular; however since partition the northern economy has stagnated and it is heavily dependent on aid from Turkey. The Turkish lira is now the official currency and Turkey pays two-thirds of the total budget. Although official unemployment figures are low there is a high degree of disguised unemployment, and lack of productivity is a problem. The civil service employs 13,000 people, a figure kept deliberately high in order to discourage emigration. The luxury hotels remain empty as no one has the confidence to run them, and the tourist industry as a whole has suffered greatly from the ban on flights into the country except by Turkish airlines, effectively excluding package holidays. There has been a gradual increase in the number of non-Turkish tourists entering the region but the industry has certainly not regained its buoyancy. *Per capita* income is much lower than in the south: US $1,100 compared to $4,400 in 1981, but some Turks have managed to do well financially by selling electrical goods to Turkey. The population of the north is given as 121,000 by the Greeks and as 153,000 by the Turks. The discrepancy is probably due to the immigration of large numbers of Turks since 1974, although many are known to have returned to the mainland, finding it hard to settle in Cyprus. In mid-1989 there were reports that the Turkish government intended settling ethnic Turkish refugees from Bulgaria in northern Cyprus.

The search for a solution

The political scene was initially dominated by Denktaş' and Kyprianou's proposals for settlement. Denktaş advocated a gradual move towards federalism. Makarios, who returned to power in December 1974, met Denktaş twice in 1977 and guidelines for future negotiations were established. These included acceptance of the idea of an independent, non-aligned Federal Republic, and the possibility of arriving at boundary lines by objective criteria rather than by population ratio. With the death of Makarios a few months later positive signs of a new Constitution ceased, however, and later talks between Makarios' successor Spyros Kyprianou and Rauf Denktaş failed to reach agreement. Various proposals put forward by the two UN Secretary-Generals Kurt Waldheim and Perez de Cuellar also failed to achieve a settlement between the two sides. Kyprianou put forward comprehensive proposals involving the complete demilitarization of the island and assisting the north to catch up economically with the south in addition to the loss to Turkish-Cypriots of 10% of the land they are now holding and a stronger system of provincial government.

The most promising chance of a workable settlement came in early 1985 when the two sides had been meeting regularly under UN auspices for five months. This plan was backed financially by the US who wished to see a settlement with its NATO allies Greece and Turkey, and also by the USSR, who wished to see a demilitarized Cyprus. Under the plan Denktaş made significant concessions, offering to reduce the Turkish-held area from 37% to 30%, agreed to accept a Greek President and a Turkish Vice-President rather than a rotating presidency, and a 70:30 ratio of Greeks to Turks in the federal cabinet and lower house of parliament. In addition the UN proposed that each side would give up 3% of its territory to form the basis of a federally administered territory. However Kyprianou made it clear that he considered these points for discussion, not agreement, and the talks collapsed amid recriminations on both sides. Denktaş called elections for June while Kyprianou was censored by his own combined parliamentary opposition.

In February 1988 George Vassiliou, campaigning on a non-party compromise platform, defeated the hard-line Kyprianou in the Cypriot presidential election. Open-ended talks began in September 1988 between leaders of the two communities, initially in Geneva and later in Nicosia, with regular reportbacks to the UN Secretary-General. But despite a promising start there appeared to be an unbridgeable gap in perceptions. While both sides agreed on the need for a federated government with a large amount of provincial autonomy in the Greek and Turkish sectors, the Greek side proposed "bi-communalism" — a demilitarized federal republic with a strong central government (which the Greeks would dominate by virtue of their numbers) — and the Turks "bi-zonalism" — with the partition of the island on ethnic lines — thus to a large extent institutionalizing the status quo. By August 1989 no agreement had been reached while there had been clashes between Greek-Cypriot demonstrators and UN soldiers across the Green Line.

The future of Cyprus

There appears to be no solution in sight to the present division of Cyprus, although it is unlikely that there will be a major new eruption of conflict. There are some factors which might support reunification: an obvious desire from ordinary people on both sides for a more permanent settlement, the use by both sides of English as an international language, and an application to join the EC, with which Cyprus already has trading arrangements. Nor is Cyprus an issue of international superpower rivalry. Huge obstacles to successful negotiations remain, however: the question of whether or not minority groups should be allowed to remain in the two provinces, the existence of large numbers of Turkish immigrants and the almost 30,000 Turkish troops in the north, the problem of trust between the two communities, and not least the fact that in any settlement both leaders will be forced to make unpopular concessions — these and other issues contribute to the difficulties involved in settling the dispute to the satisfaction of both Greeks and Turks.

(See also *Greeks of Turkey*; *Turks of Western Thrace* in **Eastern Europe**)

Druzes of Israel and the Golan Heights

Location: **Galilee, Mt Carmel, Golan Heights**
Population: **72,000 in Israel, 15,000 in Golan Heights**
% of population: **1.5% of Israeli population**
Religion: **Druze**
Language: **Arabic, Hebrew**

The Druze are a small Arab minority in Israel, part of a much larger Druze community in southern Syria and mountainous central Lebanon who form about 7% and 5% of the total populations respectively. Their religion originated in eleventh-century Egypt as a schism of a splinter of the Shi'ite branch of Islam. They do not recognize Mohammmed as the Prophet nor do they accept the infallibility of the Koran. Because of this many Orthodox Muslims consider them heretics and in response the Druze have developed a closed society, where knowledge of their beliefs is restricted both inside and outside the community and where intermarriage with other communities results in ostracism from the Druze community. There are probably about 72,000 Druze in Israel proper and another 15,000 residing in the Israeli-occupied Golan Heights.

Within Israel's 1967 borders Druze reside mainly in 17 traditional Druze villages, all in Galilee except for two in Mt Carmel. Formerly a farming and herding people the pressure of population (they have one of the highest birthrates in the world) has forced Druze men to look for work elsewhere such as the docks in Haifa, while a small group has moved south to Eilat. There are now roads leading to formerly isolated villages which are served by electricity and drinking water. Before 1948 there was 95% illiteracy; today there is an elementary school in each settlement and several secondary schools. Women still lead a largely secluded lifestyle and factories have been established in Druze villages to employ them. Like other Palestinian Israelis, the Druze live an uneasy compromise between their traditional values and the pressures of life in a comparatively westernized state and in some respects, such as their acceptance of the authority of community elders, they are more traditional than other Palestinian groups.

Druzes within Israel are Israeli citizens, although like other Arabs they do not have all the rights accorded to Jewish-Israelis. As one of the "minority communities" recognized by the Israeli government — others include Beduin, Christians and Circassians — Druzes are differentiated from other Israeli Arabs. In 1957 the Israeli government recognized the Druzes as a separate and independent religious community, in 1961 the spiritual leadership was recognized as a Religious Council and in 1962 Druze Courts, which handle matters of personal status for Druzes, were established.

Druze villages get government grants well below the levels given to Jewish-Israeli settlements and marginally higher than other Palestinian settlements. After complaints from some Druze the method of allocating grants was changed in the late 1970s and this has made the grants level *per capita* in Druze villages rise substantially. In addition Druzes receive individual grants and loans available to ex-servicemen (which in effect excludes most other Arab Israelis except some Beduin). They have also suffered land seizure as do other Palestinians; for example in Bayt Jann in 1987 there were angry clashes between Druze and police. Some younger Druze feel that few of the Druze community have gained high political or military rank and that they are considered to be second-class citizens by Jewish-Israelis. In April 1987 the Israeli government (Moshe Arens) publicly recognized that while it had preferred Druzes to other Palestinians it had not treated them equally with Jews.

The Israeli government has encouraged better treatment of the Druze than other Arabs and they are seen as more "loyal" to the Israeli state. Since 1955 Druzes have been conscripted (at the request of the Druze community) and serve in the Army, especially in certain outfits such as Border Guards, which has acquired a reputation for brutality in dealing with Palestinians in both Israel and the Occupied Territories. Druze women, unlike Jewish-Israeli women, do not have compulsory military service. Increasing numbers of Druze have refused to serve in the military and some have been jailed.

Druzes are generally perceived by Palestinians, whether living in Israel or the Occupied Territories, as collaborators. Many Israeli Druze feel that as a small heterodox minority group they have little choice but to ally themselves with whatever government is likely to protect them, their religion, culture and way of life. Not all would agree with this and during the 1970s the *Mubadira* (the Druze Initiative), a Rakah party-dominated movement which opposed Zionism and put forward an aim of a non-Zionist state in which Arabs would enjoy equality, gained popularity. However in the 1980s it seems to have declined — perhaps because of Rakah's dominating role.

Druze in the Golan Heights (on the northern sector of the border with Syria) have reacted very differently to Israeli rule. The Golan Heights was captured by Israel during the 1967 war, thus bringing some 8,000 Druze under Israeli military occupation. Some of the area was restored to Syria in 1974 but most remained with Israel thus splitting the Druze community. There was an agreement to allow family reunions under UN auspices but this collapsed in 1975. Israel annexed the Golan Heights in December 1981 but no country recognizes this annexation and therefore it remains, in international law, as Syrian territory.

During the Israeli initial occupation Druze were issued with Israeli military documents but after Israel annexed the Golan Heights, Druze were asked to return these to be replaced with Israeli identity cards (as carried by all Israeli citizens). Less than 50 Druze initially accepted the cards while 1300 handed them back. In early 1982 Druze in the Golan Heights started a strike against the imposition of cards and the annexation of the territory. The strike lasted for six months and during that time the Israeli army sealed off Druze villages from the outside world, allowing only those who wished to work in Israel to leave. A former Israeli Supreme Court judge claimed that striking Druze had been beaten, harassed and denied employment. There have been further protests and in 1986 a Druze was sentenced to six months' prison under the law of sedition for singing "anti-Israeli, pro-Syrian songs" during a demonstration in 1985. There have also been claims that the Israeli state has expropriated Druze land and restricted Druze access to irrigation water.

(See also *Beduin of Israel*; *Palestinians*)

Greeks of Turkey

Location: **Istanbul, islands of Imvros (Gökçeada) and Tenedos (Bozçaada)**
Population: **6,000-8,000 (est.)**
% of population: **0.01%**
Religion: **Greek Orthodox**
Language: **Greek, Turkish**

The Greek Orthodox minority in Turkey is a small community made up of the descendants of those who were permitted to remain in Turkey after the massive and compulsory exchange of populations agreed under the 1923 Treaty of Lausanne.

Greece and the Ottoman Empire had been in dispute over territories periodically during the nineteenth century and Greece had declared war on Turkey in 1921 in an attempt to secure the Ottoman territories it had been awarded under the Treaty of Sèvres. The Greek forces were driven from Anatolia by Kemal Atatürk in 1922 and much of the large Greek population fled, especially from Smyrna (Izmir), a largely Greek city. Under the Treaty of Lausanne Greeks were eliminated from Turkey with the exception of those in Istanbul, Imvros and Tenedos, close to the mouth of the Dardanelles, where minority rights were to be guaranteed. The Turks were similarly expelled from all Greek territory except Western Thrace. The Treaty of Lausanne was partially designed as a means of finally ending a century of murderous feuding between the two communities.

Despite assurances of continued protection from the Turkish authorities there has been a steady increase in restrictions on Greeks in Turkey. In September 1955 a Turkish mob destroyed much of the Greek business quarter of Istanbul, Greek churches, cemeteries, schools and historical monuments. Shops and warehouses were looted and burnt to the ground.

Greeks in Turkey have to live with many prohibitions such as that on the use of Greek in courts, purchase of land by social and cultural institutions and the establishment of any association based on race, language or religion. On the islands of Imvros and Tenedos land was compulsorily appropriated, schools closed and the islands declared military zones, making normal life virtually impossible for the Greek populations. In 1964 Greek Orthodox priests were forbidden to teach religion or conduct morning prayers in minority schools and Turks have since been appointed as teachers in all minority schools. Students were obliged to enrol in their nearest school rather than in a school of their choice and the teaching of the Greek language has been severely reduced. In 1971 the government closed down the Department of Advanced Religious Studies of Chalki, thus impeding preparation for office within the church. Passports are also being withheld from prominent members of the Greek Orthodox community despite the fact that they are Turkish subjects. Some of these people face restricted movement within Turkey itself.

Further restrictions were imposed after the Greek/Turkish dispute over Cyprus in 1974. At the height of the crisis the Turkish government adopted a secret decree which restricted property transactions by Greeks in Turkey, froze their assets and limited their income, although implementation of this decree appears to have begun after July 1985. Greece has protested strongly in European forums at Turkish treatment of its Greek minority.

There has been a continuous decline in the Greek population most of which remains concentrated in Istanbul. From 100,000 in 1934 it has fallen to 6,000-8,000 today. The Greek population of Imvros and Tenedos is reported to have fallen from 10,500 in the 1940s to 1,600 in 1977. However despite its decline and the restrictions it faces, the Greek minority in Istanbul is reported to be a prosperous one and, along with Armenian and Jewish minorities, to have played an important, although low-profile, role in the financial and commercial sector.

(See also *Greeks of Albania* in **Eastern Europe**; *Turks of Western Thrace* in **Eastern Europe**)

Jews of the Middle East and North Africa
(excluding Israel and Turkey)

Alternative names: **Hebrews, Musawi, Dhimmi**
Location: **various countries**
Population: **Middle East 20,000-25,000, North Africa about 20,000**
% of population: **very small in every country**
Religion: **Judaism**
Language: **Hebrew, Arabic**

The Jews are a semitic people originating perhaps in Mesopotamia whence they migrated to Egypt and then in about the mid-thirteenth century BC, to Canaan, believed by them to be the land promised them by God. Their monotheistic beliefs formed the foundations upon which Christianity and Islam were built. By 321 AD, when Christianity became the official religion of the Roman Empire, anti-semitism was already well established and Jews were legislated against; Christians viewed Jews as being collectively responsible for the death of Christ.

Before the establishment of the State of Israel in 1948 over one million Jews were living in the Muslim countries of the Near and Middle East and North Africa, but today only about 5% of this population remain in their traditional homelands.

The Middle East

Jews migrated in large numbers to Europe and throughout the Middle East and Asia. Usury or money-lending, which was an unacceptable livelihood for Muslims and Christians, became a Jewish preserve, and whilst providing an important service it heightened popular resentment against the Jews. The Jews were an unpopular minority but were treated under Islamic law as Dhimmi, subjects of the Islamic head of state and protected, as were Christians, as "People of the Book". Dhimmis were expected to pay poll tax as non-Muslims and to respect the laws and spirit of Islam, in return for which they and their property were protected and they were exempt from military service.

Syria

Some 5,600 Jews remain in Syria today of the 30,000 who were settled there before the Arab-Israeli war in 1948. 4,500 are in Damascus, which has had a large Jewish population since Old Testament times, 1,000 live in Aleppo and about 100 live in the town of Qamishli on the Turkish border. Those who remain are not permitted to leave the country. A few do manage to leave on family visits but are obliged to leave close family and large deposits as guarantees of their return. Several dozen people a year are believed to cross the border illegally, mostly into Turkey. Jews are distinguished from Arabs by stamps on official documents. Ninety-five per cent are employed as tradesmen and artisans, and university entrance is severely restricted. Jews frequently suffer beatings and extortion but despite the hostile treatment they are subjected to, many Jews hope that President Assad will remain in power, fearful of a fundamentalist Islamic revolution in Syria which might have even worse consequences for the Jewish community.

Iran

Jews have lived in Iran for 2,500 years where they have been traditionally employed as gold and silver-smiths, weavers, dyers, wine-makers and spice dealers. From the tenth century they also earned their living as moneylenders. Persecution of the Jewish community reached a height during the sixteenth century after the establishment of Shi'ism as the state religion. In 1948 28,000 Iranian Jews emigrated to Israel leaving between 70,000 and 80,000, despite the fact that conditions had been improving under the Pahlavi Dynasty (1925-1979).

With the victory of Ayatollah Khomeini's Islamic revolution Jews were reassured of their safety as "Dhimmi"; however certain Jewish leaders were executed and thousands planned their escape to Israel, although Zionism was considered a crime punishable by death. In 1982 350 Jews were believed to be in prison for "economic crimes", and many lost their jobs and property. The teaching of Hebrew was banned and Jewish schools were taken over, but the daily practice of the Jewish religion was hardly affected at all. Although very few Jews were officially permitted to leave, by 1987 between 50,000 and 55,000 had fled Iran along with hundreds of thousands of Iranians. Reports of secret airlifts to Israel and other Israeli involvement have been vigorously denied by Israel which continues to supply Iran with arms. In the second half of 1980 800 Jewish refugees arrived in Israel and 70-80 were reported to be arriving weekly at refugee centres in Vienna. How Jews will be affected by the death of Ayatollah Khomeini in 1989 is as yet unclear.

Iraq

Almost the entire Jewish community has left Iraq for Israel. Anti-Jewish outrages during the 1940s and '50s when over 600 were killed in Baghdad provoked an exodus in 1951. 120,000 left at that time and in 1972-73 most of the remaining Jews followed them, leaving only 200-300, most of whom live in Baghdad with some in Basra. The Iraq-Iran war removed much of the pressure from the Iraqi Jews and they are not believed to have been maltreated; the end of the war in 1989 leaves their future in question, however.

The Yemens

The Jewish population of both Yemen states has dropped from 16,000 to possibly several thousand, the majority of whom are believed to be living in North Yemen. They retain their Dhimmi status and are readily distinguished from the Muslims by their special dress. There have been unconfirmed reports that some Jews have been forced to convert to Islam, and contact between local Jews and Jewish communities elsewhere has been actively discouraged.

North Africa

Large-scale Jewish migration to North Africa took place after the destruction of the second Temple in Jerusalem in 71 AD, and again in the late fifteenth century. Jews settled in the cities, where many prospered as traders and moneylenders. In the twentieth century the French conferred many privileges on the Jews of North Africa, many of whom were granted French citizenship, and they attained high levels of education compared with the Arab population.

Morocco

By 1948 there were some 270,000 Jews in Morocco but thereafter the population decreased rapidly and today about 17,000-18,000 remain, the majority in Casablanca with others in Marrakesh, Meknes, Fez and Tangier. The declaration of the independence of the State of Israel and the large-scale migration of Jews provoked numerous attacks upon Jewish premises and individuals, with a number being murdered. After Moroccan independence in 1956 the situation improved. Jews were granted full suffrage and complete freedom of movement, and some became government employees, a few in positions of considerable authority. Jewish emigration was made illegal, however, although thousands did leave illegally. Morocco is at present the only Arab country in which Jews enjoy equal rights and privileges with the rest of the community, but the future of these Jews depends on events elsewhere in the Middle East.

Algeria

Jews in Algeria suffered persecution during the nineteenth century and under the Vichy regime in the 1940s. In the early 1950s the Jewish community reached a peak of 140,000 but in the 1960s Jews found themselves caught up in the War of Independence and, by 1962, 75,000 had left, most of them going to France. After 1965 with the rise of Boumedienne, Jews suffered further discrimination. Jewish property was destroyed and synagogues converted to mosques. The 1967 war increased anti-Jewish activity causing almost all remaining Jews to leave the country. Today there are thought to be about 400 left, most of whom are elderly.

Tunisia

Tunisia's Jews are thought to have arrived after the destruction of the first Temple in 586 BC. As in the other French colonies the Jews fared well under colonial rule but during the brief German occupation of Tunisia in World War II forced labour camps were set up to house thousands of Jews. Since independence in 1956 Tunisia has pursued a moderate course regarding Israel although a small Tunisian contingent was sent to support the Arab cause in the Yom Kippur war. Despite the government's liberal policies Tunisia's Jewish population has dwindled from 105,000 in 1948 to 12,000 after the 1967 war and there are now thought to be about 3,000 Jews in the country. There have been cases of attacks on Jews and Jewish property in the 1980s but the government has made efforts to allay the fears of the Jewish community and have stated that the attacks have been isolated incidents rather than part of a new anti-Jewish campaign. Jews were afraid of future developments after President Bourguiba left office in November 1987, since he had always been regarded as their protector; however the new government has supported increased human rights protection, which hopefully will ensure the continued existence of the Jewish community in Tunisia.

Egypt

Jews migrated to Egypt from Palestine in large numbers during the sixth and third centuries BC, and in 115 AD their revolt was suppressed and the Jewish community in Egypt was destroyed. By the twelfth century Jews began to re-establish themselves in the country. They experienced repression sporadically and under Ottoman rule (1517-1918) they became an oppressed minority.

In 1948 there were 65,000-70,000 Jews in Egypt, all living in the major cities. Many of these were affluent. During the 1948 war hundreds of Jews were arrested and property and businesses were confiscated; there were also bomb attacks on Jewish areas which left hundreds killed or injured. 25,000 Jews left Egypt between 1948 and 1950. Many more left after the imprisonment of thousands after the 1956 war, and again after 1967. There are now about 250 Jews, mostly elderly, living in Egypt. Jews have not returned to Egypt since the normalization of relations between Egypt and Israel and it seems likely that the community will have completely disappeared within a few years.

Kurds

Location: **Border regions of Turkey, Iraq and Iran; also Syria, Soviet Armenia, eastern Iran and Lebanon**
Population: **19.6 million; Turkey 9.6 million, Iraq 3.9 million, Iran 5 million, Syria 0.9 million, USSR 0.3 million**
% of population: **Turkey 19%, Iraq 23%, Iran 10%, Syria 8%, USSR 0.1%**
Religion: **Sunni Muslem (85%), Shi'ite Muslim, various syncretic Islamic sects e.g. Alevis, Yazidis**
Language: **Kurmanji, Kurdi (Sorani); localized variations and sub-dialects of these**

The Kurds are the fourth most numerous people in the Middle East and one of the largest minority groups in the world. They do not possess a state of their own but are found throughout the Middle East with the majority inhabiting the mountainous region where Iraq, Iran and Turkey meet. Most Kurds are probably descendants of Indo-European tribes which settled in the region some 4,000 years ago, but actual references to "Kurds" date from the seventh century AD.

Background

Few factors unify Kurdish society. Its members are probably not descended from a single ethnic group, neither are they united in their religious

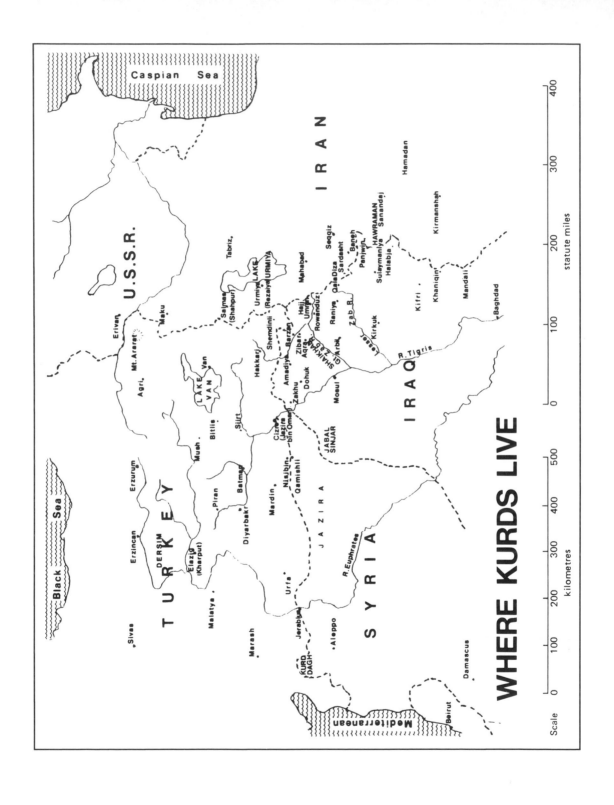

WHERE KURDS LIVE

beliefs. They do not share a single systematized written or spoken language and many Kurds are unable to communicate freely with each other although both major dialect groups stem from a north-western Iranian linguistic origin. Despite these major differences the Kurdish people do form a unique community with its own distinctive culture stemming from a tribal nomadic or semi-nomadic past, blood ties and territorial loyalty. Religious ties are also strong, and the Sheikhs or local leaders of religious brotherhoods have great influence and power within the community.

The people of Kurdistan have a history of tension, both with central government and among themselves. Until quite recently banditry was an accepted source of income for some tribes, and Kurdish revolts and plunder feature frequently in the annals of the Arab period and thereafter. For many Kurds, however, pastoralism and trade were the chief source of income, with skins, livestock, oak galls and other materials offered in exchange for basic necessities.

Kurdish tribalism is hard to classify and does not conform to any rules; many plains-dwelling Kurds are no longer tribal, and nomadism — essentially a tribal way of life — has almost completely ceased; society is nevertheless still made up of confederations, tribes and sub-tribes. The village or group of villages, led by a chief or "Agha", was the effective political unit. The Agha mediated between paramount chief and village and also between villagers and government.

The Kurds living in the foothills or plains pursue a markedly different lifestyle from those in the mountains. Theirs is a sedentary economy based on crop cultivation and some pastoralism, and most are subject to landlords to whom they are usually unrelated. Some lowland Kurds have formed sub-tribes related to tribes in the mountains, but most fear the mountain Kurds, owing to the latter's reputation for banditry.

History up to 1920

During the sixteenth century the Turkish Ottoman and the Persian Safavid empires vied with each other for regional supremacy. Most of the Kurdish Aghas supported the Ottoman cause, in exchange for which they were granted fiefdoms and in some cases principalities (emirates). Fifteen emirates were created and these formed the basis of the political structure of Kurdistan until the nineteenth century. Each emirate was ruled by an Emir, a hereditary title granted to the Aghas by government.

In the first half of the nineteenth century the Ottoman administration, alarmed by the success of the independence movement in the Balkans, extended direct control over Kurdistan, thus threatening the authority of the emirs. This led to a series of unsuccessful revolts, and secular power on a smaller scale was ultimately assumed by the many Aghas who still controlled one or two villages apiece. In the absence of the powerful emirs, rivalry and dissension broke out among the Aghas and it was the sheikhs or religious leaders — who had previously played no part in political affairs — who assumed the role of arbiter.

Calls for Kurdish autonomy began in the late nineteenth century. The Young Turk revolution of 1908 aimed at constitutional reform but failed, due — not for the first time — to inter-tribal rivalry. With the onset of World War I in 1914 the majority of Kurds fought with the Ottomans against the European powers. In the following year some Kurds were active in the killing and expulsion of Armenians from Kurdish areas, the loyalty of these Christian Armenians in the war being suspect. The support by Kurds of the government did not prevent them too from being persecuted, however. In the winter of 1916-17, the government, fearful of Russian influence on the north-eastern frontier, began to deport Kurds from the region and many died of exposure on the journey westward.

With the fall of the Ottoman empire in 1918 and the overthrow of Czarist Russia by the Bolsheviks, Turkish, Russian and British forces faced each other in the strategic zone around Azerbaijan and the Caucasus. Allied plans for postwar settlement included the apportionment of Turkish parts of the empire to Greece, Russia, Italy and France. These radical changes had a dramatic effect on the Kurdish population, but the majority of Kurds were unprepared to meet such change. They still felt themselves to be part of the Sunni community which formed the basis of Ottoman society, and were more concerned with inter-village life than with their position on the international scene.

Although the Aghas were more concerned with maintaining their position locally than uniting with other Kurdish groups, a number of intellectuals attempted to establish political groups which would further Kurdish independence or autonomy. The foremost society, the Kurdistan *Taali Djemiyeti* (Society for the Recovery of Kurdistan) soon split into factions: those who wished to see Kurdistan completely independent and those who believed in autonomy. Others were aware of Allied plans for an independent Armenian state and feared the implications for Kurds. They co-operated with Armenians to produce a joint memorandum which was presented to the Peace Conference in Paris in 1919. This resulted in the Treaty of Sèvres, which was signed on August 20, 1920. Articles 62 and 64 of this treaty stated that an Allied commission would prepare those regions with a preponderance of Kurdish inhabitants for local autonomy, leading to full independence from Turkey. However events in Turkey were to prevent the Treaty from becoming a reality.

Turkey

The Ottoman government in Istanbul was unable to sustain its credibility after (amongst other issues) the loss of its Syrian and Mesopotamian territories and the invasion of Turkey by Greece. An uprising led by Mustafa Kemal Atatürk gained the support of a significant number of Kurds who were fearful of falling within an Armenian — hence Christian — state. The revolt proved successful and Atatürk defeated the Greeks, eliminating nearly all Greeks living in Anatolia. The Allies, exhausted by the war and unable to enforce the Sèvres proposals, were no longer prepared to negotiate for the Armenians or for the Kurds. A new peace conference in Lausanne resulted in a treaty, signed in 1923, which restored sovereignty over Anatolia and Eastern Thrace to Turkey.

Kemal Atatürk was determined to establish a specifically Turkish state following the European pattern. In 1922 the Sultanate was abolished and in 1924 the Caliphate was also abolished, thus removing the temporal and spiritual bases from which the authority of the Aghas and sheikhs had derived. Kurdish associations, schools, publications, religious fraternities and teaching foundations were all banned, thus removing all public vestiges of a separate Kurdish identity. It was this clear threat to their status that finally brought about a unity, albeit a fragile one, between the politically aware urban intellectuals and the Aghas, sheikhs and their many followers.

Dissension between the tribes continued to hamper the Kurdish nationalist cause. One revolt which took place in 1925 occurred when a Turkish detachment was massacred as it tried to arrest the followers of the powerful Sheikh Said of Piran. Although Sheikh Said's followers overran about one third of Kurdish Anatolia they were unable to capture any sizeable towns, mainly because they could not amass the support of urban Kurds and because they scorned the support of those oppressed Kurds who offered to join them, considering them unfit to fight. Turkish troops took advantage of the rebels' lack of support and crushed the rising, hanging Sheikh Said and hundreds of his supporters, killing many thousands more and razing hundreds of Kurdish villages. Thousands of Kurds were then moved forcibly from their homes, leaving Kurdish Anatolia denuded of its Kurdish population.

Shortly after this rising local Aghas from the foothills of Mount Ararat led another revolt, supported by a Kurdish liberation organization, "Khoyboun", which was based in Lebanon and Syria. For the first time such a movement was not a vehicle for the personal ambitions of a sheikh or Agha; also for the first time all leading Kurdish groups cooperated in the rising, which was supported by Reza Shah, the Shah of Iran; however the Shah altered his policy and cut off support for the Kurds and the revolt failed.

In 1932 the total evacuation of Kurds from certain areas was legalized. Turks were encouraged to settle in Anatolian Kurdistan and Kurds were assimilated as far as possible into the Turkish population in other, non-Kurdish areas. Kurdish resistance was quashed and the area remained under martial law until 1946. The brutally repressive measures adopted by the Turkish government had their effect and little was heard of Kurdish nationalism for the next 30 years. Much of Anatolian Kurdistan was declared a "military zone", partly because of its proximity to the Soviet border but also so that indigenous Kurds could be displaced from the region.

In 1950 the first free general elections were held in Turkey and the Democratic Party was successful, a reaction against some 25 years of authoritarian rule under Kemal Atatürk. The election of the Democratic Party heralded the return of many exiled Aghas, sheikhs and landlords and the restoration of confiscated property. Schools, hospitals and roads were built in Kurdish areas and Kurds were elected to parliament. Members of the new Kurdish middle class espoused a movement calling for economic development in the eastern region. This movement, known as "Eastism" (doguculuk) was partly prompted by the exposure of Turkish Kurds to Kurdish-language broadcasts from neighbouring countries, and partly by news of Kurdish activism elsewhere, particularly in Iraq. Following a coup d'état in 1960 the situation improved still further for the Kurds. A new constitution permitted freedom of expression in the press and through associations. Kurds were able to voice their dissent publicly and in Kurdish if they wished although they risked imprisonment for their views since it was — and still remains — illegal for a specifically Kurdish party to be formed.

As a result of the previous policy of displacement the government was now faced with the problem of a large urban population of whom very many were Kurds, increasingly aware of liberation movements in other countries. In 1965 a separatist movement, the Kurdistan Democratic Party (KDPT), was formed and members of the left-wing Turkish Workers' Party espoused the Kurdish cause and established branches in Kurdistan. As these groups became increasingly vocal and popular the risk of a large-scale uprising grew and the government became uneasy, banning the publication of bilingual Kurdish-Turkish journals, ransacking the homes of suspected agitators and eventually sending commando groups into Kurdistan to patrol the area. In 1969 Members of the Turkish Workers' Party joined with young Kurds to form the Organization of Revolutionary Kurdish Youth (DDKO). Leftist groups became involved in violent confrontations with right-wing groups which in many cases had the backing of local police. The Turkish Workers' Party was banned for recognizing the Kurds, the first legal party to have done so.

A military coup in 1971 led to thousands of arrests throughout Turkey and numerous reports of the murder and torture of Kurds. Confrontations and repression continued sporadically throughout the decade, culminating in 1979 in the declaration of martial law in the Kurdish provinces. In September of that year it was reported that 5,000 Turkish Kurds had been recruited to fight alongside Iranian Kurds, although the report was denied by the government.

Repression continued with tens of thousands of people, mostly Leftist activists and Kurds, being arrested and interrogated. There were many reports of torture. There were clashes between the army and small groups from the Kurdistan Workers' Party (PKK), and over 600 death sentences were demanded by the state in mass trials of PKK members. In Turkey's eastern and southern provinces the military presence has been increased, partly because of sensitivity over Afghanistan-Iran-USSR relations, but also in order to control the Kurdish population more closely. A coup took place in September 1980.

In 1984 civilian authority was restored under Prime Minister Turgut Ozal. However there has as yet been little change in the conditions faced by Kurds, and PKK guerrilla attacks continue.

In the past, Kurdish rebels have used safe havens in Iranian and Iraqi Kurdistan after battles with Turkish troops but Turkey was now pursuing guerrillas into Iraqi territory by agreement with the Iraqi government. In the late 1980s the activities of the PKK increased considerably as did counter-insurgency activities by the Turkish security forces. Although most Kurdish villagers did not support the PKK they were prime targets of counter-insurgency warfare by the Turkish security forces. In January 1989 there were allegations of torture and killing of villagers in Cizre province, particularly of a mass grave, containing several hundred Kurds, who had been allegedly "disappeared" after arrest by the army. The government agreed to institute an enquiry into these allegations. Also in 1989 thousands of Alevi Turks left central Anatolia fearing persecution from both the security forces and local Sunni Muslim fundamentalists.

The civilian government apparently was willing to consider a more liberal attitude towards its Kurdish subjects, especially in the cultural field, partly in reaction to persistent criticism from member countries of the EC which it was applying to join. This appeared to be the case when thousands of Kurdish refugees fleeing from Iraq entered Turkey in 1988, although there were later reports that the Turkish authorities had forced several thousand across the border to Iran. However most of these intentions have not been translated into action and the Kurdish minority continues to face repression, such as the schoolgirl who was arrested in April 1989, after admitting to a teacher that she was Kurdish. To date most restrictions on Kurds — such as the ban on speaking, writing or publication in Kurdish — remain in force.

A major social development amongst Turkish Kurds has been the increasing number who have moved to the West over the past 30 years as a result of underdevelopment in south-eastern Turkey. There are an estimated 380,000 Kurdish workers in Europe at the present time, the majority of them guest workers in Germany. The perceptions of these Kurds have radically altered and they have contributed greatly to the development of a political ideology amongst the Kurds in Anatolia. Recently, however, considerable economic advances have been made in the region, with the electrification of villages, greatly improved communications and the construction of the largest hydro-electric dam in Turkey. This economic advance partly explains the reluctance of most Kurds to join Kurdish political activists.

The old divisions between traditionalists and

urbanized Kurds continue. Political opinion is now divided between those who support the Turkish leftist parties, tribal or religious leaders who act as intermediaries between the Turkish authorities and the Kurdish peasantry, and the traditionalist members of the Kurdistan Democratic Party of Turkey, who are suspicious of leftist ideology and talk of class war.

Iran

During World War II the USSR occupied northern Iran and the British occupied the south. The Kurdish area between the two zones was a power vacuum and the Shahpur and Urmiya regions fell under Soviet control. Both the Kurds and the Azerbaijanis began to take more direct control of their internal affairs with the encouragement of the Soviet Union. In December 1945 the Azerbaijanis captured Tabriz and declared a Democratic Republic of Azerbaijan. Within days the Kurds had declared the Republic of Mahabad. The Kurdish republic was very small, however, as the Kurdish areas which lay within the Anglo-American zone of control were not incorporated. In January 1946 a government was formed by the Kurdish Democratic Party (KDPI).

The Mahabad government had expected Soviet support to continue but in May 1946 the Soviets left Iran. Their interests lay in maintaining good relations with the Iranian government and not with supporting a secessionist movement. Government troops entered Azerbaijan and Mahabad which fell easily. Qazi Muhammad and two colleagues were publicly hanged, the teaching of Kurdish prohibited and Kurdish books burned. After this the Kurdish nationalist movement went underground but the KDPI remained active during the next 30 years.

The downfall of the Shah in January 1979 presented the Kurdish people with an opportunity to pursue their demands for autonomy; however once more Kurdish leadership was divided, this time between those who had previously received financial and political rewards for ensuring peace in their regions and those who had attempted to assert their independence. The following months were marked by a series of negotiations and armed clashes culminating in July and August 1979 in the fall of Mahabad and Sardasht to the Iranian army and the summary execution of at least seventy people by the revolutionary court.

Despite the loss of all their towns to government forces the Kurds had not been beaten decisively and they began to regain territory. The government made an offer of self-administration but not full autonomy, granting the Kurds rights as a religious, not a political minority. The offer was rejected by Kurds, who still held an area of about 192,000 square kilometres. The invasion of Iran by Iraq in September 1980 opened new opportunities for Kurds within Iran but due to divisions within the Kurdish groups these were not utilized. Instead the Iranian military presence has been tightened. By early 1984 the Kurdish controlled area of Iran had been virtually eliminated by which time 27,500 Iranian Kurds were estimated to have died, only 2,500 of whom were soldiers.

The loss of a territorial base has forced the two main Kurdish groups, the KDPI and Komala, to abandon conventional guerrilla warfare and concentrate on specific limited military actions at night, in addition to organizing among civilians. There have been clashes between the two groups and the KDPI has also split over its position towards the Iranian government. A KDPI leader in exile, Dr Abdulrahman Qassemlou, was assassinated in Vienna in mid-1989, allegedly by agents of the Iranian regime, and a Komala leader was killed in Cyprus a month later. To date Iranian Kurdistan remains under heavy military operations and there are continuing reports of arrests, torture and "disappearances".

Iraq

The Kurdish experience in modern Iraq has been dominated by the charismatic figure of Mulla Mustafa Barzani, who died in 1979. He combined the secular power of the Agha with religious leadership, and for many years his name was almost synonymous with Kurdish revolt. He established cordial relations with government whilst participating in the illegal Kurdish Democratic Party (KDP). By co-operating with government troops in the defeat of Arab nationalists and monarchists Barzani succeeded in gaining the legitimization of the KDP, but he lacked the support of many Kurds who supported instead other Kurdish tribal leaders.

With the backing of a number of disaffected Aghas Barzani gradually led the Kurds into widespread revolt against the government, gaining popular support from Kurds unhappy with agrarian reform laws and unpopular land and tobacco taxes. Throughout the 1960s war raged between the army and Kurdish forces. 300,000 people were displaced or made homeless during this period and 60,000 others were killed or wounded. There were also reports of massacres of civilians. A peace agreement reached in March

1970 recognized the bi-national character of the Iraqi state in which the Kurds were to be free and equal partners. A Kurdish Vice-President was appointed and education and economic development in Kurdish areas improved. Despite these improvements Barzani made more demands in 1972, with the support of Iran, the US and Israel, and this led to further clashes between Kurds and government troops. The situation was unstable and there were accusations by both sides of rape and the burning of villages.

In 1974 the Kirkuk oil production was nationalized. Barzani and the KDP demanded proportional distribution of oil revenues but the Ba'ath government was adamant that the revenues were national assets which should be allocated under central authority. This dispute and divisions within the KDP provoked a crisis which resulted in the declaration of a new Autonomy Law in 1974. Although the law recognized the existence of the Kurds as a distinct group it was rejected by Kurdish leadership mainly due to the dispute over Kirkuk. With strong backing from Iran the Iraqi Kurds reverted to war. Fighting intensified until in early 1975 it became clear that the army could not win unless Iranian support was cut off. In March Iraq ceded the strategic Shatt-al-Arab waterway to Iran and in return Iran withdrew its support for the Kurdish rebels. The revolt collapsed and Kurdish inhabitants of the border areas were moved to "model villages" outside a new *cordon sanitaire*. The war resulted in the displacement of approximately 600,000 people with possibly as many as 50,000 killed or wounded. Repression of Kurds continued long after this; in 1983 8,000 non-combatant members of the Barzani clan had been arrested and "disappeared".

The Iran-Iraq war 1980-88

In September 1980 Iraq invaded Iran, providing the Kurds with an opportunity of establishing independent enclaves. Lack of agreement among the Kurds on either side of the border prevented them from capitalizing on the situation, however. In 1983 Iraqi-backed Iranian Kurds were defeated by Iranian forces and expelled from Iranian territory. Iraqi Kurds were more successful in their struggle and the KDP and Patriotic Union of Kurdistan (PUK) succeeded in pinning down one quarter of the Iraqi army and inhibiting troop movements after dark. Tremendous loss of life and the use of lethal (and internationally banned) chemical weapons by the Iraqi forces persuaded Iran to accept a ceasefire which came into force on August 20, 1988.

Iraqi troops then drove KDP and PUK forces almost out of Iraqi Kurdistan using gas, massive bombardment and the threat of shooting all Kurds found in prohibited areas, in what international observers have described as an official policy of genocide. On March 16, 1988 Halabja, a mainly Kurdish city, was attacked with chemical weapons, killing 6,350 people, largely civilians. There were further attacks with the deadly gas against civilian and military targets in April and May 1989. By the end of August over 3,000 villages had been razed to the ground, over 60,000 Kurdish civilians had fled across the border into Turkey and as many had crossed into Iran where they were housed in camps along the border.

There are reports of continuing displacement of Kurdish civilians. Basically the Iraqi government appears to envisage destroying the Kurdish heartland. Up to one million Kurds are estimated to have been moved within Kurdistan and another half a million have been sent to camps in remote desert regions. Arab settlers are being encouraged to move into former Kurdish areas. Over 100,000 Kurds are in squalid refugee camps in Turkey and Iran, which are not subject to international monitoring and protection. An amnesty offered to Kurds by the Iraqi government has been widely distrusted and few Kurds have returned. There are many reports of torture within Iraq and in early 1989, Amnesty International reported cases of torture of babies and young children by the Iraqi security forces.

Syria

The Kurdish population of Syria, which numbers about 8% of the total population, is largely "arabicized", with many Kurds feeling themselves to be part of the local Arab culture. The majority of Syrian Kurds moved into the area following the collapse of the Ottoman Empire in 1918. Kurds held high rank in the army and the first three military coups in Syria were carried out by officers with part-Kurd backgrounds. By 1958 high-ranking Kurds had been purged from the army, however, possibly as a result of the union of Syria and Egypt in the United Arab Republic in that year and a mood of Arab nationalism inspired by Nasser's first successful years in office.

Following the collapse of the union with Egypt in 1961, plans to create an "Arab belt" along the border of Jazira, while never fully implemented, caused some 60,000 Kurds to leave their homes and settle in Damascus, Turkey and Lebanon. After 1963, when the Ba'ath party assumed power, persecution of the Kurds continued, but in the 1970s the situation improved. Land reforms already implemented elsewhere were now carried out in Kurdish areas and the long-standing plan to transfer Kurdish and Arab populations in these areas was officially renounced. The position of Kurds in Syria today is more secure than in neighbouring countries although thousands, stripped of citizenship, are still obliged to serve in the armed forces.

Lebanon

Before the Civil War of 1975-77 there were some 70,000 Kurds living in Lebanon, mainly engaged in unskilled and poorly paid manual labour. Most had come originally from south-east Anatolia but less than 20,000 had been awarded citizenship. Since the Civil War Kurds have suffered oppression. At least 10,000, possibly many more, are known to have left Lebanon, mostly returning to Syria.

USSR

There were about 300,000 Kurds living in the USSR according to the 1970 census, mostly in Azerbaijan, Soviet Armenia, Georgia and the Turkoman Republic. There are no Kurdish territories although there are compact Kurdish colonies. Several Kurdish tribes entered the Caucasus region during the latter part of the eighteenth century whilst others reached Central Asia when used by the Persian Shahs to guard their eastern border in the sixteenth century.

There is a strong sense of cultural identity among Soviet Kurds, for whom a measure of cultural freedom exists. There are Kurdish schools and books and there is a Kurdish radio station. Kurds also identify strongly with Kurds in neighbouring countries. Since they are not physically contiguous with Kurdish communities over the border and since they are a small minority in the Soviet Union, government recognition of their cultural freedom presents no threat to central authority.

The future of the Kurds

In their major countries of residence, Turkey, Iran and Iraq, the Kurds continue to face discrimination and persecution from repressive regimes and despite international protests against aspects of their treatment, there appear to be no forseeable real changes in their situation. As in the past, some Kurdish groups are fighting for an independent state but although they pose a threat to governments they are not a united force and the odds are against the emergence of an independent Kurdistan. Other Kurds have urged a measure of political autonomy and full cultural recognition to satisfy Kurdish aspirations. Given the present political situation in the Middle East and the lack of resources and committed political support from other nations for the Kurds, the likely scenario is for continued conflict and repression.

Lebanon

Location: **Eastern Mediterranean, 10,400 sq km in area**
Population: **3.5 million (est. 1986)**
Racial/religious groups: **(est.) Christian: Maronite 900,000, Orthodox 250,000, Greek Catholic 150,000, other 50,000; Muslim: Sunni 750,000, Shi'ite 1,100,000, Druze 200,000; also Armenians 175,000, Palestinians 325,000, Syrians/Kurds 100,000**
% of population: **Christian: Maronite 25%, Orthodox 7.1%, Greek Catholic 4.3%, others 1.4%; Muslim: Sunni 21.4%, Shi'ite 31.4%, Druze 5.7%; Armenians 5%; Palestinians 9.2%; Syrians/Kurds 2.8%**
Language: **Arabic**

Lebanon is a country wholly composed of minorities, all strongly bound by ties of loyalty based on religious confession and kinship, and since 1975 divided by civil war. The most prominent of the various groups are the Maronites, Sunnis, Shi'ites, and Druzes.

The Maronites follow the monothelete doctrine of the Maronite Church. As a result of persecution by the Byzantine Church its members retreated from Syria into the remoter part of Lebanon in the seventh century. In the thirteenth century the Maronites established relations with Rome and from the seventeenth century onward they developed an affinity for

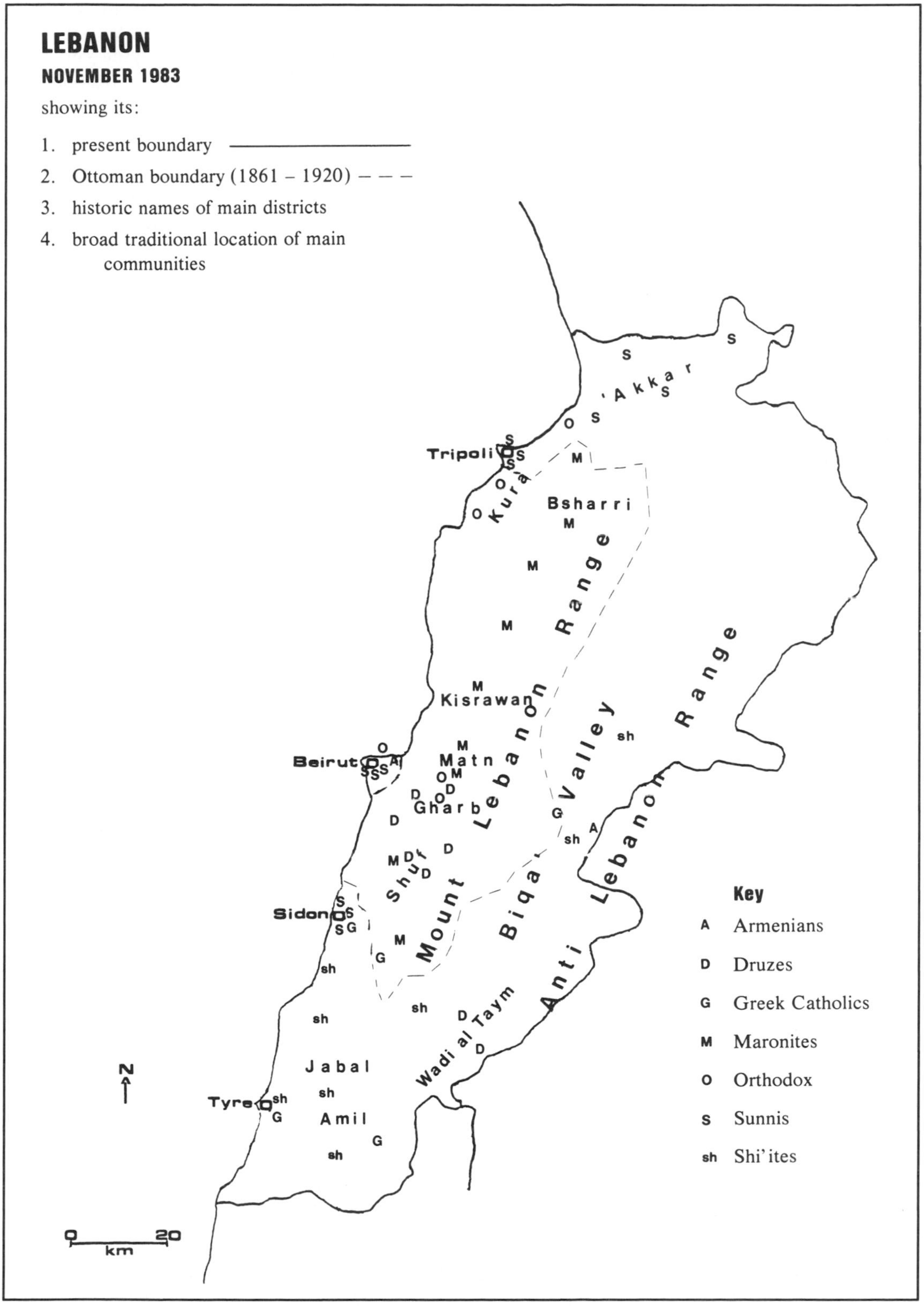

LEBANON

NOVEMBER 1983

showing its:

1. present boundary ——————————
2. Ottoman boundary (1861 – 1920) — — —
3. historic names of main districts
4. broad traditional location of main communities

S

S

S 'Akkar S

Tripoli S
S

Kura

O

M

Bsharri
M

M

M

Mount Lebanon Range

Biqaʼ Valley

Anti Lebanon Range

M
Kisrawan

sh

M
Matn
Beirut O A
S S S
M
O M
D O D
D
Gharb
D

G
A
sh

M
Shuf
D Df
D

S S
Sidon O
S G

M

G

sh

sh

sh

Wadi al Taym
D
D

Jabal
sh

Tyre sh
G

Amil
G

sh

Key

A	Armenians
D	Druzes
G	Greek Catholics
M	Maronites
O	Orthodox
S	Sunnis
sh	Shiʼites

N
↑

0   20
km

Europe and particularly France, with the result that many Maronites still use French as their first language.

The Sunnis are believers in the Quran supplemented by the traditions of the Prophet as the sole repository of the faith. Sunni Islam has traditionally been the majority faith and the faith of government in Islamic countries, including the former Ottoman Empire.

The Shi'ites (also known as Shias and in Lebanon as Mutawila) are followers of the Prophet Mohammed's son-in-law 'Ali. They believe in a succession of infallible Imams or religious leaders who were all members of the Prophet's family and who interpreted the law and doctrine. It is believed that the Imams died out in the ninth century but the last Imam, the twelfth, will one day return to rule the world. Shi'ism is the established faith in Iran, and Lebanese Shi'ites have a continuing interest in events in that country.

The Druzes broke away from mainstream Shi'ism in the eleventh century. They believe that God is composed of several principles such as universal soul, universal intelligence and God in his unity, which all become incarnate in man. They are the followers of disciples of the Fatimid Caliph of Egypt who claimed to be the emanation of God in his unity. The Druzes also believe in supernatural hierarchies and the transmigration of the soul. They form a tight-knit community which maintains strict moral standards.

Until 1920 the term Lebanon was used to designate only the mountain range inhabited mainly by Maronites in the north and centre and by Druzes in the Shuf region. The country lay within the Ottoman empire, and until the eighteenth and nineteenth centuries power within Lebanon was vested in the Druze nobility. Later the Maronite community came to the fore, largely as a result of inter-faction fighting among the Druzes. Relations between the two dominant communities were good until the 1930s when the region was briefly occupied by Egypt and then divided into separate areas. During the mid-nineteenth century notables in both groups were displaced by a Christian middle class which came to monopolize trade and had ties with Europe, especially France.

With the collapse of the Ottoman Empire in 1918 Syria and Mount Lebanon were annexed by France despite earlier assurances by the Allies that Arab independence would be guaranteed. Syrian districts such as the ports of Tyre and Sidon, Tripoli and Beirut, which had previously been under Ottoman provincial administration, were annexed and became part of the Republic of Greater Lebanon. This act greatly increased the proportion of Muslims living in the Lebanon, both Sunni and Shi'ite, and antagonized all but the Maronite community.

The National Pact

In 1943 Lebanon gained independence from France and the Maronite President and Sunni Prime Minister reached a formal understanding which became known as the National Pact. This stipulated that power would be divided between the various groups as follows: The President would always be Maronite, the Prime Minister Sunni, the Speaker of the Chamber of Deputies Shi'ite and the Deputy Speaker Greek Orthodox. The Greek Catholics and Druzes were to be represented in the Cabinet and seats in the Chamber were to be allotted proportionately to the sects, on the basis of six Christians to five Muslims, as were posts in the army and civil service. The Christian communities agreed not to seek protection agreements with the European powers, thereby threatening Lebanon's independence, and the Muslims undertook to respect the religious and cultural links between the Christians and the West and not to attempt a merger with Lebanon's Islamic neighbours. Although the National Pact was drawn up in an effort to divide power fairly between the minorities it had the effect of concentrating the real power within the two major communities. It also formalized the sectarian nature of Lebanese politics. The various factions depended almost entirely on respected families and individuals, and only the Maronite *Kata'ib* or *Phalange* party, founded by Pierre Gemayel, had a central organization and philosophy.

During the 1950s the effects of the revolution in Egypt and the rise to power of Gamal Abdel Nasser were felt throughout the Middle East and brought about a surge of Arab nationalism. In 1958 Muslim leaders suspected President Camille Chamoun of manipulating the system in order to be re-elected. This led to demonstrations and riots by Muslims and Druzes, in some cases clearly Nasserist in tone. President Chamoun attempted to retain control with the help of US military intervention in 1958 but Christians and Muslims alike called for his resignation and he was replaced by General Shihab who as commander of the army had refused to become militarily involved in internal power struggles.

The 1960s saw the meteoric rise of Beirut as the banking centre of the Arab world, with the major part of the city's wealth being created by Christian, Palestinian, Druze and Armenian entrepreneurs. Industry was undeveloped however, and agriculture was in decline; there was a great contrast between the prosperous regions and the more remote areas, where the economy stagnated. In stark contrast to the wealth of Beirut, the belt surrounding the city was a slum area inhabited largely by immigrant groups for whom the death rate and unemployment were two or three times higher than the national average; nevertheless Shi'ites from the south and Sunnis from the north flooded into the belt during the 1970s, compounding the problem of poverty and unemployment.

A further factor which contributed to the discontent in Lebanon was the influx of Palestinians, who arrived in three waves: the original refugees of 1948, those who fled the West Bank after the 1967 war, and those who arrived after the suppression of the Palestinian movement in the camps in Jordan in 1970-71. Of the 350,000 Palestinians in Lebanon, over 200,000 were registered with the UNRWA (United Nations Relief and Works Agency for Palestine Refugees); many of the remainder were illegal immigrants. Hostility towards the Palestinians was fuelled by the growing number of PLO raids across the border into Israel, especially after the 1967 war. Lebanese fears were justified as Israel began retaliatory attacks into Lebanon; there was however support for the PLO actions from many of the poorer members of the Shi'ite community in the suburbs of Beirut.

Civil war 1975-77

The civil war started in April 1975 with an attack on Palestinians by Kata'ib militia in the suburbs of Beirut and quickly developed into open conflict between rival militias, each fighting to ensure control of strategic points in Beirut. The main groups involved in the fighting were: (i) the Lebanese Front, three Maronite groups each led by a prominent Maronite family: The Kata'ib (*Phalange*), led by the Gemayel family; the National Liberation Party (*Ahrar*) led by the Chamoun family: the Zghorta Liberation Army, led by the Franjieh family; and (ii) the National Movement, largely made up of Muslim groups: the Progressive Socialist Party, a Druze organization led by Kemal Jumblat; the Syrian National Socialist Party, an Orthodox and Muslim group led by In'am Ra'd; the *Murabitun* (independent Nasserists), a Sunni group led by Ibrahim Qulaylat; the Lebanese Communist Party, a non-sectarian group led by George Hawi; the Ba'ath Socialist Party (Syria)

led by Asim Qansuh; the Ba'ath Socialist Party (Iraq) led by Abd al Majid Rafi'i, and the Amal, a Shi'ite group led by Musa al Sadr.

Although many people — Muslim and Christian — did not hold extremist views and were not otherwise alienated by poverty, they were nevertheless unavoidably caught up in the conflict and were forced to align themselves to one group or the other; others left the country to escape the situation. With the entry of the PLO into the conflict in December 1975 the war assumed even more savage proportions, with both sides eliminating potentially hostile enclaves within their zone of control. Shi'ites, Syrians, Armenians, Kurds and Palestinians were all killed indiscriminately: it has been estimated that some 50,000 people died in the fighting, most of them non-combatants.

The Syrian government was determined to keep Lebanon within its sphere of influence, afraid of either a victory by the Christian Lebanese Front which would be friendly towards Israel or the radicals with Palestinian involvement, which would undoubtedly cause Israeli intervention. At the request of the Lebanese Front Syria intervened in April 1976 and then remained to enforce the peace at the request of the Arab League. It soon became apparent that there was no unity within the two sides and the various factions were now fighting each other. Gradually the situation developed into a struggle between three groups: the Lebanese Forces (LF), the National Movement incorporating the Palestinians, and the Syrians.

Israeli invasion, 1982

On June 6, 1982 Lebanon was invaded by Israel. Within a few days the Israeli army had reached Beirut, and over 10,000 people, most of them civilians, had died. Syria was defeated and the Israelis faced the PLO and Nasserist *Murabitun* in Beirut. Here they were forced to a stop as a result of heavy casualties inflicted by the PLO. On August 19, the PLO also withdrew, with US guarantees for the safety of the Palestinian refugee camps and an Israeli undertaking not to enter West Beirut; these guarantees were not met however and US troops of the UNMNF withdrew as soon as the PLO had left West Beirut, leaving the city unprotected and open to the Israelis, who moved into the city a few days later. The Israeli government was determined to destroy the PLO and, it was believed, facilitate their annexation of the West Bank and Gaza Strip with the co-operation of the Lebanese Forces and the *Kata'ib*. The commander of the

Lebanese Forces, Bashir Gemayel, was elected President of the Republic but was assassinated on September 14, within days of his election. Israeli troops moved into West Beirut and a company of Lebanese Forces entered Sabra and Shatila camps where they are reported to have killed between 1,000 and 2,000 people, half of them Lebanese.

The shock and outrage that followed the massacres, both within Israel and internationally, led to the signing of a Withdrawal Agreement by Lebanon and Israel on May 17, 1983, and an Israeli retreat to the Awali river. The US, which had supported the Lebanese Army, although always emphasizing US neutrality, was widely mistrusted by the Muslim population and a series of suicide truck bombs directed against US targets caused nearly 300 deaths and led to the withdrawal of the American presence in Lebanon. The Israelis were replaced in Beirut by the mainly Christian-controlled Lebanese Army which began to round up and arrest members of the Palestinian community and others who lived in the shanty areas. This action fuelled Muslim anger and by July the army was engaged in armed conflict with the Shi'ites, soon compounded by battles with the Amal and Sunni *Murabitun* following a visit to Beirut by the Israeli Defence Minister.

The Israeli Army now began a series of retreats southward. They withdrew abruptly from the Gharb and the Shuf areas without any warning to the Lebanese Army. This sudden action threw the region into chaos. Israel had allowed the Christian *Kata'ib* and Lebanese Forces into the Shuf, traditional homeland of the Druzes, in the previous year, and the *Kata'ib* had separated the Jumblat and Yazbak factions of the Druze population and had reportedly committed atrocities in Kfar Matta. The Israeli withdrawal left the Druzes free to drive the *Kata'ib* out of the region which they did with an overall loss of some 600 lives, and a further 75,000 Christians who were not connected with the *Kata'ib* fled the Shuf. The Druzes drove the Maronite forces from all but a narrow coastal strip in Iqlim and by February 1984 the Lebanese army had also been driven out of West Beirut and Gemayel's predominantly Maronite government had resigned.

As the Israeli army retreated it rounded up hundreds of suspects in the Palestinian camps around Tyre and Sidon, moving many to a camp at Ansar. Attacks on the Israeli troops became more frequent, and popular demonstrations against the Israeli occupation were put down. Leaders suspected of encouraging armed resistance were imprisoned or killed and homes of resistance suspects were destroyed. In the face of growing opposition from the Muslims Israel coerced members of the various communities into collaborating, and also organized the formation of the South Lebanese Army (SLA) which soon gained a reputation for the brutal harassment of Palestinians and other opponents of Israel. In February 1985 the Israeli army withdrew from Sidon and at the same time launched its "Iron Fist operation", a sweeping attack on Lebanese villages between the Ajrani and Litani rivers, in which many died. Having then withdrawn the bulk of its troops Israel left 1,000 men inside Lebanese territory as support for the South Lebanese Army.

Syrian influence

The Syrian government, which had rejected the Lebanese-Israeli withdrawal Agreement of May 1983, quickly took advantage of the overthrow of the Maronite-dominated government by the Druzes and the Shi'ites to assemble its allies. Syria pressured Gemayel into forming a new government incorporating these allies, who included Sulayman Franjieh, the Maronite with closest relations with Syria; Walid Jumblat of the Druzes; Rashid Karami of the Sunni Tripoli and Nabih Berri of Amal. With the ousting of the Lebanese forces from the Shuf and the Lebanese Army from West Beirut the Muslims were in a strong position to negotiate with the Christians. Gemayel's government collapsed and a meeting of the Lebanese factional leaders in Geneva resulted in a significant rewording of the 1943 National Pact. Rather than "An Arab country with a Western aspect" Lebanon was now described as an Arab country and founding member of the Arab League, with all the obligations that such membership entails. The participants also agreed to the ratio of Christian and Muslim representation in parliament being altered to 1:1 rather than the 6:5 stipulated in the National Pact. Little more was decided however, and talks in Lausanne did not result in a peace agreement.

By now tension was mounting within both sides. The Druzes attacked the Sunni *Murabitun* in West Beirut, driving them out of key positions. In this they were probably encouraged by Syria, as both feared that the *Murabitun* were assisting the PLO to rebuild a power base in the refugee camps. Disagreements within the Shi'ite community were also becoming evident, with Husain Musawi's Islamic Amal — a splinter group of Berri's Amal — and an Iranian Shi'ite faction becoming mutually hostile. In May 1985

Amal, encouraged by Syria, moved against the Palestinian camps in Beirut and a savage battle ensued in which Amal and the Shi'ite sixth Brigade committed atrocities similar to those carried out in the same camps by the Lebanese Forces in 1982. The Palestinians held on to Burj al Barajneh but lost most of Sabra/Shatila. The Shi'ites of south Lebanon condemned Berri's action as did the Hizballah and Iran, and Berri lost his strong position within the Shi'ite community. Tension was high too within the Christian communities, between those who accepted Syria's strength in Lebanon and hoped to hold the Christian militias and the office of President together, and those who wished to cantonize the country and minimize Syrian influence. Since Fuad Abi Nader, a relative of Gemayel, had taken command of the Lebanese Forces in October 1984, they had been more amenable to Syria, but this displeased many within the forces and a revolt led by Samia Geagea resulted in an attack on Sunni Sidon and the Christian refugee camps. After three weeks Druze, Sunni, Palestinian and Sh'ia forces with Syrian backing counter-attacked seizing much of the region and causing its almost total abandonment by the Christian population which numbered about 70,000.

Samia Geagea was replaced by Elie Hobeiqa who had commanded the Lebanese Forces in Sabra and Shatila in 1982. Hobeiqa publicly acknowledged Syria's prime role in the conflict and on December 28, 1985 he joined Berri and Jumblat in signing an agreement calling for the secularization of Lebanon's political life, the passing of considerable powers from the President to the Prime Minister and the disbandment of the militias. This agreement, signed in Damascus, was to have formed the basis for a new constitution but it was immediately rejected by other groups which had not been consulted and Hobeiqa was ousted by Samia Geagea with the support of President Gemayel, thus ending any possibility for its implementation.

Violence increases 1986-88

After the collapse of the Damascus Agreement the situation in Lebanon deteriorated still further. There was a festering power struggle within the Maronite camp between Gemayel and Geagea and the Sunni community was in a weak position having lost Beirut which until recently was a quintessentially Sunni city. The Shi'ites were potentially very powerful but they were riven by disunity and in many southern areas Berri's Amal had been displaced by fundamentalist Hizballahis and others who drew inspiration

from Iran, and whose visionary ideology represented a real threat to less idealistic rivals and to all other factions. Only the Druzes were well placed; Jumblat remains unchallenged although he continues to call for a secular democratic state in which the Druzes, with only 7% of the population, would lose power. The Druzes have established a "United Investment Enterprise" for Druze-controlled areas, to support investment in productive enterprise. The purpose of this is partly to find employment for militiamen before they turn to crime.

In May and June 1986 there were clashes between the Amal and Druze militias on the one hand and the Palestinians in the refugee camps of south Beirut. These developed into the "battle of the camps" in which hundreds died, although it also revived world sympathy for the Palestinian cause. Although there was some relaxation of restrictions earlier, Amal's siege did not end until January 1988. By mid-1986 there was a new outburst of violence in Beirut with car bombings taking a toll of over 200 dead and 600 wounded in two weeks, while President Gemayel began to lose support among the military. The cabinet of "National Unity" had failed to meet since January but Gemayel indicated that he would consider a new formula for dividing power by calling a special parliamentary session, although nothing eventuated from this initiative.

Violence continued throughout 1987 which was also noted for the dramatic decline in the Lebanese economy when inflation reached over 700%. The two Shi'ite rivals Amal and Hizballah continued to fight their proxy war for control of the Shia population on behalf of their respective backers — Syria and Iran — not only by military means but by the provision of social services and community support. Although Hizballah was rich, Amal controlled a much larger area. From February 1988 there was a new attempt by Amal to reassert control in the south and there was fighting in April in southern Lebanon, only ended by intervention by Shi'ite clerics from both sides. Fighting between the two groups broke out again in the Shi'ite suburbs of Beirut in May and by the end of the month over 260 people had been killed and 1,100 wounded while half the population of half-a-million who had lived in the 40 square kilometre enclave had fled. There was also continuing fighting between Christian groups.

By May also Israeli troops had returned to Lebanon in greater numbers than at any time since 1985, and carried out "Operation Law and Order" with the SLA in south Lebanon, searching, raiding and sometimes destroying villages. Israeli air raids also took place over various areas of Lebanon. Israeli actions have continued in the SLA dominated areas for over two years, including an international crisis precipitated by the kidnapping of a Hizballah cleric in August 1989. Although not widely covered by the international media, there were steady and reliable reports of forced conscription of villagers into the SLA army, financed by the Israelis. For ordinary Shia villagers life became a nightmare as they were torn between fears of collaborating with any of the factions — and yet most were prevented from leaving the area while others were forcibly expelled. UN UNIFIL troops were unable to stop such violations taking place.

Military rule and the bombardment of Beirut

Gemayel's six year term as President expired on September 23, 1988, but since the Lebanese parliament failed to elect a successor, a military government took control, led by the Maronite Christian general Michel Aoun and comprising Christian and Muslim senior officers. Amid fears of a new civil war and imminent partition, Muslim factions refused to accept the Aoun government and the Geagea (LF) quietly swallowed the *Phalange* of ex-President Gemayel. In effect Lebanon was without a central government, partitioned into Christian and Muslim mini-states, a position that was confirmed in October when the Parliament failed to elect a new Speaker.

At first General Aoun gained a measure of support from all communities by his stated intention of disbanding all militias. He engaged in a war with the LF of Geagea and attempted to end the LF mini-state north of Beirut. His apparent success in this on February 24, 1989 brought him cautious support from West Beirut's Muslim communities, the Green Line crossings began to re-open and the Lebanese pound gained in value. But Aoun's intentions to disband the Muslim militias and his declaration of a "War of Liberation" against occupying Syrian forces soon alienated Muslims and the Syrians, whom the Muslims had seen mainly in the role of protectors. On March 8, 1989 Aoun began shelling and

rocketing Syrian strongholds, treatment which was soon returned in kind by the Syrians and their allies, the Muslims and the Druzes. The continued bombing turned an already battered Beirut into a ghost city — within three weeks there were 156 killed and 700 injured; by early August the figures were 530 dead and 2,000 injured. Beirut had been reduced to rubble and over 1.3 million Beirutis of all religious persuasions had fled to safety elsewhere in Lebanon or to neighbouring countries; less than 15% of the population remained. Murderous nightly bombings continued with neither side showing a willingness to either cease fire, surrender or compromise.

The future of Lebanon

By August 1989 Lebanon appeared not only to be in the process of disbandment but of depopulation and physical ruin. International mediation efforts to find a workable solution had failed. The Arab League had from late 1988 opened talks to prevent the formal partition of the country and to bring together warring communities but these failed. Another effort was made in May 1989 but this also failed and on July 31 the Arab League admitted that they had reached a "dead end". Mediation and humanitarian efforts by western powers such as France were seen as partisan towards the Christian community, but the UN Secretary-General fared no better. It was not until September that an Arab League Peace Plan was accepted by both sides. The bombardment of Beirut ceased and the population began to return.

Various proposals have been put forward for the future of Lebanon; a unitary state, a federal system, a Swiss canton-type federation on religious lines, a break-up into a series of new states, dismemberment and rule by the surrounding countries. Many wealthy or professional Lebanese have left, probably for good, but for the poor this is unlikely to be an option. Lebanon has many advantages of location and resources; whether it is now too late to regain these remains to be seen.

(See also *Palestinians*)

Palestinians

Alternative names: (in Israel: Israeli Arabs, Palestinian Israelis)
Location: Israel (including occupied East Jerusalem), Occupied Territories (West Bank of River Jordan, Gaza Strip on Mediterranean coast), Jordan (East Bank), Lebanon, Syria, other Middle Eastern countries
Population: Total 4.9 million; Israel 700,000, East Jerusalem 122,000, West Bank 890,000, Gaza Strip 500,000, Jordan 1.2 million, Lebanon 360,000, Syria 250,000, other Middle Eastern countries 720,000, elsewhere 350,000
Religion: Muslim (85%) mainly Sunni, small Shi'a and Druze communities; Christian (10%) Orthodox, Greek Orthodox, some Roman Catholic and Protestant
Language: Arabic, Hebrew

The Palestinians are the descendants of the earliest recorded residents of Palestine who intermarried with later conquerors. Among these were the Philistines, the Jews and the Arabs who conquered Palestine and Syria in the seventh century AD. From 1516 until 1917 the region was administered by Ottoman Turkey and it then came under British rule which lasted until 1948. Since that time the Palestinians have been turned from a dominant majority to a stateless minority group living under many different administrations — Israeli, Egyptian, Jordanian, Lebanese, in UN refugee camps and elsewhere. The Palestinian-Israeli conflict has continued for over 40 years and no solution which is acceptable to both sides appears to be in sight.

Palestinian society is composed of different religious and social communities. The vast majority of Muslim Palestinians traditionally lived in rural areas whereas over half of the Christian group was urban. As in the surrounding countries, leadership was divided between the notable Muslim families and the religious hierarchies of the various faiths and sects. Nomads and semi-nomads formed 5-10% of the population at the end of the nineteenth century and there was also a pre-Zionist Jewish community which by 1881 made up approximately 6% of the total population of Palestine. During most of the Ottoman period Palestine was not a single administrative unit but part of Syria. As late as World War I there was no real concept of "Palestinian", and the first "Palestinian" utterances came about only as a result of increasing Jewish immigration which had begun in the late nineteenth century but which by 1914 had become a major political issue.

The beginnings of Jewish settlement
The Jews who settled in Palestine after 1881 had little in common with the old established Jewish communities. They were a people inspired by Jewish nationalism to flee the pogroms of eastern Europe and settle in *Eretz Israel*, the kingdom of Zion and land of their ancestors. As these new immigrants arrived they began buying land and the Jewish National Fund (JNF) was formed with the purpose of facilitating land purchase. The JNF stipulated that all land purchased by the Fund would remain inalienably Jewish and that only Jews could work on it.

The British, who captured Palestine in 1917 and ruled by League of Nations mandate from 1922, actively encouraged the establishment in Palestine of a national home for the Jewish people. The government stressed, however, that no action should be taken which might jeopardize the civil and religious rights of existing non-Jewish communities in the area. The creation of a national homeland was clearly the goal of Zionists and a stipulation that a Jewish agency should assist the British authorities to develop Palestine economically further weakened the position of the Palestinian population.

Palestinian chances of moderating the effect of Jewish settlement were forfeited when both Muslim and Christian Arabs boycotted elections for a legislative council in 1923 on the grounds that British mandatory rule legitimized Zionism in Palestine. Increasingly severe attacks on Jewish settlements were taking place and the British government decided to limit Jewish immigration; however, vacillation on the part of the British resulted in the revolt of 1936 in which British troops took 18 months to suppress the attempt by Palestinian peasants to drive both the British and the Jewish settlers from their land. In 1937 a partition of Palestine was proposed by the British and when this was rejected by the Palestinians a government White Paper proposed the restriction of Jewish immigrants to 75,000 over five years. The proposal did not go far enough for the Palestinians and it was a bitter blow to the Jews in view of what was now happening in Europe.

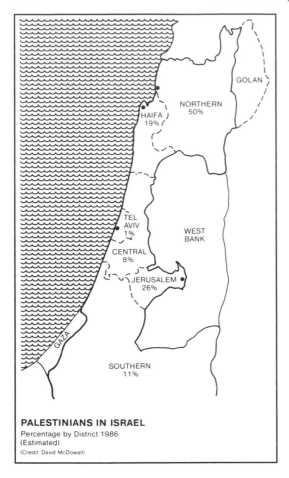

PALESTINIANS IN ISRAEL
Percentage by District 1986
(Estimated)
(Credit: David McDowall)

The Arab-Israeli War of 1948

Following the events of World War II Britain referred the Palestinian question to the United Nations. The near-extermination of European Jewry had driven survivors to a desperate search for refuge in Palestine. Palestinians were now faced with world opinion which favoured the notion of a Jewish homeland, an organized Jewish defence force which the British had helped to train during the 1936 rebellion, and a weakened fighting capacity as a result of their defeat during the same rebellion. The United Nations decided to partition Palestine, awarding 54% of the land area to the proposed Jewish state. Within that state Arabs would constitute 50.5% of the population and own three times the land area owned by the Jews; in the proposed Arab state Arabs would make up 98.7% of the population and in the proposed international zone around Jerusalem, 51.4%. The Palestine Arabs rejected the UN plan on the grounds that

it violated the principle of self-determination set out in the United Nations Charter. British relations with the Jews and the Arabs were steadily worsening. Jewish terrorist activity was increasing and official Jewry was dismayed by the British recognition of the related mandatory territory of Transjordan as an independent sovereign state in May 1946.

The British withdrawal from Palestine in 1948 was marked by fighting between Jews and Palestinians. By the time Arab armies had crossed into Palestine on May 15 the Haganah or Jewish forces had captured sizeable parts of Palestine which had been allocated to the proposed Arab state. As they advanced a number of atrocities occurred, notably at Deir Yassin, near Jerusalem, where 254 villagers died. Fear of similar atrocities caused some 725,000 Arabs to abandon their homes and flee to neighbouring countries where they were settled in refugee camps which soon acquired an air of permanency.

In 1948 Transjordanian forces crossed into Palestine and were soon in control of most of Arab Palestine. Egypt, fearing Transjordanian ambitions in the area, established a Government of All-Palestine based in Gaza but with authority in Egyptian-occupied southern Palestine. By the end of the year Israeli forces had driven southward across the Negev desert to Eilat and separated Hebron from Gaza, gaining control of most of southern Palestine. The Egyptian army maintained a hold over the narrow costal strip of Gaza on the Mediterranean and 190,000 Palestinian refugees swamped the resident population of 80,000 in an area only 45 kilometres long by six to ten kilometres wide. By 1949, when an armistice was agreed, Jewish forces were in control of 73% of Palestine.

The wars of 1956 and 1967

In April 1950 the West Bank region was formally incorporated into the "Hashemite Kingdom of Jordan" which had been created from Transjordan in 1946. The population of Jordan almost trebled to 1,280,000, of whom more than half-a-million were refugees either in West Bank or East Bank. Although the great increase in territory and population increased the power of the Kingdom of Jordan it also destabilized it and from 1948 until 1967 the Jordanian government suppressed Palestinian nationalist expression which consequently began to manifest itself in the refugee camps.

In the course of its 1956 campaign against Egypt, Israel invaded and occupied the Gaza

Strip. Its withdrawal under US pressure the following year was seen as a victory for President Nasser and for Arab nationalism. The Gazan economy began to flourish as a result both of the opening of Eastern European markets to citrus production and its new status as a tax-free port, which encouraged Egyptian holiday-makers to visit the region.

In 1967 the Arab armies were routed by Israeli forces which seized large areas including the West Bank and the Gaza Strip. Thousands of Palestinians fled their villages or refugee camps and 355,000 crossed the River Jordan into the East Bank where they were housed in emergency camps in Jordan and Syria. These temporary camps, like those erected in 1948, soon took on a permanence never intended. Whereas before 1967 some Palestinians had been living under Arab — if not Palestinian — rule, after that date all Palestine was subject to Israeli rule. The Labour government of Israel accepted Security Council Resolution 242 which states that acquisition of territory by war is inadmissible, but later stressed that in its interpretation "withdrawal of Israeli forces from territories of recent conflict" did not mean all those territories, indeed Israel had already annexed East Jerusalem.

The growth of Palestinian resistance movements

Of the various Palestinian resistance groups the following have been the most influential: (i) Fatah: The largest single group, led by Yasir Arafat, it stresses that political disagreement should be subordinate to the question of the return of refugees. Fatah is an umbrella organization which is able to withstand much internal disagreement and it has survived the split of 1983; (ii) Palestine Liberation Organization (PLO): Formed in 1964 as a result of a move within the Arab League, the PLO was seen as a means of "organizing the Palestinian people and enabling them to play their role in the liberation of their country and their self-determination". The growth of Fatah after the 1967 war led to the movement gaining control of the Executive Committee of the PLO and the election of Arafat as its chairman; (iii) Popular Front for the Liberation of Palestine (PFLP): Established by George Habash, the PFLP is the most extreme branch of Palestinian resistance. It advocates revolutionary violence and has only intermittently held a seat on the PLO executive committee because of disagreements with Fatah. The PFLP was responsible for the hijacking of international aircraft between 1968

and 1972 and the killing of 27 people at Lod airport in 1972, after which it renounced the use of terrorist tactics; (iv) Democratic Front for the Liberation of Palestine (DFLP): A left-wing breakaway group of the PFLP under the leadership of Naif Hawatmeh. Formed in 1969, the DFLP was the first group to publicly accept the right of Jews to their own state but has as its ultimate objective the formation of a popular democratic state of all inhabitants of Palestine; and (v) Fatah Revolutionary Council (Black June Organization), led by Abu Nidal, is based in Syria and is not part of the PLO. Its members left Fatah in 1976 when it became more moderate, and it was responsible for the deaths of PLO representatives in London, Kuwait and Paris and probably for the Rome and Vienna airport terrorist attacks in 1985. It also claimed responsibility for the attempted assassination of the Israeli Ambassador in London which triggered the Israeli invasion of Lebanon in 1982.

Other resistance groups include the Syrian-backed National Alliance which includes As Saiqa, PFLP-General Command (PFLP-GC), and Palestine Popular Struggle Front (PPSF): and the Iraqi-backed Palestine Liberation Front (PLF) and Arab Liberation Front (ALF).

In countries such as Jordan and Lebanon, made vulnerable by the presence of thousands of Palestinian refugees or by internal political instability, the presence of large numbers of *fedayeen*, as the resistance groups are known, affected relations between the Palestinians and the host government. In Jordan the tensions erupted in 1970-71 into a battle in which Jordanian troops drove the *fedayeen* from the country with the loss of about 3,000 Palestinian lives, military and civilian. In Lebanon the dominant Maronite community felt itself increasingly threatened by the support given the PLO by the poorer sectors of society such as the Shi'ite villagers of southern Lebanon and the large Sunni and Shi'ite population of the Beirut slums. When, following the 1969 Cairo Agreement, the state ceded control of the Palestinian refugee camps to the PLO and sanctioned PLO operations against Israel, progress towards civil war was rapidly accelerated.

Following the events of 1970-71 the majority of Palestinians in the Occupied Territories switched allegiance from Jordan to the PLO. The Arab League's decision in 1974 to recognize the PLO as the sole legitimate representative of the Palestinians was very popular amongst the Palestinians; however this optimism was short-lived as the right-wing Likud government was elected in Israel in 1977. The new government had as its aim the total integration of the territories into Israel's economy. In 1975 the US and Israel reached a formal agreement to the effect that there would be no US recognition of or negotiation with the PLO until it recognized Israel's right to exist and accepted Security Council Resolutions 242 and 338. In 1977 the peace initiative by Anwar Sadat led to the Camp David Agreement between Israel and Egypt, an agreement hailed in the West but denounced by all Arab states since it rejected the Palestinian claim to self-determination in favour of an autonomy plan for the West Bank and Gaza. Camp David in effect also freed Israel to invade Lebanon in 1982 in pursuit of the PLO.

In March 1978 an attack by Fatah commandos on Israel's coastal road resulted in the deaths of 37 civilians and caused Israel to invade Lebanon in an attempt to drive the PLO out of southern Lebanon. Israeli troops withdrew as a result of US pressure and a United Nations Interim Force in Lebanon (UNIFIL) was sent into the country to prevent border violations.

(For Israel, Syria and the PLO in Lebanon see under *Lebanon*.)

By mid-1984 the Palestine movement had divided into three factions: those who remained loyal to the PLO chairman Yasir Arafat, the Syrian-backed groups which demanded his removal from office, and the Democratic Alliance (comprising the DFLP, the Palestine Communist Party and the PLF) which called for greater democracy within the PLO but did not wish to see Syria dominate the organization. This split into factions appeared permanent until the Syrian-sponsored attacks on the Lebanese refugee camps at the end of 1986 forced the groups to unite and face the threat together. The reunited PLO still faces major problems such as the need for a permanent base.

The refugees

The position of the 2,100,000 Palestinian refugees remains precarious. They have no political rights and the enormous strain placed on the host nations has meant that they are not a welcome addition to the population. In Lebanon the refugees constitute one tenth of the total population and in West Bank and East Bank they make up almost half. The problem of cramped living conditions has been compounded by the cultural differences between the Palestinians and the native population, especially in Lebanon with its large Christian element, and in Jordan with its Beduin-dominated culture.

In 1950, two years after the first wave of evacuation, the United Nations Relief and Works Agency for Palestine Refugees (UNRWA) was formed. Its first task was to provide food for the refugees and to assist in the building of semi-permanent shelters. UNRWA also played a part in the control of major communicable diseases and provided the refugees with schooling for thousands of children (360,000 in 1985) and with vocational and teacher training for a limited number of adults; its mandate does not include development, however, and as a result the Palestinians have not taken charge of their own affairs but have remained heavily dependent on welfare. The UNRWA has not been given responsibility for the legal or physical protection of refugees either and host governments have the power to withhold travel documents.

Palestinians in the Arab world

Although Palestinians have found refuge or employment in every Arab country since 1948 their relationship has often been ambiguous. Palestinians in general have higher educational standards and are more politically aware, a fact which is of concern to repressive Arab governments. In Lebanon Palestinians represented at one stage about 10% of the population, but they have faced discrimination in employment, social security and freedom of movement. The lives of the refugees in Lebanon improved immensely as a result of PLO control of the camps but this alienated many Lebanese, and during the civil war the Christians and later the Shi'ites turned against Palestinians in the "battle of the camps".

There are over half a million Palestinians in the Gulf States, probably half of whom are in Kuwait. Most are employed on an individual basis; they provide skilled labour power and their remittances have supported both families and the Palestinian struggle. But many governments suspect them and with the oil crisis, employment and earnings have fallen. In Jordan on the East Bank there are 1.2 million Palestinians. Although they consider themselves as Palestinian and fraternize among themselves, they are recorded as Jordanians.

Palestinian Israelis

After the 1949 armistice Israel began a process of transferring most Arab land into Jewish control. The 1950 Law of Absentees legitimized the transfer of land from those who had been forced out of the Jewish state and also from those who had been displaced internally. This resulted in the loss of 40% of land to Israel under the absentee property policy. Thousands of acres of agricultural land and thousands of houses, businesses and shops were offered to newly arrived Jewish settlers. More land was lost by the Arabs when Arab citizens were required to furnish certificates of ownership issued by the British mandatory authority. The British had withdrawn from the region without completing the issue of the certificates and Israel was able to declare as State land most of the remaining Arab-held lands. Israeli expropriation of Arab lands has continued since the mid-1970s and Palestinian Arabs retain only one third of their land holdings, although their population has increased fourfold since 1948. Israel has also taken control of the water resources of the Occupied Territories. Water allocation for Arabs and Jews differs considerably, with an estimated *per capita* domestic consumption for Arabs of 35 cubic metres yearly in towns, and 15 cubic metres in villages, as opposed to 90 cubic metres for Israelis.

Israeli-subsidized agricultural produce is freely marketed in the Occupied Territories but there is no comparable reciprocal arrangement for Palestinian produce. Gaza's thriving market in citrus fruits has declined as a result of Israeli restrictions which forbade the planting of new trees except by permit, although permits were often extremely hard to obtain. Gaza had originally sold produce to Western Europe but after 1967 Israel blocked this competition with its own market and Gaza now relies on a small amount of trade with Eastern Europe and a declining amount of trade with the Arab world — although a new 1986 trade agreement with EC countries may change this.

The great increase in the Palestinian population of Israel has meant that Palestinian Israelis have rapidly changed from peasantry into a rural proletariat dependent on the Israeli economy. Few industries are sited in Arab areas and fewer still are owned by Arabs. The industries which existed before 1948 were concentrated in Haifa, Jaffa and Acre but the loss of these territories to Israel left the Arab community without any industry of its own. Many Arab villagers cannot find work locally but are not free to live elsewhere, partly because so much housing is held by the JNF and may not be occupied by non-Jews; consequently they commute to work, which is often over 50 kilometres from their homes. Palestinian Israelis are less poor than in 1948 and their standard of living is probably higher than that enjoyed in neighbouring states but it is nevertheless significantly lower than

that of the Jews, probably about 40% lower, and on average Palestinians receive about half the wages of Jewish Israelis.

Of the 112 Arab towns and villages in Israel only two have central sewage systems whilst all Jewish population centres of over 5,000 people have a central sewage system. Seventy-two per cent of Arabs are living in overcrowded conditions compared with 22% of Jews, according to a recent survey, and on average Arab households are twice as densely populated as Jewish ones. Most health facilities are situated in towns but the Arab population is 70% rural. *Per capita* health expenditure in the West Bank is only 8% of that inside Israel and in the West Bank and Gaza there are six doctors per 10,000 people compared with 29 per 10,000 in Israel.

The Ministry of Education, in common with almost all other Israeli ministries, deals with Arab affairs separately in a different department where they are dealt with by a Jewish rather than an Arab director. Arab children follow a separate curriculum and Arab schools lack classrooms, trained teachers and textbooks. There is a 50% drop-out rate for children up to the age of 14 and only one-third of children complete secondary school. The only colleges and universities in the West Bank and Gaza are private institutions and all have suffered official harassment in some form or another. Substandard education has impeded the growth of an Israeli Arab intelligentsia and ensured that Israeli Arabs are concentrated in the unskilled sector as agricultural workers, miners and construction workers.

The Intifada

The *Intifada* or "uprising" began spontaneously on 7 December 1987 in the refugee camps of the Gaza Strip, and rapidly spread throughout the Occupied Territories and within Israel. It was a protest against Israeli occupation and from the start involved large numbers of young people, including school children, but gained support from a broad cross-section of the Palestinian population. Strike action was used together with boycotts and a campaign to force Arab policemen and tax collectors to quit their posts. School children boycotted their classes, which were then closed by the Israelis; it was only after pressure by the US that schools again opened in the Occupied Territories in mid-1989. Although there were Israeli allegations of a shadowy conspiratorial Palestinian leadership, attempts to crush this leadership have failed and most Palestinian actions, although often spontaneous, have followed a regular pattern. Israeli forces responded with considerable force, often described by observers as excessive, against protestors. After a year the death toll had reached at least 320 (Palestinian sources say over 400) with thousands injured or imprisoned for either short or longer periods, among them young children. By the end of May 1989 the number of deaths had topped 600. In August 1989 the Israeli government doubled the period of detention without trial to one year. Army sources stated that 4,215 Palestinians had been held in administrative detention since the *Intifada* had commenced although unofficial Israeli sources placed the figure at over 5,000.

In August 1988 King Hussein of Jordan announced that Jordan was abandoning its claims to the West Bank, dissolving the joint Jordanian-Palestinian parliament set up in 1950, and would begin to dismantle the legal and administrative links between the two areas. In effect this was a recognition of Palestinian claims to a separate state and a renunciation of Jordanian hegemony over Palestinians although some observers noted that Palestinians on the West Bank still needed the financial and political support of Jordan (which had paid salaries to West Bank officials and issued West Bank Palestinians with Jordanian passports). Fears that the *Intifada* might spread beyond Israel into Jordan may have been a factor in the King's decision to let the PLO go ahead and search for its own diplomatic solution.

On November 14, 1988 the Palestine National Council (PNC), meeting in Algiers, issued a Palestinian Declaration of Independence and declared the creation of a Palestinian state, with a Palestinian identity but without a recognized territory, borders or government. After much debate the PNC also voted to renounce terrorism and to accept UN Resolution 242, implicitly recognizing the right of the state of Israel to exist, thus expressing on the Palestinian side a willingness to negotiate with Israel. Israel however rejected the initiative and has acted to block further initiatives by the new state, including an attempt (with the USA) to prevent Yasir Arafat from speaking before the UN in New York. In the event Arafat did address the General Assembly at a special session held in Geneva. The new state gained rapid recognition from third-world countries — within three days 22 countries had announced diplomatic relations. In April 1989 Arafat was elected the provisional President of the new Palestinian state.

The future for the Palestinians

At the present time the future remains bleak for the Palestinians. Although there have been projects aimed at increasing self-sufficiency there have been many more which have had the effect of reinforcing dependency on international aid. But demographic factors appear to be working for the Palestinians — by 2010 Jews will be outnumbered by the total number of resident Palestinian Arabs in Israel, the West Bank and the Gaza Strip. The demand for political and civil rights is bound to become more insistent and it is extremely unlikely that Palestinians will settle for anything short of self-determination.

World Powers stress the need for peace in the Middle East but continue to pour arms into the region. The appearance of Yasir Arafat at the United Nations in 1988 and the PLO's acceptance of Israel's right to exist mark a major step forward, but Israel has once again rejected the Palestinians' demand for an independent territory, and the situation appears to have reached an impasse.

(See also *Beduin of Israel*; *Druzes of Israel and the Golan Heights*)

Roma in Turkey

Location: **Especially in the west of Turkey, large cities**
Population: **545,000**
% of population: **1%**
Religion: **Muslim**
Language: **Romanes, Turkish**

There are over a half-a-million of nomadic and settled Roma in Turkey. Nomadic Roma have been accustomed to crossing the border into Greece when border restrictions have permitted.

There are about 25,000 Roma in Istanbul, living in quarters used by Roma for centuries. There are also shanty quarters in Ankara and Izmir where Roma earn their living as street-sweepers, shoe-cleaners, porters and domestic servants. Many have been reduced to scavenging paper, rags and scrap metal.

As with other minority groups in Turkey, Roma receive no special recognition and have long been deterred from forming any social or cultural organizations. Many fear persecution and conceal their Roma identity, which is only acknowledged in their homes. Despite the 1969 recommendations from the Council of Europe (of which Turkey is a member) the government appears to be unconcerned about Roma as a national minority. No legislation has been passed in their favour and efforts at self-help have met with indifference.

(See also *Roma in Western Europe* in **Western Europe and Scandinavia;** *Roma in Eastern Europe* in **Eastern Europe**)

Further References

Israel's Oriental Immigrants and Druzes, MRG Report No. 12, 1981

The Kurds, MRG Report No. 23, 1989

The Palestinians, MRG Report No. 24, 1987

Cyprus, MRG Report No. 30, 1984

The Armenians, MRG Report No. 32, 1987

The Baha'is of Iran, MRG Report No. 51, 1985

Lebanon: a conflict of minorities, MRG Report No. 61, 1986

The Jews of Africa and Asia, MRG Report No. 67, 1987

SUB-SAHARAN AFRICA

Most States in Sub-Saharan Africa are recently independent, consequent upon emancipation from colonial rule. Many of the new States would figure highly on any register of ethnic, linguistic and religious diversity. There are more than 250 distinct ethnic groups in Nigeria's 90 million population. In Uganda, the national borders cut across ethnic and language boundaries. They also place together over 40 ethnic groups which formerly had little in common and frequently do not understand each other's languages. A cursory glance at African boundaries with their lines of longitude and latitude provides the clue that the divisions between States are not coterminous with population distribution; it suggests that the States are artificial, not organic. An All-African People's Conference in 1958 passed a special resolution on Frontiers, Boundaries and Federations: The Conference " . . . (a) denounces artificial frontiers drawn by imperialist powers to divide the peoples of Africa, particularly those which cut across ethnic groups and divide peoples of the same stock; (b) calls for the abolition or adjustment of such frontiers at an early date". The revisionist approach to boundaries proved to be unrealistic. Realignments would be as disastrous in human terms as the original colonial conquests. The new States have instead chosen to develop nationality within their colonial inheritance. Arbitrary borders have been accepted as a basis for statehood and have been defended tenaciously. The Charter of the Organization of African Unity (OAU) 1963 lists the aims and purposes of the OAU, which are, among other things, "to defend the States' sovereignty, their territorial integrity and independence". The member States proclaim their adherence to principles, including "respect for the sovereignty and territorial integrity of each State and for its inalienable right to independent existence". Challenges to this principle have been unsuccessful.

All of this creates a formidable problem for minorities. Some States manifest, in effect if not in form, an "ethnocracy", rule by a particular ethnic group within the complex (this is normally, but need not be, a majority group — exceptions are the minority whites in South Africa, and the minority Tutsi in Burundi). Most States express official opposition to tribalism, particularism and chauvinism. Some look forward to a homogenous nation in terms of culture. Many socialist States — such as Ethiopia — seek to mobilize and "modernize" the nation. None will allow their constituent elements (in an ethnic/tribal sense) to join a kin-State or achieve their own independence. Self-determination stops at the point of independence from colonial rule; it cannot be conceded to minorities, however harsh their fate in the new republics. Many States in turn deny that they have any "minorities", implying that this concept is only applicable to Europe, or only outside Africa. Particular groups may not be recognized: citizenship and equality in rights and duties are proclaimed for all; opposition to the segregationist policy of South Africa reinforces this attitude. Unhappily, minorities have been "natural" victims in nation-building.

Within this broad context, particular types of minority may be recognized in terms of origins, relation with the dominant group, cultural practices and religious affiliation. Africa experienced large-scale importation of Asian labour under colonial rule and Asians have suffered considerably under "Africanization" policies since independence. Americo-Liberians represent an extraordinary example of "repatriation" of a partly assimilated group of emancipated slaves for philanthropic reasons (and because of "difficulties" in extending suffrage in the USA to ex-slaves). Many minorities "lost-out" in the rush to independence and are essentially "separatist", but the separatist ambitions of Biafrans, Ashanti and Ewe, of the Southern Sudanese, of Eritreans and Tigrayans, Baganda and Bakongo, have not prospered. Nomadism represents, as elsewhere (Roma or Gypsies in Europe) a problem for the territorial State with its impulse to control and demarcate. Some minorities — the San — exhibit cultural features which mark them out as profoundly different from neighbouring peoples. Religious groups are the object of suspicion and hostility in nationalistic States. Most of the questions that can be posed on the relations between minorities and majorities, and the State, can be illustrated with examples from Africa.

Instruments on Minority Rights

African States participate widely in United Nations bodies — they have been particularly active in proposing and supporting international instruments condemning racial discrimination and Apartheid, such as the International Convention on the Elimination of All Forms of Racial Discrimination, and the Convention on the Suppression and Punishment of the Crime of Apartheid. The Colonial Declaration of 1960 (Resolution 1514 (xv) of the UN General Assembly) elevates self-determination into a supreme principle of international law, subject to the qualification that it should not disturb the territorial integrity and political unity of States.

The concentration on self-determination and independence as supreme contemporary principles deflected attention from the post-independence human rights performance of the new States. Increasing international scrutiny drew increasing criticism from within and without the continent. The response was the adoption by the OAU Assembly of Heads of State and Government in 1981 of the African Charter of Human and Peoples' Rights (see *Appendix 6.1*). The Charter is a unique statement of collective peoples' rights and individual human rights. While there is not an explicit ranking of the two classes of rights, the preamble states that "the reality and respect of peoples' rights should necessarily guarantee human rights", which may imply some practical priority for the former class of rights. Individual rights have only lexical priority; the first 18 articles of the Charter are devoted to them, including civil and political rights, and economic and social rights. Individuals also have duties, including the duty to "preserve and strengthen social and national solidarity", and "to preserve and strengthen the national independence and the territorial integrity of their country". Peoples' rights are essentially variations on the theme of self-determination, including the right to "economic, social and cultural development". There is no reference to minorities in the Charter. The rights are guaranteed without distinction of any kind, including distinctions based upon "ethnic group" as well as those based on "race . . . colour, sex, language, religion, political or any other opinion, national and social origin, fortune, birth or other status". The Charter amplifies and strengthens the legal concept of self-determination and adapts the concept of individual rights to the African context. "People" as a term is not defined in the Charter. Although there is room for interpretation and development of the concept, it seems tolerably clear at present that the "people" is the people of the States considered as wholes, and not minority tribes, ethnic groups, races or religions. The Charter does not go far in recognising middle terms between the individual and the State — references to duties to the family, society and "other legally recognized communities" may count for little in this context. The possibility of the Charter serving to ameliorate the prospects of many minorities in Africa appears rather tentative. Much depends upon the performance of the African Commission on Human and Peoples' Rights, the body charged with implementing this major regional treaty. Africa is not deficient in human rights instruments. Many constitutions "adopt" the Universal Declaration of Human Rights, and contain extensive chapters of rights. The major abuses of rights have been little tempered by these documents. The growing maturity of the States has naturally led to the increased penetration of international standards: practice may eventually follow precept.

Treatment of minorities

The move from colonialism to independence has been momentous historically. As with all political cataclysms, wars, terror, genocide, have accompanied these changes. The new nations strive to achieve a new identity. They are hostile to remaining vestiges of colonialism or neo-colonialism — South African white rule is seen partly in this light. They are anxious to defend and strengthen independence, and are conscious that this means economic as well as political independence, to secure self-respect and the respect of the international community. Human rights can only improve as the anti-colonial ferment dies away, as South Africa changes and accommodates to political realities. Unfortunately, the colonial pattern which bites deepest may be in the very conformation of the States themselves with their inextricable mixture of peoples. It is not implausible that ethnic realignments may take place and produce greater homogeneity. It is clear that the immediate outlook for minorities as such is poor; they are menaced both by the States and dynamics of their situation. A general improvement in civil and political, and economic, social and cultural rights is the first, but not the last requirement for minority groups.

Afars and Issas of Djibouti

Alternative names: **the Afars are known in Ethiopia as the Danakils**
Location: **the republic of Djibouti and neighbouring borders of Ethiopia and Somalia**
Population: **460,000 (1986)**
% of population: **Issas about 50%, Afars 25%**
Religion: **Muslim**
Language: **the Issas are a Somali-speaking people**

The Issas are a Somali people and the Afars belong to the same ethnic group as the neighbouring Ethiopian Danakils. About two-thirds of the population of Djibouti are settled; the rest roam across the borders of Ethiopia and Somalia in search of grazing land for their cattle and goats. Djibouti itself is of great strategic value, because of its proximity to the entrance to the Red Sea, and 12 years after independence France still has a military base in the area.

In 1862 France established a small naval base at Obock and in 1884 formally annexed the area and named it French Somaliland. In 1892 the capital was transferred from Obock to Djibouti. Following severe riots during a visit by General de Gaulle in 1966, a referendum on independence was held in March 1967. This produced a majority for French rule, although there were widespread allegations of electoral malpractices. French Somaliland was then renamed the *Territoire Française des Afars et des Issas* (TFAI), some say to emphasize the existence of two disparate population groups. The local chamber of Deputies was expanded and France was represented by a High Commissioner, retaining complete control of defence, foreign policy, security and finance.

There was growing opposition to French rule, fuelled by Somali interest in the Issas' cause and perhaps in the hope of a Greater Somalia, and growing international pressures for decolonisation. Ethiopia too had an interest in Djibouti because of its port and railway which carry more than 60% of Ethiopia's trade to and from the sea. Although the French expressed concern about possible conflicts between the Afars and the Issas, Djibouti gained its independence in 1977, with Hassan Gouled as Head of State. In October 1981, a one-party system was introduced and the *Rassemblement Populaire pour le Progrès* (RPP) became the sole legal party.

Djibouti has a President (elected for a six-year term by universal adult suffrage), a Prime Minister who heads a Cabinet, and a 65-member Chamber of Deputies (also elected by universal adult suffrage) — which reportedly reflects the balance between ethnic groups. In elections held on April 24 1987 over 90% re-elected Hassan Gouled to office for a third term. No opposition candidate was permitted to stand, although several former leaders of the *Parti Populaire Djiboutien* (PPD) (the opposition party which was nullified when the one-party system was introduced in 1981) were included on the list of the 65-member Chamber of Deputies.

Before independence the smaller Afar community had a greater share of political influence, but afterwards the reverse has been true. The Government under Hassan Gouled, an Issa, tends to represent the slightly larger Issa population, who together with the Somali related tribes are in the majority, although the Prime Minister, Barkat Gourad Hamadou is Afar and there are five Afars in the politburo. The President has removed Afars from most of the administration and army: there are only two Afar permanent secretaries, whereas there are 17 from the Mamassen clan of the Issas — the presidential family clan.

In October 1981, just after an opposition group tried to register as a political party *Le Parti Populaire Djiboutien* (PPD) the government amended the constitution in order to form a one-party state and consequently illegalize PPD. The government claimed that PPD was an ethnic pressure group, although its central committee was made up of six Afars, seven Issas and one Arab.

Djibouti's President, Gouled, is now in his seventies and he has no clear successor. If he is succeeded by an Issa, then the other Issa clans will demand that the successor come from a clan other than the ruling Mamassen, and the Afars will in that case certainly expect the Prime Minister to remain an Afar. It is interesting to note that the presidential armoured squadron, the *Difaac Madaxtoyaada Maamassan* (the defender of Mamassen power), composed of 200 men, is 70% Mamassen.

There is an Ethiopian-backed Afar resistance movement, the Afar Liberation Front (*Front Afar*) (FA), which has been monitoring the treatment of Ethiopian Afar refugees in Djibouti and claims that indiscriminate arrests and imprisonment without trial are common for the Afar refugees. In 1986 Djibouti launched a formal repatriation programme for Ethiopian refugees, although Ethiopians had been deported from Djibouti since early summer 1981 and by September 1984 about 25,000 had been sent back. The FA say that Djibouti is using force to accomplish this repatriation, particularly where Afar refugees are concerned. In April 1987 *Africa Confidential* reported that a new special

security unit had been set up composed of a hundred Issa from Ethiopia.

Other minority groups

Non-Issa Somalis — the Isaaqs (Issaks) with an estimated population of 40,000, and the Gadabourse of whom there are about 45,000, resent the Issa (Mamassen clan) power. In May 1988 the government detained 500 Isaaqs who were demonstrating in favour of the Somali National Movement (SNM), and in June they detained 300 more.

There are about 18,000 Arabs in Djibouti. Arabic is officially on a par with French as a national language, but French remains the main medium for business and political affairs and is the medium of instruction in schools. There also are about 12,000 Europeans who live a luxurious expatriate lifestyle.

(See also *Eritreans*; *Oromo of Ethiopia*)

Americo-Liberians

Alternative names: **"Honorables", "Congoes"**
Location: **mainly Monrovia and coastal cities**
Population: **50,000-100,000**
% of population: **2.5-5%**
Religion: **Christian**
Language: **English**

Americo-Liberians are the descendants of ex-slaves from the USA who were settled in the area which is now Liberia from 1822 onwards by the American Colonization Society, which had been formed with the purpose of returning freed black slaves to their homeland in West Africa. In 1847 Liberia's American Governor declared it an independent republic — Africa's first — although it was not recognized as such by the US government until 1862. During the next 50 years it lost territory to British and French colonies but in the twentieth century saw the establishment of rubber plantations, diamond and iron ore mines and international shipping links to Monrovia.

Americo-Liberians have until recently formed the main elite group in Liberia, despite their very small numbers. Economic, social and political power was in the hands of the Americo-Liberian community, whose True Whig party was in power for over a century until 1980. The government was composed largely of Americo-Liberians and the civil service and diplomatic corps were almost

totally Americo-Liberian. Almost the only way in which wealth and status could be acquired was through membership of the minority elite, although there was also a small immigrant community of Lebanese and Asians who controlled much of the commercial sector.

The non-Americo-Liberian indigenous population, the vast majority of the population of Liberia, comprises 16 major tribal groups which come from three main language families, the West Atlantic, Mende and Kru. The West Atlantic group includes the Kissi and Gola tribes from the mountainous north and west of the country; the Mende group of Vai, Mono, Kpelle and Don tribes in the centre of Liberia; and the Kru and Bassa tribes from the south and the coast on the border of the Ivory Coast. The Kru are the largest single tribe.

The indigenous peoples were not given Liberian citizenship until 1904 and were not granted the right to vote until 1944. However this right was restricted to property owners or those who paid a "hut tax". The non-Americo-Liberian peoples have generally received little economic benefit from developments such as agricultural improvements and foreign investments. One area where they have dominated through sheer weight of numbers is the armed forces; however for many years any signs of unrest amongst its ranks were effectively dealt with by imprisonment. Sergeant Samuel K. Doe, an indigenous Liberian, in April 1980 seized power from the corrupt regime of President William R. Tolbert, who though pledged to give a share of "civil office" to the indigenous majority had failed to do so.

Sergeant Doe ruled Liberia through a "People's Redemption Council", dissolved in 1984, and was the first indigenous Liberian to become State Leader. Liberia was returned to civilian rule in October 1985 when elections were held but only four legal political parties were able to contest them and power is still effectively in the hands of President Doe, despite a number of coup attempts against him. An attempt was made to draft a Constitution which would provide for full equality for all peoples of Liberia and a draft Constitution was approved in a referendum of 1983. The most common criticism of the old Constitution was the restriction on the right to vote which was widely seen by indigenous Liberians as a device for continuing Americo-Liberian dominance.

Despite attempts to place indigenous Liberians in positions of power in the government and private sector, there have been reports that lack of education and skills have been instrumental in the reinstatement of the Americo-Liberian elite in vital areas. But by the late 1980s the economy had collapsed, civil liberties were non-existent and many educated Liberians — including Americo-Liberians — had fled abroad.

(See also *Creoles of Sierra Leone*)

Anglophones of Cameroon

Alternative names: **westerners**
Location: **north-west and south-west provinces in western area of Cameroon**
Population: **2-2.5 million**
% of population: **20%**
Religion: **Christianity, Islam, animism**
Language: **English, French, various indigenous languages**

The Anglophones, inhabitants of Cameroon's two ex-British provinces, make up 20% of its total population and inhabit one-tenth of the land area. Effective political and economic power lies with a government and military drawn from the Francophones who comprise the majority of the population. However the great majority of both Anglophones and Francophones speaks neither English or French but one of the many indigenous languages. There are over 100 ethnic groups in Cameroon. Sudanic-speaking people inhabit the north and Bantu-speaking groups live in the rest of the country. There are pygmy tribes in remote areas in the east.

Cameroon has been a republic since 1960 when the trusteeship territory administered by France on behalf of the United Nations became fully independent. In 1961 there was a referendum in the British-administered territory of Western Cameroon to determine whether the region should unite with Nigeria to the west or with the ex-French colony of Cameroon to the east. Voters in the north were in favour of unification with Nigeria whilst southern voters elected to merge with Cameroon. The southern region duly joined with its eastern neighbour under a federal constitution in which the ex-British and ex-French regions retained their own parliaments. In 1966 Cameroon's six legal parties were amalgamated into a single government party, the *Union National Camerounien* (UNC) under the leadership of Ahmadon Ahidjo. The federation was replaced by a more centralized system in 1972 forming the United Republic of Cameroon.

In 1982 Paul Biya, a bilingual southerner, who had been Ahidjo's Prime Minister, was elected President with a five-year mandate. There were serious threats of a coup in August 1983 and April 1984 when units of the armed forces stationed in Yaoundé attempted to overthrow the government but were defeated by forces loyal to the authorities. The UNC was the sole legal political party until 1983 and in 1984 it became the *Rassemblement démocratique du peuple camerounais* (RDPC). The UNC/RDPC claims to be working towards national unity out of tribal diversity. In February 1979 Vicor Ayissi Mvodo, the Minister of Territorial Administration, was quoted as saying "the linguistic split is healing. A major factor in the success of bilingualism is party unity". In November 1983 the Constitution was amended to allow independent candidates to seek office.

Anglophones claim that they are under-represented in governmental positions of power. When Western Cameroon joined the Republic it was as a functional state but in May 1985 Dr Yongbang and "The Elite", a joint committee of the north-west and south-west provinces, sent a memorandum to President Biya in which they objected to the fact that Western Cameroon was treated as merely two provinces out of the 10 without appropriate constitutional rights for the minority group of Anglophones. In 1985, four out of the 28 ministers in the cabinet were from the Western Cameroon.

Economically the Anglophone region has always been less advanced than the Francophone region and when they united it lost Commonwealth trade preferences and its banana crop has been progressively excluded from British markets. The opening of road and rail links and removal of customs barriers between east and west has meant in effect the rapid decline of the west's two main ports, Victoria and Tiko, and the growth of Douala in the Francophone east. There was a consequent rise in unemployment in western cities. In 1973 oil was discovered off the coast of Western Cameroon but although the Cameroon government built an oil refinery in Victoria, now renamed Limbe, and redeveloped port facilities, Anglophones claimed that this income was spent on development projects in the Francophone area and that most of the labour employed was Francophone.

Although the Republic of Cameroon is officially bilingual, without French it is impossible to pursue a good career in state administration as all administrative work must be carried out in French. There is discrimination against Anglophones in appointments to private and state corporations even when they are in English-speaking regions, and English place names are being removed (as with Victoria to Limbe) while French names remain unchanged. The two million Anglophones frequently complain of being second-class citizens. They allege that major English language newspapers are often censored by the government.

Despite the fact that bilingual teaching was introduced in primary schools in 1972 in the south-west and north-west provinces the primary school registration rate in the 1970s was 55% in 1975 compared to 82% for the country as a whole. In late 1983 there were demonstrations and strikes by Anglophone students because of cuts in the number of courses given in English at Cameroon's only university. According to "The Elite" in 1985 London GCE and City and Guilds examinations were being replaced by French-oriented exams, national inspectors of English were in fact French speakers and overseas scholarships meant for Anglophones were not announced, or awarded to "bilingual" French speakers. English students also found that their educational qualifications were considered inferior to those of Francophones and this affected their chances of employment. English-speaking lawyers from abroad have to undergo two years' further pupilage while French-speaking lawyers can go straight to the bar.

Some Anglophones favour secession from the Francophones of the east. They feel that the western region is being dominated by the east and the north and that westerners are insufficiently represented in government posts. But it appears that any moves towards secession would be strongly resisted by the central government.

Asians of East and Central Africa

Name: **East African Asians**
Alternative names: **Indians**
Location: **East Africa (mainly Kenya, Tanzania); central Africa**
Population: **Total 85,000; Kenya 40,000; Tanzania 20,000**
% of population: **Kenya 0.2%; Tanzania 0.1%**
Religion: **Hindu, Muslim (including Ismaili)**
Language: **English, Gujarati, Punjabi**

The Asian population of east and central Africa is a small but significant minority group, which is largely engaged in trade and professions. They came to Africa during the British colonial period but since independence their numbers have declined.

The colonial period

Indian contact with Africa far predates that of Europeans; for over one thousand years the Indian sub-continent engaged in trade with East Africa. In the early nineteenth century coastal settlements were established at Mombasa, Malindi and Bagamoyo and by the mid-century the Asian population of Zanzibar was estimated to be five or six thousand. A combination of famines in India and plentiful opportunities for work in Africa as indentured labour on railways, led to many thousands of Indians, mainly agricultural labourers, immigrating to east, central and southern Africa. They were followed by "free immigrants" who came to trade, often running small general stores. The majority of immigrants came from Gujarat and Punjab.

European settlers soon recognized Asians as an economic threat and developed opposition to Asian immigration. Legislation restricting Asian immigration was prevented however because of the Imperial principal of common citizenship. In Rhodesia literacy testing in a European language was introduced as a condition of entry in 1904 and this reduced Asian immigration. Similar legislation was introduced in East Africa during World War II during which there was almost complete cessation of immigration, but there was a dramatic increase in the post war years.

Indians, like Africans, were categorized on racial lines and facilities set aside for their use were inadequate and inferior to those used by Europeans. The best agricultural land was reserved for Europeans and the remainder was set aside for African use so that Indians were effectively barred from agricultural work. Asians occupied most of the lower and middle grades of the public services such as railways, as they did in the larger commercial and industrial enterprises, but were unable to rise to higher positions. Indians saw education as a way of advancement; most of the early schools were established privately by the Asian communities themselves although the colonial authorities gradually provided more funding.

After the war many Asians went overseas where they qualified as lawyers, doctors, teachers and engineers, thus changing the character of the Asian workforce. In central Africa, where the communities were less numerous, opportunities and educational facilities were considerably less and as a result there were few professionally qualified people and most Indians remained dependent on commerce.

Independence

At the time of independence East African Asians were dominant in commerce and had also begun to move into manufacturing. There was inevitably a degree of hostility from Africans, many of whom themselves aspired to these positions; many Africans also felt that they had been exploited by Asian shopkeepers. There were also religious and cultural differences between the two groups and most Asians lived in more or less exclusive communities, partly as a result of the practice of caste exclusiveness in India. Africans felt that Asians had done little to further the cause of African nationalism although in East Africa there always had been a small group of Asians active on behalf of African independence.

Unlike European residents, who were generally protected both economically and by the new constitutions, Asians lacked such security. Before independence most residents of British East and Central Africa had been either British citizens or British protected persons. After independence an individual either became a citizen of the new country automatically or had the option to do so within a specified time. Those who did not qualify for citizenship retained their pre-independence status. Many Asians

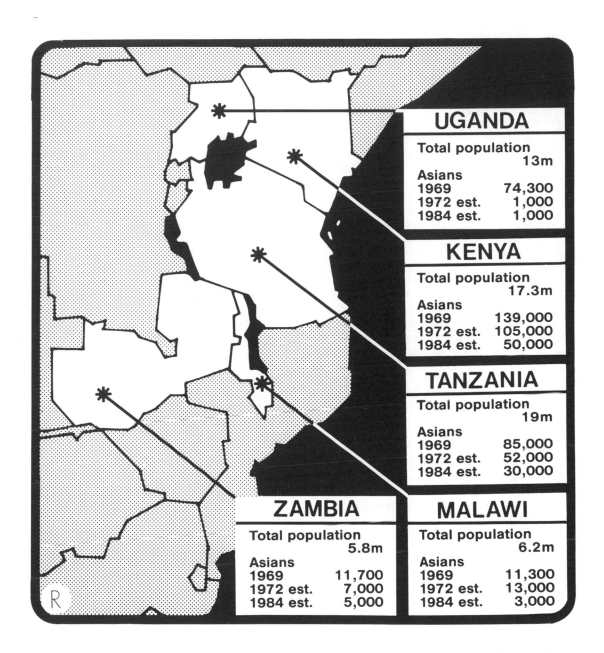

UGANDA

Total population	
	13m
Asians	
1969	74,300
1972 est.	1,000
1984 est.	1,000

KENYA

Total population	
	17.3m
Asians	
1969	139,000
1972 est.	105,000
1984 est.	50,000

TANZANIA

Total population	
	19m
Asians	
1969	85,000
1972 est.	52,000
1984 est.	30,000

ZAMBIA

Total population	
	5.8m
Asians	
1969	11,700
1972 est.	7,000
1984 est.	5,000

MALAWI

Total population	
	6.2m
Asians	
1969	11,300
1972 est.	13,000
1984 est.	3,000

All the figures quoted are estimates. It is very difficult (and in some cases impossible) to obtain accurate figures but the above figures do illustrate clearly a general trend for both the numbers of Asians in East and Central African countries and their proportion in the total population, to drop significantly over this period.

Asians of East and Central Africa

did not take up the citizenship option, partly as they felt that a British, Indian or Pakistani passport would offer protection in the event of persecution or expulsion. Africans were further alienated by the reluctance of Indians to assume African nationality.

After independence in the 1960s each country adopted different policies towards Asian residents but two common factors were the distinction between citizens and non-citizens, and "Africanization" policies whereby key areas of economic and governmental activity were gradually assumed by citizens, the vast majority of whom were indigenous Africans. Legislation was passed restricting residence, trade and employment for non-citizen employees. The Zambian government decreed that from 1970 non-citizens would not be given licences to operate in rural areas and from 1972 they were also forbidden to operate in urban areas; in Kenya and Uganda Asian trading was restricted to scheduled areas and trade in certain commodities such as staple foodstuffs was restricted to citizens only. In Tanzania the major economic institutions were nationalized, one effect of which was to make Asian private enterprise redundant. In Malawi deportation at short notice became common. The pressures placed upon non-citizens created much insecurity and caused many to look for resettlement opportunities elsewhere. Foreign exchange regulations permitted only a limited amount of capital repatriation on emigration and many of the wealthier Asians began to transfer money abroad while it was still possible.

The citizenship crisis

Most Indians had assumed that those with British nationality would be permitted free entry into the UK and in 1965 and 1966 nearly 13,000 did enter; however the British government, alarmed at the direction African governments were taking with regard to their Asian residents and fuelled by fears of increased tensions at home, introduced a new Act in 1968, the purpose of which was to restrict the entry into the UK of certain categories of British citizens overseas. The Act excluded those who, despite their British nationality, had no close connections with Britain (defined as either a father or grandfather born in Britain). The UK government introduced a quota voucher system whereby 1,500 families were permitted entry to the UK annually. Waiting lists were predictably long and this created major problems for many; in 1971 the number of annual quotas was doubled. Before the 1968 Act few Asians had opted to return to India but when many attempted to do so, the Indian government halted their policy of free entry to all Asians making it much more difficult for those Indians with UK passports to obtain access to India.

In 1971 a military coup in Uganda brought Idi Amin to power. Eight months later it was announced that all Asians, including 12,000 still awaiting citizenship, were to leave the country within 90 days. It was later stated that only non-citizen Asians were obliged to leave but subsequently some 15,000 Ugandan passport holders had their passports withdrawn and others were intimidated by Amin's soldiers. Within the last six weeks of the period of the ultimatum, 50,000 Asians left Uganda, with no property and £55 in cash each. 27,000 of them fled to Britain, which temporarily waived its immigration laws to deal with the crisis, 10,000 went to India (including 6,000 UK citizens), 6,000 to Canada, 4,000 to UN camps throughout Europe and others to the USA, Pakistan, and elsewhere including Kenya and Malawi.

In 1968 there were 344,000 Asians resident in the five countries; by 1984 the probable number had fallen to about 85,000 of whom 40,000 were in Kenya; 20,000 in Tanzania; Zambia 3,000, Malawi 1,000 and Uganda 1,000. Of these about 20,000 Asians were British citizens with about 8,000 each in Kenya and Tanzania. In 1982 the British Nationality Act was passed and UK Asian passport holders were reclassified as British Overseas Citizens with restricted rights of entry. The UK was issuing an annual 5,000 vouchers to British passport holders but there was no longer much demand for them.

The present situation

Few of the Indians who remain in East and Central Africa can expect more than middle-ranking careers in the civil service, police or armed forces, but the private sector remains open to them although it is now dominated by an African mercantile class. Since the overthrow of Idi Amin in Uganda in 1979 several Asian companies have returned to Uganda but on a corporate rather than an individual basis, and few other than Indian and Pakistani contract personnel have resided there. The Museveni government however has indicated its willingness to pay some compensation for the losses of 1972 and the Asian community has welcomed the move towards reconciliation, although few will probably wish to return on a permanent basis. Since departure of the non-citizen (and many citizen) Asians, thousands of Asian doctors, teachers, accountants, railway workers and engineers have come into the region on two year Indian and Pakistani technical assistance programmes.

Although Asians in East and Central Africa are not in general optimistic about their long-term future in the region, they cannot be described as a persecuted or harassed minority. They are however a visible one and could become a scapegoat in a violent situation or economic crisis, as appeared to happen in the abortive coup in Kenya in 1982 when some Asian women were raped and Asian shops looted. Yet Kenya also has an Asian MP, elected on a multi-racial basis. For most Asians their present situation is reasonably comfortable, their standard of living is good and they have complete religious and cultural freedom. Many Asians commute between the USA or UK and Africa and almost all have relatives established outside Africa.

(See also *Indian South Africans; Uganda*)

Bubis of Equatorial Guinea

Location: **Fernando Po/ Bioko (island off coast of Cameroon)**
Population: **20,000-25,000 (est.)**
% of population: **6%-7%**
Religion: **Catholic, indigenous beliefs**
Language: **Spanish is the official language**

The Bubis are the indigenous inhabitants of the island of Fernando Po (now Bioko) which is part of Equatorial Guinea, although the island itself is physically much closer to Cameroon. The island was "discovered" by the Portuguese in the late fifteenth century and ceded to Spain, together with trading rights over the mainland, in 1778. It was leased to the British as a naval base and was used as a refuge for freed slaves during the early nineteenth century.

Fernando Po was not administered by the Spanish until the 1890s when the world demand for cocoa increased and they recognized the island's suitability for growing the crop. Since the local labour force was too small for economic production Spain laid claim to the adjacent mainland, the north-western region of French Gabon, which was granted to Spain by the Treaty of Paris in 1900, and renamed Rio Muni. This territory and the island of Fernando Po together made up the country of Equatorial Guinea.

The Bubis are one of three groups inhabiting Fernando Po. The other two are the Fernandinos, descendants of freed slaves, and the Nigerian workforce, brought to the island when it became clear after Rio Muni labour had been introduced that there were still not sufficient numbers to grow the cocoa crop. The population of the mainland is largely made up of Fangs, a people inhabiting parts of Cameroon and Gabon as well as Rio Muni. The Bubis were originally a farming people but the Spanish amalgamated their farms into cocoa plantations; some Bubis were retained as foremen on the plantations; others received pensions and a Spanish education for their children. A few who had been educated abroad were able to borrow money from the plantation companies and establish themselves in business. The Bubis therefore initially had little interest in independence but the Spanish encouraged Bubi nationalism and separatism as a counterweight to the Fangs of Rio Muni.

Independence was granted to the colony in 1968 and a federal two-province system of government was established. Although the Bubis comprised only about 6% of the population they initially had one third of the parliamentary seats. The Spanish had made little effort to develop the country during their rule and the new government was faced with the enormous task of modernization in every sphere. It soon became apparent that the new Prime Minister, Francisco Macias Nguema, a member of the Fang tribe, was interested in accruing personal power above all else. He formed his own party and all other parties were banned. Opposition leaders, including prominent members of the Bubi community, and members of his own government and civil service were killed, tortured or exiled, together with their families and sometimes their entire village if they opposed his actions. The Deputy President, who was a Bubi, died in imprisonment as did many others. Nigerian workers began to leave the country in 1972 and diplomatic relations with that country were severed. In 1973 Equatorial Guinea was declared a unitary state. The island peoples were denied any significant rights, and islanders were forbidden to leave Fernando Po which was renamed Macias Nguema Biyong.

The entire island was turned into a giant slave labour camp.

The international community was slow to condemn the government of Equatorial Guinea despite the fact that a quarter of the population were killed or fled the country. Most countries remained silent about the atrocities committed there, whilst discreetly continuing to trade with its government. Human rights groups, such as Amnesty International and the Anti-Slavery Society, publicized the situation and in 1976 the UN Sub-Commission on the Prevention of Discrimination and Protection of Minorities decided on grounds of gross and persistent violations of human rights, to examine the situation in Equatorial Guinea.

In August 1979 the regime of Macias Nguema was overthrown by a military coup led by his cousin, Obiang Nguema Mbasago. Macias was shot and political prisoners were released. Spain was asked to return to take over the day-to-day administration of the country and later a UN Plan for the restoration of the battered economy became operative. However the country remained under military rule and the Fang tribal group continued to occupy positions of power. No political parties are allowed and opposition groups work from exile, mainly in Spain. Among these groups is the Bubi Nationalist Group, founded in 1983, which supported independence from Rio Muni for the peoples of Fernando Po (which was renamed Bioko in 1979).

Chad

Location: **Landlocked country in west-central Africa.**
Population: **5,100,000 (est.)**
% of population: **Sara 50%, Arabs 25-30%, Teda-Daza 6%**
Religion: **Muslim, 45%-55%; Christian and Animist 6%-25%; Animist**
Languages: **French and Arabic; other languages: various, including Sara.**

Like many other African countries, Chad is essentially a nation of minorities, arbitrarily grouped under one administration during the colonial period. Since its independence in 1960, Chad has been beset by internal rebellions and civil war, fuelled by the indirect financial and military support, and, periodically, the direct military intervention of external forces, notably France, Libya and the USA. Neighbouring African states, whose border peoples in many instances are ethnically linked to Chadian groups, have, willingly or otherwise, provided refuges for dissidents and armed rebels from Chad. A series of authoritarian ruling groups have failed so far to unite the diverse peoples of Chad with any lasting cohesion. For much of the period since independence, large parts of the country have been under the control of rival "warlords". Human rights abuses on a large scale have occurred during this time — detention without trial, torture, extra-legal killings and massacres of civilians — overshadowed by the larger military conflict. Numerous initiatives of the Organisation of African Unity (OAU) as well as of individual African leaders to resolve the conflict in Chad have brought only temporary peace and stability.

Geography and ethnicity

Chad is one of the poorest countries in the world, if not the poorest: a huge but landlocked nation in west-central Africa with an area of 1.25 million square kilometres, and a total of 4,000 kilometres of borders with six other states. Ecologically, the country has three main parts: desert in the far north, including the Tibesti mountains; a more populous arid Sahelian belt in the centre; agriculturally-endowed savannah, verging on forest, in the far south. It is little favoured in natural resources, cattle being the mainstay of the northern economy and cotton and other agricultural produce in the more fertile central and southern areas.

No reliable survey, let alone census, has been conducted in Chad since 1964, when population was estimated at 5.1 million. Based on this figure, today's population is projected at around 5,100,000. This population is, however, very unevenly distributed, with 46% concentrated in the five southern prefectures which constitute only one tenth of the country's area.

The Sara language and culture dominates the southern area, although there are other ethnic groups such as the Massa and Moundang, in Mayo-Kebbi. The southern people are thought to be fairly evenly divided between Christians and Animists, although the number of Christians is probably overestimated.

The northern areas of Borkou, Ennedi and Tibesti, collectively known as the BET region, are inhabited mainly by nomadic Toubou peo-

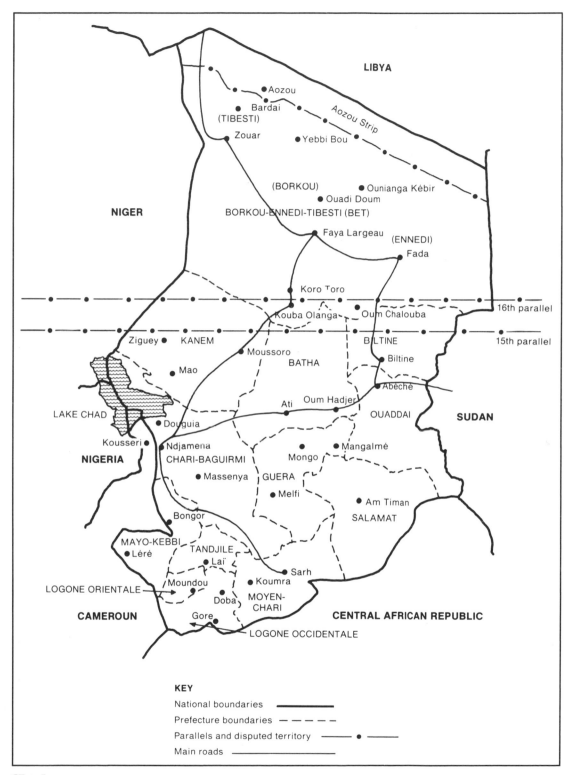

Chad

ples, who divide into the Teda and the Daza groups, the former being concentrated around the Tibesti area and the latter further south in the BET region. These groups, which are Muslim, are more ethnically related to the Kanembu than the Arabs. The Daza, who are known in Arabic as the Gorane, are the group with which Hissein Habre, of the fringe Anakaza clan, is associated. The BET area, which constitutes one third of the country, contains only 6% of the population.

There is also a major group in Chad who are considered to be Arab in origin, although they have co-existed and intermarried with African peoples of the Western Sahel for centuries. The Arabs constitute some 25% to 30% of the total population. Some are nomads or semi-nomads; others are in settlements as in the Salamat area in the south-east, or settled and assimilated as an administrative elite in most of the central prefectures. This group is distinguished by their adherence to Arabic customs and use of the Arabic language, and are also predominantly Muslim, so that the overall proportion of Muslims is 45%-55%.

The Hadjerai (Hadjeray) come mainly from the central Guera highlands. The Zaghawa, one of the Ouaddian groups, who are known as the Bidayet (Bidayat) in northern Chad, inhabit the north and east of the country straddling the Sudan-Chad border. Both groups have been Islamised. Other ethnic groups include the Buduma, who are mainly fishing people living on and around Lake Chad.

Until 1979, the military, government and administration (although not business) were dominated by Sara-speaking people, largely due to their advantage in Western-style education, brought to the area by missionaries in the nineteenth and early twentieth centuries. The level of literacy is higher generally in the south than the north — although still low at 26.8% — and is almost exclusively literacy in French (the official language at independence) rather than Arabic.

History to 1960

The borders of Chad were hastily drawn following the European "scramble for Africa" in the 1880s and 1890s, and France's failed attempt to control a continuous belt stretching from Algiers to the Red Sea. The French finally defeated the Islamic military ruler Rabeh, who then controlled the once powerful Kanem-Borno empire, in 1900, at the battle of Kousseri, just inside the present Chad-Nigerian border. The BET region was only "pacified" by the 1920s

but remained extremely hostile to domination (either by the French or by Arabic peoples to the north and south). Moreover the northern border remained in doubt after the dubious 1935 agreement between Mussolini and French Premier Laval, which pushed the Libyan border southwards to include the much-disputed Aozou strip. This agreement later formed the basis of independent Libya's continued claim to the strip.

The political movements which were formed in the French colonial territories in the build-up towards independence following the Second World War, were not as strongly rooted in Chad as elsewhere in the French territories. Gabriel Lisette, a Guadeloupian former administrator, led the local version of the *Rassemblement Démocratique Africain* (RDA) known as the *Parti du Peuple Tchadien* (PPT). Following the "balkanization" of the French territories and elections to territorial assemblies, the PPT did not have an overall majority, resulting in the fall of Lisette's government in 1959. Its immediate successor was the *Mouvement Socialiste Africain*, led by Ahmed Koulamallah, which had a Muslim base, and was more nationalistic and pan-African in outlook, but lasted only 12 days. Francis Tombalbaye, a Sara, succeeded Lisette as head of the PPT and held fresh elections which returned him with a convincing majority, based largely on southern support. He then went on to become President of independent Chad in August 1960.

The Tombalbaye Government 1960-75

Tombalbaye was regarded with suspicion by Muslim politicians, who feared the dominance of educationally advanced Sara in the administration following the withdrawal of the French. In 1962, Tombalbaye declared a one-party state, leaving Muslims no vehicle for political expression, and subsequently reduced the number of Muslims in the government. In late 1963, serious rioting between Muslims and non-Muslims broke out in the capital and more than a hundred were killed, while many future rebel leaders were jailed or went into exile. In 1965, the forcible collection of extortionate taxes in Mangalme, Batha prefecture (home of the Moubi, a subgroup of the Hadjerai) provoked riots which were brutally repressed. This was the first spark of rebellion which fired a spate of future revolts in central and eastern Chad.

At this juncture, FROLINAT was formed in Western Sudan. In 1965, the replacement of the French by the southern-dominated Chadian army, in the BET region, and disregard for some of the local practices — notably attempts to "sedentarize" the nomadic population — eventually led to Toubou armed revolt and the formation of the northern wing of FROLINAT. The French intervention in 1969 temporarily staved off the military threat from the centre and east. After a long leadership struggle, in 1971 the rebel forces split into two parts: the northern Second Army, later known as the *Forces Armées du Nord* (FAN) and the eastern First Army, led by Goukouni Weddeye and Abba Siddick respectively. A period of vicious in-fighting between the two factions of the rebel forces ensued. Eventually, in October 1972, a new figure emerged as the leader of the reconstituted FAN, now called the *Conseil de Commande des Forces Armées du Nord* (CCFAN): Hissein Habre. Habre — one of the first university educated Toubou — had displaced Goukouni who was now his deputy.

From 1972 onwards the Tombalbaye government entered its final decline, despite French-backed attempts at administrative reform and reconciliatory moves in 1971, including the release of political prisoners and the incorporation of Muslims into the ruling group. The metamorphosis of the PPT into the *Mouvement National pour la Révolution Culturelle et Sociale* (MNRCS), which stressed traditional African cultural practices such as youth initiation, created much resentment amongst the already disaffected educated Sara. When it was extended to include all candidates for the civil service, widespread discontent was engendered. Tombalbaye's relationship with key army personnel was also rapidly deteriorating. On April 13 Tombalbaye was overthrown in a coup, allegedly originating from the Sara-dominated army. However, in the long run, the coup did nothing to redress the imbalance of power and resources which was at the root of FROLINAT rebel activity.

The Malloum regime 1975-79

General Malloum emerged as the new head of state after the coup, forming the *Conseil Supérieure Militaire* (CSM), which preached reconciliation. Some dissident leaders returned, but the CSM was inevitably southern dominated and few concrete steps were taken to ensure political reconciliation, with key figures from the Tombalbaye era remaining in place. There were further strains in Chad's relations with France and Libya over the Claustre kidnapping fiasco, and the Aozou strip, which Tombalbaye had ceded to Libya in December 1972. Malloum's reluctance to engage militarily with the rebels

left large areas of the country in the centre, east and north under the control of rebel armies, who meanwhile fragmented and regrouped into at least three separate forces: CCFAN under Habre, the *Forces Armées Populaires* (FAP), an alliance between Goukouni and Acyl, who later left to form the *Conseil Démocratique Révolutionnaire* (CDR). From this position of relative strength, and with considerable external backing, the various rebels were able to push for favourable ceasefire conditions. After a FAP offensive in April 1978, Malloum had to call back the French, whom he had expelled in 1975, to save his government. French and Libyan sponsored attempts at peace treaties between the Malloum government and the various rebel groups culminated eventually in the signing of the Habre-Malloum Fundamental Charter in late August 1978.

Under the conditions of the Fundamental Charter, Habre became Prime Minister while Malloum remained Head of State. The CSM was dismantled and the *Conseil de Défense et de Sécurité* (CDS) formed, in which half the posts went to the CSM and half to Habre's CCFAN. Arabic became an official language on a par with French and the Prime Minister was to form a new government and organize elections to a Constituent Assembly. Before this could happen, however, tensions surfaced. Habre was rapidly gaining the upper hand in the allocation of posts and beginning to exclude southerners. The CDS met less and less frequently and hostilities rose, as the Sara felt increasingly isolated. Little progress was made in integrating Habre's FAN into the national army (*Forces Armées Tchadiennes* or FAT). The intra-government tensions brought about by Habre's return led to the final collapse of central authority, the end of Malloum's power, and full-scale civil war from 1979. This was a watershed, after which the control of southerners or Sara over the army and administration was rapidly eroded.

Disintegration and civil war 1979-82

The period from 1979 onwards led to increasing inter-communal violence, the virtual collapse of central authority, and the rule of large areas of the country by competing warlords. Various foreign backed attempts at establishing new coalitions were made, with external forces drawn in deeper and deeper to protect their own positions.

In February 1979, a school strike of Muslims allegedly inspired by FAN sparked off hostilities between FAN and southern troops. By this time,

Goukouni's troops had advanced from the BET region to Kanem and briefly allied to FAN. Under this pressure the Chadian army disintegrated and an exodus of refugees to the south began. This first battle of Ndjamena brought in its wake communal massacres, along ethnic, regional and religious cleavages, with FAN troops killing southerners in Ndjamena. Reprisals occurred in the south where, reportedly, between 5,000 and 10,000 mainly Arab Muslims were killed.

From March 1979 onwards, a series of meetings in Kano, Nigeria began, aiming to establish a coalition, which eventually included some elements from the *Front d'Action Commun Provisoire* (FACP) and an agreement was arrived at in Lagos, with OAU backing, to establish the *Gouvernement d'Union Nationale de Transition* (GUNT) headed by Goukouni, with Habre as Defence Minister and Acyl as Foreign Minister. OAU peacekeeping troops were to move in to guarantee the peace, and a programme of reconciliation was drawn up. GUNT was established in early November, but by the end of the year there was no progress in the reconciliation programme, the OAU troops had not yet arrived, and tensions in the coalition were surfacing. FAN-FACP fighting broke out in the build-up to the second battle of Ndjamena, which was to overshadow even the first and produce a massive wave of refugees.

As a consequence of this, Habre and his forces were excluded from GUNT, the French withdrew their troops and much to the dismay of Libya Habre, with French backing, was advancing into the BET region. On June 15, 1980, Gaddafy announced a Chad-Libyan mutual support treaty, which later emerged as a cover for Libyan military intervention. There was widespread international and internal disapproval of Libyan intervention. Under this pressure, Goukouni asked the Libyans to leave, which they did in early 1981, to be replaced by the OAU troops. However, the US had now begun to supply Habre's forces in their bid to destabilise Gaddafy. Goukouni refused to negotiate with Habre and by mid-1982, Habre was advancing rapidly towards Ndjamena. GUNT was starting to disintegrate. On June 7, 1982, Habre took Ndjamena with almost no resistance.

Habre takes power 1982 — present

After Habre took Ndjamena, the main area of remaining resistance was Kamougué's (FACP) area of support in the far south, but by clever use of dissident Sara, Habre managed to oust Kamougué and take control. By October 1982,

a "government in exile" composed of most of the old GUNT factions (FAT, FAP and CDR with Acheikh ibn Oumar having replaced Acyl) had established itself at Goukouni's northern stronghold, in Bardai, Tibesti, which was still held by his forces. With US and French backing, however, Habre's control seemed fairly solid. Doubts still remained about Habre's ability to be a truly national leader, particularly among southerners who laid the responsibility for the 1979 and 1981 massacres at his doorstep. The actions of FAN in the south after Habre's takeover did little to reassure them. In May and August 1983, there were violent clashes after Habre's attempt to impose taxation in the south. A southern rebel group, the *Codos Rouges*, had emerged opposing Habre with backing from Libya and GUNT. The Central African Republic, whose northern peoples are ethnically linked to the Sara, harboured Codos supporters and bases and may have allowed Libya and GUNT to operate within its borders.

In June 1983, Libya, increasingly isolated within the OAU which had accepted Habre as the leader of the Chad delegation, backed Goukouni in a new offensive which left GUNT in control of much of the north and east of Chad. Increased US military aid, and a massive French intervention called "Operation Manta" enabled Habre's forces to keep GUNT at bay, establishing an effective partition along the 16th parallel. This partitioning was to last until Habre's decisive push north in 1987.

The OAU's attempts to convene further peace talks in 1983 foundered but the establishment of a new national army — *Forces Armées Nationales du Tchad* (FANT) in early 1983 was a step towards broadening Habre's support. Habre made further reconciliatory moves in 1984 when — in spite of considerable objection from some of his own supporters — he dissolved the ruling FROLINAT-CCFAN coalition and replaced it with the *Union Nationale pour l'Indépendance et la Révolution* (UNIR). The executive committee of UNIR included six southerners out of 15 members (although northerners retained the key positions), and the new government which was formed in July 1984 had a former Codos leader as Defence Minister. The breakdown in negotiations with the Codos in August 1984 brought an upsurge of fighting in four out of five of the southern prefectures. In a pact with General Kolingba of the Central African Republic, who had his own domestic motives, a brutal government repression with widespread massacres of civilians and razing of villages was enacted on both sides of the border.

By early 1985, Habre had regained control over most of the south.

Habre's final push north beginning in December 1986, which eventually recovered all Chad's territory to his side, was assisted by: the large amount of military aid and back-up from the French and the US; the support of many former dissident leaders including Djogo, Kotiga (of the Codos) and Senoussi of the now split CDR; and the disintegration of GUNT. The CDR ceased collaboration with Goukouni, and formed a neo-GUNT under Acheikh ibn Oumar. When Libya switched its support to Acheikh, Goukouni's troops began to rally to Habre. FANT eventually forced the Libyans and the rump of the GUNT forces out of Faya Largeau, and into retreat back to Aozou in early 1987. A Chad-Libya ceasefire was agreed on September 12, 1987 and held well into 1988, in spite of some skirmishes on the Sudan border. In mid-1988 Gaddafy began making moves towards a peace treaty, involving Libyan aid and recognition of Habre's government and Chad's formal recognition of Libyan control over the Aozou strip. Under considerable pressure from France, Habre agreed to a formal restoration of diplomatic links with Libya in November 1988.

Meanwhile, Habre's reconciliation policy, engineered by Mahammat Ibrahim Itno, the Interior Minister, had been running into problems. The return of rebel leaders (six out of 24 had rallied to UNIR by August 1988), many taking up ministerial posts, was both alienating more long-standing supporters, and creating splits in rebel forces over the defection of their leaders. Two major groups, the Hadjerai and the Zaghawa, went successively into opposition in 1987 and 1988. Prior to 1984, the Hadjerai had supported Habre and formed a large part of the armed forces (FAN) which brought him to power in 1982. The deterioration in their relations with Habre commenced with suspicions over the death of their traditional leader Idriss Miskine in 1984. Subsequent tensions, a decrease in the number of Hadjerai in the government and army (as they were replaced by Zaghawa and Goranes) and arrests of prominent Hadjerai, spurred guerrilla

actions by the *Mouvement du Salut National du Tchad* (MOSANAT) in the Guera highlands from late 1986.

The return to Habre's government of Acheikh ibn Oumar, former leader of the pro-Libyan CDR in 1988, provoked a split among his Zaghawa supporters: 500 former CDR fighters in Darfur have joined the First Army and MOSANAT; another 200 or so were abandoned by Acheikh in Ndjamena. The remaining CDR divided into two Libyan based-groups, under Rakhis Manani and Moctar Moussa respectively.

Idriss Deby, a Zaghawa, and his relatives Hassan Djamous and Mahammat Itno, were key Habre supporters since the 1980-82 period. Under Itno, the security services and elite army units were increasingly dominated by Zaghawa while the traditional ruling group of the Zaghawa — the Haggar — was offended by Itno, Deby and Djamous' attempts to introduce relatives into the Ndjamena power structure. Meanwhile, Habre, increasingly sceptical of Zaghawa support, had removed the conventional security forces from Itno's control, created his own private security force composed of Gorane. Growing Zaghawa perceptions that they were being ousted from the power structure is said to be the cause of the failed April 1, 1989 coup attempt, led by Deby, Djamous and Itno, who subsequently fled to Sudan. A spate of Zaghawa arrests (at least 100) have occurred in Ndjamena since the coup attempt.

Although Habre, with substantial French and US backing, remains in power to date, his rule is becoming increasingly based on the backing of his own tiny ethnic group — the Goranes — at the expense of all others. Until 1987-88, attempts at reconciliation had brought dissident Arab and southern factions back into government, but old as well as newer allies have increasingly been alienated and excluded from power, thus leaving Habre's government with minimal legitimacy. Given Chad's history of political instability and ethnic division, together with its poverty and interventions by outside powers, it appears likely that conflicts will continue.

(See also *Mauritania*; *Sahelian Nomads*)

Creoles of Sierra Leone

Location: **Freetown and urban areas**
Population: **about 100,000**
% of population: **3%**
Religion: **Christian**
Language: **English, Krio**

The Creoles are the descendants of ex-slaves freed from Britain and the West Indies and who settled in Freetown after its establishment by British abolitionists in 1787. Freetown became a Crown Colony in 1808 and the interior was declared a British Protectorate in 1896. Sierra Leone gained independence in 1961.

The Creole community, descended from those ex-slaves, amounts to only about 3% of the population yet has formed the main elite group from colonial times. The Creoles are almost all Christians, with a culture that combines British and West Indian traditions with those of the indigenous groups. Although they initially intermarried with the indigenous population, they gradually acquired British education and culture and began to set themselves apart from the local majority.

Creoles are well educated professionals who have had a disproportionate degree of influence over government and the economy. The British were careful not to allow the Creole community to dominate colonial politics. The 1924 Constitution brought the tribal chiefs into the Legislative Council and in 1943 Africans were allowed into the Executive Council for the first time. The 1951 Constitution established the framework for independence ten years later but in 1964, following the death of Milton Margai, the first Prime Minister, his successor as head of the Sierra Leone People's Party (SLPP) Albert Margai began to

replace Creoles with supporters from his own southern region, the Mende. Creoles shifted their support to Siaka Stevens' All People's Congress (APC) which narrowly won the 1967 elections but was prevented from assuming power by a military coup and only returned to government after another coup in 1969. Stevens' regime, which gained the support of the Creole elite, instituted a repressive one party state, which has continued since under President Momoh. The Creoles have never had the monopoly of power of the Americo-Liberian elite in Liberia and have followed a lower profile; as a result they have retained far more influence, although this has also caused resentment and animosity from other groups.

The other major ethnic groups in Sierra Leone are the Mande and West Atlantic peoples. The Mande includes the Mende, almost one third of the total population, the Dyalanke, Koranko and Vai, whilst the West Atlantic group includes the Temne, almost about one third of the population, the Kissi and the Ballom. Other ethnic groups are the Mandingo and Peal (also called Fulani). Religions followed by these groups include Christianity, Islam and animism.

Sierra Leone also has small immigrant trading communities, mainly Lebanese and Indians. Many new Lebanese immigrants have moved to Sierra Leone following civil war from 1975 in the Lebanon.

(See also *Americo-Liberians*)

Eritreans

Location: **Northern Ethiopia**
Population: **probably 3-4.5 million**
% of population: **probably 7%-10% of Ethiopian population**
Religion: **Christian, Muslim**
Language: **Tigrinya, Danakil, Saho**

The Eritreans are the indigenous people of Eritrea, a region of some 128,000 square kilometres situated between the Ethiopian highlands, Sudan and Djibouti. It has two distinct divisions between the mountainous central plat-

eau where the capital, Asmara, is situated and the lowlands in the north and west and along the Red Sea coast. The people of the mountains are Christians and have been a part of mainstream Ethiopian culture for 2,000 years. They speak

Tigrinya, a language they share with the people of neighbouring Tigray. The lowland Eritreans are largely Muslim. Although they speak native languages such as Danakil and Saho they also use Arabic in commercial dealings and have long been exposed to foreign influence in the form of traders and explorers from expanding empires such as Egypt, Greece and Persia. In the far west there are peoples from the tribes of northern Sudan.

European colonialism

The opening of the Suez canal in 1869 transformed the Red Sea into a vital trade artery thus making Eritrea economically and strategically important to Ethiopia since, without access to the Eritrean and Somali coastline, it is a landlocked country. The unification of Eritrea and the demarcation of its boundaries did not occur until 1890 when the Italians formally declared the creation of their colony Eritrea; the highlands had previously been part of the Christian province of Tigray, and the lowlands had been penetrated successively by Turks, Egyptians and the Mahdi's forces from the Sudan.

When Italian settlers arrived they brought technological skills and encouraged economic development. They built the capital, Asmara, and schools, roads and hospitals. Under Italian occupation the borders of Eritrea were altered, and the Tigrinya-speaking peoples and the related ethnic groups of northern Ethiopia were united into one entity for the first time. Italians also helped Eritreans to develop institutions such as political parties and trade unions. While Italian colonialism had a positive impact on Eritrea in some respects it also brought hardship. During the period of colonialism the most fertile highland areas were expropriated for commercial use by Italian settlers and land below 800 metres was declared state land. Living conditions of the poorer peasants deteriorated sharply.

When the British took control in 1941 Eritrea was returned to its pre-war frontiers and placed under military occupation until 1952. A debate on Eritrea's future was held in the UN General Assembly in 1950 and a resolution was passed calling for Eritrean autonomy and Eritrean legislative, executive and judicial authority over its own domestic affairs, with all other matters falling under federal (i.e. Ethiopian) jurisdiction. In

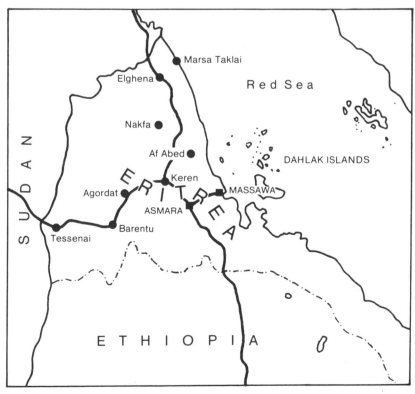

Eritrea

September 1952 after a two-year interim period during which the details of a Constitution were decided under UN direction, Eritrea became a semi-autonomous, self-governing territory in federation with Ethiopia. The UN added to the agreement the following condition: ". . . The UN resolution on Eritrea would remain an international instrument and, if violated, the General Assembly could be seized of the matter."

The first Eritrean Assembly had 68 members, half of whom were Christian and half Muslim. Top government posts were also divided up between the two faiths. Once the Emperor's representatives arrived in Asmara, separatist leaders began to be harassed. Some were arrested, others went into exile, and in 1956 the Eritrean Assembly passed a resolution accusing Ethiopia of violating political and civil rights in the region. The Chief Executive and the President of the Assembly both resigned and were replaced by men appointed by the Emperor. A campaign favouring total absorption of Eritrea by Ethiopia began, and the existing federal structure collapsed. All parties other than the Unionist Party were banned, as were trade unions and newspapers. In 1962 the Eritrean Assembly decided in favour of full integration into the Ethiopian kingdom.

Growth of Eritrean nationalist organizations

Encouraged by daily broadcasts from Cairo radio by exiled leaders, nationalist forces began to form within Eritrea with the support of students and workers. Trade unions expressed their dissatisfaction with the declining political and economic situation and in 1958 a general strike was called although it was quickly suppressed. In 1960 the Eritrean Liberation Front (ELF) was formed by students and workers in Arab countries. Membership of the ELF increased steadily despite religious and tribal differences within its ranks; however in 1969 three groups split away from the main organization and formed the Eritrean Peoples Liberation Front (EPLF). The ELF was concerned purely with the liberation of Eritrea from foreign control, while the EPLF also wanted to change the exploitative structure of Eritrean society by implementing land reforms and by mobilizing the working classes. Three years of civil war between the ELF and EPLF followed, and a ceasefire was finally agreed in 1975. Despite internal differences the EPLF continued to grow and its field forces were estimated in 1983 to number between 20,000 and 30,000. It had offices throughout the Arab world and also in Rome and New York.

On taking over full power in Ethiopia in 1975 after the fall of the empire, the Marxist military administration, commonly known as the Dergue (Amharic for Committee), found itself faced with a real threat to national unity in the form of Eritrean, Somali, Oromo, Afar and Tigrayan nationalist movements. In an attempt to prevent the collapse of military rule the administration began in 1976 to pursue a policy of conscription and enlisted 40,000 peasants to fight in its campaign against the Eritreans. This offensive proved to be disastrous for the Dergue however, as many conscripts were killed in guerrilla attacks and many more deserted to return to their crops. In late 1976 Eritrean forces launched their own offensive and within a year were in control of 80% of Eritrean territory.

Attempts at a settlement

By now the Ethiopian army was receiving large shipments of Soviet arms including MiG aircraft, gunships and tanks. A suggestion that they were receiving GA nervegas from the same source has never been substantiated although the Ethiopian airforce used napalm. Soviet and other Eastern bloc military advisers were by 1979 actively engaged in planning and executing the Ethiopian offensive. Despite its active role in the conflict however, the USSR supported the idea of a settlement between the two sides. Eager to encourage a Marxist alliance among its Red Sea allies, Moscow tried to promote a federal alliance between the Dergue and the ELF. At the same time, Arab backers of the EPLF were becoming increasingly worried by the mounting Soviet and Cuban presence in the region. They began to press for an end to internecine quarrels and a move towards a federal relationship between Eritrea and Ethiopia. Sudan, which had previously supported the Eritrean movement, now felt the need to improve its relations with Addis Ababa, closed its borders to Eritreans and in 1980 tried to promote an initiative between the EPLF and the Dergue.

Relations between the liberation fronts were by now very tense. ELF relations with the Dergue had become more open following the start of Syrian patronage, since Syria enjoyed good relations with the USSR, Ethiopia's principal ally. ELF leaders had resolved to eliminate other resistance groups and to start negotiations with Addis Ababa, and in 1980 there were several claims by the EPLF that the ELF had been waging "undeclared war" on EPLF forces.

A major reversal in official EPLF policy was announced in November 1981 at the time of Ethiopia's sixth offensive into Eritrea. A seven-point programme for a peaceful solution to the conflict was proposed. This included a referendum to determine whether Eritreans wanted independence, a regional autonomy or federation with Ethiopia. It also called for an immediate ceasefire and the holding of free elections, to be supervised by an international commission. The ELF rejected the referendum proposals however, on the grounds that they would nullify the role of the liberation fronts and place Eritreans on an unequal footing with the Ethiopian government. The Islamic Summit of January 1981 was unsuccessful in finding a solution to the deadlock, and an all-party meeting in Tunis in the same year also failed. A trilateral treaty of friendship and co-operation signed by Ethiopia, Libya and South Yemen alienated President Nimeiri of Sudan who was on extremely bad terms with Libya, and at the same time EPLF forces began pushing ELF forces back across the border into Sudan where they were disarmed and joined the 500,000 Ethiopian (mostly Eritrean) refugees in border camps.

At the beginning of 1982 the Ethiopian government launched "Operation Red Star", a three-pronged campaign comprising military, economic and organizational elements. The military element involved the drafting of some 100,000 troops to join the 30-40,000 troops already in Eritrea in a sixth major military campaign to eradicate the Eritrean guerrillas. The economic plan consisted of a three-part programme of short and long-term reconstruction to repair damaged socio-economic services, and the organizational aspect involved improving general education and production skills by establishing political structures and peasant associations throughout Eritrea. Government troops reported significant victories in their initial campaign, but within months the situation had once again reached an impasse and the EPLF began an offensive to regain territory lost during the massive Ethiopian push from 1978. At the beginning of 1984 the EPLF captured Ethiopian garrisons on vital road links to Asmara. Eritrean forces again held most of the territory.

Drought and military victories

However by this stage it was obvious that Eritrea, like all of northern Ethiopia, was severely affected by drought. The EPLF claimed that 1.2 million people within its area of administration were in urgent need of food aid after the complete failure of the crop, and that a further half million

Eritrean refugees in Sudan were also suffering. Most food aid from western governments went through the Addis Ababa regime although some agencies also sent food into EPLF areas. But the continued war, including aerial bombing, made it difficult to ensure that aid would reach into Eritrean territory. Relief operations, including feeding centres and an emergency programme of agricultural development, were largely co-ordinated by the Eritrean Relief Association (ERA). The famine therefore was not as devastating in most areas of Eritrea as in Tigray or other parts of Ethiopia nor were Eritreans part of the massive resettlement programme which took place in 1985.

In October 1985 the Ethiopian government launched another military offensive — its eighth — which pushed the Eritreans back to the mountainous area in the north of the province. However the government forces could not reach the EPLF mountain fortress at Nakfa and this provided the base from which Eritrean guerrilla forces broke out in December 1987 to again challenge the government forces. In March 1988 they overran the strategic town of Af Abed, claiming in the process to have killed or captured 18,000 government troops. The only areas to remain in government hands were four towns along the Red Sea Coast which could only be supplied by air. The Eritreans waited for yet another offensive at the end of the year — it never came and with the decisive defeats of government forces in Tigray in early 1989, it appeared that the EPLF was at last in a position to force the government to the negotiating table.

Just before the victories of 1984 the EPLF and the ELP and two smaller groups agreed to merge, after pressure from the Arab States. In practice this did not take place, and there followed in the next few years further attempts to bring together the different forces. It was clear that the EPLF was, and remains, the dominant force; it tended to remain apart from these unity efforts and had the least to gain from them. At the same time it wished to maintain good relations with the Arab world although in recent years these have become less important to them. The EPLF had held ten secret "exploratory meetings" with the Dergue between late 1982 and March 1985 but these had failed to conclude with an agreement. The Dergue attempted to hold the referendum of February 1987 to approve the new Constitution of 1986 based on " . . . administrative regions and autonomous regions . . . " in some areas of south and central Eritrea, but it was claimed by the EPLF that those who voted had been forced to do so.

As with the Tigrayan People's Liberation Front (with which it has had strained relations which sometimes broke into open fighting) the EPLF is a nationalist and Marxist group, following radical policies. The issue of access to land and the payment of rent and tribute to feudal landlords has clear priority. There were attempts to redistribute land on an equal basis, to abolish usury and to give women both land and participation in community life. Self-reliance has been vitally important to the survival of the movement over a quarter of a century of almost continuous warfare. In areas under heavy bombing many administrative functions and living quarters have simply moved underground and function in caves.

Prospects for the future

By early 1989 it was clear that the Dergue, by now under pressure from its main backer the USSR to end the war, had suffered a series of military defeats in the north. The EPLF Secretary-General, Isseyas Afeworki, stated that

(See also *Oromo of Ethiopia*; *Tigrayans*)

a settlement could only depend on "a democratic alternative and a devolution of power within Ethiopia" which some observers have interpreted as a willingness for Eritrea to maintain some form of linkage with Ethiopia. In June 1989 the Dergue offered to begin talks with the Eritreans without preconditions under neutral auspices. Talks began in early September 1989 under the chairmanship of former US President, Jimmy Carter, but there seemed little chance of an early settlement and it appeared that the first round of talks would concentrate on logistics rather than substantive issues. There is no guarantee that the outcome of the talks will result in peace or Eritrean independence and some insurgent forces within Ethiopia have stated that the talks with the EPLF are merely an opportunity for the Dergue to recover from defeat and prepare for a fresh offensive. The Eritreans have now been involved in one of the longest wars in modern history and it would be surprising if they settled for anything substantially less than independence.

Falashas of Ethiopia

Alternative names: **Ethiopian Jews, Beta Israel**
Location: **Gondar province, Semien mountains, Tigray and Wollo provinces**
Population: **28,000 before mass emigration; today about 7,000 remain in Ethiopia with remainder in Israel**
% of population: **0.065%-0.015%**
Religion: **Judaism**
Language: **Agau dialect, Amharic**

The Ethiopian Jews, more commonly known as the Falashas, are a people of ancient Cushitic descent numbering about 28,000, most of whom lived until recently in Gondar province and the Semien mountains in the north of Ethiopia. They are a branch of the Agau people, some of whom adopted the Jewish faith around 300 BC receiving it from either south-western Arabia or Elephantine in upper Egypt, both of which had important Jewish communities at the time. Jewish tradition claims that the Falashas are descendants of the lost tribe of Dan exiled to Mesopotamia; according to another tradition they are descended from the Queen of Sheba.

The Jewish Agau came to be known as Falashas, a term thought to derive from an ancient Ethiopic or Ge'ez word meaning exiles or strangers. They established an independent

kingdom in the mountains of north western Abyssinia where they managed to resist conversion or assimilation but fought several wars defending their political independence, which was finally lost in 1616. Since that date the numbers of Falashas have gradually declined. In the early nineteenth century evangelical Christian missionaries found many Falashas eager to accept the coming of the Messiah and there were many conversions.

The Falashas suffered greatly from prejudice at the hands of neighbouring peoples and were believed to practise witchcraft. There was opposition to Jewish schools, the first of which had been opened in 1924, with the help of Jacques Faitlovitch, a French Jew who devoted much of his life to the Falasha cause. When the Italians invaded Ethiopia in 1935 the anti-Semitic policies of Nazi Germany brought about a form of apartheid directed largely at the Falashas. Although they fought with Ethiopian guerrilla forces to liberate the country from the fascists during World War II, Falashas continued to face discrimination, violent attacks, eviction, and extortionate rents and taxes after the war.

Contact with Israel was established in 1954 when the Jewish Agency established a school in Asmara. Falasha leaders communicated with leading Jewish agencies asking for recognition as Jews, financial assistance and intercession with the Emperor for the right to emigrate. Initially the Israeli Chief Rabbi would not accept them as Jews, a position which was reversed in 1973, to the extent that in 1975 automatic Israeli citizenship was granted to Ethiopian Jews. Falasha hopes of resettlement in Israel were dashed, however, when Ethiopia first severed diplomatic ties with Israel in 1973, and then in 1974 underwent a violent revolution which overthrew the Emperor. Emigration under the new Marxist regime was as severely restricted as before.

During the early years of the Marxist regime the equality of all minority groups was proclaimed, and full participation of Ethiopian Jews was invited; however the eradication of tribal differences and minority cultures soon became a priority and during the period 1977-79 the Falashas, caught in the cross-fire of contending parties, became the victims of both right and left-wing groups, and many Jews were killed. Conditions steadily worsened and small groups of Falashas started fleeing into the Sudan where they joined the thousands of Ethiopians in refugee villages. Those caught trying to escape were treated as political prisoners and imprisoned without trial. In late 1983 however, the Ethiopian authorities altered their policy towards the Falashas. Certain reforms were introduced and synagogues and schools re-opened.

From the late 1970s political disturbances and, later, famine in Ethiopia caused large-scale population movements. While some Falashas were badly affected by the famine, many used the mass movements to mask their escape from the country; being highland people, however, they were unprepared for the heat in the plains. Water was scarce and many became ill and had no resistance to disease. It is estimated that at least 10% of those who left Ethiopia died from the rigours of their journey to the Sudan, and many more died in the refugee camps, leading some escapees to return to their homes.

Menahem Begin, who became Israeli Prime Minister in 1977, was committed to the idea of the "return" to Israel of the black Jews. He and President Mengistu arrived at a secret agreement according to which Israel continued to supply Ethiopia with arms in return for a limited emigration of Falashas. This policy was short-lived, however, and once it became known that a Marxist, anti-Zionist state was dealing in this way with Israel the legal emigration ended. Begin started to move Falashas to Israel by alternative means, and between 1979 and mid-1984 some 6,000 had made their way to Israel, some by sea and others by air.

It was now becoming increasingly difficult to deal with the large numbers of refugees, and with the tacit agreement of Sudan's President Nimeiri an airlift started in late 1984 with more than 7,000 Falashas being lifted to Israel in just over a month. This operation too was doomed to be short-lived, as it soon became known that an Islamic country was aiding Jews to leave Ethiopia; however the migration continues on a reduced scale, and by 1985 only 7,000 to 8,000 Falashas were thought to remain in Ethiopia, of whom most, if not all, were expected eventually to leave.

Since arriving in Israel the Falashas have been given every assistance in settlement, despite a certain amount of bigotry. They successfully fought a call for their "symbolic conversion", protesting that as they are fully Jewish such treatment is both unnecessary and insulting. They are likely to remain poorer than other Israelis for some time and it remains to be seen whether or not they will in time become fully integrated into Israeli society.

(See also *Jews of the Middle East and North Africa* in **Middle East and North Africa**; *Oromo of Ethiopia*; *Tigrayans*)

Hutu and Tutsi of Burundi

Location: **Burundi (also Rwanda)**
Population: **Total 4.2 million (1981), Hutu 3.5 million, Tutsi 670,000**
% of population: **Huti 83%, Tutsi 16% (est.)**
Religion: **Christian (Catholic 60-65%, Protestant 5-10%); Muslim**
Language: **Kirundi**

The Hutu and Tutsi are the two major peoples of Burundi together accounting for almost all the population. The Hutu are the majority people consisting of around 83% of the population and are mostly peasant farmers of southern Bantu stock. The Tutsi are around 16% of the population and are the descendants of the herdspeoples from the Horn of Africa. 1% of the population are from the Twa minority, a pygmoid group, who play little part in the mainstream society of Burundi. Burundi is a small landlocked country which was a German colony from the 1890s and a Belgian colony from 1918 to 1962, when it gained independence, first as a monarchy and, after a military coup in 1965, as a republic.

The Tutsi, Hutu and Twa are each divided between patrilineages of different social rankings which has produced considerable social differences within each ethnic group. In addition the Tutsi have been divided into two separate categories, the "lower-caste" Tutsi-Hima group and the "higher-caste" Tutsi Banyaruguru, the latter generally, although often erroneously, associated with the south and the former with the north. The Tutsi-Hima are the politically dominant group within the Tutsi. However, not withstanding divisions within ethnic groups, the major factor in Burundi, in pre-colonial, colonial and post-colonial politics, has been the continued dominance of the Tutsi group over the majority Hutu.

The killings of 1972

During the 1960s, despite their majority, the Hutu had few government or military posts and were discriminated against at all levels. In the period the Hutu made several attempts to gain majority rule, inspired by the victory of the majority Hutu population in neighbouring Rwanda. There were apparently Hutu-led coups in 1965 and 1969 which were crushed by Tutsi officers and which increased Tutsi dominance. In 1972, during the military regime of President Micombero, increasing tensions led to Hutu uprisings in Bujumbura and the provinces of Rumonge, Nyzanza Lac and Bururi, in which 2,000 Tutsi were reportedly killed. In retaliation

the Tutsi-controlled government, especially the "revolutionary youth brigades" and army, began reprisals which resulted in the deaths of between 100,000 and 150,000 Hutus, and which has been described as "selective genocide." Restrictions on travel and fear of further atrocities prevented Hutu reprisals but many thousands of people — largely Hutu — managed to flee the country and seek refuge in Zaire, Tanzania and Rwanda. These refugees totalled about 150,000.

Many Hutu still remain as refugees in these countries. The largest number are in Tanzania which is relatively underpopulated and where the Ha ethnic group speak a similar language to Kirundi. There are at least 60,000 refugees at Ulyankulu in Tabora region in addition to other settlements, and while there have been some complaints against interference by Tanzanian authorities in refugee affairs, most Hutu refugees in Tanzania have no immediate plans to return to Burundi. 35,000 Hutu refugees initially crossed to Zaire, mainly to the Ruzizi plain and the towns of Uvira and Bukavu, but some returned to Burundi after an amnesty in 1976. Of the 6,000 Hutu refugees who initially fled to Rwanda, about half left within three years, mainly for Tanzania.

During the 1972 killings particular groups among the Hutu were "targeted". These were principally educated Hutu in the civil service and students in higher education. From 1972 there appeared to be an unwritten yet widely enforced policy by Tutsi-led governments, to exclude Hutu from these positions. This succeeded partially because of Hutu memories of the killings of 1972, and many Hutu parents attempted to take children from secondary and higher education for fear of Tutsi reprisals. For example, of the 36,000 students who complete primary school education each year, only 4,000 go on to secondary education, and within this group Hutu are consistently under-represented. It has been reliably reported that the inspectors who determine entry from primary to secondary school are all Tutsis. Large numbers of Hutu secondary school students have been educated in neighbouring countries. It is also reported that only one third of students at the University

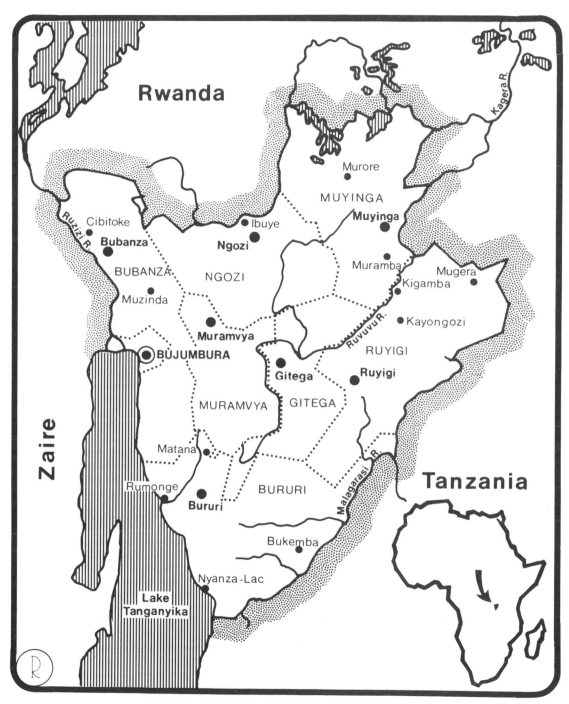

Burundi provincial borders 1962-1984

Hutu and Tutsi of Burundi

of Burundi in Bujumbura are Hutu.

After 1972 the Hutu had only a nominal representation in government. In 1987 during the Bagaza regime they held four government ministries out of 20; seven of the 65 seats in the National Assembly and two places of 65 on the Central Committee; one provincial governor out of 15.

The Bagaza regime, which came to power in a bloodless coup against Micombero in 1976, continued a series of repressive measures against the Catholic Church. The church was criticized ostensibly because of its colonial origins, but observers claim that government actions were an attempt to quash independent opposition to the Bagaza regime and to one of the few organizations where Hutu have some influence. Many foreign priests were ordered to leave the country and in 1987 some 450 had left, placing extra pressures on rural Hutus who now had to travel long distances to attend mass or see a priest.

The killings of 1988

In 1987 another bloodless coup brought to power a new military government under the leadership of Major Pierre Buyoya, under whose rule there initially appeared to be an improvement in the position of the Hutu. A number of Hutu politicians were brought into government, political prisoners were released and restrictions against the church were relaxed. Nevertheless inequalities between the two groups persisted; the President, three quarters of the cabinet, three-quarters of the National Assembly, 13 of the 15 provincial governors, two-thirds of university students, all army officers and 96% of enlisted soldiers were Tutsi.

In August 1988 reports of violent incidents between members of the two major groups were reported from the provinces of Ntega and Marangara. It has not been established which group was responsible for beginning the violence but it appears that increased expectations on the part of the Hutu and rising resentment by the Tutsi may have generated ethnic tensions, which after an initial attack, spread rapidly and violently. Killings on both sides seem to have been brutal and indiscriminate with regard to individuals, with women, children and old people among the victims. However Hutu refugees reported that government troops, including those in tanks and army helicopters, played an important role in the killings, deliberately targeting Hutus and acting on government orders. Independent reports by journalists and Amnesty International corroborate this interpretation, and comparisons were made with 1972. It is estimated that about 25,000 people, mainly Hutu, were killed, chiefly by the army, and over 50,000 fled across the border into Rwanda.

In October 1988 President Buyoya announced the formation of a new government headed for the first time by a Hutu Prime Minister, Adrian Siboana. He also announced that a National Commission composed of both Hutus and Tutsis would investigate the events of 1988 and make recommendations for furthering national unity. The Commission reported in April 1989; among its recommendations were that all forms of exclusion must be condemned and combated; that there should be a charter of National Unity; that employment and the public services should be managed objectively; and that there should be equality in the education system. Refugees began return from Rwanda at the end of 1988, under UNHCR auspices, apparently voluntarily to farm their land. While it appears that President Buyoya is anxious to improve the position of the Hutu it is unclear whether the steps needed to satisfy the Hutu can be implemented without another Tutsi backlash.

(See also *Uganda*)

Ilois of Diego Garcia

Alternative names: **Diego Garcians**
Location: **formerly in Diego Garcia island, Chagos Archipelago; now in Mauritius**
Population: **2,000**
% of population: **0.2% of Mauritian population**
Religion: **mainly Roman Catholic**
Language: **Creole**

The Ilois are a small minority of only 2,000 people, formerly the residents of the island of Diego Garcia in the Indian Ocean, who are now resident in Mauritius. The Chagos Islands were inhabited from 1776 as a fishing company and leper colony under French rule. After 1815 they (along with Mauritius) came under British colonial rule and received new immigrants from Africa and India, and a successful copra industry. These varied peoples developed a distinct culture and Creole dialect.

In December 1966, in the period preceding Mauritian independence, Britain demarcated the Chagos Islands and other isolated islands from Mauritius as the British Indian Ocean Territory (BIOT). In the same month it leased the BIOT to the USA for defence purposes for 50 years with the option of a further 20 years. From 1972 three further agreements were signed between the two, allowing for military construction and expansion on Diego Garcia island which by now had become the main US base in the Indian Ocean. These agreements in effect meant that the Ilois people had to leave. However this was done in a way which was secretive and underhand.

The Ilois had long had the custom of visiting Mauritius for visits and shopping. From 1965 until the mid-1970s the UK government did not allow those in Mauritius to return home. The Ilois were forced to squat in the slums of Port Louis, where, without money, some starved and all suffered great hardship. The copra plantations were run down and food imports were cut. From 1965 to 1971 about half the population was pressured into leaving. The remainder, about 800 people, were assembled and removed at short notice in September 1971, at first to smaller islands not required by the military and then in 1973 to Mauritius where they were left without help or compensation. The removal was carried out in secrecy until the facts became known at a US Congressional hearing in 1975 and after US and UK media coverage.

There has been a long fight for compensation by the Ilois and their supporters in Mauritius and the UK. Compensation was given to the last shipload of Ilois, who staged a demonstration on the removal ship, and a small amount of compensation was available from 1973, but the islanders did not receive it until 1978. In 1976 the UK government had paid £600,000 to the Mauritian government for the resettlement of the Ilois, but this was inadequate and there were delays by the Mauritian authorities. In 1979 the UK government offered the Ilois a further £1.25 million but stipulated that they must sign a document renouncing their right to return to the BIOT; after consultation, most Ilois rejected the offer. There were Ilois demonstrations in 1980 and 1981 and the UK government then agreed that talks between the two governments and the Ilois should take place in June 1981.

The 1981 London talks centred around the need for improved compensation. The Ilois asked for £8 million in order to give each family land, a house and some capital. The UK government offered only the original £1.25 million and an extra amount of £300,000 for technical assistance. No agreement could be reached but the Ilois, who were now desperate, decided to ask for compensation somewhere between the two sums. A final agreement was made, "a full and final settlement", in March 1982. The terms were that the Ilois were to be given £4 million in addition to the money already paid, that the Mauritian government would give land to the value of £1 million and that the money was in compensation for "all acts . . . done by or pursuant to the BIOT order of 1965 . . .". However, Mauritius saw nothing in the wording of the agreement to preclude a return of BIOT to Mauritius.

Compensation did not solve all the problems of the Ilois. There were delays in payment and although it was originally hoped to establish a job creation plan the economic situation of the Ilois was so desperate that they demanded an individual shareout. After improving their housing, many Ilois had nothing left and suffered from high unemployment in Mauritius. They attempted to gain compensation also from the US but this, to date, has been a failure. Yet the Ilois are today better organized and gaining in confidence. Although they are presently settled in Mauritius almost all express a wish to return, even if on a temporary basis to attend family graves, if not to Diego Garcia, which is now a military base with over 2,000 residents, to the other islands of the Chagos.

(See *Nauruans and Banabans* in **Oceania**)

Indian South Africans

Alternative names: **South African Indians**
Location: **80% in Natal province**
Population: **870,000 (1983)**
% of population: **3%**
Religion: **Hindu, Muslim**
Language: **various**

Indian South Africans are the descendants of indentured labourers and immigrants who came to South Africa in the nineteenth and early twentieth century. Although almost all areas of India were represented in the migration, two-thirds of immigrants were Tamil and Telugu-speaking people from Madras Presidency, a predominance which continues today. As in the past the overwhelming majority live in Natal province.

Immigration and settlement

During the course of the nineteenth century there was widespread impoverishment of the peasantry in the Indian sub-continent and this, coupled with opportunities for work in Africa at a time of colonial expansion, resulted in many Indians entering Africa as indentured labour to work on the railways, and in the case of South Africa in mines, agriculture and domestic service. Unlike the majority of Asian labourers indentured in East Africa, who returned to India after the completion of their contracts, most of those who had gone to Natal in South Africa remained, and over 90% of Asians resident in South Africa today are the descendants of those original labourers. After recruitment for labour in Natal ceased in 1911, a small number of professional people such as lawyers, teachers, accountants and priests entered under a clause permitting entry to educated Indian immigrants only. Most of this group came from Gujarat in western India.

Immigration restrictions limited freedom of movement and over 80% of Indians were concentrated in the province of Natal, where they were 12% of the population and equalled Europeans in numbers. Indians in Natal were allowed to purchase land but their trading opportunities and licences were restricted. Elsewhere they were not permitted to own land or enter certain areas without a permit. Indians began to organize, by petition, by representation and, under the leadership of M. K. Gandhi, by mass action, for greater equality with white settlers.

It was anticipated by Europeans that the Indians would eventually be repatriated to India, but Indian opposition to repatriation schemes was widespread. Initially Indians had sought to distinguish themselves from the Africans on grounds of culture and judicial status. They had not been granted equality with Europeans but their position was superior to that of Africans. As a race it was considered that they were better suited to clerical and supervisory posts, and some had already established themselves as a wealthy and influential mercantile class. Indians were also permitted to join trade unions, a right not granted to Africans.

Gradually however Indian attitudes towards equality with Africans changed, partly due to education but also to a more radical climate inspired by the events of World War II and the nationalist struggle for independence in India. Following the Durban riots of 1949 which were triggered by a minor dispute between an African and an Indian, responsible members of both communities began to realise the dangers inherent in the different treatment of the races; only by uniting could they hope to change the situation.

The Apartheid State

South Africa became a Republic and left the Commonwealth in 1961, and in the following year Indians were accepted as a permanent part of the South African population, more than a century after their arrival. A Department of Indian Affairs was established under a white minister, and a South African Indian Council was nominated in 1964 and elected in 1981.

Indians had no real power and the policy of separate development effectively restricted contact between Indians and Africans.

Indians, Coloureds and Africans have suffered equally from the enforcement of the Group Areas Act according to which each group is allocated to specific areas. In the vast demographic upheavals which followed the introduction of this Act, 40,000 Indians were moved to new locations, often already overcrowded, and much of their economic independence was destroyed. Property left behind was sold at very low prices but land shortage in the new areas forced up house prices beyond the reach of many Asians, and the majority depend on Council housing.

As was the case also in East Africa, educational facilities for Indians were limited and such schooling as was available was largely a result of financial contributions from the Indians themselves. A comprehensive survey undertaken in 1982 found that only 8% of the Indian population had passed standard 10 and only 3% had any post-school training. Other statistics also reflect the inferior position of Indians compared to the white population, as for example an Indian life expectancy in 1983 of 65 years compared to 70 for whites[1] and an infant mortality rate twice that of whites. As with the majority of the black population, most Indian South Africans lived in poverty although a few did well. Some have gained employment in the separate administrative machinery set up to deal with Indian matters, although critics point out that if there had been no restrictions on the employment of Indians, they would have been employed in all sectors of the economy.

The new South African Constitution of 1983 was presented by the South African government as benefiting the Indian community. In 1983 the then Prime Minister P. W. Botha stated: "Nowhere in Africa . . . in the world outside India, did any Indian community manage to reach this kind of constitutional recognition." The Constitution provided for an extremely powerful executive President and a tri-racial Parliament, whose powers were considerably less than the previously all-white one. An Indian House of Delegates, with its own separate Ministerial Council, was established and was responsible for Indian Affairs. Yet legislation which is concerned with residence, for example, is not within the purview of the House of Delegates. White control is secured by a 4:2:1 ratio in the Houses, the President's Council and the electoral college that chooses the President.

Indian opposition to Apartheid

The 1980s saw a marked rise in organized resistance movements and Indian South Africans played an important part in resistance activities. The growing unity of groups opposed to apartheid was given structural form in the United Democratic Front (UDF) which was formed in 1983, and in the Natal Indian Congress and Transvaal Indian Congress which were later affiliated to it. The UDF led the opposition to the Constitution, and organized the boycotts of the 1984 elections to the House of Delegates (Indians) and also the House of Representatives (Coloured) and the Local Authorities (Africans). On election day over 82% of Indian voters stayed away from the polling stations despite intimidation by police and campaign workers.

Opposition to the Apartheid system and rejection of the Constitution by all non-white groups continues, and there has been an enormous increase in the amount of organized and spontaneous opposition, which has been met by massive repression by the South African government. UDF leaders — including the Presidents of the Natal and Transvaal Indian Congresses — have been detained and charged with high treason. The majority of Indians have continued to reject the Apartheid Constitution and in the elections of September 1989 most boycotted the polls, once again despite widespread intimidation.

Some Indian South Africans are dubious about the advantages for them of possible future majority rule, looking to East Africa as an example of the difficulties faced by Asian minorities in the post-independence era, and this fear is deliberately invoked by the government. An increasing number of Indian families are preparing to emigrate, amid continuing uncertainty over South Africa's future. But this is an option available only to a small proportion of the Indian community. Increasingly Indians have politically identified themselves with the Black cause — a term used to cover Africans, Coloureds and Indian South Africans alike — and have demonstrated that their allegiance is to a non-racial democratic South Africa.

(See also *Asians of East and Central Africa*)

---

[1] The figures for African and Coloured were 57.5 and 59 respectively.

Jehovah's Witnesses in Africa

Alternative names: **Watch Tower Bible and Tract Society, Publishers**
Location: **Many African countries, especially Nigeria, Zambia**
Population: **Total 250,000**
% of population: **In Zambia 0.9%; elsewhere much smaller**
Religion: **Jehovah's Witness, millennarian Christian sect**
Language: **various**

Jehovah's Witnesses are a religous minority in every country where they are present and because of their beliefs — which includes a refusal to participate in politics or to honour nationalist symbols — have been the subject of harassment and persecution by many governments. In Nazi Germany they were rounded up and sent to concentration camps, while during World War II the Society was banned in Canada and Australia. Today there are about two million Jehovah's Witnesses world wide, of whom about one quarter of a million are in Africa.

Experiences in Africa

The Watch Tower Bible and Tract Society (WTBTS) was founded in 1884 in the United States. Watch Tower ideas were brought to Southern and Central Africa in 1908 by an Australian, Joseph Booth, and they spread rapidly, carried initially by migrant workers returning to their homes from the mines of Southern Rhodesia. For many Africans WTBTS was a means of gaining literacy, with Watch Tower commentaries in African languages being virtually the only form of reading material available in the villages during the 1920s and '30s. Autonomous sects appeared, led by local prophets, and as a result doctrines differed widely according to local conditions. The movement in Africa was led then, as now, largely by Africans. Before 1940 it was an independent organization but is now directly responsible to WTBTS headquarters in New York. Its members have been known as Jehovah's Witnesses since 1931.

One important aspect of WTBTS teaching in Africa was its emancipatory message. The original teachings, embodied in Charles Taze Russell's seven-volume "Studies in Scripture", predicted the downfall of the old order and the establishment of a new one. Believers, however severe their present sufferings, would be the inheritors of eternal life in the new order and Satan's power would be overthrown. This message, whilst religious in meaning, clearly had an appeal to those living under colonial rule at the start of the century, and also appealed to vassal peoples such as the Wiko and Luvale in Barotseland. In Tanganyika in 1917 Witnesses took a stand against conscription and collaboration with the British, and in 1926 when land was seized from the Kunda people of Eastern Province by European settlers it was the Witnesses who led protests. In these and other cases Witnesses were arrested and many were imprisoned. After World War II the Watch Tower Movement lost much of its revolutionary quality however, and was no longer a vehicle of protest, partly because it was replaced in this capacity by modern nationalist parties and labour organizations and partly because the passivist WTBTS was allowed to organize openly in the post war world and thus displaced many of the overtly rebellious independent sects. Jehovah's Witnesses have long suffered persecution in Africa, usually due to their failure to honour symbols of state such as the national flag or the national anthem. The Witnesses' attitude towards governments and political parties arises from their belief that temporal authority represents the power of Satan and that their only duty to the state should be that of paying their taxes and keeping the peace. In some countries this stand has been interpreted as a deliberate attempt to undermine the authority of the state. In certain cases Witnesses have served as scapegoats for governments which have failed to fulfil expectations raised before independence, and many governments have viewed the WTBTS as competitors to the ruling party.

Malawi

The most serious conflict between Witnesses and government occurred from 1967 in Malawi. WTBTS members, prohibited from joining political groupings by their religious convictions, refused to purchase Malawi Congress Party (MCP) membership cards. MCP is the country's sole legal political organization, to which most nationals belong. Government persecution of the sect's 18,000 members began. Leading members were deported, and Witnesses suffered assault, murder and arson. The move against the Witnesses failed, however, and members (now numbering 23,000) still refused to buy party cards. In 1972 further persecutions led some 21,000 to flee across the border to Zambia but they were forcibly repatriated, and this pattern was repeated several times with numbers also being imprisoned, tortured and killed. The situation improved considerably after international pressure brought about the liberalization of political conditions in Malawi in 1976, but the persecution is by no means over; the WTBTS is still banned and some Witnesses are still in jail.

Elsewhere in Africa

Although Witnesses have not suffered the same degree of persecution elsewhere as they experienced in Malawi, they have nevertheless suffered for their beliefs in other African countries. In Mozambique the majority of the country's 7,000 members were arrested for refusing on religious grounds to give allegiance to Frelimo shortly after independence in June 1975, and today the sect is still banned although some refugee Witnesses from Malawi are thought still to be living there. In Angola Witnesses have been persecuted by both the Portugese authorities and the MPLA regime; some have been jailed and tortured although all were freed by 1980. There have however been occasional reports of new arrests. The sect was banned in 1978.

In Zambia, which has one of the largest concentrations of Witnesses in the world, and where the WTBTS is a legal organization, members refused to register as voters in the 1968-69 general elections and were as a result subjected to widespread violence, hostility being particularly directed against European officials of the WTBTS, who were criticized as being alien and a hostile influence. However there has been no repetition of these violent incidents and Zambia today with almost 60,000 Witnesses has the highest ratio of Witnesses to population on the Africa continent (1:109 in 1982).

In South Africa white Jehovah's Witnesses have faced sanctions from the apartheid regime for their refusal to accept military conscription and in January 1983, 66 Witnesses were sentenced to three years' imprisonment. However it has since been ruled that Witnesses and others who can prove religious grounds for their refusal to serve can instead carry out a long period of alternative non-military service. In Swaziland in 1982 Jehovah's Witnesses, of whom there are about 700, refused to shave their hair in mourning after the death of the king and over the following months at least 30 Witnesses were arrested, jailed, fined and forcibly shaved by the police. However adverse publicity internationally restrained the authorities and some sentences were later quashed.

In East Africa the movement is banned in Ethiopia and Tanzania. There have been recent reports of widespread arrests in Burundi.

Jehovah's Witnesses also faced persecution in the West African state of Benin in 1976 when the country's 2000 Witnesses refused to attend political education classes, to salute the flag or to participate in ceremonies honouring the country's change of name (from Dahomey). The sect was banned in April 1976 and some of its members were arrested. Much the same process took place in Cameroon when the Witnesses were banned in 1970. By 1982 the new President had released a number of Witnesses held without trial since 1978. The largest population of Jehovah's Witnesses in Africa is found in Nigeria — 108,000 in 1983 — but there are no reports of government persecution.

(See also *Falashas of Ethiopia*)

Jews of South Africa

Location: **overwhelmingly in urban areas**
Population: **about 110,000**
% of population: **0.3%**
Religion: **Judaism**
Language: **English**

Jews have lived in South Africa from the earliest days of white settlement. Their community numbered several hundred in the 1860s and consisted mainly of British and German Jews.

Between 1882 and 1912, 40,000 Jews went to South Africa from Russia; to be joined in the next few decades by 30,000 who fled there from Lithuania, Germany and Latvia. Today the South African Jewish community numbers about 110,000 and is *per capita* among the richest in the world.

Anti-Semitism was negligible until the introduction of Nazi ideology in the 1930s. This appeared to peter out with the defeat of Germany but in 1969 the ultra-right-wing anti-reformist *Herstigte Nasionale Party* was founded to oppose any deviation from strict apartheid; it was also highly anti-semitic, identifying Jews as the founders and supporters of communism. In 1981 Eugene Terre Blanche, the leader of the *Afrikaner Weerstandsbeweging* (Resistance Movement) (AWB), threatened to deprive Jews of political rights and called for them to be expelled from South Africa. The official opposition party, the Conservative Party, has maintained that if they should form a government, Jews would be eligible for office only if they were prepared to promote Christianity publicly.

Most anti-Apartheid groups demand that Jewish groups formally denounce Zionism as a prerequisite for co-operation. There is an anti-Apartheid group, Jews for Social Justice, which is affiliated to the United Democratic Front.

Small Jewish communities were established in the twentieth century in a number of European African colonies, notably Kenya and Rhodesia, but these have tended to disintegrate with the coming of independence.

(See also *Indian South Africans*)

Mauritania

Location: **Large desert country in north-west Africa**
Population: **1,735,000 (est. 1986)**
% of population: **Bidan (white) Moors 34%, "black" Moors 26%, other blacks 40% (est.)**
Religion: **Islam (Malekite rite)**
Language: **French (official language) Arabic (Hassaniya dialect) Peul, Soninke and Wolof**

Ethnic violence in Mauritania in 1989 and the expulsion of both Senegalese and black Mauritanians in large numbers which followed, signalled a grave crisis in Senegal-Mauritania relations, and in the ethnic power balance within the country. The seeds of this crisis lie in the legacy of colonial rule, which brought ethnically diverse peoples and ecologically contrasting regions under one administration. The Sahelian drought since the early 1970s has increasingly forced nomadic Moors, who have dominated political power since independence, out of desert and arid zones into urban areas and the fertile Senegal river valley, where the country's black minorities are concentrated. Competition over the limited amount of viable agricultural land, with the ruling elite using state power to dispossess black settlers, is one major underlying cause of the crisis. Arabization policies pursued since independence, and alignment with the Maghreb, rather than black Africa, have added to the alienation of blacks from the system. Purges of blacks within the administration and army have occurred following each major outbreak of ethnic unrest. Detentions and death penalties have been imposed on blacks, who have no legitimate political voice, opposing the system by illegal means. In addition, slavery is still prevalent, and the Haratine (former slave) community suffer severe discrimination. They have often been caught in the middle of the black-Moor conflict, creating further ethnic tensions and divisions.

Ethnic and class divisions

Mauritania is a geographically large country with a small population, which is highly unevenly distributed. At least two-thirds of the country consists of desert: in some places there is not even enough vegetation to graze camels, traditionally the main livelihood of northern and central nomads. The Sahelian belt is gradually being pushed south by the desert.

The Moors, if considered as one, are probably the largest ethnic group. Of Arab and Berber origin, they speak dialects of Hassaniya related to Beduin Arabic. However, Moor society is traditionally divided on social and descent criteria. "White", Bidan or Beydane Moors historically enslaved by the "black" Moors, sometimes called Haratine, and slavery at differing levels is still much in evidence in contemporary Mauritania. (The words "black" and "white" are misleading in this context in that they do not denote colour, but rather paternal descent). The Moors are, by tradition, nomadic peoples, but the last century and particularly the last 25 years have seen a rapid decrease in nomadism. In 1963 about 83% of the population was nomadic and 17% sedentary; by 1980 only 25% remained nomadic, whilst 75% were settled, many in the larger towns.

The Bidan are further divided into warriors (Hassan) and holy men (Zawya or *marabouts*), the former said to be of Arab origin and the latter of Berber origin, although this distinction is somewhat blurred. The "warrior" role of the Moor elite has diminished since the French colonial conquest: they are now mainly traders and herders. The *marabout* strata have continued to be influential within the Muslim brotherhoods and the administration.

As well as enslaving the "black" Moors, the Bidan also dominated other groups, through exacting service or tribute. Hundreds of years of regional inter-ethnic conflict brought into being the defeated Zenaga or tributary groups. The pastoral, nomadic tributaries are considered Bidan Moors, while the Imraguen fishermen, and the Aghazazir salt miners, are clearly of mixed (probably African/Berber) origin. The common form of tribute, the *horma*, consists of goods or services handed over once a year: though imposed by one group upon another, the tribute is usually paid individually. Debt bondage also still exists in the salt-mining area. Below the tributaries in the social order, come the artisans (*mu'allmin*) and the musicians (*ighyuwn*), who were once nomadic but are now increasingly sedentary. These castes are subject to the Bidan. A few hundred white, Hassaniya-speaking hunters — the Namadi — inhabit the El Djouf desert area.

The slave community can be divided into three levels: firstly, there is the *adb*, who is a total subject. Then, there is the part-slave, who has obtained a degree of freedom by favour, payment, or other means, usually going to live in an *edebaye*, with other part-slaves, but close to the masters, for whom they cultivate, or work as herders, sometimes travelling seasonally to Senegal or Mali, or even as far afield as France. Finally, there are the true Haratine: the government has long described all forms of slave as Haratine or "newly freed" to imply the end of slavery. The Haratine become freed either by favour, by purchase, or perhaps most commonly by escape. Urbanization, internal and international migration have to some extent broken down the slave system and certain districts of Nouakchott have become "havens" for escaped slaves. These escapees form the basis of the emancipation movement *El Hor* (Freedom),

formed in 1974. In 1980, slavery was formally abolished. However, in 1981, the Anti-Slavery Society (UK) estimated that there were around 100,000 people still enslaved, plus approximately 300,000 Haratine.

Once free, however, ex-slaves are subject to continuing discrimination, by the elite moors and the smaller black elite, from whom they are distinguishable in appearance (Haratine Moors may range all the way between black and white), language and culture. The Haratine Moors share language and culture with their Bidan oppressors, although they have their own folklore. Haratine commonly find it difficult to obtain employment, and if they do, it is usually of the most menial kind. Women escapees often work as street vendors and sometimes become prostitutes. There are also numerous cases of escaped slaves being recaptured, by their masters, with discreet connivance from the Bidan-dominated police and authorities.

Other than the Haratine Moors, Mauritania also has a significant black African population. By tradition, the Peuls (Fulbe, Fellata or Fulani), are nomadic pastoralists, although this may be changing. Closely related to the Peuls in language and culture, to the extent that they are sometimes referred to as a single group, are the Toucouleur (Tukulor, Tocolor, Tekoror, Tekrur or Halphoolaren), who are basically sedentary, as are the majority of the black groups. The Sarakolle (Soninke, Swanik, Azer) are currently concentrated in Guidimakha, Assaba and Hodh in southern Mauritania, and speak their own language of the Manding group. The above-mentioned groups traditionally had highly stratified social structures, encompassing warrior, scholar, farmer, artisan and slave castes. Even today, slavery is not the exclusive preserve of the Bidan. All the black groups are at least nominally Muslim, but each has its own distinct language, culture and lifestyle.

The most densely populated area in Mauritania is the fertile Chemama land on the Mauritanian bank of the River Senegal in the south-west, where the black population is concentrated. However, in spite of substantial investment in irrigation schemes to increase the area of land available for cultivation, the river has been at record low levels in recent years and riverine cultivation is therefore reduced. Competition over these lands, brought about by the undermining of the nomadic economy during the long drought from the early seventies into the eighties, is one of the major underlying factors in ethnic conflict in Mauritania today. Many blacks claim to have been forcibly dispossessed of their lands and assert that legislation has been enacted to this end.

Another less numerous black group are the Wolof (Djolof), who are one of the major groups in neighbouring Senegal. Ethnically, the southern blacks are closer to populations across the borders in Senegal and Mali, than to other groups within their own national boundaries.

Demographic statistics are problematic in Mauritania, a common breakdown in the past being Moors (Bidan and "black"), 75%; other blacks, 25%. The 1977 census results were not. officially released, leading to suspicions among the black opposition that the ruling Bidan elite was trying to cover up for the relative decrease in their own numbers: the growth rate of the black population is known to be significantly higher than that of the "white" Moors. A new headcount was conducted in 1988 but figures are not yet available. It has been estimated that the relative proportions in 1980 may have been: Bidan 34%; "black" moors 26%; other blacks 40%. Based on the 1965 census, the populations of the various black communities were as follows: Toucouleurs 66,400; Peuls 40,000; Sarakolle 31,000; Wolofs 8,800; various 2,800.

The ethnic and social boundaries described above are not completely rigid, and economic, demographic and political factors in recent times have created new divisions and alliances, which interact with the old ones.

History

The legendary inhabitants of Mauritania are the Bafours, said to be related to the contemporary Sarakolle. It is thought that the Berbers conquered the Bafours and in the first millennium AD the Berber Sanhadja nomads controlled the area down to the Senegal River. Islam filtered southwards from the seventh century onwards. In the fourteenth century the Hassan Arabs began their invasion, and gradually gained the upper hand, imposing Arabic language and culture on the Berbers, who were already Islamised. Most nomads claim an Arab origin; however, Berber origins and words are still discernible in the people and language in some areas. From the seventeenth century onwards, the Emirates were established at Trarza, Brakna, Tagant, Adrar and Hodh, dominated by the Hassan. The Sanhadja became scholars and leaders of the Muslim brotherhoods.

The French were responsible for joining the river valley and the desert — and the Moors and black populations — under a single administration. A combination of inhospitable terrain and fierce resistance meant that large areas of Mauritania did not come under the control of the French colonisers until well into the twentieth century. The military conquest of Mauritania began in earnest around 1850, led by Faidherbe, with resistance led by El Hadj Omar, until 1860. Defeats in the 1850s and 1860s led to the signing of treaties with the Emirates of Trarza and Brakna. In 1891, the southern bank of the river was annexed to the Senegalese colony. The French military occupation as far north as Idjil began in 1901 and by 1910 most of the territory was brought under French control through a series of campaigns and punitive expeditions extending northwards. "Pacification" was not complete until 1934 however, and even after this, isolated pockets of resistance remained up until the eve of independence.

Officially, Mauritania was a French possession from 1904, administered from St Louis, in Senegal. (Nouakchott was established as the capital just before independence.) The black population of Mauritania, being sedentary, and more accessible from the south, were exposed to mission education from the early twentieth century. They thus became instrumental in assisting the French administration. In order to control the vast desert areas effectively, the French needed co-operation from the Moor and black elites, so their decrees abolishing individual slavery and inter-tribal tribute were never seriously implemented. Co-operation was also encouraged through sedentarization: land titles and financial aid were distributed to the elite who, using slave labour, set up the oases, and the dams and cultivation plots of the south, sowing the seeds for future conflict over land rights. Some slaves were able to take advantage of colonial rule to flee southwards, but more often than not ended up as slaves of the southern land-owning (primarily Toucouleur) elite. To a certain extent, the French attempted to control the ensuing struggles over slave possession, by allocating plots in groups to escaped slaves: the origin of some *edebaye* villages.

Mauritania became an independent Islamic Republic in 1960, and was ruled by Moktar Ould Daddah, who had become Prime Minister in 1959, until the bloodless coup of 1978. After independence, all parties merged with the ruling *Parti du Peuple Mauritanien* (PPM). The 1961 constitution of the Republic created an executive Presidency, to which Daddah was elected, and Mauritania became a one-party state in 1965. After 1978, a succession of unstable military governments followed. The current regime, led by Colonel Maawiya Ould Sid'Ahmed Taya, who came to power in 1984, is the fourth, and has proved more durable than previous ones. However, recent troubled experiments with local democracy, on top of the economic crisis which feeds into entrenched ethnic positions, have led to outbreaks of unrest followed by repression.

Arabization and ethnic violence (1960s)

Due to the legacy of early French contact and education, a large number of southern blacks — particularly Toucouleurs — work in the educational sector and the second level of the administration. Since the takeover of state control by the Bidan on independence, the upper echelons of the military and administration have been controlled by the Moors. Although every government has contained a minority of blacks, the southerners feared Moor domination.

The mid-1960s saw ethnic violence, in response to policies of Arabization. The first crisis came with the decision in 1966 to make Arabic compulsory in secondary schools. Strikes of black school students ensued, supported by black civil servants. The protests culminated in inter-ethnic riots in Nouakchott. Haratine were used by the Bidan to attack blacks and crush the revolt. The fighting, resulting in six dead and 70 wounded (although these official figures are thought to be underestimated), was only brought to a halt by army intervention. Several ministers and black civil servants were purged from the government and administration. At this stage, discussion of ethnic problems was banned

The Western Sahara conflict (1975-79)

When Spain withdrew from the Western Sahara in 1975, the territory was split between Mauritania and Morocco. From 1975 onwards, Mauritania was at war with the Saharawi, who are ethnically close to the Bidan. The war was unpopular in Mauritania, including with many of the Moor elite, and caused a severe drain on the ailing economy. Blacks and slaves were drafted into the army in large numbers, which expanded from a mere 1,500 to 17,000 during the war. The black population, moreover, was not generally in favour of the Mauritanian expansion into Saharawi territory, which would increase the Moor majority. The war was only popular with the conservative pro-Moroccan tendency. Moreover, the Mauritanian forces did not achieve military success despite foreign support.

The overthrow of Daddah in the July 1978 coup, by which time the economy was in ruins, ended civilian rule. The Constitution was sus-pended and the government dissolved. A military committee headed by Lt-Col Ould Salek assumed control. Less than a year later, following various reshuffles, Mohammed Khouna Haidalla took over as Prime Minister and in August 1979 he ended Mauritania's involvement in the Western Sahara conflict and renounced territorial claims. In early 1980, Haidalla assumed the presidency.

The resurgence of ethnic unrest and the opposition (1979-80)

A resurgence of ethnic unrest began in early 1979, again centring on the Arabization issue. The suppression of results from the 1977 census also led to suspicions that the Moors were trying to play down the size of the black population. The immediate issue was the poor examination results of black students in their 1979 end of year exams: the introduction of Arabic into the curriculum in the '60s and the subsequent weighting of marks in favour of Arabic subjects were blamed. Black teachers and pupils demonstrated and the police intervened. Senegal threw its weight behind demands for autonomy for Mauritania's blacks, although the motives for this were probably as much concerned with territorial expansion of Senegal into the River valley, as with solidarity. Black opposition in the form of the *Union Démocratique Mauritanienne* (UDM) was based in Senegal.

Minor concessions were made on the linguistic front, with the announcement in October 1979 that French would remain on a par with Arabic in schools, and the establishment of an Institute of National Languages, whose staff later became the targets of government repression. However, in 1980, pre-emptive arrests of blacks were made, presumably to prevent further actions. The full implementation of *Shari'a* law in Mauritania in 1980 — perhaps as a condition for financial aid from Saudi Arabia — was perceived by some members of both black and Haratine communities as an unwelcome measure, which could be manipulated to oppress the slave and poor black communities in general.

In 1980, fearing links between the Haratine movement *El Hor* and the black opposition, the government pronounced the abolition of slavery, and a system for compensation of slave owners. Despite the ban on political parties, *El Hor* was permitted a degree of freedom. However, no serious economic or social measures, such as land reform, were undertaken to back up the formal abolition, which rendered it largely symbolic and ineffective. Moreover, compensation was bitterly opposed by some members of the Haratine movement who felt that they were the ones owed some form of redress.

Rising ethnic tensions and attempted coup (1986-88)

In April 1986, the Dakar-based black opposition group, *Forces de Libération Africaine de Mauritanie* (FLAM), which was established in 1983, published the "Oppressed Black Minorities Manifesto". The distribution of this document provoked the arrest of up to 30 prominent blacks in September, 20 of whom were sentenced to prison terms. A wave of civil disturbances across the country followed in October. The military regime responded with further arrests. Eighteen of the alleged perpetrators of the violence were tried in March 1987, and 13 received prison sentences. In late 1986, municipal elections held in the 13 regional capitals raised the ethnic question again, when lists of black candidates were overruled in favour of government-sponsored lists and blacks were allegedly intimidated when trying to vote. Reports that three or four of the 1986 detainees had died at the notorious Oualata jail began circulating in 1988, as did reports of torture — although these were denied by the Mauritanian authorities.

In October 1987 an attempted coup by black officers failed and 51 Toucouleur officers were arrested. Of these, three received death sentences, while most of the others were given prison terms, some life sentences. The remaining defendants, including a former minister, Lt.-Col. Babaly, were acquitted. The executions were considered extreme in many quarters, but particularly among the black population. Riots occurred in Nouakchott, Boghe and Kaedi: for six months following the executions, a state of emergency existed in Boghe and local elections were boycotted. Purges of blacks from the police began and black candidates were barred from applying to join. According to FLAM, in early 1988, up to 500 black NCOs were dismissed from the Army.

Opposition within the ruling elite also surfaced when hundreds of pro-Iraqi (and pro-Moroccan) Ba'athists, who form one of two loose groups around the ruling military council, were arrested, and allegedly tortured, from mid-1988 onwards. The other main grouping are the dominant Nasserists, who are sympathetic to Polisario. In October 1988, a former army officer of the Ba'athist tendency, was sentenced to four years for attempting to destabilize the Bidan ruling group. By the later '80s, economic and political power were increasingly becoming concentrated among the Semassida (the northern Mauritanian Bidan) who tend to be anti-Ba'athist.

Senegal-Mauritania ethnic violence (1989)

In April and May 1989 several hundred people (estimates vary between 100 and 1,000) were killed in a spate of looting, rioting and reprisals in both the Senegalese capital Dakar and the Mauritanian capital Nouakchott, as well as in other towns on both sides of the border. In each case, local people attacked migrants or settlers from the neighbouring country. Prior to the violence, there were thought to be around 30,000 Senegalese traders, migrant workers and students in Mauritania, and between 200,000 and 300,000 Mauritanians in Senegal, who controlled up to 80% of the petty commercial sector.

The clashes were ostensibly sparked off by a border incident on April 9, at Diaware, in which two Senegalese farmers were allegedly shot by Mauritanian border guards in a dispute over grazing rights. On news of the border incident reaching Dakar, looting of Mauritanian businesses by Senegalese began. This was followed, in turn, by much larger-scale violence in Mauritania, with some reportedly very brutal attacks. When the first batch of 160 fleeing Senegalese returned from Mauritania on April 28, with graphic accounts of their experiences, looting turned to murder in Dakar, leaving 40-60 dead. By early May, as many as 100,000 people had been airlifted in both directions assisted by Moroccan, Algerian, French and Spanish aircraft, with more undertaking the perilous journey overland.

These events, which caused a drastic deterioration of Senegal-Mauritania relations, verging on fears of war at one stage, related to domestic ethnic tensions. Although the killings in Mauritania, estimated at between 100 and 400, with many more injured, affected mainly Senegalese, it is reported that Mauritanian blacks — particularly from the Peul-Toucouleur communities — were also targets. Haratines are said to be mainly responsible for the killings. Mauritanian Interior Minister Djibril Ould Abdullahi is considered the architect of repression of southern blacks in recent years and has sought the support of Haratines, promoting individuals from the Haratine community. In the aftermath, the Senegalese government accused Mauritanian authorities of encouraging, or at least not acting to prevent, the violence in Nouakchott, Nouadhibou and Rosso.

On May 3, 1989, the Mauritanian government announced that it would begin repatriating those Senegalese remaining in the country, who had settled there since 1986. However, the expulsions of Senegalese blacks seemed also to be affecting the Mauritanian black population, according to aid workers and other officials who visited refugee camps over the Senegalese border. Of around 80,000 who appeared to have fled or been forced to leave Mauritania by July 1989, at least 30,000 are thought to be Mauritanian, a minority of whom are middle-class blacks including a handful of senior government officials. The Mauritanian government claimed that all those expelled are Senegalese, some of whom had "fraudulently"

obtained Mauritanian nationality. Fleeing and forcibly repatriated people from both sides were dispossessed of property and belongings. The conflict and ensuing repatriations reportedly left 100,000 to 200,000 Bidan and Haratine Moors destitute in Mauritania. Many from the repatriated settler and migrant communities have only tenuous links in their "home" countries, having been long-term residents in the neighbouring state. In August 1989, Senegal referred grievances over the crisis to the UN Security Council, demanding a settlement which would resolve border disputes and end the expulsions of blacks.

(See also *Chad*; *Sahelian Nomads*; *Western Saharans*)

Namibia

Alternative names: **formerly South-West Africa**
Location: **Large desert country in south-western Africa**
Population: **1-1.3 million (est.)**
% of population: **Ovambo approx. 50%; no other group more than 10%**
Religion: **Christian (Lutheran, Catholic, Anglican), Indigenous African beliefs**
Language: **various**

Namibia is a multi-ethnic country, which, after having spent a century as a colony of other nations, is scheduled to achieve independence in April 1990. Although the indigenous African Namibians are the great majority of the population, they have, in effect, been treated as an underprivileged minority, and have been denied self-determination and equality. As a newly independent nation, one of the problems Namibia will face is to give equal opportunities to its various constituent peoples.

Ethnic groups

Population figures in Namibia are not especially reliable because of effects of war and refugee exodus and because there is good reason to believe that the African population has been underestimated by South African officials. In addition apartheid-type terminology has been employed dividing the African population (but not the white) into ethnic-subgroups. However Namibians are not as divided as the official classification might suggest as many of them are of mixed descent; some groups are closely related to others and many groups live in close proximity.

Over 90% of the Namibian population is

African. Of these the Ovambo are by far the largest group, comprising over half-a-million people, or about 50% of the total population. They were primarily a pastoral people who came from the north centuries ago to settle and today occupy the area of northern Namibia known as Ovamboland. The Herero are traditionally herdspeople who settled in the centre of present-day Namibia some time after the Ovambos in the north. They probably constitute between 7% and 8% of the population. The Namas are often referred to as Hottentots, a name they resent. They are related to the San (Bushmen) but settled in the area much later. They are settled in the south and probably comprise about 5% of the population. The Damara arrived with the Namas and lived among the Hereros and Namas, working for them as herdsmen. They probably comprise between 7% and 8% of the population. The Kavango are one of the largest groups living in the north-east of Namibia and may comprise anything between 6.5% and 9.5% of the population. The Orlams are a group of the Namas who returned from further south in the nineteenth century due to pressure from white colonial expansion in the Cape. Many spoke Dutch and were Christians. The Rehoboth Bastars are of mixed Nama/Afrikaner ancestry who today constitute about 2.5% of the population. There is also a larger group of about 4% of the population classified as "Coloured". Other African groups include the East Caprivians of the extreme north-east, the San (Bushmen), the Kaokovelders of the north-west and the Tswana.

The White population comprises well under 10%, but large numbers who are counted as Namibian in the census are in fact South African officials and their families. Most whites are of Afrikaner descent with 25% of German descent.

South-West Africa

The original inhabitants of Namibia were the San hunters and gatherers, who were later displaced by the Ovambos, Hereros, Namas and others. From the late nineteenth century Afrikaners began to move into the territory on a small scale and although one Herero leader urged the Cape government to stop such migration and for Britain to extend a protectorate to the territory, such warnings were not heeded. In 1885 the Germans established control over the territory and named it South-West Africa (SWA). The Germans never really established control over the northern Ovambos but launched a genocidal war on the Hereros and Namas, killing three-quarters of their population and destroying or confiscating thousands of their cattle.

Between the years 1915 to 1919 the territory was under South African military rule and the South Africans hoped to annex it after the war; however it was awarded to them to administer under a League of Nations mandate. Under the terms of the mandate they were to prepare the territory for eventual self-determination and were not to profit from its administration. South Africa was to have full powers of administration over the territory but in the case of any dispute between itself and the League, if negotiations failed, it could be settled at the International Court of Justice (ICJ). South Africa almost immediately broke the terms of the mandate, white settlers flooded in, land was stolen, and there were several African rebellions which were brutally suppressed. Ovamboland was occupied and the area split between SWA and Portuguese-ruled Angola.

In 1945 the United Nations replaced the League of Nations and established the Trusteeship Council (the UN Fourth Committee) to look after the Trust Territories. South Africa again applied to annex SWA but this was rejected. South Africa then refused to place SWA under

UN Trusteeship although it maintained that it would " . . administer the territory scrupulously in accordance with the mandate . . .". Protests from the African population to the UN went unheeded by the South Africans and the UN sought an advisory opinion from the ICJ in 1950. The Court ruled that South Africa had a legal obligation to fulfil the original mandate and could not unilaterally modify the international status of the territory. South Africa ignored this ruling and began to introduce aspects of the Apartheid system into SWA. At this time African political parties began, most notably the South West African People's Organization (SWAPO), but also others. The ICJ made several further rulings on the SWA case but after a reversal of judgment in 1965 most UN member states demanded firmer action and in 1966 the General Assembly passed a resolution terminating South Africa's mandate. It appointed a Council for Namibia (as SWA was now renamed) to seek to administer the territory until independence.

Developments since the end of the mandate

At first the new status made little difference to the territory. The South Africans had received support for their claim from many western nations, including the UK, and they consolidated their previous policies, displacing Africans into Bantustans and keeping the best land for white farmers. Namibia's considerable economic wealth remained in the hands of white South Africans of multi-national companies, despite a ICJ ruling in 1971 that South Africa's occupation was illegal and that UN member states should refrain from any acts or dealings implying recognition of the illegal occupation. Since international pressure proved ineffective African Namibians began to organize resistance; in 1966 SWAPO had formed the People's Liberation Army of Namibia (PLAN) and began guerrilla warfare against the massive South African military presence in the north. In December 1973 the UN voted unanimously to end further dialogue with South Africa and to take steps to expel South Africa from Namibia.

The period between 1974 to 1976 saw many external pressures on South Africa, most notably stemming from the ending of the Portuguese Empire in Africa and more unified pressure from the UN which passed a resolution 366/1974 calling for South African withdrawal and a satisfactory solution by May 30, 1975. The South African government under John Foster announced a Constitutional Conference, dubbed the "Turnhalle Talks", to find an internal solution to the future status of Namibia. However SWAPO and those who opposed the government were excluded from the talks and, in any case, progress was limited and painfully slow. SWAPO formed their own Namibia National Convention in opposition to the Turnhalle arrangements. During this period the South African military presence in Namibia grew, especially in the sealed-off Northern "Homelands" where SWAPO was conducting a guerrilla war. By the beginning of 1976 South African forces were facing defeat in Angola and a school children's revolt at home. The UN passed yet another resolution, 435/1976, calling among other things for free elections held under UN supervision and control; the preparations to be made by August 31, 1976. As with other UN resolutions this was not implemented but it laid the basis for a future settlement.

The Turnhalle Talks had produced proposals for independence by 1979 with an interim government in the meantime; however since the interim government was to consist of South African-approved tribal leaders and appointees it was seen by the outside world as a South African puppet state. The plan was dropped in 1977 after pressure from the "Contact Group" of western nations (the UK, France, Canada, West Germany and the USA) and instead new legislation (The South West Africa Constitution Amendment Bill) was passed by the South African Parliament giving new, almost dictatorial, powers in Namibia to the South African President and creating a new post of Administrator-General. In the meantime the Bantustan policy in Namibia had continued with "tribal homelands" becoming "self-governing". The South African-sponsored elections were held in December 1978 and were "won" by the Democratic Turnhalle Alliance, but since the elections were boycotted by SWAPO and allied parties and had been characterized by widespread irregularities and intimidation they had no recognition internationally.

Despite this, however, South African policies continued with few modifications. Under successive Administrator-Generals there has been some restructuring of government departments and functions to make them appear more autonomous; in practice Pretoria still retained considerable influence not compatible with independence. New Legislative Assemblies were created for each "population group" (the term "homelands" had become internationally unacceptable). Racially discriminatory provisions remained on the Statute Book, despite African attempts to remove them. Attempts to

foster a political alternative to SWAPO by the administration failed and the DTA retained only limited support. The South African authorities then formulated a new alternative to Resolution 435 in the Multi-Party Conference (MPC) as an anti-SWAPO front. The MPC set a deadline of December 31, 1984 for other parties to join in talks on the independence issue; otherwise it would negotiate self-government directly with South Africa. SWAPO and its allies rejected the offer.

The most serious development however had been the escalation of the bush war in the north of the country (principally Kaokoveld, Ovamboland, Kavangoland, East Caprivi) into full-scale military conflict. Conscription had been extended to the African population and there were regular incursions into Angola to break the SWAPO fighters based there. These raids also affected civilians, as in the 1978 South African bombing of the refugee camp at Cassinga, which killed over 800 civilians. A massive military presence failed to stop the guerrillas but inflicted intense suffering on the civilian population. Thousands of citizens fled from the war zone; health, education and welfare services had been disrupted while the destruction of crops was exacerbated by the severe drought of the early 1980s. Civilians who were suspected of aiding PLAN were routinely detained and tortured under sweeping laws, or under no law at all. The *Koevoet* ("crowbar") unit, a special police counter-insurgency unit, composed almost entirely of Ovambo special policemen under the command of white officers, gained particular notoriety for brutal behaviour. The South African authorities made a few attempts to restrain or punish offenders; these had little effect.

Implementation of the UN plan

From 1984 international pressure on South Africa began to intensify, especially from the USA. However South African procrastination was aided by the question of "linkage" whereby a withdrawal of South African troops in Namibia was to be paralleled by a withdrawal of Cuban troops in Angola. By the beginning of 1985 the US policy of "constructive engagement" was facing increasing frustration and new pressures from inside South Africa such as the townships' revolt, the total lack of credibility of the so-called interim government in Namibia, while US Congressional votes to begin sanctions against South Africa finally began to produce results. But it was not until November 1988, after extensive US-sponsored negotiations between

South Africa, Angola and the Cubans, that an accord was signed on proposals for Namibian independence and the implementation of UN resolution 435. SWAPO itself was not involved with negotiations and this was later to have fatal consequences in the events of April 1989. It took several months for the agreement to be ratified and the details to be established.

Eventually a timetable for the implementation of 435 was established beginning in April 1989 with the UN Representative taking over administration, the declaration of a ceasefire with both SWAPO and South African forces confined to base, with the later establishment of de-militarized zones and withdrawal and disbandment of South African troops in May; at the same time Namibian refugees would begin to return under UN supervision. In July the official election campaign would begin with elections to be held on November 1 and one week later the final withdrawal of South African troops. Namibia would become fully independent in April 1990 after the new Constituent Assembly completed its constitution.

However at the beginning the plan went disastrously wrong when several hundred SWAPO guerrillas crossed from Angola into Ovamboland, in contravention to the agreement which stated that they must be inside Angola and north of the 16th parallel. The South African forces therefore demanded that they be allowed to hunt the guerrillas and this was agreed by the UN representative. In the following week several hundred SWAPO fighters, and reportedly also civilians, were killed, at least some apparently in cold blood. SWAPO was forced to withdraw its fighters. However two errors had become clear; firstly the decision to exclude SWAPO from negotiations and secondly the UN decision in January to cut the numbers of UN monitoring troops from 7,500 to 4,500, especially as at the beginning of the projected ceasefire even these troops were not in place. Over the next few months it became obvious also that in many ways the South African forces were violating the spirit of the agreement; they initially insisted on their right to interrogate wounded guerrillas; they set up military camps beside UN assembly points; the notorious *Koevoet* forces were not disbanded but reintegrated into the police force; and there were numerous complaints of intimidation, assault and misconduct. Under the circumstances the return of refugees was postponed slightly and was also marred by allegations by former refugees of detention and torture in SWAPO camps (allegations which SWAPO has partially admitted). By September the bulk of the refugees had returned to Namibia as had the SWAPO leader Sam Nujoma. However political violence within Namibia had increased in the run-up to the elections and there were fears that state-sponsored violence would be replaced by shadowy vigilante squads. There seemed little doubt that SWAPO would win the elections, but it was problematic whether they would achieve the two-thirds majority necessary to agree a constitution.

Whatever the outcome of the elections and the composition and course of the first independent government, there are major problems ahead for Namibia. The colonial apartheid legacy has aided divisions between its diverse peoples, some of whom resent the dominance of the Ovambo (although there are also many divisions within the Ovambo which might neutralize this). There are also divisions between the returning exiles and the emerging leadership within the country. More serious however is the continuing economic dominance of South Africa. Namibia is rich in resources, with mining, fishing and agriculture. But unequal land distribution has meant that much fertile land is concentrated in white hands (for example in Ovamboland white farmers have over 200 times as much useful land *per capita* as blacks), while many thousands of Africans live in terrible conditions as contract labourers at Katutura and other black townships. Wages are highly unequal; most Africans are unskilled labourers and marginal peasant farmers. South Africa has indicated that it will retain its hold over the enclave of Walvis Bay. The country has for many years been traumatized by war, poverty and widespread violations of human rights. All of these problems will have to be challenged by the new government.

(See also *San of the Kalahari*)

Oromo of Ethiopia

Alternative names: **Galla (derogatory name rejected by Oromo)**
Location: **Southern, south-eastern, south-western Ethiopia and the Highlands; Oromo refugees have settled in Somalia, Djibouti, Kenya and Sudan**
Population: **about 18 million**
% of population: **nearly 50%**
Religion: **various**
Language: **Oromo (Oromifaa, Oromiffa, Galle)**

The Oromo people are the largest ethnic grouping in Ethiopia, which has a total of 74 ethnically diverse language groups. About 95% are settled agriculturalists and nomadic pastoralists, practising archaic farming methods and living at subsistence level. A few live in the urban centres. They are dominated by the minority tribal group, the Amhara, who have controlled the country almost continually for the past 100 years, conducting their own colonialization policies, except for a short period, from 1936 to 1941, when Ethiopia was occupied by the Italians.

In the nineteenth century the Oromos' land was forcefully annexed into Ethiopia by the Amhara emperor, Menelik II. The Oromo were also severely repressed by Amhara overlords: the majority reduced to tenancy, paying heavy tributes for the use of land; large numbers sold into slavery and thousands killed. Written Oromo texts were destroyed, education of Oromos was continued in Amharic and any social advance was only possible by way of assimilation into the dominant culture. The Oromo culture and religion were denigrated and viewed as inferior or "savage", and Oromo cultural and religious shrines and places of worship were replaced by those of the Amhara ruling class. It was even forbidden to produce religious literature in the Oromo language. From 1936-41 the Italians occupied Ethiopia, but in 1941 the Amhara administration under Haile Selassie was restored by the British. There had been certain reforms of the unequal treatment of Oromo under Italian occupation, which included land reform, but now the tenancy system was reintroduced, and persisted until 1974 despite continual resistance by the Oromo.

In 1973 Oromo discontent with their position led to the formation of the Oromo Liberation Front (OLF), which began political agitation in the Oromo areas. Also in 1973 there was a catastrophic famine in which over one quarter of a million people died from starvation before the government recognised the disaster and permitted relief measures. The majority who died were Oromos from Wollo, Afars and Tigrayans. There were strikes and demonstrations in Addis Ababa in 1974; and in February of that year, Haile Selassie's government was replaced by the Dergue, a military junta (later renamed the Provisional Military Administrative Council (PMAC)); but the Council was still Amhara-dominated, with only 25 non-Amhara members out of 125. In 1975 the government declared all rural land State-owned, and announced the end of the tenancy system. However, much of the benefit of this reform was counteracted by compulsive collectivization, State farms and forced resettlement programmes. Also in the Oromo regions 95% of the ex-landlords were Amhara, a proportion that was reflected in the police

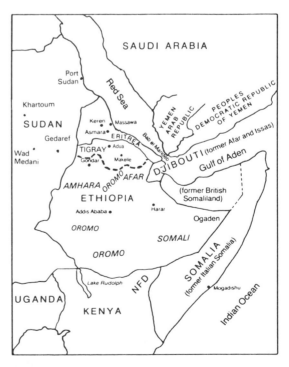

Ethnic groups in Ethiopia

force and bureaucracy, so it was relatively easy for them to take revenge on the Oromo peasants for the loss of their land, and from March 1975 to April 1976 there were fierce battles between them. This insecurity and unrest continued into 1977 and 1978. For example, in 1978, according to an OLF report, there was looting and massacre, with 80,000 Oromo peasants killed by former armed Amhara landlords in Hargarie province alone.

By this stage liberation forces were conducting armed struggles in all parts of the country: Eritrea, Tigray, Addis Ababa, southern Bale and the Ogaden and, by the beginning of 1977, Ethiopian Somaliland. Freedom fighters were in full control of large areas. The government charged Oromo peasants with collaboration with the Western Somali Liberation Front. In 1978 the government formulated a resettlement programme. The PMAC planned to resettle three million northerners, mainly Amhara, in the south, which was mainly occupied by the Oromo. After the 1983-84 drought in the north, the government announced an acceleration in this resettlement programme, planning to resettle about 1.5 million people from north and central Ethiopia to the south and west by the end of 1985. Also, at the end of 1984 the government started a villagization programme in Hargarie province, where there is much OLF guerrilla activity, and by February 1986 three million people had been moved into centralized villages, facilitating political control of the region. In late 1985 the government launched a nationwide campaign with the aim of moving 25 million people into consolidated settlements by 1995, and in December 1988 *Africa Confidential* estimated that by the end of 1989 the villagization programme would have affected nearly 15 million people.

In 1987 the PMAC was abolished and Lt.-Col. Mengistu Haile Mariam, chairman of the PMAC, was re-elected as Secretary-General of the Workers' Party of Ethiopia. Continued war with Tigray and Eritrea and failure to reach a settlement with Eritrea led to an attempted coup by most of Mengistu's senior generals in May 1989. In September 1989 peace talks between the government and the Eritrean People's Liberation Front (EPLF) began in the United States, although at present neither side seem prepared to compromise on the independence of Eritrea. The Tigrayan People's Liberation Front (TPLF), linked with the Ethiopian People's Democratic Movement (EPDM), are attempting to offer a viable alternative to Mengistu's government in their programme for an umbrella movement, the Ethiopian People's Revolutionary Democratic Front, in which OLF has shown interest.

Legal constitution

The People's Democratic Republic of Ethiopia, established on December 12, 1986, is "a unitary state consisting of administrative regions and autonomous regions based on worker-peasant co-operation". The economy is centrally planned and purportedly based on socialist principles. The Workers' Party of Ethiopia is the leading force. The National Assembly is elected by proportional representation (with reserved representation for various nationalities) and the Assembly elects the President. In 1987 the government declared an amendment to the Constitution referring to the villagization programme, which reads: "The State shall encourage the scattered rural population to aggregate in order to enable them to lead a better social life." There was a similar statement in support of the resettlement programme.

Past and present developments

The 20-year Eritrea war has been very costly for the government and the Oromo people have suffered as a result. There are reports that taxes *per capita* were levied on the Oromo three years in advance, with imprisonment or threats of imprisonment if there was no compliance. It is also common for Oromo men to be abducted to serve in the army — there are about 10,000 urban families whose breadwinners have been victims of war and political oppression. The Oromo have also had to help provide agricultural products consumed by troops in Eritrea and elsewhere and in 1980 the government forced local people from Wollo and Gondar to work on state agricultural farms. According to government sources 1,626 people died in these camps, although other estimates are that 4,000-6,000 people died or were seriously ill.

After the Land Reform of 1975 the government declared that the land was to be controlled by local Peasant Associations. One report states that these have developed into Government controlled labour organizations, with local farmers obliged to work for the militia and collective farms for two to five days a week. As a result peasant harvests have declined by two-thirds to three-quarters since 1974. Many Oromo were displaced from their land to allow for the resettlement of armed Amharas from Shoe and Wollo provinces, so that the Oromos are left with no means of subsistence.

There has been a succession of poor harvests as a result of drought (*ORA Report*). It is estimated that the number of displaced farmers reaches about 220,000. The Oromo were also forced to provide the new settlers with tools, furniture, food and even labour, while they themselves were frequently despised and denigrated by both the new arrivals and their camp officials.

By September 1987, eight million rural Ethiopians (about 20% of the total rural population) had been moved to centralized villages. *Africa Confidential* reported in December 1988 that in 1989 the government planned to collectivize nearly three million peasants into new centralized villages. This would bring the total to nearly 15 million, about 40% of the rural population. There is no conclusive evidence of forced removal of people, but the programme moves people away from arable land to areas on main roads which are easier to control politically, and there have been claims that these new settlements are in very poor condition. An eyewitness account in February 1988 states that in Gada Dissi in the Ghimbie region in western Ethiopia an estimated 1,500 people, the entire population of a new village centre, died from cold-related illnesses. There are reports of arrests, imprisonment and killing by the government of hundreds of Oromos because of their "unreliability". Thousands of Oromo have fled to land inaccessible to the government or army, but they are subject to air raids; in March 1981 the military sprayed flammable chemicals over an Oromo populated valley in southern Ethiopia and jet fighters launched rockets and incendiary devices to light the chemicals. Over 2,000 Oromo were killed, and animals, buildings and crops were destroyed. Over 20,000 Oromo fled the area. *Médecins sans Frontières* claim that 15,000 refugees, forced resettlers and displaced locals, fled to the Sudan, and Cultural Survival estimate that over 600,000 Oromo have fled to neighbouring countries.

In 1982 the government offered alphabetization programmes in five languages, but reportedly 99% of the programmes are in Amharic. There is a compulsory alphabetization campaign in the school vacation during harvest time using pupils as teachers. This has been claimed as one of the causes of starvation in West Wollega.[1] Educational discrimination has meant only a very small minority of Oromo have good jobs in skilled and professional fields. Less than 10% of Oromo children go to school, and all Ethiopian schools function in Amharic. In 1982 Cultural Survival

reported that some refugees they dealt with had fled because they were wanted by the police for teaching Oromo in village schools. A separate report states that in the summer of 1978 Oromo people were afraid to talk in their language in Addis and in 1982 Cultural Survival noted that it was now illegal to speak Oromo for public purposes.

Refugees

The main reasons for the flight of refugees, Oromo and other groups, are: Amharization; large-scale militia conscriptions with loss of strong labour leading to famine; heavy taxes to pay for the war; compulsory agricultural collectivization; displacement of indigenous non-Amharic populace in the south, east and west of the country in order to settle Amharas from the north; legal instability, arbitrary arrests, torture and religious persecution. Cultural Survival estimated in 1982 that more than half of the 2.5 million refugees from Ethiopia were Oromo.

Hundreds of thousands of Oromo refugees have sought refuge in Somalia, Djibouti, Kenya, the Sudan — in the Blue Nile or Upper Nile provinces and also in urban areas — and the Middle East. The major settlement in Sudan is in the Blue Nile. In 1984 famine conditions developed in eastern Oromo regions, but little international aid has reached these areas. There were at least 15,000 Oromo in the Sudan Blue Nile province in 1986. They had mostly fled because of the Ethiopian resettlement programme. In 1984 60,000 new refugees entered Somalia, which had 35 camps with 600,000 to two million refugees; it is estimated that there are 20,000 in Djibouti, 15%-20% of whom are Oromos. By September 1984, 26,900 Ethiopians were repatriated from Djibouti, many unwillingly. There are also a few thousand refugees in Eritrea.

Other minority groups

When the government introduced its resettlement programme, the Anuak, Berta (Barta) and Komo people were also displaced from their traditional lands. The Anuak has an estimated population of 40,000-50,000. They were agriculturalists and fishermen in the fertile Gambelo region of Western Ethiopia, when, at the end of 1979, their land was seized by the government. There were also attempts to draft them into the army. The Anuak fled to the bush

---

[1] Ironically, the alphabetization programme won the UNESCO prize in 1981.

in an attempt to reach Sudan. One report claims that the total Anuak population has halved from a generation ago.

The Berta had an estimated population of 50,000 in 1975. They comprise three language groups and are hoe cultivators of grain. Komo speakers had an estimated population of 7,000 in 1975. They practise family cultivation in Wollega and Illubabor.

(See also *Eritreans*; *Tigrayans*)

Sahelian Nomads

Alternative names: **Tuareg, Fulani and various tribal names**
Location: **across the desert and semi-desert areas of West Africa**
Population: **4 million (est.)**
% of population: **13% (est.) of population of six Sahelian countries**
Religion: **Islam**
Language: **various**

The Sahel is a belt of land which runs for 5,000 kilometers through six mainly French-speaking West African countries; Mauritania, Senegal, Mali, Burkina Faso (formerly Upper Volta), Niger and Chad. Situated between the 10 and 50 centimetre annual rainfall lines, it is a region of semi-arid steppe country bordering the Sahara desert and is inhabited largely by nomadic and semi-nomadic peoples, the best known of which are the Tuareg, a Berber-speaking nomadic group of stock breeders who have dominated much of the Sahara and the Sahel for some 800 years, and the Fulani, who are pastoralists.

The river valleys are occupied for the most part by agriculturalists who have historically traded with the Tuareg, providing corn, gold and slaves in exchange for meat, milk, salt and dates. There is difficulty in estimating the number of nomads inhabiting this region. The total population of these countries is about 31 million but many of these are the agriculturalist peoples living in more fertile irrigated areas. One survey gives the total population of the Sahel as six million of whom two-thirds are nomadic, but all figures need to be treated with caution, especially after the effects of drought, famine, local wars and large-scale migration.

The nomadic economy

The traditional Sahelian economy is based entirely upon nomadic pastoralism. Herd numbers are normally limited by the extent of grazing areas: cattle are concentrated around wells during the dry season and move out to the Sahel grassland once the harshest conditions have abated. Nomads also graze their herds on the stubble of harvested fields and are hunter-gatherers as necessity and opportunity dictate. As the dry season progresses the Tuareg diet depends increasingly upon grain and dates and as the season becomes cooler and wetter milk and meat become the staples. In bad years when the rains fail the Tuareg resort to reserves and loans.

Traditional nomadic and semi-nomadic life involves living in a delicate balance with the land and with water, a balance quite removed from the concepts of commercial cropping, stock marketing and taxation. Even so, famine and drought have always been a recurring problem in the Sahel and until recently nomads have reared as much stock as could be supported in order to protect themselves against a bad year. In good years when stock numbers were high the nomads loaned animals to farmers, reclaiming them in times of hardship.

Colonial rule led to the growth of the coastal towns in West Africa and this in turn led to a rising demand for meat, which was supplied by the pastoralists; however colonial policy also altered the ecological balance of the Sahel by introducing a money economy and also veterinary and medical facilities. Natural checks on population growth were removed and deforestation, overgrazing and insufficient fallowing of cropland gradually followed.

The 1968-1973 drought

Between 1968 and 1973 there was a major drought which caused a high death toll among the nomadic herds (estimates vary from 25%-80% of total numbers). There is evidence to suggest that people died both in the bush and in refugee camps but there are no reliable figures to indicate how many people in all were affected. There was an alarming degree of confusion and contradiction in this matter displayed by government spokesmen and aid agencies, with for example, the Director-General of the UN Agriculture and Food Organization (FAO) announcing that "millions of people are dying" in the Sahel, and an FAO magazine stating that "there's not much famine". The director of the EC's operations in Niger stated that "no-one will die of starvation in Niger" but a 1974 report by the United States Agency for International Development (USAID) estimated that 100,000 had already died and that millions still faced famine.

While the six Sahelian countries clearly suffered an economic disaster of huge proportions, the effects were not felt equally by all citizens but were borne largely by the nomadic cattle-raisers, many of whom lost most of their herds. As the drought worsened the nomads were also obliged to sell more and more animals to buy grain. Aid agencies treated the problem as one of food shortage and provided 250,000 tons of grain. It later transpired that grain was not in short supply but that some governments magnified the effects of the drought in order to obtain grain donations.

In 1974 there were reports that the Malian government was beginning to withhold food from Tuareg nomads in its refugee camps. This may have been a continuation of a dispute begun in the early 1960s, when the Tuareg living in Mali had attempted to ally themselves to Algeria but had been defeated in a violent civil war. The Malian Defence Minister now accused neighbouring governments of harbouring Malian nomads in order to obtain more drought relief. Preparations for war between Mali and Upper Volta began and a national levy on the population of Upper Volta followed. Upper Volta citizens became hostile to the Tuareg nomads who were harassed, beaten and imprisoned by local administrators. One group of Tuareg refugees living in Algeria were returned to Mali at the request of the Malian government.

The rains of 1974 reached record levels and crops were good in that year. The majority of those who survived the drought returned to pastoralism, although with much smaller herds. A few who had been settled in experimental stations remained to raise stock and grow crops. A third group remained in a state of dependency however. In Mauritania over 100,000 refugees settled outside the coastal city of Nouakchott and by the mid 1980s there had been a complete reversal of the situation of 20 years earlier — when three-quarters of children had been born in the desert — to one in which three-quarters were born in the capital. There is little employment for these people and already a second generation has been born, but with no animals to depend on and famine relief continuing there is little incentive for them to return to a nomadic or semi-nomadic existence.

The Sahelian countries began to implement development plans put forward by the UN Office for Sahelian Relief Operations (OSRO) and USAID. Some of these schemes have proved impractical, however, and have had to be abandoned, and the problems involved in maintaining the delicate ecological balance in this region have not been seriously addressed.

The drought of 1984 onwards

The 1968-73 drought was followed by a period of good rainfall and the numbers of livestock in many areas returned to pre-drought levels. However further drought threatened from 1984, after the rains failed in 1983, and governments again appealed for food aid. Between 1975 and 1980 over $7,000 million in aid had been committed to the region by the *Club de Sahel* of western nations, but much was inappropriate and in any case desertification had continued for a number of complex reasons. By 1984 nomads were again threatened, along with agriculturalist peoples. However unlike the previous drought there was now no market for cattle and thus nomads could not even sell their assets in order to survive. By mid-1985 aid workers stated that tens of thousands of Tuareg and Tamashek nomads were starving to death in the remote interior of Mali. An estimated 40%-80% of livestock was lost, the grain harvest had failed and millions of people were reported to have moved into already over-exploited agricultural areas or into towns where there was still no work available. Some national borders were closed to nomads. Traditionally Tuareg structures began to break down as men left to work in the cities of the south and villages were populated only by women and children.

Once again emergency aid flooded in and experimental agricultural projects started in several refugee settlements; unless they take into account the true needs of the nomads these can only serve to upset still further the delicate ecological balance in the Sahel, causing problems of over-population, over-grazing and deforestation. Most aid however did not go to increase food production; one analysis stated that one third of aid went on food imports from abroad, one third to infrastructure and only 4% to grow rainfed crops and 1.5% on tree-planting and soil and water conservation. Drought continued into 1985 and although the situation has since improved somewhat there are also new problems including plagues of locusts, increased fuel needs in the cities and threats to wildlife from big game hunters. Most Sahelian countries have adopted World Bank "restructuring programs" which have cut public spending and helped to further impoverish dependent peoples. Gradually nomadic strategies for dealing with the ecology are being destroyed and the problem of desertification is becoming more severe.

(See also *Chad*; *Mauritania*; *Western Saharans*)

San of the Kalahari

Alternative names: **Bushmen, Masarwa, Basarwa**
Location: **Kalahari desert in Botswana and Southern Namibia**
Population: **Total about 50,000: Botswana about 20,000, of whom less than 1,000 live a hunter-gatherer lifestyle; Namibia 29,000**
% of population: **Botswana 1.8%, Namibia 2-3%**
Religion: **animist**
Language: **Khoi "click languages"**

The San or Bushmen are by tradition hunter-gatherers. The term "Bushmen" was first used by early Dutch settlers in the Cape and still holds emotive connotations, either contemptuous or affectionate in tone; the Bushmen themselves have no generic term to cover all their socio-linguistic groups, but the Hottentot people, who have a similar language, refer to them as the San, or Hunter-Gatherers. The term "Khoisan" refers to the Bushmen-Hottentot group of peoples as a whole. The San speak a tonal, monosyllabic language which includes four "click" consonants. Today San are a tiny minority in both Botswana and Namibia.

The traditional San lifestyle is distinguished by a remarkable adaptation to a hostile environment. The basic social unit is the band, a small group which moves constantly within its own hunting territory and within which all scarce resources are shared. There is no formal system of government amongst the San and no single authoritative figure within the band, all decisions affecting the group being jointly taken after general debate.

Before the seventeenth century, the San inhabited much of the present-day Central and Southern Africa. With the gradual arrival of white colonists during the eighteenth century and the simultaneous arrival of southward-moving Bantu agriculturalists, the San were increasingly deprived of their food sources, and many resorted to stealing Dutch and Bantu cattle. Some became absorbed into the Bantu community whilst others were employed by the white settlers as servants or herdsmen;

most moved to the regions where older San communities had been living for generations.

Botswana

The administration of the British Protectorate of Bechuanaland had shown some concern for the San; an 1885 report had suggested that the San were being enslaved by the Tswana. However it was not until the end of the colonial period that action was taken on their behalf. In 1961 all "tribesmen" were granted the right to hunt in their "tribal areas" whilst land was granted to the majority population, the Tswana but not specifically to the San. In 1963 a Central Kalahari Game Reserve was established partly to provide a reserve for those San who still pursued their traditional lifestyle; the *Bushman Survey Report*, published in 1965, provided the basis for action taken by the independent government of Botswana which succeeded the colonial administration in the following year. Using 1964 government census figures the report estimated that the San population was 24,652 of which some 14,000 lived in or near Bantu villages, about 4,000 lived in the Ghanzi area on European-owned ranches, and only 6,000 still pursued the traditional hunter-gatherer life-style.

Despite being formally recognized as full and equal citizens of the new state, the San had no rights to land, as they had not been classed as tribesmen in the Tribal Lands Act of 1968. A Bushmen Settlement Officer was appointed in 1971 but non-governmental action had the most far-reaching effects in the first half of

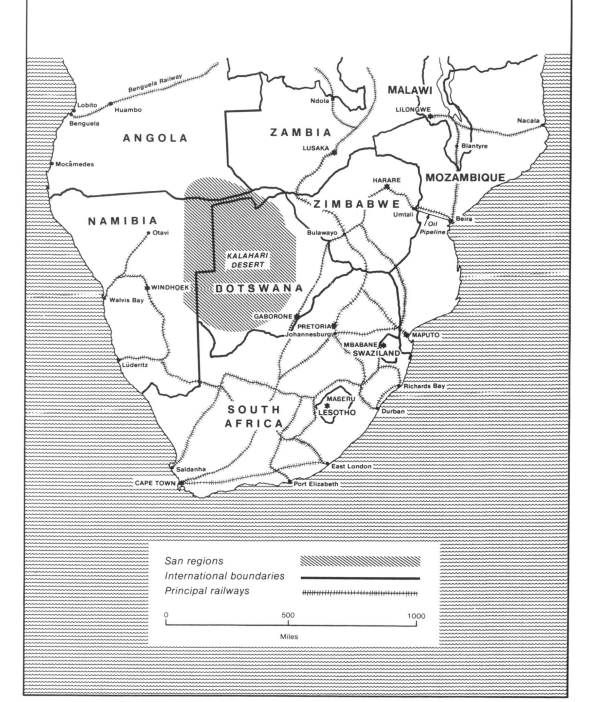

SOUTHERN AFRICA

Benguela Railway

Lobito
Huambo
Benguela
Mocâmedes

ANGOLA

ZAMBIA

Ndola

LUSAKA

MALAWI

LILONGWE

Blantyre

Nacala

MOZAMBIQUE

HARARE

ZIMBABWE

Umtali
Oil
Pipeline
Beira

Bulawayo

NAMIBIA

Otavi

WINDHOEK

Walvis Bay

KALAHARI
DESERT

BOTSWANA

GABORONE

PRETORIA
Johannesburg

MBABANE
SWAZILAND

MAPUTO

Lüderitz

Richards Bay

SOUTH
AFRICA

MASERU
LESOTHO

Durban

Saldanha

CAPE TOWN

Port Elizabeth

East London

San regions

International boundaries

Principal railways

0   500   1000

Miles

the decade. In addition to a Dutch Reformed Church project at D'kar, a school, workshop, shop, reservoir and borehole were established at Bere and the Kalahari Peoples' Fund was set up by a team from Harvard University in 1973. The government reactivated resettlement plans in the Ghanzi district to help those San living in poverty around the farms and villages of the Kalahari by resettling them in underdeveloped parts of the area as stock owners; however in 1971 it was decided that government focus should be on "hunter-gatherers" rather than specifically "bushmen". This was partly because the government wanted to avoid creating ethnic or racial categories similar to those used in the Republic of South Africa, and partly because it did not want to single out one group for special attention at the expense of other groups. A decision was taken to spend government funds only on policies beneficial to "all citizens", and it was agreed that only funds from foreign donors should be expended on projects involving the San. In 1973 funds were granted to several educational projects in Ghanzi District and in 1974 a "Bushmen Development Officer" was appointed.

In the latter half of the 1970s there was a huge increase in expenditure on rural development in Botswana. This had a considerable effect on the traditional San areas: between 1975 and 1978 26 different projects were started which were, as far as possible, under the control of and in tune with the needs of the San. More than 1,000 San children were admitted to schools in this period, boreholes were drilled and boarding hostels opened. In 1978 the Bushmen Development Programme was restructured and became the Remote Area Development Programme (RADP). This heading covered "all those living outside organized village settlements", although emphasis on the San remained.

A 1973 report recommended the expansion of Botswana's beef exports by the opening up of new grazing lands for commercial breeding primarily by large individual owners as well as smallholders. These moved into San territory, forcing the San in some cases to become dependent on Tswana or white ranchers for their livelihood, tending cattle in exchange for food or access to water. It was thought that the San should also own cattle while not necessarily abandoning their hunter-gatherer lifestyle. More water holes were bored to facilitate the herding of cattle by San. The expansion of the beef industry created unforeseen problems for the San. Much of the land intended for commercial grazing was not in fact available, either because

of conservation measures, lack of water or the presence of bands of San; as a result, although numbers of cattle have steadily increased, they are concentrated in the hands of a few large-scale breeders, large areas have been fenced in, and the movement of game and thus the mobility of the San has been affected.

In 1980 a report evaluating the achievements of the RADP recorded a considerable fall in the numbers of San inhabiting the Central Kalahari Game Reserve. Numbers had dropped from the estimated 3,000 to 6,000 of 1965 to only 1,125. By 1982 there were thought to be about 800, and many of those now living in the Kalahari region were of mixed Bantu and Khoisan origin. The report put forward a programme of development involving small scale self-help projects and further provision of water. Apart from those few San still pursuing a hunter-gatherer way of life within the Kalahari reserve area the majority of the San have become sedentarized. Their children attend school, there is access to health care and social services and many are now part of the cash economy. There is greater interaction with the dominant Botswana culture and many San have adopted a Tswana diet and Tswana-style housing.

San were also affected by the drought which affected Botswana from 1981 and many sought employment in towns or construction camps or became dependent on feeding stations. The San diet also suffered from the lack of game as wild animals died; this created international concern and the Botswana government announced that it hoped to extend wildlife protection by relocating over 1,000 San from the Central Kalahari Game Reserve. Critics say that alternative lands for resettlement simply do not exist and this action, if carried out, will result in the end of the traditional San lifestyle in Botswana.

Namibia

Namibia, like South Africa, is organized on the basis of "racial" classification, with a total population of around one million being divided into eight population groups. In 1980 there were estimated to be about 29,000 "Bushmen" in Namibia, some 2%-3% of the total population. Land for grazing and other uses was allocated to the various groups in 1968 and 1969. Under these acts "Bushmanland", the area allotted to the San, was smaller than that which they had previously occupied, and whereas plans existed for limited rights of self-government for the other groups, such plans were not envisaged for the San. In 1976 the Advisory Board for Bushmen was established and San representatives participated in South African sponsored talks on the future of the territory.

Although "Bushmanland" has not played any great part in the guerrilla war in Namibia, the San have been recruited as soldiers by the South African Defence Forces (SADF). The "Bushman" unit, established in 1974, is the oldest of the ethnic units, with two battalions in the South West Africa Territory Force (SWATF). About 5,000 San soldiers and their families are based at the Omega military base, thus becoming completely dependent on the army for facilities. One report stated that while engaged in military service "Bushmen" have been taught basic hygiene, schools have been built and health services have been established; others see the relationship between armed forces and the San as one of exploitation. Plans for the establishment of a nature reserve of about 6,000 square kilometres put forward by the South-African dominated government in

1978 have also been heavily criticized by anthropologists as leading to the complete demise of the San as a viable community. The plans would affect the 200 Juwasi who have been involved in a development project aimed at creating a viable mixed economy.

The military presence has apparently encouraged the San in their feelings of hostility towards the majority Ovambos and assumed that in the event of a victory of the South West African Peoples' Organization (SWAPO) any freely elected government would represent Ovambo needs at the expense of minority groups such as the San. Whatever the future for the San in Namibia it seems certain that if internationally supervised elections do result in SWAPO being elected, the present ethnic-based system would be abolished and the position of the San would change. Under such circumstances similar issues to those being faced in Botswana might well be raised.

Southern Sudan

Name: **Southerners**
Alternative names: **Equatorians (pol.), various ethnic groups: Dinkas, Nuers, Anuaks, Shilluks, Equatorians, Latukas, Taposas, Turkanas, Moru, Madi, Azande**
Location: **southern area of Sudan, in towns and camps in north and central Sudan; in exile, especially in Ethiopia**
Population: **in total about six million**
% of population: **about 28%**
Religion: **animist, Christian**
Language: **various indigenous languages, English (lingua franca)**

"Southerners" is a general name given to the varied peoples who live in the southern area of Sudan, about one third of Africa's largest country. Although the current war is generally described as a conflict between the "Arab Muslim" north and the "Christian and animist" south, this is misleading and simplistic. Sudan is a nation of several hundred ethnic and religious groups and sub-groups and the concept of a north-south divide in the Sudan is a relatively recent one.

The peoples of the southern third of Sudan divide into four main linguistic groups as follows: (i) the Western Nilotes, who are the largest linguistic group. The major tribes are the Dinka, Nuer, Anuak and Shilluk and they inhabit the northern and central area of southern Sudan; (ii) the Eastern Nilotes, often referred to as Equatorians, who include the Bari-speakers, Latuka, Taposa and Turkana, and who inhabit the southern regions bordering East Africa; (iii)

the Central Sudanic group, who include the Moru and Madi, and (iv) the Azande, who are related to West African peoples.

The colonial period

There was no north-south division in the area of modern Sudan before the nineteenth century when, after the Turco-Egyptian conquest of Sudan in 1821-23, Egyptian forces moved south into the region and opened it up to traders. During the seventeenth and eighteenth centuries the northern regions of the Sudan had been subject to strong Islamic influence and some rulers in the region had adopted an Arab identity. These Muslim leaders expanded their authority southward and conducted raids to provide slaves for their armies and for the international slave market. In the wake of the Egyptian forces followed European and Sudanese merchants, and

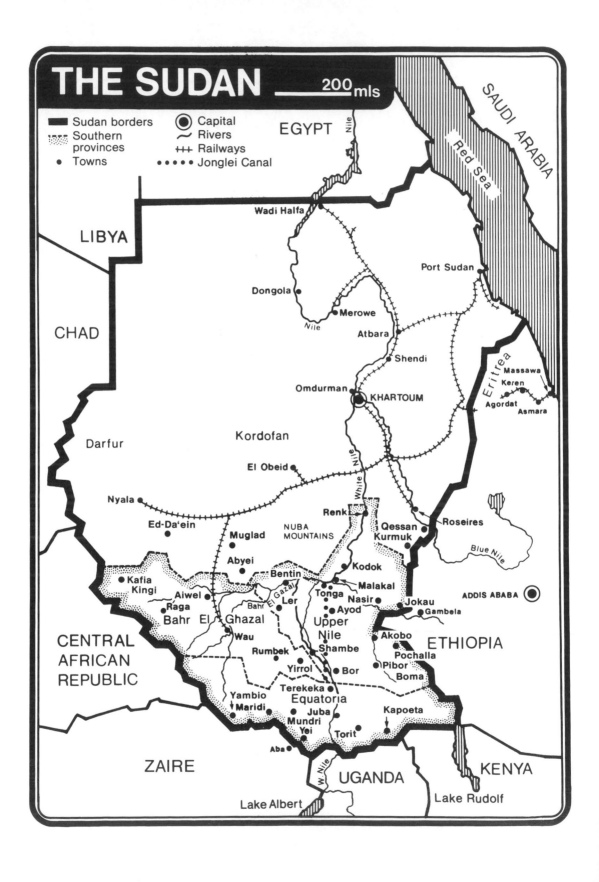

THE SUDAN

200 mls

- ▬ Sudan borders
- ⠿ Southern provinces
- • Towns
- ◉ Capital
- ∿ Rivers
- +++ Railways
- •••• Jonglei Canal

EGYPT

SAUDI ARABIA

Red Sea

LIBYA

CHAD

Wadi Halfa

Port Sudan

Dongola

Merowe

Nile

Atbara

Shendi

Massawa

Keren

Omdurman

KHARTOUM

Eritrea

Agordat

Asmara

Darfur

Kordofan

El Obeid

Nyala

Renk

White Nile

Qessan

Kurmuk

Roseires

Ed-Da'ein

NUBA MOUNTAINS

Muglad

Abyei

Kodok

Bentin

Blue Nile

ADDIS ABABA ◉

Kafia Kingi

Aiwel

Raga

Bahr El Ghazal

Bahr El Gazal

Ler

Tonga

Nasir

Malakal

Jokau

Gambela

Wau

Upper Nile

Ayod

Akobo

ETHIOPIA

CENTRAL AFRICAN REPUBLIC

Rumbek

Shambe

Pochalla

Pibor

Yirrol

Bor

Boma

Yambio

Maridi

Terekeka

Equatoria

Juba

Mundri

Yei

Torit

Kapoeta

Aba

ZAIRE

W. Nile

UGANDA

KENYA

Lake Rudolf

Lake Albert

itinerant northern traders who captured slaves for the Egyptian territories and northern Sudan. This trade in slaves destroyed the independence of the southern Sudanese people who, with no internal cultural or political unity, were unable to resist the threat posed by the Muslim state to the north.

The Anglo-Egyptian Condominium, which came into force in 1898, accepted the by now traditional definition of the south as a single region. A policy of devolution was introduced and rural areas were administered by tribal leaders who ordered internal affairs according to traditional law, guided by British officials. This system of administration effectively halted the southward movement of Islam, since the northern rural communities followed a combination of local custom and Islamic law (*Shari'a*), and the two administrative structures necessarily developed along different lines.

Although the British-run administrative system in the south did emphasize tribal values, hence causing the minimum of disruption to the way of life, it failed to prepare the people of the region for independence. Education was neglected, economic development severely restricted, and commerce left under the control of northern Sudanese merchants and companies. While regional exploitation had been halted, the inequalities caused by the lack of regional development had increased. The south now lacked an educated elite capable of administering the country after independence. Awareness of this problem led southern leaders to propose first a delay in independence and, when that failed, a federal system of government for the entire country. This option too was rejected in 1958 and the only recourse left to the south appeared to be a call for secession.

The first civil war 1955-72

In August 1955 a series of mutinies on the part of southern police and troops of the Equatorial Corps marked the start of the first civil war, which continued until 1972. Independence followed five months later on January 1, 1956. After independence Muslim sectarian domination in the north and weak political organization in the south led to the formation in 1958 of a military government which ruled with civilian assistance until 1964. During this time several guerrilla armies were formed, dedicated to fighting for self-determination in the south.

Although southern Muslims had been among the earliest supporters of southern opposition to Khartoum, northern leaders believed this sup-

port to be the result of foreign interference, and they initiated changes designed to lessen foreign influence in the south. Arabic was introduced as the administrative and educational language, Christian missionaries were expelled from the south and Friday replaced Sunday as the weekly day of rest. The British administration had not in fact placed much emphasis upon Christian education in the Sudan, believing it to be disruptive of tribal life. The effect of these new measures now actually increased the popularity of Christianity in the region, creating a feeling of southern Sudanese unity in the face of northern hegemony.

In 1964 general discontent brought about a return to parliamentary politics, but an all-party Round Table Conference held in the following year failed to reach a solution to the southern problem. In the north, the Democratic Unionist Party (DUP) and the Umma Party were amongst those calling for a unitary national government without southern regional government, and they also joined another group, the Muslim Brothers, in their call for an Islamic state. The 1968 Constituent Assembly, elected to draft a permanent Constitution, failed to reach agreement on these points.

By 1969 the civil war had spread to all three southern provinces. On 25 May 1969 a military coup led by Colonel Nimeiri replaced the civilian government. The Constituent Assembly was dissolved and political parties banned. A secular, socialist State was declared, with regional autonomy proposed for the south. In 1971 negotiations began between the government and the Southern Sudan Liberation Movement (SSLM) which had been formed in the previous year.

The Addis Ababa Agreement

The war ended in March 1972 with the Addis Ababa Agreement which led to the formation of regional government in the south and guaranteed its autonomy. The agreement provided for a single southern region with a regional Assembly which had legislative and revenue powers and which elected a President for its own High Executive Council (HEC), responsible for internal administration and security. The Agreement also provided for the absorption of some of the guerrillas into the national police, army and prison service. But neither the members of the Sudan government of the day or the main guerrilla movement were involved in the negotiations and this undermined its future. In practice government policy was frequently decided in Khartoum however, without reference to the regional government, particularly in the fields of education and economic planning, and regional autonomy was severely curtailed by financial dependence.

Internal divisions in the south

Although the first government, under the leadership of Abel Alier, did make progress in establishing an administrative and governmental structure, many felt that progress was not rapid enough. This led to a smooth transfer of power in 1978 when Joseph Lagu was elected President of the National Assembly. Lagu was ineffective as a government leader, however. Despite his powers of oratory he lacked administrative and political skills and antagonized many of his own supporters. President Nimeiri was asked to dissolve the regional Assembly which he did, appointing an interim regional government. In 1980 a new Assembly returned Alier to office. A growing rift was now apparent between the regional government and the politicians of the Equatoria region and this, combined with a general feeling of unrest in the south, ultimately led to the outbreak of the second civil war.

In addition to problems relating to administration and development, southern leaders were concerned about several major border disputes. Under the Addis Ababa Agreement mineral-rich Kafia Kingi district was to have been returned to the south and the inhabitants of border areas allowed to decide whether they wanted to be included in the southern or northern parts of the country. These stipulations had not so far been met, and central government had taken the decision to site the nation's first oil refinery in the north and not in the south where most of the nation's oilfields are.

The question of Equatoria had now become a pressing issue. The people of that region are mostly agriculturalists. They had been subject to British administration long before the Western Nilotes, who inhabit a seasonally swampy area inaccessible to British administrators; as a result such educational and economic development as there was in the Sudan under British administration had been mainly concentrated in Equatoria. Equatoria had provided the impetus for the 1955 mutiny and Equatorians had controlled the Nilotic pastoralists in other parts of the south.

The balance had altered after the civil war, however. During the war Equatorians had crossed the border and joined related peoples outside the Sudan, particularly those in Uganda, where they were welcomed into Idi Amin's army and administration. In their absence from the Sudan, increasing numbers of Nilotic people had entered the guerrilla forces. Many had also joined the Anyanya movement, and when that party was absorbed into the national army in 1972 the number of Nilotic people in the forces became far greater than it had been in 1955. Although many exiled Equatorians elected to remain abroad, a substantial number returned to the Sudan after the fall of Amin in 1979. On their return they found a majority Nilotic population and few employment opportunities, and many embarked upon an anti-Nilotic campaign similar to that previously waged in Uganda.

Equatorians were divided over the issue of regional autonomy, which had been proposed by central government; however in 1981 Nimeiri dissolved both national and regional Assemblies, appointed an interim government and held new national and regional elections on the issue of further regionalization. The southern constituencies rejected division by a two to one majority and Nimeiri announced that elections would now be held within the framework of a united region.

The second civil war

Between 1972-77 several units mutinied and escaped into Ethiopia where they joined forces with small groups opposing the Addis Ababa Agreement. In 1976 the Ethiopian government protested to Nimeiri about the Sudan's support for Eritrean and anti-Dergue forces and threatened to aid the Sudanese dissenters if this support did not stop; however as the Arab states, still closely linked to the Sudan, were providing strong backing to the Eritreans, Nimeiri could not risk pursuing a contrary policy; as a result Ethiopia began to aid anti-Nimeiri groups. In 1982 more northern soldiers were sent to the south and by early 1983 there was armed conflict in many parts of the region.

The Sudan Peoples' Liberation Army (SPLA) and its political wing, the Sudan Peoples' Liberation Movement (SPLM), were formed in 1983 by mutinous army units and Anyanya II groups in Ethiopia. Fighting broke out between the SPLA/SPLM and breakaway groups, whose members favoured complete secession rather than a restructuring of the south. The dissidents, mostly Nuer and members of Anyanya II, were defeated, and their leaders killed in the fighting.

Regionalization did not prove successful in Equatoria and after the announcement of *Shari'a* law in 1983 there was the constant Islamic threat from the north. The economy was in ruins, famine was becoming a major problem, there was corruption within the government and the war continued in the south. All these factors, together with an increasingly severe application of *Shari'a* law in the north, finally brought about the fall of Nimeiri in April 1985.

A Transitional Military Council was formed and a civilian cabinet appointed. The 1973 Permanent Constitution was abolished but *Shari'a* law was retained without its harsher punishment laws. The SPLA refused to recognize the council but in 1986 they agreed to a meeting with the National Alliance, a group of trade unions and political parties which together had brought about Nimeiri's removal. At this meeting eight points were agreed, including proposals that the state of emergency and all laws restricting freedom be lifted and an effective ceasefire established, that regional government be recognized by the council, which should agree to dissolve itself in favour of an interim government including the SPLA/SPLM, that all military pacts with other countries should cease, and a constitutional conference be convened to discuss major points of disagreement between the parties.

In 1986 elections were held and a Muslim coalition government formed in Khartoum under the leadership of Sadiq al-Mahdi. The strength of southern opinion had forced Sadiq to accept in principle the notion of reunification of the south, but this decision was criticized by Islamic parties favouring an economically weak and dependent south and, by implication, the expansion of Islam into these non-Muslim areas.

Effects of the war

Past associations of the south with "paganism", slavery and servility persist in the minds of many northerners and it is partly for this reason that southern opposition to *Shari'a* law is deeply felt. It is feared that the expansion of Islam into the south will threaten the cultural traditions and values associated with tribal religions, and that racial antagonism on the part of the northern Muslims will place southerners in an inferior position in their own land.

In 1986 the SPLA base was moved from Ethiopia to the Boma plateau overlooking Eastern Equatoria and operations were extended into the Blue Nile and Kordofan provinces. Despite some army successes the SPLA had by early 1988 captured much of the region along the Ethiopian border and also a large area in the centre of the country. Yet the fighting between the forces of the government and the SPLA has produced relatively few casualties while civilian deaths have been high. The Khartoum government

has made increasing use of Arab militias in their fight against the SPLA, although in practice it is Dinka civilians who are the main victims. These militias operate for the most part independently of the army and are provided with arms and ammunition but are unpaid. There have been reports of looting and slave-trading, mainly directed at Dinka civilians in Kordofan and Darfur provinces. In March 1987 over 1,000 Dinka and other southern civilians were massacred by Arab militias from the Rizeigat ethnic group in southern Darfur. Wholesale massacres took place in Wau in August and September 1987, resulting in the deaths of thousands of Dinkas. In its turn the SPLA is reported to have encouraged rival tribal militias to aid their cause.

The activities of the militias have greatly contributed to the numbers of homeless and to the destruction of food supplies in the south. Both army and SPLA units have requisitioned food from civilians and independent armed groups are also active, capturing relief food outside major towns. By the end of 1988 it was reported that at least one quarter of a million people in the south had died of starvation. Three million, perhaps half the population of the south, had fled or had been internally displaced. Over 300,000 refugees had fled to Ethiopia, a large proportion being young Dinka men trying to escape conscription into the SPLA. At least one million refugees lived in makeshift camps on the outskirts of Khartoum; these were the chief victims of the disastrous flood of August 1988. The government in Khartoum ignored and sometimes denied the scale of the problem, leading to allegations of genocide against southerners. Attempts by international agencies to get food aid to the south largely failed in 1988.

Worldwide publicity at the scale of the disaster in the south and diplomatic pressure from the US among others led to increasing pressure on both the government and the SPLA to begin peace talks. The Democratic Unionist Party (DUP), one of three parties in the government coalition, began to make contact with the SPLA after consultation with the Prime Minister, and on 16 November a peace agreement was signed between John Garang of the SPLA and the DUP. The agreement provided for a constitutional conference, the suspension of the state of emergency (imposed in 1985) as a prelude to a ceasefire, and of the imposition of Islamic law. The last in particular fuelled the anger of the National Islamic Movement (NIM) which had been brought into the government coalition in May; its members took to the streets of Khartoum, indiscriminately attacking southerners. The Prime Minister vacillated, on the one hand indicating that he was in favour of concessions for peace, but on the other procrastinating in bringing the accord before parliament. At the last moment he refused to sign it and the DUP left the coalition while the Umma Party and the NIM continued in government. The war in the south continued.

By this stage the government of Sadiq al-Mahdi was losing much of its support in the north, there were riots over food prices at the end of the year, and in early 1989 open talk of an army coup. There was a further attempt in March 1989 by Sadiq al-Mahdi to renew negotiations with the SPLA, but again the NIM and the *Shari'a* issue proved to be stumbling blocks and there was further delay, although one round of talks with the SPLA was held. It was therefore no surprise when a successful military coup took place in Khartoum on June 30, 1989 and General el-Beshir and a 15-member junta took power.

The General declared that all previous peace efforts were null and void and although there were several announcements to the effect that fresh negotiations would take place, this in fact had not begun by August 1989. Meanwhile the grip of the SPLA on the south had tightened with the fall of the government garrison at Torit in July 1989, resulting in 30,000 refugees entering Uganda in search of food and sanctuary.

The immediate future is unclear. By August 1989 there had been no progress in lifting the state of emergency, implementing a ceasefire or ending the war. Although prompt action by relief agencies, aided by international pressure on both government and rebels to allow food supplies into war zones, has prevented famine on the same scale as in 1988, the situation is effectively at a stalemate. The northern government appears to be still committed to an Islamic state, and until this issue is resolved there is unlikely to be peace in the Sudan.

Tigrayans

Location: **Tigray province, parts of Wollo and Bergemir provinces, northern Ethiopia**
Population: **about 5 million**
% of population: **about 12%**
Religion: **Christian, Muslim**
Language: **Tigrinya, minority languages**

The Tigrayans are the chief inhabitants of Tigray province in Northern Ethiopia and in some adjoining areas in Wollo and Bergemir provinces. Seventy per cent of its estimated population of five million are Christians, members of the Ethiopian Orthodox Church, while one-and-a-half million people are Muslims. Eighty per cent of the population speak Tigrinya and the remainder is made up of minority groups such as the Afar, Agew, Saho and Kunama. Most Tigrayans are peasant farmers.

Background and history

Tigray is made up of a central highland plateau bordered on the east and west by lowland plains. The highland region has the highest population density in the country owing to its favourable climate, although the western plains have a more fertile soil. The eastern region is the site of the Danakil depression, one of the hottest places on earth. It is dry and infertile and supports only small numbers of nomadic and semi-nomadic pastoralists. Tigray has frequently undergone catastrophic drought, famine and locust plagues,

the effects of which have been exacerbated by economic underdevelopment, an oppressive land tenure system and the lack of an administrative infrastructure.

Tigray has been under the control of various dynasties since the founding of the first Axumite empire in the first century AD. An Amhara emperor led a successful campaign against the Italian invasion of 1896; however the cost of the campaign was high and the country was left in a poor economic state which deteriorated further after the accession of the new Amhara emperor, Haile Selassie in 1930. A Tigrayan National Movement composed of peasant armies revolted in 1943 both against the emperor's soldiers garrisoned throughout the country and the Tigrayan feudal lords who held taxation rights over much of the cultivated land. The rebellion was halted with the help of British warplanes, and soon after thousands of people living in the southern and western regions were dispossessed of their land and crippling taxes were imposed. Under Haile Selassie's rule Tigray was administered by Tigrayan feudal lords although few Tigrayans held government office.

War with the Dergue

The Tigrayan National Organization (TNO) was formed in the early 1970s with the aim of improving literacy and promoting political debate, and it also played a part in bringing about the overthrow of the Emperor in 1974. With the ascendance of the new military regime, the Dergue, the TNO opposed military rule, especially after it became clear that national self-determination would not be granted to Tigrayans and after the use of Amharic, declared the official language of Tigray in 1958, was retained by the predominantly Amhara Ethiopian government and publications in Tigrinya were suppressed.

In 1975 the Tigray People's Liberation Front (TPLF) was formed. Its objective was self-determination for the Tigrayan people. Its ideology had much in common with that of the Eritrean People's Liberation Front (EPLF); however whereas the EPLF is fighting an anti-colonial battle with Eritrean independence as it goal, the TPLF sees its struggle as one of national liberation against an undemocratic central regime which has allowed their country to stagnate economically. Like the EPLF, the Tigrayan movement recognized the importance of major change for the most oppressed groups in society: the landless, poor peasants and women.

The Ethiopian government launched a series of military campaigns in Tigray. The sixth such campaign, waged in 1980-81, was aimed at disrupting agricultural production and the economy of the densely populated central region. Government troops were heavily armed and were successful in their aim; however the major damage done to vast areas of cropland at a time of prevailing famine had the effect of causing an upsurge of popular support for the TPLF, and by 1983 it controlled about 85% of Tigrayan countryside and was administering several sizeable towns. Government troops remained in urban garrisons and government convoys were heavily protected. Despite the successes of the TPLF many people fled over the border into neighbouring Sudan, most of them during the period of the "Red Terror", when thousands of young people were shot or tortured on suspicion of having opposed the military regime.

The TPLF has gained the active support and participation of the majority of the Tigrayan population. Land reforms were implemented and a campaign to promote women's interests was mounted. The Relief Society of Tigray (REST) has undertaken education, health, agricultural, craft and resettlement programmes and by 1983 was administering over 40 schools, over 35 clinics, 70 mobile medical teams, eight resettlement schemes and a nationwide literacy programme.

Drought and famine

The drought from 1983 in northern Ethiopia was equal to that of 1970-73 in which an estimated 200,000 people died in Tigray and northern Wollo province. According to REST officials, in early 1983 two million people were living in drought-affected areas under the TPLF's control, of which at least 1.2 million were in urgent need of assistance. There was a large-scale displacement of people and, by February 1983, 400,000 had arrived in western Tigray. REST launched an appeal for food supplies and set up reception centres and collection points for food. Because of the slowness and limited amounts of aid these were later disbanded and the affected people distributed to villages in the west. There were logistic problems also with transport. Tigray was frequently unable to have access to food supplies donated by Western governments and agencies, most of which went through the Addis Ababa regime, which also attempted to deal with the famine by resettlement schemes to send people from the north to the relatively unpopulated areas in the south. There were allegations that the resettlement programme aimed to depopulate the rebellious northern areas, including Tigray, and there were well attested reports of forced resettlement and human rights abuses both during the movement of people and in camps in the south. Some Tigrayans managed to escape from the camps, and after a hazardous journey, to reach the Sudan. Despite the devastating effects of the drought of 1983-5, in which hundreds of thousands of people died throughout Ethiopia, the TPLF retained its support in Tigray and continued the war against the Dergue.

From early 1988 fighting intensified, leading to large scale casualties. By the end of May the TPLF had gained control of most of Tigray including the historic centre of Axum and the area surrounding the regional capital of Makelle. Government forces counter-attacked, beginning a ruthless aerial bombardment of the main TPLF towns, including the use of napalm. This bombing seriously disrupted economic activity, as towns, villages and fields had to be evacuated during the day, and killed and injured large numbers of civilians. But the TPLF remained largely intact and confident and in early 1989, acting in co-ordination with forces in Eritrea and Afar areas, decisively defeated Ethiopian government forces, taking the strategic garrison at Endaselassie, and Makelle. The TPLF claimed that 26,000 government troops had been killed, wounded or captured.

There was now intense pressure on the Addis Ababa regime, by the USSR among others, to make peace with the Tigrayans and Eritreans. There was internal disaffection also which resulted in an attempted coup by military officers in May. On June 5 the government announced that it would be prepared to enter into unconditional negotiations with the TPLF. In March the TPLF had issued an eight-point peace plan as a basis of discussion. Among other things it proposed an immediate ceasefire as soon as a peace agreement was reached, restoration of democratic rights and the establishment of a provisional government made up of all political organizations. It also insisted that a mediator or third party should be present at the talks. However, no talks took place and by September 1989 the TPLF and allied forces were advancing rapidly southwards through Gondar and Wollo provinces towards Addis Ababa.

(See also *Eritreans*; *Falashas of Ethiopia*; *Oromo of Ethiopia*)

Uganda

Population: **14.3 million (est. 1988)**
% of population: **two-thirds of population are Bantu-speakers from various ethnic groups; remainder are Nilotic and Central Sudanic speakers from the north**
Religion: **Christian (Catholic, Anglican), Muslim, animist**
Languages: **three main groups: Bantu, Nilotic, Central-Sudanic plus colonial link language of English**

Uganda, a small landlocked nation in Eastern Africa, contains over 40 ethnic groups, speaking many languages. It is literally a nation of minorities as no one group has a majority of the population, although the various Bantu-speaking peoples account for about two-thirds of the population. The greatest differences and therefore conflicts have been between southerners (mainly Bantu speakers) and northerners (mainly Nilotic speakers). From the time of the monopoly of power of the first Obote regime from 1966 to the military victory by Museveni's NRA in early 1986 the majority southerners were dominated by northerners, especially through the army. Ethnic conflict since independence, whether under Amin, Obote, Museveni or the short-lived transitional regimes, has been persistent and tragic.

Uganda encompasses peoples of three distinctive language families, the Bantu; Nilotic; and Central Sudanic. Bantu-speakers, who are primarily but not exclusively agricultural, are found in the south, south-east and west of Uganda. Together they constitute about two-thirds of the population and occupy about half the land area. They can be divided into three main types: (i) centralized, hierarchical societies, once governed by royal families, These are the Baganda,[1] Banyankole, Banyoro, and Batoro; (ii) less centralized societies, whose social organization varies from local chieftainships to extended family units. These include the Basoga, Bagisu, Bagwere, Banyoli, Basamia and Bagwe in the south-east; the Bakiga in the south-west; and the Baamba and Bakonjo in the west; and (iii) specialized pastoralists, the Bahima and the Batutsi. Both groups established supremacy over the agriculturalists in the areas where they settled — the Bairu and the Bahutu respectively. Bahima and Bairu are collectively termed the Banyankole; the Batutsi and Bahutu[2] are known as the Banyarwanda.

Nilotic-speakers are in two main groups: (i) Western Nilotes from the north-west, related to the Kenyan Luo. They are mixed agriculturalists, organized in chiefdoms. They include the Acholi, Langi, Alur and Jonam; and (ii) Southern Nilotes from the east, related to the Kenyan Turkana,

---

[1]Baganda refers to the ethnic group; Buganda to the region; Muganda to an individual; Luganda to the language. The same set of prefixes applies to the other Bantu groups.
[2]The Tutsi and Hutu are the major ethnic groups in Rwanda and Burundi, where a similar hierarchical relationship exists between the two, which has led to conflict in both countries. See *Hutu and Tutsi of Burundi*.

Uganda

originally pastoralists, with a social organization based on clans and age sets. They include the Karamojong and Iteso.

Central Sudanic-speakers occupy the north of West Nile province and also extend across the border into Sudan and Zaire. They are agricultural peoples with a non-hierarchical social organization. They include the Lugbara, Kakwa and Madi.

Colonial history

British exploration and missionary work in the area of present day Uganda began in the latter half of the nineteenth century. There was much competition for converts and political power between Catholic and Protestant missionaries and Muslims, especially at the court of the most powerful local ruler the Kabaka (or king) of Buganda. The British East African Company was formed subsequent to the Berlin Conference of 1884-5 to administer an area roughly that of present-day Uganda, and attempted to consolidate the Protestant faction. There followed a tightening of British control; in 1893 a British Protectorate, in 1897, the deposition of the then Kabaka and his replacement by a British-dominated regency, and in 1900 rccognition of the special position of Buganda within the Ugandan Protectorate.

British colonial policy emphasized ethnic divisions. The Native Authority Ordinance of 1919 "exported" the Buganda model, together with Buganda civil servants, to other regions, while the Local Government Ordinance of 1949 drew provincial boundaries to include only one ethnic group, with a few exceptions, with overall government still in British hands. The introduction of cash crops benefited the peoples from the fertile southern areas, while the less developed North provided the main source of recruits to the colonial prisons, army and police. The Bantu peoples and especially the Baganda benefited most from western-style missionary education and provided the bulk of the civil service. They tended to look down on the "backward" Nilotic and Central Sudanic peoples.

The years leading to internal self-government in March 1962 and independence in October 1962 were stormy ones. The British administration deported the Kabaka after he refused to reform the *Lukiiko* (traditional forum) and although the Kabaka later agreed to change, this was resented by the largely Catholic Baganda peasantry. Political parties were formed, chiefly the Democratic Party (DP), which gained its main support from Catholic Bagandas, its main rival the Uganda People's Congress (UPC), lead by Apollo Milton Obote, and the *Kabaka Yekka* (King Alone Party — KY) the main support of the king and Bugandan autonomy. The first government of independent Uganda was a coalition between the UPC and the KY, with Obote as Prime Minister, and, a year later, the Kabaka as President.

The first Obote regime (1962-1971)

Without traditional authority, Obote was forced to manoeuvre to maintain his power. In the early years there were reports of discrimination against Muslims and Catholics in public office, but this was overshadowed by the growing rift between Obote and the Kabaka and KY. The coalition was dissolved in 1964 but Obote continued in power with the support of political factions. In 1966 the "Buganda crisis" resulted in Obote ordering the Army Chief-of-Staff Colonel Idi Amin to attack the Kabaka's palace. Many hundreds died in the attack and the Kabaka fled into exile. Buganda was placed under a State of Emergency which lasted until 1971, while in 1967 Obote declared Uganda a Republic and abolished the special status of the Buganda kingdom. Obote's continuing political repression of political opponents and pursuance of State-directed economic policies, which were intensely disliked by the Bantu peoples, led to opposition coalescing around the most viable alternative, the army commander Amin, who had been actively recruiting Central Sudanics from his own area of the West Nile into the Army in preference to the Nilotics favoured by Obote. In January 1971, while Obote was at the Commonwealth Conference in Singapore, Amin staged a military coup, which was greeted with widespread Baganda support.

The Amin regime (1971-1979)

Amin began his regime with popular moves such as the lifting of the State of Emergency, the release of political prisoners, and the proper burial of the Kabaka who had died in exile: yet within a few months he had suspended all democratic rights, the army had been given dictatorial powers and Amin became both President (later "President for Life") and Army Chief. His "Africanization" programme of 1972 resulted in the expulsion of the Asian trading community (see *Asians of East and Central Africa*). In the eight years of the Amin dictatorship, between 100,000 and 500,000 Ugandans lost their lives or "disappeared". Among them were very large numbers of the Nilotic speakers, especially the Langi and Acholi. These were massacred in the aftermath of the coup, after the abortive invasion by Nilotic exiles of 1972, after the arrest and murder of an Acholi Archbishop in 1977, and during Amin's regular purges of the army.

The resulting economic and administrative chaos led to opposition from within the army, from which Amin attempted to divert attention by invading Tanzania. The Tanzanian army, with the assistance of an Ugandan National Liberation Army (UNLA) of exiles, counterattacked. There were several Ugandan fighting groups already involved in warfare inside the country, notably *Kikosi Malumu* (KM) of Obote and FRONESA of Yoweri Museveni. The political initiative came from the Unity Conference held at Moshi in March 1979, which resulted in the formation of the Uganda National Liberation Front (UNLF). Its programme was based on national unity, the avoidance of ethnic, religious and political divisions, and the promise to hold national elections within two years. The elected Chairman was Yusufu Lule, from Buganda. When Kampala fell on April 11, 1979 it was the UNLF which took power, with Lule as President.

The second Obote regime (1979-85)

Lule was President for only two months before being replaced by Godfrey Binaisa. Binaisa from Buganda, was at first seen as a supporter of Obote but seemed to follow an independent course, expanding the National Consultive Council (NCC) and encouraging UNLF grass-roots organization. But his own position was weak and the militias which made up the UNLA grew at a rapid rate, especially the KM and FRONASA. His downfall came with a decision of the UNLF in April 1980 to limit the December elections to individual rather than party candidates. Binaisa faced particular opposition from Major-General Tito Okello and Brigadier David Oyite-Ojok and they were leading figures in the coup of May 1980, which resulted not only in the arrest and incarceration of Binaisa but the erosion of democratic rule. The new interim leader was Paulo Muwanga, a supporter of Obote. In the following months the position of the UPC was consolidated.

The 1980 elections, widely regarded by many independent observers as intimidating and fraudulent, resulted in a victory for the UPC. Obote became President and appointed Paulo Muwanga as Vice-President and Defence Minister. Of 50 posts in the cabinet, 42 went to Protestants.

After the elections the scene was set for confrontation. A number of guerrilla groups and opposition parties in exile were formed to fight the UNLA and UPC. They included the Uganda National Rescue Front (UNRF), composed of Amin supporters, and based in the West Nile region; the National Resistance Army (NRA) of Yoweri Museveni, based in areas of Buganda and with largely Bantu support, and the Uganda Freedom Movement (UFM), based around Kampala, along with a number of other smaller groups. Obote and the UPC during these years depended heavily on the support of the UNLA, by now dominated by Acholi, Langi and Iteso officers and troops. One of its features was increasing rivalry between the Acholis, the largest single group in the army, and the Langis and Iteso — rivalries which resulted in assassination attempts, arrests and attacks. Even more serious was the increasing indiscipline of the many factions within the UNLA, which resulted in indiscriminate attacks on and brutal mass killings of civilians, especially of Bantus and ethnic groups who were considered to have been supporters of Amin.

The second Obote period was marked then by the same series of killings, arrests, tortures and "disappearances" as the Amin regime. Unlike under Amin however there was little knowledge or publicity given to these massive violations of human rights. There are understandably no accurate figures for the numbers killed, but the numbers might range between 100,000 and 500,000 from 1981 to 1985, similar to those of the Amin period. Some of the main campaigns and targets of military violence were the following:

West Nile: Both Lule and Binaisa had prevented Acholi troops from entering the West Nile area, the power base of Amin. After Binaisa's overthrow Muwanga transferred the Tanzanian troops based there and replaced them by UNLA troops from Kitgum (Acholi) and Apac (Langi). After attacks by ex-Amin supporters these troops began to exact revenge upon the peoples of the area, principally the Kakwa, Lugbara and Madi, firstly in August 1980 and later in October 1980, resulting in the deaths of 5,000 to 30,000 civilians. An attack in February-March 1981 by the Acholi militia on East Madi resulted in an exodus of 50,000 refugees to UNRF areas. UNLA mutiny in June 1981, and killings by the retreating troops, led to further deaths. UNRF guerrillas who held most of the northern area of West Nile, and a group of ex-Amin soldiers from Zaire, also harassed civilians and from March 1982 many thousands began crossing the borders to refugee camps in the Sudan. By mid-1983 there were 60,000 refugees in Zaire and over 200,000 in Sudan.

The "Chasing" of the Banyarwanda: In September 1982 began the forcible evictions from Ankole in the south-west of Uganda of three related ethnic groups, the Batutsi and Bahutu — known collectively as the Banyarwanda — and the Bahima. The Banyarwanda had commenced migration from Rwanda and Burundi from the nineteenth century but most were Ugandan citizens, while the Bahima originated from Uganda. The three groups were mainly Catholics and politically aligned to the Democratic Party. In the days that followed over 75,000 people were collectively evicted from their homes, 35,000 took refuge in existing UNHCR camps in the south of Ankole and another 40,000 fled to Rwanda. In December 1983 a further 20,000 Banyarwanda were evicted from Rakai and Masaka districts. The decision to evict this group appears to have been made by certain UPC ministers.

The Suppression of the Baganda: The heartland of the Baganda peoples, especially that known as the Luwero Triangle, north and west of Kampala, was a natural base for the two opposition guerrilla armies, the UFM and the NRA. As such it was a major target of the government's counter-insurgency campaign in 1982-83. The UFM was infiltrated and defeated during mid-1982 but the NRA continued to attack the government from within the Luwero Triangle. Counter-insurgency attempted to cut off the material and moral support for the guerrillas given by the local population. From September 1982 civilians living along the Bombo road were driven systematically from their homes. The army campaign was stepped up from the end of 1982 and by June 1983 there were 13 battalions involved. Since by this time the NRA had strategically retreated, the army concentrated on the control of trading centres and the eviction of civilians, who after January 1983 were placed in camps "protected" by the army. The non-camp areas were "free-fire zones" in which anyone found at large could be shot as a bandit. Most of the camps contained women, children and the elderly — most of the young men had fled, been removed for interrogation or killed. Aid agencies became aware of the situation in March 1983 and began to provide food aid and other assistance. At the height of the crisis in mid-1983 there were known to aid workers to be 36 camps containing a population of between 100,000 and 140,000. Despite outside assistance conditions in the camps remained appalling, with serious malnutrition and disease. At some camps there were massacres either by troops or "bandits", such as that at Kikyusa camp in May 1983 where up to 200 may have died. The government began disbanding the camps in November 1983 and most of the camps were closed in a haphazard manner over the next five months, depriving villagers of even minimal protection and food supplies. Civilians were forced to hide in swamps and forests during the day to escape troops, returning to their homesteads only at night. As a result of the government's actions much of the fertile Luwero Triangle was turned into a desolate waste ground and its inhabitants into "zombies". Reports of the army's excesses and indiscipline were instrumental in turning international opinion against the Obote government.

Operations in Karamoja: Karamoja, the remote north-eastern area, was not assimilated into Uganda until 1921 and was, like Kenya's Northern Frontier District, kept as a closed area. Cattle raids were an integral feature of Karamoja society, and despite some disruption by the colonial and independence governments, continued, despite attempts to develop the area's potential. After the fall of Amin many thousands of automatic weapons passed into the hands of Karamojong, aiding cattle raids against rival ethnic groups such as the Teso, Acholi and Langi. Insecurity increased dramatically in 1983 as Karamojong launched raids on neighbouring districts. Revenge attacks, such as the ones by Langi militia near Mohoto, joint operations by UNLA and Kenyan troops in March 1984, and counter-attacks by Karamojong, have made it difficult to understand a complex and volatile situation but one interpretation was that the fighting in Karamoja offered an opportunity to remove Acholi-Langi factionalism within the army away from Kampala to a distant area. As a result of the fighting thousands fled from Karamoja.

The Okello interlude (July 1985-January 1986)

By the end of 1984 the Obote regime had begun to fall apart, the immediate cause being quarrelling within the army between the Acholi, the largest group in the military, and the Langi. The appointment of a Langi officer and kinsman of Obote as Commander-in-Chief angered senior Acholi officers, especially Basilo Okello and Tito Okello (no relation to one another). The army was also demoralized by defeats by the NRA. Langi-Acholi clashes took place in Kampala in July 1985, leading to an Acholi victory as Obote fled the country. Tito Okello was sworn in as head of state and an interim military council set up.

There were attempts to give the new government a broad base by the inclusion of Paulo Muwanga — ousted three weeks after his appointment — Otema Allimadi, and also Paul Ssemogerere of the Democratic Party. Peace talks with the NRA began in September 1987 in Nairobi under the chairmanship of President Moi of Kenya, but agreement could not be reached on the composition of the government. Meanwhile insecurity increased, the UNLA continued to commit atrocities against civilians, the NRA moved towards Kampala and the Okello junta fell apart. Although a peace agreement was eventually signed on December 17, 1985, there was no effective attempt to implement it, and on January 26, 1986 the NRA seized control in Kampala while the remnants of the Okello regime and the remainder of the UNLA fled north.

The Museveni (NRM) regime (1986-1989)

Museveni and his officers had a more clearly-thought-out programme than had Obote or

Amin. Their 10-point plan was and remains the basis of their programme. It emphasized the restoration of democracy, beginning with the village councils; the security of persons; the unity of Uganda and the elimination of conflicts based on tribalism and religion; and the overcoming of backwardness through planned economic and social development. The National Resistance (later Revolutionary) Movement had initially consolidated its rule before the taking of the capital in the Bantu-speaking areas of the south west, where they established village councils, called "Resistance Councils". For the first time since independence the Bantu-speaking southerners were in control of the government and it became important to win over the northern areas, either by peaceful or military means.

These have taken two forms. Firstly, amnesties and talks aimed at negotiating peace settlements. In August 1987 an amnesty was offered to ex-soldiers and to rebels and it was claimed that 25,000 people had availed themselves of such offers. The most successful negotiations have been with factions of the UPDA and there have been attempts to negotiate with other factions both inside and outside Uganda. Of those who have surrendered themselves and their weapons some have been well treated and immediately released while others have been held in detention, sometimes for a considerable period and without outside knowledge of their whereabouts. Apparently conditions in the military prisons where many ex-combatants were held had improved, partly as a result of monitoring and supplies by the International Committee of the Red Cross.

There have also been attempts at a military solution in some areas, where insurgents, rebels and cattle-raiders were operating, principally in the north of the country. While by 1987/8 the NRA appeared to have defeated most opponents, the cost has sometimes been high on both military and civilians, and in Acholi especially, military discipline, for which the NRA had been noted for its high standards, had deteriorated. This deterioration has been commented on by organizations such as Amnesty International, and the government has made efforts to improve military discipline and legal and administrative processes to protect civilians, which have however been made less effective by lack of resources to strengthen these processes.

The main areas of insurgency to date faced by the government are as follows:

Acholi: After the fall of Kampala in January 1986 the UNLA troops, largely Acholis, had fled northwards looting and massacring the civilian population, in particular in Lango district, where Acholi troops took revenge on Langi citizens. By April 1986 the NRA had taken most areas of the north, largely without heavy fighting and by persuading northern civilians to hand over stockpiled arms. The Okello faction fled to Sudan, where they were reported as attacking refugee camps. Later some soldiers returned to Uganda; while some surrendered to the NRA others fought against the government. Two factions emerged; the Uganda People's Democratic Movement (UPDM) of Basilo Okello operated from bases in the Sudan; and a pro-Obote group which operated in Bosgoga and in Teso. The 35th Battalion of the NRA which had little experience as a standing army moved into garrison the area. There were reports of a breakdown in NRA discipline, of detention and torture of civilians, and this alienated many Acholi, some of whom gave their support to the UPDM and others to a new messianic religious fighting movement, Alice Lakwena's Holy Spirit Movement, which engaged in suicidal attacks on the NRA. The movement suffered a massive defeat by the NRA in January 1987 and was finally wiped out in November 1987, after which Alice Lakwena fled to Kenya. Two new religious movements then emerged, *Lakwena 2* and *Lubanga Won*, which together with the UPDA, harassed civilians. NRA discipline improved after October 1986 when the 35th Battalion was replaced and orders were issued to cease the use of torture and harassment. In 1988 some civilians had taken refuge with the NRA, which set up camps to protect them. By May 1988 large numbers of civilians in Gulu and Acholi districts were being further harassed by cattle-raiders, rebels and government troops fighting them. By 1989 the insurgency in Acholi, although still serious, was being contained. However the fighting and disruption had produced a condition of serious and continuing food shortage and by mid-1989 there were reports that one million people in the north, especially in Gulu district, faced famine conditions, unless aid was forthcoming.

Teso: The Teso were the chief victims of the cattle-raiding Karamojong, their neighbours to the east. During the second Obote regime the Teso had organized an armed militia to keep the Karamojong at bay but because the Teso had supported Obote and were thought to be hostile to the NRA the militia was disarmed. After the Karamojong began raids, resulting in the deaths of many people and cattle, the Teso lost any faith they had in the NRA (who were mainly engaged in counter-insurgency in

Acholi — see above) and turned to the Uganda People's Front/Army led by Peter Otai, from exile in Kenya. In July 1988 the UPFA suffered a major defeat by the NRA.

Karamoja: The NRA began a major campaign against the Karamojong from late 1986 but were able to do little to contain their raids. The Karamojong, who pose a security threat to any established government, have conducted cattle raids across northern Uganda as far as Nebbi on the West Nile, destroying homes and causing havoc. In March 1989 the Kenya government accused the Uganda government of supporting a cross-border raid by armed Karamojong cattle raiders but in reply the Uganda government pointed out that cross-border raids had gone on for decades and that the previous month had seen a large-scale incursion by Kenyan tribesmen which the Ugandan army had been obliged to repel.

West Nile: Unlike during the Obote regime, the West Nile remained fairly peaceful despite the presence of ex-UNLA soldiers in Sudan who sometimes returned to harass the population. Over 250,000 refugees returned from Sudan in 1987 and 1988 while by May 1988 they had been joined by 20,000 refugees from southern Sudan escaping the increasingly bitter civil war there.

Ruwenzori Mountains: This remote area on the border of Zaire is populated by the Bakonjo people. Since the 1960s a movement among them had demanded autonomy, but this has been largely ignored since the first Obote regime failed to suppress it by the use of force. The Bakonjo clashed with the government when they became involved in coffee-smuggling into Zaire, which deprived the government of much

needed foreign exchange. In 1987 there was a harsh government clampdown and the area was sealed off.

The Museveni government has made considerable efforts to express its support for the protection of human rights, the restoration of the rule of law, the establishment of mechanisms for the investigation of past and present abuses and the restoration of security and confidence in the army and police. In February 1989 elections for resistance councils were held throughout Uganda (except in Gulu district, which was still unsettled). Candidates were restricted to standing as individuals and no party candidates were allowed. Compared to the election of 1980 there was no violence or ballot rigging. At the highest level 14 government ministers were voted from office while some government opponents became MPs.

The most serious problems the government faces are those of security and Uganda's poverty. Although a rich agricultural country, Uganda has been impoverished by the years of dictatorship and civil war, and as in other African countries now faces severe problems of debt service and IMF restructuring plans. Inflation, the flight of capital and professional skills and more recently AIDS, add to the burden. Attempts to establish legal and human rights machinery have been largely thwarted by lack of resources while the military and police structures are lacking in trained personpower. There need to be continuing attempts to bring all ethnic groups into consultation and participation in national institutions such as the government, administration, army and police, if peace and stability is to be gained.

(See also *Asians of East and Central Africa*; *Southern Sudan*)

Western Saharans

Alternative names: **Saharawis, Beiden**
Location: **former Spanish Western Sahara, in exile in southern Algeria**
Population: **150,000 (est.) including 100,000 (est.) in Algeria**
% of population: **virtually 100% are Bidan Moors**
Religion: **Muslim**
Language: **Arabic (Hassaniya dialect)**

The Western Saharans, or more traditionally Saharawis, are a branch of the Bidan or Moorish people, who are nomads of mixed Berber, Arab and black African descent. They inhabit the harsh desert region stretching from southern Morocco to the valleys of the Niger and Senegal and traditionally lived a nomadic life, trading animals, wool, skins and salt for foodstuffs and other essentials. Saharawis divide their society into tribes and castes, and tribes are organized by assemblies of respected family heads under the authority of a sheikh. Since 1975 they have been fighting a bitter war against occupying Moroccan and (until 1978) Mauritanian forces.

Colonial history

The first European contact with Western Sahara was made by Portuguese traders in the fifteenth century, and a lucrative trade in slaves and gold was begun. In the late nineteenth century Spain laid claim to the territories and in 1934 the French succeeded in gaining the border regions of north-western Sahara while the Spanish continued to govern Spanish Sahara as an appendage of the protectorate in northern Morocco.

Until the late 1950s almost all Saharawis were still nomadic. Their lives began to change radically however when the territory's rich mineral resources became known to the western world. Western Sahara has large oil reserves, both onshore and offshore; it also has rich iron ore and phosphate deposits, and one of the best fishing zones in the world, unexploited by the Saharawis themselves. The economic changes of the 1960s and early 1970s brought about a rapid modernization of Saharawi society: the majority of the population became sedentarized and the urban population trebled in seven years.

Inspired by the example of Moroccan radicals, who had brought about Moroccan independence in 1956, Saharawis rebelled against the French and Spanish in the region. However it was not until 1971-72 that the anti-colonial movement was effectively organized, largely by Saharawis living in Morocco and Mauritania, and on 10 May 1973 the Polisario Front was formed. Polisario rapidly grew to become a mass movement and in 1975 thousands of pro-Polisario demonstrators took to the streets to greet a UN mission of enquiry, which found there to be "an overwhelming consensus among (West) Saharans . . in favour of independence".

In 1966 the UN General Assembly adopted a resolution calling for a referendum in Western Sahara over the issue of self-determination. This proposal was repeatedly adopted in subsequent resolutions and in 1974 the Spanish authorities agreed to the holding of a referendum and assisted in the establishment of a moderate Saharawi political party to counter Polisario's influence in the region.

The Moroccan claim

Since 1956 Morocco had laid claim to a vast portion of the Algerian Sahara, the whole of western Sahara and Mauritania, and the north-west tip of Mali. The Mauritanian government, however, viewed any loss of western Saharan territory to Morocco as a grave threat to their security in view of the 1,570-kilometre border between the two countries, almost half of which was within 50 kilometres of the strategic iron-ore railway upon which Mauritania depended for some 85% of export earnings.

In response to the UN resolution on a referendum, King Hassan II of Morocco determined to thwart what was clearly a prelude to independence. Hoping to force Spain to cede the territory to Morocco he launched a patriotic crusade to recover the "Moroccan Sahara", and aroused enormous enthusiasm among the Moroccan people. He massed 20,000 troops near the Western Saharan border and forced a postponement of the referendum pending a decision on the dispute by the International Court of Justice (ICJ) at The Hague. The referendum was never held and in 1975 the ICJ found that neither Mauritania nor Morocco had ties of sovereignty with Western Sahara.

Within hours of the publication of the ICJ's findings King Hassan launched his Green March, named after the holy colour of Islam. 350,000

Moroccan volunteers marched across the Western Saharan border to assert Morocco's territorial claim. This manoeuvre was something of a gesture as Morocco and Mauritania had already reached an agreement with Spain, according to which Spain would cede Western Sahara to both countries in return for fishing and other interests. On April 14, 1976 Western Sahara was formally partitioned, with two-thirds of the territory going to Morocco, including the phosphate deposits and the two principal towns.

The division of Western Sahara between neighbouring countries had been carried out without consideration of the strength of Saharawi determination to resist annexation. Polisario had consistently rejected any settlement which did not grant the territory, within its pre-1975 borders, full independence. Refugees began to leave the disputed areas and within six months 50,000 were living in camps on Algerian territory. These camps were soon populated almost entirely by women and children as men left to enlist in Polisario's Saharawi People's Liberation Army (SPLA). An independent Western Saharan state, the Saharan Arab Democratic Republic (SADR) was proclaimed by Polisario on February 27, 1976.

The war

Mauritania proved to be a weak opponent and had only a small army. Polisario forces determined to knock Mauritania out of the war and so destroy the Mauritania-Morocco alliance. They were highly successful in this aim, partly because it was virtually impossible for Mauritanian troops to police the one million square kilometres of territory in which the guerrillas operated and partly because the war was in any case unpopular with most Mauritanians, many of whom were Moors related to the Saharawis, and others of whom were black African minorities to whom the conflict was a purely inter-Arab affair. In order to prevent defeat at the hands of the SPLA, Mauritania signed a defence pact with both France and Morocco. Moroccan troops were sent into the country and French military personnel also arrived. French air strikes failed to stop the SPLA's offensive however, and in July 1978 there was a military coup, and peace agreement was signed, according to which Mauritania abandoned all claims to Western Saharan territory.

On August 14, 1978 Morocco seized Dakhla and named Tiris el-Gharbia a Moroccan province. Polisario, backed by Algeria, continued its offensive and was soon assaulting towns in southern Morocco. In March 1980 Hassan began the building of a "Great Wall of the Sahara" which within two years had stretched some 400 kilometres in length, from the Algerian border in the north-east to the Atlantic coast. He later extended it to form a continuous defence line over 640 kilometres long in 1984. The wall was constructed of sandbanks, minefields, and barbed wire, with intermittent artillery placements and observation posts, underground quarters, electronic ground sensors and radar equipment to detect guerrilla vehicles. It effectively prevented the guerrillas from executing the lightning raids for which they had become known, forcing them to withdraw further into the desert and skirt around the wall. Despite the presence of the wall, in 1984 Morocco controlled less than one quarter of West Sahara's land area, although this area included the phosphate mines at Bou-Kraa.

The war continued on much the same lines until mid-1988 with Morocco continuing to expand its wall defences so that by 1988 it was 1,600 kilometres long and covered an area of perhaps two-thirds of the territory. Morocco maintained a presence of between 100,000 and 200,000 troops in the area and received military backing from France and the USA. Polisario troops, although only a fraction of the numbers of the Moroccan army and relying on arms from Algeria and those captured from the Moroccans, continued to operate a guerrilla war behind the wall, making surprise attacks and capturing Moroccan soldiers — captives were estimated to number between 2,000 and 3,000. Exhaustion began to set in on both sides and it appeared that only a diplomatic settlement rather than a military victory could bring peace to the region.

The international dimension

The situation in Western Sahara placed the Western Powers in a dilemma. The French Socialist Party maintained relations with Polisario while the Mitterrand government supplied arms to Morocco; the Spanish government has tried to preserve good relations with both Morocco and Algeria as has the USSR, which supplies arms to Polisario via Algeria rather than openly antagonize Morocco, with which it has a growing economic relationship. The USA, while officially remaining neutral in the conflict, has allied itself to Morocco for strategic reasons despite the importance of US-Algerian business interests.

Third-World countries have generally favoured Polisario which sought diplomatic recognition for the SADR. By 1989 over 70 countries, mainly in Africa, Asia and Latin America, had given SADR diplomatic status. The OAU, which had continued to call for a referendum, agreed to give a seat to the Polisario Front at its 20th Conference in November 1984; Morocco withdrew in protest. But Morocco began to become increasingly diplomatically isolated, and in October 1985 at a meeting of the UN General Assembly the Moroccan government made an offer of a ceasefire and referendum under UN auspices, while continuing to refuse any recognition to Polisario. This was rejected by Polisario and the war continued. But Polisario was also facing pressure from its chief ally Algeria and the former colonizer Spain, and hopes for a diplomatic settlement grew. This was facilitated by the harsh austerity measures the Moroccan government has been forced to adopt, which have led to civilian unrest and internal instability.

The UN became more actively involved in the search for peace and the UN Secretary General made several visits to the area in an effort to get talks under way. This resulted in the acceptance of UN proposals for a referendum, by both Morocco and Polisario in August 1988, but no date was set for a ceasefire and the precise details of the plan were not made public. Fierce fighting, resulting in 250 deaths, took place only three weeks after the agreement of the plan. But it was not until January 1989 that King Hassan agreed to meet Polisario leaders directly for the first time, although he maintained that this was for discussions not for negotiations, conditions agreed to by Polisario. There has been little progress since then and some fighting has occurred but both sides seem war weary and there is strong diplomatic pressure on both sides to reach an agreement.

(See also *Mauritania*)

Prospects for the future

There are many problems to be faced both in relation to the plan itself and on the ground. The referendum will be carried out within Moroccan-held West Sahara and in the Polisario base at Tindouf in southern Algeria. Only 74,600 Saharawis whose births were recorded by the Spanish colonial authorities will be allowed to vote. This excludes those who were born outside the area (not unusual given the nomadic nature of Saharawi society) and those whose births were not recorded. There are fears by Polisario that Morocco will attempt to inflate the numbers to include the Moroccans resident behind the wall; there are now at least 100,000 Moroccan settlers and a probable 150,000 troops. The policing of a ceasefire and withdrawal of troops before a referendum takes place has still to be determined; one proposal was for the deployment of a UN force of 2,000 to oversee the process. Morocco is confident that the area will vote to stay within Morocco but has said that it will recognize an independent Western Saharan state if the majority vote for it, but many observers, and also Polisario, are sceptical as the Moroccan regime has placed a great deal of its prestige and a large amount of resources into its West Sahara campaign.

Adversity has made the Western Saharans a determined and resourceful people. In their 24 tent camps in Algeria they have developed new skills, have established income-generating projects and have given priority to education. A number of campaigns have ensured almost universal literacy and young Western Saharans have been sent to schools in Algeria, Cuba and (at one stage) Libya. Despite their small numbers and inhospitable environment Western Saharans are well equipped to run an independent nation.

Zimbabwe

Alternative names: **formerly Rhodesia/Southern Rhodesia**
Location: **independent state within the Commonwealth, southern Africa**
Population: **9.9 million (est.)**
% of population: **Shona 75%, Ndebele 16%**
Religion: **about 25% Christian (40% Roman Catholic, 36% independent apostolic churches), 75% indigenous religions**
Language: **ChiShona (Shona), Sindebele (Ndebele), English**

Zimbabwe is a multi-ethnic state, created in 1980 from the former British colony of Southern Rhodesia, which had been ruled as an illegal white dominated state from 1965. Since independence there has been considerable ethnic and political conflict between its two major groups.

The majority group is the Shona (Mashona) who form about 75% of the population. There are two main dialect clusters, the Zezuru and the Karanga (the largest single group) who live in the areas around Harare and Masvingo respectively. The Manyika live in the east, near Mutare; the Korekore in the north towards the Zambezi, the Kalanga in the south-west and the Ndau in the east. The Kalanga, although ethnically Shona, are politically oriented towards the Ndebele.

The Ndebele live in the western third of Zimbabwe, Matabeleland, and comprise about 16% of the population. They originally came from South Africa and in the nineteenth century conquered and controlled a portion of the Shona.

Other groups are much smaller in number and generally poorer. They include the Tonga in Hwange in the extreme north of Matabeleland, the Venda and the Shangaan in the extreme south.

The European population, who once controlled the country, are very small in numbers. Their number/percentage has dropped considerably since independence.

The colonial period

The colony of Rhodesia came into being under the auspices of Cecil Rhodes' British South Africa Company which gained a charter to administer the area and followed this by military conquests of Matabeleland in 1893 and Mashonaland in 1897. The area was seen as favourable to white settlement and farming, and immigration from South Africa and Europe was encouraged. In 1923 the area became the self-governing colony of Southern Rhodesia after the white settlers had rejected the idea of union with South Africa, and in 1953 part of the Federation of Rhodesia and Nyasaland; which however broke apart a decade later, primarily because of the opposition of the white supremacist Rhodesian Front, which had won the 1962 elections in Rhodesia, to African advancement. It was this issue also which prompted Ian Smith, the white Prime Minister, to announce a Unilateral Declaration of Independence (UDI) for Southern Rhodesia in illegal rebellion against the British government. African nationalist agitation had begun when Joshua Nkomo set up the African National Congress in 1957 and the Zimbabwe African People's Union (ZAPU) in 1961. Within two years a rival organization had been set up by Reverend Sithole called the Zimbabwe African National Union (ZANU). UDI marked the beginning of armed struggle by the nationalists, which ZANU claims to have inaugurated. Robert Mugabe replaced Sithole as leader of ZANU in the early 1970s and for a brief period all resistance groups came together under Bishop Abel Muzorewa's African National Council (ANC). However by 1976 the old parties and personal splits had reappeared.

In 1979 Bishop Muzorewa's ANC was elected to government under the short-lived government of Zimbabwe-Rhodesia, but the war did not abate as many Africans felt that Muzorewa was Smith's puppet. But by this time the long-running bush war and the effects of economic sanctions, along with diplomatic pressure from various sources, finally brought Smith to the negotiating table. A constitutional conference was convened at Lancaster House by the UK government, and was attended by delegations led by Muzorewa, Mugabe and Nkomo. By mid-October 1979 the joint "Patriotic Front" delegation (ZANU and ZAPU) had agreed on the independence Constitution and on December 21, 1979 a ceasefire was finally reached. ZANU and ZAPU contested the elections separately, ZANU under the name of ZANU-PF and ZAPU under the name Patriotic Front.

In the 18 April 1980 elections Rhodesia, now named Zimbabwe, gained its independence when Robert Mugabe of the ZANU (PF) was elected

Prime Minister with 63% of the vote and 57 seats. Nkomo's Patriotic Front won 20 seats and Muzorewa's ANC won three. The 20 seats reserved for whites under the Lancaster House Agreement were all won by the Republican Front led by Ian Smith.

Disaffection in Matabeleland

From 1980 to 1987 there were growing strains between the Shona majority and the Ndebele/Kalanga minority. (The Kalanga are Shona-speaking but are geographically and politically allied to the Ndebele. Nkomo is himself a Kalanga). Despite his majority in Parliament, Mugabe's cabinet also included ZAPU and white independents — in 1982 these filled four and two posts respectively. There were attempts to build a Zimbabwean National Army (ZNA) by integrating the former combatants from the Zipra and Zanla — the military wings of ZAPU and ZANU. Out of the 40 odd battalions formed since independence, three have collapsed and three been badly damaged by tribal animosity and desertions. Apart from the all-Shona Fifth Brigade and Presidential Guard, the army is roughly one third Ndebele.

Soon after independence dissident guerrillas — whose numbers have been variously estimated as ranging from 300 to 3,000 — took to the bush in Matebeleland and parts of the Midlands. The majority were disaffected ex-combatants of Zipra, many of whom deserted the ZNA in 1982 when Nkomo was sacked from the cabinet after the discovery of an arms cache on ZAPU-owned land. In order to combat the guerrillas, government troops were sent into largely Ndebele areas, and reports began to filter through of troops torturing, harassing and killing local people and burning down villages on the pretext that they were harbouring or helping the guerrillas. Particularly prominent in these reports were the Fifth Brigade, trained by North Korean advisors in 1981, and the Presidential Guard. In 1983 about 1,500 Ndebele civilians were killed by security forces while thousands of others were beaten and hundreds detained without charge.

From February to April 1984 there was a three-month curfew in Matabeleland, affecting about 400,000 rural Ndebele. The government imposed food rationing with a view to depriving the guerrillas of supplies. This restriction was all the more severe due to the effects of the drought of the previous three years. The provision of extension work and transport became almost impossible in the eastern fringe of Matabeleland and white farmers abandoned their land. The guerrillas then resorted to destroying clinics, schools and boreholes or preventing the creation of new infrastructure. It is reported that they were responsible for several hundred deaths, mainly civilians, but also over 100 ZANU officers and about 40 white farmers or their relatives. Some of these deaths however are suspected to have been perpetrated by ZANU security forces — reminiscent of the tactics of Rhodesian troops before independence. The Zimbabwe media publicized the dissidents' activities but little of the government response, and journalists were barred from the curfew area until May 1984 when it was estimated that there were 6,000 internal refugees in Bulawayo. In late 1983 a special Commission of Inquiry was set up to investigate charges of brutality against the Fifth Brigade, but the findings were never made public.

Tensions were high in the period before the 1985 elections. ZAPU supporters were detained from 1984 while in the last half of the year and in the months before and after the elections hundreds of Ndebele civilians were rendered homeless when gangs of ZANU-PF ransacked their homes. In the Midlands province, which is two-thirds Shona and one third Ndebele, many Ndebele changed their names to Shona names in order to escape such intimidation. In a sweep by the Police Internal Security and Intelligence Unit (PISI) in Bulawayo in March 1985, 1,300 people were arrested because of their supposed sympathy with ZAPU — only 39 were detained and only one was reckoned to be a dissident guerrilla. These divisions were reflected in the election results which saw ZANU-PF winning 77% of the seats and ZAPU winning all 15 seats for Matabeleland. In August five ZAPU MPs were detained and in September and October there were two purges of ex-Zipra army officers in the ZNA. Nkomo claimed that 350 ZAPU activists had disappeared and there were allegations that prisoners were beaten and tortured.

In December 1987, after lengthy talks between Mugabe and Nkomo, the government declared a one-party state, with the declared aim of wiping out all tribal divisions. Mugabe had earlier abolished the 20 seats (out of 100 in total) reserved for "whites, Coloureds and Asians" although the vacancies had been filled by white businessmen and ZANU officials rather than ZAPU representatives. The 1988 New Year cabinet reshuffle of government posts included Nkomo as one of three senior ministers and installed several other ZAPU members in the cabinet. It appears that violence in Matabeleland has abated since the merger — some ex-guerrillas in North Matebeleland have accepted an amnesty and laid down their arms — and some of the divisions between the Shona and Ndebele are healing. However, memories of the brutalities of 1983 and 1984 remain strong in Matabeleland, which still suffers from inequalities within Zimbabwe, being overcrowded and its people often poor and malnourished. In 1985 UNICEF reported that 45% of the participants in its National Child Feeding Programme were from Matabeleland.

The position of the Ndau

The Ndau only make up 3% of the Shona group and are traditionally looked down upon by other Shona speakers. They live in the area along the Mozambique border where they have affinities with the Ndau of Mozambique. The South Africa-backed Mozambique Resistance Movement (RMN), which is engaged in a civil war with the FRELIMO government of Mozambique, was set up by the Rhodesian government in the early 1970s, and has recruited mainly from the Mozambiquan Ndau. RMN attacks have taken place on the Zimbabwean side of the border and in 1989 the government reported that there had been 420 such attacks in the previous six months, with 932 civilians killed. In response the army has placed people into "protected villages" and there are complaints by villagers that these villages are too far from their homes and lands and that they are not adequately protected by the army. The Ndau of the Chipinge district are also discontented with what they claim is unsatisfactory land allocation and since land pressure is severe there are many landless squatters, who are sometimes dealt with harshly. Chipinge is the only seat held by Sithole's ZANU Party in the 1987 elections and since Sithole is in exile and is reportedly allied with RMN, this increases suspicion of the Ndau and also of the many Ndau Mozambiquan refugees in this region.

Other minority groups

The Tonga and the Shangaan in south-east Zimbabwe, the Venda in the south-west, and the Sotho, Chikunda, Barwe and Korekore in the Zambezi valley, are some of the poorest and least developed peoples in Zimbabwe. The Tonga, numbering about 70,000, once lived in the Kariba Valley but were moved in the late 1950s to make way for the Kariba Dam. The 40,000 resident in the Nyaminyami district have the highest infant mortality rates in Zimbabwe, and malnutrition is endemic. They live in one of the largest wildlife reserves in Africa and up to 50% of their maize and sorghum crops are destroyed by wildlife predatory raids, yet if they kill the animals they face heavy fines and imprisonment. They cannot raise cattle because of tsetse fly infestation. In 1988 the Nyaminyami district set up a Wildlife Development Trust with the aim of lobbying the government for direct access to the funds generated by wildlife tourism in order to enable the Nyaminyami to become self-supporting, to fence off the farmers' land and to develop the wildlife industry through hide-tanning, crafts and a crocodile farm.

The white minority on the other hand is the richest group in Zimbabwe, controlling over 80% of the wealth, owning 34% of the land, dominating export agriculture and the industrial and corporate sector based in Harare. They also earn 40% of the nation's foreign exchange although there is evidence that small African peasant farmers are contributing an increasing share of this. Mugabe has followed a policy of reconciliation towards the white minority, inviting white businessmen to take up some of the extra 20 parliamentary seats and dividing the white Conservative Alliance of Zimbabwe. But political control now lies with the African majority.

Future developments

With advent of the Unity Agreement in 1987 the conflicts between the Shona and the Ndebele appear to be decreasing. However there is still antipathy within the Shona group between the Karanga (Masvingo province) and the Zezuru (Harare province) tribes, who are the two major tribes within the government. The administration is dominated by the Zezuru in alliance with the Manyika (Eastern Highlands) while the army is dominated by the Karanya. Mugabe is Zezuru but is generally considered to be above tribal divisions, but many of his ministers are not and when there are political disagreements or scandals, tribalist divisions frequently arise.

Further References

Eritrea and Tigray, MRG Report No. 5, 1983

Inequalities in Zimbabwe, MRG Report No. 8, 1981

The new position of East Africa's Asians: problems of a displaced minority, MRG Report No. 16, 1984

Burundi since the genocide, MRG Report No. 20, 1987

Jehovah's Witnesses in Africa, MRG Report No. 29, 1985

Peoples of the Sahel, MRG Report No. 33, 1990

Indian South Africans, MRG Report No. 34, 1985

The Western Saharans, MRG Report No. 40, 1984

Diego Garcia: a contrast to the Falklands, MRG Report No. 54, 1985

The San of the Kalahari, MRG Report No. 56, 1982

Uganda, MRG Report No. 66, 1989

The Falashas: The Jews of Ethiopia, MRG Report No. 67, 1985

The Jews of Africa and Asia, MRG Report No. 76, 1987

The Southern Sudan, MRG Report No. 78, 1988

Chad, MRG Report No. 80, 1988

SOUTH ASIA

South Asia is the location of some of the most spectacular and publicized conflicts involving minorities in the modern world. The colonial era, with British India as the pivotal creation, was succeeded by States with large and rapidly increasing populations, divided partly along sectarian lines. The partition process was accompanied by considerable loss of life and displacement of populations. The separation did not finish in 1947. The establishment of the State of Bangladesh in place of the former East Pakistan in 1971-72 remains the outstanding example of a post-colonial exercise in self-determination, and this, too, was accompanied by tragic loss of life and the creation of an enormous refugee problem. The contemporary legal/political theory of self-determination does not allow for separation of fragments of new States which are deemed to have exercised their rights through the achievement of independence. Separation has not succeeded in Africa (see Introduction to Sub-Saharan Africa) and has been resisted both there and in Asia. The fact that separation inevitably involves what, until a successful "new" independent entity is created, is an ethnic minority, creates formidable problems for ethnic relations. The secession of Bangladesh may have set a destabilizing precedent in this respect, since a number of groups in the area — Kashmiris, Sikhs, Tamils — have agitated for self-determination or secession. South Asia is characterized by many different types of minorities. If there are outstanding themes, they are religion and the very particular social/religious institutions of caste. Recurring tensions exist between Muslims, Hindus, Sikhs and Buddhists in various permutations. Within this area of primordial and great religious inspiration, tensions within religious systems also exist. Ahmadis and other Muslims disagree on the interpretation of Islam. The Scheduled Castes, the "Untouchables" of the Hindu caste system, represent perhaps the world's largest minority; the scourge of Untouchability condemns the existence of some 110 million persons, sufficient for the population of a large state. Tribal peoples in India and Bangladesh constitute sizeable groups in uneasy relationship with neighbours. Besides its legacy of partition, colonialism produced "planted" groups such as Indian Tamils in Sri Lanka, and mixed-race Anglo-Indians. The scale of minority problems in the area is great, but considerable thought and effort has also gone into devising appropriate structures towards the achievement of social harmony.

Instruments on Minority Rights

The record of State adherence to general international instruments on human rights is variable. The most noticeable lacuna concerns the position of Pakistan, which is not a party to either of the two International Covenants on Human Rights, but is a party to the Conventions Against Racial Discrimination and Apartheid; in reports on its implementation of the former treaty, Pakistan has claimed to have no ethnic minorities. India has made a unique reservation to the Covenants on Human Rights, both of which allow the right of self-determination to "all peoples": ". . . the Government of the Republic of India declares that the words 'the right to self-determination' apply only to the peoples under foreign domination and that these words do not apply to sovereign independent States or to a section of the people or nation — which is the essence of national integrity". This clearly curtails the scope of the right, and, in effect, serves as a warning to ambitious minority groups claiming self-determination that the State will resist them. The reservation is difficult to equate with India's action in assisting the emergence of Bangladesh, but has never been withdrawn. Bangladesh, India and Pakistan are parties to the International Labour Organization's Convention on Indigenous and Tribal Populations.

Besides general treaties, specific agreements on minorities have been concluded between States in the region, as might be expected in an area of few States but many large minority groups. The earliest is the Agreement between Pakistan and India (see *Appendix 7.1*), signed at New Delhi in 1950 in the light of the horrendous events which accompanied partition; the opening paragraph reads: "The Governments of India and Pakistan solemnly agree that each shall ensure to the minorities throughout its territory, complete equality of citizenship, irrespective of religion, a full sense of security in respect of life, culture, property and personal honour, freedom of movement within each country and freedom of occupation, speech and worship, subject to law and morality. Members of the minorities shall have equal opportunity with members of the majority community to participate in the public life of their country, to hold political or other office, and to serve in their country's civil and armed forces. Both Governments declare these rights to be fundamental and undertake to enforce them effectively." Other notable agreements include the New Delhi Agreement of 1973 between India and Pakistan with the concurrence of Bangladesh, and the Tripartite Agreement of 1974 concerning, among other things, the transfer of large numbers of Biharis and other non-Bengalis from Bangladesh to Pakistan.

The most recent case of an international agreement designed to cope with an ethnic crisis is the Colombo Accord of July 1987 between India and Sri Lanka to establish peace and normality in Sri Lanka (see *Appendix 7.2*). Both the rights of minorities and the rights of the State are underlined; the preamble recites the parties' desire "to preserve the unity, sovereignty and territorial integrity of Sri Lanka", "acknowledging that Sri Lanka is a multi-ethnic and a multi-lingual plural society consisting, *inter alia*, of Sinhalese, Tamils, Moslems (Moors) and Burghers . . . recognizing that each ethnic group has a distinct cultural and linguistic identity which has to be carefully nurtured". The Agreement provides for referenda and elections on the status of the Tamil area, an amnesty and other procedures designed to satisfy "the imperative need of resolving the ethnic problem of Sri Lanka". Specific constitutional protection of minority rights is a strong feature in the region. That most complex of all constitutions, the Constitution of India, recognizes the claims of communities and individuals on the State. The Constitution combines provisions on equality of individuals with principles designed to protect and consolidate the identity and integrity of groups. Elements of positive discrimination for certain groups are present — "for the advancement of . . . socially and educationally backward classes of citizens or for the scheduled castes and scheduled tribes". For group identity, Article 29(1) of the Constitution provides that "any section of the citizens residing in the territory of India . . . having a distinct language script or culture of its own shall have the right to conserve the same". Whereas Article 29 refers to citizens, Article 30(1) describes minorities: "All minorities, whether based on religion or language shall have the right to establish and administer educational institutions of their choice." Article 350A provides that it is the goal of every State and local authority "to provide adequate facilities for instruction in the mother tongue at the primary stage of education to children belonging to minority groups". Linguistic group rights are balanced against the general direction of State policy — it is deemed to be the duty of the Union to promote Hindi "so that it may serve as a medium of expression for all elements of the composite culture of India". Broad guarantees are provided in respect of religion, and there are extensive sections in the Constitution devoted to the Scheduled Castes and Scheduled Tribes.

India is a secular State, but Pakistan is an Islamic State according to Article 2 of its Constitution. Article 222 commences in a very unpromising manner for non-Muslims: ". . . all existing law should be brought into conformity with the injunctions of Islam . . . ." However, the rest of the Article recites that "nothing in this part shall affect the personal laws of non-Muslim citizens or their status as citizens". Pakistan, like many Islamic States, is not governed entirely by principles of legal territoriality, but also by the principle of personality: members of religious groups may be legally subject to the demands and benefits of their religions as well as to State law in general (see introduction to the Middle East and North Africa). Other articles of the Constitution deal positively with minorities and their rights. Rights are for individuals as well as religious communities; linguistic groups are also catered for — Article 28 recites the right of "any section of the citizens speaking in a distinct language . . . to preserve and promote the same . . . ". Despite a much more draconian approach to non-Muslim religious minorities in Bangladesh, the validity of religious laws and customs of religious minorities has been recognized in such matters as personal and family laws. The Constitution of Afghanistan recognises the equality of citizens, recognizes human rights and refers specifically to ethnic groups — the Government is committed to raising the standard of living for all nationalities, tribes and ethnic groups in Afghanistan. Emphasis is also placed on realizing the unity of all of Afghanistan's people.

Treatment of minorities

The retreat of colonialism from South Asia left major minority problems in its wake. Minorities in this area are often large, organized groups inhabiting specific historical territories. Their ambitions are frequently seen to threaten the stability of States, creating situations of considerable tension. Difficulties are compounded by *de facto* discrimination against minorities, despite the proliferation of admirable accommodating structures and principles of non-discrimination and equality — untouchability has been "abolished" by law but clearly exists. Further questions are raised by "confessional" States such as Pakistan; in a region of intense religious division, perhaps the secular State stands a greater chance of delivering liberty and justice to its citizens. States do not conform to the ideal of one nation or one creed; it should be a principle of politics that they do not act as if the ideal were real — a narrow vision produces real difficulties for those who do not share it. The rise of religious fundamentalism creates the most acute difficulties in a State officially given over to a particular religion. The situation of Ahmadis in Pakistan illustrates these points. Finally, the "internationalization" of minority conflicts in the region is a mixed blessing; kin-State interest in a group can result in interference in a State's internal affairs and escalate conflict. On the other hand, it can result in consolidation of a group's position in that the host-State's conduct is subject to close and continuing scrutiny.

Adivasis of India

Alternative names: **Scheduled Tribes, various tribal names e.g. Santhals, Hos, Mundas, Oraons, Gonds, Konds, Bhils etc.**
Location: **throughout India but especially in central India and north-eastern states**
Population: **51.5 million (1981)**
% of population: **7.5% of Indian population**
Religion: **Indigenous beliefs, Hinduism, Christianity**
Language: **various**

The Adivasis (original inhabitants) is the collective name used for the many tribal peoples of India. Officially they are termed "Scheduled Tribes" but this is a legal and constitutional term which differs from state to state and area to area and therefore excludes some groups who might be considered tribal. Adivasis are not an homogenous group — with over 200 tribes speaking over 100 languages, which vary greatly in ethnicity, culture and language; however there are similarities in their way of life and generally perceived inferior position within Indian society. There are over 50 million Adivasis constituting 7.5% of the Indian population, thus making it the largest tribal population in the world.

Adivasis are found throughout India but are primarily based in the mountain and hill areas, away from the fertile plains. The greatest concentration is in the central states of India, notably Madhya Pradesh, Orissa, southern Bihar, the western *ghats* (hills) of Gujarat and Maharastra and northern Andhra Pradesh; where over 85% of the Tribal population is to be found. However in no peninsula state does the Tribal population reach more than one quarter of the population. There are smaller groups in the mountain areas

of the south, notably in Kerala, Tamil Nadu and Karnataka. The other concentration is found in the north-eastern states, the "seven sisters" (Assam, Manipur, Nagaland, Mizoram, Tripura, Megalaya and Arunchal Pradesh) but here the situation is significantly different as in most of these states (the exceptions are Assam and Tripura) Adivasis are a majority and are likely to remain so since regulations restrict settlement by outsiders.

The Indian government has a special programme for the welfare of tribes it classes as "primitive" tribes. These are Adivasis engaged in pre-agricultural technology and shifting cultivation with either a static or declining population. In 1988 there were 73 such tribes totalling over one million people.

Background and history

Adivasis are some of the earliest inhabitants of the sub-continent and once inhabited much greater areas than at present. However little is known of their history although it appears that many were pushed into the hill areas after the invasions of the Indo-Aryan tribes 3,000 years ago. Tribals were not integrated into Hindu caste society; they stood outside it but nevertheless there were many points of contact. Tribal religious beliefs contain many aspects of Hinduism (and vice-versa); Tribals traded with settled villages on the plains and sometimes paid tribute to Hindu rulers. In turn some Tribal rulers conquered and ruled over non-tribals and some Tribals permanently settled and entered caste society.

It was not until the unifying political rule of the British from the late eighteenth century that government made substantial inroads into Adivasi society. British rule brought money, government officials and moneylenders into tribal areas, beginning the process of encroachment of Adivasi land by outsiders. As a result there were tribal revolts from the mid-nineteenth century in several parts of eastern India and this forced the administration to recognize the vulnerable position of Tribals and pass laws to protect their lands from outsiders. These laws (some of which are still on the Statute Book) completely barred the sale of Tribal lands to non-Tribals and made provisions to restore alienated land. However in practice most of these laws were widely disregarded and unscrupulous merchants and money-lenders found ways to circumvent them. These problems still face Adivasis today although their opponents are as likely to be large companies and state corporations as small traders and moneylenders. Christian missions began to proselytize in some tribal areas where (in contrast to Hindu and Muslim areas) they achieved a degree of success and also, most notably in the north-east, began the process of education and political awareness. Tribal peoples played little role in the run-up to independence and it was only in the north-east that they had enough political consciousness to make demands for separation or autonomy. (See *Nagas of India*.)

Constitution and law

Under the constitution of the Republic of India of 1950, Tribal peoples along with so-called "Untouchables" became subject to special protective provisions. The vast majority of tribes were classified as "Scheduled Tribes". Article 341 authorizes the President of India to specify "castes, races or tribes which shall for the purposes of this constitution be deemed to be Scheduled Tribes". The first amendment to the Constitution passed in 1951 allowed the state to make special provision for the advancement of socially and educationally backward classes of citizens of the Scheduled Castes and Scheduled

Tribes. The central Government has a special Commission for Scheduled Castes and Scheduled Tribes which issues an Annual Report. These reports give accounts of illegal actions against Adivasis and makes recommendations to improve their position.

There are reservations for the Scheduled Tribes in legislatures in the central and the state governments. In the two houses of Parliament, the Lok Sabha and the Rajya Sabha, 7% of the seats are reserved for Scheduled Tribe members and similar representation occurs in the state assemblies in proportion to the percentage of Scheduled Tribes in the state's population. However since the "Scheduled Tribe" voters are always a minority (except in the north-eastern states where they are a numerical majority) in the reserved constituencies and in the assemblies as a whole, favourable legislation can be blocked by vested interests. Furthermore the system does not encourage Scheduled Tribe organization by separate parties but facilitates organization and representation by the major parties, especially the Congress Party which has been in a dominant position since independence. Governments normally have Scheduled Tribe Ministers and sometimes Cabinet Ministers but to date in peninsula India there has been only one Chief Minister from a Scheduled Tribe (in Gujarat) although in the five predominantly Tribal north-eastern states the Chief Minister invariably comes from a Scheduled Tribe.

There have been very few attempts to found distinctive Scheduled Tribe political parties, apart from those in the north-eastern states. Perhaps the most notable example in peninsula India has been that in eastern and southern Bihar, where a tribal regionalist movement known as the Jharkhand movement has been a factor since independence. The roots of this movement lie in the Santhal peoples of eastern Bihar and western Bengal, the scene of one of the early tribal revolts against land alienation under British rule. Some of this area also contains India's richest mineral deposits and mining, and subsequent industrialization and deforestation has added to Tribal grievances.

The Jharkhand Party was first formed in 1950 and had as its main demands the formation of a separate state or territory in the traditional Adivasi areas of Santhal Paganas and Chotanagpur and areas in West Bengal, Orissa and Madhya Pradesh. The party went into decline after its leader joined the Congress Party but was revived in 1973 when a new party the *Jharkhand Mukti Mocha* (JMM) was formed, led by a charismatic Santhal leader, who, despite his arrest during the Emergency, later worked closely with and eventually joined the Congress Party. This factionalized the JMM into several smaller groups but in 1987 a new co-ordinating organization the Jharkhand Co-ordinating Committee (JCC) was formed, with over 50 constituent organizations. This group has led a number of *bandhs* (strikes) and mass demonstrations in support of its demands and also tried to set up a parallel government although with little success, and both the central and state governments have consistently refused to consider a Jharkhand state. Were such a state to be granted it would not have a majority of Adivasis although they would probably be the largest single group if the different tribes were totalled together.

Land and economic factors

Over 95% of Scheduled Tribes still live in rural areas and economic exploitation remains their most acute problem. Less than 10% are shifting hunter-gatherers but more than half depend on forest produce for their livelihood, many in the form of the tendu leaf, used for the production of *bidis* (local cigarettes). From the time of the British administration there have been laws regulating the ownership and use of the forests and today most forest land is effectively nationalized or in the hands of state governments, and large areas are contracted to outside commercial interests. This has progressively deprived Adivasi communities of rights in the land and they can be fined or imprisoned for taking forest produce which has traditionally been theirs. The ostensible reason for state intervention has been to stop the destruction of forest land which has continued throughout this century. There are a number of reasons for deforestation which is often blamed on Adivasi shifting cultivation practices; one has been the increase in demand for firewood as fuel; another is the impact of commercial, sometimes illegal, cutting down of forests. Although many Adivasis already have a similar lifestyle to small peasant farmers, farming marginal plots of land, they are even less likely to have the traditional agricultural skills to exploit such land, or the knowledge of government to enable them to get the loans and grants to which they may be entitled.

Another threat to Adivasis is large-scale dam building, for irrigation and hydro-electricity. A number of such schemes have been carried out since independence but the largest is the giant World Bank-financed Narmada Valley project which involves 30 major, 135 medium and 3,000 minor dams and which will flood 350,000 hectares of land, including 11% of the forests of the Narmada Valley. Up to 300,000 people, the majority of them Tribals, may be forced to relocate to make way for the dam. Furthermore compensation is limited to landowners (which is difficult for many Adivasis to prove) and is normally given in money rather than land. There have been campaigns by organizations within India and internationally to at least give compensation in the form of an equal amount of land to the displaced but, although these schemes have achieved a limited amount of success in delaying the project and gaining better compensation terms, the dams will still go ahead. Furthermore it is doubtful whether sufficient land for resettlement is available in such a densely populated country, where pressures on land are already high.

Social developments

As with the Scheduled Castes, members of Scheduled Tribes are beneficiaries of "positive discrimination" provisions laid down in the constitution, reserving places in education, the civil service and nationalized industries. Problems of remoteness, poverty and prejudice mitigate against Adivasis exploiting these provisions however. For example, in Andhra Pradesh the Tribal literacy rate is only 11% against an all-India level of 29% (in the north-east, however, Tribal literacy is considerably higher). Because few Adivasis finish their schooling, few are able to use the reserved places in higher education or the civil service. Nevertheless some Adivasis do manage to achieve positions of responsibility in government and education, although they continue to be under-represented in almost every field.

Some Adivasis have been organized by left-wing groups, known commonly in India as "Naxalites", to press for higher wages and payments for forest produce. As a result Adivasis may become victims of both Naxalite pressures and government counter-insurgency campaigns. More commonly police, forest guards and officials frequently cheat, bully and intimidate Adivasis and large numbers are routinely arrested and jailed, often for petty offences. In such circumstances many Adivasis prefer to bribe officials to escape harassment or flee into the jungles when they appear.

Although Adivasis are not, as a general rule, regarded as "unclean" by caste-Hindus in the same way as Untouchables are, they continue to face prejudice and often violence from society. They are at the lowest point of almost every socio-economic indicator. The majority of the population regards them as primitive and government programmes aim to "integrate" them with the majority society, rather than to emphasize their distinctiveness. While the larger tribal groups and languages will survive as a result of numbers, the destruction of their economic base and environment poses grave threats to those who are still able to follow the basis of a traditional way of life and may result in the cultural extinction of many of the smaller Adivasi peoples.

(See also *Andaman Islanders; Chittagong Hill Tract Tribes of Bangladesh; Nagas of India*)

Ahmadis of Pakistan

Alternative names: **Qadianis, Lahori group**
Location: **Pakistan, mainly Punjab and Sind**
Population: **3-4 million**
% of population: **3.1%-4.2%**
Religion: **Ahmadi**
Language: **Punjabi, Sindhi, Urdu**

The Ahmadis are a Muslim sect which was founded in Qadian, Punjab, in the nineteenth century. Its founder was Mirza Ghirlam Ahmad, a Muslim who claimed prophetic status as the Mahdi or Messiah, in succession to Krishna, Jesus Christ and Mohammed. The Ahmadis accept four of the five basic principles of Islam, namely prayer five times a day, the Ramadan fast, the Pilgrimage to Mecca (*Haj*) and alms-giving. They do not accept the fifth principle, that of the *Jihad* or Holy War against non-believers. Many Muslims regard them as heretics and refuse to accept them as a legitimate part of Islam.

Today Ahmadis are found all over the world[1] but the core community is in Pakistan: estimates vary from half a million to six million people out of a total population of over 96 million, but three million to four million is the most commonly accepted figure. During British rule of undivided India many were employed in government service and after partition many crossed the border from Indian Punjab into Muslim West Pakistan, where they continued to play a prominent part in the civil and diplomatic services and in industry and commerce.

Like many successful minorities the Ahmadis attracted hostility. It was felt by many that their influence in society was out of all proportion to their numbers and there was agitation calling for them to be declared non-Muslim on the grounds that they did not accept the principle of the Jihad. In 1953, several newspapers, which had allegedly been paid by conservative parties, waged a campaign of anti-Ahmadi sentiment culminating in riots in Lahore; however, the subversion involved was publicly exposed and for some years there was little overt hostility towards the Ahmadis.

In the election of 1970 the Ahmadis supported President Bhutto and Ahmadi members were returned to the National Assembly and the Provincial Assembly of the Punjab. Despite their influence in government affairs they were unable to prevent the government voting with the majority at the Islamic States Conference in 1974, when the Ahmadi community was formally declared non-Muslim and forbidden to perform the Haj Pilgrimage to Mecca. There was a wave of sectarian riots during April and May 1974 and President Bhutto agreed to a re-examination of the Ahmadis' position. In September of that year the National Assembly adopted a constitutional amendment to the effect that those persons not believing in the absolute and unqualified finality of the prophethood of Mohammed were not Muslims under the law and would not be eligible to become president or prime minister or indeed to marry Muslims; further, the practice or propagation of such a heretical creed would

[1]Worldwide there are about 10 million Ahmadis, including 10,000 in the UK where the leader, Mirza Tahir, has been in exile. There is a growing Ahmadi community in the USA, especially among Black Americans.

be punishable by law. However the Ahmadis, who consider themselves to be faithful Muslims, continued in their beliefs.

After the overthrow of President Bhutto by General Zia ul-Haq, and the imposition of martial law in July 1977, pressure on the Ahmadi community increased. This was given institutional form in Ordinance No. 20 of 1984, which came into effect on April 26, 1984, and forbade Ahmadis from describing themselves as Muslims, from using any Islamic terminology to describe any of their buildings or from using the *azan* or public call to prayer. Ahmadis who were convicted of violating these prohibitions could be punished by fines or prison sentences of up to three years. Ahmadis were disenfranchized unless they agreed to register with the electoral authorities as non-Muslims. These restrictions resulted in the spiritual leader of the Ahmadi, Mirza Tahir, leaving Pakistan for London. There was also public violence against Ahmadis by extreme Muslim fundamentalists, both against property, such as mosques, and people; 10 leading Ahmadis were murdered between 1983 and 1985.

Martial law was lifted on December 30, 1985 but the Ordinance remained in force, becoming part of the Constitution of Pakistan. Therefore, arrests and detentions of Ahmadis who professed their faith or displayed the article of their faith, the *Kalema,* continued. According to Ahmadia sources, in the 18 months following the lifting of martial law 228 people were arrested under these provisions. In February 1986, after a violent attack on an Ahmadi mosque in Sahiwal, which resulted in the deaths of two people, a military court sentenced two Ahmadis to death; a similar death sentence was passed only weeks later on two Ahmadis in the town of Sukkar. These sentences aroused worldwide protests to the Pakistan government. In 1986 the punishment for making supposedly derogatory remarks about the prophet Mohammad was changed to include the death penalty, and this was seen as aimed especially at the Ahmadia community.

In August 1988, the sudden death of General Zia in an air crash completely altered the course of Pakistani politics and, after elections in November 1988, Benazir Bhutto of the Pakistan People's Party took office. There were Ahmadi hopes that the discriminatory laws operating against them would be lifted; however to date this has not happened, although a general advance in human rights practice should give Ahmadis some protection against arbitrary arrest and the death penalty. Ahmadi prisoners were not among those amnestied after Bhutto's election and in 1989 Ahmadis continued to be arrested and imprisoned as before. Nor does it appear that the government is committed to the repeal of the ordinance.

In the general elections of November 1988 the system of separate electorates for minority groups gave the Ahmadis one of the 10 seats reserved for minorities (although the Ahmadis are certainly greater in numbers than the Christians or Hindus who were each awarded four seats). This implies a degree of recognition of the Ahmadis as a separate minority group; however it also ensures that it is highly unlikely that any Ahmadi will ever reach high office as has happened in the past. Increasing ethnic violence and economic difficulties, however, may once again place the Ahmadi as convenient scapegoats, and their future status in Pakistan is problematic.

(See also *Hindus of Pakistan; Baha'is of Iran* in **Middle East and North Africa**)

Andaman Islanders

Alternative names: **Andamans, Jarawa, Onges, Sentinelese**
Location: **Andaman Islands, Indian Ocean**
Population: **500-600 in total**
Religion: **indigenous beliefs**
Language: **Negrito languages**

There are four distinct tribal peoples living in the Andaman Islands—the Andamanese, the Onges, the Jarawa and the Sentinelese. The Andaman Islands are a chain of over 500 islands, 27 of which are inhabited, in the Bay of Bengal. Although they are closer to the south-east Asian archipelago the islands, along with the Nicobar islands to the south, are an Indian Union Territory, under the jurisdiction of the Home Ministry in New Delhi.

Little is known about the history and development of the indigenous peoples of the

Andamans, since they are small groups of hunter-gatherers, have no written language and have fallen drastically in numbers over the last two centuries. Although the islands were known to outsiders the first attempts to colonize them came from the British at the end of the eighteenth century although these were soon abandoned. The islands were again colonized in the aftermath of the "Indian Mutiny" of 1857 when a penal colony and jail was established on South Andaman which housed over the years both political and other prisoners. In addition settlers from the Indian mainland, especially from East Bengal/Bangladesh, have settled in the islands and today total 180,000. As a result there has been a permanent, and most probably irreversible, decline in the numbers of indigenous people.

The Andamanese have suffered most drastically. In 1858, when the penal settlement was started, there were 4,800; in 1901, 625; in 1930, 90; and in 1988, 28. Initial casualties came from warfare with colonizers, later ones from diseases such as pneumonia, measles and syphilis. Today the survivors have been resettled by the administration on the 603-hectare Strait Island. The Jarawa were the next group to face colonization of their lands. At first, in desperation, they moved away from the settlements but later they began to attack them. The British retaliated and organized punitive expeditions. The Jarawa today number about 300 and live on the 742 square kilometre Jarawa reserve in South and Middle Andaman islands. The Onge of the remote Little Andaman islands were the next to be contacted by outsiders in 1867 when they killed eight sailors. In retaliation a punitive mission took 70 Onge, about 10% of the total population. Although friendly relations were established in 1887, the Onges were infected by disease and numbers declined from 670 in 1901 to 250 in 1930 and 103 in 1984. The exact numbers

of the Sentinelese of remote North Sentinelese Island remains unknown but they probably number about 50 to 150. Outsiders who have attempted contact have been met by flights of arrows and the official policy is to leave the Sentinelese alone.

Like other Tribal Peoples in India the indigenous peoples of the Andamans are classed as "Scheduled Tribes" and have special protection under the Indian Constitution. The four tribes are among those classed as "primitive tribes" — the subject of special government programmes. But the odds against their survival as viable peoples are overwhelming. The main threat comes from development of the islands by large-scale settlement and deforestation. This was recognized by the late Prime Minister, Indira Gandhi, who stated in 1975: " . . . Neither resettlement nor development should be made an excuse to uproot tribal groups or cut down forests. The Tribals are the original inhabitants and any disturbance may threaten their survival." In 1960 the total population was 50,000 and is today approaching 200,000. Over 100,000 hectares of forest have been cleared and the Andamans Grand Trunk Road will eventually link the main islands.

Tribal resistance continues today, especially by the Jarawa, to those who encroach on their reserve as happened when several road building crew died in 1976 and two settlers died in 1985. Some attempts have been made to contact these Jarawa with gifts, and sometimes these have been successful, but many anthropologists have warned that such contact is intrinsically harmful and will only result in the destruction of the few tribespeople who still survive. Recent proposals by the Indian government to give the Andaman and Nicobar islands the status of a Free Port and to encourage the tourist and communications industries may be the final blow for the original Andaman Islanders.

(See also *Adivasis of India; Veddas of Sri Lanka*)

Anglo-Indians

Location: **India, especially Calcutta; UK, Australia**
Population: **100,000**
% of population: **0.01%**
Religion: **Christian**
Language: **English**

The Anglo-Indian community is the smallest officially recognized minority group in India. Article 366(2) of the Indian Constitution of 1950 defines an Anglo-Indian as "a person whose father or any of whose male progenitors in the male line is or was of European descent but who is domiciled within the territory of India and is or was born within such territory of parents habitually resident therein and not established there for temporary purposes only".

The Anglo-Indian community originated soon after 1639 when the British East India company founded a settlement in Madras. The community identified itself with, and was accepted by, the British, until 1791 when they were excluded from positions of authority in the civil, military and marine services in the East India Company. During the Indian Rebellion of 1857 the Anglo-Indians sided with the British, and consequently received favoured treatment from the British government in preference to Indians, serving in large numbers in the strategic services of the Railways, Post and Telegraph, and Customs. In 1919 the Anglo-Indian community was given one reserved seat in the Central Legislative Assembly in Delhi. The English-speaking Anglo-Indians identified themselves with the British against the nationalist Congress Party, despite British attitudes of superiority.

After independence in 1947 the Anglo-Indians faced a difficult choice — to leave India or to integrate. Many Indians distrusted their pro-British attitudes and western-oriented culture. Large numbers did leave, mainly for Britain and Australia. Those who remained were allowed reserved representation in the Central Legislative (Article 331 — in practice one seat in the lower house) and there are similar provisions in state legislatures. There were also stipulations for reservations in some government posts for a period of 20 years.

In many ways the Anglo-Indians who remain in India are a protected and relatively well-off community. They are literate, urbanized and are well represented in the military, sports and some areas of the civil service. But they are also an ageing community and declining in numbers. Most younger members emigrate, if possible, and those who remain are unlikely to have the numbers or social cohesion to continue as a dynamic community.

Baluchis

Alternative names: **Brahuis (in Kahat plateau)**
Location: **western Pakistan, eastern Iran, south-western Afghanistan**
Population: **Total about 5 million**
% of population: **Pakistan 4.2%; Iran 2%; Afghanistan 1%**
Religion: **Sunni Muslim**
Language: **Baluchi, Brahui, also Punjabi, Urdu, Farsi, Dari, Pashto**

The Baluchis are tribal pastoralists inhabiting the remote and inhospitable mountain and desert region of the border areas of Pakistan, Afghanistan and Iran. The majority are found in the Baluchistan province of Pakistan, with smaller numbers in Iran and Afghanistan. There are significant numbers of Baluchis who live outside their traditional homelands in the three countries and also in the Gulf States. The Baluchis are not a homogenous group and are divided between the Sulemani or Eastern Baluchis in Iran, the Makrani or Western Baluchis in Pakistan and south-western Afghanistan, and the Brahuis of the central Kalat plateau of Pakistani Baluchistan, who speak the Brahui language which is not related to Baluchi, but which often has a heavy Baluchi admixture.

Baluchis are Sunni Muslims of the Hanafi school. They share elements of a cultural and linguistic heritage despite variations in lifestyle and environment. Originally a warrior people, they are divided into tribes, clans and sub-clans which fall under the authority of powerful chiefs, but no leader has been able to create a lasting political framework encompassing all of Baluchistan. Cultivable land is very limited, and most families live by combining subsistence farming with semi-nomadic pastoralism.

Background and history

The Baluchis are a racial amalgam of peoples whose language belongs to the Iranian branch of the Indo-European language family and they claim descent from ancestors who left Aleppo in modern Syria at the time of the ninth century Arab conquests. Linguists believe them to be descended from Indo-Europeans settled around the southern coast of the Caspian Sea in north-west Iran; by the thirteenth or fourteenth century they are believed to have settled in their present homeland. Persian, Sindhi, Afghan, Sikh and other conquering armies repeatedly overran Baluchistan in the following centuries but neither they nor Baluchi chiefs were able to establish permanent control.

The British gained control of most of the region in the nineteenth century, at first through political agreements and subsidies negotiated with tribal leaders and, by the 1870s, by direct control over Baluchi territory or through four princely states. Customary tribal law was retained and enforced by tribal councils under the authority of the Frontier Crimes Regulations (FCR). In 1893 the Durand Line — an official boundary between Afghan and British territory — was created. In the Baluchi areas of Persia, between 1928 and 1930, Reza Khan launched a series of pacification campaigns with the aim of ending tribal raiding of settled villages and controlling general lawlessness. The campaign was successful and after 1935 Iranian Baluchis had lost much of their power to defy the state.

Pakistan

There are an estimated 2.5 million Baluchis and about one million Brahuis in Pakistan, together accounting for less than 5% of the total population. Approximately 56% live in the province of Baluchistan, about 40% of the total area of Pakistan, where there are also increasing numbers of Sindhi, Pashtu and Punjabi speakers, and Baluchis are often in a minority; a further 43% have settled outside their tribal homeland in Sind and Punjab provinces, where they have adopted the local vernacular and sedentarized way of life. As with most of the Pakistani population, they are Sunni Muslims, following the Hanafi school.

In Pakistan, as also in Afghanistan and Iran, the Baluchis are being gradually integrated into the market-oriented economy. Communications were improved, land reform programmes instituted and modern technology introduced. More and more Baluchis are moving to the cities to find work as their economic autonomy has diminished. Tribal chiefs are now acting as middlemen and brokers, dealing with both government and tribespeople. Although the aim of governments is to integrate the Baluchis and other tribes into the mainstream of economic life, there are very few Pakistani Baluchis working in the small manufacturing sector of Baluchistan which is based in Quetta, the regional capital, and largely owned and controlled by non-Baluchis. The province of Baluchistan produces most of Pakistan's natural gas and coal but the Baluchis themselves have little control over these industries. They are also poorly represented in the armed forces, government and bureaucracy. Many tribal leaders have welcomed modernization and have rapidly adapted to the accompanying change in lifestyle, but others have felt their authority being eroded and have resisted change.

At independence in 1947, British Baluchistan and the four Baluchi princely states were merged with Pakistan. But this arrangement ended in 1955 when West Pakistan was amalgamated in one province. In July 1970 Baluchistan was restored to separate provincial status, its boundaries incorporating the former British Baluchistan and the Baluchistan States, a union of four princely states given semi-autonomous status between 1952 and 1955. After East Pakistan (Bangladesh) gained its independence, a new Pakistani constitution, drafted in 1973, contained numerous guarantees of the rights of ethnic minorities, reaffirming their separate legal status and right to their own language and culture; however there was no devolution of power under the leadership of Zulfikar Ali Bhutto and the provinces became increasingly subordinate to central authority despite their lack of support for Bhutto's People's Party of Pakistan (PPP).

The years 1973 to 1977 were marked by a major Baluchi and Brahui tribal rebellion against the Pakistani government, backed by the opposition National Awami Party (NAP). The crisis developed when Bhutto dismissed the NAP coalition government in 1973 on the grounds that they had patronized and encouraged violence and smuggling and had opposed modernization efforts. NAP and other opposition leaders were arrested and jailed and the NAP banned in 1975. In 1976 the *sardari* (tribal chief) system was abolished. Meanwhile the war had escalated; by 1974 there were reported to be as many as 55,000 tribesmen fighting some 70,000 government troops armed with sophisticated weaponry. It is estimated that over 5,000 insurgents and 3,000 government troops were killed, large quantities of livestock destroyed and the interruption of food supplies to civilians in insurgent-controlled areas caused great suffering. Some tribal rebels surrendered under a general amnesty and others fled to Afghanistan where they were housed in government camps. The insurgency continued fitfully until the fall of Bhutto's government in 1977 and the subsequent release of the imprisoned NAP leaders.

After the declaration of martial law by General Zia ul-Haq there was relative peace in Baluchistan. The government posted military and para-military forces throughout the region and greatly increased government expenditure on communications and economic and social programmes. In 1979 Baluchi and Pathan leaders formed the Pakistan National Party (PNP) as a successor to the NAP, and in 1982 this joined with the Movement for the Restoration of Democracy (MRD). Violence which erupted in Sind province in late 1984 led to the meeting in London of leaders of the three minority provinces and the formation of the Sindhi-Baluch-Pashtun Front, aimed at achieving a confederal form of government. Martial law, which was not lifted until 1985, had dampened much autonomous political activity within Baluchistan. In 1986 riots broke out in many cities throughout Pakistan with ethnic groups demanding decentralization and ethnic autonomy.

The political situation changed radically with the election of the PPP under Benazir Bhutto to central government in November 1988. In Baluchistan the PPP formed a coalition government but had a majority of only one seat and soon after its election the Assembly was dissolved by the state governor, allegedly to prevent a vote of no confidence in the state government. There were strikes and protests in the province but in January 1989 the Baluchistan High Court declared the dissolution to be unconstitutional and later the Baluch Nationalist Alliance (BNA) took power with Akbar Bugti as Chief Minister. By August 1989 the central and provincial governments continued to oppose each other with the BNA halting central government development programmes.

Baluchistan and the NWFP have been greatly affected by the movement of over three million refugees from Afghanistan to Pakistan, 20% of them to Baluchistan. Resistance groups moved freely across the border, their successful attacks on Afghan forces frequently provoking retaliatory action. The spillover of the war into Baluchi territory has caused many Baluchis to call for the return of the refugees to Afghanistan and they express fears that the refugees, together with the non-Baluchi immigrants from other areas of Pakistan, have made the Baluchis into a minority within their homeland.

Iran

There are between 500,000 and 750,000 Baluchis in Iran, comprising less than 2% of the population. The majority live in the province of Baluchistan and Seistan with considerable numbers also in neighbouring Kerman and Khorasan provinces. The Sunni Baluchis are set apart not only linguistically and culturally but also by religion from the majority Shia Iranians. The situation of the Baluchis since the declaration of the Islamic Republic in 1979 has been one of uneasy passivity. Under Pahlavi rule the loyalty of the tribal minorities had been assured by government patronage even though Baluchi identity had been suppressed; under Ayatollah Khomeini, an anti-reformist policy was pursued and many of the Baluchis' economic advantages were removed. Federalism seemed as remote as ever under Khomeini, and religious differences were more important in a fundamentalist Islamic Republic. In 1980 a non-Baluchi Shi'ite Muslim Governor was appointed to the province of Baluchistan and Seistan.

Afghanistan

There are about 100,000 Baluchis in Afghanistan, less than 1% of the population, occupying a sparsely-settled and little developed desert area on the southern frontier. The 1980s saw changes for the Baluchis following the pro-Soviet coup of 1978. A minorities programme pledged itself to raising the status of minority groups (including the Baluchis) by improving educational standards and increasing tribal participation in government. A Baluchi-language weekly paper began publication in 1978 and there were plans to open Baluchi-language schools in some areas. Baluchi was one of the four languages newly recognized as official languages of Afghanistan. This emphasis on tribal matters continued with the increased Soviet involvement in Afghan affairs and direct Soviet intervention in December 1979. On paper

therefore the Baluchis had become one of the most protected minorities in Afghanistan.

(See also *Pathans*)

Biharis of Bangladesh

Alternative names: **"Stranded Pakistanis"**
Location: **66 camps in Bangladesh, mainly in urban areas**
Population: **250,000-300,000**
% of population: **0.25%**
Religion: **Muslim**
Language: **Urdu, Bengali**

"Biharis" is the term given to a group of non-Bengali residents and citizens of the former East Pakistan, most of whom originated from the Indian state of Bihar. Today, many "Biharis" live in Pakistan and India in addition to Bangladesh, where many remain in refugee camps and are without citizenship.

After the Mogul conquest, north Indians in Bihar and elsewhere became Muslims and, along with others who came with the Moguls as soldiers and officials, adopted Urdu as their first language. Prior to Partition in 1947, Muslims numbered about four million or 13% of the total Bihari population of 30 million; after Partition, Bihar was assigned to India and many Bihar Muslims migrated to East Pakistan. Another sizeable group of Biharis moved to East Pakistan from Calcutta, where they had gone in search of work and where they began to feel insecure because of communal killings. During Partition, there was a mass movement of peoples between India and Pakistan. Of the eight million who moved from India into Pakistan, about 1.3 million moved into the Eastern wing. Of this group, one million were Muslims from Bihar, and thus these refugees came to be known collectively as the Biharis.

On arrival in East Pakistan, the Biharis found work as small traders, clerks, civil service officials, skilled railway and mill workers and doctors. The majority were hard-working and successful and many were appointed by the Pakistani authorities to replace educated Hindus in administrative jobs and in the mills. The success of the Biharis, at the expense of the Bengali community, created a climate of hostility. The Urdu-speaking Biharis became increasingly unpopular, and were seen by Bengalis as symbols of Pakistani domination.

In the December 1970 elections, most Biharis

supported the pro-Pakistan Muslim League rather than the Awami League which was largely a Bengali nationalist movement. In 1971, the promised National Assembly was postponed, and in retaliation, over 1,000 Biharis, who were seen as symbols of Pakistani domination, were reported to have been killed by Bengalis. Many Biharis fled to the Mirpur suburb of Dacca and more followed when Sheikh Mujibur Rahman, the Awami League leader, was imprisoned and the Awami League was banned, causing a further wave of retaliatory killings. One wing of the Razakars, an auxiliary force in the Pakistani army, was made up almost entirely of Biharis, and many of these used their military position for revenge attacks on Bengalis when civil war broke out in 1971. From March to December 1971, there was widespread bloodshed, and a possible three million people were killed, most of them apparently victims of the Pakistani army. In December the Pakistani army capitulated, but this did not prevent the massacre of several hundred Bengali intellectuals, an act of violence for which the Bihari community is widely blamed.

When the independent state of Bangladesh was formed in December 1971 and the Pakistani army and civilians were evacuated to India, the Biharis were left behind. Most took refuge in enclaves and were protected, as far as possible, by the Indian army, while their shops and houses were occupied or looted and several thousand Bihari leaders were arrested. Following the withdrawal of Indian troops in January 1972, Bangladeshi troops were ordered to gather all weapons and they entered the Bihari enclave at Mirpur where they met fierce resistance. At least 100 people on either side were killed, and following this incident, several thousand Biharis were arrested as alleged collaborators and imprisoned or "disappeared", and there were many cases of retaliation against Biharis. Sheikh Mujib had formerly called for tolerance and reconciliation but from this time on took a harder line towards the Biharis.

By mid-1972, the number of Biharis in Bangladesh was approximately 750,000. Some 278,000 of these were living in very poor conditions in camps on the outskirts of Dacca; another 250,000 were living around Saidpur in the north-west where conditions were better as Biharis outnumbered Bengalis. Reconciliation programmes were initiated and Urdu-speakers were being taught Bengali in an effort to overcome the most obvious obstacle to their acceptance by the Bengalis. However, there was a deep psychological depression and much fear of further Bengali retaliations.

The majority of the Biharis in Bengal have consistently expressed a wish to be repatriated to Pakistan. The Pakistani government initially agreed to take 83,000 Biharis — former civil servants, military and those with family in Pakistan — but later took some others. By 1974, 108,000 had been transferred to Pakistan, mainly by air, and by 1981, about 163,000. As a result, between 250,000 and 300,000 were left in camps in Bangladesh. Describing themselves as "stranded Pakistanis" some were organized into the Stranded Pakistani General Repatriation Committee which advocates militant action, such as a walk across India to Pakistan. In 1980, such a walk was stopped at the Bangladeshi frontiers. Some observers have alleged that elements in the camps have a vested interest in keeping the Biharis as a separate and distinct community, nurturing dreams of repatriation rather than constructive improvements. Conditions in the camps were still very bad for these Biharis although they were increasingly able to leave the camps in search of work.

Many feel that Pakistan has a moral obligation to take in the remaining Biharis or at least those who had remained loyal to Pakistan during the war; however, the conditions under which many Biharis live in Pakistan, mainly at Orangi outside Karachi, the lack of adequate housing or work and the growing hostility felt towards them by many Pakistanis, indicate that another large-scale influx of Biharis might create serious problems. Pakistan has agreed, in principle, to take in as many of the refugees as possible provided funds could be made available for their transport and resettlement. At a conference of the United Nations High Commission for Refugees (UNHCR) held in 1981, 12 national and international organizations agreed to form a working party to assist the resettlement programme in collaboration with Pakistan and Bangladesh. Several Islamic states have also expressed willingness to aid in financing the operation.

However, despite these promising developments, delays in the provision of finance and political procrastination by successive Pakistani governments has prevented large-scale repatriation. Pakistan's President Zia signed an agreement with the World Muslim League in mid-1988 providing for resettlement for the Biharis but he was assassinated one month later. The new government of Benazir Bhutto confirmed that it would agree to repatriation; however, after intense pressures from Sind nationalists these plans were shelved.

For those Biharis who remained in Bangladesh there are still difficulties. It has not been forgotten that they willingly entered into government service under the Pakistanis and as a result they came to symbolize Pakistani dominance. Most Biharis are afraid of trying to integrate into the Bengali community; yet after two generations they probably have closer cultural and economic ties with that community than they do with Pakistan. This integration cannot take place without determination on the part of the Biharis and increased good-will from the Bengalis; however, perhaps the most crucial determining factor in Bihari development will be the Bangladeshi government's need for the skills acquired by the Biharis under Pakistani rule. Economic necessity has meant that many have left the camps but those who remain — possibly 250,000 in all — face a bleak future.

(See also *Chittagong Hill Tract Tribes of Bangladesh*)

Chittagong Hill Tract Tribes of Bangladesh

Name: **Chittagong Hill Tract Tribals**
Alternative names: **Chakmas, Marmas, Tripuras, "Jummas" (collective name)**
Location: **Chittagong Hill Tracts, south-western Bangladesh**
Population: **about 500,000**
% of population: **0.5% of Bangladesh population, 0.66% of CHT population**
Religion: **Buddhist, animist, Christian**
Language: **various**

The Tribals of the Chittagong Hill Tracts (CHT) are part of a much larger tribal minority in Bangladesh. Some of these tribal peoples, such as the Santals, Oraons, Hos, Mundas and Rajbansis, who are found along the border of West Bengal in the east of Bangladesh, are of Australoid and Dravidian stock and have affinities with Hinduism; others, such as the Chakmas, Marmas, Tripuras, Garos, Manipuris and Khasis, are of Mongoloid stock and are Sino-Tibetan in origin. Most of these groups live in the Bandaran, Chittagong Hill Tract and Khagrachari Districts along the eastern border of Bangladesh adjoining Burma and the Indian states of Mizoram and Tripura. The Khasis and the Garos are predominantly Christian while the Chakmas and the Maghs are Buddhists. Most of the other groups have animistic beliefs. The tribes which live close to West Bengal have strong affinities with Bengali society but those in the CHT are more isolated and so retain a very distinctive culture.

The peoples of the Chittagong Hill Tracts are composed of 13 main tribes of which the Chakmas, Marmas and Tripuras (Tipperas) total approximately 90%. The Chakmas are the largest single tribe in Bangladesh, with a population of 300,000; they account for over half of the tribal population of the Hill Tracts. They are unique among the tribes in having sacred Buddhist texts written in both their own language and in Pali, the language of Buddhist scriptures. Their ancestors are believed to have migrated west from Arakan in present-day Burma and their alphabet is related to early Burmese alphabets. Culturally the Chakmas have affinities with the Chin tribes of western Burma.

Most of the CHT peoples migrated into the area from the south from the sixteenth to the nineteenth centuries, but, from the seventeenth century, when Bengali settlers arrived on the coast, they retreated into the hills. The CHT tribal groups remained largely undisturbed by British rule. The Chittagong Hill Tracts Regulation 1900 left them to govern themselves according to their traditions and non-tribals

were not permitted to settle in tribal areas. After partition in 1947, however, the Pakistani government allowed Bengali Muslims to move into Chittagong and the CHTs and this caused resentment among the hill tribes. There was a gradual movement of tribal peoples into India and the proportion of non-tribals living in tribal areas grew, but after the establishment of military rule in 1958 non-tribals were once again barred from settling in the region. The special status of the CHTs was abolished in 1964. The huge Kaptai Dam built in the 1960s submerged 40% of the cultivable land of the tracts and displaced one sixth of the population. In the general election of 1970 the CHTs elected two tribal independents to the Provincial Assembly of East Pakistan and one to the National Parliament of Pakistan. However, the popular uprising of 1971 and the subsequent breakup of Pakistan and formation of Bangladesh meant that their status was again problematic.

When the Chakmas petitioned the new government for a restoration of autonomy for the CHT they received an unsympathetic response, the government considering such a request as secessionist. Some Tribals had sided with the Pakistanis and thus all were so branded, and the government launched retaliatory raids into the CHT in 1972 with the result that thousands of Marmas and Tripuras fled to India and their lands were given to Bengalis. The People's Solidarity Association (JSS) and its military wing, the Shanti Bahini, were formed to resist the government forces. Numbering between 2,000 and 15,000, it was mainly staffed by Chakmas, but contained also Marmas and Tripuras and conducted a guerrilla war against Bengali settlers and government troops throughout the 1970s and into the 1980s. The government launched counter-insurgency campaigns against the Shanti Bahini producing fresh waves of refugees into India, most notably in 1979, 1981, 1984 and 1986, and by 1987 50,000 refugees — about 10% of the tribal population of the CHT — were living in Indian camps or in bush settlements.

The CHT and the north-east of India are

remote strategic areas which are normally closed to foreigners; therefore, independent information on the continuing war in the CHT is not easy to obtain. However there are some well-attested accounts of human rights violations against Tribals by both military and government personnel and Bengali settlers. Amnesty International has documented cases of deliberate killings and executions, torture and ill-treatment, and detentions although it appears that stricter controls over military personnel may have led to a decrease in such reports after 1987.

The main reason behind the Shanti Bahini attacks is the continuing encroachment of Bengalis onto tribal lands. The CHT contains about 10% of the total land area of Bangladesh which is one of the world's poorest and most densely populated countries. Consequently for many years the government saw the CHT as a major opportunity to resettle Bengali peasants and between 1977 and 1987 about 300,000 ethnic Bengalis moved into the area and now constitute about one third of the total population, leading to fears by the Tribals that they will soon become a minority in their own land. From the end of 1982 the government claimed that it had ceased to allot land to non-tribals and it appears that official efforts to decrease migration have made some impact on population growth; however, landless peasants from the plain still migrate of their own volition. The CHT are not suitable for wet-rice cultivation and attempts to build industries and development projects have benefited settlers rather than Tribals. Some western development agencies have terminated projects in the area because of the effects of these projects and the government's human rights record.

There have been attempts by the government to make a settlement with the Shanti Bahini. In 1987 a National Committee was formed to look into the problem and held talks with tribal leaders from the JSS and Shanti Bahini between October 1987 and February 1988 with the hope of creating a permanent settlement and allowing the return of the refugees from Tripura. The JSS made a number of demands contending that these were the only way of protecting the interests of the Tribals; these include the withdrawal of Bengali settlers and prohibition of future settlement by non-Tribals; constitutional guarantees that these provisions will never change without a plebiscite; economic development aimed at Tribals; dismantling of model villages and release of JSS prisoners; and involvement of international agencies such as UNHCR or ICRC in the implementation of such an agreement. However, the government contends that many of these demands are not possible without violating the present constitution. A lull in fighting was broken with renewed attacks on settlers by the Shanti Bahini in April 1988.

Perhaps 50,000 Tribal refugees remain in five refugee camps inside India. India does not accept UNHCR or other international assistance for these camps, which precludes international inspection or aid. Conditions are reputed to be poor; nevertheless the JSS has managed to keep some sense of continuity and to organize schools, medical facilities and temples. Some observers see the Indian decision to isolate the camps as being deliberately obstructive of attempts by the Bangladeshi government to settle the situation; while others maintain that it is a way of defusing possible tensions with the tribal peoples of its own north-eastern states (Tripura, formerly a tribal area is now predominantly a Bengali settler state). In 1982 there was a repatriation agreement between the Indian and Bangladeshi governments, but the JSS says that Bangladeshi promises to the returning refugees of rehabiliation and protection were not met and that many were forced to flee to other areas. In 1988 the two governments agreed to seal the borders between the two, preventing infiltration by guerrilla groups on both sides, but at the same time preventing refugees from crossing the border to safety. An agreement to repatriate refugees was reached between the two countries in November 1987; however, after pleas from international human rights organizations, the Indian government suspended the plans. Apparently refugees had refused to return, fearing violence against them.

(See also *Adivasis of India; Nagas of India*)

Hindus of Pakistan

Location: **Sind province, Pakistan**
Population: **approximately 1.5 million**
% of population: **1.6% of population of Pakistan; 7.5% of Sind population**
Religion: **Hindu**
Language: **Sindhi**

The Hindus of Pakistan are a religious minority in an overwhelmingly Muslim society. They constitute about one-and-a-half-million or about 1.6% of the population of 96 million. They live primarily in the urban areas of the province of Sind in the lower Indus valley and over half are concentrated in the south-east district of Thar Parkar which borders India. For the most part Hindus in Pakistan are well educated and active in commerce, trade and the civil service.

Sind at one time had a Hindu majority; however, invasion and later settlement by Arabs, Persians and Turks and conversion by Sindhis to Islam led to a decrease in the proportion of Hindus. Prior to Partition in 1947 a quarter of the population of Sind was Hindu but after widespread inter-religious violence in the North West Frontier Province and in the Punjab the great majority of Hindus living in Pakistan elected to migrate to India. Sindhi Hindus joined in the migration, fearful that violence might spread to their province after Partition. By late 1948 most had left Sind for India, where large numbers settled in Rajasthan, Delhi and Bombay.

Those Hindus who elected to stay in Pakistan after Partition were faced with constitutional and other limitations imposed generally on all non-Muslims. The Preamble to the Constitution of Pakistan states that "adequate provision shall be made for the minorities to freely profess and practise their religions and develop their cultures" and that "adequate provision shall be made to safeguard the legitimate interests of the minorities and backward and depressed classes". Although barred from holding the highest offices, the religious freedom of Hindus has not been threatened; nevertheless there is an element of distrust towards the Hindus, who are believed by many to be pro-India, and during the Indo-Pakistani wars of 1965 and 1971 many Hindus were suspected of being Indian informers. Some students have suffered discrimination as a result of the government quota scheme whereby only a certain number from minority groups are accepted into higher education.

Under the leadership of Zulfikar Ali Bhutto, who came to power in 1971, the provinces of Pakistan became increasingly subordinate to central authority despite assurances of their continued autonomy. Greater constitutional powers were given to the central executive, and the country's economic, political and administrative institutions were reorganized with the aim of centralizing power further. The process continued after 1977 after the rise of Zia ul-Haq and in 1982 Sindhis joined with other minority groups in forming the Movement for the Restoration of Democracy (MRD). In 1984 the MRD led anti-government demonstrations in a movement which erupted into widespread violence. Thousands of protestors were imprisoned. In late 1985 Sindhi leaders met leaders of the Baluchi and Pashtoun groups in London and set out demands for a confederal form of government. A few months later the radical Awami National Party was formed. While Hindus were not in the forefront of these political movements they tended to be sympathetic to moves both for greater religious tolerance and provincial autonomy, including linguistic autonomy. Their interests were however opposed to the Mohajirs — Muslim immigrants who came from India during and after 1947 — and who tend to speak Urdu or Punjabi.

In the "partyless" elections of 1985, held by President Zia after the lifting of martial law, Hindus and other religious minorities were allocated separate electorates in nationwide minority constituencies. Previously, the minority groups had voted in general electorates in which they resided and members of the National Assembly subsequently elected members from the minority communities to sit in the legislature. The system of separate electorates was retained in the November 1988 elections — the first general elections since 1976. Ten of the 207 seats in the National Assembly were set aside for minorities. This included four seats for Hindus, four for Christians, one for Ahmadis and one for smaller groups such as Parsis, Sikhs, Baha'is, Jews and the Kalash tribe. Some Hindus were opposed to the system of the separate electorates, which they maintain dilutes the influence of the community and paves the way for further segregation. Most Hindu candidates concentrated their efforts on the Thar Parkar district and neglected smaller Hindu communities. Other Hindus defend the system as giving them a direct minority voice in the Assembly.

(See also *Ahmadis of Pakistan; Muslims of India*)

Jews of India

Alternative names: **Cochinis, Bene Israel, Baghdadis, Manipur Jews**
Location: **Bombay, west coast, Manipur**
Population: **5,000+**
Religion: **Judaism**
Language: **various**

There are three main Jewish communities in India, each of a different origin and with different characteristics; Cochinis, the Bene Israel and the Baghdadis. None has faced persecution but they are all declining in numbers due to immigration to Israel.

The Malayalam-speaking Jews from the city of Cochin in Kerala claim to have arrived in the sub-continent after the destruction of the Temple, although the earliest documentary evidence dates from the ninth century. They are divided into three endogamous groups; the White Jews, a mixture of indigenous Indian Jews and Middle Eastern and European Jews; the Black Jews, who are in most ways indistinguishable from local Indians; and the Meshuhrarim, descendents of Indian slaves who were attached to both groups. The Cochin Jews maintained trading and religious links with Middle Eastern Jewish communities but, although they numbered 2,500 in 1948, immigration to Israel has reduced them to a handful.

The Bene Israel lived for centuries on the Konkan coast and, later, in Bombay, isolated from Jews elsewhere but maintaining some Jewish religious practices. From the nineteenth century they made efforts to bring their customs into line with Orthodox Jewish practices. In 1951 there were 20,000 Bene Israel but today there are no more than 5,000. Also based in Bombay is the most recent Jewish community of Middle Eastern and Iraqi origin who came to India from the early nineteenth century. As white non-Indians the Baghdadis enjoyed a special status and much prosperity under the British, but after independence most left for Israel or other countries and today there may be no more than 300-400.

More recently, tribal groups in the north-east of India have claimed themselves to be Jewish. These belong to the Shinlung tribes, usually called Kuki in India and Chin in Burma. They claim to be the descendants of one of the lost tribes of Israel and to have maintained Jewish practices until their conversion to Christianity in the last century. These "Manipur Jews" have established a number of synagogues and have gained thousands of converts. Some observers have seen this conversion as a way of escaping the constraints of the caste system.

(See also *Jews of the Middle East and North Africa* in **Middle East and North Africa**)

Kashmiris

Alternative names: **Jammu and Kashmir, "Azad Kashmir"**
Location: **north-west India, north-east Pakistan**
Population: **Jammu and Kashmir (Indian administered) 6.1 million**
% of population: **0.9% of Indian population**
Religion: **Muslim 66%, Hindu 30%, Buddhist 1%**
Language: **Kashmiri, Urdu, Hindi**

The Kashmiris are the inhabitants of a region in the extreme north-west of India. The constitutional position of this area is complex as about two-thirds is presently administered as the Indian state of Jammu and Kashmir and one third ("Azad Kashmir") is under Pakistani administration, although this is not recognized by India and the effective border between the two areas is the ceasefire line agreed in 1949 modified in places by the line of control resulting from the war of 1971. In addition, parts of the unpopulated mountainous areas in the north and east are disputed between India and China.

The total area of Jammu and Kashmir is about 220,000 square kilometres with about 132,000 square kilometres under Indian administration as the state of Jammu and Kashmir. This state has a population of about 6.1 million, of whom approximately two-thirds are Muslim and most of the others are Hindu, with small minorities of Buddhists and Sikhs. Slightly over half of the state's population lives in the Vale of Kashmir where 90% are Muslim, while in the lowlands of Jammu only 37% are Muslim and there is an overall Hindu majority.

The mountainous northern frontier region of Ladakh is sparsely populated and its population has close cultural and linguistic ties with Tibet. The various areas of the state are often referred to collectively as Kashmir and their inhabitants as "Kashmiris" although it can also be used to refer only to the inhabitants of the Vale of Kashmir. Jammu and Kashmir is the only state in the Indian Union with a Muslim majority. In addition, it is the only Indian state which borders the two countries with which independent India has been at war — Pakistan and China.

History

In the fourteenth century the Vale of Kashmir was invaded by Muslims from the west who brought to an end centuries of Hindu and Buddhist rule. In 1587 the region became part of the Mogul Empire and in the mid-seventeenth century it was conquered by Afghans who ruled there for over 60 years until the Sikhs took control in 1819; by this time the majority of the population had converted to Islam. In 1846 the British defeated the Sikhs in the First Sikh War and founded the modern state of Jammu and Kashmir which they turned over to the Hindu Maharaja of Jammu in exchange for seven million rupees. Kashmir then was never part of the British empire, a crucial point for advocates of Kashmiri independence. By making this transaction the British gained a buffer state between British India and Russia and China, one which they did not have to administer; however, by setting a Hindu ruler over a largely Muslim population they also set in motion events which later caused conflict in the region.

The Hindu dynasty continued to rule over Kashmir until the partition of the sub-continent in August 1947. During this time the Muslim majority lived under orthodox Hindu law and was excluded from the civil service and the military. In the 1930s two popular movements were formed by Kashmiris agitating against Hindu rule. These movements did not share a common goal, however, as one was Islamic and favoured the inclusion of Kashmir in the new state of Pakistan while the other, the Kashmir National Conference lead by Sheikh Mohammed Abdullah, was secular and demanded independence for Kashmir.

Partition

Under the terms of the Partition agreement the rulers of the various princely states were given the choice of acceding either to Pakistan or to India. The Maharaja vacillated over his decision and at Partition had still not decided on the matter. His lack of commitment to either country provoked revolts in the south-west of the province in October 1947 and led to the formation by Muslim deserters of the "Azad Kashmir Army" in central Kashmir and an invasion of Pathan tribesmen from Pakistan. This was followed by accusation and counter-accusation from the Kashmir ruler and the Pakistani government and, under the pressure of these events, the Maharaja acceded to India. India accepted the

accession on condition that a referendum be held
to determine the wishes of the people once order
had been restored, and Indian troops were sent
into Kashmir to deal with the tribal invasion.

Both India and Pakistan accepted the principle
of self-determination for Kashmir but they were
unable to agree on the conditions of a referendum. India would not agree to the holding of a
plebiscite until Pakistani forces had been withdrawn from Kashmir, and Pakistan stressed the
geographical and cultural continuity of Pakistan
and Kashmir, and called for the establishment
of an impartial Kashmir government before the
holding of a referendum. In January 1948 India
appealed to the UN Security Council and, after
investigation by a UN Commission, the Security
Council passed a resolution according to which
Pakistani troops and nationals would withdraw,
the evacuated territory would be administered
by the local authorities under the surveillance of
the commission, and India would withdraw its
forces in stages; the two sides would then hold
consultations with a view to holding a referendum
in the future. Although both sides agreed to the
resolution it was never implemented. Neither
side wanted to be the first to withdraw and risk
the other side remaining in control.

Integration with India

Over the next 20 years Kashmir was gradually
integrated into India. There was no referendum
and Kashmiris were denied free and open state
elections; in 1957 the pro-India state assembly
proclaimed Kashmir an integral part of India.
Sheikh Abdullah — undoubtedly the most popular symbol of Kashmiri identity — spent much of
this time in detention. In the mid-1960s there was
widespread protest within Kashmir — much of it
with a strongly Islamic refrain — and anti-Indian
guerrilla activity, combined with a non-violent
campaign of civil disobedience, exacerbated
tension between India and Pakistan, leading in
August 1965 to the second Indo-Pakistani war
over Kashmir. Talks between the two countries
led to a ceasefire in September and a withdrawal
to the 1949 ceasefire line.

In the aftermath of the 1965 war there was
an upsurge of protest by militant Muslim
students. In order to curb this the Indian
government invoked the Defence of India
Rules, instituting censorship, jailing all advocates of self-determination and prohibiting
gatherings of more than five people without
prior permission. These measures were later
relaxed somewhat. The 1971 Indo-Pakistani war
over Bangladesh weakened Pakistan, leaving it

less able to challenge Indian control of Kashmir
by force, and India began a programme of heavy
investment in Kashmir's economic development
which, it was hoped, would help to make the
Indian presence more acceptable to Kashmiris.

Sheikh Abdullah was released from detention
in 1972 and in 1974 he and the Indian Prime
Minister, Indira Gandhi, concluded an agreement on the constitutional status of Kashmir in
which Sheikh Abdullah accepted Kashmir's accession to India. Under this agreement relations
between the two would continue to be governed
under Article 370 of the Indian constitution. This
article limited the Union Parliament's power to
legislate for Kashmir to only three areas; those
of defence, communications and foreign policy,
and such subjects as the President might by order
specify with the concurrence of the Kashmiri
government. The Union Parliament would,
however, continue to have powers to make laws
relating to the prevention of activities directed
towards the secession of any part of the Indian
Union. Thus, Kashmir had considerably greater
autonomy than other Indian states although, in
practice, such autonomy was severely limited by
the centralizing trends of Indira Gandhi's rule
and, of course, the strategic position of Kashmir
in relation to Pakistan.

Sheikh Abdullah's government proved to be
corrupt and inefficient; nevertheless his National
Conference Party won an election victory in
1977 and after he died in 1982 his son Farooq
Abdullah took over as leader. The National
Conference government was re-elected in 1983,
partly because of fears that Kashmir's special
status would be changed. By this time, however,
Indira Gandhi had turned against Abdullah,
had repeatedly criticized him for encouraging
"anti-national" activities and had encouraged
defections from the National Conference so that
it finally lost its majority. A Congress Party
government, headed by Abdullah's brother-in-
law, took over in July 1984, despite widespread
protests. To some extent these protests were part
of the growing number of Muslim-Hindu communal clashes throughout India, but in Kashmir
they also reflected the desire of many Muslims
for either union with Pakistan, independence,
or greater autonomy, or were simply against
increasing dominance from Delhi.

Although Farooq Abdullah again won power
at the next election, there were further violent protests throughout the late 1980s against
Kashmir's integration within India. This was
particularly so from mid-1988 when there was
a series of bomb blasts, arson attacks, shootings
and strikes, organized by various Islamic sepa-

ratist organizations, to which the government responded by police and military action. The Indian government contends that the separatists are organized and financed by Pakistan, and there is evidence that this is at least partly true, but it is also aware that such sentiment reflects the frustration of many poor Kashmiri Muslims, especially in the slums of Srinagar, who feel that their position within India is inevitably an inferior one. Many of the secessionist gunmen are educated unemployed Muslim youths. On the other hand, critics of the government contend that the situation in Kashmir has been deliberately allowed to fester and that a situation, similar to that in the Punjab, is developing. By September 1989 more than 80 people had died and several hundred Kashmiris had been detained (some without trial under administrative detention) and legislation had been introduced imposing press censorship.

Divisions within Kashmir

Apart from the position of Kashmir *vis à vis* India there is also considerable diversity within the state, most notably between the 3.2 million highlanders from Kashmir proper, 90% of whom are Muslims, and the lowlanders from Jammu, the majority of whom are Hindu. Most of the state's industry is concentrated in Jammu but most of the development funds are spent in the Valley, where 60% of the population is engaged in horticulture, although tourism flourishes around Srinagar Lake. The two areas compete for economic resources and a delicate balance is maintained between them, paralleled in the state administration moving to Jammu in winter and Srinagar in the summer. When Farooq Abdullah announced in 1987 that his government would take steps to discontinue the practice and that some departments would be stationed permanently in Srinagar, there were protests in Jammu, followed by counter-protests in the Valley throughout November 1987.

(See also *Muslims of India; Sikhs*)

More recently there have been tensions in the remote northern area of Ladakh between the Muslims (who are a minority in the area) and the majority Buddhists. Ladakh occupies about one third of the area of Kashmir but contains only 135,000 people. The Buddhist Ladakhis claimed that they did not have adequate political representation in the Jammu and Kashmir state legislature, that there were few Ladakhis in the administration, and that commerce was dominated by traders from the Vale of Kashmir. In addition there were religious tensions, fanned by the Muslim separatist feelings in Srinagar. There were demands that Ladakh be separated from Jammu and Kashmir and be given the status of a Union Territory, i.e. ruled directly from Delhi, and also that Ladakhis be classified as a Scheduled Tribe. Violent clashes between Ladakhis and Muslims took place in mid-1989 and Buddhists began a campaign of civil disobedience in support of their demands.

"Azad Kashmir"

In Pakistani-ruled Azad ("Free") Kashmir there has also been tension between Kashmiris and the Pakistani authorities. Its constitutional status is anomalous since Pakistan, in theory, still regards the whole state as disputed territory; consequently, it has never been represented in the Pakistan National Assembly, although in practice it is administered as Pakistani territory. Some structures were put in place in order to allow for a certain measure of local rule; however these were abolished, along with the National and Provincial Assemblies' in 1977, after General Zia had assumed power, and the holder of the post of "President of Azad Kashmir" was dismissed and replaced by Zia's own nominee in 1982, despite protests. As with Indian Kashmir there is a geographic and ethnic division within the area between the lowlands and the mountainous "Northern Territories" of Gilgit, Hunza and Skardu.

Koochis of Afghanistan

Alternative names: **various tribal names**
Location: **Afghanistan, Pakistan**
Population: **2.5 million (est. 1978)**
% of population: **15%-20%**
Religion: **Muslim**
Language: **various**

The Koochis are the nomadic herding peoples of Afghanistan, who have followed a nomadic way of life for perhaps 2,000 years. They are from a variety of ethnic groups as is the country as a whole. The exact population of Afghanistan is not known due to the geographical remoteness of the country, while the continuing state of war since the Soviet invasion of 1979 has driven many into exile. In 1978 a UN-sponsored study of nomads estimated that there were about 2.5 million Koochis. Since then the numbers have probably decreased as the effects of war have forced large numbers of Koochis into internal or external exile.

Koochi tribes can be divided into three types; pure nomads, semi-sedentary and nomadic traders. Pure nomads, whose movements are determined by the availability of pasture, are finding their way of life increasingly precarious. Even before the war, border restrictions, agricultural irrigation schemes and droughts limited their freedom; today there are minefields, bombing raids and fighting between rival forces which kill both people and animals. Koochis are often forced to camp near urban areas where the men can find labouring jobs. The development of roads suitable for motors made the caravans of Koochi traders obsolete in many areas. The semi-sedentary Koochis have tended to become more sedentary as they can no longer live off their livestock. The war has also limited their traditional treks between summer pastures and winter habitation.

Koochis are organized within a patriarchal tribal structure and live communally. Male and female roles are rigidly adhered to, but Koochi women are responsible for many important economic functions within the tribe and go unveiled, unlike most rural Afghan women. Illiteracy is high and access to health, education and social services is minimal. Each tribe is a self-contained unit and none, either separately or in conjunction with others, has political power or representation within the national government. Large numbers have become refugees and others have been forced to give up a nomadic life. As a silent minority within Afghanistan their future appears bleak.

Muslims of India

Location: **throughout India**
Population: **75-80 million**
% of population: **about 10%-11%**
Religion: **Muslim**
Language: **various, most notably Urdu**

The Muslims of India are the major religious minority within India and one of the largest Muslim communities in the world, certainly the largest Muslim minority in the world. They are the second largest minority group within India (after the Scheduled Castes); however they are a relatively small group, comprising only 10% to 11% of the population or about 75 to 80 million people, in an overwhelmingly Hindu society.

Muslims are not an homogenous group, divided as they are by language, ethnicity, culture and economic position. The great majority are Sunni Muslims, the remainder are Shia and diverse sects. They are a majority only in one state in India, Jammu and Kashmir, everywhere else they are a minority although often concentrated in Muslim residential areas. The largest numbers are found in Uttar Pradesh, Bihar, West Bengal and the southern state of Kerala.

Background and history

Although Islam had reached India much earlier, it was not until the Muslim invasions of the eleventh and twelfth centuries that Islam became a force in northern India, and even so it did not establish itself until the time of the Mogul Emperors in the sixteenth century. In general, the Moguls did not try forcibly to convert their Hindu subjects and the greatest of the Moguls, Akbar, tried to merge aspects of the two religions, but granted a large degree of tolerance to the majority religion. With the Moguls came large numbers of Central Asian soldiers and officials but the bulk of Muslims were converts from indigenous Indians, mainly from the lower castes, who saw it as a way of escaping the restrictions of caste inferiority. The greatest concentrations of Muslims were in the north-west (present-day Pakistan) and the east (present-day Bangladesh) where Hinduism had been weakest (and Buddhism strongest), but there were substantial numbers of Muslims throughout north and east India. The south (with the exception of the Malabar coast) was, and remains, predominently Hindu.

By the time of the British domination of India in the nineteenth century the Muslims comprised perhaps one quarter of the total population. Although there was sometimes animosity between Hindus and Muslims, there were also grounds for co-operation; as had happened during the uprising against the British in 1857. There was also, in practice, a considerable amount of syncratic mixing on either side, especially in areas with an admixture of the two religions. The British administration of India inevitably relied heavily on Indian co-operation and collaboration; as a result caste Hindus (especially Bengalis) took posts in the civil service and as middlemen. The Muslims tended to be less likely to learn English or to take these roles; consequently, they lost much of their remaining power and influence, as was most notably symbolized by the British takeover of the Muslim-ruled kingdom of Oudh and later the deposition of the Mogul Emperor (although he was a powerless figurehead). At the end of the nineteenth century some Muslims had began to challenge these attitudes; they organized Muslim social and educational associations (most notably the founding of Aligarh Muslim University in Uttar Pradesh) and the beginnings of political associations.

The British were able to use the divisions between the Hindu and Muslim communities to "divide and rule". In general, Muslims were considered to be more conservative, loyal and reliable. At times there was some commonality between Hindu and Muslim aspirations; increasingly, however, Muslims feared the dominant Hindu influence; they demanded separate electorates for Muslims and these were embodied in the Government of India Act of 1909. Although at first there was little demand for a separate state for Muslims, the growth of the Congress Party with its Hindu symbolism alienated some Muslims, and the Muslim League under Jinnah was able to step into the gap. After World War II Partition appeared inevitable and finally took place in 1947, with consequent and tragic loss of life on both sides.

Ironically the creation of Pakistan (later to become Pakistan and Bangladesh), ostensibly in order to give the Muslim minority a state of its own, created a new minority problem within India. While the Muslim majority areas became separate (with the exception of Kashmir) the Muslims living as a minority in Hindu areas were left more isolated than previously. From being one quarter, Muslims were now only about 10% of the total population of newly partitioned India. The greatest population transfers were in the areas close to the borders, but some of the Muslim elite, principally from Uttar Pradesh, left for Pakistan. In the south of India, there was little movement of peoples; to this day Muslim-Hindu relations are better there than in the north — even when there is a large Muslim population as in Kerala. The Muslims of the north were therefore left without their previous leadership.

Perceptions and issues

Many Hindus were embittered by the Partition and Muslims were blamed collectively for this. Although India has fought three wars with Pakistan and there has been no collective disloyalty to India by Muslims, nevertheless Muslims are seen generally as "anti-Indian" and "anti-national", which in turn affected their own perceptions of themselves. It was only in the 1970s that Indian Muslims began to reassess their own position within India. A generation was growing up which had no personal experience of Partition and the breakup of Pakistan in 1971 demonstrated that a Muslim state in itself did not necessarily ensure equality. The Emergency of 1975-77 was also a watershed, as Indian Muslims, particularly in the north, suffered from forced sterilization campaigns. From this time Muslims began to shake off some of their previous passivity and demand rights.

Indian Muslims are not granted the same constitutional safeguards as the Scheduled Castes or Scheduled Tribes and they are not entitled to reservations in employment or education. Although Hinduism is the majority religion it is not an official or state-sponsored one; India is a secular state and there is complete religious freedom guaranteed. A Minorities Commission, set up after the election of a Janata government in 1977, monitors the position of non-Scheduled Caste and non-Scheduled Tribe minorities, such as Muslims, although it has no power to implement changes. Nor are Muslims entitled to reserved constituencies in the central or state government assemblies although all, except the explicitly communal parties, will have Muslim parliamentary representatives in their group and governments try to ensure that there is at least one Muslim in the Cabinet. There have been several Muslim Chief Ministers in various states. However the number of Muslims in legislatures is less than their numbers would warrant. To date there have been two Muslim Presidents of India, a highly visible post, although with little real power.

Despite their large numbers, Muslims in fact do badly in some areas of employment and administration. For example, at the beginning of the 1980s Muslims comprised only 1.5% of the officers and 1% of the clerks of the central civil service, and 3% of the elite Indian Administrative Service. Less than 2% of the army officer corps is Muslim (although a Muslim has been appointed as Commander-in-Chief of the Indian Air Force). This pattern extends beyond government however. A recent survey of 800 senior positions in 86 major companies showed only five Muslims. Some commentators have blamed the poor showing on traditional Muslim attitudes to education and the emphasis on Urdu and religious education, rather than on science or marketable skills. In any case the effect is reinforcing; Muslims are by necessity employed or self-employed in small businesses, artisanship, fishing and unskilled work and few are willing to try to break this circle if it exposes them to further discrimination.

Another problem is language, especially in the north of India where most Muslim communities speak Urdu, a Persian-derived language, using a Persian script but which in its spoken form has similarities to Hindi (Hindi also has a considerable Urdu influence). Once the language of the elite, Urdu is not a recognized official language in India. This is, in part, not because of the numbers who speak it (which actually totals more than many recognized languages) but because of its lack of a distinct majority population in a specific area; apart from Kashmir, Muslims are everywhere a minority. Uttar Pradesh, the state with the largest population in India and where approximately 15% of its 110 million people

are Muslims — 17 million in all — did not recognize Urdu as an official language. Muslims have campaigned for Urdu to receive the status of an official language (alongside Hindi). When this was granted in Uttar Pradesh in September 1989 there were clashes between Hindu and Muslim students in which at least 23 died. Urdu has also received official language status in Bihar.

There have been frequent, and sometimes violent, communal clashes between Muslims and Hindus in India. Ostensibly about religion, the root causes are often deeper; unemployment, poverty, discrimination etc. Hindu extremist groups such as the Shiv Sena or the RSS still consider Muslims to be disloyal. On the other hand, Muslim extremist groups preach a militant Islam and maintenance of a separate Muslim way of life. Some of the tensions that can result can be seen in the Shah Bano case when an elderly Muslim woman sued her divorced husband for maintenance. Muslim traditionalists, apparently backed by a majority of Muslims, saw the court ruling in the woman's favour as state interference in Islamic personal law which governs the community (Hindu personal law applies to Hindus). Less traditionalist Muslims saw the case as an important breakthrough for women's rights in Islam. More explosive, however, was the contention about a shrine at Ayodhya in Uttar Pradesh which Muslims claimed was a mosque and Hindus claimed was the birthplace of the god Rama. There have been many major communal disturbances concerning this shrine. Muslims allege that the police and army see Muslims in a discriminatory way; the single most serious incident being the killing of several hundred Muslims at Meerut in May 1987 by the UP Provincial Armed Constabulary.

Muslim expectations are rising. In the 1970s and early 1980s hundreds of thousands of Muslims worked in the Gulf countries and their new wealth put them directly into competition with Hindus; this has been a factor in some clashes. Even within the small business sector in the north there is a slow improvement in the Muslim economic position. But in many ways this has made Muslims more conscious of their perceived inferior position and gives them a new determination to change it. How such change is likely to come about is problematic. The Muslim League and various other Muslim Parties are unlikely to be anything more than an irritant to governments. There is no all-Indian Muslim party and attempts to found a common front with Scheduled Castes have yet to come to fruition. Before 1977 the Congress Party was the favoured choice. Today many Muslims still vote for Congress but no longer is it an automatic choice, and unless Muslims find a new way out

(See also *Hindus of Pakistan; Kashmiris*)

Nagas of India

Alternative names: **various tribal names, Angami, Sema, etc.**
Location: **Nagaland, north-eastern India**
Population: **700,000**
% of population: **0.1% of Indian population**
Religion: **Christian, indigenous beliefs**
Language: **Naga languages, English**

The Nagas are a hill people numbering about 700,000 inhabiting the remote and mountainous country between the Indian state of Assam and Burma (Myanma). There are also Naga groups in Burma. The Nagas are divided into 16 main tribal groups, each with its own name and mutually unintelligible language, but their sense of national identity, forged during the years of British administration and reinforced by resistance to Indian government domination, now largely overrides the differences that separate them.

The Nagas traditionally are a tribally-organized people with a strong warrior tradition, with their villages sited on the hill tops, and making frequent raids onto the plains below. The British first came into contact with the Nagas when they took over Assam and the Brahmaputra Valley in the 1820s and moved into the hill areas in order to stop Naga raids, especially from the Angami tribe. In 1878 the Angamis rose as a tribe and were severely suppressed. After this the British gradually took over the whole area; however, in effect, British administration was limited in scope and effect. It was made a rule that no Indian official should be posted to the hills, that traders and speculators from the plains should be excluded and that most officials were drawn from the Nagas themselves. Missionaries converted many Nagas to Christianity and this facilitated literacy and the use of English, all of which encouraged a Naga sense of a separate identity.

In the run-up to Indian independence Nagas presented their own case for independence and when Assam (with other Indian provinces) was granted a large measure of self-rule in 1937, the Naga areas were under direct British administration. In World War II Nagas aided the British and harassed the Japanese. The Nagas set up the Naga National Council (NNC) to discuss matters of future status and in 1947

of this impasse, it is unlikely that they will feel secure and equal within India.

an NNC delegation led by Z. A. Phizo went to Delhi to press for Naga independence, a demand that was refused by Nehru, although he stated that autonomy for the Nagas would be considered. Therefore the NNC declared unilateral independence in August 1947 (at the time of Indian and Pakistani independence), although this was ignored by the outside world. However the Governor of Assam held talks with NNC leaders in 1948 and reached a nine-point agreement with them which recognized "the right of Nagas to develop themselves according to their freely elected wishes" although the agreement could be extended or negotiated after 10 years. The Nagas interpreted this as giving them the right to opt out of the Indian Union after 10 years. This was not the interpretation of the Indians however, and in practice they treated the nine-point agreement as a dead letter.

From 1948 the administration of the Naga areas began to change. Indians took over the administration and the posts which in the past had been held by Nagas. After the Chief Minister of Assam had been given a hostile reception by Nagas he ordered that a police force be placed in the hills. The Nagas again declared independence in January 1950 after they had conducted their own plebiscite which showed an almost unanimous vote in favour but this was not recognized by the Indian government which gave the Naga Hills the status of part of the tribal areas of Assam. In 1952 Nehru himself visited the Naga Hills but refused to meet the NCC while he was there or to receive their demands, and the Nagas were suspected of being manipulated by foreigners who wished to break up the Indian union. Soon after, the Baptist missionaries were expelled from the Naga areas.

The Nagas then launched a campaign of civil disobedience, similar to that used to achieve Indian independence, withdrawing from schools

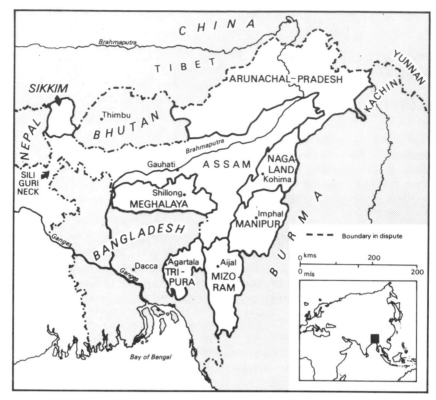

North-East India

and the administration and refusing to pay taxes. The NNC leaders were arrested, the 16 tribal councils — all under the control of the NCC — were abolished and armed police and, later, the Indian army, were moved into the area. In 1956 the NCC proclaimed the establishment of a Federal Government of Nagaland (FGN) with its own constitution and Naga Home Guard. From 1956 to 1958 a bitter guerrilla war was conducted in the Naga Hills, with alleged atrocities on both sides. According to government figures 1,400 Nagas were killed against 162 Indians. Nagas and others have alleged that the Indian forces engaged in torture, rape and murder, burned villages and destroyed crops and while not all of these reports can be substantiated (because of restricted access to independent observers) it does appear that many violations did take place.

Divisions began to emerge in the Naga movement with the formation of the Naga People's Convention led by Dr Imkongliba Ao, which favoured Indian statehood as a practical alternative to complete independence, and this received a more favourable response in Delhi, although the new state of Nagaland — at that

time the smallest state in India with an area of 15,360 square kilometres and a population of 350,000 — came into being only in 1963. But the war continued with the Indian army using counter-insurgency tactics of rehousing villagers away from their villages in order to separate them from the insurgents. Phizo of the NNC had managed to reach London where his efforts on behalf of the Nagas began to attract world attention and sympathy, forcing the Indian government to let some journalists visit and report on Nagaland.

A breakthrough appeared to come with the appointment of a three-man Peace Commission, of the Rev. Michael Scott, B. P. Chaliha (the Chief Minister of Assam), and J. P. Narayan, which was able to negotiate a ceasefire beginning in May 1964. However efforts to bring about a permanent settlement failed as the two sides could not agree on a formula for settlement. The ceasefire continued in name until September 1972 when it was unilaterally terminated by the Indian government, but in practice fighting had continued and by the late 1960s the situation in Nagaland had reverted almost to what it had been before the ceasefire. Further allegations of brutalities were made against the Indian army. However it appeared that the Indian forces had been strengthened and the NCC guerrillas weakened during these years. There were divisions within the guerrilla forces, with one breakaway group in a much publicized surrender in August 1973, and perhaps more importantly a well entrenched Nagaland state government of the Naga National Organization (NNO) which had joined with the Indian government and which supported measures against the guerrillas. Many NCC guerrillas had taken refuge on the Burmese side of the border while Phizo remained in exile in London. A new state government in Nagaland, the United Democratic Front (UDF) elected in 1974, attempted to negotiate a ceasefire, but this was refused by the Indian government, which was now in a position finally to defeat the much depleted NCC forces, who by 1975 were surrendering in significant numbers.

Some Nagas, while supporting the ideal of independence, nevertheless argued that armed conflict against the full power of the Indian state could only lead to suffering for Nagas and ultimate defeat, and that resistance should be on the political plane, with the search for maximum autonomy within the Indian Union. The Naga Peace Council, a continuation of the body which had brought about the ceasefire of the 1960s, made contact with the underground forces. The result was the Shillong Accord signed between the governor and the representatives of the FGN in November 1975. The provisions of the Accord stated that the signatories accepted the binding extent of the Indian constitution, that weapons would be surrendered to the Peace Council, that security operations would be suspended and that the curfew would be lifted. This Accord reflected the strong desire for peace within Nagaland but it was not accepted by all of the Naga resistance; Phizo in London repudiated it as did the Chinese-influenced *Alle*

command led by J. H. Muivah based in Burma, which introduced a new ideological note into the formerly heavily Christian Naga movement. This group became the National Socialist Council of Nagaland (NSCN) and carried on its struggle from Burma for many years, although heavily outnumbered by Indian forces.

By the 1980s most of Nagaland was at peace in contrast to the various insurgent movements active in the other Tribal States and Territories of the north-east and the growing conflict within Assam between Assamese and Muslim immigrants from Bangladesh. The NSCN, however, was still active not only in Nagaland but among the Nagas of neighbouring Manipur, and there were continuing clashes between the NSCN based in Burma and the Indian army, and allegations of human rights violations by military forces. Within constitutional politics there had been growing dissidence in the ruling Congress I Party (the NNO had merged with the Congress Party in 1976) but its future appeared secure when it was re-elected in November 1987; however it lost its majority in August 1988 and, rather than allow the newly formed opposition group, the Joint Regional Legislature Party, form a government, the legislature was dismissed and the state was placed under President's rule (i.e. direct rule from Delhi).

Notwithstanding the many problems that continuing insurgency has created, Nagaland's future will depend on how well government can fulfil the expectations of its people — at 42% its literacy rate is higher than that of India as a whole yet jobs are scarce, especially outside the civil service. Nagas have successfully resisted the imposition of Hindi by the central government in favour of English, but a knowledge of Hindi is necessary to function in the north of India at least and this may limit opportunities outside the state.

(See also *Adivasis of India; Chittagong Hill Tract Tribes of Bangladesh*)

Pathans

Alternative names: **Pashtuns, Pashtouns, Pakhtuns, Afghans**
Location: **North and West Frontier Province, Baluchistan and elsewhere in Pakistan, eastern Afghanistan**
Population: **Pakistan 12 million (est., not including refugees); Afghanistan 6.5 million (est., including refugees in exile in Pakistan)**
% of population: **Pakistan 13%; Afghanistan 50% (of pre-war population)**
Religion: **Sunni Muslim (Hanifi school)**
Language: **Pashtu**

The Pathans (most of whom identify themselves as "Afghans") are the main inhabitants of the mountainous areas straddling the present Pakistan/Afghanistan border, presently occupying one quarter to one third of Afghanistan's territory, and the North West Frontier Province (NWFP) of Pakistan. The Pathans are speakers of Pashtu, an Indo-European language, in one of its two major dialects, Pashto (Pushto) or Pakhto (Pukhto); the "soft" Persian-influenced and "hard" dialects spoken in the south-west and north-east of the area respectively.

The many Pathan tribes fall into three divisions: the Western Afghans, Persian-influenced and often Persian-speaking and settled mainly in Afghanistan (such as the Durranis and Ghilzaris); the Eastern Afghans, Indian-influenced and mainly settled in the trans-Indus plains of Pakistan, such as the Yusufzais; and between these two the highlanders of the tribal belt, sometimes considered the "true" Pathans such as the Wazirs, Mahsuds, Afridis, Mohmands, Bangash, Orakzai and others.

Background and history

The precise origins of the Pathans are impossible to establish and they are almost certainly an amalgam of the various peoples who have passed through the area from both the east and west. The Pathans occupied a strategic position astride the highway between Central Asia and the Punjab plain, thus leading the sixteenth century Mogul emperors of India to attempt to subjugate the Pathan tribes of the frontier. They largely failed in this as did many others who followed them including the Durrani kings in Kabul, the Sikhs under Ranjit Singh and the British in India.

The British annexed the trans-Indus area in 1849 thus facilitating the cultural divide between the Eastern Afghans and the highlander Pathans who waged a long and bitter struggle to retain their autonomy; a division which was later formalized in the Durand Line which became (and remains) the border between Afghanistan and British India (Pakistan). At first the British were prepared to tolerate a degree of tribal independence beyond the settled areas but after the Second Afghan War (1878-80) there was a shift in policy which, by the beginning of the twentieth century, resulted in an extensive military presence and road construction. In 1901 the area was designated as the North West Frontier Province and Tribal Territories ruled directly from Delhi. There was fierce Pathan opposition to this encroachment and a number of major tribal rebellions against the British, the most serious occurring in Waziristan in 1936-38.

The Pathans played a major, though rather anomalous, role in the struggle for Indian independence, when Abdul Gaffar Khan, the "frontier Gandhi", founded a Pathan nationalist organization, the Khundai-Kidmatgars (also known as the Red-Shirts) formally aligned with the Indian National Congress against the British. It remained the most popular political movement in the NWFP until the eve of independence when Hindu-Muslim violence made a secular stand impossible and the Muslim League became the leader of most of the Pathan masses. There was an attempt by Ghaffar Khan to put forward the idea of an independent Pathan state ("Pashtunistan"), but after a British supervised referendum in June 1947, in which voters were given the choice of joining either India or Pakistan (but not independence or union with Afghanistan), there was a 99% vote in favour of Pakistan.

Pakistan

There are an estimated 12 million Pashtu-speaking people in Pakistan, most of whom live in the plains, and a minority of 2.2 million (18%) in the highlands of the semi-autonomous Federally Administered Tribal Area (FATA). Substantial numbers are also found in Baluchistan (25% of the population) and migration to urban areas means that there are probably over one million Pathans living in greater Karachi.

They are the second largest ethnic community in Pakistan (after the Punjabis) and are in no immediate danger of being reduced to a minority in their homeland. As with most of the Pakistani population they are Sunni Muslims of the Hanafi school. Pathans have been relatively successful in preserving intact traditional cultural values and forms of social organization based upon fragmented but decentralized clans in which values of male individuality and equality are valued above all else and leaders compete for followers. Pathan society is essentially anarchic and this has meant that it has been difficult to build up the idea of a Pathan identity above that of tribal loyalties.

As in the case of Baluchistan, the NWFP is economically weak, especially compared to the Punjab. What little industry exists is concentrated in the regional capital, Peshawar, and outsiders exercise disproportionate influence. Economic development is generally welcomed but some tribal leaders have attempted to impede road construction as this would erode their own autonomy. Large amounts of opium are produced in Pathan areas and are an important economic factor; the government of Zia ul-Haq attempted a massive crackdown on opium production and consumption without much success. There has also been severe class conflict between landlords and tenants among Swat Pathans.

Many aspects of British policy towards the Pathans continued in post-independence Pakistan. Although the princely states of the NWFP area were abolished there continue to be 11 designated tribal areas comprising the FATA which remain primarily under central administration. These are, however, only a small part of the total Pathan population. These tribal areas retain a fair amount of ethnic autonomy; central and provincial laws generally do not apply and they are ruled by customary laws and the Frontier Crimes Regulations (FCR). The British made special efforts to recruit and retain Pathans in the military and they continue to be disproportionately represented, although most tend to come from the two districts of Kohat and Mardan.

In the immediate post-independence period a policy of "benign neglect" was followed, but under Ayub Khan (1958-69) authority was centralized and West Pakistan was amalgamated into one unit which resulted in minority disaffection. Zulfikar Ali Bhutto (1971-77) reconstituted the provinces and guaranteed their autonomy in the 1973 constitution; but in practice, power was centralized even more than previously. This continued after Bhutto was overthrown by Zia ul-Huq who ruled for 11 years before his death in a plane crash, allegedly a result of sabotage. The Zia government was initially wary of asserting its influence in the NWFP but the Soviet military occupation of Afghanistan led to increased attempts to control the tribal areas, most notably in 1985-86, with regard to heroin and arms smuggling. The large numbers of refugees from Afghanistan (largely Pashtuns) also helped to destabilize the area. Over three million Afghan refugees came to Pakistan of which 75% were in the NWFP, with a special impact on FATA, where one out of three of the population were refugees. Apart from humanitarian and economic considerations the refugees posed a security dilemma as Afghan resistance groups operated from Pakistan and Mujahidin fighters moved freely across the border, while there were attacks on Afghan refugees, allegedly by agents of the Afghan government. Pathan opposition leaders were active in the formation of the Sindhi-Baluch-Pashtun Front in 1985, although this later broke apart and the opposition National Awami Party was formed in 1986.

The situation again changed with the election of the Pakistan People's Party (PPP), under Benazir Bhutto, to central government in November 1988. In the NWFP no one party won a majority in the provincial assembly although the PPP was the largest single party and entered into a coalition with the ANP under Abdul Wali Khan, the son of Abdul Gaffar Khan (who had died in 1988 aged 99), but the alliance has been a shaky one and there have been considerable differences between the coalition partners on various issues, including the policy towards Afghanistan. However, in January 1989, 10 members of the opposition Islamic National Alliance formed a "democracy group" to support the government and thus for the time being ended opposition attempts to topple the provincial government. The NWFP has not, however, seen the large-scale ethnic violence which has affected Sind province although some observers see possibilities for renewed Pathan nationalism for "Pashtunistan".

Afghanistan

The Pashtuns (Pathans) are the largest single ethnic group and the dominant political group in Afghanistan, probably comprising about one half of the population. Most are sedentary or semi-sedentary farmers and perhaps two million or more are nomads. Afghanistan is still largely a tribal society, divided into many tribes, clans and other sub-divisions and to a large extent the internal politics of Afghanistan is the intra-tribal politics of the Pashtuns. This has been the case since the time of the indigenous Durrani dynasty established in Kabul in 1747 and there have been conflicts between (western) Durrani and (eastern) Ghilzai Pashtuns and between Pashtuns and the Tajiks, Uzbeks or other people north of the Hindu Kush. The Durranis initially ruled over most of modern Afghanistan and Pakistan but lost territory in the external attempts to control or destroy them, notably in the adoption of the Durrand Line of 1893. This demarcated the border between Afghanistan and British India and marked the Durrani's loss of Baluchistan and the division of the Pathan/Pashtun peoples roughly in half (although the hill tribes paid little heed to the official boundary). Attempts to impose modernization, for example by King Amanullah (1919-29), or the Marxist coup of 1978 and subsequent Soviet military intervention, have been strongly resisted by large parts of Pashtun tribal society. The war itself has produced a large-scale refugee exodus from Afghanistan and the vast majority of the over three million Afghan refugees in Pakistan are Pathans/Pashtuns from eastern Afghanistan. There are Pashtuns on both sides of the ideological divide; President Najibullah and others in the present Marxist-oriented Afghan government are detribalized Pashtuns.

(See also *Baluchis*)

Scheduled Castes of India

Alternative names: **"Untouchables", "Harijans", various caste names, "Dalits"**
Location: **throughout India, also Pakistan, Sri Lanka, Nepal, Bangladesh**
Population: **110 million (1989 est.)**
% of population: **14.5%**
Religion: **Hinduism, Buddhism, Christianity**

The "Scheduled Castes" is the legal and constitutional name collectively given to the groups which have traditionally occupied the lowest status in Indian society and the Hindu religion which provides the religious and ideological basis for an "untouchable" group, which was outside the caste system and inferior to all other castes. Today, untouchability is outlawed, and these groups are recognized by the Indian Constitution to be especially disadvantaged because of their past history of inferior treatment, and are therefore entitled to certain rights and preferential treatment.

The Scheduled Castes are not an homogenous group and are divided into many castes and sub-castes, as well as by language and geography. Collectively they are best known outside India as "Untouchables" but this term is not used in official Indian terminology where the word *harijan* is more likely to be favoured. Politically-aware members of the Scheduled Castes are likely to use the term *dalit*. At an everyday level specific caste names are more likely to be used. Some derogatory names have been banned by law; in practice they are commonly used. Members of the Scheduled Castes are found all over India in some areas rising to over 25% of the population. With total numbers of over 100 million, they are the largest minority group in the world — indeed one person in 40 is born "untouchable".

Background and history

There is controversy on the origin of untouchability with some accounts stating that it was a feature of ancient Indian society and others that it was introduced with the Aryan invaders in the third century BC. The philosophy of caste is contained in the *Manusmiriti*, a sacred Hindu text dating from the second century BC and is related to the theory of transmigration of the soul and of *karma* (rebirth) and *dharma* (duty). "Untouchable" outcast communities were forbidden to join in the religious and social life of the community and were confined to menial "polluting" tasks such as slaughtering animals and leatherworking. The introduction of Islam from the thirteenth century AD led to widespread conversions by many low caste and "untouchable" groups and by the mid-nineteenth century about one quarter of the population was Muslim.

The period of British rule from the late eighteenth century brought little change and attempts to ensure that public facilities, such as government schools, would be open to all castes

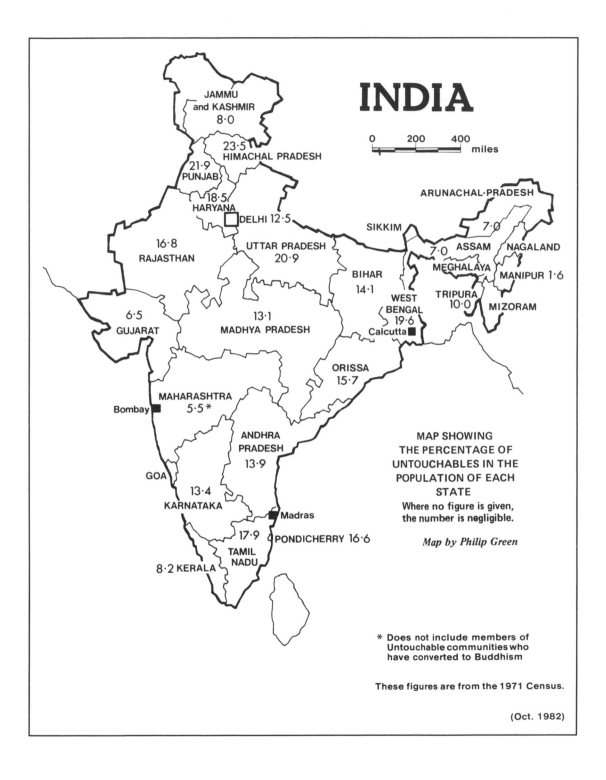

INDIA

0   200   400 miles

JAMMU and KASHMIR 8·0

23·5 HIMACHAL PRADESH

21·9 PUNJAB

18·5 HARYANA

DELHI 12·5

ARUNACHAL-PRADESH 7·0

SIKKIM

16·8 RAJASTHAN

UTTAR PRADESH 20·9

7·0 ASSAM

MEGHALAYA

NAGALAND

MANIPUR 1·6

BIHAR 14·1

WEST BENGAL 19·6

TRIPURA 10·0

MIZORAM

6·5 GUJARAT

13·1 MADHYA PRADESH

Calcutta

ORISSA 15·7

MAHARASHTRA 5·5 *

Bombay

ANDHRA PRADESH 13·9

MAP SHOWING THE PERCENTAGE OF UNTOUCHABLES IN THE POPULATION OF EACH STATE

Where no figure is given, the number is negligible.

Map by Philip Green

GOA

13·4 KARNATAKA

Madras

17·9 PONDICHERRY 16·6

TAMIL NADU

8·2 KERALA

* Does not include members of Untouchable communities who have converted to Buddhism

These figures are from the 1971 Census.

(Oct. 1982)

had little impact. During the first half of the twentieth century the British Indian government began to take an interest in the condition of "untouchable groups" and "depressed classes" and their special position was recognized under the term "Scheduled Castes". Among Indian politicians two main approaches emerged, typified by two political and religious leaders who have by their ideas and actions made most impact on "Untouchable" advancement.

M. K. (Mahatma) Gandhi, whose chief aim was liberation from colonial rule within a distinctive philosophical system based upon *amhinsa* (non-violence), believed in raising the status of "Untouchables" while retaining elements of the traditional caste system but removing the degrading stigma and manifestations of untouchability, and coined the term *harijan* (Children of God) to describe them. This term is still used widely today by the non-Scheduled Caste communities although many Scheduled Caste members have now rejected it. The other approach came from Dr B. R. Ambedkar, a brilliant "Untouchable" lawyer, who believed that only by destroying the caste system could untouchability be destroyed. Ambedkar became the chief spokesperson for Scheduled Castes who demanded recognition as a separate entity similar in status to Muslims, Sikhs and Christians. Ambedkar was forced to drop this demand after Gandhi threatened a hunger strike, but as a consequence Scheduled Castes were granted increased electoral representation and a guarantee of special protection and rights for them. Ambedkar also rejected Hindu values and in 1956 converted to Buddhism, later followed by about three million converts.

Constitution and law

After Independence for a partitioned India in 1947, Ambedkar became Law Minister in the government of Jawaharlal Nehru and the drafter of the Indian Constitution of 1950. The Constitution states that no citizen should be discriminated against because of religion, race, or caste among other attributes, and should not be denied access to and the use of public services. Article 341 authorizes the President of India to specify "castes, races or tribes which shall for the purposes of this constitution be deemed to be Scheduled Castes". The First Amendment to the Constitution passed in 1951 allowed the state to make special provision for advancement of socially and educationally backward classes of citizens of the Scheduled Castes and Scheduled Tribes.

The Untouchability Offences Act of 1955 outlaws discrimination on "the ground of untouchability" in regard to public facilities, eating places, temples, residential choice etc. and provides for fines and imprisonment of offenders. However, relatively small numbers of convictions were made under the Act. In 1976 the Act was strengthened by the Protection of Civil Rights Act which increases punishment and allows for collective fines to be imposed on the offending community and for punishment of civil servants who neglect to investigate the offence. State governments were directed to introduce new measures such as providing officers, police stations and special courts to deal with offenders, to provide legal aid to victims and to identify special areas where there is a high incidence of untouchability. The central government has a special Commission for Scheduled Castes and Tribes which issues an Annual Report outlining processes, problems and violations of the law as regards the Scheduled Castes. However, despite these measures, there is still evidence that the law is often ignored and that untouchability continues, especially in rural areas.

The central and state governments have from time to time appointed Commissions of Enquiry to investigate the situation of the Scheduled Castes, especially after riots and violent incidents. After a series of attacks against Scheduled Caste communities which resulted in many deaths in Tamil Nadu in 1968, Scheduled Caste MPs compiled the Elaperumal Report, which detailed continuing untouchability in villages across India. Incidents of violence and discrimination, especially from the states of Bihar, Uttar Pradesh, Madhya Pradesh and Andhra Pradesh, continue to be regularly reported in the national press.

In Bihar during the 1980s many Scheduled Caste landless labourers in the central plains supported left-wing trade union and peasant groups, some of which used armed opposition to the state government and advocated land reform and standard wages. (Most of these demands were actually already on the Statute Book but had never been enforced.) As a result, landlord armies or *senas* have organized and used counter-violence against the *lal senas* or "red armies". Some estimates give a total of 2,000 deaths each year in land disputes in Bihar, most of the victims being landless labourers or small farmers. Landlord *senas* have been responsible for violent attacks on Scheduled Caste communities and there have been allegations that these attacks have been implicitly supported by police and leading politicians in the state government. After the most publicized of these incidents, politicians descend upon the village and many promises are made of compensation and justice. Yet few of the perpetrators of violence against Scheduled Caste communities are prosecuted by the government, and even fewer are convicted or sentenced.

Politics

The Congress Party has dominated Indian politics from before independence and has been out of office at the centre only once — from 1977 to the beginning of 1980. However, from the mid-1980s, it has lost power in many of the states to regionally-based parties, while the Communist Party (Marxist) is the dominant party in the states of West Bengal and Kerala. Almost all political parties actively pursue their Scheduled Caste voters, and in some states there is reported to be widespread ballot-rigging. There is no one Scheduled Caste "vote bank", as was once thought to have existed in relation to the Congress Party, and there are Scheduled Caste voters for all parties, with probably the largest number of votes going to the Congress Party. Congress was reported to have lost much of its traditional Scheduled Caste support during the Emergency of 1975-77. Almost all parties have had Scheduled Caste politicians among their leading figures although few have gained real power. To date there have been no Scheduled Caste Prime Ministers, but the late Jagivan Ram served as Deputy Prime Minister in the brief Janata government of 1977-79 and at least three Chief Ministers in northern India have been from the Scheduled Castes.

There are also reservations for the Scheduled Castes in legislatures in the centre and the states. In the two houses of Parliament, the *Lok Sabha* and the *Raiya Sabha*, 15% of the seats are reserved for Scheduled Caste members and similar representation occurs in the state assemblies in proportion to the percentage of Scheduled Castes in the state's population. However, since the Scheduled Caste voters are always a minority in the reserved constituencies and in the assemblies as a whole, favourable legislation has been often blocked by vested interests. Furthermore, the system does not encourage Scheduled Caste organization by separate parties but facilitates organization and representation of Scheduled Castes by the major parties, especially the Congress Party, which has been in a dominant position since independence. On some occasions, however, Scheduled Caste legislators have been able to act and influence policies across party lines.

There have been several attempts to found distinctive Scheduled Caste political parties, among them the Republican Party of Ambedkar, which still exists but which has little political significance. In the early 1970s a new radical political movement in Maharashtra took the form of the Dalit Panther Party, which was inspired by the American civil rights movement and "black power". *Dalit* means the "oppressed ones" and the movement embraces not only Scheduled Castes but also Adivasis (Tribal peoples), low caste groups, Muslims, workers and women. The party later splintered and has since had only sporadic success. More durable was the accompanying literary and cultural movement which has spanned poetry, theatre, music and film, and the sense of pride and identity brought about by the *Dalit* movement. The *Dalit* movement has been concentrated in the Western states of Maharashtra and Gujarat and some of the larger Indian cities. Buddhism has also been a major influence in forming a new sense of identity, once again mainly in the western states. In the southern states there have recently been attempts by Christian groups, who have come from traditionally untouchable communities but who are not recognized as Scheduled Castes by the government, to organize within and outside the Christian community.

Economic factors

Almost 90% of the Scheduled Castes still live in rural areas and economic exploitation remains their most acute problem. They are overwhelmingly marginal farmers or landless labourers. Large numbers migrate to cities or labour-scarce rural areas such as Punjab. Many are in debt and are obliged to work off their debts through debt-bonded labour despite the fact that this practice was abolished by law in 1976. In these cases a labourer takes a loan from a landlord or moneylender and in return agrees to work for that person until the debt is repaid. In practice it is difficult to repay the debt as interest payments are high and cumulative, and poverty forces the labourer deeper into debt. The debt can be passed onto the next generation and thus it is impossible to escape the cycle. In some areas many high-caste landlords pay their Scheduled Caste labourers minimum wages in cash or food, or nothing at all, and any resistance is frequently met by violence, sometimes resulting in the death or injury of the victim. Sexual harassment against Scheduled Caste women is frequent. Mob violence against Scheduled Caste communities is frequently reported, sometimes led by landlords or community leaders, and has been especially noticeable in situations where Scheduled Caste workers have joined labour unions or made progress in gaining education and economic mobility.

Many Scheduled Caste families have left rural areas and come to live in slums and on the pavements in the rapidly growing cities. Here also they tend to do the worst jobs for the lowest wages. However in some cities, traditional occupations such as sweepers have been organized in municipal unions and have the advantage of regular work and wages. Most Scheduled Caste workers are casual day labourers, in small factories, quarries and brick kilns or on construction sites, or work as cycle rickshaw drivers or in petty trade. Women and children as well as men work in such jobs but at lower wages. In the large textile mills of Bombay, Scheduled Caste workers have been generally confined to less skilled and less well-paid work. There are, however, growing numbers of Scheduled Castes in relatively secure areas such as the public service, banking and railways and sometimes in private industry. Those resident in the cities have greater access to secondary and higher education and a growing middle class has evolved within the Scheduled Caste community. Discrimination is less evident in the urban areas but residential patterns, particularly in poorer areas, are often on a caste basis.

As a result of the official policy of "positive discrimination" in favour of the Scheduled Castes in the civil service there have been growing numbers of Scheduled Caste public servants. To date there has been some improvement in the levels of Scheduled Caste recruitment in the central civil service. From 1949 to 1979 this rose from 0.71% to 4.5% in Class I posts, from 2.01% to 7.3% in Class II posts, and from 7.03% to 12.35% in Class III posts. There has been a similar slow process in public-sector and nationalized industry posts, where positive discrimination did not begin until the 1970s. In private business and industry, however, there are no positive discrimination provisions and, therefore, progress has been limited. Members of the Scheduled Castes, however, are frequently over-represented in the lower Class IV posts and occupy almost all Class V posts (i.e sweepers — a traditional "Untouchable" occupation).

There has also been positive discrimination in education, but the poverty of many Scheduled Caste families often prevents utilization of education facilities. In 1977-78 only 75% of Scheduled Caste children in the age group six to eleven attended school, compared to 88% for other children, and the disparity becomes greater at older ages with the respective figures for the 11 to 14 age group as 26% to 42%. Places for Scheduled Castes in higher education, and especially for post-graduate posts, are sometimes not filled, either because of lack of qualified candidates or prejudice against qualified candidates. In 1981 there were riots in the state of Gujarat by high-caste students protesting against the system of reservation in education institutions, in which 42 people died.

However, despite the overwhelming odds against them, former "Untouchables" are gaining increasing access to education and their expectations and aspirations are rising. Increasingly they are refusing to accept their former degraded and subservient position and, if they are able to organize across barriers of language and sub-caste, should present a formidable challenge to government.

(See also *Adivasis of India; Burakumin of Japan* in **East Asia**)

Sikhs

Location: **Punjab state, north-western India, Delhi and elsewhere in India**
Population: **India 13 million; Punjab 10.2 million (1981)**
% of population: **1.9% of Indian population, 60% of Punjab population**
Religion: **Sikhism**
Language: **Punjabi**

The Sikhs are an Indian minority living, for the most part, in the north-western state of Punjab. They comprise one of the most visually distinctive groups in India, notably because of the beard and turban adopted by orthodox male Sikhs, and also because of their conspicuous presence in the transport sector and the military. They number over 14 million, of whom over one million live outside India. The 13 million living in India comprise less than 2% of its total population, although 80% are concentrated in their home state, Punjab, where they are a majority of 60%.

History

The founder of Sikhism was Guru Nanak, a Hindu of the high-ranking Khattri caste who lived from 1469-1539. Dissatisfied with the teachings of Hinduism and Islam he formulated an egalitarian doctrine which transcended both, and could be summarized in the commandment to "adore the Divine Name, practise one's livelihood and share its fruits". The Guru established a community of Sikhs or "disciples" who were mostly Hindu in origin. In contrast to the ascetic ideals prominent at the time, the practical existence of the householder was held to be the ideal, and devotion consisted of private prayer and the congregational singing of hymns written by Guru Nanak and the embodiment of his teachings in poetic form. Sikhism, from the first, laid strong emphasis upon equality within the community, between castes and between men and women. Temples are open to all and there is no priestly hierarchy.

Guru Nanak appointed a successor to himself who was to be a spiritual guide, and between 1469 and 1708, a period known to Sikhs as the age of the Gurus, there were 10 such leaders; during this period the authoritative scriptures of Sikhdom, a collection of hymns known as the Adi Granth or "Original Book" was compiled and a new community named the Khalsa or "Company of the Pure" was formed by the tenth Guru. Members of this company assumed unshorn hair, beard and turban and were given the martial name of Singh or "lion". The creation of this community marked a change of emphasis which led Sikhdom away from its traditional peaceful course into a more war-like stance, and although not all Sikhs adopted the baptismal tokens, bearded and turbanned members of the Khalsa came to be recognized as guardians of Sikh orthodoxy.

Throughout the next 150 years the Sikh Khalsa was involved in conflict with the invading Afghans and the Muslim governors of Lahore. In 1746 the city of Amritsar was sacked, the Golden Temple defiled, and Sikh forces massacred by one such governor, and another massacre occurred in 1762, this time perpetrated by the Afghans. The Afghans were unable to conquer the Punjab, however in 1799 a Sikh chieftain became Maharajah of the Punjab. Some Sikh states maintained a separate existence under British rule but elsewhere in the Punjab the Sikh Khalsa remained independent. Factional fighting gave the British a chance to intervene and after two Anglo-Sikh wars in the mid-nineteenth century the British gained control of the whole of the Punjab, and the Khalsa army was disbanded, although its actions during the "heroic" age have never been forgotten by the Sikhs.

Sikhs in British India

The British were impressed by the fighting qualities and loyalty of the Sikh troops and began to recruit Sikhs into its forces. By the time of World War I, Sikhs made up 20% of the Indian army. The Jat peasantry, which formed the core of the Sikh community or Panth, were especially eager to take up newly irrigated land in the western Punjab,[1] and many prospered through working the now fertile region. The Jats have given Sikh society its traditional rural bias, although there is a small but influential urban Sikh minority. Many Sikhs took advantage of their British citizenship to emigrate to other

[1]This refers to the undivided Punjab which covers the approximate areas of the Indian states of Punjab and Haryana and the Pakistani province of Punjab.

PUNJAB AND ITS NEIGHBOURS

0   50   100   miles

Srinagar

Islamabad

JAMMU AND KASHMIR

CHINA

PAKISTAN

HIMACHAL PRADESH

R. Beas

R. Sutlej

Amritsar

Lahore

Bhakra

Jullundur

Anandpur

Nankana

Ludhiana

Chandigarh

PUNJAB

R. Sutlej

Fazilka

Patiala

Abohar

UTTAR PRADESH

HARYANA

RAJASTHAN

Delhi

Population of principal cities (1981) in thousands

	Hindus	Sikhs	
Amritsar	348	241	(40%)
Chandigarh	323	84	(20%)
Jullundur	308	94	(23%)
Ludhiana	386	209	(34%)
Patiala	118	85	(41%)

parts of the Empire where, for the most part, they prospered although enduring prejudice and initial hardship.

Elected provincial governments began to exercise more power and as independence approached Sikhs put forward proposals for alterations to the Punjab's boundaries in order to exclude the largely Hindu and Muslim areas to the south-east and west; or alternatively for increased Sikh representation to protect their interests. These proposals had little effect, however, and the largely Muslim Unionist party retained control over the province. During the 1940s there were increasing demands made by the Muslims for a separate Muslim state after independence. Muslims urged the Sikhs to join with them in the new state but there were too few cultural or religious links between the two groups to make this a feasibility. Afraid of their numbers being split up between India and Pakistan, Sikh leaders, in 1946, called for the creation of their own independent Sikhistan or Khalistan but without success. The situation deteriorated rapidly into violent outbreaks between the Muslims on the one hand and Hindus and Sikhs on the other.

Partition and independence

Independence came to India in August 1947 and the Punjab was divided into two parts, with the larger, western portion being allocated to Pakistan, now a Muslim state. In the terrible holocaust that followed, hundreds of thousands of Punjabis were killed and millions fled from one part of the province to the other. The Sikh community had been split down the middle and over 40% were forced to flee Pakistan for India, leaving behind them homes, land and many sacred shrines. The majority of Sikh refugees settled in the Indian part of Punjab although many moved to Delhi and other neighbouring regions.

Sikhs quickly established themselves as a successful and enterprising section of Indian society; nevertheless many felt they had somehow been cheated by the partition of the country. The Hindus had India, and the Muslims Pakistan, but the Sikhs had not been granted a state of their own, and in India they were a small minority. In only one of the Punjabi states — that of the former princely states, known as PEPSU — were they a majority. In the south-eastern districts they were hardly represented and in the rest of the eastern (i.e. Indian) Punjab they constituted one third of the population. In the north-west they were in the majority in the rural areas but were outnumbered by Hindus in the principal cities. In order to promote local political autonomy Sikhs called for the creation of a new state, a combination of the Sikh majority districts of Punjab and PEPSU. Since the government of India was opposed to meeting any such demands made on purely religious grounds, the Sikhs' demand was for the creation of a state for Punjabi speakers, the majority of people in the Punjab speaking either Hindi or Urdu.

In 1955, mass demonstrations in favour of separatism provoked a police invasion of the Golden Temple at Amritsar; however, the demonstrations also resulted in the merging of PEPSU into a large new Punjab and the regulated use of Punjabi and Hindi in their respective regions. In 1966 the state of Punjab was divided into the new states of Punjab (Punjabi-speaking and mainly Sikh), Haryana (Hindi-speaking and mainly Hindu) and Himachal Pradesh (the mountainous areas to the east). The Sikhs now constituted a 60% majority in Punjab state but various complex issues remained unresolved. Firstly, the city of Chandigarh, which lay on the border between the two new states, was now the capital of both, and the water supply from the Punjab rivers was divided between them in what the Sikhs saw as an unfair manner. As was the case in 1947, many religious and linguistic groups found themselves on the wrong side of the boundary after the division, with Punjabi Hindus constituting a majority of the urban population in the Punjab and a sizeable Sikh minority remaining in Haryana. Nor were the majority Sikhs politically united. The Akali Dal represented for the most part the Jat Sikh farmers but the state Congress Party attracted many Sikh voters in addition to Hindus. The Punjab was now declared a unilingual Punjabi state with safeguards for the use of Hindi.

Between 1966 and 1984 these conflicts were not resolved. Relations between Sikh political leaders became strained and there were disputes between the Punjab and neighbouring states, especially Haryana. These were exacerbated by Indira Gandhi's domination of the Indian political scene and her centralization of power rather than granting greater autonomy to many of the country's regional movements, including that of the Sikh Akalis. In 1969 there was tension over the status of Chandigarh. One Sikh fasted to death in order to gain Chandigarh for the Punjab and, after another threatened fast, Indira Gandhi awarded the city outright to the Punjab in 1970, after a five-year interim period, in return for which Haryana was awarded the Hindi-dominated areas of Abohar and Fazilka.

Economic developments

The Punjab has seen remarkable economic and
agricultural growth in the second half of this
century, largely as a result of the introduction
of high-yielding strains of wheat, chemical fertili-
zation and tubewell irrigation schemes during the
1960s. Despite their relative wealth, old grievances had not been forgotten. Sikhs believed
that there should have been greater acknowl-
edgement of their huge economic contribution
to India's growing prosperity. Small-scale industries expanded rapidly and *per capita* income was
higher than that of any other Indian state. The
Punjab was contributing half its grain production
to India's protected economy and it was felt
that this contribution had not been sufficiently
recognized in economic terms, neither had the
allocation of river waters been altered as a result
of earlier complaints.

Many Sikhs who had left India for Britain,
North America and the Middle East were sending
remittances to relatives in the Punjab and these
funds were of help in the expansion of small
industry in urban areas. The labour shortage
created by this emigration was filled by Hindu
labourers from other regions, and this pattern of
immigration affected Sikh perceptions of the balance between communities. Increasing numbers
of young Sikhs from poorer Jat families found
themselves without work in a society moving
from an agricultural to an urban-based economy
at a time when military recruitment of Sikhs was
declining.

Political developments

Although most Sikh politicians started their
political careers as members of the Akali Dal
many later turned to the Congress Party which
offered more opportunity for those with political
ambitions; the Congress Party was successful in
the state elections of 1972. In the following year,
the Akali Dal issued a manifesto known as the
Anandpur Sahib Resolution (ASR) which was
designed to protect Sikh interests in India and
called for increased autonomy within a larger
Punjab, extended to include Sikh communities
in adjoining regions of neighbouring states.
The ASR also aligned the Akali Dal with
other autonomy-seeking minorities in India.
During the Emergency of 1975 many Akali
leaders were arrested, but after elections in
1977 the Akalis formed part of an anti-congress
coalition government, which remained in office
until Indira Gandhi's return to power in 1980.

The youth wing of the Akali Dal, the All-India
Sikh Students' Federation (AISSF), had become
active during the 1970s. In 1978 a radical Sikh
named Sant Jarnail Singh Bhindranwale, who
had been involved in a number of violent
incidents, became popular amongst members
of the AISSF. Increasingly bitter relations were
developing between the Akali Dal, the Delhi
government — which now had a Sikh as its
President, and Bhindranwale's extreme nationalists. Negotiations between Indira Gandhi and
Akali leaders were held in 1981 and 1982 to
discuss the questions of more autonomy for
the Punjab and guarantees of minority status;
however, these discussions proved fruitless and
the Akalis launched a "Holy War Agitation"
supporting the ASR. The campaign was met by
repression from the Punjab government which in
turn provoked more extreme action by the Akali
Dal. Threats made by Sikhs to disrupt the 1982
Asian Games staged in Delhi were countered
by blatant discrimination directed at prominent
Sikhs who were travelling to the Games.

"Operation Bluestar"

As tensions grew, Bhindranwale's role became
ever more central. By late 1982 he and his young
followers were established in the Golden Temple
complex from where he directed "hit squads"
mounted on motorcycles. One such squad was
responsible for the death of a senior Sikh police
officer in 1983. Because Bhindranwale so publicly espoused the Sikh cause, it was difficult
for many more moderate Sikhs to oppose him
directly and the Indian government had soon
labelled all Sikhs as extremists who posed a
threat to national integrity. In 1983, following
the hijacking of a bus and murder of its Hindu
passengers, the state government was dismissed
and President's rule was imposed. Within the
refuge of the inner sanctum of the Golden
Temple, Bhindranwale continued his operations
secure from police action. There was increasing
violence against police officers or Sikhs hostile to
his cause which in turn generated Hindu support
for militant Hindu organizations. In addition
there were anti-Sikh riots.

In June 1984, the army was sent into Amritsar
in "Operation Bluestar" with orders to eliminate
the Sikh extremists from the Golden Temple. It
was unprepared for the fortifications within the
Temple precincts and many of Bhindranwale's
supporters escaped. Some 150 were arrested and
imprisoned and the remainder were killed after
the army had resorted to the use of tanks which
damaged many of the Temple buildings. Many
innocent victims died in the crossfire as the attack
took place during one of the most important festi-

vals of the Sikh year when pilgrims were present. The storming of the Golden Temple caused outrage among Sikhs throughout the world. Even those who had previously felt no sympathy for the Akali movement now felt obliged to make public their fury. Bhindranwale, who had been killed in the attack, was increasingly seen as an heroic martyr, and there was an upsurge of support for the demand for a separate Khalistan. A mutiny by Sikh troops throughout the country was quickly suppressed and those involved were imprisoned, provoking further resentment among Sikhs. Several hundred Sikhs, including Sikh pilgrims to the Golden Temple, were taken into police custody and there were allegations of torture, later substantiated by a government enquiry.

After the assault on the Golden Temple, the army presence in the Punjab was increased and the level of terrorist activity was reduced. Work was rapidly started on the restoration of the Temple; however, while the Indian government was in control of the Temple it was not possible to find members of the Sikh community willing to carry out voluntary manual labour according to traditional practice, and work was eventually undertaken by the leader of a minority sect hostile to the Akalis. Although the restoration work was quickly and efficiently executed, considerable ill-feeling had been caused by the flouting of Sikh law by the use of paid-labour under a compliant Sikh figurehead.

On October 31, 1984, Indira Gandhi was assassinated by two of her Sikh bodyguards. Some Sikhs felt that this was just revenge for the storming of the Golden Temple; many others were shocked. A wave of Hindu violence was unleashed against the Sikh community, in many cases allegedly with the compliance of the police and the political support of Congress Party politicians. There was massive destruction of Sikh property and at least 2,150 Sikhs, mainly males, were killed in Delhi and over 600 in other parts of India. Some 50,000 left Delhi and other places to return to the Punjab. The army took over after three days and restored order but the killings created a deep and residing bitterness among Sikhs. As the Punjab was at this time still under President's Rule Sikhs were now effectively without a political voice. In June 1985 an explosion on an Indian airliner was ascribed to pro-Khalistan Sikhs in Canada — an indication of the, by now, international dimensions of the conflict.

The "Punjab Accord"

On July 24, 1985, an agreement was reached between Rajiv Gandhi, the new Indian Prime Minister who had been elected by an overwhelming majority in December 1984, and Longowal, the Akali leader who had been initially taken into custody and later released. According to the Punjab Accord of July 1985, which granted many of the demands of the ASR, Chandigarh was given to the Punjab, whilst the issue of river water was to be decided by a commission; Sikh control of their religious affairs was to be extended, release of detainees was to be speeded up and fresh investment was promised for the Punjab. These measures did not go far enough to meet the demands of many Sikhs and Longowal was assassinated shortly afterwards by an extremist Sikh group. Although many called for a boycott of elections due in September there was a substantial turnout and the Akalis, under Surjit Singh Barnala, were returned to power with a large majority — an indication that most Sikhs supported a negotiated political situation.

In 1986, a group of AISSF members took over the Golden Temple and started to demolish the Akal Takht on the day before traditionally-organized labour was due to begin. On this same day, Chandigarh was to have been handed over to the Sikhs but the provision was hampered on a technicality; three months later the zealots in the Temple declared an independent Khalistan. The police then moved in and cleared the Temple.

President's Rule

In the months that followed, terrorist attacks on both sides increased, with extremist Hindi groups organizing counter-violence against Sikhs, and in May 1987 Rajiv Gandhi dismissed the Barnala government on the grounds of its alleged inability to deal effectively with the violence. He then instituted President's Rule. The army and police presence was intensified and emergency powers of search, arrest and detention were used extensively, resulting in allegations of police and army brutality and harassment of civilians. None of these measures, however, stopped terrorist activity; in fact it increased over the next two years with armed gangs of Sikhs and Hindu extremists deliberately targeting innocent civilians. Between May 1987 and March 1989 almost 3,000 lives were lost, the vast majority of whom were civilians, although the targets of police killings were invariably described as "terrorists". There were also divisions between the extremist groups; by early 1989 at least 15 such Sikh groups had been identified. In May 1988 some of these groups were again established in parts of the

Golden Temple, resulting in yet another siege, "Operation Black Thunder", which, however, was conducted with considerably more sensitivity than "Operation Bluestar", and resulted in much less public alienation.

There have been tentative moves by the central government to reach a political solution to the crisis in the Punjab. From March 1988 Rajiv Gandhi began to release some of the "Jodhpur detainees" who had been held for over four years after "Operation Bluestar" without trial, although some were later re-arrested. However, appeals to commute the death sentences of the two Sikhs found guilty of Indira Gandhi's assassination were not heeded, and the two were hanged in Delhi in January 1989. Announcements were made to the effect that local government elections would be held between May and September 1989 (to date these have not taken place). However, the general consensus was that these measures were too little and too late and that the situation in the Punjab would

continue to fester, with polarization of both Sikh and Hindu communities. No date has been set for the restoration of elected government.

The Sikhs however remain as a majority within the Punjab, a majority that is likely to increase as other communities move from the area. Especially poignant is the situation of the low-caste migrant labourers who came to the Punjab during the boom years of the 1970s and early 1980s when Jat Sikhs were more likely to expand into farm management and small-scale industries than agricultural labour. These labourers generally come from the poverty-stricken regions of Bihar, Orissa and Uttar Pradesh and can earn far higher wages in the Punjab than in their home areas. There have been deliberate terrorist attacks on these labourers, forcing them to flee. Nearly 15,000 had left the Amritsar District by May 1988 and the resulting labour shortages are likely to affect agricultural productivity.

(See also *Kashmiris; Muslims of India*)

Tamils of Sri Lanka

Alternative names: **"Ceylon Tamils", "Indian Tamils"**
Location: **north and east: central highlands**
Population: **Total 2.7 million; Ceylon Tamils 1.9 million; Indian Tamils 825,000**
% of population: **total 18.2%**
Religion: **Hindu, Muslim**
Language: **Tamil**

The Tamils of Sri Lanka can be divided into two groups: the indigenous or "Ceylon" Tamils who number 1.9 million, and the 825,000 "Indian" Tamils, plantation workers descended from labourers indentured by the British during the nineteenth and twentieth centuries. Both groups are mainly Hindu and together they make up about one fifth of the population of 14.85 million, the majority of whom are Sinhalese Buddhists. The Tamils of Sri Lanka are part of a much larger Tamil community — over 50 million strong — in the state of Tamil Nadu, southern India.

Background and history

Both Tamils and Sinhalese have been living in Sri Lanka from as early as the sixth or fifth century BC. The Sinhalese are traditionally believed to be the descendants of migratory Aryans from Northern India. According to tradition, their

race was created at the time of the Buddha's death in order that his message might be continued, and they regard the island of Sri Lanka as a place of special sanctity, enshrining as it does relics of the Buddha's person. The Tamils are descended from Dravidian settlers who may have reached Sri Lanka even earlier than the Sinhalese. In the sixteenth century Portuguese invaders found quite separate kingdoms of Hindu Tamils in the north and Buddhist Sinhalese in the south, which remained separate under both the Portuguese administration and that of the Dutch, who succeeded them. Only under British rule in the nineteenth century were the two kingdoms brought under a single administration.

During the nineteenth century, the British imported thousands of Tamils from southern India to work on coffee, tea and rubber plantations. By 1911, there were 530,000 "Indian" Tamils, more than the number of indigenous "Ceylon" Tamils of whom there were 528,024. The spread of the

SRI LANKA

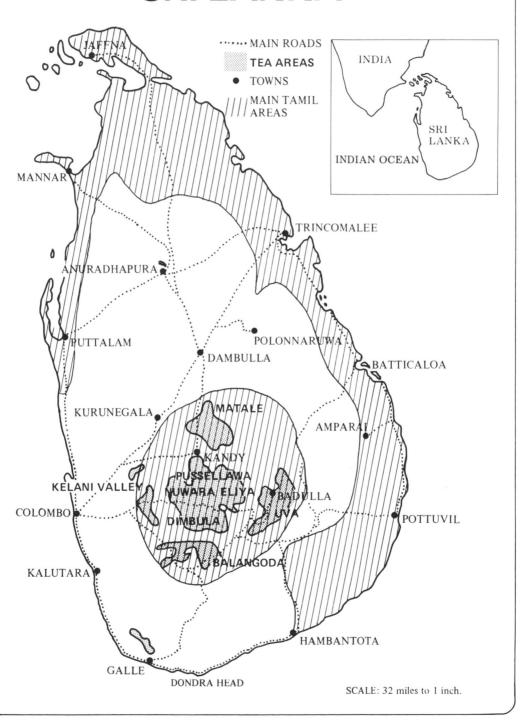

MAIN ROADS
TEA AREAS
TOWNS
MAIN TAMIL AREAS

INDIA

INDIAN OCEAN

SRI LANKA

JAFFNA

MANNAR

TRINCOMALEE

ANURADHAPURA

PUTTALAM

POLONNARUWA

DAMBULLA

BATTICALOA

KURUNEGALA

MATALE

AMPARAI

KANDY

PUSSELLAWA

KELANI VALLEY

NUWARA ELIYA

BADULLA

UVA

COLOMBO

DIMBULA

POTTUVIL

BALANGODA

KALUTARA

HAMBANTOTA

GALLE

DONDRA HEAD

SCALE: 32 miles to 1 inch.

estates around Kandy in the heart of Sinhalese hill country created a shortage of land among the Sinhalese who, in some cases, were financially worse off than the indentured labourers, the latter being for the most part provided with housing, medical care and schools, however minimal.

The British government relied upon English as the language of the administration and this produced a small elite class of English-speaking civil servants and professional people. Because agriculture and industry were less developed in the Tamil areas in the north of the country than in largely Sinhalese regions, proportionally more of the "Ceylon" Tamils entered public service and the professions. At the time of independence in 1948, the "Ceylon" Tamils, who made up 10% of the population, held 31% of university places and in 1956, 60% of professional people (engineers, doctors and lecturers) were "Ceylon" Tamils. Many Sinhalese resented the fact that Tamils had enjoyed disproportionate educational advantages and prosperity, and they were also uncomfortably aware of the presence of the 50 million strong Tamil community across the narrow straits in Tamil Nadu, feeling threatened by its size and proximity.

Independence

Before independence in 1948, the Tamil minority had been assured by the future Sinhalese president that it would not be discriminated against with regard to representation and legislation. However, under two Acts passed by the new government, citizenship was granted only to those persons who could prove that they had been born in Ceylon and who had been resident there since 1936. Since most "Indian" Tamils did not have access to relevant documents, the Acts effectively rendered them stateless. The Electoral Amendment Act of 1946 disenfranchised most "Indian" Tamil plantation workers in the uphill Kandyan regions by omitting their names from the revived electoral registers, leaving the onus on individuals to have their names reinstated if they could furnish proof of Ceylonese nationality.

Sinhalese nationalism was growing and as vernacular education gradually replaced English, there was a motion for the adoption of Sinhala as the only official language of Ceylon. The *swabasha* or "own language" movement became a central part of the nationalist cause and although the government wavered over this issue, it did finally adopt the motion in 1955. S. W. R. D. Bandaranaike's People's United

Front was returned to office in 1956 and, under the Official Language Act, it was declared that the Sinhala language should be the one official language of Ceylon. The new government was the first not to include a Tamil in its Cabinet. After the Tamil Federal Party threatened to launch nationwide peaceful protest, the Prime Minister, in an attempt to restore Tamil confidence, proposed plans for preferential treatment of Tamils in the Northern and Eastern provinces. The Bandaranaike-Chelvanayakam Pact of 1957 was a statesmanlike compromise; the Tamils gave up their demand for parity between the languages in return for "recognition of Tamil as the language of a national minority in Ceylon", but agitation by extremist Buddhist nationalists led to rioting in which several hundred people were killed, and the proposals were never implemented.

In 1959, Bandaranaike was assassinated by a leader of the Eksath Bikkhu Peramuna, the Buddhist extremist group which led to the strengthening of the Tamil Federal Party, which called for parity of status for Tamils, citizenship on the basis of residence, and the creation of one or more linguistic states. Elections held in 1960 saw the Federal Party gain most of the seats in the Northern Province and all seats in the Eastern Province. It held the balance in parliament for a short period, but fresh elections were held later in the year, and Sirimavo Bandaranaike, widow of the assassinated leader and head of the United Front, became Prime Minister.

During the 1960s, the previously impartial Marxist LSSP and Communist parties yielded to Sinhalese pressure and abandoned their support for the Tamil Language Act, and the "Sinhala-only" policy was retained and broadened to include court proceedings, previously conducted in English. In 1964, an agreement between Sri Lanka and India provided for the repatriation to India over a period of 15 years of some 975,000 Tamils; 300,000 others would be granted Ceylon citizenship. In 1968, the Federal Party left the government and the new United Front government, which came to power in 1970, wrote a new constitution, enforcing the "Sinhala-only" rule. The Republican Constitution of 1972 did away with the safeguards for minorities in the original section 29.

In the same year a system of "standardization" was introduced in the universities, according to which disadvantaged candidates were given priority. In practice, this meant that the Kandyan Sinhalese were given a better chance of admission than many highly educated Tamils. The Tamils felt that they were being squeezed out of the (admittedly privileged) position they had occupied in the civil service; between independence and 1973 the percentage of Tamil admissions fell from 30% to 6%. State-sponsored colonization schemes put many Sinhalese settlers into Tamil areas.

Gradually, groups from both communities were moving towards extremism. In 1976 the Tamil United Liberation Front (TULF) passed a resolution demanding complete independence. Among several resistance groups formed at this time was the Tamil New Tigers, later renamed the Liberation Tigers of Tamil Eelam (LTTE), which claimed responsibility for several killings. Similarly on the Sinhalese side groups were formed to resist the Tamil demands.

The Government of
J. R. Jayawardene (1977)

In 1977 the United National Party (UNP), led by J. R. Jayawardene, came to power. The TULF, which was now pledged to achieving a separate state, gained all 14 seats in the Northern Province and three of the 10 seats in the Eastern Province, and thus became the principal opposition party. At first, the change of government seemed to augur well for moderate people of both sides. Standardization in university admission was abolished and Tamil was recognized in the Constitution as a national language; talks were planned on the subject of removing discrimination in employment and education. Within a month of the elections, however, violence broke out in the Northern Province and quickly spread to the south. It was believed by some that the rioting had been deliberately instigated with the aim of preventing agreement between Sinhalese and Tamils, and several known Sinhalese extremists were among the 1,500 people arrested. There had also been an increasing number of attacks on Tamils by Sinhalese police and armed forces. The government extended legislation renewing special police powers; from this time there was a steady erosion of democratic government and human rights protection which affected all communities, but most particularly the Tamils.

During the upheavals the Indian Tamils, who had not previously been involved in the troubles, came under Sinhalese attack and several thousand families sought refuge in the north, where they made their first significant link with the "Ceylon" Tamils. Conditions on the estates had deteriorated sharply after a slump in the export trade and increased domestic inflation. Medical and educational facilities were poor and there was high infant mortality due partly to poor

sanitation and lack of knowledge about hygiene. Nationalization of the estates in 1975 had made conditions worse rather than improving them, and many Indian Tamils were now becoming militant.

After the violence of 1977 the Tamil and Sinhalese communities were scarcely on speaking terms. A planned round table conference failed to take place and, on the Tamil side, the ideal of Tamil Eelam, a separate and independent state, became dominant. Yet most Tamils would probably have accepted less than this ideal; a reasonable autonomy in running their own administration, security from the fear of being dominated or overrun as a minority in their own areas through colonization, and a fair share of economic and educational opportunity.

The events of 1983

Between 1979 and 1983 Sri Lanka was severely affected by the continuing world recession and the prices of its principal exports remained low, the effects of which exacerbated communal feeling. A scheme put forward by President Jayawardene in 1981 which offered Tamils some degree of autonomy under an all-island system of district development councils was far too little to satisfy Tamil aspirations. Sinhalese hard-liners opposed any concessions to Tamils and Jayawardene instituted a series of measures which effectively curtailed civil liberties. A State of Emergency and censorship of the press was imposed in 1981 while, in late 1982, a referendum was used to extend the government's term of office until 1989. Extremist actions had increased and in July and August 1983 inter-communal violence reached a new pitch of intensity in Colombo when Sinhalese mobs turned on Tamils. Government figures state that the number of deaths, mainly of Tamils, was 384, but independent observers believed that it was much higher. By mid-August 100,000 refugees had been evacuated to Jaffna.

Tamil militant groups were formed during the 1970s, but really consolidated themselves in the early 1980s. In 1983 four Tamil militant groups came together under the umbrella of the Tamil Eelam Liberation Front (TELF) with the goal of complete independence. A series of attacks and counter-attacks by security forces and Tamil guerrillas resulted in the deaths of hundreds of civilians and "disappearance" of several hundred Tamils. Assassination of experienced moderate Tamil leaders only strengthened the position of the militants. Fighting between members of the Liberation Tigers of Tamil Eelam (LTTE —

commonly referred to as the "Tamil Tigers") and other Tamil militant groups resulted in deaths and confusion, and the various groups agreed to form a new coalition of Tamil militants from which the LTTE would be excluded. Nevertheless the LTTE gradually assumed a dominant position, aided by its fanatical fighting cadre, support in India and abroad and, it later transpired, financial assistance from the Indian government. As the government tightened its counter-insurgency campaign in the north, all Tamils were seen as suspect, thousands of young Tamil men were routinely detained and tortured; thus increasing the belief among the Tamil population that only the Tigers could protect them.

Indian intervention

Fighting between the security forces and the Tigers continued throughout the first half of 1987. Attacks on guerrilla bases were countered by Tamil attacks on buses and trucks in the eastern Trincomellee district. In May a large-scale offensive against LTTE positions in the north-east resulted in the detention of over 2,500 Tamils and the deaths of between 200 and 1,000 people, many of them civilians. By this time, there were over 130,000 Tamil refugees living in camps in Tamil Nadu, southern India, and the Indian government was coming under increasing domestic pressure to intervene on behalf of the Sri Lankan Tamils. A flotilla of unarmed vessels carrying relief supplies and Red Cross personnel to the Jaffna peninsular set out from Tamil Nadu but was turned back when intercepted by Sri Lankan naval patrol boats. An airlift of supplies was parachuted into the area two days later and complaints by the Sri Lankan government led to talks which resulted in agreement allowing the delivery of relief supplies by sea but not by air. At talks held in New Delhi, Vellupillai Prabakharan, the leader of the Tamil Tigers, rejected settlement proposals put forward by Rajiv Gandhi, but his stance was criticized by four of the Tamil militant groups as being too narrow.

In July 1987, India and Sri Lanka signed an agreement giving autonomy to the north and east of the island. The agreement made provision for the merging of the Northern and Eastern Provinces into one regional council which could later be divided again if the Eastern Province wished to withdraw. Provincial councils were to be largely autonomous and would consist of a governor, chief minister and board of ministers. Tamil, Sinhala and English were to

be given equal status as administrative languages. Hostilities would officially cease on July 31, 1987, and an amnesty would be granted to all political prisoners after the lifting of the State of Emergency in mid-August. Three thousand Indian troops, designated Indian Peace Keeping Forces (IPKF), were sent to the Jaffna peninsula to undertake peace-keeping duties and a further 6,000 were reportedly stationed on standby in southern India. Six hundred Sri Lankan troops were moved from Jaffna to Colombo where they assisted police in controlling Sinhalese demonstrators. Detention camps were opened and thousands of Tamil prisoners were released.

The negotiators failed to anticipate the reaction of the Sinhalese community to the accord. It was condemned by the opposition leader and provoked widespread mob violence which was directed mainly at trains, courtrooms and other government buildings. More than 40 people were killed and over 100 injured in two days. Not only did the Sinhalese reject the accord, but the Tamil Tigers, who had at first accepted the proposals, now also resumed their demand for independence. It was later claimed that the Tigers had only accepted the agreement because they had been paid to do so by the Indian government which had also promised economic aid to the Jaffna peninsular if the Tigers would stop imposing their own taxes on the people of Jaffna. The Tigers now felt that the agreement had been compromised by the policy of settling Sinhalese in the east, thereby altering the demographic balance. The LTTE had in any case only agreed to the proposals in view of the threat posed by the Indian army; its members did not believe that the accord went far enough towards meeting their demands, neither did they believe that the changes could be satisfactorily enforced once Indian troops had departed.

In September, Tamil groups failed to heed an Indian warning that they should stop feuding after at least 100 people had died in clashes. In October there was a massacre by Tamils of hundreds of Sinhalese civilians, and Indian troops launched an offensive in Jaffna, gaining almost total control of the region. In one month of fierce fighting, tens of thousands of refugees had been left homeless. The Tigers demanded that the Indian forces withdraw to their original position and cease patrolling the region but instead more Indian troops were brought in. By mid-1988 there were an estimated 70,000 of them including paramilitary police, air force, naval and support personnel, and over 1,000 civilians had died in addition to more than 1,000 troops and guerrillas.

In November 1987, a constitutional amendment granting Tamils substantial autonomy in the north and east gained an overwhelming parliamentary majority, and an administrative link between the two regions was also approved; however, there was still considerable resistance to the moves on the part of many Tamils and Sinhalese. India wished to return 120,000 Tamil refugees to Sri Lanka and elections for the newly merged province were to be put off until they had returned to vote. The Indian government promised withdrawal of its troops from Sri Lanka once the proposals were in operation, but there were doubts about the degree of unity possible between the Northern and Eastern Provinces since in the Eastern Province the Tamils were outnumbered by Sinhalese and Muslims. Since order had not been restored the security forces were allowed greater freedom to protect the population. The District Minister had been assassinated by Sinhalese, and both Sinhalese and Tamil guerrillas carried out numerous attacks, killing several hundred people, many of them civilians.

The 1988 elections

In June 1988, the Indian troops began a limited withdrawal from Sri Lanka although the situation was far from settled. Although initially popular in India, the intervention had begun to turn sour; Indian troops were being killed in large numbers and indiscipline was creeping in, sometimes in the form of violations against civilians. Yet there were also fears that if they were withdrawn fratricidal war would be fully unleashed. Provincial elections were held in November 1988 in the north and the east and, despite boycott calls and intimidation by the Tigers, over 60% of eligible voters turned out. In the north the Tigers' two main rivals, the Eelam People's Revolutionary Liberation Front (EPRLF) and the Eelam National Democratic Liberation Front (ENDLF) shared power without a vote, while in the east the EPRLF, the ruling United National party and the Sri Lanka Muslim Congress put up candidates. The new Councils had only modest powers but many saw them as a chance to establish peace and stability.

By now, however, the focus had shifted to the south and centre of the country as extremists of the majority Sinhalese community organized armed opposition to the Indian presence. The main organization was the People's Liberation Front (JVP), an extremist leftist Sinhalese group which used terror tactics against those it claimed had betrayed Sri Lanka, in this case primarily the new government of President Ranasinghe Premadasa, elected in December 1988. Death squads of the JVP and, allegedly, the government began a campaign of killings and counter-killings. By mid-1989 government forces had rounded up at least 10,000 people and killed hundreds of innocent civilians and in June the government re-imposed the State of Emergency. President Premadasa called for Indian withdrawal, which the Indians initially refused to do; eventually, however, it was agreed that the Indians would begin a phased withdrawal of the 45,000 strong Indian contingent, with all leaving by the end of 1989.

The situation in the north and the east was also far from stable. The Tigers continued their attacks against both the Indians and the new provincial government. In early August 1989 troops from the IPKF were alleged to have gone on a rampage in the Tamil village of Valvettiturai, killing over 50 civilians in cold blood; two weeks later Tamil Tigers retaliated by killing 24 Indian soldiers. In Sri Lanka the situation had developed from being a situation of the denial of rights to the Tamil minority to one of conflict between extremists of both minority and majority communities and an embattled and precarious government, itself engaging in massive violations of citizens' rights. In the year from September 1988 to September 1989, 10,000 people had been killed in Sri Lanka and there appeared to be no end in sight to the violence.

Veddas of Sri Lanka

Alternative names: **"Wanniya-Laato" (jungle dweller)**
Location: **south/central Sri Lanka, eastern coast**
Population: **2,000 living traditionally**
% of population: **0.01%**
Religion: **animist beliefs, ancestor spirits**
Language: **Vedda**

The Veddas are a Dravidian people and probably, historically, the oldest group in Sri Lanka. They are distinguished by their lifestyle of hunting and gathering, by their unwritten language which is closely related to but different from Sinhalese, their beliefs in Vedda gods and ancestor spirits, and the importance of ancestral lands to all aspects of their life. Since Veddas are not counted separately in the census it is difficult to estimate their numbers but there are probably about 2,000 living a relatively traditional lifestyle.

The Vedda lived on the island before both Sinhalese and Tamils arrived in the sixth century AD. Legend has it that Vijaya, the leader of the original colonists from Northern India, who is said to have founded the first Sinhalese kingdom, married a Vedda princess as his first wife. Gradually, the Veddas were pushed from the fertile agricultural lands into the remote jungle areas where they could continue hunting and gathering. Cultural assimilation of Veddas into other groups has been occurring for hundreds of years and continues today. Increased population pressure has meant that Vedda hunting grounds have become seriously depleted, placing further pressures on the traditional economy. As a result some Veddas now practise cultivation or settled agriculture — these groups are generally known as the "village" Veddas compared to the "jungle" Veddas. There is a small group known as "coastal" Veddas who live near Batticaloa on the east coast and are Tamil-speaking. Whatever their economic situation all Veddas live a marginal existence on the periphery of the market economy.

There are no special laws in Sri Lanka relating to the protection of the Veddas. Their title to land, being unwritten and based on communal ownership, was not recognized either by the colonial authorities or by the post-independence governments. The official view is that the Veddas' hunting and gathering grounds are Crown Land, although on occasions Veddas have been paid compensation (as when they had to move from their lands to make way for the Gal Oya irrigation project). A more recent case has been the relocation of Veddas from the Madura Oya National Park in south-central Sri Lanka in 1985, ostensibly to preserve wildlife, although it appears that the real threats came from professional poachers and not the hunting and gathering Veddas. From 1982 Vedda delegations made pleas to remain but these were disregarded by the authorities and eventually most Veddas were removed, although some were reported to have returned. The relocated Veddas were placed in a village where they intermix with other groups and children are educated in Sinhalese. They have asked for the preservation of their language, forests to hunt in and compensation for the lands they have lost. The UN Working group on Indigenous Populations invited three Vedda representatives to attend the August 1985 session in Geneva; they were unable to obtain travel documents but 42 indigenous and non-governmental organizations supported a statement on Vedda land rights, to be forwarded to the UN Commission on Human Rights. The World Wildlife Fund is also reported to have expressed support for their case. To date, however, the Veddas do not appear to have been allowed to move back to the Madura Oya National Park.

(See also *Andaman Islanders*)

Further References

The Biharis of Bangladesh, MRG Report No. 11, 1982

India, the Nagas and the North-East, MRG Report No. 17, 1980

The Tamils of Sri Lanka, MRG Report No. 25, 1988

The Untouchables of India, MRG Report No. 26, 1982

The Baluchis and Pathans, MRG Report No. 48, 1987

The Sikhs, MRG Report No. 65, 1986

The Jews of Africa and Asia, MRG Report No. 76, 1987

EAST ASIA

East Asia includes, in the Peoples' Republic of China (PRC) and Japan, two of the world's largest States. According to the 1982 census, the population of the PRC exceeded 1,000 million and the 55 distinct national minorities totalled 67 million, or 6.7% of the total. The population of Japan in 1986 was almost 122 million. The spatial extent of the PRC, and the variety of climate and topography, coincides with a considerable range of ethnicity, language and religion, including, according to the census, 15 minorities of more than one million people each. The census claimed only 3,870,000 Tibetans; the true figure is more probably of the order of six million. Approximately 90% of the PRC's border is inhabited by minority nationalities. There are smaller numbers of minorities in Japan but together they form 4% of the population.

The principal descriptive characteristics and human rights issues raised by the groups are, as always, a variable. Questions of international law have persistently been raised by the Chinese occupation of Tibet. On one view, the case is a simple example of the violation of Tibet's right to self-determination and independence; the Chinese view is that Tibet is an integral part of China, and the Chinese mission is to assist the region in getting rid of poverty and backwardness. Another feature of Chinese minority culture is the very large number of religious groups: there are reputed to be some 15 million practising Muslims, millions of practitioners of Buddhism (including those of Tibet) and Daoism, and anywhere from six to 20 million Christians (many of these religious minorities are ethnically Han Chinese). This creates peculiar tensions in a Communist State, which, despite greater openness since the ending of the Cultural Revolution in 1976, is still highly authoritarian. China has also been greatly concerned with security issues in its relations with the USSR; this affects the minorities considerably, since they, in effect, guard the borders of the PRC. Thus, for example, the Sinkiang region has experienced considerable Han immigration and "sinification" pressures have at times been intense. The profile of the PRC is therefore that of a State dominated by a Han "core" people, which has attempted to control a vast and ethnically heterogeneous area of Asian territory.

Japan provides a rather different profile. Japanese education tends to emphasize the homogeneity and uniqueness of the culture. There are, however, groups such as the Koreans, who, despite being designated as foreigners, clearly constitute a well established ethnic minority in Japan; the Ainu of Hokkaido are another much smaller group, in many ways different from the majority Japanese. But the most characteristic minority group of Japan are the Burakumin, products and victims of the hierarchical nature of traditional Japanese society, with its conceptions of acceptable and unacceptable castes and clean and unclean occupations — the closest analogy to this group is the caste of Untouchables in Hindu society. Discrimination against this group, much of it hidden, continues to exist throughout Japanese society.

Relations of mutual hostility between Japan, China and the USSR in this century have produced other minorities such as the Koreans of Sakhalin; intra-Chinese disputes between Communists and Nationalists have led to rival forms of authoritarian government in the PRC and Taiwan, creating problems for the Taiwanese, including its minority tribal Mountain Peoples.

Instruments on Minority Rights

The record of adherence to human rights instruments by the States in the region shows notable gaps. The PRC is not a party to either of the UN Covenants on Human Rights. Japan is a party to the UN Covenants, but not to the Convention against Racial Discrimination, nor the Genocide Convention. The position of Taiwan is bedevilled by questions of recognition and representation at the United Nations. Until 1971, China was represented at the United Nations by the Nationalist government of Chiang Kai-shek; since that time, China has been represented by its effective Communist government, excluding Taiwanese representatives. As with other regions, the absence of a regional human rights treaty means that constitutions assume singular importance (as well as general human rights procedures at the UN).

The PRC Constitution of 1982 represents by far the most interesting attempt to create a participatory regime for minorities. In terms of state structure, Article 1 of the Constitution describes a ". . . Socialist State under the people's democratic dictatorship". It is the people ". . . of all nationalities in China . . ." who are invoked as the creators of a glorious revolutionary tradition in the Preamble to the Constitution. The PRC is envisioned in the Preamble as ". . . a unitary multinational State built up jointly by the people of all its nationalities . . .", with the goal of safeguarding this unity by combating ". . . big-nation Chauvinism, mainly Han Chauvinism, and . . . local-national Chauvinism". Further, "The State does its utmost to promote the common prosperity of all nationalities in the country". The PRC is in concept a unitary State with democratic centralism (Article 3) tempered by a degree of regional autonomy in areas inhabited by minority nationalities. The Constitution recognizes the right of equality between citizens (Article 33), and refers specifically to minorities being guaranteed equality in this area: "All nationalities in the PRC are equal. The State protects the lawful rights and interests of the minority nationalities and upholds and develops the relationship of equality, unity and mutual assistance among all of China's nationalities. Discrimination against and oppression of any nationality are prohibited; any acts that undermine the unity of the nationalities or instigate their secession are prohibited. The State helps the areas inhabited by minority nationalities to speed up their economic and cultural development in accordance with the peculiarities and needs of the different minority nationalities" (Article 4). The same article promises that "The people of all nationalities have the freedom to use and develop their own spoken and written languages, and to preserve or reform their own ways and customs". The concessions to autonomy, it may be noted, are coupled with a warning against encouraging secession, and this is reinforced by Article 52 by which citizens have a duty to safeguard the unity of all China's nationalities.

There is some tension on the issue of minority languages in the Constitution. Article 4 (above) is reinforced by Articles 22 and 34 regarding minority languages in cultural activities and official proceedings. But the State Council is empowered by Article 19 §5 to promote the official common language. Freedom of religious belief is guaranteed by Article 36. The freedom is modified by the requirement that religious activities do not disrupt "the public order", and are not subject to "foreign domination". Minority nationalities are entitled to "appropriate representation" in the National People's Congress and its standing committees which has a nationalities committee as one of its responsibilities (Articles 59, 65 and 70). The State Council, or highest organ of State administration, has as one of its purposes, to ". . . direct and administer affairs concerning the nationalities, and to safeguard the equal rights of minority nationalities and the right of autonomy of the national autonomous areas" (Article 39 §11). Local people's congresses of nationality townships may, to a limited degree, tailor certain legal measures to the peculiarities of the nationalities concerned (Article 99). Article 121 provides that "in performing their functions, the organs of self-government of the national autonomous areas, in accordance with the autonomy regulations of the respective areas, employ the spoken and written language or languages in common use in the locality". The implementing text for the constitutional provisions, the law on regional autonomy for minority nationalities of the PRC, was adopted by the second session of the National People's Congress on May 31, 1984 (see *Appendix 8.1*).

Treatment of minorities

The PRC provides a major example (as also does Yugoslavia) of an attempt to combine Marxist-Leninist principles with respect for local ethnic, religious and linguistic characteristics. The theory did not have a great deal to say about associative factors based on ethnicity as opposed to class, but Marxist States have in practice made considerable claims for their structures and policies in this area. The Soviet and Yugoslav experiments are showing signs of considerable strain in the wake of the new motifs of *glasnost* and *perestroika* and renewed ethnic consciousness. China does not appear to be experiencing a similar scale of ethnic unrest, though such dissatisfaction is always difficult to gauge in a closed society. The reaction of the Chinese authorities to student demonstrations in Beijing and other major cities gives substance to previous reports of the ferocity of reaction to minority disaffection in Tibet and elsewhere. It is unclear how and to what extent the broad guarantees in the Constitution and autonomy laws are being implemented, but it is apparent that most powerful posts in the Communist Party committees in autonomous regions are occupied by Han Chinese, and the same appears to be true of the People's Liberation Army.

Japanese attitudes to minorities stem more from the continuation of social attitudes under the Tokugawas than from official state policy and ideology. Japan provides evidence of a liberal, human rights constitution but maintains regressive attitudes to many of its own citizens. There is also a strong element of racialist attitudes in the treatment of Koreans. In neither case can these attitudes be put down to economic pressures in one of the world's most economically advanced societies.

The East Asian cases reinforce the truth that racialist attitudes resulting in oppression of minority groups are not a variable depending on the particular political system, but rather to some degree underlie all societies. The worth of a system may be gauged by the intensity and sincerity of the efforts it makes to combat such prejudice.

Ainu of Japan

Location: **eastern Hokkaido, Tokyo and other cities**
Population: **18,000-25,000**
% of population: **0.02%**
Religion: **indigenous Ainu and Japanese beliefs**
Language: **Japanese, Ainu**

The Ainu are a small indigenous minority group, who were probably once distributed throughout Japan but whose villages are now confined to Eastern Ezo Territory on the island of Hokkaido, the northernmost island in the Japanese group. Today many also live in Tokyo and other Japanese cities. There has been much speculation on the possible proto-Caucasoid origins of the Ainu and they are somewhat different in appearance to majority Japanese, although these differences are fairly small and there are no more than a few hundred "pure" Ainu at most. The Ainu population is estimated at between 18,000 and 25,000 although there may be 25,000 more who have not declared their Ainu identity.

The Ainu were traditionally known as fierce warriors and military campaigns were waged against them during the eighth and ninth centuries, but gradually they were brought under the control of the Japanese, with whom there has been much intermarriage. Japanese migration northward resulted in the outnumbering of the Ainu people; in 1701 the Japanese population of Hokkaido was only 20,000; by 1873 150,000; and today over five million.

The Ainu have suffered to a certain extent from Japanese prejudice. While they have not been regarded as actually unclean (as have some minorities in Japan) they have been viewed with a certain condescension. Ainu culture has been com-mercialized, perhaps as a means of preserving something of its past, and Japanese tourists visit Ainu reservations to witness traditional dances and purchase examples of native crafts. While this has helped to keep the minority culture alive, it has also reduced the dignity of a once-proud people still further.

In the 1970s, Ainu activists began to put pressure on the government to improve the status and conditions of their people. Although Ainu officially enjoyed the status of Japanese citizens, their living standards had been low and work opportunities poor. Between 1973 and 1978, however, schemes were initiated to help the Ainu, and approximately 15 billion yen was set aside for this purpose. Increased welfare payments were made available to Ainu families as were subsidies to purchase farming and fishing equipment. Extra funds were also put into Ainu schooling and today 80% of Ainu children finish compulsory middle school, 10% more than in 1970.

Despite the improved status of the Ainu, most of them remain landless, and only a small portion of their original tribal lands has been restored to them. Many Ainu have been absorbed into the mainstream of Japanese society. In recent years there have been efforts by Ainu activists to publicize their situation internationally through the UN Working Group on Indigenous Populations and elsewhere.

Burakumin of Japan

Alternative name: **eta (derogatory historical term)**
Location: **Kinki, 40%; other areas around Inland Sea**
Population: **2-3 million**
% of population: **1.6%-2.5%**
Religion: **various**
Language: **Japanese**

The Burakumin are the largest minority group in Japan today but to a large extent they are physically the least visible. They are ethnically, culturally and linguistically similar to the majority Japanese population but they have been distinguished from them by their origins in the lowest castes of traditional Japanese society. Although Japan has since that time been transformed from a hierarchical, feudal society into one of the world's richest and most powerful industrial nations, many former prejudices against the Burakumin have persisted and they remain a discriminated minority group.

The Burakumin are descended from the two lowest castes of Japanese feudal society: the "hinin" and the "eta". The "hinin" formed a heterogenous group of people who had left the four-tiered class system of "acceptable" castes, namely samurai or warrior administrators, farmers, artisans and merchants. The hinin might have been beggars, prostitutes, itinerant entertainers, mediums and diviners, religious wanderers or fugitives from justice. Others had been officially reduced to hinin status as a punishment for certain offences against the penal code. The eta performed tasks which were considered ritually polluting, such as animal slaughter and disposal of the dead. From 1600 AD, outcaste status became firmly established and eta were required to wear special clothing which made them instantly recognizable. Anyone who performed tasks connected with death was traditionally considered to be intrinsically subhuman and in Western Japan, where 80% of Burakumin live, historical myths about the inferiority and "unjapaneseness" of eta are still current and, although there is no appreciable physical difference between the majority Japanese population and Burakumin, the latter were generally felt to be racially inferior. Both hinin and eta, but particularly the latter, were forbidden to intermarry with members of the "acceptable" castes.

In 1871, the new Meiji government passed the Emancipation Edict which officially abolished discrimination against hinin and eta. In 1903, the Greater Japan Fraternal Conciliation Society was formed with the aim of raising the status and conditions of the Burakumin. Other more militant organizations such as the *Suiheisha* (Levellers'

Association) were formed after World War I, and after 1930 the movement took a clear leftist turn and established links with other workers' movements and with the Communist Party. As Japan moved towards World War II under militarist leadership, these trends were curbed and the movement was forced underground; however, members of the leftist movements regrouped after the war to form the *Buraku Kaiho Domei* (Buraku Liberation League). In the immediate postwar period, ten Burakumin were elected to either the House of Councillors or the House of Representatives, including one Buraku leader, Matsumoto Jiichiro, who was then further elected to the position of Vice-President of the House of Councillors, although he was later removed by the American military authorities at the instigation of Japanese conservatives.

The Kaiho Domei has pressed strongly for slum clearance, nurseries, clinics and welfare legislation amongst other things. It has proved more effective in its campaigns than any other agency, including the federal government. Another organization, the *Dowakai* (Integration Association), is a fairly moderate and conservative organization whose members tend to be upper-status Burakumin who seek self-improvement by appealing to the sympathies of the Liberal Democratic Party. Another group, allied to the Communist Party, is the *Zenkoku Buraku Kaiho Undo Rengokai* (National Buraku Liberation Movement Federation). Although government attempts at tackling the problems of the Burakumin have proved largely ineffective, actions taken by local government have produced noticeable results in the field of urban redevelopment and education. The delinquency rate in Burakumin ghettos is often higher than other areas, truancy is higher and employment levels are markedly lower. Since there are no physical features to distinguish them from majority Japanese, some Burakumin who have entered major colleges and universities have tried to conceal their low status.

During the 1970s and 1980s, there was further progress in the move towards equality with the majority Japanese. Over 270 billion yen is spent annually on jobs, housing, education and health programmes in *Dowa* programmes; when viewed against the changes occurring nationwide, however, these improvements are on a small scale, and funding of such projects is decreasing. However, the programmes — under another name — have been continued and externally there is little to distinguish a Buraku neighbourhood from a similar non-Buraku area. The Burakumin remain disadvantaged in most areas and many are unemployed — for example in 1980 in some districts unemployment was 30-50% as compared with the national average of 2.2%. Most large large firms require prospective employees to provide evidence of good, i.e non-Burakumin, birth before engaging them, as do many banks, schools and universities,

and lists of Buraku addresses have circulated in large companies.

The *Kaiho Domei* continues to campaign on behalf of the Burakumin and has branches throughout Japan. But despite its successes, progress remains slow in the face of age-old prejudices. The Buraku have been active in fighting for human rights for other minority groups in Japan and internationally, and the International Movement Against All Forms of Discrimination and Racism (IMADR) was formed in 1988 to express some of these concerns. They have actively lobbied for Japan to accede to the Convention on the Elimination of All Racial Discrimination.

Koreans of Japan

Location: **Kinki region, 48%; Kanto region, 20%; Chubo region, 14%**
Population: **about 700,000**
% of population: **0.6%**
Religion: **various**
Language: **Japanese, Korean**

The Koreans are the major foreign community in Japan, comprising about 85% of Japan's total resident alien population.[1] The majority — about 75% — were born and brought up in Japan, speak Japanese as their first language and have Japanese names which they use in public life, and are in most cases visually indistinguishable from the majority Japanese population. But within Japan they are seen, and see themselves, as a distinct ethnic and cultural group. Their population is probably about 700,000.

There have been links between Korea and Japan for centuries, and as early as the seventh century over one third of the Japanese nobility apparently claimed Korean or Chinese ancestry, while archaeological evidence supports a Korean presence. There were numerous Japanese incursions into Korea from Japan from the thirteenth century until the late sixteenth century when they were forbidden by the Japanese authorities. In 1904, at the start of the Russo-Japanese War, Japan again invaded Korea, which was forced to enter into an alliance with Japan and become a protectorate of the Meiji state. Violent reaction to these developments on the part of the Koreans resulted in the total annexation of Korea in 1910 and the establishment of military rule. After a decade the military

government was replaced by a civilian administration which had to deal with the problems of civil disturbance, chronic unemployment and a rapid population increase. Because many Japanese had been given Korean land to farm, thousands of Koreans — who were now Japanese citizens — were obliged to emigrate to Japan in order to find work which was generally the hardest and most lowly paid. Koreans living in Japan increased from 40,000 in 1920 to 419,000 by 1930 and 2,400,000 by 1945, although after the war repatriation reduced the numbers to 345,000.

In 1952 Koreans in Japan were officially designated as foreigners since Korea was no longer a Japanese territory. Korea had now been divided into the People's Democratic Republic (North) and the Republic of Korea (South). Although nearly all the Koreans had emigrated from the South, both North and South had claimed their allegiance, and the North succeeded in attracting a good deal of support due to its emphasis on ethnic education and national identity. Koreans in Japan became sharply divided over this issue. In 1959 the Japanese government entered into an agreement with North Korea as a result of which some 100,000 Koreans were repatriated over the following eight years. In 1965 it became possible by law for

---

[1]This estimate may now be outdated with recent reports of several hundred thousand migrants — many illegal — entering Japan over the last few years. Most of these workers are from Asian countries such as Bangladesh and the Philippines; many have previously worked in the middle east and gulf countries and the vast majority work in low paying jobs, normally occupied by Koreans and Burakumin.

Koreans residing in Japan to apply for permanent residence status and over half of them applied, many of them in order to be eligible for National Health Insurance benefits and the advantages of free compulsory education.

Despite the fact that the majority of Koreans are born and brought up wholly in Japan, they are mostly classified as "resident aliens" as citizenship is granted on the basis of Japanese parentage, although they may apply for citizenship through naturalization, a lengthy and complicated procedure. Koreans in Japan face many social and economic problems. Although most second- and third-generation students are now completing junior high school the numbers entering higher education are low. The majority of those Koreans in work are employed as labourers, restaurant staff and production-line workers. Few major Japanese companies offer work opportunities to foreign nationals on a permanent basis, and government-related jobs also require Japanese citizenship; as a result many Koreans are engaged in family or community businesses.

The Korean community remains strongly divided over the question of alliance to South and North Korea. Those favouring the South number about 350,000, while some 300,000 claim allegiance to the North. The principal pro-South organization is *Mindan* (Korean Resident Association in Japan). It has many members or sympathizers but is politically weak, due partly to lack of support from the South Korean government. The main North organization, *Ch'ongnyon* (General Federation of Koreans in Japan), is more effective and has sponsorship of the North Korean government. It is recognized by North Korea as the sole representative of Koreans in Japan and is used as an informal channel of communication with the Japanese government with whom North Korea does not have diplomatic relations. With financial backing from North Korea *Ch'ongnyon* maintains its own school system which is attended by almost one quarter of Korean children in Japan. Teaching is in Korean and emphasis is laid on the importance of Korean history and culture. In 1968, after a lengthy campaign, a Korean university in Tokyo was fully accredited.

While the Korean community has received the help and support of a variety of groups in Japan, Koreans still suffer prejudice. Aliens over 16 years of age have to carry alien registration cards at all times and there is compulsory fingerprinting of all aliens, the majority of whom are Korean. There has been much opposition to fingerprinting, which Koreans feel has placed them in the same category as criminals. In this they have been supported by teachers, community workers and some prefecture and local government bodies. Since that time the campaign has continued and in 1983, for example, 29 Koreans were facing jail sentences for their refusal to accept fingerprinting. These and other cases have been brought several times before UN Human Rights bodies.

One group of Koreans who are in a particularly difficult position are the remnants of the 45,000 who were forcibly removed to the island of Sakhalin during the war and who were abandoned in 1946 when half a million Japanese residents were repatriated. Many have since become Soviet or North Korean citizens, but others have elected to remain stateless. In 1956, 2,200 Koreans who were married to Japanese citizens were allowed to return to Japan. Since then a persistent campaign has been waged to allow the remaining refugees — by now elderly — to return.

Mountain Peoples of Taiwan

Alternative names: **various tribal names: Amis, Tayal, Taroko, Saisiat, Tsao (Tsou), Bunun, Paiwan, Rukai, Punuma, Yami**
Location: **mountains and plains on eastern side of Taiwan**
Population: **350,000 (est.)**
% of population: **2%**
Religion: **75% Christian**
Language: **Indigenous languages, Japanese, Chinese**

The "Mountain Peoples" are the indigenous tribal inhabitants of the island of Taiwan. They once occupied the entire island, but today are a small minority of about 350,000 people, or less than 2% of the majority Chinese population. They are divided into 10 tribal groups, each with its own language, living mainly in scattered communities in the mountains in the east of Taiwan. There are some exceptions to this; for example the Amis (the largest single group comprising about one third of the Tribal population) live on the eastern plains, and the Yami on the island of Lanya (Orchid Island).

Although the aboriginal languages of Taiwan are Austronesian, the origins of the tribes are diverse, and they probably migrated to Taiwan from the Philippines over hundreds of years. There was little contact with the Chinese until the seventeenth century when Dutch attempts to establish a plantation economy led to the importation of thousands of Chinese labourers from Fukkien. The Dutch were driven out by Chinese pirates and settlers and in 1683 western Taiwan became part of the Chinese Empire. Immigration of Chinese continued for the next 200 years and by the end of the nineteenth century had reached three million. The administration followed two distinct policies towards the tribal people; one towards the "Pingyu" (flat land) tribes of the plains who were integrated into Chinese society and the other towards the "Sheng Fan" (Raw Savages) of the mountains. The mountain areas were not regarded as part of the Chinese Empire until 1874, and Chinese were forbidden to enter them. But even before this Chinese had penetrated the mountains in search of campourwood. There were conflicts between the two groups, both on the plains and in the mountains, especially after the policy had changed, expressed in the slogan "Open up the Mountains and Pacify the Savages".

In 1894 the Sino-Japanese War resulted in the ceding of Taiwan to Japan leading to 50 years of Japanese rule. Taiwan was economically developed as a plantation economy; roads and railways were built and Chinese immigrated to the eastern plains. Tribal groups of the eastern plains, such as the agricultural Amis, were able to compete economically with the Chinese and were able to some extent to retain a separate identity. In the mountain areas Japanese police handled administration. In the south a policy of village consolidation and road building was successful in tribal areas, but in the north, abuses involving the recruitment of forced labour led to conflicts. Most notable of these was the Wushe incident of 1930 when Tayal and Bunun tribes united to massacre Japanese residents, and over 900 Tribal peoples were killed by the Japanese in retaliation (300 Japanese also died in the two months it took to suppress the uprising). After this, Japanese policy in the mountain areas was reformed somewhat; schools and medical establishments were created in tribal areas and education in Japanese was promoted, with the result that even today Japanese is the lingua franca among the different tribes, while many Mountain People maintain links with Japan.

At the end of the war, the Chinese under the Kuomintang (KMT) Nationalist regime regained Taiwan. After its defeat by Chinese communist forces in 1949, the KMT leadership and one-and-a-half million mainland refugees fled to the island which became the only substantial area of China not under communist rule. There had been almost immediate tensions between the KMT and Chinese Taiwanese; a protest in 1947 against corruption and misrule had been severely repressed and martial law remained in force from 1949 to 1987. The KMT followed the previous policy of restricting access to the mountain peoples but allowed missionaries to enter the area. Although the Japanese had forbidden missionary activity in the mountains there were indigenous Christian movements and after the war the missionaries laid the basis for rapid religious conversion. Today, about 75% of the Mountain People are Christians, mainly Catholics (27% of Tribal population) and Presbyterians (21%). The KMT government followed a largely protective and paternalist policy towards the Tribal groups, seeing in them potential allies against the Taiwan Chinese. The term "savage" was replaced by that of "mountain brethren"; mountain reserves of state land were established, along with indigenous "mountain townships", where administration was in the hands of mainland Chinese officials. All education was to be in Mandarin Chinese, and Japanese and indigenous languages were forbidden despite the difficulties this caused. Economic development resulted in rapid social changes and, despite the restrictions on land sale, mountain land was sold to Taiwanese and many young Mountain People moved to the cities to work. As a result by 1977 over one quarter of the tribal population was resident in cities.

As a group the Mountain Peoples are poorer than Taiwanese and face many social problems such as unemployment and prostitution. New restrictions on movement came in 1985 when Mountain Peoples were required to have entry permits from the police if they wish to travel to areas outside their own township. Indigenous land rights are not recognized as the government maintains that all land belongs to the state, not to the Tribal communities. But there have also been positive developments, one of which is the growth of indigenous participation in the Christian churches, especially of the Mountain Tribe Presbyteries of the Presbyterian Church. Both major churches have supported community development initiatives, such as credit unions and co-operatives, in the mountain areas, while Church missions have developed alphabetical scripts for aboriginal languages. But the government has restricted the use of such scripts to Bibles and hymnbooks and allows their use only if Chinese characters appear together with the aboriginal script. Only Mandarin Chinese is taught in schools. Mountain Peoples still face a great deal of discrimination from the Taiwanese and are seen as a quaint tourist attraction rather than as a living culture.

Okinawans

Alternative name: **Ryukyu Islanders**
Location: **Japanese island chain**
Population: **about 1 million**
% of population: **0.8%**
Religion: **various**
Language: **Japanese**

The Okinawans are the indigenous inhabitants of the Ryukyu Islands, about 600 kilometers south of the Japanese mainland and equidistant from Taiwan and China. The main island, Okinawa, is small — 60 kilometers by 20 kilometers — but contains the majority of the total population of one million. For over 700 years the Ryukyus were a semi-independent kingdom paying tribute first to China, and then to the Satsuma clan based in Kyushu, but retaining their distinctive language and culture. In 1872 the islands were forcibly invaded and annexed by the new Meiji regime, the Okinawan king was deposed, and forcible assimilation policies imposed.

During World War II Okinawa was the major battleground on Japanese soil and over 150,000 Okinawans died after US forces invaded in 1945, many massacred by the Japanese forces. Like the Japanese mainland Okinawa was under direct US military rule in the immediate postwar years but Okinawa was placed under direct US administration in 1951 and this continued until 1972. During these years there were significant social and economic changes, most notably the establishment of large-scale military bases and the effects of a large foreign presence on what had formerly been an isolated rural society. Some of the best arable land was taken for military bases and facilities, and farmers who had lost their land emigrated or worked in the new service industries.

Okinawa reverted to Japanese control in 1972, although the US bases remain and today occupy about 20% of the land. There were cutbacks in military spending, especially after the ending of the Indo-China War, which increased Okinawan unemployment. By the early 1980s this was two or three times as high as on the mainland, while average income was only 65%. The islands were more integrated into the Japanese economy, thus placing pressures on local businesses, while the main growth industry was tourism which grew fivefold between 1972 and 1982. Although most Okinawans welcomed the return of the islands to Japan in an attempt to escape foreign control, many still feel that they are regarded as a "backward" group and there have been movements to revitalize local culture and to fight ecological destruction.

Within Okinawa, one group which faces particular problems are the children of mixed Okinawan and American unions, who are likely to face problems of family instability and poverty in addition to discrimination. In the early 1980s there were estimated to be 3,500 mixed-race people in Okinawa, a small number of whom were stateless as they could claim neither Japanese nor American citizenship.

Tibetans

Alternative names: **Champas**
Location: **Tibetan Autonomous Region, Sichaun, Yunnan, Qinghai, Gansu, India, Nepal**
Population: **3.87 million (official 1982); 6 million (unofficial estimate); India, 100,000**
% of population: **0.38%-0.6%**
Religion: **Buddhism**
Language: **Tibetan**

The Tibetans are the indigenous inhabitants of the traditional "Three Provinces" of Tibet which are currently part of the People's Republic of China (PRC) and which have been divided into six Chinese regions, most notably the Tibetan Autonomous Region (TAR). Tibetans also live in the Chinese provinces of Sichuan, Yunnan, Qinghai and Gansu. According to the last Chinese census there were 3.87 million Tibetans, but other sources claim that these figures are seriously flawed and the true numbers of Tibetans are about six million. In addition there are about 100,000 Tibetans in exile in India and elsewhere.

The history of the Tibetans has been shaped by

their harsh and isolated environment. Tibet is a vast plateau encircled by the Himalayas, the Karakoram, Kumlun and Altya-tagh mountain ranges. Stretching for over 1,500 miles from east to west and 500 miles from north to south, its average elevation is about 12,000 feet. The Tibetans are believed to be descendants of the nomadic Chiang tribes of eastern central Asia, and their language belongs to the Tibet–Burman group. The higher region, with its extreme climate and few inhabitants, supports a largely nomadic and semi-nomadic population and the river valleys are inhabited by agriculturalists, traders and forest dwellers.

History

During the earliest periods of Tibetan history, Tibetan leaders pursued an expansionist policy until by the eighth century they controlled Swat, Hunza, Nepal, the Himalayas and Upper Burma. They also controlled much of Sichuan and northern Yunnan and were in contact with the Arab rulers of Western Central Asia. Buddhism was introduced to Tibet from India in the seventh century and the Tibetan script, which derives from an Indian script, was introduced at the same time; thus the Buddhist scriptures could be written in the indigenous language. By the mid-eighth century a form of Tantric Buddhism had penetrated much of the country. For several centuries there was no political unity within Tibet and in 1244 the Mongols took control of the region and the highest ranking Lama was appointed Kublai Khan's spiritual advisor. Tibet at this time held a curious position in relation to China since it was part of the Mongol Empire, but was definitely not a part of China. After the fall of the Yuan dynasty in 1368 the relationship ceased.

The tradition of the Dalai Lama began in the late sixteenth century, and in 1640 the whole of Tibet was unified under the spiritual leadership of the fifth Dalai Lama. He is believed by most Tibetans to be the reincarnation of Chenresi, the Buddha of Mercy, and he traditionally ruled Tibet from the capital Lhasa, assisted by a hierarchy of Lamas, or monks. When a Dalai Lama died, a search was instituted to find his reincarnation who was always found in infancy and taken to the Potala Palace in Lhasa where he received his education. From then on he was treated with the greatest reverence by Tibetans. Until recently, Buddhism was all-pervasive in Tibet and about one fifth of the male population were monks. There were thousands of monasteries and the largest, Drepung, had about 10,000 monks.

Chinese domination

The Chinese had always considered Tibet to be a province of China, but although there were two representatives of the Chinese Emperor present in Lhasa from 1720 onwards, they had almost no say in internal policy matters. The British had signed several trade and border agreements with China towards the end of the nineteenth century and at the turn of the century they began to fear that Russian influence in the region might threaten British India. The Younghusband expedition was despatched in 1904; the Tibetans refused to negotiate with the British and the Mission became an armed expedition which penetrated to Lhasa. A treaty was eventually concluded with the British representative and this prompted the Chinese in turn to invade Tibet. At a conference in Simla in 1913 Chinese "suzerainty" over Tibet was acknowledged by representatives of Britain, China and Tibet, although China refused to sign the treaty. Despite this, Tibet remained in effect an independent country for the next 38 years.

In 1931 Mao Tse Tung declared the right of self-determination, complete separation and the formation of an independent state for each nationality within the "Motherland"; in 1945 he further stated that Communists should help the nationalities "to fight for their political, economic and cultural liberation and development". Despite these pledges the Chinese state viewed Tibet as a remote province whose people were in need of liberation from their feudal lifestyle. In October 1950 the People's Liberation Army entered Tibet and routed the Tibetan army at Chamdo. In May 1951, a Seventeen Point Agreement was signed under Article 3 of which the Tibetans agreed "to return to the big family of the Motherland" in return for certain guarantees, one of which was that the central authorities would alter neither the existing political system in Tibet nor the established status, functions and powers of the Dalai Lama. The religious beliefs and practices of the Tibetans were to be respected, as was their written and spoken language.

Little change was felt initially within Tibet except by those who lived close to the Chinese border. In Chamdo, the first area to be occupied, a Liberation Committee was set up under the nominal leadership of the young Panchen Lama, the second highest reincarnation in Tibet. Membership consisted of Chinese soldiers and cadres and Tibetan dignitaries. Large numbers of Chinese were brought into the region and the increased numbers brought about severe inflation as stocks of food were brought up by the Chinese. Roads were built with Chinese labour and taxes were imposed. Atrocities began to be reported, including the public execution of hundreds of so-called "serf-owners" and "reactionaries". Reports of events in the east soon reached Lhasa and in 1952 the "People's Movement" and the first Tibetan National Party were formed. Massive anti-Chinese demonstrations followed, after which the leaders of the People's Movement were arrested and the movement dissolved.

Revolt and repression

In 1956 the Chinese authorities began to levy high taxes on traders returning from India. They also began listing the property holdings of all landlords and monasteries. This provoked hostility amongst the monks and villagers alike and a series of uprisings known as the Lithang Revolt began. The number of refugees reaching Lhasa from Kham and Lithang increased rapidly. Resentment in the capital erupted in 1959 into a popular uprising which was brutally suppressed, during which the Dalai Lama fled to India and thousands of Tibetans died. The Tibetan government was dissolved and property redistributed. The population was divided into classes such as rich, land-owning, reactionary, and poor; monasteries were dissolved and monks were set to work with only elderly monks being allowed to remain. Of the 3,000 to 4,000 monasteries and religious monuments existing in Tibet before 1959, only thirteen remained in 1981 and the majority of these were apparently destroyed between 1959 and 1961. After the revolt many men were arrested and taken to Nachen valley to work on the building of a hydro-electric complex. Peasants' associations were set up in the countryside and former landlords were denounced and punished for their former lifestyles. According to a report by the Dalai Lama, 65,000 died between 1955 and 1959 and at least 10,000 children were deported to China; in 1960 Chinese-controlled Radio Lhasa announced that in the preceding year 87,000 Tibetans had been executed in Central Tibet alone, and thousands more are believed to have died over the next few years.

The Cultural Revolution

With the onset of the Cultural Revolution in China, conditions in Tibet continued to deteriorate. In 1966 Red Guards entering the region were critical of the slow rate of progress in Tibet. Many called for immediate change without regard for local conditions, whilst others preferred the current policy of gradual transformation. Many young Tibetans also belonged to the Red Guard and there were Tibetans on each side in the resulting conflicts. The two factions were soon involved in open fighting and the Gyenlog, who had called for instant change, were victorious. Young Red Guards, many of them Tibetan, went through the villages destroying prayer wheels, shrines and scriptures; the object being the destruction of the "Four Olds", namely old thought, old culture, old habits

and old customs. Those major monasteries which had not previously been destroyed were now demolished, leaving only a handful of the most important standing.

As in the rest of China, communes were introduced to Tibet during the Cultural Revolution. Although food production undoubtedly increased as a result of collective farming, Tibet experienced difficulties not encountered in other regions. Whereas land is in short supply throughout China and communal farming methods can be effective, Tibet is sparsely populated and vast tracts of uncultivated land lie unused. Many Tibetans are nomadic and live by bartering goods but barter was forbidden by the Chinese and nomads were obliged by law to sell their produce to the state at less than market rates. The presence in Tibet of nearly 400,000 Han Chinese, both military and civilian, meant that much grain had to be purchased locally and Tibetans were obliged to sell it at artificially low prices. Since Han Chinese eat wheat rather than barley — the Tibetans' staple food — wheat had to be grown, and there was frequently insufficient barley for Tibetan consumption.

Tibetan reaction to the various measures adopted during the Cultural Revolution was predictably hostile. Increasing numbers of refugees followed the Dalai Lama into India and others entered Nepal. There were several revolts which resulted in the deaths of the ringleaders; by 1969, however, the worst excesses of the Cultural Revolution were over. Leading members of the Gyenlog faction were arrested, funds were released for the restoration of monuments where possible, and religion, while still discouraged, was now treated with slightly more leniency.

There have been Chinese claims of significant advances in industry and agriculture since 1959. By 1976 there were 252 industries in Tibet including a dairy plant, leather factories and woollen mills; however 75-80% of the workforce is Chinese and the produce of these industries is exported to China and elsewhere. Most Tibetans cannot afford to buy what they produce. The lumber industry is also thriving, but the amount of deforestation is alarming and once again the lumber is exported to China. Although large areas of uncultivated land have been opened up for cultivation and produce has increased, there have been persistent reports of food shortages, and in 1980 it was admitted by the authorities that Tibet, which was once self-sufficient, now had to import over 30,000 tonnes of food annually.

Recent developments

By the end of the 1970s the Chinese leadership had began to admit to some of the damage caused by their policies and the party chief who had been in charge for the last decade was removed. The Dalai Lama was invited by the Chinese government to send a number of fact-finding delegations to Tibet. In 1980 the first such delegation reported some of their findings; only 44% of school students and 30% of teachers were Tibetan; in some regions the Tibetan language was not taught at all and in others it was taught for up to three years at primary school level only; there were almost no books in Tibetan (although a number of Tibetan classics have been reprinted with heavy emphasis on Marxist-Leninist thought); the standard of health care was noticeably lower than in China and such hospitals as existed appeared to serve Han Chinese or Tibetan officials. These and other criticisms were acknowledged by the Chinese leadership which instituted reforms including allowing peasants to grow barley rather than wheat and lifting taxes. There were further reforms in 1984 intended to encourage private ownership and initiative. There were also attempts to persuade the Dalai Lama to visit Tibet and he initially stated that he hoped to do so in 1985; however there were disagreements as to the conditions of the visit and it was later cancelled.

For the first time western tourists, scholars and media were able to visit Tibet in large numbers and the flow of information improved dramatically. From 1987 there were a series of protests by Tibetans in Lhasa against continuing Chinese occupation, some of which were brutally suppressed by Chinese forces in full view of the Western media. The first was in October 1987 when pro-independence demonstrations by Tibetan monks erupted into riots in which at least a dozen people died. There were further disturbances in March 1988, once again resulting in deaths on both sides, and in December 1988, when Tibetan monks demonstrating on the 40th Anniversary of the UN Declaration of Human Rights were shot at point blank range by police. The worst violence came in March 1989 at the time of the 30th anniversary of the 1959 uprising when police again fired on protesters and riots resulted. The Chinese claimed that 12 people died but other sources put the figure much higher. Martial law was declared in Lhasa and the surrounding areas and foreigners were expelled. There were also reports of violence in other areas. It had become apparent that resentment had evolved into something like a popular, although uncoordinated, uprising.

There have been many reports of human rights violations in Tibet, not only shootings and beatings by police and security forces but arrests, detention without trial and torture. These reports have been confirmed by organizations such as Amnesty International and Asia Watch among others. There has been a constant stream of refugees escaping to India or Nepal.

In September 1987 the Dalai Lama issued a five-point plan for Tibet as a basis for negotiation with the Chinese government. The basic points were the transformation of Tibet into a zone of peace; abandonment of the policy of population transfer of Han Chinese into Tibet; respect for human rights; environmental protection; and commencement of negotiations on the future status of Tibet. In a speech to the European Parliament in Strasbourg in June 1988 he put forward more specific proposals of a self-governing Tibet in association with China, giving Beijing the right to station troops there and control foreign policy. This was a radical departure from previous statements, as it acknowledged Chinese sovereignty. While some Tibetan exiles expressed strong disapproval of this stance, the Chinese government initially appeared favourable to some aspects of the offer, but insisted that there should be no discussion of Tibetan independence and that talks should take place only in Beijing. Later, this second condition was dropped, and the Dalai Lama offered to begin direct talks in Geneva in January 1989. To date, however, no talks have taken place and it appears unlikely that they will do so in the light of the present repression within China.

Tibetans in exile

About 100,000 Tibetans are now living in exile, mostly in India and Nepal. The Chinese government is embarrassed by their presence and has made several attempts to persuade the Dalai Lama to return to Tibet, thus legitimizing the political situation in Tibet. So far these attempts have been unsuccessful, since the Dalai Lama insists on the right of the Tibetan people to decide how they should be governed whereas the Chinese maintain that Tibet is part of China and must therefore be governed by the Chinese. The exiled Tibetans have created a thriving community and built a number of schools and several institutions of education and culture, such as the Central Institute of Higher Tibetan Studies in Sarnath and the Library of Tibetan Works and Archives in Dharamsala. There are several museums, libraries and medical centres and there is also a Tibetan Institute for the Performing Arts. Smaller groups of Tibetans have settled throughout Europe, Canada and the United States and many have now received university education in these countries.

Further References

Japan's Minorities: Burakumin Koreans, Ainu and Okinawans, MRG Report No. 3, 1983

The Tibetans, MRG Report No. 49, 1983

SOUTH-EAST ASIA

South-East Asia has seen more than its share of devastation since 1945. The retreat of the colonial powers — Britain, France, the Netherlands, the United States — did not herald an era of peace and stability but ushered in fearful conflicts. Both the mainland and insular areas have suffered. South-East Asia has been used by the superpowers as a testing ground for rival ideologies and military competition. The Cold War became by proxy the Vietnam war, with its enormous death toll. The Vietnam war indirectly produced the monstrous regime of Pol Pot in Kampuchea; genocide was the result, then invasion by Vietnam. Communist insurgency in Indonesia was put down with, again, huge loss of life. Dictatorships and authoritarian regimes have flourished in the region in response to the lack of political consensus and factional struggles for dominance. Instability continues to threaten in the revival of Kampuchea and the re-emergence of the Khmer Rouge. Human rights remain under stress.

Minorities have been affected by these developments, and by other factors stemming from the mix of races and religions in the various States. Apart from broad questions about general standards of human rights, ideological conflict has a specific effect on many groups. The various hill and border tribes often straddle the frontier between rival nations, and are thus objects of suspicion. This results in oppression as States like Thailand devote energies to fighting Communist insurgency. Ethnic or religious discontent can become confused with right-left polarities when dictators such as President Marcos discern a "red threat" in the activities of Philippine Muslims. The rather negative position of many Chinese in South-East Asia has stemmed in part from a perception that they exhibit a dual loyalty: to the host-State but also to the Beijing or Taipei regimes. This adds an extra dimension to inter-ethnic tensions.

There are many inter-ethnic problems. The minority types seen elsewhere are also found in South-East Asia. There are the indigenous and the non-indigenous, hill and lowland groups. Religion is also a separate focus of identity, with or without ethnic differences: Thailand and Burma are great Buddhist States; the Philippines represents the largest concentration of Christians in Asia. The area is rife with autonomist or separatist movements of various kinds. Separatism has placed even the existence of States such as Burma under serious threat as Karens, Shans and Kachins form "liberation armies". A particular regional feature of these and other minority groups is their involvement with large-scale drug smuggling, which enables governments to classify them as criminals, thus submerging the other, nationalist dimensions of their activities. The result is that military power buttresses or intertwines with the state structure in many cases, lending a rather fragile and evanescent quality to constitutions and laws.

Instruments on Minority Rights

Participation in international human rights instruments is frequently lacking in the various States. Of relevant treaties, Burma is a party only to the Genocide Convention; Indonesia has not even ratified that Convention. There is a similar absence in the cases of Malaysia and Thailand. On Malaysia, the American commentator Vernon Van Dyke writes that: "Malaysia has not ratified the International Convention on the Elimination of Racial Discrimination, which may or may not suggest a fear that policies pursued do not fully meet the standards prescribed."[1] The Philippines stands out as an exception to the "rule" of not adhering to human rights instruments, though Vietnam and Laos have a reasonable record in this respect.

[1] *Human Rights, Ethnicity and Discrimination*, Westport, Conn. 1985, p. 113.

In general, the constitutions of the various States have attempted to incorporate some role or voice for minorities to participate in the state structure. Successive Burmese constitutions have accorded forms of autonomy to its various minorities, though between the Constitution of 1947 and that of 1974 there was a considerable reduction in the scope of the autonomy offered to the "national races" of Burma. Successive constitutions in the Philippines have also accorded a place to constituent communities. Article II(22) of the 1986 Constitution declares that the State ". . . recognizes and promotes the rights of indigenous cultural communities within the framework of national unity and development". Even the superseded Constitution of 1973 declared in Article XV (9(2)) that "Filipino culture shall be preserved and developed for national unity", a provision interpreted by the government before the UN Committee on Racial Discrimination to mean that "the goal is not uniformity, but unity in diversity, so that the Philippines truly represents a mosaic of cultures". For all its problems, the Philippines is at least relatively free from the pressures exerted on minorities by heavily ideological States. On the other hand, Indonesia, which is, if anything, more diversified than Burma or the Philippines, describes itself simply as an "independent and sovereign republic . . . a democratic, constitutional State of unitary structure" (Article 1 of the 1950 Constitution). The generally straightforward individualist human rights constitution nonetheless recognizes minority representation in the House of Representatives in specified percentages. The official state philosophy is *Pancasila*, one strand of which is belief in one God, but without a grant of exclusivity to any one monotheistic religion.

While the actual human rights situations in the States of the region have been subject to scrutiny by various international bodies, probably the most challenging constitutional structure in terms of anti-discrimination policies is, as Van Dyke's comment suggests, that of Malaysia. The Constitution reflects a doctrine described as the *Bumiputra* (sons of the soil) doctrine, and implies a certain pre-eminence in legal arrangements for Malays, considered as indigenous inhabitants of the Federation. Article 160 describes a Malay as one ". . . who professes the religion of Islam, habitually speaks the Malay language, [and] conforms to Malay custom". Many aspects of life in Malaysia appear to be matters of Malay privilege to the detriment of the Chinese, Indians and other groups. Privilege applies in the public services, in university scholarships and places, in business permits and licences and many other areas, apart from the adoption of Islam as state religion and Malay as official language. On the other hand, there is some latitude for other groups: Article 3(1) of the Constitution provides that "Islam is the religion of the Federation; but other religions may be practised in peace and harmony in any part of the Federation"; Article 11(1): "Every person has the right to profess and practise his religion". Further, by Article 11(3), "Every religious group has the right (a) to manage its own religious affairs, (b) to establish and maintain institutions for religious and charitable purposes and (c) to acquire and own property and hold it in accordance with the law". Help from the State, however, in the field of religion, leans towards Muslims: thus Article 12(2) provides: "Every religious group has the right to establish and maintain institutions for the education of its children and provide therein instruction in its own religion and there shall be no discrimination on the ground only of religion in any law relating to such institutions; but Federal law may provide for special financial aid for the establishment or maintenance of Muslim institutions or the instruction in the Muslim religion of persons professing that religion." The basis of Malay identity is not racial, but religious, linguistic and customary: an attempt is made to distinguish between the indigenous and the immigrants such as the Chinese. Nonetheless, to quote Van Dyke again vis-à-vis the Chinese and Indians ". . . the Malays are the *Bumiputra*, and the intimation is that the country really belongs to them, the others being outsiders if not intruders".[2] The measures, with an original benign aim of affirmative action to benefit indigenous Malays, result in discrimination against other well established communities in the Federation. The nearest analogy — promoting the indigenous peoples — is probably that of Fiji. Both raise questions about the proper balance to be achieved in society when particular groups are singled out for special favour, even if a degree of affirmative action is historically and morally justified.

Treatment of minorities

Many States in South-East Asia have not recovered from the ravages of war. The first priority is therefore the achievement of a measure of stability. Evidence of overcoming difficulty is provided

[2]*op. cit.* p. 114.

by the experience of the Philippines, which has surmounted dictatorship to the general benefit of human rights for all. Other peoples are not so fortunate and the general level of deprivation in terms of civil, political, economic and social rights is severe. The future stabilization of Kampuchea in a regime of respect for human rights should be matched by similar developments in Burma, Laos and Vietnam. The gradual disengagement of the superpowers is welcome, though the potential for continued rivalry is there. The lessening of ideological tensions holds out some promise for minorities. But the experience of many other States is that ethnic differences can persist when other causes of conflict are removed. The chances of final consolidation of States such as Burma must be regarded as problematic, though other States are not so besieged. However, authoritarian solutions to minority issues are not likely to succeed, and such are the solutions frequently chosen by States. Both States and minorities require guarantees that their rights will be respected. Perhaps only protracted efforts by the international community to raise all-round levels of development and underpin mutual respect of rights will achieve this aim.

Burma (Myanma)

Population: **38 million (est. 1989)**
% of population: **two-thirds of population are Burman, remainder are from indigenous ethnic minorities, e.g. Mon, Shan, Karen, Chin, Arakanese etc., and immigrant minorities — mainly Chinese, Bengali and Tamil**
Religion: **mainly Buddhist**
Language: **Burmese and various minority languages**

There are estimated to be 67 separate indigenous racial groups speaking numerous languages and dialects in Burma. Of these the principal minorities are the Mon, Shan, Karen, Kachin, Chin and Arakanese, who live for the most part in separate minority states surrounding the central Irrawaddy plains, the chief settlement area of the majority Burmans. These various tribal groups belong to three racial categories: the Mon-Khmer, the Tibeto-Burman and the Thai, all of whom moved gradually south into the region over long periods.

The Mons entered the region before the Burmans in the early centuries of the Christian era. It was the Mons who first received Buddhism and they possessed a rich and sophisticated culture which was profoundly to affect the later Burman tradition. There are now about 1.3 million Mons who are well assimilated into the mainstream of Burmese culture. The majority live in the south-east of Burma where they cultivate wet-rice, yams and sugar cane.

The Shans are closely connected linguistically and culturally to the neighbouring Thais. They dominated lowland Burma politically from the thirteenth to the sixteenth century and they are Theravadha Buddhists like the Burmans and the Mons. The Shan state was traditionally divided into more than 30 smaller states, each under the authority of a hereditary prince. The Shans now probably number slightly under three million and inhabit the upland valleys of the Shan plateau where they practise wet-rice cultivation.

The Karens are Burma's largest minority group, estimated at over three million, or 10% of the population. Linguistically they belong to the Tibeto-Burman group and large numbers live in the Irrawaddy division around Bassein and in Kayah state and Tenasserim. The majority, however, live in Kawthule state in the eastern part of Burma bordering Thailand. Originally a hill-dwelling people, many were forced to move into the Irrawaddy delta by pressure from Burmans. The various tribal Karens such as Sgaw, Pa-O and the Kayah, or Red Karen, of Kayah state are quite distinct culturally. Some are animists, others have adopted Buddhism and a large proportion are Christians who were influenced by the American Baptist mission in the nineteenth and twentieth centuries. Some cultivate dry-rice in the hills, others are wet-rice cultivators and many work the tin mines or are *mahouts* (elephant riders) around the border areas.

The Kachins share Kachin state in the mountainous north with members of many other tribal groups. More properly called the Jinghpaw, they are hill people who practise shifting cultivation and also use hill-terraces where possible. The majority of the Kachins are animist although many are Christians and a small number of lowland dwellers are Buddhists. Kachin culture is deeply concerned with the veneration of ancestors and with the propitiation of the spirit world.

The Chins, who live in the hill regions bordering India and Bangladesh, number about 350,000, although another 800,000 live on the other side of the border. The northern Chins have hereditary chiefs and an aristocracy, and their economy is more elaborate than that of the southern Chins who have a more democratic type of traditional village government and a less developed agricultural system, largely of the shifting variety. Most — about 70% — are animist, and the remainder are Christian and Buddhist.

The Arakanese are a Tibeto-Burman group living in the coastal strip along the Bay of Bengal. There is known to have been a powerful Arakanese kingdom during the fourth century AD. They are of a slightly darker complexion than the Burmans, probably because of their close ties with Muslim India; from the fifteenth to the seventeenth centuries the Arakanese controlled Chittagong and although Buddhism remained the dominant religion in Arakan, Islam was widely adopted in the state, which has the highest concentration of Muslim inhabitants in Burma.

Other minority groups include the Nagas of the Assam hills and the Wa of the Shan state-Yunnan border region, both of whom were formerly head-hunting peoples; the Palaung of Shan state, the Padaung, whose women are known for the brass rings they wear about their necks and legs; and the Akha, Lahu and Lisu people who are more numerous in the hills of Thailand.

National unity and insurgency

The relationship between the minority peoples and the Burman majority has been very uneasy for many years. The British made a distinction between "Burma Proper" and "Outer Burma". "Burma Proper" was placed under the direct rule of British India whilst "Outer Burma", the settlement areas of the minorities, remained more or less autonomous under indirect rule. The central plains region was brought under a regular system of administration and code of law, leaving the frontier regions more or less undisturbed. Several of the hill tribes served with the British during World War II, gaining a reputation as fierce and dependable fighters who remained loyal to the Allies when the Japanese were in the ascendant, whilst the Burmans for the most part accepted Japanese rule. The Kachins, Chins and Karens were particularly distinguished fighters.

The current administrative divisions — based on the model devised by the British — were built into the 1948 constitution at the time of independence. In February 1947 General U Aung San, the leader of the Burma independence movement, successfully obtained the agreement of the frontier peoples to participate in an independent Burma, an event still celebrated on Union Day each year. The minorities were offered their own states with in some cases the option to secede from the union after 10 years. A 125-seat Chamber of Nationalities was also established in an attempt to ensure the full participation of minority groups in the decision-making process. The Karens rejected all such proposals, however, demanding an autonomous state or complete independence. Within six months of independence the Karens were in armed rebellion and they were soon followed by other minorities. Although government forces were able to push back the various resistance groups, which at one point controlled about 40% of Union territory, insurgency has continued to a greater or lesser degree since that time.

In March 1962 General U Ne Win took over government from U Nu, maintaining that a firm treatment of the insurgents was necessary. The elective state councils in frontier areas were abolished and replaced by appointed state supreme councils. A military-led hierarchy of security and administrative committees was set up. However, despite a great increase in government funds channelled into the border areas and spent on modest agricultural, educational and health improvements, hostilities continued unabated.

Under General Ne Win missionaries were ordered to leave Burma and mission schools and hospitals were nationalized. In 1973 a new constitution swept away the whole apparatus of states for the minority peoples, placing less weight on their separate identities and needs, and emphasizing their common membership of the Union. Reaction to these moves was predictably hostile and more than two-thirds of the country was soon subject to insurgency. Much of government funding has been allocated to combating the various insurgent groups and the Burma Army is active throughout the year.

Recent developments

The various communist groups have become much smaller over the past 15 years and now present little threat to the government, but the complication of the opium traffic, which provides funds for insurgent activity in addition to a livelihood for many hill-dwellers, has added greatly to the difficulty of finding a solution to the question of regional autonomy. A National

Democratic Front (NDF) of 10 ethnic minority organizations was set up in 1976 and reformed in 1986 with the aim of greater autonomy for ethnic minorities within a federal system. Increased Karen guerrilla activity in 1982-3 lead to a series of military offensives against the Karen areas and by 1987 30,000 Karen and other refugees had fled across the Thai border. The popular uprising by the Burmese people in 1988 led to many Burmese students fleeing into the hill regions where they underwent military training in Karen insurgent camps and in some cases participated in insurgent attacks on government forces. The effect on the minorities of the change of government and the promise of democratically run elections in 1989 has not yet been gauged, but it would seem that they have been encouraged in their anti-government stance by the dissatisfaction of most of the Burmese people.

(See also *Hill Tribes of Northern Thailand; Nagas of India* in **South Asia**)

Chinese of Indonesia, Malaysia and the Philippines

Name: **Overseas Chinese**
Alternative names: **Nanyang**
Location: **throughout South-East Asia**
Population: **Malaysia 4,816,000; Indonesia 3,922,000; Philippines 692,000 (1981)**
% of population: **Malaysia 34.5%; Indonesia 2.6%; Philippines 1.4%**
Religion: **Mahayana Buddhism; rituals connected with veneration of ancestors**
Language: **Mandarin, Hokkien, Hakka and Cantonese**

There are people of ethnic Chinese origin in all South-East Asian countries, most of whom are the descendants of those who migrated there in the nineteenth century, although some communities are considerably older. They are a minority in every country with the exception of the island state of Singapore where they form 77% of the population and are the dominant community, politically and economically. From 1979 the large-scale movement of "boat people", many of them Chinese, into Malaysian and Indonesian waters has both heightened sensitivities on race relations there, especially in Malaysia, and created the genesis of a new underprivileged Chinese minority.

Background

The Chinese have been migrating southward from China for centuries, driven from their homeland by economic necessity, political disturbance, flood and drought. As early as the fourth century AD Chinese traders were settling in Sumatra, and during the fourteenth and fifteenth centuries they were engaging in considerable maritime activity, travelling as far afield as East Africa. During the seventeenth century the Chinese population in Siam (Thailand) grew rapidly and many Chinese became highly assimilated, in some cases losing mastery of their own language.

The main wave of Chinese immigration into South-East Asia began just over a century ago at a time of colonial domination and economic development throughout the region, resulting in a demand for cheap imported labour — largely Chinese but also from the Indian sub-continent. For many Chinese, migration was not at first intended to be permanent, and many left their families in China. However, in most cases settlement did become permanent and there was frequent intermarriage with indigenous women. Most descendants of these immigrants did not speak Chinese and absorbed a high degree of the indigenous culture. The situation altered in the twentieth century when Chinese women began to migrate in significant numbers. Parity between the sexes was reached in 1930, and as a result mixed marriages became much less common and Chinese language and culture were preserved to a much greater extent. Large-scale Chinese immigration came to a halt in the early 1930s during the worldwide economic depression and the controls imposed at that time remained in place after it ended. The effect of war and independence restricted immigration still further. As a result the proportion of locally born Chinese has risen steadily and today is probably around 85% of the Chinese population in Indonesia, Malaysia and the Philippines.

Overseas Chinese have formed a number of voluntary associations such as speech-group associations, sports clubs, occupation groups and chambers of commerce, which provide their communities with schools, health and recreational facilities. Voluntary associations have replaced the powerful clans or descent groups of China which were often very wealthy and protected their members, caring for older members, mediating in disputes and paying burial expenses. The Chinese immigrant will usually be met on arrival in a new country by a representative of the appropriate group and will be helped to establish himself in work and to find accommodation. In the larger Chinese communities there is a temple or ancestral hall which becomes the focus for community life. Thus in areas with large Chinese communities and the minimum of intermarriage the Chinese community remains exclusive and traditional in outlook.

Indonesia, the Philippines and Malaysia are all new states established after World War II. All three shared the experience of Japanese invasion and occupation during the war, and although many factors divide the countries, the indigenous cultures and languages have much in common. Each country experienced different colonial regimes and different transitions to independence and as a result they have inherited different forms of government and different laws governing citizenship. The distinction between the Chinese born in South-East Asia and those born in China is important for reasons of nationality status, nationality being acquired either by birth or by naturalization.

In all three countries the Chinese have experienced a degree of economic success out of all proportion to their numbers, many of them being involved in commerce and many others being small traders. This success has aroused the antagonism of a large number of poor Indonesians, Filipinos and Malays. The loyalties of the Chinese have also been questioned, especially during the upheavals in China and the communist insurrections in South-East Asia. As a result South-East Asian nationalism has been directed against the Chinese as much as against Western capitalism, and Chinese have had to struggle for equal treatment and have not been granted citizenship as a right. In each country the laws governing citizenship have been altered several times during the past 50 years, usually in response to changing relations between the host country and the People's Republic of China (PRC). Whereas in Islamic Indonesia and Malaysia there was little inducement for the Chinese to assimilate into indigenous society, there was much assimilation in the Philippines.

Indonesia

Before 1960 dual nationality was legally accepted in Indonesia but by 1962 it had become established that an Indonesian Chinese could be either Indonesian or a Chinese national, but not both; the law was complicated by a regulation prohibiting aliens from retail trading in rural areas. At least two-thirds of the Chinese with dual nationality accepted Indonesian citizenship and between 1960 and 1962 600,000-800,000 Chinese became or were confirmed as Indonesian citizens. Perhaps as many as 100,000 others left Indonesia for China, but many were unable to secure a passage to China and were forced to remain in various Indonesian cities without jobs, since as aliens they were not permitted to work.

Following the attempted coup of 1965 the Chinese fell under suspicion once again. Thousands are reported to have been killed, although exact numbers are impossible to establish. (This however was only a small proportion of the total numbers killed, most of whom were Indonesians from Java and Bali. Chinese were not special targets.) Diplomatic relations between Indonesia and the PRC were broken in 1967, Chinese schools were closed and measures were taken to restrict Chinese businesses. Many thousands of Chinese left Indonesia for China or elsewhere. The treaty governing nationality was rescinded in 1969 and thereafter citizenship could only be acquired by naturalization, which was a much slower process.

In 1980 there was a new drive to naturalize the one million remaining alien Chinese — 900,000 of whom were PRC citizens and 120,000 classified as "stateless" — in a bid to eradicate the nationality problem and secure the loyalty of the Chinese community. The government has also espoused a policy of assimilation and Chinese are encouraged to adopt Indonesian names and to intermarry with indigenous Indonesians.

Assimilation has been easier in some Indonesian islands than in others. In strongly Islamic Sumatra and Kalimantan (Borneo), for instance, where a higher proportion of Chinese are China-born and where the prosperous Chinese communities of Singapore and Malaysia loom large, anti-Chinese prejudice remains strong. In Medan in Sumatra in 1972 there were about 5,000 Chinese refugees who were forcibly expelled from their homes in Banda Atjeh in northern Sumatra during army and

Muslim-led violence in 1966 which resulted in several hundred deaths. Other Chinese returned to the Banda Atjeh area apparently without problems. There has also been considerable violence in West Kalimantan region, when Dayaks turned on a largely rural Chinese community in retaliation for the murder of Dayaks by ethnic Chinese communist guerrillas in 1967. About 1,000 Chinese were killed and over 60,000 were forced to flee to coastal centres. However these people have adapted to their new circumstances as did those 17,000 Chinese who were cleared from a remote region by the Indonesian army in 1971 in order to end guerrilla incursions from Sarawak.

The position of Indonesian Chinese has improved considerably in the last 20 years. They are a relatively prosperous community and a small number are very wealthy. Some private schools now teach Mandarin in addition to the standard Indonesian curriculum, many Chinese children attend private schools and Chinese students at one stage probably held about 10% of university places although the Chinese comprise less than 3% of the population. More preference has been given to ethnic Indonesian students recently, however, and as a result since the 1970s many more Chinese students enrolled at private universities such as the Protestant university in Djakarta, while others are educated at universities outside Indonesia.

Malaysia

Malaysia is multi-ethnic and has the second highest proportion of ethnic Chinese of any South-East Asian state. The main ethnic groups are Malays — about 50%, Chinese about 35% and Indians about 10%. In Malaysia any person born in the territory after September 1962 is entitled to citizenship provided he or she was not born the citizen of another country and provided at least one of his or her parents was at the time of the birth a citizen of the Federation of Malaya or permanently resident in it. By virtue of this law and previous citizenship legislation almost all Chinese in the Federation are Malaysian citizens.

Citizenship does not mean Chinese citizens have equal rights with indigenous Malayans, however. The high proportion of Chinese, their relative wealth as a community and the proximity of ethnic-Chinese Singapore have fuelled fears of the ethnic Malays of Chinese domination. There is also suspicion of Chinese loyalties and the role of thousands of Chinese communist sympathizers during the Malayan emergency in the 1950s has

not been forgotten. The crucial point came after race riots in May 1969 in Kuala Lumpur in which over 100 people died and which led to the suspension of parliamentary government and the imposition of emergency rule for two years. The government, headed by the largest ethnic Malay party, the United Malays National Organization (UMNO), formulated its New Economic Policy (NEP), the professed target of which was to eliminate poverty, regardless of race, but which had as a target that 30% of equity capital in all businesses should be in Malay hands by 1990. The government was required to safeguard the special position of the Malays — bumiputras — and to ensure the reservation for Malays of what was considered to be a reasonable proportion of public service positions, scholarships, university places and trade or business permits and licences. Quotas limiting the proportion of non-Malays admitted to higher education have now driven many Chinese into study overseas, and Chinese voting-power, potentially considerable, has been curtailed by the redistribution of electoral boundaries in favour of rural constituencies — where Malays are better represented — rather than urban constituencies.

In the 1980s there were reports of growing ethnic tensions between the various communities, but to date these have not resulted in disturbances along the lines of 1969. Recession has increased unemployment and, therefore, competition between groups, while the growth of Islamic fundamentalism among some sections of the Malay community has led to fears among non-Muslims of the extension of Islamic personal laws to non-Muslims (presently personal Islamic law is applied only to Muslims). However, given the consensus nature of Malaysian parliamentary rule this seems unlikely. In 1987 an Education Ministry decision to promote non-Mandarin speakers to Chinese primary schools led to protests and a threatened school boycott by Chinese. The government responded by making over 100 arrests of opposition leaders under the Internal Security Act, including many ethnic Chinese, on the grounds that racial harmony was threatened; however critics maintain that this was not so and see the arrests as evidence of growing authoritarianism in Malaysia.

The Philippines

In the Philippines the Chinese community is much smaller in number, and proportionately, than in either Indonesia or Malaysia. Discrimination against Chinese is comparatively rare as they do not constitute any sort of threat to the indigenous community. In the nineteenth century, the Chinese of mixed ancestry (*mestizos*) were forced out of the wholesale and retail trade by the new Chinese immigrants and into landholding and the production of export crops. As a result their lifestyles became closer to those of indigenous Filipinos than to those of the ethnic Chinese. By the turn of the century the majority of Chinese *mestizos* had been absorbed into Filipino society, and many members of the country's elite today can claim Chinese ancestry.

Under the constitution adopted in 1973 citizenship was granted to those who were Philippine-born and their descendants and to those who had been naturalized "by decree". Over 38,000 applications (representing perhaps 120,000 people) for naturalization were received by mid-1976, the majority from Chinese. By 1978, 21,000 applicants had been naturalized.

Hill Tribes of Northern Thailand

Alternative names: **Karen, Hmong, Yao, Lahu, Akha, Lisu**
Location: **northern border areas of Thailand**
Population: **total about 415,000**
% of population: **about 1% of Thai population**
Religion: **indigenous beliefs, Christian (Karen)**
Language: **various**

The hill tribes of Thailand live for the most part in the upland areas of the north, in the region known as the Golden Triangle. There are six main groups recognized by the Thai government. These fall into three linguistic categories as follows: (i) the Lahu, Akha and Lisu belong to the Tibetan-Burman family of languages. These tribes migrated in stages from Southern China into Burma and began entering Thailand at about the beginning of the twentieth century; (ii) the Meo (Hmong) and Yao (Mien) belonging to the Sino-Tibetan language group. These people migrated from south-central China into Laos and thence across the Mekong River into Thailand. Many of them were forced to flee to Thailand after the Communist takeover of Laos in 1975; and (iii) the Karen, the most numerous of the groups, who probably originated in south-west China although there are none living there today.

There are also a number of smaller groups such as the Lawa, Kha Mu, Kha Htin, Thai Lue and Yumbri. In 1983 the total number of hill tribals in Thailand was estimated at 415,000 of whom over half were Karen. This is only a small percentage of the total number of hill tribes peoples living in the Golden Triangle of Burma, Thailand, Laos and China.

Most hill tribes practise slash and burn cultivation which causes them to migrate gradually from place to place. The majority live at high elevations, above 1,200 metres, although the Karen, who have probably lived in the region longer than other groups, are more settled and prefer to live at lower levels. Hill rice is the principal food crop although some tribal groups are now cultivating lowland irrigated rice. Maize and a variety of vegetables are also grown and the most prized cash crop among all but the Karen and Akha is the opium poppy. The government has made efforts to curb the cultivation of the poppy by substituting alternative crops such as coffee, tea and peanuts, but it is difficult to control due to the inaccessible nature of the terrain and the power of the heavily armed opium traffickers who maintain a monopoly of the traffic between the villages and markets. It is also a crop which hill people can cultivate without competition from valley-dwelling farmers. Apart from their work in the fields, all the tribal groups are skilled weavers and embroiderers, each tribe has a distinctive costume, and produces fine carving, silverware and basketware. These handicrafts are increasingly sold in market towns and to tourists.

The majority of tribal peoples have a strong belief in a powerful spirit world and their lives are surrounded by ritual. The village shaman and the priest are highly respected as having some influence over the spirits. Tribal beliefs are not uniform. However, Yao religious beliefs have marked Chinese connections and there are many Christian Karens.

Until the mid-nineteenth century the hill tribes had a high degree of autonomy and this continued after the unification of Siam (Thailand) in 1873 as the new kingdom consolidated its hold in the south and the lowlands of the north. But this changed as government exerted its control over hill tribes. One aspect which is hedged with difficulties is the granting of Thai citizenship and although the number of tribal people gaining citizenship is growing, the majority remain stateless. They are unable to own their own fields and may be fined if they cannot produce citizenship papers at checkpoints. They are unable to obtain vehicle licences — required by law — for the motorcycles and trucks which some villagers are now purchasing. Stateless children are unable to sit for school examinations.

The Thai government has made great efforts to settle the hill tribes. It is uneasily conscious of the fact that they are frequently manipulated by drug traffickers, warlords and communist insurgents who provide them with medicines, cigarettes and guns in return for message-carrying, opium and shelter. Conflicts, with the hill tribes fighting on the sides of both the communists and security forces were most active in the 1960s and 1970s, but are much less prominent in the 1980s. Many thousands of Hmong became internal refugees during and after the Red Meo War from 1967 to 1973. Government schools and health services have been established and a housing programme is available to those who are prepared to give up opium cultivation and settle permanently. Radio stations have become an important link between the hill peoples and the outside world and every village now has a radio. Roads are being constructed, mainly to assist forestry and mining industries but also in order to facilitate national integration: however, the roads have also opened up the areas to lowlanders and tourists who treat the tribespeople as curiosities and have no real respect for their traditions.

Valley-dwelling Thai are also beginning to move into the hill areas, claiming territory which the hill peoples consider to be theirs but to which they have no legal rights. Deforestation has also become a major problem partly as a result of the demands for firewood and the shifting agriculture practised by hill peoples but also due to commercial cropping, timber and mining. Many men have ceased to wear traditional tribal costume although women continue to weave and wear theirs. Gradually tribal peoples are being exposed to modern Thai and western culture and their own traditions and values are threatened. It seems unlikely that they can maintain their lifestyles in the face of such change, although it is probable that the majority of hill people will always prefer to live at higher and cooler elevations and so retain some degree of isolation and distinctiveness.

(See also *Burma* (*Myanma*); *Hmong of Laos*)

Hmong of Laos

Alternative names: **Meo, Miao, various tribal and clan names**
Location: **northern Laos, Thai refugee camps, USA**
Population: **about 400,000 (est.)**
% of population: **10% (est. of Laos population)**
Religion: **indigenous beliefs**
Language: **related to Chinese**

The Hmong, also called Meo or Miao, of Laos are a hill-dwelling people numbering some 400,000 or 10% of the population of Laos. They are closely related to the Chinese (and sometimes referred to as "Aboriginal Chinese") who entered Laos from Yunnan province only during the 1840s. Although there are over five million Meo remaining in China, and others in Thailand and Vietnam, the groups have gradually become separate.

The Hmong are agriculturists and pig herders who also cultivate the opium poppy. Soil erosion causes villages to move to new areas several times in each generation. Hmong society is strongly hierarchical and there are firm clan loyalties; during the French colonial period the French were able to control the entire tribe by favouring and educating members of the dominant family, and volunteer battalions of mountain tribesmen fought with the French until the fall of Dien Bien Phu in 1954.

In 1959, the American CIA found these dispersed former soldiers and began to form the "clandestine army". In all 30,000 full-time soldiers and 40,000 reserves of village militiamen were trained and supplied with weapons by the CIA and Green Berets and came under the leadership of the commander of the ex-French-Meo troops, Vang Pao. Allegiance to Vang Pao was expected from all Meo troops and this created difficulties between the various clans as it upset the hierarchy of clan loyalties. The territory controlled by this army at one stage exceeded that of the legitimate Lao government.

In 1967, the communist offensive pushed the Hmong from their territory in the north back to the area around the Plain of Jars which was taken by the Pathet Lao and then bombed intensively by the Americans. Many Hmong fled while others were evacuated; by the ceasefire of 1973 there were about 200,000 Meo refugees crowded into American camps in the valleys of the Mekong river and many abandoned their allegiance to Vang Pao who had lost 25% of his army. American influence was strong in the camps and Hmong traditions were further weakened.

A coalition government formed in 1974 placed emphasis on the unity and equality of all minorities with the majority Lao people. However, plans to return the refugees to their homes and rehabilitate them were thwarted when Vang Pao refused admission to the census teams. No longer supported by the CIA, Vang Pao had sided with the anti-Pathet Lao element and when the Pathet Lao took over Laos in 1975 he fled to Thailand with some 25,000 Meo. Vang Pao's forces maintained guerrilla resistance for several years before disintegrating into small bands. There have been reports of Hmong guerrillas operating in northern Laos and allegations of atrocities from both sides.

It is difficult to evaluate the situation of Hmong in Laos today, as it is a largely closed society and the area is not easily accessible. Reports state that in recent years a more conciliatory approach towards them is being taken by the Laotian government and that conditions are improving but that the majority lowland culture is predominant, education is in Lao and that "model villages" have been built.

Large numbers of Hmong live in exile, mainly in Thailand, the USA and France. After 1975 many Hmong fled to Thailand fearful of Pathet Lao reprisals. In 1975 there were 25,000 refugees, in 1976 45,000 and by 1979 60,000 refugees in the camps in Thailand while many thousands of others were thought to have died while attempting to leave. In 1986 there were probably 40,000 Hmong refugees in Thailand, 40,000 resettled in the USA and between 6,000 and 8,000 in France. The Hmong in exile remain a dispossessed people who have suffered almost total social disruption and largely lack the education and skills to integrate in western society.

(See also *Hill Tribes of Northern Thailand; National Minorities of Central Vietnam*)

National Minorities of Central Vietnam

Alternative names: **"Montagnards", various tribal names: Bohnar, Sodang, Mnong, Ma, Sre, Rhade, Jarai**
Location: **Gia Lai-Kontum, Dac Lac, Lam Dong provinces**
Population: **about 800,000**
% of population: **about 1.5% of total Vietnamese population**
Religion: **indigenous beliefs, Christian**
Language: **various**

The indigenous tribal peoples (Autochthons) of Central Vietnam are concentrated in three provinces of Gia Lai-Kontum, Dac Lac and Lam Dong — a largely forested plateau between the Mekong valley to the west and coastal plains to the east. The French termed the minorities Montagnards or mountain-dwellers, but the term is not strictly accurate since they actually live in the high valleys. The present government of Vietnam terms them "National Minorities" and the groups call themselves either by a proper or generic name e.g. *cau sre* (rice people). They are not a homogenous group but share a similar lifestyle. The various groups, numbering in total about 800,000 fall into two categories: (i) the Mon-Khmer linguistic group (Austroasiatics), who are related to the Khmer and live at elevations of about 500 metres. They include the Bohnar and Sodang in the north and the Mnong, Ma and Sre to the south; and (ii) the Malayo-Polynesian linguistic group (Austronesians) who are related to the Malays and Indonesians and live on fertile lower lands. They include the Rhade and Jarai, the largest single group with a population of about 200,000. There are other tribal minority groups in the

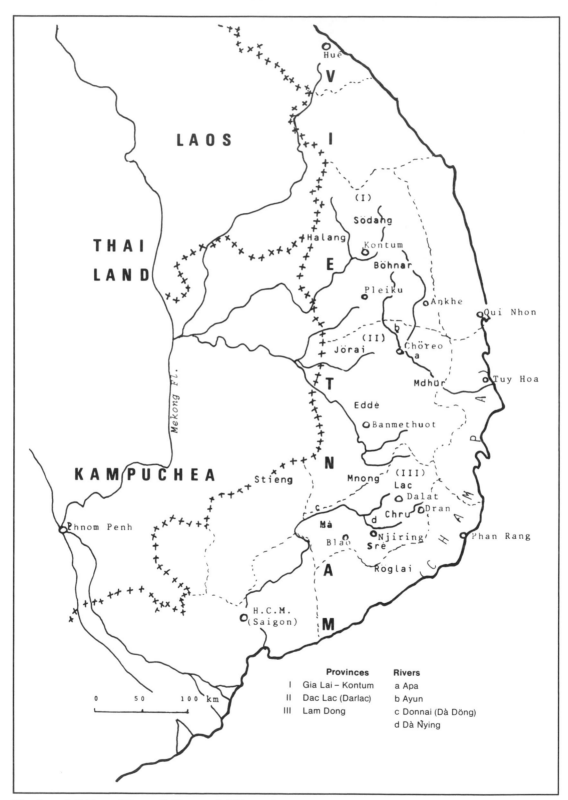

National Minorities of Central Vietnam

Within the map:

LAOS

THAILAND
LAND

KAMPUCHEA

Hué

V

I

(I)
Sôdang
Halang
Kontum
Bôhnar
E
Pleiku
Ankhe
Qui Nhon
(II)
Jörai
Chöreo
b
a
T
Mdhur
Tuy Hoa
Eddé
Banmethuot
N
Stieng
Mnong
(III)
Lac
c
Dalat
Phnom Penh
Mà
Chru
Dran
d
Blao
Njiring
Phan Rang
Srê
A
Roglai
H.C.M.
(Saigon)
M

Mekong Fl.

C H A M P A

Provinces	Rivers
I Gia Lai – Kontum	a Apa
II Dac Lac (Darlac)	b Ayun
III Lam Dong	c Donnai (Dà Döng)
	d Dà Ñying

0   50   100 km

north of Vietnam including the Hmong, Yao, Nung and Tay.

The traditional lifestyle of the highland peoples was one of hunting and gathering; however, in their more recent history they have lived mainly by farming, either the slash and burn method or by cultivating flooded rice fields. Maize, vegetables and fruit are grown and the diet supplemented through hunting, fishing and gathering. All the groups have strong religious beliefs in a spirit world which is approached through shamans and healers. Their oral literature makes use of rich imagery and many individuals are skilled in crafts such as weaving and basketry.

The French colonial period

For several centuries the Vietnamese had been expanding from the north, conquering and displacing Khmer and Cham peoples. However Vietnamese influence in the interior of the country was limited, although the tribal people themselves made occasional incursions to the coastal plains and returned with Vietnamese slaves. In 1850 a French Catholic mission was established in Bohnar territory. Although the missionaries showed little respect for traditional culture and religion they built hospitals, nurseries and leper colonies. By the 1890s the French had established a protectorate over the three-fold territory of Cochin-China, Annam and Tonkin. The people of the interior found themselves surrounded by the colonial power and military outposts were erected in their territory. The Pays Montagnards du Sud (PMS) were created as part of a development plan and numerous schools were opened, especially around Kontum and Banmethout. Minority children were taught to read and write in their own language and by 1949 the schools register of the PMS contained 3,500 Montagnard pupils. "Montagnard battalions" were formed which were later to be used against the Vietnamese. Rubber, tea and coffee plantations were established and Vietnamese were brought in to work on them. As the Vietnamese were moved into the minority areas the indigenous groups themselves began to be pushed away from their homelands. However, while the French were in charge this process was relatively limited.

During World War II Indo-China was occupied by the Japanese and Vietnamese resistance was organized by the Viet-Minh, under the leadership of Ho Chi Minh, and it was this movement which in 1945 declared Vietnam to be an independent republic. The French were determined to regain their colonial possessions and began a savage eight year war which lasted until the final French defeat at Dien Bien Phu in 1954. Vietnam was partitioned with the north becoming the Democratic Republic of Vietnam and the south the Republic of Vietnam. Initially minority insurgents aided and abetted the Vietnamese revolutionaries while most of the plateau area became the scene of a guerrilla war with the French controlling the main towns and roads. In 1949 the PMS were converted into Crown Possessions and the French set up an autonomist movement, the United Front of Liberation of the Oppressed Races (FULRO) which was restructured under Montagnard leadership in 1958. This movement, ostensibly aimed at improving relations between the French and the minorities, was led by the Rhade and some Bohnar but initially gained little popular support, and only succeeded in making the Vietnamese suspicious of the minority groups and regarding them as collaborators.

The Vietnam War

By now, the Americans had become fearful for their interests in the region, believing that South-East Asia as a whole was in danger and that if South Vietnam were to fall to the Communists other countries would follow. The USA therefore supported the anti-communist governments of first Diem and later Thieu, both of whom showed little respect for the minority population. Under Diem tribal peoples were concentrated in roadside camps and many of their lands were given to Catholic refugee settlers from the north. In 1953 there had been only 20,000 Vietnamese in the highlands but twenty years later the number had reached half a million. New laws effectively deprived the Montagnards of legal ownership of lands while the separate courts and administrative systems set up by the French were abolished, as was the use and teaching of tribal languages. In some areas traditional dress was banned while the general attitude of the Vietnamese authorities was that the tribals were savages who had to be integrated into Vietnamese society. As a result there was a FULRO-led revolt against the government, which continued for several years in the mid-1960s, and sought autonomy for the highland areas. The USA, who had enlisted many Montagnards in the CIA-sponsored "Special Forces", managed to dampen some of these demands and after US pressure, negotiations began with the government. Thieu established a Ministry for the Development of Ethnic Minorities, seats were reserved for Montagnards in the legislature and the Montagnard courts were reopened.

The USA entered Vietnam on the basis of economic assistance and help with building up its armed forces; however, over the next few years the number of US military personnel in South Vietnam grew until by 1963 there were some 16,000. In 1965 US troops were sent into Vietnam, the numbers reaching 550,000 by 1968. During the war Montagnards were forced into fortified villages or "strategic hamlets", surrounded by triple stake fences. Later villages were regrouped along the main roads and populations were hurriedly moved so that families were frequently separated between different camps. In the camps conditions were bad and mortality rates increased. Many of the tribals — especially the Austronesians — refused to be housed in camps, remaining in their villages or hiding in caves in the bush. Between 1968 and 1973 the numbers of Montagnards dropped drastically; perhaps 80,000 were killed in war or died of hunger or disease. Many Montagnard troops of the South Vietnamese army mutinied or deserted. Others joined the Vietcong in areas occupied by the Provisional Revolutionary Government (PRG), who however were also responsible for acts of terror and coercion against the tribals. In late 1968 North Vietnamese troops had entered the South to support the Vietcong, a process which eventually lead to the fall of Saigon in 1975 and the reunification of Vietnam. The contribution of the minorities to this struggle was an important one: they supported the resistance movement, feeding and sheltering insurgents and allowing them to travel through the forests towards the South.

(See also *Hmong of Laos*)

Post-1975

Although the right to self-determination was recognized as early as 1935 by the Vietnamese Communist movement, this was modified in 1960 to a call for "autonomous zones" where there was a "concentration of national minorities" and minorities were invited "to catch up within the shortest possible timescale" with the Vietnamese. An autonomous zone was established in Viet Bac in the North but it was announced in 1978 that the autonomous zones were to be abolished in order to advance socialism. No such zones were established in the South although the Montagnards were promised a degree of autonomy by the PRG, and most of the new officials appointed in the highlands were apparently drawn from tribal groups. Some FULRO resistance to the government continued into the late 1970s and in 1981 a Thai report announced the formation of the National Front for the Liberation of the Highlands. This group claimed to have formed a provisional government in Dac Lac province among the Rhade tribes.

Since 1975 Vietnam has largely been a closed country and information on minority groups has been scarce. It appears that the present government is following a similar policy to the previous South Vietnamese regime in encouraging large-scale settlement on tribal lands and it was reported in 1979 that 57,000 North Vietnamese were settled in Lam Dong Province in the years 1976-79. Many thousands of Vietnamese have spent time in "re-education camps" and it seems probable that at least some tribals, regarded as collaborators, were among them.

Orang Asli of the Malayan Peninsula

Alternative names: **Kensiu, Kintak, Lanoh, Jahai, Mendriq, Bateq, Temiar, Semai (Semang), Che Wong, Jahut, Semoq Beri, Mah Meri, Jakun, Temuan (Balandas), Semelai, Temoq (Temok), Orang Kanaq (Kanak), Orang Laut, Selitar**
Location: **Highland and rain-forest jungles of Malay peninsula**
Population: **75,000 (est.)**
% of population: **0.55% of Malayan peninsula**
Religion: **indigenous animist beliefs, Christian**
Language: **various**

The Orang Asli "original people" are the aboriginal tribes inhabiting the rain forests of the Malay peninsula. Most are believed to have migrated to the region over a long period between 8,000

and 3,000 years ago, following the southward movement of peoples throughout South-East Asia. Numbers are difficult to ascertain but the 1970 census gave an overall figure of nearly

71,000. The Orang Asli belong to 19 various tribes and sub-tribes, difficult to distinguish clearly, as tribal and linguistic boundaries have become somewhat blurred. The major groups are Negrito, Sengoi and Proto-Malay, as follows: (i) the Negrito are small in stature, averaging five feet or less in height with dark skin and woolly hair. The Negrito language is distantly related to the Mon-Khmer group. They live in the forested hill regions of the north and north eastern Malaya and southern Thailand and are hunter-gatherers. Negrito tribes are the Kensiu, Kintak, Lanoh, Jahai, Mendriq and Bateq; (ii) the Sengoi are larger in stature although still small. They are less dark than the Negrito and have wavy hair. Their language is also related to the Mon-Khmer and they practise shifting cultivation — mostly tapioca and hill rice — in addition to hunting and gathering activities. They are known for being a peaceable people and live in the remoter areas of the central highlands. Senoi tribes are the Temiar, Semai (Semang), Che Wong, Jahut, Semoq Beri and Mah Meri, and (iii) the Proto-Malay group embraces people who are similar in appearance to the Malays but who are of diverse origins, some probably having entered the region by sea in recent centuries whilst others may have been living in the peninsula for over a thousand years. Proto-Malays live among the straits of Malacca and in Southern Jahore and some have been absorbed into the Malay community and have adopted Islam. Proto-Malay tribes are the Jakun, Temuan (Balandas), Semelai, Temoq (Temok), Orang Kanaq (Kanak), Orang Laut and Selitar.

The Malays inhabiting the lowland valley and coastal areas traditionally regarded the Orang Asli as inferior; the term commonly used in reference to them was *Sakai*, which carries the connotation of "slave", and indeed they were exploited by the Malays as slaves, causing them to retreat even deeper into the jungle areas. They were largely ignored by the British authorities although there was a certain amount of Christian missionary work in the aboriginal regions. The Catholic Church established a small community in Negri Sembalan in 1847 and Methodists began work with the remote Sengoi people in 1930. This work was resented by the Malay royalty who saw it as an infringement of their authority over the Orang Asli. The Methodists agreed not to baptise any Orang Asli for a period of ten years although they continued to run medical and educational services; however, the 10-year period was ended by the Japanese invasion of Malaya and the situation was left unresolved.

Because of traditional antipathy between the Orang Asli and the Malays, the Orang Asli have tended towards better relations with the Chinese, with whom they engaged in a certain amount of small trade. This relationship made it relatively easy for Chinese guerrillas to recruit them into the Malayan People's Anti-Japanese Army, a guerrilla organization formed by Malay Chinese in response to the Japanese invasion; however, it was the Orang Asli who bore the brunt of the Japanese retaliation.

In 1948, the Chinese who advocated a Communist Revolution again entered the jungles in order to enlist the support of the Orang Asli. The British Government now realized their importance in the war and began a concerted effort to prevent Communist influence over them. Many were moved to "protected settlements" in the lowlands but the large numbers of deaths and social disruption meant that the policy was changed to one which advocated the extending of administrative and social services to the Orang Asli in their own environment. A Department of Aborigines was established in 1953 and a series of forts was built to protect the region from communist infiltration. Schools and clinics were established in these forts, which also acted as centres for administration.

Malayan independence was declared in 1957 by which time most of the Communists had been defeated. The Department of Aborigines passed to Malay control and was renamed Jabaton Orang Asli and with the end of the Emergency in 1960 the official policy towards the Orang Asli was reassessed. In 1961 a "blue book" was issued according to which existing social services would be continued and a long-term programme of development was pursued. The aim of this programme was to prepare the Orang Asli for eventual integration into the Malay community, and conversion to Islam. This latter aim has proved extremely difficult as tribal customs and laws are far removed from those of Islam and most Orang Asli have strong objections to conversion. There are a number of Christian converts however, although Christian missionary work has been prohibited in aboriginal areas since Christianity is viewed by the government as a foreign religion.

Life in the deep jungle regions is becoming increasingly difficult for the Orang Asli. The programme of medical aid and primary education has continued, although there is apparently a substantial element of Islamic instruction in the curriculum and in any case many Orang Asli do not attend school either because of poverty or the prejudice they frequently face from teachers and officials. Although many Orang Asli live on traditional lands they have no legal title to them or control over them. Legally land belongs to the state and the Orang Asli are squatters, although they are normally allowed to occupy state land which is not currently being used. The greatest threats to their livelihood have come from appropriation of land for cultivation of cash crops by Malays and logging. Environmental destruction is destroying the basis of the Orang Asli hunting and gathering way of life and may force many of them into a sedentary life in government settlements or urban areas.

(See also *Orang Ulu of Sarawak*)

Orang Ulu of Sarawak

Alternative names: **Natives, Dayaks, various tribal names: Iban (Sea Dayaks), Bidayuh, Kenyah, Kayan, Kedayan, Murat, Punan, Bisayah, Kalabit**
Location: **throughout Sarawak**
Population: **540,000 (1980)**
% of population: **44% of Sarawak population**
Religion: **indigenous animist beliefs, Christian**
Language: **various Dayak languages**

The Orang Ulu "peoples of the interior" is a name used by most of the native Dayak ethnic groups of Sarawak to describe themselves. Numerically they are the largest grouping in Sarawak, in 1980 accounting for 540,000 or 44% of the population. Other ethnic groups are Malays (22%), Melanau (6%) and Chinese (29%). The Dayaks are a diverse group, with many different tribes and sub-tribes, and are part of the much larger Dayak community of the island of Borneo, three-quarters of which is the Indonesian provinces of Kalimantan.

Iban, or Sea Dayaks, are the largest single group, which in 1980 had a population of 368,000. They do not consider themselves to be Orang Ulu although they have many affinities with interior peoples. There are many smaller groups who live in the forests, often only accessible from the rivers which are the main lines of communication. These groups include the Bidayuh (105,000), the Kenyah (15,500), Kayan (13,400), Kedayan (10,700), Murat (9,500), Punan (5,600), Bisayah (3,800) Kalabit (3,700) and some smaller groups. Most Dayak in Sarawak practise shifting cultivation (*swiden*), others such as the nomadic Punan rely on hunting and gathering. The Olang Ulu live in villages based around communal longhouses beside the rivers. Regulation of land use and resources in addition to personal and religious matters is governed by *adat* — customary law.

Sarawak joined the Federation of Malaysia in 1963, after a century of colonial rule by the Brooke family (the "white rajas") and as a British colonial possession from 1946. During the Brooke period customary native tenureship and rights over the land were recognized along with government and private ownership but restrictions on native tenure were introduced and land laws were continually refined and consolidated with the intention of restricting shifting cultivation which was considered wasteful. After the British took over, the 1948 land classification ordinance placed land in one of five categories, which along with later legislation, made all land the property of the crown and attempted to register all land. Much land in the Seventh and Fourth divisions in the interior has yet to be surveyed or adjudicated. While the categories of Native Area Land, Native Customary Land and Interior Area Land appeared to protect indigenous rights, titles to these lands can be changed or extinguished under some circumstances. Given that most Orang Ulu live in remote areas and are not literate, customary rights can be removed without their knowledge.

The major threat to Orang Ulu land and way of life comes from large-scale economic development in the form of timber logging and hydro-electric dams. Sarawak is the largest state in the Malaysian federation, containing 38% of the land area, and is also the state richest in natural resources. Tropical rainforest covers 75% of the state and its exploitation produces profits for logging contractors and revenue for the state. Between 1963 and 1985 about 30% of Sarawak's total forest area was logged by companies, who frequently pay chiefs to allow them to log on traditional lands.

Opposition to logging has come from many

communities, including the Kenyah, Kayan and Iban peoples in the Fourth division, but most notably from the hunting and gathering Punan people, who from March 1987 have erected blockades across strategic roads and rivers in the forests. Pleas by Punan people to the Malaysian Prime Minister and the establishment of a special committee to investigate their grievances appeared to have no effect and in October 1987, as part of a sweeping government crackdown on dissidents throughout Malaysia, resulted in the arrests of 42 Orang Ulu, including an indigenous Kayan organizer of *Sahabat Alam Malaysia* (Malaysian Friends of the Earth) who was arrested under the Internal Security Act although released two months later. In November the Sarawak government passed a new law making all interference with logging a criminal offence punishable by fines and imprisonment. Many Orang Ulu have consequently faced court cases. By this stage environmental groups and others had co-ordinated a worldwide protest against logging, including the European Parliament, which unanimously passed a resolution to suspend the import of tropical hardwoods from Malaysia. Despite the new law, blockades continued through 1988 and 1989, perhaps most significantly in August 1989 when nine Iban communities in the Bintulu division set up a blockade to protect their communal land. As the largest native community the Iban have potential political strength.

Another threat comes from hydro-electric projects. The Batang Ai Dam, completed in 1985, led to the flooding of 21,000 acres of land and the resettlement of 3,000 Iban who, as a result, were forced to give up shifting cultivation for settled farming. During the construction of the dam some 1,500 Iban were employed but after its completion most were retrenched and no other employment prospects are available. An even greater threat is that of the Bakun Hydro Project in the Seventh division which is planned to be South-East Asia's largest dam and will generate power mainly for the Malay peninsula. Perhaps 5,000 Orang Ulu will be displaced, mainly from the Kenyah and Kenyah Badang and Kayan groups.

There is an Iban political party among the three main political parties (the other two predominantly represent Malays and Chinese). The natives of Sarawak are especially protected under Article 161A of the federal constitution and their special status is equivalent to that of the Malays of peninsula Malaysia. However, in practice within Sarawak, the Orang Ulu are a marginalized group and generally treated as inferior by the other communities.

(See also *Orang Asli of the Malayan Peninsula*)

South Moluccans

Alternative names: **Amboinese**
Location: **Moluccas Islands, eastern Indonesia**
Population: **about 1-1.5 million**
% of population: **0.6%-1% of Indonesian population**
Religion: **Protestant**
Language: **Malay, Amboinese**

The South Moluccans or Amboinese are a people of Melanesian-Australoid origin who inhabit the islands of the Moluccas, formerly known as the Spice Islands, which today form the 25th province of the Republic of Indonesia. Despite the vast area covered by the islands they form only about 4% of the total land area of Indonesia and contain perhaps 1.5 million of Indonesia's population of over 150 million. In the Northern Moluccan islands most people are Muslims and in the interiors many are animists. Unlike most of the other ethnic groups in the Indonesian archipelago many South Moluccans are Christian, converted by Dutch Protestants who conquered the region from the early seventeenth century.

The Dutch had dislodged the Portuguese from the islands and ruthlessly cultivated spices on a forcible basis. The Amboinese were recruited into the KNIL, the Dutch colonial army, which in consequence became disproportionately Amboinese. They chose to identify themselves with the Dutch rulers rather than with other ethnic groups and many were interned with the Dutch after the occupation of the former Netherland Indies by the Japanese in 1942.

In mid-1945 after the Japanese surrender,

Dr Sukarno, the nationalist leader, proclaimed Indonesian independence. The Dutch returned, hoping to regain control of the former colony and in the ensuing armed struggle the Amboinese fought on the side of the Dutch. The Dutch eventually ceded sovereignty to an independent Federal Republic of Indonesia in 1949 in which the South Moluccas formed part of the state of Eastern Indonesia. However, when Sukarno rapidly began to dismantle the federal structure and impose a unitary state in 1950, the Moluccans, who felt themselves betrayed by the Dutch, formed a Republic of the South Moluccas (RMS) in April 1950 with the aim of separation from the Indonesian Republic. The movement was militarily suppressed by Indonesian forces by November but guerrilla elements remained active on the island of Ceram. On the demobilization of the KNIL some 4,000 Amboinese refused to demobilize on Moluccan soil which they considered to be enemy-occupied territory. Their reaction provoked hostility from Indonesians and, in order to improve relations with Indonesia, the Dutch offered temporary residence in the Netherlands to the former soldiers and their families. 12,500 Amboinese travelled to the Netherlands where their population rapidly increased and today numbers about 40,000.

These Moluccans maintained that they were forcibly relocated and therefore considered their stay in the Netherlands to be temporary. Most refused to return to the Moluccas until a free RMS was established. They maintained the RMS in exile and attempted to petition the UN and elsewhere. During the 1970s there were attacks on Indonesians by Amboinese in the Netherlands and there were a number of terrorist actions, such as the attempted kidnapping of Queen Juliana and most spectacularly the capture of hostages in a school and a train in 1977, which attracted world attention. Most of these actions were perpetuated by the militant Free South Moluccan Youth, the majority of whom were born in the Netherlands and had never seen their homeland. The Dutch government has since made special efforts to integrate the Moluccans within Dutch society, increasing spending and improving housing and to a large extent this seems to have worked and there have been no further violent incidents. The focus of political action has changed; few South Moluccans look to the Dutch government to change the situation but see their future in joining with other dissident and minority groups within Indonesia. South Moluccans still face problems in the Netherlands; in 1982 for example their unemployment rate was twice the Dutch average and there were estimated to be 1,000 heroin addicts. Most South Moluccans were citizens of the Netherlands but 20% to 30% choose to remain stateless.

Despite the strength of feeling among some young Moluccans in the Netherlands, support for an independent RMS seems to be limited in the South Moluccas where very few Amboinese guerrillas remain. There was some resistance in the 1960s but the "President" of the RMS was arrested in 1963 and executed in 1966 and his successor has since been in exile in the Netherlands. Culturally, the dominant Javanese consider the Amboinese as derogatory "*orang hitam*" (black men) and their languages and culture *kasar* (impolite and uncivil). (However the Amboinese are noted for being both good warriors and acute businessmen.) The governor and most officials and military are Javanese and there is undoubtedly some hostility towards them, but since there are few material resources and the territory consists of scattered islands, most Moluccans realize that the creation of an independent state is impractical and in any case would be strongly resisted by the Indonesians. There have been increasing numbers of Javanese immigrants being sent to the islands in transmigration schemes — they may now number one third of the total population of the Moluccas — while the island of Buru was notorious as being the main prison for thousands of political prisoners held after the attempted coup of 1965.

(See also *East Timorese* in **Oceania;** *West Papuans* in **Oceania**)

Further References

The Chinese in Indonesia, Malaysia and the Philippines, MRG Report No. 10, 1982.

Minorities of Central Vietnam (autochthonous Indo-Chinese people), MRG Report No. 18, 1980.

OCEANIA

Oceania, comprising the Australian continent and the islands, large and small, to the north and east across the Pacific, is vast in its spatial extent but small in population relative to other parts of the globe. It is, nonetheless, rich and diverse in language, culture and religion. Scattered islands, impenetrable mountain terrain, ancient and modern migrations, have all contributed to this intricate pattern of peoples. Inhospitable or specific climatic conditions contribute to the localization of cultures. On the island of New Guinea alone upwards of 700 languages are spoken. Pre-invasion Australia contained some 500 languages belonging to 31 language groups. The colonial period has also left an indelible imprint. European colonizers in Australia and New Zealand reduced the indigenous peoples to minorities, resulting in the widespread destruction of cultures. The importation of Asians into Fiji is the origin of Fiji's current ethnic conflict. Further, unlike most regions, the colonial presence is still remarkably strong. A variety of non-Oceanic powers hold sway through various forms of association with the region's territories: Australia, Britain, Chile, France, Indonesia, New Zealand and the USA maintain links with the Pacific in colonies, trust territories, association agreements or simple integration with the metropolis. Self-determination is therefore a major issue, though demands for its application do not always amount to demands for complete separation; for small peoples the burdens of independence may be heavy.

There are various minority situations. Whole States such as Papua New Guinea are, in effect, composed of minorities. The indigenous peoples are a minority in Australia and New Zealand. The extensive colonization produces what is the region's strongest characteristic minority issue: the relationship between the indigenous and the colonizers, although this is not always straightforward, as in Fiji. Nonetheless, in the great majority of cases, it is the indigenous who have suffered, and continue to suffer, deprivations of human rights.

The intensity and scope of minority deprivation varies. Where the original colonization was on the basis of the doctrine of *terra nullius* (a pretence that the land was uninhabited), the indigenous group has no basis for the reactivation of historic treaties, since none existed. On the other hand, such treaties as the Treaty of Waitangi (below) can act as a starting point for land and other claims. The position of the indigenous minority is thus considerably stronger in the latter than in the former case. This depends, of course, on the willingness of the state apparatus to countenance contemporary claims. Australia and New Zealand do not now appear to pursue policies of assimilation of their indigenous peoples in contrast to the recent past and attempt to recognize their contribution to the wider society. Indonesia continues to practise policies of forced assimilation and displacement of minorities, and probably genocide, in the case of East Timor. The violation of East Timor's right of self-determination is a clear transgression of international law, declared to be such by the United Nations; regrettably, its illegal occupation may eventually be accepted as a *fait accompli* by the international community as indignation is replaced by considerations of Indonesia's political and economic importance. The East Timorese may suffer the fate of many other small minorities in large and aggressive States.

Instruments on Minority Rights

There is no specific regional treaty on Human Rights and adherence to multilateral treaties on human rights is uneven. Small States such as Samoa, Tuvalu and Vanuatu are not parties to any relevant human rights treaty. Fiji is not a party to either International Covenant on Human Rights, although it has signed the UN Convention on the Elimination of All Forms of Racial Discrimination. Of the larger States, Australia and New Zealand have an excellent record of participation in treaties, though they have declined to become parties to the ILO's Indigenous and Tribal Populations Convention on the ground that it represents an outdated, patronising view. The non-participation in much of international human rights law by Indonesia is a serious blemish. Indonesia has neither signed nor ratified the UN Covenants on Human

Rights. It is not a party to the Racial Discrimination Convention (although it has signed the UNESCO Convention against Discrimination in Education); nor the Convention on the Prevention and Punishment of the Crime of Genocide. Indonesia is party to bilateral agreements with the Netherlands and the Peoples' Republic of China regarding choice of nationality by the Chinese of Indonesia.

The constitutional and sub-constitutional law of Oceania is the product of local conditions. The treaty between the colonial power and indigenous groups along the model of treaties in North America (see introduction to that section) makes an appearance in the New Zealand Treaty of Waitangi of 1840 (see *Appendix* 9.1) and the Treaty of Rapanui (1888) concerning Chile and the Easter Islanders. Such instruments may have contemporary relevance. Thus the treaty of Waitangi purported to hand over sovereignty (the British view) or government (the Maori text) in return for guarantees that the Maori would retain undisturbed possession of their lands, estates, forests and fisheries. This forms a basis for the enforcement of various land and resource claims currently active in the New Zealand courts. In broad constitutional terms, while some States adopt a basic non-discrimination/human rights for all formula, the use of separate electoral rolls for different groups is also represented. New Zealand adopts a system which allows for Maoris to choose the roll on which they wish to register, but the system in Fiji raises questions in terms of its rigidity (individuals do not have a choice about the roll on which they are inscribed) and preferences towards indigenous Fijians. Forms of communalism are adopted to deal with ethnic relations, and membership of particular groups carries legal consequences. Fiji has been questioned by the UN Committee on Racial Discrimination (CERD) about its legal arrangements. Various forms of autonomy are also in evidence, sometimes as a substitute or temporising measure in the face of claims to self-determination: the case of Bougainville in relation to Papua New Guinea is one instance.

Treatment of minorities

States such as Indonesia consciously implement policies of forced assimilation, in this case "Indonesianization". Such policies are generally correlated with overall low standards in human rights, a point that is amply confirmed by other cases of minority oppression, from Ethiopia and Iran to Paraguay and Turkey. Nor can past policies of assimilation and genocide be undone; the Aborigines of Australia are a case in point. The imperatives must be to preserve and develop what remains of a unique culture, and provide full citizenship and human dignity to degraded people on the edge of society. Fiji provides a different issue: how far are indigenous people entitled to go in defence of their authenticity and self-determination when the non-indigenous settlers are victims? For the rest, the imperative of autochthonous rule confronts the remnants of colonialism with an uncertain outcome: is independence always the best, most rational policy for a small people? Will economic imperialism outlast old-fashioned colonialism? The fate of the indigenous minorities and small peoples are central issues in the future politics and development of Oceania.

Aboriginal Australians

Alternative names: **Aboriginals (official), Korris, Murris, Noongars, various tribal and clan names**
Location: **throughout Australia**
Population: **250,000-300,000**
% of population: **1.5%**
Religion: **indigenous beliefs, Christianity**
Language: **various indigenous languages, English**

The Aborigines are the indigenous inhabitants of Australia. Although it is difficult to estimate their numbers accurately there are probably between 250,000 and 300,000, most of whom live in the rural areas, many in and around the fringes of country towns. In the north and west of Australia many have been able to retain their languages and aspects of their traditional lifestyles although this is generally not true of those in the east and the large cities. The Torres Strait Islanders who live in the islands to the north of Queensland are related to the Papuan peoples of Papua New Guinea and comprise about 10% of the total indigenous population of Australia.

Aboriginal beliefs and way of life

Knowledge of Aboriginal myths and customs comes for the most part from tribal people living in the north and western desert areas where traditional social structures remained largely intact until well into the twentieth century, but their experiences may not reflect accurately those of other Aboriginal peoples. Aborigines entered Australia between 40,000 and 125,000 years ago and gradually came to settle the whole continent. Most were hunter-gatherers, although the remains of sophisticated artificial drainage systems in the state of Victoria suggest that some led a more sedentary lifestyle. At least 500 languages belonging to 31 language groups were spoken. One language group, Pama-Nyungan, was used over about 80% of the continent while the remaining 20% of languages were concentrated in the north-west and on the island of Tasmania.

Aborigines in the north migrated with the monsoons between the plains and the high ground whereas the movements of those in the southern coastal areas were dictated more by the movements of the fish on which they largely depended. Authority was vested in the older men of the group whilst the young men hunted and fished and women managed the family, cooked and gathered edible plants. Aboriginal life was dominated by an awareness of the Dreamtime, a period when beings with super-human powers formed the continent and became the Aboriginal ancestors, controlling the land and human destiny. Aborigines were acutely aware of their oneness with natural forces. They believed in a spirit which exists for all time and which assumes one human form after another. Their way of life seems to have remained largely unchanged for thousands of years.

European colonization

This way of life was effectively brought to an end by the beginnings of permanent European settlement on January 26, 1788, when the British landed on the east coast of Australia at the site of what was to become the city of Sydney. As the white settlers advanced inland European diseases such as smallpox, colds and measles decimated the Aboriginal population, and one smallpox epidemic in 1789 killed almost half of the Aborigines living between Botany Bay and Broken Bay. Despite a proclamation by King George III that the Aborigines should be treated with kindness and respect it was impossible for the settlers to avoid appropriating Aboriginal land and food, and the scarcity of women settlers meant that Aboriginal women were frequently the victims of rape. Neither at this time or later were treaties or acknowledgements of Aboriginal ownership made between whites and Aborigines.

During the nineteenth and early twentieth centuries most of the coastal and eastern Australian tribes were destroyed in violent confrontations with white settlers. In Tasmania almost the entire Aboriginal population was systematically killed. In 1926 tribal Aborigines were killed in retaliation for cattle spearing in the Kimberleys, and there were many other such cases. The Aboriginal population decreased from an estimated one million in 1788 to about 30,000 in the 1930s, although the part-Aboriginal population increased to about 40,000. After this period the decline in population levelled off. The Aborigines inhabiting the north and west sometimes worked on the cattle stations since white labour was scarce and expensive; in return for labour at near slave-rates Aborigines were permitted to visit their sacred places at certain times of year and could continue their customs and ceremonies.

"Assimilation"

The poverty of the Aborigines living in urban areas became more noticeable and something of an embarrassment to the government and gradually support grew for the establishment of Aboriginal reserves in remote areas and for welfare services. Various organizations and individuals were instrumental in bettering the position of Aborigines and by the 1940s Aborigines themselves were forming associations such as the Aborigines Progressive Association which campaigned vigorously to improve their status. The employment of over 1,000 Aborigines by the army in northern Australia during World War II also had an impact on perceptions of Aboriginal status since Aborigines were paid wages and shared equal accommodation and canteen facilities with whites. They still had no legal or political status, however, neither did they figure in census surveys. Government response was to settle for a policy aimed at eliminating any sense of separate Aboriginal identity, and in 1951 "assimilation" was adopted as the main strategy of the Commonwealth and State governments which were responsible for Aboriginal affairs. In 1959 a federation of Aborigines and white sympathizers was formed under the name of the Federal Council for the Advancement of Aboriginals and Torres Strait Islanders (FCAATSI).

The "assimilation" policy which had seemed acceptable in the 1940s and '50s came under increasing criticism during the 1960s as it had been decided upon with no thought for Aboriginal wishes regarding the preservation of their culture and languages. The various states controlled their own Aboriginal policies, with the exception of the Northern Territory which was under Commonwealth control, and thus policy varied markedly from state to state which made a uniform approach to Aboriginal issues difficult. In 1967 it was decided as a result of a national referendum that the Com-

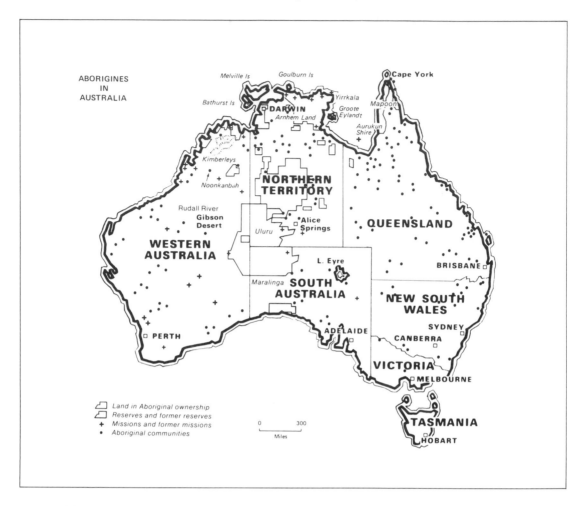

ABORIGINES
IN
AUSTRALIA

Melville Is   Goulburn Is   Cape York
Bathurst Is   Yirrkala
                DARWIN   Groote   Mapoon
            Arnhem Land   Eylandt
                              Aurukun
                              Shire
Kimberleys
Noonkanbah   NORTHERN
              TERRITORY
Rudall River
Gibson   QUEENSLAND
Desert
            Uluru   Alice
                    Springs
WESTERN
AUSTRALIA   L. Eyre
                                    BRISBANE
        Maralinga   SOUTH
                    AUSTRALIA   NEW SOUTH
                                    WALES
                        ADELAIDE   SYDNEY
                                    CANBERRA
PERTH
                                    VICTORIA
                                    MELBOURNE

⬜ Land in Aboriginal ownership
⬜ Reserves and former reserves
+ Missions and former missions   TASMANIA
• Aboriginal communities
                    0   300   HOBART
                    Miles

monwealth government should have the power to legislate for all Aborigines and Aborigines were at last counted in population censuses. Although individual states retained the right to legislate and implement their own laws, Commonwealth law could in theory now override state laws.

Land rights

During the 1960s many of the laws which discriminated against Aborigines were repealed. Aborigines gained entitlement to state benefits and the right to vote; however the living conditions, health, life expectancy and education of Aborigines remained markedly lower than that of other Australians. There were several widely publicized cases of gross exploitation of black labourers which revealed that large successful companies were employing Aborigines for near slave-rates and housing them in extremely poor living conditions. In one famous case in 1966 Aboriginal stockmen of the Gurindji tribe went on strike to protest against their exploitation by the multi-

national Vestey empire. Although the company would not act to improve conditions for Aborigines, the strike action did focus white Australian attention on the plight of the black workforce. It also marked the beginning of the land rights movement, as Gurindji demands increased to embrace not just improved wages and living conditions but self-determination and land rights. An unsuccessful action brought against the Nabalco mining company by Aborigines in the Northern Territory in 1968 convinced activists of both races that the law would have to change before Aborigines could gain access to land rights. Public attention was once more brought to the question of racial injustice with the demonstrations against the Springbok tour of 1971, and the victory of the Labor party at the 1972 elections promised further action to better the status of the Aborigines, with government concentrating on the Federal sphere and on attempts to legislate land rights.

The most significant step forward came with the Aboriginal Land Rights Bill of 1976 which handed over former reserve land in the Northern Territory to be held in trust by three Aboriginal Land Councils. Although there are deficiencies in the Act (especially concerning mineral rights) and there has been considerable opposition from elements of the white population, it has provided a basis for the long-term security and economic development of the Aboriginal community. To date about 30% of the land in the Northern Territory has passed into Aboriginal hands. Some states such as South Australia also enacted progressive legislation and 10% of the state, largely desert, has now passed in perpetuity to the Pitjantjatjura people, although many other Aboriginal communities still have to achieve land rights. But most states have been reluctant to act on behalf of Aboriginal land rights and there has been a well organized and funded campaign against the granting of such rights by mining interests. The Hawke Labor government, elected in 1983, was committed to national land rights legislation and enacted the Aboriginal and Torres Strait Islander Heritage Act in 1984, but disagreements over the form and content of policy led to the collapse of the national model, which embittered many Aborigines.

In the state of Queensland the position of Aborigines has been consistently bad and Aborigines continued to suffer discrimination under the conservative National Party–Liberal coalition, especially after the extensive mineral finds on reserve land. Some communities have been forcibly evicted and two reserves abolished in the course of working these mines, thus destroying the social and economic basis of their traditional lifestyle. The Queensland Aboriginal and Islanders Act of 1971 prevented Aborigines from living or visiting reserves of their choice and forced them into work at lower than minimum wages. Although this act was later repealed, its legacies remain, and some Aboriginal communities are governed by discriminatory local government laws. There is no land rights policy in Queensland, despite the fact that it has the largest Aboriginal population in Australia.

Social and economic developments

In almost every index of social wellbeing Aborigines score lower than other Australians. Their life expectancy is 20 years lower, infant mortality rates are four times higher and in the north and north-west trachoma and leprosy have been rife, although health programmes are now beginning to make some impact in this area. Aboriginal housing conditions are poor and this in turn has affected Aboriginal access to education and employment. There have been some improvements in these areas during the 1980s, both because of government programmes and Aboriginal self-help groups; the impact is greatest when there is maximum government commitment and Aboriginal participation. The 1972 Labor government which established a Department of Aboriginal Affairs and increased spending was a watershed; after its defeat in 1975 there were cutbacks in spending. In 1988 it was announced that the Department would be replaced by a new structure, the Aboriginal and Torres Strait Islanders Commission, which would allow for greater indigenous participation in policy-making.

The high rates of Aboriginal arrests and imprisonment, and especially of Aboriginal deaths in police custody, have been a major issue. In 1988 Aborigines accounted for 15% of the prison population and 21% of deaths in custody. The Muirhead Royal Commission set up in 1987 investigated over 100 Aboriginal deaths in custody occurring since 1980. Most of those who died were young men arrested on trivial offences such as drunkenness. The interim report issued at the end of 1988 stated that the deaths were caused by "appalling neglect", and urged reforms to the prison, legal and medical services.

The period has also been marked by an upsurge of Aboriginal interest in Aboriginal language and tradition. Aborigines have produced their own magazines and newsletters; there is now Aboriginal broadcasting and television, and an Aboriginal and Islander Dance Theatre. The Aboriginal and Islander Legal Service (NAILS) and Aboriginal Health Services have continued to operate and expand despite financial restraints. There have been several attempts to found a national Aboriginal organization whether by governments or by Aborigines; these have not always been successful partly because of differing political priorities and partly for financial and organizational reasons. Perhaps the most impressive movement has been the formation of the Land Councils, organized in the Federation of Land Councils, and ranging from the large and collectively wealthy Councils of the Northern Territory to the unfinanced and unrecognized organizations in some states. Aboriginal organizations have participated in the UN Working Group on Indigenous Populations and in other international fora.

1988 was the bicentennial year of white settlement in Australia. On January 26, 1988, 30,000 Aborigines marched through the streets of Sydney in protest at the invasion of their land and ill-treatment of their people. Although awareness by Australians of the Aboriginal situation has greatly improved in the past 20 years the issue of land and mineral rights remains a major problem and there will have to be further legal and political initiatives if the status and well-being of Aborigines is to be raised further. The negotiation of a Treaty between Aborigines and the Australian government — as promised by Prime Minister Hawke — is seen as a vitally important symbolic and practical acknow-ledgment of the Aboriginal position as the owners of the land.

(See also *Maori of New Zealand*)

Chamorros of Guam

Alternative names: **Guamians**
Location: **Guam, western Pacific**
Population: **57,000**
% of population: **45%**
Religion: **Christian**
Language: **Chamorro, English**

The Chamorros are the indigenous inhabitants of Guam, the largest of the islands of the Marianas archipelago and the most populous American possession in the Pacific. In 1984 Guam had a population of 115,000 of which about half were Chamorros and the remainder US military personnel, other US citizens and immigrant contract labourers from the Philippines and elsewhere in the Pacific.

Guam became part of the Spanish Empire after its "discovery" by Ferdinand Magellan in 1521. In the late seventeenth century, after Jesuit missionaries arrived and were met with resistance, Spanish policy shifted to a war of extermination. Between 1668 and 1740 the Chamorro population fell from over 80,000 to less than 5,000. Guam became a US possession in 1898. During World War II Guam was held by the Japanese between 1941 and 1944. Chamorros were rounded up and held in concentration camps by the Japanese occupiers while some later died in battles between the opposing forces.

Unlike the other islands of Micronesia, Guam has not been a UN Trust Territory but is an unincorporated territory, governed since 1950 under an Organic Act which gives it a local legislature and governor. Guamians are US citizens but do not have the right to vote in US national elections while they are resident on Guam although the territory has a non-voting delegate, presently a Chamorro, in the US House of Representatives. Recently there have been moves to give Guam Commonwealth status in the US in order to promote a greater degree of local autonomy.

The Chamorros were until recently a majority of the population but today are a steadily decreasing minority. In 1978 they were 62% of the population but by 1984 were less than 50% and today may be less than 45%. Despite a young population the Chamorro birthrate has been declining since 1973 and large numbers of Chamorros emigrate in search of employment. Conversely large numbers of US citizens and Asians now work in Guam for the largest employers, the military and government, and also in the tourist and construction industry. There is considerable pressure on land as one third is owned by the military and a further 20% by the government. The remaining 50% is divided between 10,000 Chamorro landowners who have an average plot of less than two hectares. There are estimated to be less than 100 active farmers. In the mid-1970s 1,400 Chamorros brought a class action against the US for land appropriation during World War II. The claim was settled for US$39.5 million in 1984 although some aspects are still being debated.

Recent years have seen the growth of a Chamorro indigenous rights movement. In 1978 Chamorros demonstrated against a local newspaper which refused to publish an advertisement in the Chamorro language. Activists have also campaigned for a restricted franchise in referenda on Guam's future status, as every eligible US citizen resident in Guam, including military personnel stationed there, can vote in such referenda. The newly formed Guam National Party of Chamorros is campaigning on this and other issues concerning future status. Most Chamorros wish to retain an association with the USA, most probably a Commonwealth status, but the exact form this will take still has to be determined.

(See also *Micronesia*)

Cocos (Keeling) Islanders

Location: **Indian Ocean, north-west of Australia, south-west of Java**
Population: **about 600 in the islands, others elsewhere**
% of population: **100% of islands' population**
Religion: **Islam**
Language: **Malay dialect**

The Cocos Malay people are the descendants of the original settlers who came to the Cocos islands from 1826. The 27 coral islands in the Cocos (Keeling) Island group are an Australian Territory in the Indian Ocean, 2,752 kilometres north of Perth, Western Australia, but closer to the main Indonesian islands of Java and Sumatra. Today there are about 600 inhabitants of the islands, while since World War II many other Cocos Islanders have migrated elsewhere — to Singapore, Sabah, Christmas Island and to four towns in Western Australia.

The Cocos Keeling Islands, originally uninhabited, were occupied by Captain John Clunies Ross in 1827 when he established a trading and plantation settlement there. Indentured labourers from Malaya and elsewhere were brought to the islands during the nineteenth century. For five generations the Clunies Ross family dominated the islands, importing Malays to work on the coconut plantation and dominating their lives completely. Queen Victoria granted the islands to the Clunies Ross family "forever" in 1886 although officially the islands were administered by the crown, from Ceylon and Singapore and, from 1955, by Australia, which bought one of the islands for a military base.

In 1972 an official report had severely criticized the rule of Clunies Ross, claiming that his rule was "feudal", that he controlled the only industry and the only store, while islanders were forbidden to speak to outsiders and faced banishment if they left the islands. The new Australian Labor Party government attempted to oust Clunies Ross, offering to buy the islands for Australia, but this was refused by Clunies Ross. The later Conservative government initially confirmed that it would support the status quo; however in 1978 Australia compulsorily acquired the islands from Clunies Ross for $A6.25 million and in 1979 instituted the Cocos (Keeling) Islands District Council and Co-operative Society. Clunies Ross continued to dominate the islands in what a UN Observer called a "subversive influence on peace and good order".

In 1984 islanders voted in a referendum between independence, free association with Australia or to merge with Australia and become Australian citizens. They overwhelmingly voted for the last option, completely breaking all links with the Clunies Ross family. The islanders also requested that the UN continue to monitor developments on the islands. The Australian government and the island's district council announced that they would fight through the courts to remove Clunies Ross permanently from the islands.

East Timorese

Alternative names: **various Tribal and clan names**
Location: **Eastern half of Timor Island, between Indonesia and Australia**
Population: **522,500 (1979)**
% of population: **c. 90% (est.)**
Religion: **Catholic, indigenous animist beliefs**
Language: **Timorese, Tetum, Portuguese**

East Timor is the eastern half of the island of Timor, part of the Lesser Sundras archipelago to the east of Java. The Timorese-speaking Atoni are believed to have been the original inhabitants of the island and today occupy most of the western half of Timor. There have been successive waves of migration including the other main group, the Tetum-speaking Belu who live in the south and east. The population of East Timor in 1970 was 610,541; nearly all indigenous except for a few Chinese traders and expatriate Portuguese and soldiers. Today the Portuguese have gone, to be replaced by Indonesian administrators and troops (who according to a recent estimate numbered at least 15,000).

Colonial rule

Portuguese traders landed in Timor in about 1520 and by the end of the century the territory was Portuguese and a thriving sandalwood industry was under way. Jesuit missionaries followed and as a result many Timorese today are Catholics. In 1859, after two centuries of attempting to gain control of Timor and the surrounding islands, the Dutch finally gained control of the western half of Timor which was incorporated into the Dutch East Indies. The present boundaries between the two areas were settled in the Luso-Hollandesa treaty of 1904. During World War II, Timor was occupied by Japanese troops and over 40,000 Timorese died in the conflict. The Dutch continued their rule in West Timor until Indonesian independence was granted in 1949; the Portuguese continued to occupy East Timor and an enclave in West Timor known as Oecusse Ambeno. As a result, the two halves of the island developed along totally different lines, the languages of administration were different and the economies, although undeveloped and peripheral to the ruling power, were unintegrated.

Portuguese colonial rule continued through the next two decades, becoming more oppressive under the Salazar dictatorship. Timor was a minor part of the huge Portuguese Empire, mainly in Africa, which was slowly disintegrating as a result of colonial wars. In April 1974 the Armed Forces Movement took control in Portugal and brought to an end the country's colonial policy which had become an expensive anachronism to one of the poorest European countries. However the Portuguese government had underestimated the strength of feeling within Timor. Political parties had existed before 1974, but in the period following the coup in Portugal three main parties emerged; the *União Democrática Timorense* (UDT) which wanted a certain amount of continued Portuguese control; the *Associação Popular Democrática Timorense* (APODETI); and *Frente Revolucionária do Timor Leste Independente* (FRETILIN), which advocated complete independence. During this time there was in East Timor far more freedom

for parties to organize and campaign than in neighbouring West Timor or Indonesia itself. The Portuguese government, led by the Armed Forces Movement, had as its aim to found a transitional government, broadly reflecting the will of the Timorese people pending a referendum on independence or integration with Indonesia, and free from outside coercion. In local elections FRETILIN collected the vast majority of the votes and in January 1975 formed a coalition with the UDT. In mid-1975 it was announced by the Portuguese administration that elections would take place in October 1976 and that complete independence would be granted within two years.

In the meantime Indonesia, who maintained that East Timor should integrate with West Timor and thus Indonesia, launched "Operation Komodo" in order to achieve this aim. At first it tried propaganda, then persuasion and bribery as in April 1975, when the leaders of all Timorese parties were invited to Jakarta, FRETILIN refused to go along with these overtures, but the UDT was more pliable, and in August 1975 attempted a takeover when it seized the main installations in East Timor's two major urban centres of Dili and Bacau. This triggered a civil war lasting about six weeks in which 2,000 died. The UDT and APODETI leaders were forced into Indonesian Timor while the Portuguese government removed itself to a small offshore island. FRETILIN emerged victorious from the civil war and became the *de facto* government.

The achievements of the government over the next three months were impressive; agricultural co-operatives were formed, literacy campaigns were established in rural areas, and an emphasis placed on reviving Timorese culture. On November 28, 1975, FRETILIN declared the Democratic Republic of East Timor. However the Portuguese did not recognize the new government and in early December 1975 Indonesia invaded East Timor, thereby preventing any further advancement on the independence issue.

The Indonesian occupation[1]

The invasion was part of "Operation Komodo" and was apparently part of a long-term Indonesian plan to gain control over the eastern part of the island. However the plan had been given concrete form after the events of 1974 and there is evidence that

[1] For example, in September 1974, President Suharto of Indonesia and Prime Minister Gough Whitlam of Australia had both agreed that "an independent East Timor would be an unviable state and a potential threat to the area". In addition Australia was at this time in a constitutional crisis with the Whitlam government dismissed and new elections taking place which resulted in the election of a conservative coalition. Subsequently it apparently covered up the deaths of two Australian TV teams shot by the Indonesian military near the border. On the US side, President Ford and Henry Kissinger had been visiting Indonesia and left Jakarta only a few hours before the invasion started.

both Indonesia's main military backer, the USA, and the regional power, Australia, knew and approved of Indonesian intensions. Military incursions into East Timor had begun in September, but a full-scale military invasion was launched on December 7. Eyewitnesses of the first hours of the invasion reported widespread indiscriminate killings, including that of a group of Chinese who had come to welcome the Indonesians.

Within days the UN General Assembly and the Security Council had passed resolutions calling on Indonesia "to withdraw without delay its forces from the territory in order to enable the people of the territory freely to exercise their right to self-determination and independence". This and other resolutions since have been ignored by Indonesia, which continues to occupy East Timor and, on May 31, 1976, staged an "Act of Self-Determination" and on July 17, declared East Timor to be the 27th Province of Indonesia.

The loss of life as a result of the Indonesian occupation has been great. It is not possible to calculate numbers accurately, in part because of the remoteness of the region, but much more as a result of the deliberate attempts by the Indonesian government to exclude foreign journalists, medical teams and other independent observers, including the Red Cross. The minimum credible estimate is 100,000 dead — 15% of the pre-invasion population — and some accounts give higher figures of perhaps one third of the population. The deaths were the result of military killings, injuries, famine, exposure and disease. In addition there were many allegations of torture and political murder of Timorese by Indonesians both at the time of the invasion and later. Some observers have described the situation as "genocidal".

At present the Indonesian army appears to be in control of almost all the island, except for small pockets of FRETILIN fighters in the east of the island. FRETILIN itself continues to exist, whether in the jungles or in exile, but it is unlikely that militarily it could be much more than an irritation to the Indonesian military, which has at least 15,000 troops in East Timor. Instead new opposition groups, some of them linked to the Church, are beginning to emerge. Well attested accounts of imprisonment and torture have continued to come from East Timor. One human rights organization estimated that one Timorese out of 125 had been arrested, tortured or assassinated in 1985 and 1986. In addition, by promoting "integration" with Indonesia, the minority rights of the Timorese were ignored. Timorese are said to be second-class citizens compared to the Indonesian elite that dominates the economy. According to one informant, only one educational institution in the capital (Dili) taught in Portuguese rather than Indonesian. East Timorese must carry travel passes even to go to neighbouring villages. Access to the islands has been restricted to outsiders for many years; however in early 1989 some foreign tourists and others were allowed to enter East Timor, albeit under heavy restrictions.

In international law the UN continues to refuse recognition to the Indonesian occupation and continues to call for an independent referendum on self-determination for the people of East Timor. Portugal has led the movement to refuse recognition but the Resolution has to be reaffirmed annually and each year the numbers voting against or abstaining increases. Some nations have recognized the Indonesian annexation and in September 1988 Indonesia and Australia reached an agreement over the "Timor Gap", an oil-rich area in the seas south of East Timor.

(See also *West Papuans*)

Indian Fijians

Location: **Fiji, western Pacific**
Population: **350,000**
% of population: **49%**
Religion: **Hindu, Muslim**
Language: **Hindustani, English**

The islands of Fiji are inhabited by Melanesians and by descendants of Indians from the Indian subcontinent who were brought to the country to work the sugar plantations. More than 320 islands, of which less than half are inhabited, are spread over some 259,000 square kilometres of ocean and mark a crossing point between the Polynesian and Melanesian cultures of the South Pacific. According to a 1987 estimate, the population totalled about 715,000. Of these 350,000 were Indian, 336,000 were Fijians and Rotuman Islanders and the remaining 29,000 people were European, part-

European, or Chinese. Around 51% of the population was Christian, 40% Hindu and 8% Muslim.

European contact with Fiji began in the seventeenth century; in 1774 the islands were visited by Captain Cook and British merchants soon followed. Inter-tribal fighting and fears of domination by European traders led Fijian leaders to appeal to various European powers to assume control of the region, and a deed of cession to Britain was signed in 1874.

Introduction of indentured labour

Fiji's modern history has been irrevocably marked by the decision to introduce Indian migrants to work the sugar plantations between 1879 and 1916. Native Fijians showed little enthusiasm for the extremely harsh conditions of plantation labour and preferred to continue their subsistence agriculture. Indian immigration to Fiji was stopped in 1931 but the beginnings of inter-racial conflict had by then been established. The first Governor of Fiji, Sir Arthur Gordon, took specific measures to protect the Fijians from the disruptive impact of immigrant traders and planters. A prohibition was placed on the purchase of Fijian land by outsiders and a provincial and village based system of native administration was created. A limited amount of land was given to the Australian Colonial Sugar Refining Company which after a time found it more economical to abandon its plantations and rely on the produce of Indian labourers who had formerly been indentured. The Indians thus became the major producers of sugar as independent farmers, but they depended for their livelihood upon the availability of leaseholds on Fijian-owned land.

Independence and after

By the 1960s Indians had become the majority race in Fiji accounting for 51% of the population. This was due in part to the earlier age of marriage and thus higher birthrate amongst Indians, and was also a result of the earlier decimation of the Fijian population by European diseases such as measles and influenza. When Fiji became independent in 1970 the new constitution specifically safeguarded the interests of the Fijian minority: Fijians retained ownership of some 83% of land, which could be leased out by the Native Land Trust Board only if not required by its Fijian owner; Fijians were guaranteed a majority in the upper house (the Senate) and the electoral system ensured that Fijians would be assured of almost half the seats in the lower house (the House of Representatives), since an equal number of members from each race were to be separately elected by Indians and Fijians. The balance of seats were to be held by representatives of the other racial communities. Fijians were also assured of fair treatment in recruitment to the civil service. The army was almost totally Fijian since Indians had earlier refused to join the army unless paid at the same rate as Europeans.

Despite these safeguards many Fijians continued to fear Indian dominance. Their fears were given political voice by the Fijian Nationalist Party (FNP), formed in 1975. This was explicitly anti-Indian and called for the repatriation of Indians. The native vote was split between the Alliance Party, which called for recognition of the distinctiveness of the two communities, and the FNP. The Indian-led National Federation Party (NFP) was thus enabled to win a majority in parliament in 1975 but internal disputes led to new elections and the Alliance Party soon regained power.

During the 1980s it became apparent that the Indian population was declining relative to the Fijian. This was due in part to an increased rate of Indian emigration and also to a rise in the age of marriage amongst Indian women. It was estimated in 1976 that of approximately 715,000 people living in the islands, slightly less than 50% were now Indians for the first time since censuses began.

The coups of 1987

In 1985 the multiracial Fiji Labour Party was formed by Dr Timothy Bavandra, a native Fijian. After winning the 1986 municipal elections it went on to win the general election of April 1987 in an alliance with the NFP. Although sensitive posts relating to land and education were retained by Melanesians, some remained hostile to the government, fearing Indian domination both politically and economically. On May 14, 1987, a military coup led by the Melanesian Fijian nationalist, Col. Sitveni Rabuka, failed to achieve immediately its more extreme aim (that the constitution be changed to prevent Indians from ever controlling government), but resulted in the formation of an interim government in which most of the posts were held by Melanesian members of the Alliance Party.

Fluctuating prices on the sugar, copra and fish markets, along with a decline in tourism, led to a recession in the Fijian economy during 1987, a situation exacerbated by the six week strike by Indian plantation workers. There were attacks on supporters of the Bavandra government and Indian-owned businesses by Melanesian youths, allegedly at the behest of the militant Melanesian *Taukei* movement. In September 1987 the Governor-General succeeded in organizing a caretaker coalition government of the Indian-based former government coalition and the Melanesian Alliance

Party, but this was aborted when a second coup was quickly staged by Colonel Rabuka. Leaders of other parties were arrested and, reportedly, were also at times ill-treated. On October 1, Rabuka declared a Fijian republic despite the likelihood of expulsion from the Commonwealth and condemnation of his actions by several governments.

Again the Governor-General tried for a compromise solution. However Rabuka proposed that there should be a single-chamber parliament with 36 seats reserved for Melanesians, 22 for Indians and eight for other communities, thus giving the Melanesians a permanent majority. The Alliance Party accepted these terms but the Labour Party and the NFP did not. In the weeks following there were reports of torture, rape and harassment of Indian citizens by Fijian soldiers, while the dismissal of the judiciary (which had remained independent of Rabuka) and the imposition of an Internal Security Decree (in 1988) removed some basic human rights protection from all communities. In December 1987 an interim civilian government was installed by the military with the former Alliance prime minister as Prime Minister, the former Governor-General as President and Colonel (now Major-General) Rabuka as Home Affairs Minister. It was proposed to hold elections at an unspecified time within two years but to date these have not taken place.

The future for Indians in Fiji is problematic. Large numbers of Indian professionals have emigrated, most commonly to Australia, New Zealand and Canada. Half the lawyers, 40% of the doctors, 30% of the accountants and 20% of the school teachers have left, as have managers and skilled tradesmen from the Fijian Sugar Corporation. This has had grave effects on the Fijian economy. Yet most Indian Fijians are poor and unskilled and are unlikely to be accepted as immigrants. Few wish to return to India where their links are weak after a century of exile. Unlike Melanesians, Indians do not have land or a native village to return to. In addition, Indians feel increasingly threatened by the growth of militant Methodist fundamentalism which General Rabuka wishes to enshrine in the new Fijian constitution. Ironically the same forces of repression, religious intolerance and economic decline also threaten indigenous Melanesian Fijians, many of whom are increasingly opposed to the present regime.

(See also *East Indians of the Caribbean* in **South and Central America**)

Kanaks of New Caledonia

Alternative names: **various clan and tribal names**
Location: **New Caledonian islands in south-western Pacific**
Population: **63,000**
% of population: **43%**
Religion: **Catholic and Protestant, indigenous Kanak beliefs**
Language: **Kanak languages**

The Kanaks are the indigenous Melanesian peoples of New Caledonia or Kanaky, an island group of one large island and several smaller ones, lying mid-way between Australia and New Zealand. The Kanaks are the largest ethnic group in New Caledonia with a total population of about 63,000; about 43% of the population of 145,000. Other groups are French (about 37%), Wallis and Futuna Islanders, Tahitians, Indonesians and other Asian settlers. New Caledonia is an Overseas Territory of France and will be the last of the Melanesian island nations to attain independence. As a result the 1980s have seen conflict between the Kanaks who seek independence and the French settlers who wish to retain the status quo.

French Colonial domination

The Kanaks have inhabited the islands for about 6,000 years, living in autonomous tribal communities in the narrow valleys between the mountains. New Caledonia was so named by Captain Cook who landed there in 1774. He was followed by traders and missionaries from both the UK and France and it was competition between the two which led to French annexation in 1853. New Caledonia was established as a penal colony and ruled by military administration. The French settlers, convicts and cattle took much of the best land while the administration legalized the alienation of Kanak land and replaced traditional chiefs with more docile men. The Kanaks resisted and in 1878 launched a major revolt against the French, in which over 1,000 Kanak lives were lost. Repression continued with further restrictions on land ownership, Kanak tribes were forced onto reservations and subject to the *Indignat* — a code of "native regulations" also used in other French colonies. In addition Kanaks died from the introduction of new diseases, alcohol and guns. As a result the Kanak population declined from 42,500 in 1887 to only 28,000 in 1901. Meanwhile French and other immigrants settled in New Caledonia, either to farm, to trade or to work in the new nickel mining industry. There was a further Kanak revolt in 1917, partially as a result of the forcible conscription of Kanak men into the French army.

During World War II New Caledonia was of strategic importance in the Pacific theatre and had thousands of American troops based there. Employed by the US forces, the Kanaks for the first time received standard pay for their labour and better treatment than they had from the settlers. The end of the war and an emerging worldwide trend towards decolonization saw reforms in the status of New Caledonia as it became an Overseas Territory with representation in the French National Assembly. Most adult Kanaks obtained the franchise and Kanak political parties began to be formed, most notably the *Union Calédonienne* (UC). In 1957 a Territorial Assembly was created in which the UC won the majority of the seats. Reactionary French settlers, known as *caldoches*, opposed the UC, and in 1963 prevailed upon the French government to enact the *loi Jaquinot*, and later other laws, which restricted the scope of the Territorial Assembly to a purely consultative status. At the same time there was large-scale immigration from France and elsewhere, including French settlers from newly independent Algeria, who tilted the ethnic balance against the Kanaks, who had been beginning to gain in numbers. While the "nickel boom" brought wealth to the French, the Kanaks missed out on the new prosperity and New Caledonia was, and remains, a society divided on race and class lines.

The Kanak independence movement

The 1970s saw the growth of a number of Kanak political parties, many of which sought greater autonomy from France but most of which eventually decided that independence was their goal. Some of these parties were jointly organized by Kanaks and left-wing Europeans but others were formed by radical Kanak youth who had been educated in the French system and were influenced by the events of 1968. Demonstrations and protests against the French presence were violently dispersed by the French police. Conservative French settlers formed their own parties which opposed Kanak demands. Two developments in 1975 intensified Kanak pro-independence feelings. Firstly, there was a rightward shift in French policies with a more rigid colonial policy, and secondly, an increase in settler organization and activities. French

policy initially aimed to undermine the Kanak movement by promoting pro-government Kanaks and repressing independence supporters. When this failed there were attempts to improve the economic situation of Kanaks but the pro-independence parties rejected these reforms as too little and too late. The Dijoud plan of 1979, which promoted economic development, was one such example in which attempts were made to diversify the economy while keeping it under French control. After attempts were made to disenfranchise small parties most of the Kanak parties formed the Independence Front (FI) which won 34.4% of the total votes (and 80% of the Kanak votes) and 14 of the 36 seats in the July 1979 territorial elections. Demonstrations, protests and counter-protests, some of them violent, continued.

The election of the Socialist government in May 1981 appeared to favour new initiatives towards independence. However, once in power, the Socialists appeared to renounce immediate independence in favour of minor reforms. In an effort to defuse the escalating conflict the French government invited the different political parties to round-table talks in France. The French government then recognized "the innate and active right of the Kanak people . . . to independence" while the FI offered to accommodate the "victims of history", i.e. *caldoches* who had resided in New Caledonia for several generations. The French government then proposed a new statute which incorporated a transitional period of internal autonomy, culminating in a referendum on New Caledonia's future status in 1989. The FI pointed out that the statute did not incorporate its two major concerns; firstly that the electoral register should be restricted to Kanaks and long-term settlers (all French citizens who had been in the territory for six months or longer had the right to vote there) and secondly to move independence forward, preferably to 1985, within the term of the Socialist government. As the French government would not agree to these points, the FI decided to boycott the 1984 Territorial Assembly elections and to confront the government directly.

In the summer of 1984, seeking to broaden its support, the FI reconstituted itself as the *Front de Libération Nationale Kanak et Socialiste* (FLNKS) from four political parties, a labour union and a women's organization. It organized grassroots committees and at the elections co-ordinated a series of actions — setting up roadblocks, occupying polling stations, setting municipal buildings alight etc. — which for the next few weeks brought the country to a standstill. Eighty per cent of Kanaks abstained from the elections. In December the FLNKS declared a provisional government. There was violence from settlers, backed by right-wingers in France, who organized counter-violence, including the deaths of 10 Kanaks in a settler ambush, which came close to bringing the territory to civil war. The French government announced that there should be an "acceleration of the process of self-determination which must lead to a choice, including independence" and appointed Edgard Pisani as Special Envoy to New Caledonia. After further murders and violence on both sides, Pisani declared a State of Emergency in January 1985, bringing in further military forces. Many Kanaks saw these forces as acting with French settlers against Kanaks.

In May 1985 Pisani was recalled to France and became Minister for New Caledonia while the Prime Minister, Laurent Fabius, presented a new status proposal for the territory. This involved a referendum for self-determination in December 1987; the creation of four regions governed by regional councils; economic and other reforms to alleviate inequalities; and the reinforcement of the French military presence. Although these demands did not satisfy FLNKS, after much debate it decided to participate in the elections and embarked on an electoral registration drive. When the elections took place in September 1985 the FLNKS won a majority in the three areas of North, Centre and Loyalty Islands. However, because of the greater weight given to the capital, Noumea, they won only 35.2% of the votes and 16 of the 46 seats in the Territorial Assembly (which had a purely consultative function) compared to anti-independence parties with 60.8% and 26 seats respectively. Eighty per cent of Kanaks had voted for pro-independence parties. Despite continued violence, many Kanaks found the experience of government in the Regional Councils a valuable one, the first time that they had been able to exercise power under French rule. However it was short-lived, since the new Conservative government in France, elected in March 1986, announced in May 1986 that it would transfer to the Territorial Assembly most of the powers granted to the Regional Councils.

This created great bitterness among the Kanaks as did the French government decision to hold a referendum on the future of the colony. FLNKS called for a boycott of the referendum, which was finally held in September 1987, under heavy military protection. Of the 59% of the electorate who voted in the referendum, 98% voted for retention of links with France. However, 31%, or 82% of the Kanak population, boycotted the referendum in protest. South Pacific Forum countries stated that they did not consider the referendum a genuine act of self-determination. FLNKS leaders stated that they could not rule out further violence. This reached a flashpoint in May 1988 when Kanak militants took 23 French gendarmes hostage in a cave at Ouvea, resulting in the deaths of 19 Kanaks by French troops; some apparently had been killed while in military custody.

The Accord de Mantignon and after

The situation was in part resolved by the new elections in France which resulted in a victory for the Socialist Party. The new Prime Minister, Michel Rocard, immediately began a process of negotiation and reconciliation between representatives of FLNKS and pro-French groups. The Accord de Mantignon was signed on June 26, and the protocol on the draft agreement on August 20, 1988 by Jean Maire Tjibaou on behalf of the FLNKS. It had as its main provisions (i) a one-year period of direct rule of New Caledonia from France, followed by (ii) the creation and transfer of powers to three new regional assemblies for a 10 year period, after which (iii) a new and final referendum on future status would be held in which the options would be independence or continued association as part of France (with only those who had been living in New Caledonia since 1988 to take part in voting); (iv) increased French economic aid to disadvantaged Kanak regions; and (v) the promotion of Melanesian culture. Despite criticisms of the Accord by extremists on both sides, it was accepted by the FLNKS, and by the majority of Kanaks in a later referendum. However, only 40% of non-Kanaks voted in favour.

There are difficulties in implementing of the Accord. Since most non-Kanaks remain opposed to it and many Kanaks are impatient with the 10-year period, it is probable that the Accord will face considerable strains. It faced a severe test in May 1989 when Kanak leaders Jean Maire Tjibaou and Yeweine Yeweine were assassinated as collaborators by Kanaks at Ouvea, the scene of the previous year's confrontation.

Economic and social inequalities

Kanaks are a disadvantaged minority within New Caledonia. There are marked disparities between the capital Noumea, where most whites live, and the rural areas. Kanaks are discriminated against in employment, holding low-paid unskilled jobs, and many are unemployed. Few are employed in the nickel industry, the main economic asset of the island. Land is at the heart of Kanak grievances. Eighty per cent of Kanaks live on the reservations where they were herded by French colonialists. The area of the reservations has increased by only 15% since that time but the Kanak population has more than doubled. Programmes to redistribute land to the Kanaks have largely failed. There is particular resentment against French domination of language and education. The foundation of the Kanak newspaper "Bwenando" and the Kanak radio station "radio Djiido" in 1985 marked major breakthroughs, as did the formation of the *écoles populaires kanaks* (EPK) — Kanak alternative schools movement, established by the FLNKS in 1985. Kanaks have been continuously disadvan-

taged in French schools, although they comprise over half the school population, because of the use of the French language and curriculum. The EPK, operating in Kanak languages and promoting Melanesian culture, remains the most impressive example of continuing Kanak organization.

(See also *Tahitians of Polynesia*)

Maori of New Zealand

Location: **New Zealand (Aotearoa)**
Population: **400,000 (est.)**
% of population: **12%-13%**
Religion: **Christianity, indigenous Maori beliefs**
Language: **Maori, English**

The Maori are a people of Polynesian origin who inhabit New Zealand or Aotearoa, "the land of the long white cloud". They make up 12%-13% of the total population of just over three million.

The origins of the Maori people are unclear. They almost certainly came from East Polynesia and the first settlers probably arrived in Aotearoa during the eighth century AD or earlier. Archaeological evidence suggests that the ancestors of the Polynesians moved southward from the South China coast over hundreds of years since cultural influences can be traced back to South-East Asia and China. It is probable that there were two major waves of immigration into the islands; scholars of Maori history and legend believe that the ancestors of most of the present-day tribes arrived in about 1350 AD in a Great Fleet of Polynesian vessels. Oral tradition lists the names of canoes and the navigators and priests aboard them; the Maori were a sedentary tribal people who cultivated crops, snared birds and fished the sea and rivers. They engaged in tribal warfare on a seasonable basis and lived in fortified villages built on hill-tops. There was a strong sense of the presence of the ancestors of whom carvings were made, and all natural objects such as trees, rocks and water, were believed to contain a spiritual essence or power.

European settlement

European navigators first landed in New Zealand in the eighteenth century. Captain Cook's expedition returned to Europe with news of great forests of tall straight trees suitable for ships' timbers, and sailing ships were soon arriving to take on cargoes of timber. As was the case in Australia the most immediate effect of white traders and settlers arriv-

ing in New Zealand from the early nineteenth century was the rapid spread of western disease and illness such as influenza and TB which had previously been unknown amongst the Maori. A second dramatic effect of contact with the European was the introduction of muskets, first purchased on a visit to London by a tribal chief in 1820. The scale of warfare escalated rapidly as tribes were forced to obtain guns to defend themselves and used them against their enemies. Warfare became much more drawn-out and a period known as the Musket Wars began, a period during which perhaps one quarter of the Maori population was killed and some parts of New Zealand were depopulated. Weakened by the disruptive effects of war the Maoris accepted the mediation of Christian missionaries and became receptive to European influence.

In 1840 the Treaty of Waitangi was signed by Maori chiefs and representatives of the British Crown. Sovereignty was ceded to the British in return for the guaranteed continued possession by Maoris of their lands, forests, fisheries and other properties, and the Maori granted the sole right of purchasing their lands to Queen Victoria. Not all Maori chiefs were enthusiastic about the treaty, however. During the 1840s and 1850s white settlers arrived in New Zealand in large numbers until by 1858 they outnumbered the Maoris. There were clashes throughout the country between settlers and tribesmen. It soon became evident that the Maori benefited materially by the immigration: a variety of new crops such as wheat, potatoes and apples were grown successfully and traded with Europeans; literacy spread rapidly and Maori schools were built.

Many Maori felt nevertheless that the advantages gained by the contact were outweighed by the

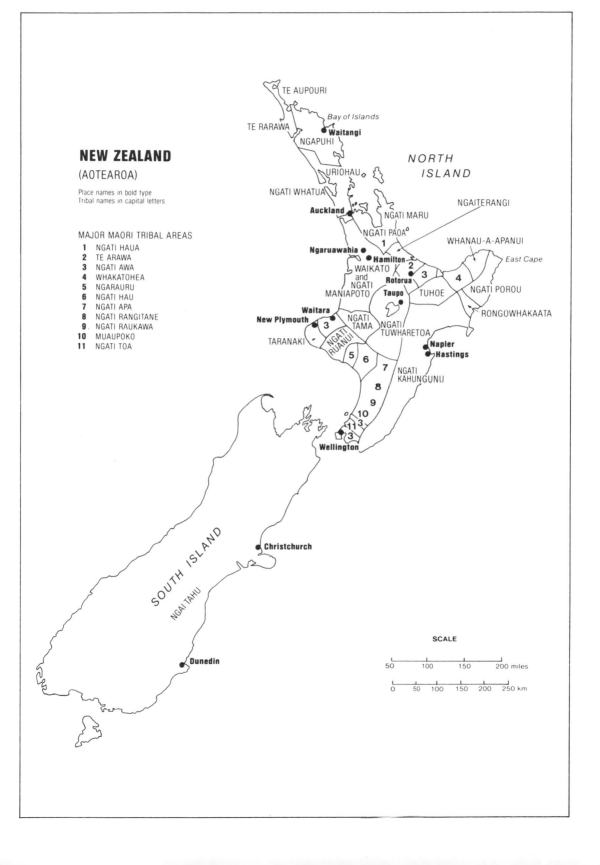

NEW ZEALAND
(AOTEAROA)

Place names in bold type
Tribal names in capital letters

MAJOR MAORI TRIBAL AREAS
1   NGATI HAUA
2   TE ARAWA
3   NGATI AWA
4   WHAKATOHEA
5   NGARAURU
6   NGATI HAU
7   NGATI APA
8   NGATI RANGITANE
9   NGATI RAUKAWA
10 MUAUPOKO
11 NGATI TOA

TE AUPOURI

Bay of Islands

TE RARAWA

● **Waitangi**

NGAPUHI

URIOHAU

*NORTH
ISLAND*

NGATI WHATUA

Auckland ●

NGATI MARU

NGATI PAOA

NGAITERANGI

Ngaruawahia ●

1

WHANAU-A-APANUI

East Cape

Hamilton ●

2

WAIKATO
and
NGATI
MANIAPOTO

Rotorua

3

4

Taupo

TUHOE

NGATI POROU

RONGOWHAKAATA

Waitara

New Plymouth

3

NGATI
TAMA

NGATI
TUWHARETOA

Napier

Hastings

TARANAKI

NGATI
RUANUI

5

6

7

NGATI
KAHUNGUNU

8

9

10

11 3

3

Wellington

SOUTH ISLAND

NGAI TAHU

● **Christchurch**

SCALE

50   100   150   200 miles

0   50   100   150   200   250 km

● **Dunedin**

loss of Maori culture. In 1858 they elected a Maori king in a move to establish their own system of ordered government. Two years later the Maori Wars began after the Governor of New Zealand attempted to take possession of a fertile region at Waitara and his troops were resisted by a local chief. The conflict escalated and the government decided to punish the tribes by confiscating tribal lands. In all almost three-and-a-quarter million acres were seized; much of it good, fertile land. Although some land was later returned to the Maori, most of it remained in the hands of the white settlers. Partly to allay criticism in Britain, the government introduced the Maori Representation Bill of 1867. According to the terms of this bill the Maori were able to elect four Maori members of Parliament. One other result of the disastrous Maori Wars was the emergence of a pacifist movement led by a Maori prophet who established a settlement based on principles of non-violence similar to those espoused by Mahatma Gandhi in the twentieth century.

Throughout the remainder of the nineteenth century and for much of the twentieth century government policy encouraged the Europeanization of the Maori. English became the only language of instruction used in the schools and Maori pupils were taught to respect European culture rather than their own. Maoris obtained full adult franchise along with Europeans in 1893, although since Maoris held land on a communal rather than an individual basis, few qualified to vote. Several politically moderate Maoris rose to high government office, but any attempts to regain the lands lost after the Treaty of Waitangi were unsuccessful, including one attempt made during a deputation to London.

In 1928, as a result of much agitation from Maoris, a Royal Commission was established with the purpose of investigating Maori grievances regarding the confiscated territory. The Commission, led by the Prime Minister, Gordon Coates, found in favour of the Maori, stating that they had been forced to fight in self-defence and that the Maori War had been "an unjust and unholy war". Compensation was offered to the various tribes but the Waikato people refused the offer, demanding instead the return of their lands.

In the 1930s an alliance was forged between the Labour Party and the Ratana Members of Parliament representing Maori seats. This alliance has continued until the present day and in several elections Maori support has been crucial for maintaining the Labour Party in office. After the elections of 1935 the Labour government began to create a welfare state which was to have a great impact upon the living conditions of the Maori people. In 1946 the government made a revised offer of compensa-

tion to the various aggrieved tribes. Maori Trust Boards were established to administer the payments which were NZ$5,000 per annum in perpetuity. Whilst this payment was of help to some tribes, the problem of Maori alienation from the land remained.

During the 1950s and 1960s there was a marked drift of Maoris into the cities and problems previously avoided began to surface. Many were young, unemployed and of low economic status, and race relations in the cities deteriorated. Under the Maori Affairs Act of 1953 anyone who was more than half Maori had to enrol on the Maori electoral roll, whilst those of half-Maori blood were given the choice of enrolling on either the Maori or the general roll.

Maori protest

In the early 1970s a Maori protest movement began to develop, led by young militants belonging to *Nga Tamatoa*, a group which campaigned on several major issues such as language teaching in schools. In 1975 the great Land March of Maoris, led by older Maori activists, moved down the length of North Island to the Parliament Buildings in Wellington. Attention was focused once more on the Treaty of Waitangi, and Maori protests became more persistent, to the increasing consternation of many whites (*pakehas*) who had previously believed New Zealand society to be a model of egalitarian and non-racist principles.

A Waitangi Tribunal was set up in order that all breaches of the Treaty of Waitangi should be investigated. During the 1970s and 1980s several cases involving land and fishing rights were brought before the tribunal and won by Maoris. Public attention was focused on the traditional customs of the Maori and their complex food-gathering procedures. Maori interests were not taken into account in the planning of industrial developments, but Maori protests about the threat to the Waitara fishing reefs from a proposed synthetic fuel plant gained much support from the large body of New Zealanders concerned about environmental issues. Government policy towards the Maori was now changing and the emphasis was no longer on assimilation but on greater awareness of Maori land rights and their relationship with the environment. The Electoral Amendment Act of 1974 recognized the fact that many people of part-Maori descent felt themselves to be Maori. It directed that a Maori was a person of Maori race and so was anyone descended from such a person. Maoris were permitted to transfer their names from one roll to the other if they so wished.

Demonstrations against the Springbok Tour of 1981 marked a watershed in New Zealand's race relations. There was unprecedented violence in the cities and a test match was halted by anti-apartheid protesters. Another march, the *Hikoi* or peace march, took place in 1984. Maoris from all over New Zealand marched to Waitangi to present their grievances at the Treaty commemoration ceremony, but they were prevented from presenting their case and their mood became increasingly militant, with many marchers calling for Maori sovereignty. There have been increasing calls for Maori control over the funds spent by government in administering Maori affairs.

Inequalities

In 1985 the Labour Party returned to office. The Prime Minister, David Lange, immediately announced that a White Paper for a proposed Bill of Rights had been prepared. The government proposed to increase the powers of the Waitangi Tribunal which would be empowered to investigate Maori land grievances going back to 1840, when the treaty was signed. Although there was discussion about increasing the number of Maori seats in parliament the number remained fixed at four. This means that although the Maori now make up as much as 13% of the population, they still have only 5% of parliamentary seats.

The problem of under-development remains for the Maori people. According to "Race Against Time", a report published by the Human Rights Commission in Wellington in 1982, only 4.7% of professional people are Maori, and they are concentrated in the fields of teaching, medical work and social work. Sixty-four per cent of Polynesians hold non-skilled jobs compared with 38% of whites, and 67% of Maoris leave school with no qualifications compared with 28.5% of whites. Crime is much higher amongst Maoris, as is alcoholism, whereas health standards are lower. The government is now committed to a community-based health scheme which concentrates on a holistic approach to health. Maori are being encouraged to develop projects themselves which will meet the needs of the community. In the field of education, four more bilingual primary schools

(See also *Aboriginal Australians*)

are being opened and Maori language classes are more widespread than before.

Recent developments

There have been several important precedents established under the Lange Labour government. In 1987 the Treaty of Waitangi faced one of its most important cases when the NZ Maori Council sought to restrain the government from transferring certain assets to state-owned enterprises, alleging that this was inconsistent with the principles of the Treaty. The court upheld the Maori case and the judges placed emphasis on the Treaty as a partnership requiring "utmost good faith". The interests in the case were later settled by agreement and given legislative form in the Treaty of Waitangi (State Enterprises) Act 1988. There has been a rush of claims to the Tribunal which is expected to be reviewing claims until the end of the century. The Department of Maori Affairs began implementing its "Devolution Programme" *(Tukua Te Rangatiratanga)* to return many of its functions to *Iwi* (or Tribal) authorities, and other Maori programmes were instituted, including the Maori Language Act of 1987, which established the Maori Language Commission to promote Maori as an official language of New Zealand.

Many of these developments produced strains within New Zealand society. There was a backlash as many whites felt threatened by the new Maori militancy and Maori claims to land. Many Maoris were also critical of what was regarded as the slowness or bad faith of the government in implementing pro-Maori policies. There was controversy in 1987 as some Maoris supported the military coup by Colonel Rabuka in Fiji. The 150th anniversary of the Treaty of Waitangi in February 1990 was expected to highlight these tensions.

Yet in many ways there are signs of optimism also. There is a high rate of inter-marriage between the two communities; many whites as well as Maori are learning the Maori language, and the possibilities for co-operation and reconciliation are good. In 1985, Sir Paul Reeves was sworn into office as the first Governor-General of Maori descent.

Micronesia

Alternative names: **Marshall Islands; Northern Marianas; Federated States of Micronesia (Yap, Truk, Ponape, Kosrae — Eastern Caroline Islands); Palau (Belau — Western Caroline Islands)**
Location: **Western Central Pacific**
Population: **180,000**
% of population: **mainly indigenous**
Religion: **Christianity, indigenous beliefs**
Language: **Nine major Malayo-Polynesian languages, English**

Micronesia comprises three main island archipelagos — the Marshalls, the Carolines and the Marianas — covering an area of approximately 7.8 million square kilometres of the western Pacific. Of this less than 2,000 square kilometres is land, consisting of over 2,000 islands and low lying coral atolls. The total estimated population in 1977 was 126,239, growing at an annual rate of 4.5%; thus the population today may have reached 180,000 although there is high migration to the USA and elsewhere in the Pacific. Most of Micronesia, with the exception of Guam, has been part of the US administered Trust Territory of the Pacific Islands.

The people of Micronesia are an amalgam, reflecting the mongoloid, polynesian and melanesian emigration from South-East Asia which began around 1000 BC. This, along with later migration, resulted in the cultural, ethnic and linguistic divisions which persist today. There are nine major languages, which are mutually unintelligible, although English is widely spoken. The first contacts with the west came with Spanish explorers and missionaries and the Spanish presence continued in the western Pacific until the Spanish–American War of 1898. Following the Spanish defeat the US took control of Guam and the rest of Micronesia was sold to Germany. After the defeat of Germany in World War I, the islands were occupied by Japan, and the Japanese presence was later regularized under a League of Nations mandate. The Japanese saw the islands as areas for Japanese settlement and by 1938 it was estimated that 58% of residents were Japanese. After the withdrawal of Japan from the League of Nations in 1935 the islands were fortified and later became a strategic Pacific battlefield in World War II with the result that many Micronesians were killed and injured.

At the end of the war Micronesia was in US hands. In 1947 a trusteeship agreement between the UN and the US placed the area under US administration as the Trust Territory of the Pacific Islands (TTPI). Unlike the 10 other UN Trust Territories, the administering power was able to establish military bases and employ armed forces in the islands, and reported directly to the Security Council (where the US had a veto) rather than the General Assembly. The US agreed to act in accordance with the UN Charter to "promote the development of the inhabitants of the Trust Territory toward self-government or independence as may be appropriate to the particular circumstances of the Trust Territory and its peoples and the freely expressed wishes of the peoples concerned".

Military considerations have played an important part in the US administration of the TTPI. Between 1946 and 1958, Bikini and Enewetak atolls, located in the Marshalls, were used by the US as sites for nuclear tests. This resulted in extensive damage including radiation fallout on a number of islands, resulting in the involuntary evacuation of indigenous peoples from Bikini in 1946, from Enewetak in 1947 and from Rongalap in 1954. Since the mid-1940s the US Army missile range located in Kwajalein Atoll in the Marshall Islands has been an important testing ground for US missiles fired from Vandenburg Air Force base in California. This has resulted in protests by some Marshallese who have demanded an end to testing, the renegotiation of the terms of a lease signed in 1964 for the use of the land, and improved social and economic conditions for the Marshallese people. As a result of employment opportunities on the base, there has been a large influx of Marshallese into Kwajalein Atoll, but since islanders working at the base are not allowed to reside there after hours, they are forced to commute daily from nearby Ebeye Island. In 1978 a UN Visiting Mission commented on the contrast between slum conditions on Ebeye and those on the US base. As a result of protests there have been some improvements in living conditions on Ebeye.

The Constitutional evolution of the TTPI has been slow. Some governmental functions were transferred to the people at a municipal and district level, but it was not until 1964 that certain restricted legislative powers were granted to the people on a Territory-wide basis in the elected legislature of the Congress of Micronesia. In 1967, the Congress created a commission on its future status, which in 1969 recommended that the TTPI become either a self-governing state in Free Association with the USA or be completely independent. In April 1978 all parties negotiating accepted a "Statement of

Agreed Principles for Free Association" which provided that the Micronesians shall "enjoy full internal self-government" while the US will maintain "full authority and responsibility for security and defence matters" for a period of at least 15 years, subject to renegotiation. However, if the relationship was terminated other than by the US, or unilaterally by the Micronesians without US consent, then the US "shall be no longer obligated to provide the same amount of economic assistance ... initially agreed upon".

The Congress of Micronesia was abolished in 1978 following the referendum after which (in 1980) the TTPI was divided into four units — the Marianas, the Federated States of Micronesia, the Marshalls and Palau. The four entities were encouraged to write their own constitutions and all had done so by 1980 with the exception of Palau. In 1976 the US had signed a separate commonwealth agreement with the representatives of the Northern Marianas. Their convenant grants them exemption from some American legislation, notably the Jones Act (regarding the use of American ships between American ports), and laws on immigration and minimum wages. The USA gives the islands about US$33 million a year as budgetary aid and there is substantial income from Japanese tourism. The Federated States of Micronesia and the Marshall Islands have entered into Compacts of Free Association with the USA. This has led to an ambiguous status for the two former Trust Territories, since the TTPI has not yet been dismantled by the UN Security Council, and this is seen as a prerequisite to diplomatic recognition by the bulk of the world community. For example, the Federated States of Micronesia won self-government in Free Association with the USA in 1986 and declared its independence in 1987, but to date has been recognized as an independent state by only

11 countries. However, it has been able to obtain membership of the 15-nation South Pacific Forum.

Palau, also called Belau, has yet to finalize its acceptance of a Compact of Free Association with the USA and attempts to do so have resulted in political conflict within the island group of 15,000 people. The Palauan Constitution of 1980, often described as the world's first nuclear-free constitution, had a provision prohibiting the use, testing, storage or disposal in Palauan territory of "harmful substances such as nuclear, chemical, gas or biological weapons" without the express approval of voters in a referendum. The USA, which saw Palau as a strategic military option, insisted that the nuclear-free clause was incompatible with the Compact of Free Association and both before and after the adoption of the Constitution has made repeated attempts to change it, mainly by repeated referenda, and also allegedly by illegal intimidation of individuals and unfair electoral practices. To date, six referenda have failed to reach the 75% level of voters needed to change the Constitution. As with the other former TTPI territories, Palau is in an ambiguous position as the USA has announced that it will unilaterally terminate the Trusteeship; however, since the Trusteeship is the responsibility ultimately of the Security Council, this does not appear to be possible in international law. In the meantime there have been efforts to cut US assistance to Palau, which resulted in widespread retrenchment of public sector workers in 1987.

Economically all the former TTPI entities are underdeveloped territories in which a money economy in urban centres operates alongside a more traditional subsistence way of life in outlying areas. The weakness in the economy is largely made up by US economic assistance and there is a heavy dependence on imported food and materials.

(See also *Chamorros of Guam*)

Nauruans and Banabans

Alternative names: **Ocean Islanders (Banabans)**
Location: **western Pacific, 350 km apart**
Population: **Nauru, 4,100; Banaba (Kiribati), 3,500**
% of population: **Nauru, 50% of population; Banaba, 5% of Kiribati population (includes Banabans on Rabi)**
Religion: **Christian (Protestant)**
Language: **Indigenous languages, English**

Nauru and Banaba (Ocean Island) are two small islands in the Pacific, both of which have possessed rich phosphate deposits and both of which have

fought legally and politically for increased economic benefits from phosphate mining and for political independence. Both island communities are from similar ethnic backgrounds, but have different colonial experiences and present political status.

Both Nauru and Banaba are isolated islands and were not "discovered" by Europeans until the early nineteenth century. There was initially little European interest in either island, but the division of the Western Pacific in 1886 between Germany and the UK placed Nauru with Germany and Banaba (Ocean Island) with the UK. Nauru was made part of the German Marshall Islands protectorate in 1888. Ocean Island was ignored, although the Gilbert and Ellice Islands became a UK protectorate in 1892. In 1899, after phosphates were discovered on both islands, Ocean Island was incorporated into the protectorate in 1900 and by 1910 the Pacific Islands Company had mined heavily on both islands. At the end of World War I Germany lost its Pacific possessions and Nauru became a Trust Territory jointly administered by the UK, Australia and New Zealand under a League of Nations mandate. The three governments combined to buy all rights from the phosphate company on the islands and to work them jointly under the title of the British Phosphate Commission.

During the Japanese occupation both communities suffered. Of 1,200 Nauruans deported to Truk in the Carolines, over one third died. Over 150 Banabans were massacred by the Japanese in one incident. Both war and the despoliation of the islands by mining meant that it was difficult to return to live there; nevertheless many of the Nauruans did so while the Banabans were moved to Rabi Island in north eastern Fiji. Both communities received small royalties, but as a result of mining, 80% of Nauru and Banaba is now uninhabitable.

Nauru became independent in 1968 under Chief Hammer DeRoburt, and took over control of the phosphate industry. As one of the world's smallest states, with a total population of about 7,000, of whom 4,100 are citizens and the remainder Filipinos and other Pacific islanders, it is also the richest state *per capita*, with an income per head of about US$30,000. Much of the income from phosphates has been invested in Australia and elsewhere. However, the phosphates are expected to run out around 1995 and there are fears for the future, especially as few Nauruans now follow a traditional agricultural lifestyle and almost all goods are imported. At the end of 1988 Nauru announced that it would ask the UK, Australia and New Zealand to pay US$34 million in compensation after the release of an independent committee of enquiry set up by the Nauruan parliament in 1986 which stated . . . "Entrusted by the world community . . . with this 'sacred trust of civilization' the three powers failed to act in accordance with that trust and acted for their own benefit".

Banabans have had two main demands relating to their future; firstly to gain a more equitable share of the mining royalties, and secondly for a different political status. The struggle for compensation started in the mid-1960s with demands for royalties, and continued in the 1970s with proceedings in the UK High Court. Judgment was delivered in December 1976 after a long and involved court case. This ruled in effect that the courts had no power to order monetary damages for actions carried out by the UK colonial authorities even though they may have been in the wrong or against the financial interest of the community. However, it provided a strong moral base for compensation and in May 1977 the UK government offered the islanders US$6.5 million in compensation, on condition that the Banabans would give up legal proceedings against the government. Although the Banabans through their eight-man Council of Elders were unhappy about the decision, they agreed after legal advice to accept the offer.

Banabans were also opposed to their continued incorporation in the Gilbert and Ellice Islands and urged instead that they be allowed to become an Associated State in conjunction with Fiji. As a prelude to independence for the Gilbert and Ellice group it was agreed that the two would be separated because of their considerable ethnic and cultural differences. In 1979 the two became independent as Kiribati and Tuvalu respectively. Despite protests, Banaba remained with Kiribati. The Kiribati constitution offers Banaba a parliamentary seat; guarantees Banabans land rights on Banaban; gives Banabans inalienable rights to land and to live on their own island, and guarantees a review of these arrangements three years after independence. Although mining stopped in 1979, Banabans were also concerned that the Kiribati government might wish to restart mining operations. In 1982 there were 400 Banabans living on Banaba and attempting to revive traditional subsistence agriculture, although they were still relying on funds and supplies from Rabi Island.

Papua New Guinea

Location: **eastern half of New Guinea and islands**
Population: **3.6 million**
Religion: **animist beliefs, Christianity**
Language: **pidgin, motu, English, 700 local languages**

Papua New Guinea (PNG) comprises the eastern half of the island of New Guinea and a number of smaller islands extending north-east to Bougainville Island at the northern end of the Solomon Archipelago. The population of about 3.6 million is divided into about 10,000 tribes each with varying social and cultural characteristics and over 700 distinct languages; in fact Papuan society is composed only of minorities. In addition there is a small community of Chinese traders and many expatriate foreigners, most of whom are on short term contracts.

The colonial period

Little is known about New Guinea before the arrival of Europeans in the area. Its island and coastal peoples participated in the well-established trading cycles in the area while those in the mountainous interiors were more isolated and technologically unsophisticated. From the nineteenth century the European powers staked their claim to the islands; the Dutch to the western half, which was incorporated into the Dutch East Indies, the Germans to the north-east and the islands; and successively, the UK, the Queensland government and (after 1901) the Australian government, to the south-eastern section. After the end of World War I the German section passed to Australia as a Trust Territory under the League of Nations and later the United Nations mandate. Both the Germans and the Australians had confined themselves to the coastal areas and the islands, sometimes expropriating land for copra plantations and trading. It was not until the 1930s that Europeans began penetrating the unknown interiors in the search for gold. There they found highland peoples — later estimated to number a total of one million — living in the large valleys. However it was many years before there were effective road or transport communications in these remote areas; even today they are limited and air is the most accessible means of transport.

After the Japanese occupation of Papua New Guinea during World War II, the Australians made efforts to improve administration and increase development. However it was not until the 1960s and the commencement of more critical UN scrutiny that a programme of rapid economic development began, with priority being given to education and political development. The war had brought large numbers of indigenous people into contact with the world outside the narrow limits of the Australian administration and for the first time they received more equitable treatment. The material wealth of the Allied armies, and apparent prosperity of black American soldiers in particular, helped to fuel expectations to acquire money and material goods. By the mid-1960s there were the beginnings of an educated independence movement, drawn from an emerging urban elite of civil servants, students, urban workers, trade unionists and the church. In the villages developments took a number of forms ranging from the outright conservatism of the Highlanders, fearful of rapid change and post-independence domination by the coastals, through to various cargo cults, to a number of ethnically based, sub-regional movements seeking a greater economic stake.

During the late 1960s opposition movements were formed, most significantly in the islands. Chief among these were the Mataungan Association of New Britain and the Kabiswali Movement in the Trobriand Islands. Much more serious, in retrospect, was the discontent being expressed in Bougainville. Incorporated into the German adistration from 1899 to 1914 Bougainville was a late addition to the nation. Bougainvillians have closer ethnic ties to the northern Solomon Islands than to the other islands of PNG. They are taller and darker than the "redskins" from the mainland and Bougainville leaders have often used the term *mungkas* (black) to create a sense of unity. They suffered as coastal land was expropriated for plantations. Later Australian administration was indifferent. By the late 1960s Bougainvillians could centre their protest around the working of a large copper mine in central Bougainville owned by Conzinc Riotinto Australia (CRA), disputing land ownership and the payment of royalties which were paid not to local land owners but to the administration. After repeated demands for a share of the royalties it was agreed in 1967 that 5% of royalties (of the 1.25% of the value of the minerals paid to the administration) should be paid to the village land owners. Further disputes over the administration's compulsory acquisition of land for the development of mine and port facilities resulted in the formation of *Napidakoe Navitu*, an association of local language groups which negotiated greatly improved terms for the land-owners.

Independence

In 1972 in the first elections the Pangu Party came to power in a coalition government under the leadership of Michael Somare. This government appointed a Constitutional Planning Committee (CPC) to draw up a constitution for the newly independent Papua New Guinea. The CPC found that there should be decentralization of power to the new provincial level and that villagers should have real control over local affairs and a framework within which their rights and interests could be protected.

In the run up to independence set for September 1975, two movements announced their secession from PNG. The first was a Papuan separatist movement which announced its independence from PNG in January 1975. Papua, at least in part linked by a lingua franca called *motu*, claimed that it was less developed than the interior areas and had received less than its fair share of government spending. The government ignored the movement, which in any case had confused objectives and no real ethnic basis, and it seemed to fade away. Papuans in turn were resented by the more conservative Highlanders, largely operating through the United Party.

The Bougainville secession movement

A more serious challenge came from the revival of the Bougainville separatist movement. The copper mine was by far the largest foreign exchange earner for the PNG government and therefore it was determined to hold onto it, especially after it appeared that Australian budgetary aid would be cut after independence. In December 1972 the murder of two Bougainvilleans by highlanders hardened secessionist feelings, which had previously considered the options of joining the then British Solomons or forming a federation with other islanders. The secessionist movement came to a head two weeks before PNG independence when the former District Commissioner, supported by an MP and the local Roman Catholic Church, declared unilateral independence as the Republic of the North Solomons. Neither the PNG government nor Australia recognized the new republic, but after PNG independence, talks between the two sides began. The national government, under Somare, agreed on revitalized proposals for decentralization in provincial government and further concessions were made on royalties, while the Bougainville leaders withdrew their more radical demands, and in August 1975 signed an Agree-

ment (the North Solomons Agreement) which marked their return to membership of PNG. Within the agreement was recognition of the principles of decentralization at the national, provincial and local levels, and for the need for provincial governments to have certain exclusive areas in legislation and taxation.

Early in 1977 an Organic Law on Provincial Government was passed. The act embodied full details of devolution, and after Bougainville had been granted full provincial government status in 1977, other provinces rapidly followed. To date it has appeared that this has not damaged national unity (in many ways a new and foreign concept) and no one provincial government has been able to determine policy or dominate others.

In Bougainville itself local dissatisfaction with the policies of the administration was never really resolved. The main cause was the presence and exploitation of the giant Bougainville Copper Ltd (BCL) mine. The Nasioi people felt continuing resentment against the low level of royalties accruing to themselves, especially as the renegotiation of 1974 mainly benefited the provincial government. The mine has had devastating environmental effects; roads have torn through the jungles, almost 8,000 acres is used as the mine site and dump and the ore waste is emptied into a nearby river, polluting the sea. Although the mine employs local people, ethnic tensions arise from the presence of mainlanders who stay in the area after their contracts expire.

In late 1988 the Bougainville Revolutionary Army (BRA), led by a former employee of the mine, was formed. Despite being poorly equipped it appeared to benefit initially from strong local support and successfully launched attacks on the mine and its employees, culminating in an attack on the BCL's electricity supply in May 1989 which resulted in the closure of the mine. After the failure of negotiations, the central government declared a State of Emergency and brought in 1,600 non-Bougainvillian troops, who have killed rebels, burnt villages and forcibly relocated hundreds of villagers to detention centres on the coast. The Deputy Premier of the province was himself beaten by police. In mid-September BRA militants murdered the Provincial Minister of Commerce, a move which led to the postponement of a US$300 million landowner's package due to be signed on September 12, 1989.

The Highlanders

There have always been potential sources of friction between the peoples of the coastal lowlands and those of the high valleys in the interior. At the time of independence, some Highlanders were considered backward and conservative, and some of their leaders urged the Australian government to delay independence in order to allow them to catch up with coastal groups. To a large extent these fears have been alleviated as more Highland peoples have been drawn into the political system of parliamentary government at central and provincial levels, partly through the adoption of the traditional system of the rule of "big men". In 1985 Paias Wingti became the first Prime Minister from the Highlands. The rise in the prices of coffee and other highland commodities, grown substantially on small plots and marketed by local organizations, has encouraged highland enterprise and initiative, while the continuing development of the Highlands Highway to the coast and air services elsewhere has drawn the Highlanders into national life. However, economic and social changes have also produced strains. In some areas land shortages have developed and thousands of young Highland men migrate to coastal cities where their lack of education and urban skills has led many into crime and anti-social behaviour. There are occasional clashes between Highlanders and coastal peoples; states of emergency were declared in Port Moresby in 1986 and in Lae and the Eastern Highlands in 1987 and clashes took place in Port Moresby in 1989. Traditional, inter-tribal warfare remains a regular feature of dispute settlements in the Highlands. Such conflicts are resolved by a mixture of military and police intervention, administrative measures and traditional conciliation and compensation.

(See also *West Papuans*)

The future

Apart from the continuing secessionist movement in Bougainville, PNG has not been faced with long-term ethnic unrest but rather with civil unrest as a result of social changes and economic factors. In some ways there have been encouraging moves towards greater unity. An indigenous lingua franca has emerged in Pidgin, sometimes called neo-Melanesian, which is a combination of English, Malay and local vocabulary and Melanesian grammar, and which exists alongside the other lingua franca of motu. Over one million Papua New Guineans speak Pidgin today and it is the main language in the country's national parliament. A national paper, *Wantok* ("One Talk"), is published in Pidgin. There is great national pride in the role played by the PNG army in the transition to independence of the Melanesian state of Vanuatu (formerly New Hebrides). There has been a growing sense of PNG's role in support of the Kanaks of New Caledonia and leadership of the Melanesian Spearhead Group, a regional grouping. PNG remains a lively parliamentary democracy with political allegiances based on shifting factional or personality-based alliances, rather than ethnic or ideological ones. The human rights record is generally a good one. PNG's future well-being rests on its ability to reconcile the rising expectations of its young population, to channel mining revenues into productive sectors and to manage the volatile relationship with its giant neighbour Indonesia.

Rapa Nui (Easter Island)

Location: **Easter Island (south-east Pacific Ocean)**
Population: **1,500**
% of population: **80%**
Religion: **Indigenous Rapanui beliefs**
Language: **local Polynesian, Spanish**

The inhabitants of Rapa Nui, known more widely as Easter Island, are a Polynesian people who for the past century have lived under Chilean administration. Rapa Nui is a small Pacific island to the west of the South American mainland. In 1982 Rapa Nui's population was 1,936, of which about 1,500 were classified as "indigenous" by Chile's Office for Indian Affairs.

Rapa Nui was first occupied by Polynesian and/or Pre-Incan peoples over one thousand years ago. They produced the *moai*, or giant stone statues, for which the island is famous, during what is known as the "Golden Era". The *moai* continue to play an important role in the religious and political life of the Rapanui. There was only sporadic contact with Europeans until 1862 when Peruvian slavers took 1,500 people to the mainland. Rapanui who escaped and returned to the island carried infectious diseases which by 1877 had reduced the population from several thousand to 110. In 1888 the Rapanui were forced to sign a treaty with an officer of the Chilean navy under which the Government of Chile assumed administrative responsibilities in return for respect of Rapanui lands and culture. Despite this, however, the Rapanui were forced to work on Chilean plantations; in 1933 their lands were taken in the name of the state and by 1977, as a result of Decree Law 2885, they were left in possession of only 7% of the total land, the remainder becoming a National Park or in the ownership of an agricultural corporation.

Rapa Nui is administered as a Chilean province with a Governor, appointed by the Chilean President. The present governor is reported to have assumed a large amount of personal control over the island's resources, including tourism, the major source of income. The Chilean government does not recognize as a representative body, the Rapanui Council of Elders, whose 35 members represent each of the Rapanui families. The Chilean authorities are reported to have increased their presence on Rapa Nui in response to recent efforts to regain land in accordance with the 1888 treaty. Before the 1988 national plebiscite in Chile the government made new subsidized housing available to islanders; in return the contract of purchase required that the buyers had to agree to vote for Pinochet. When the Chilean Navy visited the islands in September 1988 — the 100th anniversary of annexation — the Chairman of the Council of Elders was detained and islanders reportedly intimidated to prevent a boycott of the visit, which however was poorly attended. Apparently the Rapanui do not seek independence from Chile but a degree of cultural autonomy and control over land and cultural resources.

Tahitians of Polynesia[1]

Alternative names: **Maohis**
Location: **French Polynesia, eastern Pacific**
Population: **115,000**
% of population: **72%**
Religion: **Protestant Christian**
Language: **Maohi and other indigenous languages, French**

The Polynesian peoples of Tahiti and the other islands of French Polynesia come from five archipelagos, each with its own distinctive culture and language — the Society Islands, which contain the largest island Tahiti; Tuamotu Archipelago; Marquesas Islands; Mangareva Islands and the Austral Islands. Although their land area is tiny (3,265 square kilometres, together with over 5 million square kilometres of ocean in the eastern Pacific), they make up the territory of French Polynesia, presently an Overseas Territory of France. It has a population of about 160,000; 115,000 of whom are indigenous Polynesians, about 20,000 French settlers and 30,000 Chinese and *demis*, those of mixed ancestry.[2]

Polynesians have lived in these islands for thousands of years. Tahiti island came into contact with European explorers from 1767 and from 1790 onwards whaling vessels called there regularly for rest and trade. Foreign contact proved disastrous for Tahitians and by the beginning of the nineteenth century only around 10% of the population survived. At the same time missionaries from the London Missionary Society arrived, who not only succeeded in converting most of the remaining inhabitants of the Society Islands over the next 20 years, but also laid the beginnings of a plantation society. Tahiti was annexed by the French in 1842 and despite Tahitian resistance in the following years became a French protectorate, and later in 1880 a colony called French Oceania. The French presence was always fairly small and confined to a few islands, as was the Chinese; as a result traditional Polynesian life on most of the islands remained relatively unaffected by the outside world well into the twentieth century.

Three hundred Tahitian volunteers fought in the European theatre with the Free French Forces. After their return to Tahiti some formed a group around a war veteran, Pouvanaa a Oopa, who founded the first Polynesian Political Party, the *Rassemblement Démocratique des Populations*

[1]Tahiti is the name of the largest island in French Polynesia. In this entry we use the name to denote all the indigenous inhabitants of French Polynesia in order not to confuse them with other Polynesian peoples such as Maoris in New Zealand or native Hawaiians.
[2]*Demis* quite frequently identify themselves as indigenous Polynesians in culture and political affiliation; thus for example Pouvanaa a Oopa, Francis Sanford and Charlie Ching, three Tahitian nationalists, are of *demi* ancestry. Many Tahitians also have French, English or Chinese names.

Tahitiennes (RDPT) and was several times elected as Polynesian representative to the French National Assembly. Political reforms in 1957 extended the numbers in the local Territorial Assembly and created a local executive body, the Government Council, of which Pouvanaa became vice-president and minister of the interior. In the referendum on the future of the French colonies, held in 1958, local politicians were banned from electioneering by radio; thus while most of French Polynesia voted to stay with France, Pouvanaa's RDPT gained a majority "no" vote in Tahiti and Moorea where they had been able to hold meetings against the option of staying with France. Soon after, Pouvanaa and other RDPT ministers were dismissed from the Government Council, arrested and, after a year, charged, tried and found guilty of the unauthorized use of weapons and attempted destruction of buildings. Pouvanaa was sentenced to eight years of solitary confinement followed by 15 years' banishment. This ended effective Polynesian opposition to the French presence for many years.

In 1966 France began its atmospheric nuclear testing programme in French Polynesia at Moruroa and Fangataufa atolls. These tests drew protests from other Pacific nations and in 1974 France, who had not signed the 1963 Test Ban Treaty, announced that it would continue future tests underground. To date there have been 41 atmospheric nuclear tests and 107 underground. The military and nuclear industry have played a major part in the Polynesian economy and employed around 15% of the workforce, although critics say that little of the income generated goes to indigenous Polynesians and that it has seriously distorted the local economy, drawing people away from an agricultural and fishing livelihood on the islands to the capital Papeete. There are fears of radiation contamination, although to date there have been no authoritative health surveys of the effects of the tests. Protests against testing have continued from other Pacific nations and environmental groups.

Pouvanaa was allowed to return to Tahiti in 1968 and was later elected to the French Senate. Meanwhile an Autonomist Movement had sprung up, led by a younger generation of Polynesians, most notably Francis Sanford and John Teariki. The Autonomists were a loose coalition of parties and factions; however all wished to see an end to nuclear testing and greater powers of self-government, and sometimes also complete independence. The Autonomists had first gained a majority in the Territorial Assembly in 1962 and won several times thereafter. Elections to the Territorial Assembly in 1977 resulted in the Autonomists retaining their majority, following which increased autonomy was granted; but in the elections of 1982 the pro-autonomy parties lost their overall majority to a Gaullist party, which opposed further loosening of ties with France. From 1985 pro-independence activities increased, partly in response to the situation in New Caledonia, although opposition parties tended to remain fragmented and some small groups apparently advocated violence. The Protestant Church, to which most Polynesians belong, has also spoken out against testing. In October 1987 a dispute at Moruroa docks led to a strike in Papeete and, after riots and arson, the French government declared a State of Emergency. Troops were brought in from France and New Caledonia and trades unionists were jailed (and later released). As a result the ruling coalition in the Territorial Assembly split and a new majority coalition, which included pro-independence parties, was formed. In August 1988 Tahiti's first political coalition to oppose nuclear testing was launched, but it was not until July 1989 that the President of the Territorial Assembly agreed to call a special session to discuss whether the tests should be allowed to continue and whether independent health surveys should take place. While the open discussion is considered a step forward there appear to date to be no positive moves by the French government to grant further autonomy or independence to French Polynesia, although recent announcements state that nuclear testing may be downgraded or moved elsewhere.

Although Polynesians still comprise the majority of the population within French Polynesia[3] (unlike New Caledonia) they are a disadvantaged majority. The extensive military construction programme initially raised employment and wages for Polynesians but it also resulted in the abandoning of the coconut and vanilla plantations, along with traditional agriculture and fishing, and brought people from the outlying islands to Tahiti island, whose population doubled in 10 years with most of the newcomers settling in hillside slums in Papeete. Unemployment has since risen and wages have fallen. Most Tahitians work as unskilled labourers and almost 40% of the population work in the public sector. Imports outnumber exports by 10 to one, further increasing Polynesian dependence and undermining self-sufficiency.

(See also *Kanaks of New Caledonia*)

[3]Polynesians fear that the integration of the EC after 1992 will lead to an influx of settlers from other EC countries. Ninety per cent of the Polynesian electorate boycotted the June 1989 European Parliament elections in protest against integration.

West Papuans

Alternative names: **West Irianese, various tribal names**
Location: **Western half of island of New Guinea**
Population: **800,000**
% of population: **65%**
Religion: **Indigenous animist beliefs, Christianity**
Language: **various, Indonesian**

Irian Jaya[1] is the Indonesian name for the western half of the island of New Guinea and is presently the easternmost province of Indonesia. Politically aware indigenous people generally prefer to think of the territory as West Papua. Like the rest of New Guinea it is largely inhabited by small clans separated from each other by terrain, language and customs who live for the most part by subsistence agriculture, hunting and gathering. There are perhaps 250 languages in the territory. Because of the mountainous terrain and limited communications, and also because independent outside access to Irian Jaya is severely restricted by the Indonesian authorities, it is difficult to find reliable and independent first-hand information on the area. There is probably a total population of about 1.2 million of whom 800,000 are indigenous, mainly living in the central highlands, and the remainder are from elsewhere in Indonesia, either civil servants, traders, military or settlers on transmigration schemes.

The Dutch colonial period

The Dutch laid claim to the territory in 1848. Although it became part of the Dutch East Indies, which became Indonesia at independence, geologically and geographically it was more closely related to Australasia than to Java or other Indonesian islands, and the people are related racially and culturally to Australasia and Melanesia. The Dutch devoted little attention to the region and penetrated no further than the coast. During World War II the area was under the control of the Japanese but was regained by the Dutch at the end of the war.

When Indonesia became independent in 1949, Western New Guinea was excluded and remained under Dutch control, since there was considerable international debate about its legal status. The Indonesians rested their claim as being the inheritors of the whole former Dutch East Indies. The Dutch postponed the question and during the 1950s made some efforts to develop the territory so

that by the end of the decade one third of all government posts were held by indigenous peoples. Missionary groups were also active in the development of the country, building hospitals and clinics, schools and some agricultural projects. (Most missionary activities were severely curtailed by the Indonesian authorities in 1978.) Indonesia threatened a full-scale invasion if the Dutch did not hand over the colony. Eventually the Dutch handed it over to the UN in 1962 which then passed it on to Indonesia in 1963, with the proviso that a plebiscite be held in 1969 and the views of the people of West Irian regarding their country's status should be ascertained. In the event there was no such referendum, but a so-called "Act of Free Choice" of mid-1969 which involved the assessment of the opinions of pro-Indonesian tribal leaders. However, despite questions as to the fairness and legality of this method of determination in international law, there was little opposition on the international scene when the territory became part of Indonesia.

Indonesian rule

Some observers felt that after the territory had passed to Indonesian control the population would come to identify itself with the Indonesian Republic, but while many groups living in inaccessible areas remain largely oblivious to the changes, there has also been a protracted period of resistance to Indonesian rule led by the *Organisasi Papua Merdeka* (OPM) or Free Papua Movement, formed in 1963. The OPM was reorganized in 1971 when it proclaimed a "Provisional Revolutionary Government of West Papua New Guinea". Aware of the threat to Indonesia's presence from either economic success or civil war in Papua New Guinea (PNG), across the border from the new Indonesian territory, the government determined to pursue a policy of "Indonesianization" and to invest a disproportionate share of development funds in the area.

Resistance to this policy, and in particular to the transmigration policy where thousands of settlers

[1]The Indonesian name of the province was Irian Barat (West Irian) but in 1973 it was changed to Irian Jaya (Greater Irian) — a name which some commentators see as indicating Indonesian aspirations to the eastern half of the island (i.e. Papua New Guinea).

are moved from overpopulated regions elsewhere in Indonesia, such as Java and Bali, has resulted in widespread hostility. Thousands of people, mainly indigenous tribal peoples, but also Indonesian soldiers and settlers, are believed to have died in violent clashes, although allegations and accounts are difficult to verify. For example, there were reports of indiscriminate napalm bombings of remote valleys and the dropping of tribal leaders from helicopters to their deaths by the Indonesian air force in an effort to destroy the guerrilla army. There was a major rebellion in April/May 1971 which was crushed by Indonesian troops after six weeks of fighting. Inevitably those who were mostly affected by military operations were non-combatants.

As a result of continuing fighting several thousand refugees have crossed the borders into PNG; for example between 1984 and 1988 over 12,000 West Papuans fled there. Although most PNG politicians felt sympathy for the rebels they also felt threatened by the closeness of their giant Indonesian neighbour (which has over 150 million people to PNG's less than four million). There have been a number of accounts of Indonesian forces crossing into PNG to pursue OPM fighters and refugees. In some cases PNG has sent OPM members back to Irian Jaya and as a result the rebels were almost certainly executed by the Indonesians. Later it followed a more cautious policy, limiting access to the camps and moving them further away from border areas. More prominent refugees have not been granted asylum in PNG, but are more likely to be in exile in the Netherlands and elsewhere.

Hostility to the Indonesian settlers has mounted and a number have been killed by West Papuans. The settlers — many of whom migrated against their wishes — sometimes face poverty and hunger, as they have not always received the assistance promised by their government and the areas in which they have settled are not always fertile nor suited to the cultivation of rice. Despite these problems the Indonesian government has continued with the transmigration programme and in 1986 announced that it planned to settle three-quarters of a million people by 1989. To date, between 200,000 and 300,000 transmigrants have come to Irian Jaya, but not all stay. There are also at least 100,000 Indonesians who are not transmigrants — traders from Sulawesi (Celebes) are reported to be a prominent group. Transmigration has also had negative consequences for the environment, as

for example with logging in Asmat province. A number of human rights and environmental organizations have consistently expressed opposition to the transmigration programme[2] with the result that the World Bank, a major funder of the scheme, has been forced to be more strict in its monitoring. There are allegations that West Papuans have been deprived of compensation for their land and have been forced to work without pay on highways and public works; that travel passes are needed for travel from one village to another; and that West Papuans have been forced to use birth control against their will. Some observers fear that if transmigration continues the West Papuans will become a minority in their own country.

To date transmigration has mainly affected coastal areas but there are increasing indications that attention is turning to the more fertile Highland valleys. These valleys contain some of the largest ethnic groups such as the Dani. These groups initially suffered disastrously from outside intervention, not only by the introduction of infectious diseases but by attempts by the Indonesian authorities to change their "primitive" lifestyles, such as forcing them to give up traditional penis gourds and pigs' grease in favour of clothing, which rapidly resulted in the spread of skin diseases. Although the Dani and other tribes are technologically a "stone-age people" their culture has been one which has, over thousands of years, been adapted to their remote environment. By attempting to destroy local languages, cultures and lifestyles the government apparently hopes to destroy political aspirations also.

Yet OPM has managed to survive against all the odds. It has never been a large fighting force; present estimates are of about 500 hard-core fighters, and it was initially equipped with little more than bows and arrows. Today it has weaponry and its knowledge of the terrain and local sympathies have enabled it to conduct guerrilla operations against the Indonesian Army. There have been several military operations to counter it, such as *Operasi Sate* ("Operation Skewered Meat"), which in the last quarter of 1986 involved aerial bombardments, raids and house-to-house searches. There are also reports of widespread violations of human rights such as executions, "disappearances", detentions and torture. For example, in late 1983 Arnold Ap, a distinguished indigenous anthropologist, who had gained much local support for his efforts to promote Melanesian culture, was detained and tortured, and later died in police custody.

(See also *East Timorese; Papua New Guinea*)

---

[2]The Transmigration Programme also operates elsewhere in outlying islands such as Sumatra and Kalimantan, where indigenous tribal peoples have also been displaced.

Further References

Aboriginal Australians, MRG Report No. 35, 1988

East Timor and West Irian, MRG Report No. 42, 1982

The Maori of New Zealand, MRG Report No. 70, 1985

The Kanaks of New Caledonia, MRG Report No. 71, 1986

Fiji, MRG Report No. 75, 1987

APPENDIX 1.1

UNITED NATIONS CHARTER
(EXTRACTS)

TEXT

WE THE PEOPLES OF THE UNITED
NATIONS DETERMINED

to save succeeding generations from the scourge of war,
which twice in our lifetime has brought untold sorrow to
mankind, and

to reaffirm faith in fundamental human rights, in the
dignity and worth of the human person, in the equal rights
of men and women and of nations large and small, and

to establish conditions under which justice and respect
for the obligations arising from treaties and other sources
of international law can be maintained, and

to promote social progress and better standards of life
in larger freedom,

AND FOR THESE ENDS

to practise tolerance and live together in peace with one
another as good neighbours, and

to unite our strength to maintain international peace
and security, and

to ensure, by the acceptance of principles and the
institution of methods,

that armed force shall not be used, save in the common
interest, and

to employ international machinery for the promotion
of the economic and social advancement of all peoples.

HAVE RESOLVED TO COMBINE OUR EFFORTS
TO ACCOMPLISH THESE AIMS

Accordingly, our respective Governments, through
representatives assembled in the City of San Francisco,
who have exhibited their full powers found to be in good
and due form, have agreed to the present Charter of the
United Nations and do hereby establish an international
organization to be known as the United Nations.

CHAPTER X
The Economic and Social Council
Composition

Article 61

1. The Economic and Social Council shall consist of
   twenty-seven Members of the United Nations elected
   by the General Assembly.
2. Subject to the provisions of paragraph 3, nine members
   of the Economic and Social Council shall be elected
   each year for a term of three years.[1] A retiring member
   shall be eligible for immediate re-election.

   [1]General Assembly Resol. 1991 (XVIII). B. para.
   3. '*Further decides* that, without prejudice to the
   present distribution of seats in the Economic and
   Social Council the nine additional members shall be
   elected according to the following pattern:

   (*a*) Seven from African and Asian states;
   (*b*) One from Latin American states;
   (*c*) One from Western European and other states.'

3. At the first election after the increase in the membership of the Economic and Social Council from eighteen

to twenty-seven members, in addition to the members
elected in place of the six members whose term of
office expires at the end of that year, nine additional
members shall be elected. Of these nine additional
members, the term of office of three members so
elected shall expire at the end of one year, and of
three other members at the end of two years, in
accordance with arrangements made by the General
Assembly.

4. Each member of the Economic and Social Council
   shall have one representative.

Functions and Powers

Article 62

1. The Economic and Social Council may make or initiate
   studies and reports with respect to international
   economic, social, cultural, educational, health, and
   related matters and may make recommendations with
   respect to any such matters to the General Assembly,
   to the Members of the United Nations, and to the
   specialized agencies concerned.
2. It may make recommendations for the purpose of
   promoting respect for, and observance of, human
   rights and fundamental freedoms for all.
3. It may prepare draft conventions for submission to
   the General Assembly, with respect to matters falling
   within its competence.
4. It may call, in accordance with the rules prescribed
   by the United Nations, international conferences on
   matters falling within its competence.

Procedure

Article 68

The Economic and Social Council shall set up commissions
in economic and social fields and for the promotion of
human rights, and such other commissions as may be
required for the performance of its functions.

Article 69

The Economic and Social Council shall invite any Member
of the United Nations to participate, without vote, in its
deliberations on any matter of particular concern to that
Member.

Article 70

The Economic and Social Council may make arrangements for representatives of the specialized agencies
to participate, without vote, in its deliberations and in
those of the commissions established by it and for its
representatives to participate in the deliberations of the
specialized agencies.

Article 71

The Economic and Social Council may make suitable
arrangements for consultation with non-governmental
organizations which are concerned with matters within
its competence.

Such arrangements may be made with international
organizations and, where appropriate, with national
organizations after consultation with the Members of
the United Nations concerned.

Article 72

1. The Economic and Social Council shall adopt its own
   rules of procedure, including the method of selecting
   its President.

2. The Economic and Social Council shall meet as required in accordance with its rules, which shall include provisions for the convening of meetings on the request of a majority of its members.

CHAPTER XI
Declaration Regarding Non-Self-Governing Territories

Article 73

Members of the United Nations which have or assume responsibilities for the administration of territories whose peoples have not yet attained a full measure of self-government recognize the principle that the interests of the inhabitants of these territories are paramount, and accept as a sacred trust the obligation to promote to the utmost, within the system of international peace and security established by the present Charter, the well-being of the inhabitants of these territories, and to this end:

(*a*) to ensure, with due respect for the culture of the peoples concerned, their political, economic, social, and educational advancement, their just treatment, and their protection against abuses;

(*b*) to develop self-government, to take due account of the political aspirations of the peoples, and to assist them in the progressive development of their free political institutions, according to the particular circumstances of each territory and its peoples and their varying stages of advancement;

(*c*) to further international peace and security;

(*d*) to promote constructive measures of development, to encourage research, and to co-operate with one another and, when and where appropriate, with specialized international bodies with a view to the practical achievement of the social, economic, and scientific purposes set forth in this Article; and

(*e*) to transmit regularly to the Secretary-General for information purposes, subject to such limitation as security and constitutional considerations may require, statistical and other information of a technical nature, relating to economic, social, and educational conditions in the territories for which they are respectively responsible other than those territories to which Chapters XII and XIII apply.

Article 74

Members of the United Nations also agree that their policy in respect of the territories to which this Chapter applies, no less than in respect of their metropolitan areas, must be based on the general principle of good neighbourliness, due account being taken of the interests and well-being of the rest of the world, in social, economic, and commercial matters.

CHAPTER XII
International Trusteeship System

Article 75

The United Nations shall establish under its authority an international trusteeship system for the administration and supervision of such territories as may be placed thereunder by subsequent individual agreements. These territories are hereinafter referred to as trust territories.

Article 76

The basic objectives of the trusteeship system, in accordance with the Purposes of the United Nations laid down in Article 1 of the present Charter, shall be:

(*a*) to further international peace and security;

(*b*) to promote the political, economic, social, and educational advancement of the inhabitants of the trust territories, and their progressive development towards self-government or independence as may be appropriate to the particular circumstances of each territory and its peoples and the freely expressed wishes of the people concerned, and as may be provided by the terms of each trusteeship agreement;

(*c*) to encourage respect for human rights and for fundamental freedoms for all without distinction as to race, sex, language, or religion, and to encourage recognition of the interdependence of the peoples of the world; and

(*d*) to ensure equal treatment in social, economic and commercial matters for all Members of the United Nations and their nationals, and also equal treatment for the latter in the administration of justice, without prejudice to the attainment of the foregoing objectives and subject to the provisions of Article 80.

Article 77

1. The trusteeship system shall apply to such territories in the following categories as may be placed thereunder by means of trusteeship agreements:

(*a*) territories now held under mandate;

(*b*) territories which may be detached from enemy States as a result of the Second World War; and

(*c*) territories voluntarily placed under the system by States responsible for their administration.

2. It will be a matter for subsequent agreement as to which territories in the foregoing categories will be brought under the trusteeship system and upon what terms.

Article 78

The trusteeship system shall not apply to territories which have become Members of the United Nations, relationship among which shall be based on respect for the principle of sovereign equality.

Article 79

The terms of trusteeship for each territory to be placed under the trusteeship system, including any alteration or amendment, shall be agreed upon the States directly concerned, including the mandatory power in the case of territories held under mandate by a Member of the United Nations, and shall be approved as provided for in Articles 83 and 85.

Article 80

1. Except as may be agreed upon in individual trusteeship agreements, made under Articles 77, 79 and 81, placing each territory under the trusteeship system, and until such agreements have been concluded, nothing in this Chapter shall be construed in or of itself to alter in any manner the rights whatsoever of any States or any peoples or the terms of existing international instruments to which Members of the United Nations may respectively be parties.

2. Paragraph 1 of this article shall not be interpreted as giving grounds for delay or postponement of the

negotiation and conclusion of agreements for placing mandated and other territories under the trusteeship system as provided for in Article 77.

Article 81
The trusteeship agreement shall in each case include the terms under which the trust territory will be administered and designate the authority which will exercise the administration of the trust territory. Such authority, hereinafter called the administering authority, may be one or more States or the Organization itself.

Article 82
There may be designated, in any trusteeship agreement, a strategic area or areas which may include part or all of the trust territory to which the agreement applies, without prejudice to any special agreement or agreements made under Article 43.

Article 83
1. All functions of the United Nations relating to strategic areas, including the approval of the terms of the trusteeship agreements and of their alteration or amendment, shall be exercised by the Security Council.
2. The basic objectives set forth in Article 76 shall be applicable to the people of each strategic area.
3. The Security Council shall, subject to the provisions of the trusteeship agreements and without prejudice to security considerations, avail itself of the assistance of the Trusteeship Council to perform those functions of the United Nations under the trusteeship system relating to political, economic, social, and educational matters in the strategic areas.

Article 84
It shall be the duty of the administering authority to ensure that the trust territory shall play its part in the maintenance of international peace and security. To this end the administering authority may make use of volunteer forces, facilities, and assistance from the trust territory in carrying out the obligations towards the Security Council undertaken in this regard by the administering authority, as well as for local defence and the maintenance of law and order within the trust territory.

Article 85
1. The functions of the United Nations with regard to trusteeship agreements for all areas not designated as strategic, including the approval of the terms of the trusteeship agreements and of their alteration or amendment, shall be exercised by the General Assembly.
2. The Trusteeship Council, operating under the authority of the General Assembly, shall assist the General Assembly in carrying out these functions.

CHAPTER XIII
The Trusteeship Council
Composition

Article 86
1. The Trusteeship Council shall consist of the following Members of the United Nations:
   (*a*) those Members administering trust territories;
   (*b*) such of those Members mentioned by name in Article 23 as are not administering trust territories; and

(*c*) as many other Members elected for three-year terms by the General Assembly as may be necessary to ensure that the total number of members of the Trusteeship Council is equally divided between those Members of the United Nations which administer trust territories and those which do not.
2. Each member of the Trusteeship Council shall designate one specially qualified person to represent it therein.

Functions and Powers

Article 87
The General Assembly and, under its authority, the Trusteeship Council, in carrying out their functions, may:
   (*a*) consider reports submitted by the administering authority:
   (*b*) accept petitions and examine them in consultation with the administering authority;
   (*c*) provide for periodic visits to the respective trust territories at times agreed upon with the administering authority; and
   (*d*) take these and other actions in conformity with the terms of the trusteeship agreements.

Article 88
The Trusteeship Council shall formulate a questionnaire on the political, economic, social, and educational advancement of the inhabitants of each trust territory, and the administering authority for each trust territory within the competence of the General Assembly shall make an annual report to the General Assembly upon the basis of such questionnaire.

APPENDIX 1.2

THE UNITED NATIONS UNIVERSAL DECLARATION OF HUMAN RIGHTS

Whereas recognition of the inherent dignity and of the equal and inalienable rights of all members of the human family is the foundation of freedom, justice and peace in the world.
Whereas disregard and contempt for human rights have resulted in barbarous acts which have outraged the conscience of mankind, and the advent of a world in which human beings shall enjoy freedom of speech and belief and freedom from any fear and want has been proclaimed as the highest aspiration of the common people.
Whereas it is essential, if a man is not to be compelled to have recourse, as a last resort, to rebellion against tyranny and oppression, that human rights should be protected by the rule of law.
Whereas it is essential to promote the development of friendly relations between nations.
Whereas the peoples of the United Nations have in the Charter reaffirmed their faith in fundamental human

rights, in the dignity and worth of the human person and in the equal rights of men and women and have determined to promote social progress and better standards of life in larger freedom.

Whereas Member States have pledged themselves to achieve, in co-operation with the United Nations, the promotion of universal respect for and observance of human rights and fundamental freedoms.

Whereas a common understanding of these rights and freedoms is of the greatest importance for the full realization of this pledge.

Now, Therefore,

THE GENERAL ASSEMBLY
proclaims

THIS UNIVERSAL DECLARATION OF HUMAN RIGHTS as a common standard of achievement for all peoples and all nations, to the end that every individual and every organ of society, keeping this Declaration constantly in mind, shall strive by teaching and education to promote respect for these rights and freedoms and by progressive measures, national and international, to secure their universal and effective recognition and observance, both among the peoples of Member States themselves and among the peoples of territories under their jurisdiction.

Article 1.
All human beings are born free and equal in dignity and rights. They are endowed with reason and conscience and should act towards one another in a spirit of brotherhood.

Article 2.
Everyone is entitled to all the rights and freedoms set forth in this Declaration, without distinction of any kind, such as race, colour, sex, language, religion, political or other opinion, national or social origin, property, birth or other status.
Furthermore, no distinction shall be made on the basis of the political, jurisdictional or international status of the country or territory to which a person belongs, whether it be independent, trust, non-self-governing or under any other limitation of sovereignty.

Article 3.
Everyone has the right to life, liberty and security of person.

Article 4.
No one shall be held in slavery or servitude; slavery and the slave trade shall be prohibited in all their forms.

Article 5.
No one shall be subjected to torture or to cruel, inhuman or degrading treatment or punishment.

Article 6.
Everyone has the right to recognition everywhere as a person before the law.

Article 7.
All are equal before the law and are entitled without any discrimination to equal protection of the law. All are entitled to equal protection against any discrimination in violation of this Declaration and against any incitement to such discrimination.

Article 8.
Everyone has the right to an effective remedy by the competent national tribunals for acts violating the fundamental rights granted him by the constitution or by law.

Article 9.
No one shall be subjected to arbitrary arrest, detention or exile.

Article 10.
Everyone is entitled in full equality to a fair and public hearing by an independent and impartial tribunal, in the determination of his rights and obligations and of any criminal charge against him.

Article 11.
(1) Everyone charged with a penal offence has the right to be presumed innocent until proved guilty according to law in a public trial at which he has had all the guarantees necessary for his defence.
(2) No one shall be held guilty of any penal offence on account of any act or omission which did not constitute a penal offence, under national or international law, at the time when it was committed. Nor shall a heavier penalty be imposed than the one that was applicable at the time the penal offence was committed.

Article 12.
No one shall be subjected to arbitrary interference with his privacy, family, home or correspondence, nor to attacks upon his honour and reputation. Everyone has the right to the protection of the law against such interference or attacks.

Article 13.
(1) Everyone has the right to freedom of movement and residence within the borders of each state.
(2) Everyone has the right to leave any country, including his own, and to return to his country.

Article 14.
(1) Everyone has the right to seek and to enjoy in other countries asylum from persecution.
(2) This right may not be invoked in the case of prosecutions genuinely arising from non-political crimes or from acts contrary to the purposes and principles of the United Nations.

Article 15.
(1) Everyone has the right to a nationality.
(2) No one shall be arbitrarily deprived of his nationality nor denied the right to change his nationality.

Article 16.
(1) Men and women of full age, without any limitation due to race, nationality or religion, have the right to marry and to found a family. They are entitled to equal rights as to marriage, during marriage and at its dissolution.
(2) Marriage shall be entered into only with the free and full consent of the intending spouses.
(3) The family is the natural and fundamental group unit of society and is entitled to protection by society and the State.

Article 17.
(1) Everyone has the right to own property alone as well as in association with others.
(2) No one shall be arbitrarily deprived of his property.

Article 18.

Everyone has the right to freedom of thought, conscience and religion; this right includes freedom to change his religion or belief, and freedom, either alone or in community with others and in public or private, to manifest his religion or belief in teaching, practice, worship and observance.

Article 19.

Everyone has the right to freedom of opinion and expression; this right includes freedom to hold opinions without interference and to seek, receive and impart information and ideas through any media and regardless of frontiers.

Article 20.

(1) Everyone has the right to freedom of peaceful assembly and association.

(2) No one may be compelled to belong to an association.

Article 21.

(1) Everyone has the right to take part in the government of his country, directly or through freely chosen representatives.

(2) Everyone has the right of equal access to public service in his country.

(3) The will of the people shall be the basis of the authority of government; this will shall be expressed in periodic and genuine elections which shall be by universal and equal suffrage and shall be held by secret vote or by equivalent free voting procedures.

Article 22.

Everyone, as a member of society, has the right to social security and is entitled to realization, through national effort and international co-operation and in accordance with the organization and resources of each State, of the economic, social and cultural rights indispensable for his dignity and the free development of his personality.

Article 23.

(1) Everyone has the right to work, to free choice of employment, to just and favourable conditions of work and to protection against unemployment.

(2) Everyone, without any discrimination, has the right to equal pay for equal work.

(3) Everyone who works has the right to just and favourable remuneration ensuring for himself and his family an existence worthy of human dignity, and supplemented, if necessary, by other means of social protection.

(4) Everyone has the right to form and to join trade unions for the protection of his interest.

Article 24.

Everyone has the right to rest and leisure, including reasonable limitation of working hours and periodic holidays with pay.

Article 25.

(1) Everyone has the right to a standard of living adequate for the health and well-being of himself and of his family, including food, clothing, housing and medical care and necessary social services, and the right to security in the event of unemployment, sickness, disability, widowhood, old age or other lack of livelihood in circumstances beyond his control.

(2) Motherhood and childhood are entitled to special care and assistance. All children, whether born in or out of wedlock, shall enjoy the same social protection.

Article 26.

(1) Everyone has the right to education. Education shall be free, at least in the elementary and fundamental stages. Elementary education shall be compulsory. Technical and professional education shall be made generally available and higher education shall be equally accessible to all on the basis of merit.

(2) Education shall be directed to the full development of the human personality and to the strengthening of respect for human rights and fundamental freedoms. It shall promote understanding, tolerance and friendship among all nations, racial or religious groups, and shall further the activities of the United Nations for the maintenance of peace.

(3) Parents have a prior right to choose the kind of education that shall be given to their children.

Article 27.

(1) Everyone has the right freely to participate in the cultural life of the community, to enjoy the arts and to share in scientific advancement and its benefits.

(2) Everyone has the right to the protection of the moral and material interests resulting from any scientific, literary or artistic production of which he is the author.

Article 28.

Everyone is entitled to a social and international order in which the rights and freedoms set forth in this Declaration can be fully realized.

Article 29.

(1) Everyone has duties to the community in which alone the free and full development of his personality is possible.

(2) In the exercise of his rights and freedoms, everyone shall be subject only to such limitations as are determined by law solely for the purpose of securing due recognition and respect for the rights and freedoms of others and of meeting the just requirements of morality, public order and the general welfare in a democratic society.

(3) These rights and freedoms may in no case be exercised contrary to the purposes and principles of the United Nations.

Article 30.

Nothing in this Declaration may be interpreted as implying for any State, group or person any right to engage in any activity or to perform any act aimed at the destruction of any of the rights and freedoms set forth herein.

APPENDIX 1.3

UNITED NATIONS COVENANT ON CIVIL AND POLITICAL RIGHTS 1966 (EXTRACTS)

Article 27

In those States in which ethnic, religious or linguistic minorities exist, persons belonging to such minorities shall not be denied the right, in community with the other members of their group, to enjoy their own culture, to profess and practice their own religion, or to use their own language.

APPENDIX 1.4

UNITED NATIONS CONVENTION ON THE PREVENTION AND PUNISHMENT OF THE CRIME OF GENOCIDE, 1948 (EXTRACTS)

The Contracting Parties

Having considered the declaration made by the General Assembly of the United Nations in its resolution 96 (I) dated 11 December 1946 that genocide is a crime under international law, contrary to the spirit and aims of the United Nations and condemned by the civilized world;

Recognizing that at all periods of history genocide has inflicted great losses on humanity; and

Being convinced that, in order to liberate mankind from such an odious scourge, international co-operation is required,

Hereby agree as hereinafter provided:

Article I
The Contracting Parties confirm that genocide, whether committed in time of peace or in time of war, is a crime under international law which they undertake to prevent and to punish.

Article II
In the present Convention, genocide means any of the following acts committed with intent to destroy, in whole or in part, a national, ethnical, racial or religious group, as such:

(*a*) Killing members of the group;
(*b*) Causing serious bodily or mental harm to members of the group;
(*c*) Deliberately inflicting on the group conditions of life calculated to bring about its physical destruction in whole or in part;
(*d*) Imposing measures intending to prevent births within the group;
(*e*) Forcibly transferring children of the group to another group.

Article III
The following acts shall be punishable:

(*a*) Genocide;
(*b*) Conspiracy to commit genocide;
(*c*) Direct and public incitement to commit genocide;
(*d*) Attempt to commit genocide;
(*e*) Complicity in genocide.

Article IV
Persons committing genocide or any of the other acts enumerated in Article III shall be punished, whether they are constitutionally responsible rulers, public officials or private individuals.

Article V
The Contracting Parties undertake to enact, in accordance with their respective Constitutions, the necessary legislation to give effect to the provisions of the present Convention and, in particular, to provide effective penalties for persons guilty of genocide or of any of the other acts enumerated in Article III.

Article VI
Persons charged with genocide or any of the other acts enumerated in Article III shall be tried by a competent tribunal of the State in the territory of which the act was committed, or by such international penal tribunal as may have jurisdiction with respect to those Contracting Parties which shall have accepted its jurisdiction.

Article VII
Genocide and other acts enumerated in Article III shall not be considered as political crimes for the purpose of extradition.

The Contracting Parties pledge themselves in such cases to grant extradition in accordance with their laws and treaties in force.

Article VIII
Any Contracting Party may call upon the competent organs of the United Nations to take such action under the Charter of the United Nations as they consider appropriate for the prevention and suppression of acts of genocide or any of the other acts enumerated in Article III.

Article IX
Disputes between the Contracting Parties relating to the interpretation, application or fulfilment of the present Convention, including those relating to the responsibility of a State for genocide or for any of the other acts enumerated in Article III, shall be submitted to the International Court of Justice at the request of any of the parties to the dispute.

APPENDIX 1.5

CANADA: THE CONSTITUTION ACT 1982: THE CANADIAN CHARTER OF RIGHTS AND FREEDOMS (EXTRACTS)

Section 15
(1) Every individual is equal before and under the law and has the right to equal protection and equal benefit of the law without discrimination and, in particular, without discrimination based on race, national or ethnic origin, colour, religion, sex, age or mental or physical disability.
(2) Sub-section (1) does not preclude any law, program or activity that has as its object the amelioration of conditions of disadvantaged individuals or groups including those that are disadvantaged because of race, national or ethnic origin, colour, religion, sex, age or mental or physical disability.

Section 16
(1) English and French are the official languages of Canada and have equality of status and equal rights and privileges as to their use in all institutions of the Parliament and Government of Canada.

Section 35
(1) The existing aboriginal and treaty rights of the aboriginal peoples of Canada are hereby recognized and affirmed.
(2) In this Act, 'aboriginal peoples of Canada', includes the Indians, Inuit and Metis peoples of Canada.

APPENDIX 1.6

THE GREENLAND HOME RULE ACT
ACT. NO. 577 OF 29 NOVEMBER 1978
(EXTRACTS)

We, Margrethe the Second, by the Grace of God Queen of Denmark make it known:

Recognizing the exceptional position which Greenland occupies within the Realm nationally, culturally and geographically, the Folketing has in conformity with the decision of the Greenland Provincial Council passed and We by Our Royal Assent confirmed the following Act about the constitutional position of Greenland within the Realm:

CHAPTER 1
HOME RULE AUTHORITIES

Section 1
(1) Greenland is a distinct community within the Kingdom of Denmark. Within the framework of the unity of the Realm, the Greenland home rule authorities shall conduct Greenland affairs in accordance with the provisions laid down in this Act.
(2) The Greenland home rule authorities shall consist of an assembly elected in Greenland, to be called the Landsting, and an administration headed by a Landsstyre (Executive).

Section 2
(1) Members of the Landsting shall be elected for a four-year term in general, direct and secret elections.
(2) Detailed rules on elections, including such matters as the franchise, eligibility for election, and the number of members of the Landsting, shall be laid down by Act of the Landsting.
(3) The Landsting shall make its own standing orders.

Section 3
The Landsting shall elect the Chairman and the other members of the Landsstyre. The Chairman of the Landsstyre shall assign responsibilities between its members.

CHAPTER 2
Powers of the Home Rule Authorities

Section 4
(1) The home rule authorities may determine that jurisdiction in any field listed in the Schedule to this Act, or in part of such field, shall be transferred to the home rule authorities.
(2) The home rule authorities shall exercise legislative and executive power in fields transferred under subsection (1), and shall assume responsibility for expenditure associated with them.
(3) The same shall apply where the central authorities of the Realm, after negotiation with the home rule authorities, determine that jurisdiction in such fields or parts of such fields shall be transferred to the home rule authorities.
(4) Bills regarding such fields of jurisdiction as are passed by the Landsting and signed by the Chairman of the Landsstyre shall be called Acts of the Landsting.

Section 5
(1) Where jurisdiction over a field or part of a field listed in the Schedule to this Act has not been transferred to the home rule authorities under section 4, the central authorities of the Realm may after negotiation with the home rule authorities by statute determine that the home rule authorities shall assume regulatory jurisdiction for and administer it. Subsidies to be paid in such fields shall be fixed by statute.
(2) Draft regulations regarding such fields of jurisdiction as are passed by the Landsting and signed by the Chairman of the Landsstyre shall be called Landsting Regulations.

Section 6
(1) Landsting Bills and draft Landsting Regulations which have been passed cannot be carried into force until they have been signed by the Chairman of the Landsstyre and promulgated in accordance with the provisions laid down by the Act of the Landsting.
(2) Within a period of 8 days the Landsstyre may resolve that a Bill or draft Regulation is not to be signed until passed by the following session of the Landsting. Should that session fail to pass it unamended it shall lapse.

Section 7
(1) The central authorities of the Realm may after negotiation with and having secured the consent of the home rule authorities by statute determine that jurisdiction in fields not listed in the Schedule to this Act shall be transferred to the home rule authorities, section 4 (2) and (4) or section 5 applying correspondingly.
(2) In determining in which fields jurisdiction should be transferred to the home rule authorities under sub-section (1), regard shall be had to the unity of the Realm and to the desirability of the home rule authorities' receiving an extensive role in matters which particularly affect Greenland interests.

Section 8
(1) The resident population of Greenland has fundamental rights to the natural resources of Greenland.
(2) To safeguard the rights of the resident population in respect of non-living resources and to protect the interests of the unity of the Realm, it shall be enacted by statute that preliminary study, prospecting and the exploitation of these resources are to be regulated by agreement between the Government and the Landsstyre.
(3) Before any agreement under subsection (2) is entered into, any member of the Landsstyre may demand that the matter be laid before the Landsting, which may determine that the Landsstyre may not consent to an agreement of the proposed content.

Section 9
(1) Greenlandic shall be the principal language. Danish must be thoroughly taught.
(2) Either language may be used for official purposes.

Section 10
(1) The home rule authorities shall be subject to such obligations arising out of treaties and other international rules as at any time are binding on the Realm.
(2) The powers delegated to international authorities under section 20 of the Constitution shall at all

times prevail over the powers of the home rule authorities.

(3) The Government may order the home rule authorities to take such measures as may be necessary to ensure the observance of subsections (1) and (2).

CHAPTER 3
Relations with the central authorities

Section 11

(1) The central authorities of the Realm shall have jurisdiction in questions affecting the foreign relations of the Realm.

(2) Measures under consideration by the home rule authorities which would be of substantial importance for the foreign relations of the Realm, including participation by the Realm in international cooperation, shall be discussed with the central authorities before any decision is taken.

Section 12

(1) Bills which include provisions which exclusively concern Greenland shall be referred to the home rule authorities for their comments before they are introduced in the Folketing.

(2) Draft administrative orders which include provisions which exclusively concern Greenland shall be referred to the home rule authorities for their comments before they are issued.

(3) Statues and administrative orders which are of particular importance to Greenland shall be referred to the home rule authorities for their comments before being put into force in Greenland.

Section 13

Treaties which require the assent of the Folketing and which particularly affect Greenland interests shall be referred to the home rule authorities for their comments before they are concluded.

Section 14

(1) Unless the central authorities in individual cases otherwise determine, the home rule authorities' comments shall be submitted within six months after the date on which the proposals were referred to them under sections 12 and 13.

(2) If proposals cannot be referred to the home rule authorities due to compelling circumstances, the statute, administrative provision or treaty shall be referred to the home rule authorities for their comments as soon as possible.

Section 15

(1) Within the framework of section 11 the Government shall after consultation with the Landsstyre lay down guidelines for the handling of matters of particular interest to Greenland in the European Community Institutions.

(2) The home rule authorities shall be kept informed of proposed legislation before the Council of European Communities which particularly affects Greenland interests.

Section 16

(1) The home rule authorities may demand that in countries in which Greenland has special commercial interests Danish diplomatic missions employ officers specifically to attend to such interests. The central authorities may determine that expenditure to this end be borne by the home rule authorities.

(2) The central authorities may after negotiation with the home rule authorities empower the home rule authorities to advance special Greenland interests by taking part in international negotiations of special importance for Greenland's commercial life.

(3) Where matters of particular interest to Greenland are at issue, the central authorities may on a request by the home rule authorities authorize them to negotiate directly, with the cooperation of the Foreign Service, provided such negotiation is not considered incompatible with the unity of the Realm.

Section 17

(1) The central authorities' chief representative in Greenland shall be the Rigsombudsmand (Commissioner).

(2) The home rule authorities may invite the Rigsombudsmand to take part in debates in the Landsting or the Landsstyre.

(3) The home rule authorities shall inform the Rigsombudsmand as soon as possible of new Acts of the Landsting and Landsting Regulations, and of other legislation of general application made by the home rule authorities.

Section 18

(1) Should any doubt arise between the central authorities and the home rule authorities concerning their respective jurisdictions, the question shall be laid before a board consisting of two members nominated by the Government, two members nominated by the home rule authorities and three judges of the Supreme Court nominated by its President, one of whom shall be nominated as Chairman.

(2) If the four members nominated by the Government and the home rule authorities reach agreement the question shall be considered settled. If these four fail to reach agreement the question shall be decided by the three Supreme Court judges.

(3) The Government may suspend an enactment or decision of the home rule authorities which has been placed before the board until such time as the board's decision is taken.

CHAPTER 4
Entry into force and transitional provisions

Section 19

(1) Statutory provisions and regulations applicable to Greenland shall remain in force subject to such changes as arise out of this Act, until amended or repealed by the appropriate authority.

Section 20

(1) The date on which this Act is to enter into force shall be fixed by statute.

(2) The Rigsombudsmand shall take up the duties formerly exercised by the Governor of Greenland, with such changes as arise out of this Act.

APPENDIX 1.7

US JOINT RESOLUTION

Passed October 1988 to acknowledge the contribution of the Iroquois Confederacy of Nations to the Development of the United States Constitution and to Reaffirm the Continuing Government-to-Government Relationship Between Indian Tribes and the United States Established in the Constitution.

It was resolved by the Senate (the House of Representatives concurring), that:

Whereas, the original framers of the constitution, including most notably, George Washington and Benjamin Franklin, are known to have greatly admired the concepts, principles and government practices of the Six Nations of the Iroquois Confederacy; and

Whereas, the Confederation of the original thirteen colonies into one Republic was explicitly modeled upon the Iroquois Confederacy as were many of the democratic principles which were incorporated into the Constitution itself; and,

Whereas, since the formation of the United States, the Congress has recognized the sovereign status of Indian Tribes, and has, through the exercise of powers reserved to the Federal Government in the Commerce Clause of the Constitution (art.I, s8, cl.3), dealt with Indian Tribes on a government-to-government basis and has, through the Treaty Clause (art.II, s2, cl.2), entered into 370 treaties with Indian tribal nations; and

Whereas from the first treaty entered into with an Indian nation, the Treaty with the Delaware Indians of September 17, 1778, and thereafter in every Indian Treaty until the cessation of treaty-making in 1871, the Congress has assumed a trust responsibility and obligation to Indian Tribes and their members to "exercise the utmost good faith in dealings with the Indians" as provided for the Northwest Ordinance of 1987 (I Stat.50); and

Whereas, Congress has consistently reaffirmed these fundamental policies over the past 200 years through legislation specifically designed to honor this special relationship; and

Whereas, the judicial system of the United States has consistently recognized and reaffirmed this special relationship;

Now, therefore be it Resolved by the Senate and House of Representatives of the United States in Congress assembled, that:

1) The Congress, on the occasion of the 200th anniversary of the signing of the United States Constitution, acknowledges the historical debt which this Republic of the United States of America owes to the Iroquois Confederacy and other Indian Nations for their demonstration of enlightened, democratic principles of government and their example of a free association of independent Indian Nations;
2) The Congress also hereby reaffirms the constitutionally recognized government-to-government relationship with Indian Tribes which has historically been the cornerstone of this nation's official Indian Policy;
3) The Congress specifically acknowledges and reaffirms the trust responsibility and obligation of the United States Government to Indian Tribes, including

Alaska Natives, for their preservation, protection and enhancement, including the provision of health, education, social and economic assistance programs as necessary, to assist Tribes to perform their governmental responsibility to provide for the social and economic Well-being of their members and to preserve tribal cultural identity and heritage; and
4) The Congress also acknowledges the need to exercise the utmost good faith in upholding its treaties with the various Tribes, as the Tribes understood them to be, and the duty of a great nation to uphold its legal and moral obligations for the benefit of all its citizens so that they and their posterity may also continue to enjoy the rights they have enshrined in the United States Constitution for time immemorial.

APPENDIX 2.1

ILO CONVENTION 107 (EXTRACT) CONVENTION CONCERNING THE PROTECTION AND INTEGRATION OF INDIGENOUS AND OTHER TRIBAL AND SEMI-TRIBAL POPULATIONS IN INDEPENDENT COUNTRIES

The General Conference of the International Labour Organisation,

Having been convened at Geneva by the Governing Body of the International Labour Office, and having met in its Fortieth Session on 5 June 1957 and

Having decided upon the adoption of certain proposals with regard to the protection and integration of indigenous and other tribal and semi-tribal populations in independent countries, which is the sixth item on the agenda of the session, and

Having determined that these proposals shall take the form of an international Convention, and

Considering that the Declaration of Philadelphia affirms that all human beings have the right to pursue both their material well-being and their spiritual development in conditions of freedom and dignity of economic security and equal opportunity, and

Considering that there exist in various independent countries indigenous and other tribal and semi-tribal populations which are not yet integrated into the national community and whose social, economic or cultural situation hinders them from benefiting fully from the rights and advantages enjoyed by other elements of the population, and

Considering it desirable both for humanitarian reasons and in the interest of the countries concerned to promote continued action to improve the living and working conditions of these populations by simultaneous action in respect of all the factors which have hitherto prevented them from sharing fully in the progress of the national community of which they form part, and

Considering that the adoption of general international standards on the subject will facilitate action to assure the protection of the populations concerned, their progressive integration into their respective national communities, and the improvement of their living and working conditions, and

Noting that these standards have been framed with the co-operation of the United Nations, the Food and Agriculture Organisation of the United Nations, the United Nations Educational, Scientific and Cultural Organisation and the World Health Organisation, at appropriate levels and in their respective fields, and that it is proposed to seek their continuing co-operation in promoting and securing the application of these standards,

adopts this twenty-sixth day of June of the year one thousand nine hundred and fifty-seven the following Convention, which may be cited as the Indigenous and Tribal Populations Convention, 1957:

PART I. GENERAL POLICY

Article 1

1. This Convention applies to—

    (a) members of tribal or semi-tribal populations in independent countries whose social and economic conditions are at a less advanced stage than the stage reached by the other sections of the national community, and whose status is regulated wholly or partially by their own customs or traditions or by special laws or regulations;

    (b) members of tribal or semi-tribal populations in independent countries which are regarded as indigenous on account of their descent from the populations which inhabited the country, or a geographical region to which the country belongs, at the time of conquest or colonisation and which, irrespective of their legal status, live more in conformity with the social, economic and cultural institutions of that time than with the institution of the nation to which they belong.

2. For the purposes of this Convention, the term 'semi-tribal' includes groups and persons who, although they are in the process of losing their tribal characteristics, are not yet integrated into the national community.

3. The indigenous and other tribal or semi-tribal populations mentioned in paragraphs 1 and 2 of this Article are referred to hereinafter as 'the populations concerned'.

Article 2

1. Governments shall have the primary responsibility for developing co-ordinated and systematic action for the protection of the populations concerned and their progressive integration into the life of their respective countries.

2. Such action shall include measures for—

    (a) enabling the said populations to benefit on an equal footing from the rights and opportunities which national laws or regulations grant to the other elements of the population;

    (b) promoting the social, economic and cultural development of these populations and raising their standard of living;

    (c) creating possibilities of national integration to the exclusion of measures tending towards the artificial assimilation of these populations.

3. The primary objective of all such action shall be the fostering of individual dignity, and the advancement of individual usefulness and initiative.

4. Recourse to force or coercion as a means of promoting the integration of these populations into the national community shall be excluded.

Article 3

1. So long as the social, economic and cultural conditions of the populations concerned prevent them from enjoying the benefits of the general laws of the country to which they belong, special measures shall be adopted for the protection of the institutions, persons, property and labour of these populations.

2. Care shall be taken to ensure that such special measures of protection—

    (a) are not used as a means of creating or prolonging a state of segregation; and

    (b) will be continued only so long as there is need for special protection and only to the extent that such protection is necessary.

3. Enjoyment of the general rights of citizenship, without discrimination, shall not be prejudiced in any way by such special measures of protection.

Article 4

In applying the provisions of this Convention relating to the integration of the populations concerned—

    (a) due account shall be taken of the cultural and religious values and of the forms of social control existing among these populations, and of the nature of the problems which face them both as groups and as individuals when they undergo social and economic change;

    (b) the danger involved in disrupting the values and institutions of the said populations unless they can be replaced by appropriate substitutes which the groups concerned are willing to accept shall be recognised;

    (c) policies aimed at mitigating the difficulties experienced by these populations in adjusting themselves to new conditions of life and work shall be adopted.

Article 5

In applying the provisions of this Convention relating to the protection and integration of the populations concerned, governments shall—

    (a) seek the collaboration of these populations and of their representatives;

    (b) provide these populations with opportunities for the full development of their initiative;

    (c) stimulate by all possible means the development among these populations of civil liberties and the establishment of or participation in elective institutions.

Article 6

The improvement of the conditions of life and work and level of education of the populations concerned shall be given high priority in plans for the over-all economic development of areas inhabited by these populations. Special projects for economic development of the areas in question shall also be so designed as to promote such improvement.

Article 7

1. In defining the rights and duties of the populations concerned regard shall be had to their customary laws.
2. These populations shall be allowed to retain their own customs and institutions where these are not incompatible with the national legal system or the objectives of integration programmes.
3. The application of the preceding paragraphs of this Article shall not prevent members of these populations from exercising, according to their individual capacity, the rights granted to all citizens and from assuming the corresponding duties.

Article 8

To the extent consistent with the interests of the national community and with the national legal system—

   (*a*) the methods of social control practised by the populations concerned shall be used as far as possible for dealing with crimes or offences committed by members of these populations;
   (*b*) where use of such methods of social control is not feasible, the customs of these populations in regard to penal matters shall be borne in mind by the authorities and courts dealing with such cases.

Article 9

Except in cases prescribed by law for all citizens the exaction from the members of the populations concerned of compulsory personal services in any form, whether paid or unpaid, shall be prohibited and punishable by law.

Article 10

1. Persons belonging to the populations concerned shall be specially safeguarded against the improper application of preventive detention and shall be able to take legal proceedings for the effective protection of their fundamental rights.
2. In imposing penalties laid down by general law on members of these populations account shall be taken of the degree of cultural development of the populations concerned.
3. Preference shall be given to methods of rehabilitation rather than confinement in prison.

PART II. LAND

Article 11

The right of ownership, collective or individual, of the members of the populations concerned over the lands which these populations traditionally occupy shall be recognised.

Article 12

1. The populations concerned shall not be removed without their free consent from their habitual territories except in accordance with national laws and regulations for reasons relating to national security, or in the interest of national economic development or of the health of the said populations.
2. When in such cases removal of these populations is necessary as an exceptional measure, they shall be provided with lands of quality at least equal to that of the lands previously occupied by them, suitable to provide for their present needs and future development. In cases where chances of alternative employment exist and where the popu-

lations concerned prefer to have compensation in money or in kind, they shall be so compensated under appropriate guarantees.
3. Persons thus removed shall be fully compensated for any resulting loss or injury.

Article 13

1. Procedures for the transmission of rights of ownership and use of land which are established by the customs of the populations concerned shall be respected, within the framework of national laws and regulations, in so far as they satisfy the needs of these populations and do not hinder their economic and social development.
2. Arrangements shall be made to prevent persons who are not members of the populations concerned from taking advantage of these customs or of lack of understanding of the laws on the part of the members of these populations to secure the ownership or use of the lands belonging to such members.

Article 14

National agrarian programmes shall secure to the populations concerned treatment equivalent to that accorded to other sections of the national community with regard to—

   (*a*) the provision of more land for these populations when they have not the area necessary for providing the essentials of a normal existence, or for any possible increase in their numbers;
   (*b*) the provision of the means required to promote the development of the lands which these populations already possess.

PART III. RECRUITMENT AND CONDITIONS OF EMPLOYMENT

Article 15

1. Each Member shall, within the framework of national laws and regulations, adopt special measures to ensure the effective protection with regard to recruitment and conditions of employment of workers belonging to the populations concerned so long as they are not in a position to enjoy the protection granted by law to workers in general.
2. Each Member shall do everything possible to prevent all discrimination between workers belonging to the populations concerned and other workers, in particular as regards—

   (*a*) admission to employment, including skilled employment;
   (*b*) equal remuneration for work of equal value;
   (*c*) medical and social assistance, the prevention of employment injuries, workmen's compensation, industrial hygiene and housing;
   (*d*) the right of association and freedom for all lawful trade union activities, and the right to conclude collective agreements with employers or employers' organisations.

PART IV. VOCATIONAL TRAINING, HANDICRAFTS AND RURAL INDUSTRIES

Article 16

Persons belonging to the populations concerned shall enjoy the same opportunities as other citizens in respect of vocational training facilities.

Article 17
1. Whenever programmes of vocational training of general application do not meet the special needs of persons belonging to the populations concerned governments shall provide special training facilities for such persons.
2. These special training facilities shall be based on a careful study of the economic environment, stage of cultural development and practical needs of the various occupational groups among the said populations; they shall, in particular, enable the persons concerned to receive the training necessary for occupations for which these populations have traditionally shown aptitude.
3. These special training facilities shall be provided only so long as the stage of cultural development of the populations concerned requires them; with the advance of the process of integration they shall be replaced by the facilities provided for other citizens.

Article 18
1. Handicrafts and rural industries shall be encouraged as factors in the economic development of the populations concerned in a manner which will enable these populations to raise their standard of living and adjust themselves to modern methods of production and marketing.
2. Handicrafts and rural industries shall be developed in a manner which preserves the cultural heritage of these populations and improves their artistic values and particular modes of cultural expression.

PART V. SOCIAL SECURITY AND HEALTH

Article 19
Existing social security schemes shall be extended progressively, where practicable, to cover—

  (*a*) wage earners belonging to the populations concerned;
  (*b*) other persons belonging to these populations.

Article 20
1. Governments shall assume the responsibility for providing adequate health services for the populations concerned.
2. The organisation of such services shall be based on systematic studies of the social, economic and cultural conditions of the populations concerned.
3. The development of such services shall be co-ordinated with general measures of social, economic and cultural development.

PART VI. EDUCATION AND MEANS OF COMMUNICATION

Article 21
Measures shall be taken to ensure that members of the populations concerned have the opportunity to acquire education at all levels on an equal footing with the rest of the national community.

Article 22
1. Education programmes for the populations concerned shall be adapted, as regards methods and techniques, to the stage these populations have reached in the process of social, economic and cultural integration in the national community.

2. The formulation of such programmes shall normally be preceded by ethnological surveys.

Article 23
1. Children belonging to the populations concerned shall be taught to read and write in their mother tongue or, where this is not practicable, in the language most commonly used by the group to which they belong.
2. Provision shall be made for a progressive transition from the mother tongue or the vernacular language to the national language or to one of the official languages of the country.
3. Appropriate measures shall, as far as possible, be taken to preserve the mother tongue or the vernacular language.

Article 24
The imparting of general knowledge and skills that will help children to become integrated into the national community shall be an aim of the primary education for the populations concerned.

Article 25
Educational measures shall be taken among other sections of the national community and particularly among those that are in most direct contact with the populations concerned with the object of eliminating prejudices that they may harbour in respect of these populations.

Article 26
1. Governments shall adopt measures to the social and cultural characteristics of the populations concerned, to make known to them their rights and duties, especially in regard to labour and social welfare.
2. If necessary this shall be done by means of written translations and through the use of media of mass communication in the languages of these populations.

PART VII. ADMINISTRATION

Article 27
1. The governmental authority responsible for the matters covered in the Convention shall create or develop agencies to administer the programmes involved.
2. These programmes shall include—

  (*a*) planning, co-ordination and execution of appropriate measures for the social, economic and cultural development of the populations concerned;
  (*b*) proposing of legislative and other measures to the competent authorities;
  (*c*) supervision of the application of these measures.

PART VIII. GENERAL PROVISIONS

Article 28
The nature and the scope of the measures to be taken to give effect to this Convention shall be determined in a flexible manner, having regard to the conditions characteristic of each country.

Article 29

The application of the provisions of this Convention shall not affect benefits conferred on the populations concerned in pursuance of other Conventions and Recommendations.

APPENDIX 2.2

INTERNATIONAL CONVENTION ON THE ELIMINATION OF ALL FORMS OF RACIAL DISCRIMINATION, 1966 (EXTRACTS)

PART 1

Article 1

1. In this Convention, the term, 'racial discrimination' shall mean any distinction, exclusion, restriction or preference based on race, colour, descent, or national or ethnic origin which has the purpose or effect of nullifying or impairing the recognition, enjoyment or exercise, on an equal footing, of human rights and fundamental freedoms in the political, economic, social, cultural or any other field of public life.

2. This Convention shall not apply to distinctions, exclusions, restrictions or preferences made by a State Party to this Convention between citizens and non-citizens.

3. Nothing in this Convention may be interpreted as affecting in any way the legal provisions of States Parties concerning nationality, citizenship or naturalization, provided that such provisions do not discriminate against any particular nationality.

4. Special measures taken for the sole purpose of securing adequate advancement of certain racial or ethnic groups or individuals requiring such protection as may be necessary in order to ensure such groups or individuals equal enjoyment or exercise of human rights and fundamental freedoms shall not be deemed racial discrimination, provided, however, that such measures do not, as a consequence, lead to the maintenance of separate rights for different racial groups and that they shall not be continued after the objectives for which they were taken have been achieved.

Article 2

1. States Parties condemn racial discrimination and undertake to pursue by all appropriate means and without delay a policy of eliminating racial discrimination in all its forms and promoting understanding among all races, and, to this end:

   (*a*) Each State Party undertakes to engage in no act or practice of racial discrimination against persons, groups of persons or institutions and to ensure that all public authorities and public institutions, national and local, shall act in conformity with this obligation;

   (*b*) Each State Party undertake not to sponsor, defend or support racial discrimination by any persons or organization;

   (*c*) Each State Party shall take effective measures to review governmental, national and local policies, and to amend, rescind or nullify any laws and regulations which have the effect of creating or perpetuating racial discrimination wherever it exists;

   (*d*) Each State Party shall prohibit and bring to an end, by all appropriate means, including legislation as required by circumstances, racial discrimination by any persons, group or organization;

   (*e*) Each State Party undertakes to encourage, where appropriate, integrationist multi-racial organizations and movements and other means of eliminating barriers between races, and to discourage anything which tends to strengthen racial division.

2. States Parties shall, when the circumstances so warrant, take, in the social, economic, cultural and other fields, special and concrete measures to ensure the adequate development and protection of certain racial groups or individuals belonging to them, for the purpose of guaranteeing them the full and equal enjoyment of human rights and fundamental freedoms. These measures shall in no case entail as a consequence the maintenance of unequal or separate rights for different racial groups after the objectives for which they were taken have been achieved.

Article 3

States parties particularly condemn racial segregation and *apartheid* and undertake to prevent, prohibit and eradicate all practices of this nature in territories under their jurisdiction.

Article 4

States Parties condemn all propaganda and all organizations which are based on ideas or theories of superiority of one race or group of persons of one colour or ethnic origin, or which attempt to justify or promote racial hatred and discrimination in any form, and undertake to adopt immediate and positive measures designed to eradicate all incitement to, or acts of, such discrimination and, to this end, with due regard to the principles embodied in the Universal Declaration of Human Rights and the rights expressly set forth in Article 5 of this Convention, *inter alia*:

   (*a*) Shall declare an offence punishable by law all dissemination of ideas based on racial superiority or hatred, incitement to racial discrimination, as well as all acts of violence or incitement to such acts against any race or group of persons of another colour or ethnic origin, and also the provision of any assistance to racist activities, including the financing thereof;

   (*b*) Shall declare illegal and prohibit organizations, and also organized and all other propaganda activities, which promote and incite racial discrimination, and shall recognize participation in such organizations or activities as an offence punishable by law;

   (*c*) Shall not permit public authorities or public institutions, national or local, to promote or incite racial discrimination.

Article 5

In compliance with the fundamental obligations laid down in Article 2 of this Convention, States Parties undertake to prohibit and to eliminate racial discrimination in all its forms and to guarantee the right of everyone, without distinction as to race, colour, or national or ethnic origin, to equality before the law, notably in the enjoyment of the following rights:

(*a*) The right to equal treatment before the tribunals and all other organs administering justice;

(*b*) The right to security of person and protection by the State against violence or bodily harm, whether inflicted by government officials or by any individual, group or institution;

(*c*) Political rights, in particular the rights to participate in elections—to vote and to stand for election—on the basis of universal and equal suffrage, to take part in the Government as well as in the conduct of public affairs at any level and to have equal access to public service;

(*d*) Other civil rights, in particular:

(i) The right to freedom of movement and residence within the border of the State;

(ii) The right to leave any country, including one's own, and to return to one's country;

(iii) The right to nationality;

(iv) The right to marriage and choice of spouse;

(v) The right to own property alone as well as in association with others;

(vi) The right to inherit;

(vii) The right to freedom of thought, conscience and religion;

(viii) The right to freedom of opinion and expression;

(ix) The right to freedom of peaceful assembly and association;

(*e*) Economic, social and cultural rights, in particular:

(i) The rights to work, to free choice of employment, to just and favourable conditions of work, to protection against unemployment, to equal pay for equal work, to just and favourable remuneration;

(ii) The right to form and join trade unions;

(iii) The right to housing;

(iv) The right to public health, medical care, social security and social services;

(v) The right to education and training;

(vi) The right to equal participation in cultural activities;

(*f*) The right of access to any place or service intended for use by the general public, such as transport, hotels, restaurants, cafés, theatres and parks.

Article 6

States Parties shall assure to everyone within their jurisdiction effective protection and remedies, through the competent national tribunals and other State institutions, against any acts of racial discrimination which violate his human rights and fundamental freedoms contrary to this Convention, as well as the right to seek from such tribunals just and adequate reparation or satisfaction for any damage suffered as a result of such discrimination.

Article 7

States Parties undertake to adopt immediate and effective measures, particularly in the fields of teaching, education, culture and information, with a view to combating prejudices which lead to racial discrimination and to promoting understanding, tolerance and friendship among nations and racial or ethnical groups, as well as to propagating the purposes and principles of the Charter of the United Nations, the Universal Declaration of Human Rights, the United Nations Declaration on the Elimination of All Forms of Racial Discrimination, and this Convention.

PART II

Article 8

1. There shall be established a Committee on the Elimination of Racial Discrimination (hereinafter referred to as the Committee) consisting of eighteen experts of high moral standing and acknowledged impartiality elected by States Parties from among their nationals, who shall serve in their personal capacity, consideration being given to equitable geographical distribution and to the representation of the different forms of civilization as well as of the principal legal systems.

Article 9

1. States Parties undertake to submit to the Secretary-General of the United Nations, for consideration by the Committee, a report on the legislative, judicial, administrative or other measures which they have adopted and which give effect to the provisions of this Convention: (*a*) within one year after the entry into force of the Convention for the State concerned; and (*b*) thereafter every two years and whenever the Committee so requests. The Committee may request further information from the States Parties.

2. The Committee shall report annually, through the Secretary-General, to the General Assembly of the United Nations on its activities and may make suggestions and general recommendations based on the examination of the reports and information received from the States Parties. Such suggestions and general recommendations shall be reported to the General Assembly together with comments, if any, from States Parties.

Article 11

1. If a State Party considers that another State Party is not giving effect to the provisions of this Convention, it may bring the matter to the attention of the Committee. The Committee shall then transmit the communication to the State Party concerned. Within three months, the receiving State shall submit to the Committee written explanations or statements clarifying the matter and the remedy, if any, that may have been taken by that State.

2. If the matter is not adjusted to the satisfaction of both parties, either by bilateral negotiations or by any other procedure open to them, within six months after the receipt by the receiving State of the initial communication, either State shall have the right to refer the matter again to the Committee by notifying the Committee and also the other State.

APPENDIX 2.3

THE ATLANTIC COAST
AUTONOMY LAW (EXTRACTS)

WHEREAS

Imperialism, the oligarchy and the Somoza dictatorship brought about a divided nation whose people were strangers among themselves and mutually mistrusted one another; while the ruling class kept for itself the right to the enjoyment, use and benefit of the resources of both the Atlantic and Pacific coasts of Nicaragua.

WHEREAS

Only through the war of liberation and the victory of the Sandinista Popular Revolution has Nicaragua been able to dignify the laws of its history, to develop an awareness of its identity and to recognize that it is a multi-ethnic and multi-cultural nation.

WHEREAS

As a consequence of its interpretation of Nicaraguan history and the recognition of a resulting social dichotomy, as well as its awareness of political, economic, and cultural injustice, the Sandinista Popular Revolution has always set the unification of the nation as one of its main goals.

WHEREAS

The Communities of the Atlantic Coast have demanded autonomy as a historical right, in order to achieve genuine national integration based on their cultural characteristics and the use of their national resources, for their own benefit and that of the nation.

WHEREAS

Our Political Constitution holds that Nicaragua is a multi-ethnic nation (Art. 8) and recognizes the right of the Atlantic Coast communities to preserve their cultural identity, their languages, art and culture, as well as the right to use and enjoy the waters, forests and communal lands for their own benefit. It also recognizes their rights to the creation of special programmes designed to contribute to their development (Art. 89 and 90), while respecting their right to live and organize themselves according to their legitimate cultural and historical traditions (Art. 180).

THE GOVERNMENT OF NICARAGUA PROCLAIMS THE FOLLOWING LAW CONCERNING THE AUTONOMOUS REGIONS OF THE ATLANTIC COAST

Title I
Fundamental Principles

CHAPTER 1
About the Autonomous Regions

Article 1

This law establishes an autonomous regime for the Regions where the communities of the Atlantic Coast live, in accordance with the Constitution of the Republic (Art 89, 90, 180 and 181) and establishes specific rights and duties for their inhabitants.

Article 2

Nicaragua is a Unitary State, of which the communities of the Atlantic Coast are an integral part, being entitled and subject to all the rights and duties of Nicaraguans.

Article 3

The Communities of the Atlantic Coast have a common history, and it is a principle of Autonomy to promote unity, fraternity and solidarity among their inhabitants.

Article 4

The regions where the Communities of the Atlantic Coast live will benefit from a regime of Autonomy which, within the framework of national unity and faithful to the principles, policies, and judicial system established in the Constitution of the Republic, will guarantee its inhabitants and the real use of their legitimate historical rights.

Article 5

In order to ensure full use of the autonomy rights of the Atlantic Coast Communities, two Autonomous Regions will be established in what is currently known as the Department of Zelaya.

1. Autonomous Region "North Atlantic" will exercise jurisdiction over the territory of Special Zone I and the adjacent islands.
2. Autonomous Region "South Atlantic" will exercise jurisdiction over the territory of Special Zone II and the adjacent islands.
3. Other zones that have traditionally been considered part of the Atlantic Coast, while remaining at this time under the jurisdiction of other authorities, will be incorporated into their respective Autonomous Regions as soon as the circumstances allow for this incorporation. These circumstances will be defined and determined by the respective Region.

Article 6

The administrative seat for Autonomous Region "North Atlantic" will be Puerto Cabezas, while Bluefields will be the seat for Autonomous Region "South Atlantic". Under very special circumstances the administrative seat of the Autonomous Regions may be transferred to other locations in their respective territories.

Article 7

Spanish is the official language of the Nicaraguan state. The languages of the Communities of the Atlantic Coast of Nicaragua will be official within the Autonomous Regions.

Article 8

The Autonomous Regions established by the present law are legal entities and as such, in accordance with national policies, plans and guidelines, will have the following general functions:

1. To participate effectively in the planning process and programmes of national development within the Region.
2. To administer in coordination with the corresponding ministries, the programmes related to health, education, culture, basic goods distribution and communal services, as well as the establishment of economic, social, and cultural projects in the Region.
3. To promote the rational use of the waters, forests, and communal lands for the benefit and enjoyment

of their peoples, and the overall preservation of the ecological system.

4. To promote national culture, as well as the study, preservation, promotion, development, and dissemination of the different cultures and traditions of the Atlantic Coast's Communities, including their historical, artistic, linguistic, and cultural heritage.

5. To promote the traditional exchange with the Caribbean countries in accordance with the national laws and established procedures regulated to this matter.

6. To establish regional taxes in accordance with the established laws related to this matter.

Article 9
The rational exploitation of the mining, forestry, and fishing resources as well as other natural resources in the Autonomous Regions of the Atlantic Coast, must benefit its inhabitants in just proportions, in accordance with agreement between the Regional Government and the Central Government.

CHAPTER TWO

About the internal territorial divisions of the Autonomous Regions

Article 10
For administrative purposes, the territory of the Autonomous Regions will be divided into municipalities. These municipalities will be ruled according to established laws concerning this matter. Such administrative subdivisions will be organized and established by the corresponding Regional Councils, in accordance with the traditions of each Autonomous Region.

CHAPTER THREE

About the rights and duties of the inhabitants of the Communities in the Auonomous Regions

Article 11
Within the territory of the Autonomous Region, all Nicaraguan citizens will benefit from the rights and guarantees granted by the Constitution and those stated in the present law.

Article 12
The inhabitants of the Atlantic Coast Communities are entitled by law:

1. To full equality of rights.
2. To promote and develop their languages, religions and cultures.
3. To use and benefit from their waters, forests, and communal lands, in accordance with national development plans.
4. To organize their social and productive activities according to their own values.
5. To be educated in their own languages, through programmes that take into account their historical heritage, their traditions and the characteristics of their environment, all within the framework of the national education system.
6. To their own forms of communal, collective, or individual ownership and transfer of land.

Article 13
The members of the Atlantic Coast communities have the right to define and to determine their own ethnic identity.

Article 14
The defence of life, homeland, justice, and peace for the integral development of the nation is an essential duty of the inhabitants of the Communities of the Autonomous Region.

Article 15
In Nicaragua, the defence of the Nation is based on the organized power of the people. In the Autonomous Regions, the Atlantic Coast Communities will hold the main responsibility for the defence of the nation within the framework of the Sandinista Popular Army, the Security Forces, and the Ministry of the Interior.

Title IV

Consolidated Chapter
About the patrimony of the Autonomous Regions and communal property

Article 34
The patrimony of the Autonomous Regions will be constituted by its possessions, rights and obligations acquired through any legal means as a public legal entity.

Article 35
The Autonomous Regions have the full and legal capacity to obtain, administer, and own the possessions comprising their patrimony, in accordance with the law.

Article 36
Communal property is constituted by the communal lands, waters and forests that have traditionally belonged to the Communities.

Communal property is subject to the following provisions:

1. Communal lands cannot be sold, seized, or taxed; their communal status cannot expire.
2. The inhabitants of the Communities will have the right to work on communal plots of land and are entitled to the benefits generated therefrom.

Article 37
The remaining form of property in the region are those recognized by the Constitution and the laws of the Republic.

Title V

Consolidated Chapter
About Law Reform

Article 38
Two thirds or more members of both Regional Councils may request that the National Assembly reform the present law through the established constitutional channels.

Title VI

Consolidated Chapter
Final and tentative provisions

Article 39
Once the present law has been passed, the National Assembly will call for the elections of the Regional Council in each Autonomous Region. The Supreme Electoral Council will then proceed to organize and direct the elections, to announce and publicize their results, and to give credentials to the elected Regional representatives.

Article 40

The National Assembly will set the date of investiture for each Regional Council. The President of the Supreme Electoral Council will take the oath of office and invest the regional representatives. He will also preside over the meeting where the President of the Council and the Board of Directors are elected.

Article 41

An especially appointed commission of each Regional Council will organize a solemn inaugural ceremony in the presence of the President of the Republic, or his representatives from the National Assembly and the Supreme Court of Justice.

Article 42

The present law will be widely publicized throughout Nicaragua, both in Spanish and in the languages spoken in Nicaragua's Atlantic Coast Communities.

Article 43

Those officials who are engaged in their duties at the time this law comes into force will continue in their positions until the newly elected authorities take office, in accordance with the new provisions.

Article 44

The present law will take effect, from the date of its publication in the official newspaper, "La Gaceta".

APPENDIX 2.4

UNITED NATIONS
DRAFT DECLARATION OF PRINCIPLES
FOR INDIGENOUS RIGHTS

1. Indigenous nations and peoples have, in common with all humanity, the right to life, and to freedom from oppression, discrimination and aggression.
2. All indigenous nations and peoples have the right to self-determination, by virtue of which they have the right to whatever degree of autonomy or self-government they choose. This includes the right to freely determine their political status, freely pursue their own economic, social, religious and cultural development, and determine their own membership and/or citizenship, without external interference.
3. No State shall assert any jurisdiction over an indigenous nation or people, or its territory, except in accordance with the freely expressed wishes of the nation or people concerned.
4. Indigenous nations and peoples are entitled to the permanent control and enjoyment of their aboriginal ancestral-historical territories. This includes surface and subsurface rights, inland and coastal waters, renewable and non-renewable resources, and the economies based on these resources.
5. Rights to share and use land, subject to the underlying and inalienable title of the indigenous nation or people, may be granted by their free and informed consent, as evidence in a valid treaty or agreement.
6. Discovery, conquest, settlement on a theory of *terra*

nullius and unilateral legislation are never legitimate bases for States to claim or retain the territories of indigenous nations or peoples.
7. In cases where lands taken in violation of these principles have already been settled, the indigenous nation or people concerned is entitled to immediate restitution, including compensation for the loss of use, without extinction of original title. Indigenous peoples' desire to regain possession and control of sacred sites must always be respected.
8. No State shall participate financially or militarily in the involuntary displacement of indigenous populations, or in the subsequent economic exploitation or military use of their territory.
9. The laws and customs of indigenous nations and peoples must be recognized by States' legislative, administrative and judicial institutions and, in case of conflicts with State laws, shall take precedence.
10. No State shall deny an indigenous nation, community, or people residing within its borders the right to participate in the life of the State in whatever manner and to whatever degree they may choose. This includes the right to participate in other forms of collective actions and expression.
11. Indigenous nations and peoples continue to own and control their material culture, including archeological, historical and sacred sites, artifacts, designs, knowledge, and works of art. They have the right to regain items of major cultural significance and, in all cases, to the return of the human remains of their ancestors for burial in accordance with their traditions.
12. Indigenous nations and peoples have the right to be educated and conduct business with States in their own languages, and to establish their own educational institutions.
13. No technical, scientific or social investigations, including archeological excavations, shall take place in relation to indigenous nations or peoples, or their lands, without their prior authorization, and their continuing ownership and control.
14. The religious practices of indigenous nations and peoples shall be fully respected and protected by the laws of States and by international law. Indigenous nations and peoples shall always enjoy unrestricted access to, and enjoyment of sacred sites in accordance with their own laws and customs, including the right of privacy.
15. Indigenous nations and peoples are subjects of international law.
16. Treaties and other agreements freely made with the indigenous nations or peoples shall be recognized and applied in the same manner and according to the same international laws and principles as treaties and agreements entered into with other States.
17. Disputes regarding the jurisdiction, territories and institutions of an indigenous nation or people are a proper concern of international law, and must be resolved by mutual agreement or valid treaty.
18. Indigenous nations and peoples may engage in self-defense against State actions in conflict with their right to self-determination.
19. Indigenous nations and peoples have the right freely to travel, and to maintain economic, social, cultural and religious relations with each other across State borders.

20. In addition to these rights, indigenous nations and peoples are entitled to the enjoyment of all the human rights and fundamental freedoms enumerated in the International Bill of Rights and other United Nations instruments. In no circumstances shall they be subjected to adverse discrimination.

APPENDIX 3.1

CONCLUDING DOCUMENT OF THE VIENNA MEETING 1986 OF REPRESENTATIVES OF THE PARTICIPATING STATES OF THE CONFERENCE ON SECURITY AND CO-OPERATION IN EUROPE, HELD ON THE BASIS OF THE PROVISIONS OF THE FINAL ACT RELATING TO THE FOLLOW-UP TO THE CONFERENCE (EXTRACTS)

The representatives of the participating States of the Conference on Security and Co-operation in Europe (CSCE), Austria, Belgium, Bulgaria, Canada, Cyprus, Czechoslovakia, Denmark, Finland, France, the German Democratic Republic, the Federal Republic of Germany, Greece, the Holy See, Hungary, Iceland, Ireland, Italy, Liechtenstein, Luxembourg, Malta, Monaco, the Netherlands, Norway, Poland, Portugal, Romania, San Marino, Spain, Sweden, Switzerland, Turkey, the Union of Soviet Socialist Republics, the United Kingdom, the United States of America and Yugoslavia met in Vienna from 4 November 1986 to 17 January 1989 in accordance with the provisions of the Final Act relating to the Follow-Up to the conference, as well as on the basis of the other relevant CSCE documents.

PRINCIPLES

The States confirm that, by virtue of the principle of equal rights and self-determination of peoples and in conformity with the relevant provisions of the Final Act, all peoples always have the right, in full freedom, to determine, when and as they wish, their internal and external political status, without external interference, and to pursue as they wish their political, economic, social and cultural development. . . .

5. They confirm their commitment strictly and effectively to observe the principle of the territorial integrity of States. They will refrain from any violation of this principle and thus from any action aimed by direct or indirect means, in contravention of the purposes and principles of the Charter of the United Nations, other obligations under international law or the provisions of the Final Act, at violating the territorial integrity, political independence or the unity of a State. No actions or situations in

contravention of this principle will be recognized as legal by the participating States.

16. In order to ensure the freedom of the individual to profess and practise religion or belief the participating States will, *inter alia*,

16a take effective measures to prevent and eliminate discrimination against individuals or communities, on the grounds of religion or belief in the recognition, exercise and enjoyment of human rights and fundamental freedoms in all fields of civil, political, economic, social and cultural life, and ensure the effective equality between believers and non-believers;

16b foster a climate of mutual tolerance and respect between believers of different communities as well as between believers and non-believers;

16c grant upon their request to communities of believers, practising or prepared to practise their faith within the constitutional framework of their states, recognition of the status provided for them in their respective countries;

16d respect the right of religious communities to
establish and maintain freely accessible places of worship or assembly,
organize themselves according to their own hierarchical and institutional structure,
select, appoint and replace their personnel in accordance with their respective requirements and standards as well as with any freely accepted arrangement between them and their State,
solicit and receive voluntary financial and other contributions;

16e engage in consultations with religious faiths, institutions and organizations in order to achieve a better understanding of the requirements of religious freedom;

16f respect the right of everyone to give and receive religious education in the language of his choice, individually or in association with others;

16g in this context respect, *inter alia*, the liberty of parents to ensure the religious and moral education of their children in conformity with their own convictions;

16h allow the training of religious personnel in appropriate institutions;

16i respect the right of individual believers and communities of believers to acquire, possess, and use sacred books, religious publications in the language of their choice and other articles and materials related to the practice of religion or belief;

16j allow religious faiths, institutions and organizations to produce and import and disseminate religious publications and materials;

16k favorably consider the interest of religious communities in participating in public dialogue, *inter alia*, through mass media;

17. The participating States recognize that the exercise of the above-mentioned rights relating to the freedom of religion or belief may be subject only to such limitations as are provided by law and consistent with their obligations under international law and with their international commitments. They will ensure in their laws and regulations and in their application the full and effective implementation of the freedom of thought, conscience, religion or belief;

18. The participating States will exert sustained efforts to implement the provisions of the Final Act and of the

Madrid Concluding Document pertaining to national minorities. They will take all the necessary legislative, administrative judicial and other measures and apply the relevant international instruments by which they may be bound, to ensure the protection of human rights and fundamental freedoms of persons belonging to national minorities within their territory. They will refrain from any discrimination against such persons and contribute to the realization of their legitimate interests and aspirations in the field of human rights and fundamental freedoms.

19. They will protect and create conditions for the promotion of the ethnic, cultural, linguistic and religious identity of national minorities on their territory. They will respect the free exercise of rights by persons belonging to such minorities and ensure their full equality with others.

APPENDIX 4.1

SECTION III OF THE TREATY OF LAUSANNE (JULY 21, 1923) CONCERNING PROTECTION OF MINORITIES

Article 37
Turkey undertakes that the stipulations contained in Articles 38 to 44 shall be recognised as fundamental laws, and that no law, no regulation, nor official action shall conflict or interfere with these stipulations, nor shall any law, regulation, nor official action prevail over them.

Article 38
The Turkish Government undertakes to assure full and complete protection of life and liberty to all inhabitants of Turkey without distinction of birth, nationality, language, race or religion.

All inhabitants of Turkey shall be entitled to free exercise, whether in public or private, of any creed, religion or belief, the observance of which shall not be incompatible with public order and good morals.

Non-Moslem minorities will enjoy full freedom of movement and of emigration, subject to the measures applied, on the whole or on part of the territory, to all Turkish nationals, and which may be taken by the Turkish Government for national defence, or for the maintenance of public order.

Article 39
Turkish nationals belonging to non-Moslem minorities will enjoy the same civil and political rights as Moslems.

All the inhabitants of Turkey, without distinction of religion, shall be equal before the law.

Differences of religion, creed or confession shall not prejudice any Turkish national in matters relating to the enjoyment of civil or political rights, as, for instance, admission to public employment, functions and honours, or the exercise of professions and industries.

No restrictions shall be imposed on the free use by any Turkish national of any language in private intercourse, in commerce, religion, in the press, or in publications of any kind or at public meetings.

Notwithstanding the existence of the official language, adequate facilities shall be given to Turkish nationals of non-Turkish speech for the oral use of their own language before the Courts.

Article 40
Turkish nationals belonging to non-Moslem minorities shall enjoy the same treatment and security in law and in fact as other Turkish nationals. In particular, they shall have an equal right to establish, manage and control at their own expense, any charitable, religious and social institutions, any schools and other establishments for instruction and education, with the right to use their own language and to exercise their own religion freely therein.

Article 41
As regards public instruction, the Turkish Government will grant in those towns and districts, where a considerable proportion of non-Moslem nationals are resident, adequate facilities for ensuring that in the primary schools the instruction shall be given to the children of such Turkish nationals through the medium of their own language. This provision will not prevent the Turkish Government from making the teaching of the Turkish language obligatory in the said schools.

In towns and districts where there is a considerable proportion of Turkish nationals belonging to non-Moslem minorities, these minorities shall be assured an equitable share in the enjoyment and application of the sums which may be provided out of public funds under the State, municipal or other budgets for educational, religious, or charitable purposes.

The sums in question shall be paid to the qualified representatives of the establishments and institutions concerned.

Article 42
The Turkish Government undertakes to take, as regards non-Moslem minorities, in so far as concerns their family law or personal status, measures permitting the settlement of these questions in accordance with the customs of those minorities.

These measures will be elaborated by special Commissions composed of representatives of the Turkish Government and of representatives of each of the minorities concerned in equal number. In case of divergence, the Turkish Government and the Council of the League of Nations will appoint in agreement an umpire chosen from amongst European lawyers.

The Turkish Government undertakes to grant full protection to the churches, synagogues, cemeteries, and other religious establishments of the above-mentioned minorities. All facilities and authorisation will be granted to the pious foundations, and to the religious and charitable institutions of the said minorities at present existing in Turkey, and the Turkish Government will not refuse, for the formation of new religious and charitable institutions, any of the necessary facilities which are granted to other private institutions of that nature.

Article 43
Turkish nationals belonging to non-Moslem minorities shall not be compelled to perform any act which constitutes a violation of their faith or religious observances,

and shall not be placed under any disability by reason of their refusal to attend Courts of Law or to perform any legal business on their weekly day of rest.

This provision, however, shall not exempt such Turkish nationals from such obligations as shall be imposed upon all other Turkish nationals for the preservation of public order.

Article 44

Turkey agrees that, in so far as the preceding Articles of this Section affect non-Moslem nationals of Turkey, these provisions constitute obligations of international concern and shall be placed under the guarantee of the League of Nations. They shall not be modified without the assent of the majority of the Council of the League of Nations. The British Empire, France, Italy and Japan hereby agree not to with-hold their assent to any modification in these Articles which is in due form assented to be a majority of the Council of the League of Nations.

Turkey agrees that any Member of Council of the League of Nations shall have the right to bring to the attention of the Council any infraction or danger of infraction of any of these obligations, and that the Council may thereupon take such action and give such directions as it may deem proper and effective in the circumstances.

Turkey further agrees that any difference of opinion as to questions of law or of fact arising out of these Articles between the Turkish Government and any one of the other Signatory Powers or any other Power, a member of the Council of the League of Nations, shall be held to be a dispute of an international character under Article 14 of the Covenant of the League of Nations. The Turkish Government hereby consents that any such dispute shall, if the other party thereto demands, be referred to the Permanent Court of International Justice. The decision of the Permanent Court shall be final and shall have the same force and effect as an award under Article 13 of the Covenant.

Article 45

The rights conferred by the provisions of the present Section on the non-Moslem minorities of Turkey will be similarly conferred by Greece on the Moslem minority in her territory.

2. No privileges or restriction of rights based on nationality, origin, creed, sex, race, education, social and material status are allowed.
3. The state secures the equality of the citizens by creating conditions and opportunities for the exercise of their rights and the fulfilment of their obligations.
4. The propagation of hate or humiliation of man because of race, national or religious affiliation is forbidden and shall be punished.

Article 45 (paragraphs 1 and 7)

1. Citizens are entitled to free education in all types and grades of educational establishments under conditions determined by law.
7. Citizens of non-Bulgarian extraction, in addition to the compulsory study of the Bulgarian language, are entitled to study also their own language.

Article 48

1. The freedom and inviolability of the person is guaranteed.

Article 52, paragraph 1

1. Citizens may form organizations for political, professional, cultural, artistic, scientific, religious, sports and other non-economic purposes.

Article 53

1. The citizens are guaranteed freedom of conscience and creed. They may perform religious rites and conduct anti-religious propaganda.

Article 54

1. Citizens enjoy freedom of speech, press, meetings, associations and demonstrations.
2. These freedoms are guaranteed by placing the necessary material conditions for the purpose at the disposal of the citizens.

Bulgarian legislation provides for equal rights of all citizens in the constitution (articles 35, etc.), and also prescribes penalties for crimes against racial and national equality.[11] Section I of the Criminal Code "Crimes against national and racial equality" and section III "Extermination of population groups (genocide and apartheid)" are the appropriate sections that prescribe these penalties.

APPENDIX 4.2

CONSTITUTION OF BULGARIA
(EXTRACTS)

The present constitution, adopted in 1971, established the Council of State as the supreme body of the National Assembly, with both legislative and executive functions.[10] The legal framework for the prevention and elimination of racial discrimination does exist in the Bulgarian constitution. Articles 35, 45, 48 and 52–54 of the constitution are the portions relevant to minority groups.

Article 35

1. All citizens of the People's Republic of Bulgaria are equal before the law.

APPENDIX 5.1

CONSTITUTION (FUNDAMENTAL LAW) OF THE UNION OF SOVIET SOCIALIST REPUBLICS

Adopted at the Seventh (Special) Session of the Supreme Soviet of the USSR, Ninth Convocation, on October 7, 1977 (EXTRACTS)

CHAPTER 8
THE USSR—A FEDERAL STATE

Article 70

The Union of Soviet Socialist Republics is an integral, federal, multinational state formed on the principle of socialist federalism as a result of the free self-determination of nations and the voluntary association of equal Soviet Socialist Republics.

The USSR embodies the state unity of the Soviet people and draws all its nations and nationalities together for the purpose of jointly building communism.

Article 71

The Union of Soviet Socialist Republics unites:

the Russian Soviet Federative Socialist Republic,
the Ukrainian Soviet Socialist Republic,
the Byelorussian Soviet Socialist Republic,
the Uzbek Soviet Socialist Republic,
the Kazakh Soviet Socialist Republic,
the Georgian Soviet Socialist Republic,
the Azerbaijan Soviet Socialist Republic,
the Lithuanian Soviet Socialist Republic,
the Moldavian Soviet Socialist Republic,.
the Latvian Soviet Socialist Republic,
the Kirghiz Soviet Socialist Republic,
the Tajik Soviet Socialist Republic,
the Armenian Soviet Socialist Republic,
the Turkmen Soviet Socialist Republic,
the Estonian Soviet Socialist Republic.

Article 72

Each Union Republic shall retain the right freely to secede from the USSR.

Article 73

The jurisdiction of the Union of Soviet Socialist Republics, as represented by its highest bodies of state authority and administration, shall cover:

1. the admission of new republics to the USSR; endorsement of the formation of new autonomous republics and autonomous regions within Union Republics;
2. determination of the state boundaries of the USSR and approval of changes in the boundaries between Union Republics;
3. establishment of the general principles for the organisation and functioning of republican and local bodies of state authority and administration;
4. the ensurance of uniformity of legislative norms throughout the USSR and establishment of the fundamentals of the legislation of the Union of Soviet Socialist Republics and Union Republics;
5. pursuance of a uniform social and economic policy; direction of the country's economy; determination of the main lines of scientific and technological progress and the general measures for rational exploitation and conservation of national resources; the drafting and approval of state plans for the economic and social development of the USSR, and endorsement of reports on their fulfilment;
6. the drafting and approval of the consolidated Budget of the USSR, and endorsement of the report on its execution; management of a single monetary and credit system; determination of the taxes and revenues forming the Budget of the USSR; and the formulation of prices and wages policy;
7. direction of the sectors of the economy, and of enterprises and amalgamations under Union jurisdiction, and general direction of industries under Union-Republican jurisdiction;
8. issues of war and peace, defence of the sovereignty of the USSR and safeguarding of its frontiers and territory, and organisation of defence; direction of the Armed Forces of the USSR;
9. state security;
10. representation of the USSR in international relations; the USSR's relations with other states and with international organisations; establishment of the general procedure for, and co-ordination of, the relations of Union Republics with other states and with international organisations; foreign trade and other forms of external economic activity on the basis of state monopoly;
11. control over observance of the Constitution of the USSR, and ensurance of conformity of the Constitutions of Union Republics to the Constitution of the USSR;
12. and settlement of other matters of All-Union importance.

Article 74

The laws of the USSR shall have the same force in all Union Republics. In the event of a discrepancy between a Union Republic law and an All-Union law, the law of the USSR shall prevail.

Article 75

The territory of the Union of Soviet Socialist Republics is a single entity and comprises the territories of the Union Republics.

The sovereignty of the USSR extends throughout its territory.

APPENDIX 6.1

AFRICAN CHARTER ON HUMAN RIGHTS AND PEOPLES' RIGHTS (EXTRACTS)

The Heads of State of the Organisation of African Unity at their meeting in Nairobi in July 1981 approved the Charter unanimously. The text printed here is that which was approved at the OAU Ministerial Conference in Banjul, the Gambia, in January 1981 and is believed to be the correct text of the Charter as approved at Nairobi.

PART I: RIGHTS AND DUTIES

CHAPTER I
Human and Peoples' Rights

Article 1
The Member States of the Organization of African Unity parties to the present charter shall recognize the right, duties and freedoms enshrined in this Charter and shall undertake to adopt legislative or other measures to give effect to them.

Article 2
Every individual shall be entitled to the enjoyment of the rights and freedoms recognized and guaranteed in the present Charter without distinction of any kind such as race, ethnic group, colour, sex, language, religion, political or any other opinion, national and social origin, fortune, birth or other status.

Article 3
1. Every individual shall be equal before the law.
2. Every individual shall be entitled to equal protection of the law.

Article 4
Human beings are inviolable. Every human being shall be entitled to respect for his life and in the integrity of his person. No one may be arbitrarily deprived of this right.

Article 5
Every individual shall have the right to the respect of the dignity inherent in a human being and to the recognition of his legal status. All forms of exploitation and degradation of man particularly slavery, slave trade, torture, cruel, inhuman or degrading punishment and treatment shall be prohibited.

Article 6
Every individual shall have the right to liberty and to the security of his person. No one may be deprived of his freedom except for reasons and conditions previously laid down by law. In particular, no one may be arbitrarily arrested or detained.

Article 7
1. Every individual shall have the right to have his cause heard. This comprises:

   (a) The right to an appeal to competent national organs against acts violating his fundamental rights as recognized and guaranteed by conventions, laws, regulations and customs in force;

   (b) the right to be presumed innocent until proved guilty by a competent court or tribunal;
   (c) the right to defence, including the right to be defended by counsel of his choice;
   (d) the right to be tried within a reasonable time by an impartial court or tribunal.

2. No one may be condemned for an act or omission which did not constitute a legally punishable offence at the time it was committed. No penalty may be inflicted for an offence for which no provision was made at the time it was committed. Punishment is personal and can be imposed only on the offender.

Article 8
Freedom of conscience, the profession and free practice of religion shall be guaranteed. No one may, subject to law and order, be submitted to measures restricting the exercise of these freedoms.

Article 9
1. Every individual shall have the right to receive information.
2. Every individual shall have the right to express and disseminate his opinions within the law.

Article 10
1. Every individual shall have the right to free association provided that he abides by the law.
2. Subject to the obligation of solidarity provided for in Article 29 no one may be compelled to join an association.

Article 11
Every individual shall have the right to assemble freely with others. The exercise of this right shall be subject only to necessary restrictions provided for by law in particular those enacted in the interest of national security, the safety, health, ethics and rights and freedoms of others.

Article 12
1. Every individual shall have the right to freedom of movement and residence within the borders of a State provided he abides by the law.
2. Every individual shall have the right to leave any country including his own, and to return to his country. This right may only be subject to restrictions, provided for by law for the protection of national security, law and order, public health or morality.
3. Every individual shall have the right, when persecuted, to seek and obtain asylum in other countries in accordance with the laws of those countries and international conventions.
4. A non-national legally admitted in a territory of a State Party to the present Charter, may only be expelled from it by virtue of a decision taken in accordance with the law.
5. The mass expulsion of non-nationals shall be prohibited. Mass expulsion shall be that which is aimed at national, racial, ethnic or religious groups.

Article 13
1. Every citizen shall have the right to freely participate in the government of his country, either directly or through freely chosen representatives in accordance with the provisions of the law.

2. Every citizen shall have the right of equal access to the public service of his country.

3. Every individual shall have the right of access to public property and services in strict equality of all persons before the law.

Article 14

The right to property shall be guaranteed. It may only be encroached upon in the interest of public need or in the general interest of the community and in accordance with the provisions of appropriate laws.

Article 15

Every individual shall have the right to work under equitable and satisfactory conditions and shall receive equal pay for equal work.

Article 16

1. Every individual shall have the right to enjoy the best attainable state of physical and mental health.

2. State Parties to the present Charter shall take the necessary measures to protect the health of their people and to ensure that they receive medical attention when they are sick.

Article 17

1. Every individual shall have the right to education.

2. Every individual may freely, take part in the cultural life of his community.

3. The promotion and protection of morals and traditional values recognized by the community shall be the duty of the State.

Article 18

1. The family shall be the natural unit and basis of society. It shall be protected by the State.

2. The State shall have the duty to assist the family which is the custodian of morals and traditional values recognized by the community.

3. The State shall ensure the elimination of every discrimination against women and also ensure the protection of the rights of the woman and the child as stipulated in international declarations and conventions.

4. The aged and the disabled shall also have the right to special measures of protection in keeping with their physical or moral needs.

Article 19

All peoples shall be equal; they shall enjoy the same respect and shall have the same rights. Nothing shall justify the domination of a people by another.

Article 20

1. All people shall have the right to existence. They shall have the unquestionable and inalienable right to self-determination. They shall freely determine their political status and shall pursue their economic and social development according to the policy they have freely chosen.

2. Colonized or oppressed peoples shall have the right to free themselves from the bonds of domination by resorting to any means recognized by the international community.

3. All peoples shall have the right to the assistance of the States Parties to the present Charter in their liberation struggle against foreign domination, be it political, economic or cultural.

Article 21

1. All peoples shall freely dispose of their wealth and natural resources. This right shall be exercised in the exclusive interest of the people. In no case shall a people be deprived of it.

2. In case of spoliation the dispossessed people shall have the right to the lawful recovery of its property as well as to an adequate compensation.

3. The free disposal of wealth and natural resources shall be exercised without prejudice to the obligation of promoting international economic cooperation based on mutual respect, equitable exchange and the principles of international law.

4. States Parties to the present Charter shall individually and collectively exercise the right to free disposal of their wealth and natural resources with a view to strengthening African unity and solidarity.

5. States Parties to the present Charter shall undertake to eliminate all forms of foreign economic exploitation particularly that practised by international monopolies so as to enable their peoples to fully benefit from the advantages derived from their national resources.

Article 22

1. All peoples shall have the right to their economic, social and cultural development with due regard to their freedom and identity and in the equal enjoyment of the common heritage of mankind.

2. States shall have the duty, individually or collectively, to ensure the exercise of the right to development.

Article 23

1. All peoples shall have the right to national and international peace and security. The principles of solidarity and friendly relations implicitly affirmed by the Charter of the United Nations and reaffirmed by that of the Organization of African Unity shall govern relations between States.

2. For the purpose of strengthening peace, solidarity and friendly relations, States parties to the present Charter shall ensure that:

   (a) any individual enjoying the right of asylum under Article 12 of the present Charter shall not engage in subversive activities against his country of origin or any other State party to the present Charter;

   (b) their territories shall not be used as bases for subversive or terrorist activities against the people of any other State party to the present Charter.

Article 24

All peoples shall have the right to a general satisfactory environment favourable to their development.

Article 25

States parties to the present Charter shall have the duty to promote and ensure through teaching, education and publication, the respect of the rights and freedoms contained in the present Charter and to see to it that these freedoms and rights as well as corresponding obligations and duties are understood.

Article 26

States parties to the present Charter shall have the duty to guarantee the independence of the Courts and shall allow the establishment and improvement of appropriate national institutions entrusted with the promotion and protection of the rights and freedoms guaranteed by the present Charter.

CHAPTER II
Duties

Article 27
1. Every individual shall have duties towards his family and society, the State and other legally recognized communities and the international community.
2. The rights and freedoms of each individual shall be exercised with due regard to the rights of others, collective security, morality and common interest.

Article 28
Every individual shall have the duty to respect and consider his fellow beings without discrimination, and to maintain relations aimed at promoting, safeguarding and reinforcing mutual respect and tolerance.

Article 29
The individual shall also have the duty:
1. To preserve the harmonious development of the family and to work for the cohesion and respect of the family, to respect his parents at all times, to maintain them in case of need;
2. To serve his national community by placing his physical and intellectual abilities at its service;
3. Not to compromise the security of the State whose national or resident he is;
4. To preserve and strengthen social and national solidarity, particularly when the latter is threatened;
5. To preserve and strengthen the national independence and the territorial integrity of his country and to contribute to its defence in accordance with the law;
6. To work to the best of his abilities and competence, and to pay taxes imposed by law in the interest of the society;
7. To preserve and strengthen positive African cultural values in his relations with other members of the society, in the spirit of tolerance, dialogue and consultation and, in general, to contribute to the promotion of the moral well being of society;
8. To contribute to the best of his abilities, at all times and at all levels, to the promotion and achievement of African unity.

PART II: MEASURES OF SAFEGUARD

CHAPTER I

Establishment and Organization of the African Commission on Human and Peoples' Rights

Article 30
An African Commission on Human and Peoples' Rights, hereinafter called "the Commission", shall be established within the Organization of African Unity to promote human and peoples' rights and ensure their protection in Africa.

CHAPTER II
Mandate of the Commission

Article 45
The functions of the Commission shall be:
1. To promote Human and Peoples' Rights and in particular:
   (a) To collect documents, undertake studies and researches on African problems in the field of human and peoples' rights, organize seminars, symposia and conferences, disseminate information, encourage national and local institutions concerned with human and peoples' rights, and should the case arise, give its views or make recommendations to Governments.
   (b) To formulate and lay down, principles and rules aimed at solving legal problems relating to human and peoples' rights and fundamental freedoms upon which African Governments may base their legislations.
   (c) Co-operate with other African and international institutions concerned with the promotion and protection of human and peoples' rights.
2. Ensure the protection of human and peoples' rights under conditions laid down by the present Charter.
3. Interpret all the provisions of the present Charter at the request of a State Party, an institution of the OAU or an African organization recognized by the OAU.
4. Perform any other tasks which may be entrusted to it by the Assembly of Heads of State and Government.

CHAPTER IV
Applicable Principles

Article 60
The Commission shall draw inspiration from international law on human and peoples' rights, particularly from the provisions of various African instruments on human and peoples' rights, the Charter of the United Nations, the Charter of the Organization of African Unity, the Universal Declaration of Human Rights, other instruments adopted by the United Nations and by African countries in the field of human and peoples' rights as well as from the provisions of various instruments adopted within the Specialised Agencies of the United Nations of which the parties of the present Charter are members.

Article 61
The Commission shall also take into consideration, as subsidiary measures to determine the principles of law, other general or special international conventions, laying down rules expressly recognized by member States of the Organization of African Unity, African practices consistent with international norms on human and peoples' rights, customs generally accepted as law, general principles of law recognized by African states as well as legal precedents and doctrine.

Article 62
Each State party shall undertake to submit every two years, from the date the present Charter comes into force, a report on the legislative or other measures taken with a view to giving effect to the rights and freedoms recognized and guaranteed by the present Charter.

Article 63

1. The present Charter shall be open to signature, ratification or adherence of the member states of the Organization of African Unity.
2. The instrument of ratification or adherence to the present Charter shall be deposited with the Secretary General of the Organization of African Unity.
3. The present Charter shall come into force three months after the reception by the Secretary General of the instruments of ratification or adherence by a simple majority of the member states of the Organization of African Unity.

APPENDIX 7.1

AGREEMENT BETWEEN INDIA AND PAKISTAN 1950 CONCERNING MINORITIES (EXTRACT)

The Governments of India and Pakistan solemnly agree that each shall ensure to the Minorities throughout its territory complete equality of citizenship, irrespective of religion, a full sense of security in respect of life, culture, property and personal honour, freedom of movement within each country and freedom of occupation, speech and worship, subject to law and morality. Members of the minorities shall have equal opportunity with members of the majority community to participate in the public life of their country, to hold political or other office, and to serve in their country's civil and armed forces. Both Governments declare these rights to be fundamental and undertake to enforce them effectively. It is the policy of both Governments that the enjoyment of these democratic rights shall be assured to all their nationals without distinction.

Both Governments wish to emphasize that the allegiance and loyalty of the minorities is to the State of which they are citizens, and that it is to the Government of their own State that they should look for the redress of their grievances.

APPENDIX 7.2

INDO-SRI LANKA AGREEMENT TO ESTABLISH PEACE AND NORMALCY IN SRI LANKA (EXTRACT)

The President of the Democratic Socialist Republic of Sri Lanka, His Excellency Mr. J. R. Jayewardene, and The Prime Minister of The Republic of India, His Excellency Mr. Rajiv Gandhi, having met at Colombo on July 29, 1987.

Attaching utmost importance to nurturing, intensifying and strengthening the traditional friendship of Sri Lanka and India, and acknowledging the imperative need of resolving the ethnic problem of Sri Lanka, and the consequent violence, and for the safety, well-being and prosperity of people belonging to all communities in Sri Lanka.

Have this day entered into the following agreement to fulfil this objective.

In this context,

1.1 desiring to preserve the unity, sovereignty and territorial integrity of Sri Lanka;
1.2 acknowledging that Sri Lanka is a multi-ethnic and a multi-lingual plural society consisting, *inter alia*, of Sinhalese, Tamils, Muslims (Moors), and Burghers;
1.3 recognising that each ethnic group has a distinct cultural and linguistic identity which has to be carefully nurtured;
1.4 also recognising that the northern and the eastern provinces have been areas of historical habitation of Sri Lankan Tamil speaking peoples, who have at all times hitherto lived together in this territory with other ethnic groups;
1.5 conscious of the necessity of strengthening the forces contributing to the unity, sovereignty and territorial integrity of Sri Lanka, and preserving its character as a multi-ethnic, multi-lingual and multi-religious plural society in which all citizens can live in equality, safety and harmony, and prosper and fulfil their aspirations;

2. resolve that:
2.1 since the government of Sri Lanka proposes to permit adjoining provinces to join to form one administrative unit and also by a referendum to separate as may be permitted to the northern and eastern provinces as outlined below:
2.2 during the period, which shall be considered an interim period, (i.e. from the date of the elections to the provincial council, as specified in para 2.8 to the date of the referendum as specified in para 2.3, the northern and eastern provinces as now constituted, will form one administrative unit, having one elected provincial council. Such a unit will have one Governor, one Chief Minister and one Board of Ministers.
2.3 there will be a referendum on or before 31st December, 1988 to enable the people of the eastern province to decide whether:

(a) the eastern province should remain linked with the northern province as one administrative unit and continue to be governed together with the northern province as specified in para 2.2 or
(b) the eastern province should constitute a separate administrative unit having its own distinct provincial council with a separate Governor, Chief Minister and Board of Ministers.
The President may, at his discretion, decide to postpone such a referendum.

2.4 all persons who have been displaced due to ethnic violence, or other reasons, will have the right to vote in such a referendum. Necessary conditions to enable them to return to areas from where they were displaced will be created.
2.5 the referendum, when held, will be monitored

by a committee headed by the Chief Justice, a member appointed by the President, nominated by the government of Sri Lanka, and a member appointed by the President, nominated by the representatives of the Tamil speaking people of the eastern province.

2.6 a simple majority will be sufficient to determine the result of the referendum.

2.7 meetings and other forms of propaganda, permissible within the laws of the country, will be allowed before the referendum.

2.8 elections to provincial councils will be held within the next three months, in any event before 31st December 1987. Indian observers will be invited for elections to the provincial council of the north and east.

2.9 the emergency will be lifted in the eastern and northern provinces by August 15, 1987. A cessation of hostilities will come into effect all over the island within 48 hours of the signing of this agreement. All arms presently held by militant groups will be surrendered in accordance with an agreed procedure to authorities to be designated by the government of Sri Lanka.
Consequent to the cessation of hostilities and the surrender of arms by militant groups, the army and other security personnel will be confined to barracks in camps as on 25 May 1987. The process of surrendering of arms and the confining of security personnel moving back to barracks shall be completed within 72 hours of the cessation of hostilities coming into effect.

2.10 the government of Sri Lanka will utilise for the purpose of law enforcement and maintenance of security in the northern and eastern provinces same organisations and mechanisms of government as are used in the rest of the country.

2.11 the President of Sri Lanka will grant a general amnesty to political and other prisoners now held in custody under the prevention of terrorism act and other emergency laws, and to combatants, as well as to those persons accused, charged and/or convicted under these laws. The government of Sri Lanka will make special efforts to rehabilitate militant youth with a view to bringing them back into the mainstream of national life. India will co-operate in the process.

2.12 the government of Sri Lanka will accept and abide by the above provisions and expect all others to do likewise.

2.13 if the framework for the resolutions is accepted, the government of Sri Lanka will implement the relevant proposals forthwith.

2.14 the government of India will underwrite and guarantee the resolutions, and co-operate in the implementation of these proposals.

2.15 these proposals are conditional to an acceptance of the proposals negotiated from 4.5.1986 to 19.12.1986. Residual matters not finalised during the above negotiations shall be resolved between India and Sri Lanka within a period of six weeks of signing this agreement. These proposals are also conditional to the government of India co-operating directly with the government of Sri Lanka in their implementation.

2.16 these proposals are also conditional to the government of India taking the following actions if any militant groups operating in Sri Lanka do not accept this framework of proposals for a settlement, namely,

(a) India will take all necessary steps to ensure that Indian territory is not used for activities prejudicial to the unity, integrity and security of Sri Lanka.

(b) the Indian navy/coast guard will co-operate with the Sri Lanka navy in preventing Tamil militant activities from affecting Sri Lanka.

(c) in the event that the government of Sri Lanka requests the government of India to afford military assistance to implement these proposals the government of India will co-operate by giving to the government of Sri Lanka such military assistance as and when requested.

(d) the government of India will expedite repatriation from Sri Lanka of Indian citizens to India who are resident here, concurrently with the repatriation of Sri Lankan refugees from Tamil Nadu.

(e) the governments of Sri Lanka and India will co-operate in ensuring the physical security and safety of all communities inhabiting the northern and eastern provinces.

2.17 the government of Sri Lanka shall ensure free, full and fair participation of voters from all communities in the northern and eastern provinces in electoral processes envisaged in this agreement. The government of India will extend full co-operation to the government of Sri Lanka in this regard.

2.18 the official language of Sri Lanka shall be Sinhala. Tamil and English will also be official languages.

3. This agreement and the annexure thereto shall come into force upon signature.
In witness whereof we have set our hands and seals hereunto.
Done in Colombo, Sri Lanka, on this the twenty ninth day of July of the year one thousand nine hundred and eighty seven, in duplicate, both texts being equally authentic.

Junius Richard Jayewardene
President of the Democratic
Socialist Republic of
Sri Lanka

Rajiv Gandhi
Prime Minister of
the Republic of
India

ANNEXURE TO THE AGREEMENT

1. His Excellency the President of Sri Lanka and the Prime Minister of India agree that the referendum mentioned in paragraph 2 and its sub-paragraphs of the agreement will be observed by a representative of the election commission of India to be invited by His Excellency The President of Sri Lanka.

2. Similarly, both heads of government agree that the elections to the provincial council mentioned in paragraph 2.8 of the agreement will be observed by a representative of the government of India to be invited by The President of Sri Lanka.

3. His Excellency The President of Sri Lanka agrees that the Home Guards would be disbanded and all para-military personnel will be withdrawn from the eastern and northern provinces with a view to creating conditions conducive to fair elections to the council.

The President, in his discretion, shall absorb such para-military forces, which came into being due to ethnic violence, into the regular security forces of Sri Lanka.

4. The President of Sri Lanka and The Prime Minister of India agree that the Tamil militants shall surrender their arms to authorities agreed upon to be designated by The President of Sri Lanka. The surrender shall take place in the presence of one senior representative each of the Sri Lanka Red Cross and The Indian Red Cross.

5. The President of Sri Lanka and The Prime Minister of India agree that a joint Indo-Sri Lankan Observer Group consisting of qualified representatives of the government of Sri Lanka and the government of India would monitor the cessation of hostilities from 31 July 1987.

6. The President of Sri Lanka and The Prime Minister of India also agree that in terms of paragraph 2.14 and paragraph 2.16 (C) of the agreement, an Indian peace keeping contingent may be invited by The President of Sri Lanka to guarantee and enforce the cessation of hostilities, if so required.

APPENDIX 8.1

SESSION OF CHINA'S NATIONAL PEOPLE'S CONGRESS (EXTRACTS)

Law on Regional Autonomy for Minority Nationalities 'People's Daily' 4th June 84

Text, as published of "The law on regional autonomy for minority nationalities of the PRC (adopted by the second session of the sixth NPC on 31st May 1984)":

Preamble

The PRC is a unified and multinational country jointly founded by people of various nationalities throughout the country. Regional autonomy for minority nationalities is a basic policy of the CCP for solving the problem of nationalities on the basis of Marxism-Leninism, and an important political system of our country.

Regional autonomy for minority nationalities means that under the unified leadership of the state, in regions where minority nationalities live in compact communities we carry out regional autonomy, and establish autonomous organs which exercise autonomous power. The implementation of regional autonomy for minority nationalities has demonstrated the spirit that the state fully respects and protects the rights of minority nationalities to handle their internal affairs, and that the state upholds the principles of equality, unity and common prosperity for various nationalities.

The implementation of regional autonomy for minority nationalities will play a great role in arousing the enthusiasm of people of various nationalities as the masters of their own affairs, in developing socialist national relations characterised by equality, unity and mutual help, in consolidating the unification of the state, and in promoting the development of socialist modernisation in the autonomous areas of minority nationalities and the entire country. In future, the system of autonomy for minority nationalities will play a greater role in the course of socialist modernisation of the state.

Practice has proved that to persist in implementing autonomy for minority nationalities, we should ensure the enforcement of the law and policies of the state in light of the practical conditions of the areas concerned, and train a large number of cadres of minority nationalities at various levels, and various kinds of specialised personnel and skilled workers. The national autonomous areas should carry forward the spirit of self-reliance and hard struggle, work hard to develop their own socialist modernisation, and make contributions to the construction of the state. The state should make efforts to help national autonomous areas speed up economic and cultural development in accordance with their plans for economic and social development. In the struggle to uphold unity among nationalities, we should oppose big nationality chauvinism, Han chauvinism in particular. In the meantime, we should also oppose local nationalism.

Under the leadership of the CCP and the guidance of Marxism-Leninism-Mao Zedong Thought, people of various nationalities in the national autonomous areas should work together with the people throughout the country to adhere to the people's democratic dictatorship, stick to the socialist path, concentrate their efforts to carry out socialist modernisation, speed up economic and cultural development in national autonomous areas, promote unity and prosperity in the national autonomous areas, strive for the common prosperity of various nationalities, and build our motherland into a highly civilised and highly democratic socialist country.

The law on regional autonomy for minority nationalities of the PRC is a basic law on autonomous system in the areas of minority nationalities prescribed by the constitution.

CHAPTER I

General principles

Article 1
The law on regional autonomy for minority nationalities of the PRC is enacted in accordance with the Constitution of the PRC.

Article 2
Regional autonomy shall be implemented in areas where minority nationalities live in compact communities.

The areas of national autonomy shall be divided into autonomous regions, autonomous prefectures and autonomous counties. The various areas of national autonomy are the inalienable parts of the PRC.

Article 3
The areas of national autonomy shall establish their own autonomous organs which are local organs of state power.

The principle of democratic centralism shall be implemented by autonomous organs as in the areas of national autonomy.

Article 4
Autonomous organs in the areas of national autonomy shall exercise their own functions and power as local organs of state power in accordance with the stipulations contained in section five of chapter 3 of the Constitution. In the meantime, they shall also exercise their own autonomous power in accordance with the jurisdiction defined by the Constitution, and with legal provisions on regional autonomy for minority nationalities. They shall enforce the law and policies of the state in light of their local practical conditions.

Autonomous organs in prefectures shall exercise their own functions and power like local organs of state power in prefectures, counties and cities. At the same time, they shall also exercise their autonomous power.

Article 5
Autonomous organs in the areas of national autonomy should uphold the unification of the state, and ensure the implementation and enforcement of the Constitution and laws in their regions.

Article 6
Autonomous organs in the areas of national autonomy should lead people of various nationalities to concentrate their efforts to carry out socialist modernisation.

Autonomous organs in the areas of national autonomy shall have the right to implement special policies and adopt flexible measures in the light of their own practical conditions in order to promote economic and cultural construction in their areas, provided that their policies and measures do not run counter to the Constitution and the law.

Under the guidance of the state plan, autonomous organs in the areas of national autonomy should constantly enhance labour productivity and economic results, develop the productive forces of society, and gradually improve the level of material life of the people of various nationalities in light of their own local conditions.

Autonomous organs in the areas of national autonomy should inherit and carry forward the fine tradition of national culture, build socialist spiritual civilisation with national characteristics, and constantly enhance the socialist consciousness of the people of various nationalities, and their scientific and cultural level.

Article 7
Autonomous organs in the areas of national autonomy should put the interests of the state in the first place, and actively accomplish various tasks assigned to them by the state organs of the higher level.

Article 8
State organs at the higher level should ensure that autonomous organs in the areas of national autonomy can exercise their autonomous power, and make efforts to help areas of national autonomy speed up their socialist construction in the light of the characteristics and needs of the areas concerned.

Article 9
State organs at the higher level and autonomous organs in the areas of national autonomy should uphold and develop socialist national relations characterised by equality, unity and mutual help among nationalities. Any action discriminating against or suppressing minority nationalities, undermining national unity or creating national disunity should be prohibited.

Article 10
Autonomous organs in the areas of national autonomy should ensure that minority nationalities living in their areas enjoy the freedom to use and develop their own spoken and written languages, and the freedom to maintain and change their customs and habits.

Article 11
Autonomous organs in the areas of national autonomy should protect the freedom of religious belief of citizens of various nationalities.

State organs, social organisations and individuals are not allowed to compel citizens to believe or not to believe in religions. They are not allowed to discriminate against citizens who believe in, or do not believe in religions.

The state protects normal religious activities. No person is allowed to make use of religion to disrupt social order, harm the health of citizens, or obstruct the educational system of the state.

Religious organisations and religious affairs should not be controlled by any foreign force.

CHAPTER II

The Establishment of the areas
of national autonomy and autonomous organs

Article 12
In places where minority nationalities live in compact communities, national autonomous areas can be established on the basis of one or more minority nationality areas in light of the local national conditions, economic development, and history.

In a place of national autonomy, if there are some other minority nationalities living there, relevant national autonomous areas or national villages can be established.

National autonomous areas may include localities and townships inhabited by some people of the Han nationality and other nationalities.

Article 13
The names of national autonomous areas shall be rendered in the order of the names of the localities, the names of the nationalities concerned, and their administrative status, except under special circumstances.

Article 14
The establishment of national autonomous areas, the delineation of the areas, and the rendering of the names shall be decided by the state organs at the higher level on the basis of full consultations with local organs and representatives of the nationalities concerned. The decision should be submitted to the higher authorities for approval in accordance with legal provisions.

Once the delineation of the national autonomous areas has been defined, it cannot be arbitrarily changed. When a change is needed, it should be decided by state organs at the higher level on the basis of full consultation with the departments concerned, and the autonomous organs in national autonomous areas. The decision should be submitted to the State Council for approval.

Article 15
The autonomous organs in national autonomous areas shall be the people's congresses and people's govern-

ments of autonomous regions, autonomous prefectures and autonomous counties.

The people's government of a national autonomous area shall be responsible to, and report on its work to, the relevant people's congress. If the people's congress is not in session, it shall be responsible to, and report on its work to, the standing committee of the relevant people's congress. People's governments in various national autonomous areas shall be administrative organs of the state under the leadership of the State Council. They shall be subordinate to the State Council.

The organisations and work of the autonomous organs in national autonomous areas shall be defined by autonomy regulations or specific regulations enacted in accordance with the Constitution and the law.

Article 16

In the people's congress of a national autonomous area, in addition to the deputies of the nationality or nationalities exercising regional autonomy in the administrative area, the other nationalities inhabiting the area shall also be entitled to appropriate representation.

In the people's congress of a national autonomous area, the number and proportion of the people's deputies of the nationality or nationalities exercising regional autonomy in the administrative area, and the other nationalities inhabiting the area should be decided by the standing committee of the provincial or regional people's congress in accordance with law. The decision should be submitted to the NPC Standing Committee for the record.

The chairmanship and vice-chairmanships of the standing committee of the people's congress of a national autonomous area should include a citizen or citizens of the nationality or nationalities exercising regional autonomy in the area concerned.

Article 17

The administrative head of a national autonomous region, prefecture or county should be a citizen of the nationality, or of one of the nationalities, exercising regional autonomy in the area concerned. As many members as possible of the nationality or nationalities exercising regional autonomy should be assigned to work in the people's governments and other organisations of the autonomous regions, prefectures and counties concerned.

The administrative heads of autonomous regions, prefectures and counties should follow a system of personal responsibility. They should preside over the work of the relevant people's governments.

Article 18

As many cadres as possible of the nationality or nationalities exercising regional autonomy should be assigned, as many as possible, to work in the autonomous organs in the national autonomous areas concerned.

CHAPTER III

Autonomous organs and autonomous power

Article 19

People's congresses of the national autonomous areas shall have the power to enact autonomy regulations and specific regulations in the light of the political, economic and cultural characteristics of the nationality or nationalities in the areas concerned. The autonomy regulations and specific regulations of autonomous regions shall be submitted to the NPC Standing Committee for approval before they go into effect. The regulations of autonomous prefectures and counties shall be submitted to the standing committees of the people's congresses of provinces or autonomous regions for approval before they go into effect, and they shall be reported to the NPC Standing Committee for the record.

Article 20

If the resolutions, decisions, orders and instructions of the state organs at the higher level are not suitable for the practical conditions in the national autonomous areas, autonomous organs may report the situation to the state organs at the higher level and seek their approval to adopt flexible measures to implement those resolutions, decisions, orders and instructions, or to suspend the implementation of them.

Article 21

In performing their functions, the autonomous organs of the national autonomous areas, in accordance with the autonomy regulations of the respective areas, shall employ the spoken and written languages or languages in common use in the locality. If, in performing its functions, the autonomous organ of a national autonomous area employs several spoken and written languages in common use in the locality, it may select one common spoken and written language in the locality as its main spoken and written language.

Article 23

When enterprises and establishments in national autonomous areas recruit workers, they should give special consideration to the people of the nationality or nationalities in those areas. They may recruit workers from among the people of the nationality or nationalities in the rural areas and pastoral areas. When autonomous prefectures and autonomous counties recruit workers from the people of the nationality or nationalities in the rural areas or pastoral areas, they should report this to the people's government of the province or autonomous region for approval.

Article 32

In accordance with the stipulations of the state and with the approval of the State Council, autonomous organs of the national autonomous areas may carry out economic and trade activities with foreign countries, and open up ports for foreign trade.

With the approval of the State Council, the national autonomous areas bordering foreign countries may carry out border trade.

If autonomous organs of the national autonomous areas carry out economic and trade activities with foreign countries, the state will give them special treatment with regard to the amount of retention of foreign exchange.

Article 36

In accordance with the educational policy of the state and legal provisions, autonomous organs of the national autonomous areas may decide on the establishment of various kinds of schools, education system, guiding principles for running schools, contents of courses, languages of instruction and admission system of those schools in the areas concerned.

Article 37
Autonomous organs of the national autonomous areas should independently develop education for nationalities, wipe out illiteracy, run various kinds of schools, popularise primary education, develop secondary education, and run teachers' training schools for nationalities, vocational schools for nationalities, and institutes for nationalities in order to train specialised personnel of minority nationalities.

Autonomous organs of the national autonomous areas should also run primary and secondary boarding schools in economically backward and sparsely populated minority nationality mountain areas. Students should be provided with stipends.

In schools which mainly recruit students of minority nationalities, textbooks in languages of the minority nationalities concerned should be used where conditions exist. Languages for instruction should also be the languages of the minority nationalities concerned. Primary school students of higher grades and secondary school students should learn the Chinese language (hanyu 3352 6133). Putonghua, which is commonly used throughout the country, should be popularised among them.

Article 38
Autonomous organs of the national autonomous areas should develop in their own ways national cultural undertakings such as literature, art, press publication, broadcasting, film, television and other things characterised by national features.

Autonomous organs of the national autonomous areas should collect, collate, translate and publish books for minority nationalities. They should also protect scenic spots and historical sites, precious cultural relics and other aspects of the important historical and cultural heritage of minority nationalities.

Article 42
Autonomous organs of the national autonomous areas should take active measures to promote exchanges and co-ordination with other localities in the fields of education, science, technology, culture, art, public health, sports etc.

In accordance with the stipulations of the state, autonomous organs of the autonomous regions and autonomous prefectures may carry out exchanges with foreign countries in the fields of education, science, technology, culture, art, public health, sports etc.

Article 43
In accordance with legal provisions, autonomous organs of the national autonomous areas should adopt methods to exercise control over floating population.

CHAPTER IV

The people's courts and the
people's procuratorates in the national autonomous areas

Article 47
The people's courts and the people's procuratorates in the national autonomous areas should conduct hearings in the language or languages in common use in the areas concerned. The right of the citizens of all nationalities to use their own spoken and written languages in court proceedings should be protected. Translations should be provided for any party to the court proceedings who is not familiar with the spoken and written languages in common use in the areas concerned. Legal documents should be written in the language or languages in common use in the areas concerned.

CHAPTER V

Relations between the nationalities
in the national autonomous areas

Article 48
Autonomous organs in the national autonomous areas should ensure that various nationalities in their areas enjoy equal rights.

Autonomous organs in the national autonomous areas should unite with cadres and masses of various nationalities, fully arouse their enthusiasm, and exert joint efforts to promote construction in the national autonomous areas.

Article 49
Autonomous organs in the national autonomous areas should educate and encourage cadres of various nationalities to study each other's spoken and written languages and cadres of the Han nationality should study the spoken and written languages in common use in the localities concerned. While using their own spoken and written languages, cadres of minority nationalities should also study Putonghua and the Chinese language in common use throughout the country.

State personnel in the national autonomous areas who have a good command of more than two local spoken and written languages should be encouraged and rewarded.

Article 50
Autonomous organs in the national autonomous areas should help other minority nationalities living in compact communities in their areas to establish their own relevant autonomous localities or villages of nationalities.

Autonomous organs in the national autonomous areas should help various nationalities living in their areas to develop their own economic, educational, scientific, cultural, public health and sports undertakings.

Autonomous organs in the national autonomous areas should pay attention to the characteristics and needs of the nationalities scattered throughout their areas.

Article 51
When autonomous organs in the national autonomous areas are dealing with special problems involving various nationalities in their areas, they should fully consult the representatives of those nationalities and respect their views.

Article 52
Autonomous organs in the national autonomous areas should ensure that citizens of various nationalities in their areas enjoy their citizen's rights prescribed by the Constitution, and should educate these citizens to perform their duties.

Article 53
Autonomous organs in the national autonomous areas should advocate the social ethics of loving the motherland, the people, labour, sciences and socialism. They should provide education for citizens of various nationalities in their areas in patriotism, communism and policy for nationalities. They should also educate cadres and masses

of various nationalities so that they mutually trust, learn from and help each other, and mutually respect each other's spoken and written languages, customs and habits and religious beliefs, and exert joint efforts to uphold the unification of the state and the unity of various nationalities.

Article 62
When the state is exploiting natural resources and carrying out construction in the national autonomous areas, it should pay attention to the interests of the national autonomous areas and make arrangements in the interests of the economic construction in the areas. The state should also pay attention to the production and livelihood of the minority nationalities in the areas.

When enterprises and establishments of the state organs at the higher level, which are located in the national autonomous areas, are recruiting workers, they should give priority to recruiting workers from among the people of the minority nationalities in the areas concerned.

Enterprises and establishments of the state organs at the higher levels, which are located in the national autonomous areas, should respect the autonomy of the autonomous organs in the areas, and accept their supervision.

Article 64
State organs of the higher level should help national autonomous areas train a great number of cadres of various levels, various kinds of specialised personnel and skilled workers from among minority nationalities living in the areas concerned. They should employ various methods to send appropriate numbers of teachers, doctors, scientific and technical personnel as well as management personnel to work in the national autonomous areas in accordance with the needs of the areas concerned. Appropriate consideration shall be given to their pay and conditions.

Article 65
State organs at the higher level should help national autonomous areas speed up the development of their educational undertakings and enhance the scientific and cultural level of the people of various nationalities.

The state should establish institutes for nationalities. Universities and colleges should run special classes and open preparatory courses for the students of minority nationalities. They can adopt the method of recruiting students from the national autonomous areas and sending the students back to the areas they came from after their graduation. When universities, colleges and secondary vocational schools are recruiting new students, they may lower the criteria for the admission of the students of minority nationalities.

Article 66
State organs at the higher level should provide more education for the cadres and masses of minority nationalities in the policy towards minority nationalities, and constantly examine the implementation and enforcement of the policy for minority nationalities and the law concerned.

APPENDIX 9.1

THE TREATY OF WAITANGI (ENGLISH TEXT) (EXTRACT)

Article 1
The Chiefs of the Confederation of the United Tribes of New Zealand and the separate and independent Chiefs who have not become members of the Confederation cede to Her Majesty the Queen of England absolutely and without reservation all the rights and powers of Sovereignty which the said Confederation or Individual Chiefs respectively exercise or possess, or may be supposed to exercise or to possess over their respective Territories as the sole sovereigns thereof.

Article 2
Her Majesty the Queen of England confirms and guarantees to the Chiefs and Tribes of New Zealand and to the respective families and individuals thereof the full exclusive and undisturbed possession of their Lands and Estates Forests Fisheries and other properties which they may collectively or individually possess so long as it is their wish and desire to retain the same in their possession; but the Chiefs of the United Tribes and the individual Chiefs yield to Her Majesty the exclusive right of Preemption over such lands as the proprietors thereof may be disposed to alienate at such prices as may be agreed upon between the respective Proprietors and persons appointed by Her Majesty to treat with them in that behalf.

Article 3
In consideration thereof Her Majesty the Queen of England extends to the Natives of New Zealand Her royal protection and imparts to them all the Rights and Privileges of British Subjects.

[signed] W. Hobson Lieutenant Governor

INDEX

This index is intended to refer to all the minority groups mentioned in the entries by any of their names or designations used in the text. The introduction to each region also contains information on some minorities and aspects of minority rights but these are not included in the index.